Handbook of Research
Sustainable Careers

Edited by

Ans De Vos

Antwerp Management School and University of Antwerp, Faculty of Economics, Antwerp, Belgium

Beatrice I.J.M. Van der Heijden

Radboud University, Institute for Management Research, Nijmegen, Open University of the Netherlands, Heerlen, the Netherlands and Kingston University, London, UK

Edward Elgar
PUBLISHING

Cheltenham, UK • Northampton, MA, USA

Published by
Edward Elgar Publishing Limited
The Lypiatts
15 Lansdown Road
Cheltenham
Glos GL50 2JA
UK

Edward Elgar Publishing, Inc.
William Pratt House
9 Dewey Court
Northampton
Massachusetts 01060
USA

Paperback edition 2017

A catalogue record for this book
is available from the British Library

Library of Congress Control Number: 2015930150

This book is available electronically in the Elgaronline
Business subject collection
DOI 10.4337/9781782547037

MIX
Paper from
responsible sources
FSC® C013056

ISBN 978 1 78254 702 0 (cased)
ISBN 978 1 78254 703 7 (eBook)
ISBN 978 1 78643 757 0 (paperback)

Typeset by Servis Filmsetting Ltd, Stockport, Cheshire
Printed and bound in Great Britain by TJ International Ltd, Padstow

Contents

Contributors

Teun Aalbers, Radboud Alzheimer Centre, Radboudumc, Nijmegen and Department of Geriatric Medicine, Radboudumc, Nijmegen, the Netherlands. Teun Aalbers holds a Master's degree in Human Movement Sciences and a Bachelor's degree in Sport and Health Management. He is currently doing a PhD on the relationship between healthy living and brain ageing at the Department of Geriatric Medicine at the Radboudumc in Nijmegen. His main research interests are healthy living, behaviour change, cognition and applied gaming. His work has been published in international peer-reviewed journals including the *Journal of Medical Internet Research* and *Ageing Research Reviews*.

Michael B. Arthur, Suffolk University, Boston, USA. Michael B. Arthur is a Professor at Suffolk University, Boston, and an advocate of an interdisciplinary approach to career studies. His books include the *Handbook of Career Theory* (1989, Cambridge University Press), *The Boundaryless Career* (1996, Oxford University Press), *The New Careers* (1999, Sage), and *Knowledge at Work* (2006, Wiley-Blackwell). He is a co-developer of the Intelligent Career Card Sort® (ICCS®), and serves on the editorial boards of *Career Development International*, the *Journal of Organizational Behavior* and the *Journal of Vocational Behavior*.

P. Matthijs Bal, University of Bath, UK. P. Matthijs Bal is Reader at the School of Management, University of Bath. He obtained his PhD *cum laude* at VU University Amsterdam with research on psychological contracts of older workers. He worked at Erasmus University Rotterdam and VU University Amsterdam prior to moving to Bath. His research interests concern the ageing workforce, individualization of work arrangements, psychological contracts, and the impact of fictional narratives in the workplace. He has published in a wide range of journals, including the *Journal of Management Studies*, *Journal of Vocational Behavior* and *PLOS ONE*.

Yehuda Baruch, Southampton Business School, University of Southampton, UK. Yehuda Baruch (DSc Technion, Israel, PostDoc at City University and London Business School) is a Professor of Management and Research Director of the School of Management at the University of Southampton. His research interests and writing have been extensive and wide ranging, with particular focus on careers and global HRM, including over 115 refereed papers, including in *Journal of Management*, *Human Resource Management*, *Organizational Dynamics*, *Journal of Vocational Behavior*, *Human Relations* and *Organization Studies* and over 45 books and book chapters. He is Associate Editor of *Human Resource Management* (US), former Editor of *Group & Organization Management* and *Career Development International* and former Chair, Careers Division, Academy of Management.

Claudia Bernhard-Oettel, Stockholm University, Sweden. Claudia Bernhard-Oettel, PhD, is Associate Professor in Psychology and senior lecturer for Research Methods at the Department of Psychology, Stockholm University and researcher in the field of Work and Organizational Psychology. Her focal research interests relate to changing employment contracts and job transitions in relation to individual employability, well-being, justice perceptions and possibilities for competence transfer. Her work has been published in international peer-reviewed journals including *European Journal of Work and Organizational Psychology*, *Career Development International*, *Work & Stress*, *Applied Psychology: An International Review*, and the *International Journal of Human Resource Management*.

Tanja Bipp, Open University of the Netherlands, Heerlen, the Netherlands. Tanja Bipp, PhD, is Associate Professor of Work and Organizational Psychology at the Faculty of Psychology and Educational Sciences of the Open University of the Netherlands. Her research interests include the effects of individual differences at work, work motivation, the consequences of goals and feedback, job design, as well as work and health. Her work has been published in international peer-reviewed journals including *Journal of Occupational and Organizational Psychology*, *European Journal of Work and Organizational Psychology*, *Journal of Personnel Psychology*, *Personality and Individual Differences* and *International Journal of Selection and Assessment*.

Nikos Bozionelos, Audencia, Nantes, France. Nikos Bozionelos is Professor of Organizational Behavior and Human Resources Management and Head of the Research Axis Organization and Value Chain Management in Audencia School of Management, Nantes. He holds visiting positions in institutions that include Renmin University of PRChina and Hull University Business School (UK). He is Senior Editor for *Asia Pacific Journal of Management*, and his research interests include careers, individual differences, social capital and organizational politics. He has published in excess of 50 articles – the vast majority of them single or first-authored – in journals indexed by Thomson Reuters, and his individual research impact, indicated by the h_I index (www.harzing.com), exceeds 20.

Jon P. Briscoe, Northern Illinois University, USA. Jon P. Briscoe is Professor of Management in the College of Business at Northern Illinois University. He is a co-founder of the Cross-Cultural Collaboration on Contemporary Careers (the 5C Group) and a past president of the Careers Division of the Academy of Management. His research centres around managing new careers from both employee and employer perspectives, with emphasis primarily upon the 'protean' career. In addition he studies cross-cultural differences in career success and career management as well as leadership and leadership development. He teaches in undergraduate as well as graduate business programmes and has been recognized by his students with several teaching awards. He is Co-Editor of *Careers Around the World: Individual and Contextual Perspectives* and has published his work in peer-reviewed journals such as *Career Development International*, *Journal of Occupational and Organizational Psychology*, *Journal of Vocational Behavior* and *Personnel Psychology*.

Maximilian B.W. Buyken, Justus Liebig University Giessen, Germany. Maximilian B.W. Buyken is a PhD student in the Department of Work and Organizational Psychology at Justus Liebig University Giessen. His research focuses on career development, (adults') career adaptability in the face of economic stressors, career exploration in particular, and the effects of career-related behaviour on well-being. He has presented his work at conferences such as the annual meeting of the Academy of Management and is co-author of a book chapter on career adaptability as a form of proactive coping.

An De Coen, IDEA Consult, Belgium. An De Coen is researcher in Labour Market and Socio-Economic Policy at IDEA Consult. After finishing her PhD on the role of age and employability regarding job search and retirement intention at the KU Leuven in 2012, she joined IDEA Consult and continued working as a research fellow at the Research Centre for Organisation Studies, Faculty of Business and Economics, KU Leuven. Her main research interests focus on the labor market participation of different age groups, employability and factors contributing to individuals' employability, such as training and education.

Nele De Cuyper, research group Work, Organizational and Personnel Psychology, KU Leuven, Belgium. Nele De Cuyper is Assistant Professor at the research group Work, Organizational and Personnel Psychology (WOPP). The research group is part of the Research Unit Occupational and Organisational Psychology and Professional Learning (O2L) from the Faculty of Psychology and Educational Sciences, KU Leuven. Her main research areas are: employability and job insecurity in relation to both occupational well-being and careers, and with a focus upon precarious employment (for example, temporary employment, outplacement). She has published her work in, for example, *Journal of Organizational Behavior*, *Journal of Vocational Behaviour*, *Journal of Occupational and Organizational Psychology*, *The European Journal of Work and Organizational Psychology* and *Work & Stress*.

Sara De Hauw, Vlerick Business School, Belgium. Sara De Hauw, PhD, currently works as a Post-Doctoral Research Associate at the Area People and Organisation of the Vlerick Business School. She obtained her PhD in 2014 at KU Leuven, Belgium. In her dissertation she investigated the individual and contextual antecedents, and the career consequences of work–home balance. In her current research she focuses on work–home balance, well-being and careers. Her work has been published in international peer-reviewed journals, including *Journal of Vocational Behavior* and *Journal of Business and Psychology*.

Annet H. De Lange, Department of Human Resource Management, HAN University of Applied Sciences, Nijmegen, the Netherlands. Dr Annet De Lange works as Professor of Human Resource Management (Lector) at the HAN University of Applied Sciences in Arnhem and Nijmegen, and as Visiting Professor at the faculty of Social Sciences of the University of Stavanger in Norway. Moreover, she is director of a Dutch Knowledge Centre focusing on sustainable work ability (NKDI; including representatives from the Dutch government, municipalities, unions, large-scale and medium-sized companies, Healthy Ageing Northern Netherlands, temporary agencies, and researchers) which aims to develop evidence-based interventions to facilitate healthy ageing at work. Her research activities have been focused on 'HRM and sustainable work ability of ageing workers'. Her research has been successful, culminating in a *cum laude* doctorate, several honorary prizes (IBM Frye Stipendium, André Büssing Memorial Prize, Stichting Praemium Erasmianum Prize, the *Journal of Occupational Health Psychology* Best Paper of Past Ten Years Award), national and international grants, and publications in occupational health journals.

Peggy De Prins, Antwerp Management School, Belgium. Peggy De Prins, PhD, is Academic Director of the Master's in HRM programme and Professor in various Master's classes at Antwerp Management School and the University of Antwerp, Faculty of Economics and Business Administration. Her research interest crosses the borders of labour sociology, HRM, organizational behaviour and sustainability, that is, sustainable HRM, quality of work, employee engagement and positive organizational behaviour.

Ans De Vos, Antwerp Management School and University of Antwerp, Faculty of Economics, Antwerp, Belgium. Ans De Vos, PhD, holds the SD Worx chair 'Next generation work: Creating sustainable careers' at the Antwerp Management School, Antwerp and is Full Professor at the University of Antwerp, Faculty of Economics, Department of Management. She is also a research fellow at the Faculty of Business and Economics, KU Leuven. Her focal areas of interest are career development, sustainable career management and psychological contracts, which she approaches both from an individual and organizational perspective. She is academic director of the 'Leadership and Career Development' track of all full-time Masters programmes organized at the Antwerp Management School. Her work has been published in international peer-reviewed journals including *Journal of Organizational Behavior*, *Journal of Vocational Behavior*, *Journal of Occupational and Organizational Psychology*, *European Journal of Work and Organizational Psychology* and *Career Development International.*

Hans De Witte, Research Group Work, Organizational and Personnel Psychology, KU Leuven, Belgium; Optentia Research Focus Area, North-West University, South Africa; Vanderbijlpark Campus, North-West University, South Africa. Hans De Witte is Full Professor in Work Psychology at the Faculty of Psychology and Educational Sciences of KU Leuven, where he is a member of the research group Work, Organizational and Personnel Psychology (WOPP) – part of the broader Research Unit Occupational and Organisational Psychology and Professional Learning (O2L). He is also Extraordinary Professor at the Optentia Research Programme at the North-West University of South Africa (Vanderbijlpark Campus). His research includes the study of the psychological consequences of job insecurity, unemployment, temporary employment and downsizing, as well as mobbing and job stress (for example, burnout) versus well-being at work (for example, work engagement). He has published in journals such as the *European Journal of Work and Organizational Psychology*, *Work & Stress*, *Journal of Occupational and Organizational Psychology* and *Applied Psychology: An International Review*. He is a member of the European Network of Work and Organizational Psychologists (ENOP) and of the executive board of the Scientific Committee Unemployment, Job Insecurity and Health of ICOH.

Nicky Dries, KU Leuven, Belgium. Nicky Dries is a Professor of Organizational Behaviour at KU Leuven and a Research Fellow at Vlerick Business School. She held visiting appointments at VU Amsterdam, University of Tilburg, Wirtschaftsuniversität Vienna, Reykjavik University, and a Fulbright scholarship at Boston University. Her primary research interests are talent, potential and success – specifically, the interplay of organizational-strategic and individual-psychological factors in shaping careers. Nicky is on the board of the *Journal of Vocational Behavior*, *Journal of World Business* and

European Journal of Work and Organizational Psychology. She supervises four research projects on talent management, co-supervises the Flemish Policy Research Centre for Work and Social Economy, and is involved in two cross-cultural projects on careers: the 5C Project and the Career Adaptability/Life Design project.

Nikolai Egold, Psychology School, Fresenius University of Applied Sciences, Frankfurt, Germany. Nikolai Egold is Professor of Applied Social and Work and Organizational Psychology in the Department of Health and Social Sciences at the Fresenius University of Applied Sciences. After his PhD in Work and Organizational Psychology at Goethe University, he worked at the Goethe University and at the Fresenius University of Applied Sciences. Nikolai's research interests focus on social identity processes in organizations, customer orientation and customer satisfaction as well as forms of organizational citizenship behaviour. He has published in academic journals such as the *Journal of Change Management*, *Journal of Occupational and Organizational Psychology*, *Journal of Personnel Psychology* and *European Journal of Work and Organizational Psychology*.

Chen Fleisher, Utrecht University School of Economics (USE), Utrecht University, and Faculty of Economics and Business Administration, VU University Amsterdam, the Netherlands. Chen Fleisher is a researcher in Organizational Behavior and Entrepreneurship. He is currently a Postdoctoral Research Fellow at Utrecht School of Economics, and a Lecturer at Amsterdam Business Research Institute, where he also completed his Doctoral degree. His PhD research on individual and organizational outcomes of self-directed career management was funded by a prestigious research grant from the Netherlands Organisation for Scientific Research (NWO). Chen possesses a combination of extensive commercial experience and immersion in the research environment as an entrepreneur and human resources specialist. His current work revolves around talent management, intrapreneurship, employee engagement, organizational development and community involvement.

Anneleen Forrier, KU Leuven, Belgium. Anneleen Forrier, PhD, is Associate Professor at the University of Leuven, Faculty of Economics and Business. Her research interests include employability, careers, (re)employment and ageing. She published her research in leading scholarly journals such as the *Journal of Occupational and Organizational Psychology*, *Journal of Vocational Behavior*, *Career Development International*, *Journal of Management Studies* and *Ageing & Society*.

Franco Fraccaroli, University of Trento, Italy. Franco Fraccaroli is Professor of Work and Organizational Psychology at Trento University. His research interests include ageing and late careers in organizations, work stress and psychosocial risks in the workplace. He is a fellow of SIOP (Society for Industrial and Organizational Psychology) and IAAP (International Association of Applied Psychology) and a member of several editorial boards for international scientific journals. He served as President of the European Association of Work and Organizational Psychology. He is Co-Editor (with L. Finkelstein, D. Truxillo and R. Kanfer) of the book *Facing the Challenges of a Multi-age Workforce: A Use-inspired Approach*, (Psychology Press, in press).

Ariane Froidevaux, University of Lausanne, Switzerland. Ariane Froidevaux, MA, is a doctoral candidate and graduate teaching assistant at the Institute of Psychology at the

University of Lausanne. Her doctoral thesis aims to develop a relational perspective on identity challenge and adjustment during transition to retirement. Her research interests include transition to retirement, social support, identity, and meaningful work and meaning in life during the second half of career development. She also works as a career counsellor psychologist at the Counselling Service of the University of Lausanne.

Jeffrey H. Greenhaus, Drexel University, Philadelphia, USA. Jeffrey H. Greenhaus, PhD, is Professor of Management and William A. Mackie Chair at Drexel University's LeBow College of Business. His research, which focuses on career dynamics and work–family relationships, has been published in many of the field's leading journals, including *Academy of Management Review*, *Academy of Management Journal*, *Organizational Behavior and Human Decision Processes*, *Journal of Management*, *Journal of Organizational Behavior*, *Human Relations*, and *Journal of Vocational Behavior*. He is author or editor of five books and is currently preparing a book on the work–family interface with Gary N. Powell that will be published by Routledge Press.

David E. Guest, King's College, London, UK. David E. Guest is Professor of Organizational Psychology and Human Resource Management in the Department of Management at King's College, London. His main research interests concern the relationship between human resource management, organizational performance and employee well-being; the individualization of employment relations and the role of the psychological contract; flexibility and employment contracts; and the impact of the changing nature of careers. He sits on several editorial boards and has published in a wide range of journals including the *Journal of Organizational Behavior*, *Journal of Occupational and Organizational Psychology*, *Journal of Vocational Behavior*, *Human Relations*, *British Journal of Industrial Relations* and *Academy of Management Journal*.

Douglas T. Hall, Boston University, USA. Douglas T. (Tim) Hall is the Morton H. and Charlotte Friedman Professor of Management in the School of Management at Boston University. He has held faculty positions at Yale, York, Michigan State and Northwestern Universities, as well as visiting positions at Columbia, Minnesota, the US Military Academy at West Point, Boston College, the University of Canterbury (NZ), and the Center for Creative Leadership. His research deals with careers, work–family dynamics, and leadership development.

Andreas Hirschi, University of Bern, Switzerland. Andreas Hirschi, PhD, is Full Professor and Chair of Work and Organizational Psychology at the University of Bern. He obtained his PhD from the University of Zurich and subsequently worked at the Pennsylvania State University, the Leuphana University of Lueneburg, Germany, and at the University of Lausanne, Switzerland. His major research interests are career counselling, career development and well-being at work.

I.M. Jawahar, Office of the Provost, Illinois State University, Normal, USA. I.M. 'Jim' Jawahar (PhD, Oklahoma State University) is Associate Provost of Illinois State University. His main areas of research include performance appraisal, fairness perceptions, stress and work–life balance, academic integrity, citizenship and counterproductive work behaviors. Jim's research has appeared in the *Journal of Applied Psychology*, *Academy of Management Review*, *Journal of Management*, *Labor Relations*, and *Personnel*

Psychology. Jim is the Editor of *Career Development International* and serves on editorial boards of several journals, including *Group and Organization Management* and *Journal of Managerial Psychology*.

Clare Kelliher, Cranfield University, UK. Clare Kelliher, BSc, MA, PhD, is Professor of Work and Organisation at Cranfield School of Management, Cranfield University. Clare holds a PhD in Organisational Behaviour from the London Business School, an MA in Industrial Relations from the University of Warwick and a first degree in Management from the University of Surrey. Her research interests centre around the organization of work and the management of the employment relationship. Clare is the author of many published papers and book chapters and regularly speaks at national and international conferences.

Svetlana N. Khapova, Faculty of Economics and Business Administration, VU University Amsterdam, the Netherlands. Svetlana N. Khapova is a Professor of Careers and Organization Studies at the Faculty of Economics and Business Administration of the VU University Amsterdam and the Scientific Director of Amsterdam Business Research Institute (ABRI). Her research focuses on the link between careers and institutions. She studies individual careers as a resource upon which both individuals and organizations draw to innovate. She has published her research in journals including the *Journal of Vocational Behavior*, *Journal of Organisational Behavior*, *Human Relations*, and *Career Development International*, among others. She was the 2011–2012 Division Chair of Careers Division of the Academy of Management.

Ulla Kinnunen, University of Tampere, Finland. Ulla Kinnunen, PhD, is Professor of Psychology at the School of Social Sciences and Humanities in the University of Tampere. Her present research interests focus on occupational well-being from the perspectives of stress, burnout and recovery, including research on job insecurity and temporary employment, leadership and the work–family interface. She has published extensively in these areas both internationally and nationally, and serves as an Associate Editor of *Work & Stress*.

Ute-Christine Klehe, Justus Liebig University Giessen, Germany. Ute-Christine Klehe is head of the Department of Work and Organizational Psychology at Justus Liebig University Giessen. Her research interests lie in the areas of career adaptability (especially as a form of proactive coping among adults), personnel selection, as well as typical vs. maximum performance. She is Associate Editor of *Applied Psychology: An International Review* and consulting Editor of the *Journal of Applied Psychology*. Her work has been published in, among others, the *Journal of Applied Psychology*, *Personnel Psychology*, *Journal of Vocational Behavior*, *Human Performance*, and *International Journal of Selection and Assessment*.

Dorien Kooij, HR Studies, Tilburg University, the Netherlands. Dorien Kooij is Assistant Professor at the Department of Human Resource Studies of Tilburg University. Her research focuses on ageing at work, and in particular on HR practices for older workers, on how work motivation changes with ageing, and on job crafting. She has published in international peer-reviewed journals such as the *Journal of Organizational Behavior*, *Work & Stress* and *Psychology and Aging*.

Markus Latzke, WU Vienna University of Economics and Business, Interdisciplinary Institute for Management and Organizational Behaviour, Austria. Dr Markus Latzke is Assistant Professor at the Interdisciplinary Institute of Management and Organisational Behaviour, WU Vienna. He conducts research in the field of safety climates in health care organizations, where, for example, he investigates the potential of interventions such as Critical Incident Reporting Systems for organizational learning. His research interest in career studies focuses on stability and change, and currently centres on Bourdieu's theory of practice, which he mainly applies in the context of a longitudinal study on changes in managerial careers (Vienna Career Panel Project). His research has been published in various academic journals, including the *German Journal of Research in Human Resource Management* and the *Journal of Vocational Behavior*.

Barbara S. Lawrence, UCLA Anderson Graduate School of Management, UCLA, USA. Barbara S. Lawrence is Professor of Human Resources and Organizational Behavior at the Anderson Graduate School of Management, UCLA. Her current research examines organizational reference groups, internal labour markets, organizational norms, career expectations and the accumulation of disadvantage. In 2009 she received the Everett Cherrington Hughes Award for her contributions to interdisciplinary research on careers. She received the 1998 Outstanding Publication in Organizational Behavior Award from the Academy of Management. She serves on the editorial board of *Organization Science*.

Anne Mäkikangas, University of Jyväskylä, Finland. Anne Mäkikangas, PhD, is an Adjunct Professor in Work Psychology. She received her PhD from the University of Jyväskylä in 2007. Among other posts she has held, she has since worked as an Associate Professor of Work Psychology. Currently, she is an Academy Research Fellow for the Academy of Finland. She has experience in examining occupational well-being from the perspectives of personality, job stress and positive psychology. In addition, she has expertise in research methodology, especially in person-centred methodology and longitudinal data analysis. She has published over 50 national and international papers and book chapters on these topics.

Saija Mauno, University of Jyväskylä, and University of Tampere, Finland. Saija Mauno, PhD, is Professor of Psychology at the School of Social Sciences and Humanities at the University of Tampere and researcher at the University of Jyväskylä, Finland. Her research interests cover the work–family interface, temporary employment, job insecurity, and stress and coping from the perspectives of employee well-being and health. She has published extensively, including in the *European Journal of Work and Organizational Psychology*, *Work & Stress*, *International Journal of Stress Management*, *Community, Work & Family*, and the *Journal of Business and Psychology*.

Wolfgang Mayrhofer, WU Vienna University of Economics and Business, Interdisciplinary Institute for Management and Organizational Behaviour, Austria. Wolfgang Mayrhofer is Full Professor and Head of the Interdisciplinary Institute of Management and Organisational Behaviour, WU Vienna. He has previously held full-time positions at the University of Paderborn and at Dresden University of Technology, Germany. He conducts research in comparative international human resource management and leadership, work careers, and systems theory and management and has received national and international rewards for outstanding research and service to the academic community.

He has authored, co-authored and co-edited 27 books, more than 110 book chapters and 70 peer-reviewed articles. Wolfgang Mayrhofer is a member of the editorial or advisory board of several international journals and research centres.

Anke Milissen, KU Leuven, Belgium. Anke Milissen graduated in Business Economics at the KU Leuven and completed her education with a Master-after-Master's degree in Human Resource Management at the Antwerp Management School. She is currently working as a Business Analyst in an international consultancy firm, a job which perfectly combines her passion for Human Resources with her curiosity in business.

Katharina Näswall, Canterbury University, New Zealand. Katharina Näswall, PhD, works as Senior Lecturer at the Department of Psychology, University of Canterbury. Her primary research interests concern employee resilience, well-being, and performance in uncertain working conditions, the role of unions and organizations in creating healthy workplaces, as well as employability and career transitions in an increasingly boundaryless working life. Her work has been published in international peer-reviewed journals including the *Journal of Occupational Health Psychology*, *Stress & Health*, *Work & Stress*, *Career Development International*, *European Journal of Work* and *Organizational Psychology*.

Katharina Pernkopf, WU Vienna University of Economics and Business, Interdisciplinary Institute for Management and Organizational Behaviour, Austria. Dr Katharina Pernkopf is Assistant Professor at the Interdisciplinary Institute of Management and Organisational Behaviour, WU Vienna. Her research projects are located in the wider field of organizational institutionalism and comparative HRM. She is interested in how work practices are influenced by the interaction of organizational rules and demands of the institutional environment. Currently she is exploring 'talent management' and related concepts as well as their implications for individuals in their everyday employment situation from a French pragmatist perspective (convention theory). Her work has been published in the *Journal of Management Inquiry*, *ESEEN*, *Personnel Review* and the *European Journal of Cross-Cultural Competence and Management*.

Pascale Peters, Radboud University, Institute for Management Research, Nijmegen, the Netherlands. Pascale Peters is Associate Professor at Radboud University, Nijmegen (IMR). Her main area of expertise relates to flexible work arrangements, in particular part-time work, home-based telework, New Ways to Work, and working carer arrangements. She is a member of the editorial board of *Community, Work & Family* and the *International Journal of Work Innovation*. She has participated in several internal research projects and has published in international books and journals (for example, *Work, Employment & Society*, *Human Resource Management*, *Human Relations*, *Equality, Diversity and Inclusion*, *Community, Work & Family*, *The International Journal of Human Resource Management*, *Human Resource Management Journal*, *International Journal of Employment Studies* and *International Journal of Manpower*) and Dutch books and journals (for example, *Gedrag & Organisatie*, *Tijdschrift voor Genderstudies*).

Johanna Rantanen, University of Jyväskylä, Finland. Johanna Rantanen, PhD, is currently working as Adjunct Professor in the field of guidance and counselling in the Department of Teacher Education, University of Jyväskylä. Her research has focused on the work–family interface, occupational well-being and personality from psychological and longitudinal study perspectives. She has published in, among others, the *Journal of Vocational Behavior, Journal of Occupational and Health Psychology* and *Work & Stress*.

Julia Richardson, York University, Canada. Julia Richardson, PhD, is Associate Professor of Organizational Behavior at York University, Toronto, Canada. Her main areas of research are internationally mobile professionals, flexible work practices, and career identities and callings. She is currently Associate Editor for *Career Development International* and the *International Journal of Management Reviews*. Julia has published her work in a wide range of journals including *Management International Review, British Journal of Management, Journal of World Business, Career Development International* and the *International Journal of Human Resource Management*.

Ricardo Rodrigues, Kingston University, UK. Ricardo Rodrigues, PhD, is a senior lecturer in the Department of Management at Kingston Business School, London. He is also co-director of the Centre for Research on Employment, Skills and Society. His main areas of research are boundaryless careers, career boundaries and career orientations. His work has been published in the *Journal of Vocational Behavior, Human Relations* and *Career Development International*.

Carina Rohr, WU Vienna University of Economics and Business, Institute for Human Resource Management, Austria. Carina Rohr is a Research Assistant at the Institute for Human Resource Management at WU Vienna. Her research interests include career transitions with a Bourdieuian lens, sustainable HRM and ethical perspectives in international HRM. In one ongoing research project she is investigating the role of HRM and HR practices concerning human rights issues in international sustainability reporting of MNEs. Further research is located in the field of critical management studies and focuses on organizational discourses in organizational changes processes with an institutional theoretical framework.

René Schalk, HR Studies, Tilburg University, the Netherlands. Professor René Schalk is a faculty member of the Department of Human Resource Studies at Tilburg University and holds a special chair in Social Work at Tilburg University in the Netherlands. He is Extraordinary Professor at the School for Human Resources Sciences at the Potchefstroom Campus of North West University in South Africa. His research focuses on organizations and employees, with a special interest in psychological contracts, international differences, policy issues and social work. He is Associate Editor of the *Journal of Managerial Psychology*. His research has been published in journals such as *Journal of Organizational Behavior, Management and Organization Review, Human Resource Management Review* and *Journal of Occupational and Organizational Psychology*.

Mette M. Schipper, Faculty of Economics and Business Administration, VU University Amsterdam, the Netherlands. Mette M. Schipper is an entrepreneur in the hospitality and hotel industry. She has a Bachelor of Applied Science degree in Hospitality Management and a Master's degree in Human Resource Management. Her research areas include corporate volunteering and employees' career development, and the influence of these on organizational development. In November 2013 she started her own business and opened a small boutique hotel in Amsterdam.

Thomas M. Schneidhofer, University of Seeburg Castle (USC), Austria. Dr Thomas M. Schneidhofer is Full Professor for Organisation and HRM at the USC. He is also a research fellow at the WU Vienna and the AAU Klagenfurt. His focal areas of interest are career theory and research on power/domination, both of which are flavoured with the theory of practice inspired by Pierre Bourdieu. His work has been published in international peer-reviewed journals including the *Journal of Vocational Behavior, German Journal of Research in Human Resource Management, Management Revue, Equality, Diversity and Inclusion – an International Journal* and the *Journal of Occupational and Organizational Psychology.*

Jesse Segers, Antwerp Management School and University of Antwerp, Belgium. Jesse Segers, PhD, is Professor of Leadership and Organizational Behaviour at the Antwerp Management School. His research interests are leadership and leadership development with a special interest in coaching and identity development, postmodern careers, and age effects on motivation, personality and values at work. He is the Academic Director of The Future Leadership Initiative.

Luc Sels, KU Leuven, Belgium. Luc Sels, PhD, is Dean of the Faculty of Economics and Business at KU Leuven. He is full professor at the Research Centre for Organisation Studies at KU Leuven, and part-time professor at the Simon School of the University of Rochester, where he teaches in the Rochester-Bern EMBA. Luc Sels is actively involved in labour market policy research and policy advice. He serves on the Belgian High Council for Employment and is Director of the Policy Research Centre for Work and Social Economy. His primary substantive research interests centre around labour market dynamics, active ageing, and workforce differentiation. His research has been published in journals such as the *Journal of Management, Journal of Management Studies, Journal of Applied Psychology, Journal of Organizational Behavior, Human Resource Management Journal* and *Labour Economics.*

Judith H. Semeijn, Faculty of Management, Science and Technology, Open University of the Netherlands, Heerlen, the Netherlands. Judith H. Semeijn, PhD, is an Associate Professor in Strategic Human Resource Management in the faculty of Management, Science and Technology at the Open University of the Netherlands. She is also Chair of the Organisation Department in the faculty of Management, Science and Technology. She obtained her PhD at Maastricht University. Her focal areas of research are: sustainable employability and labour participation, HRM and careers. Her research has been published in national and international peer-reviewed journals, including *Human Resource Management* and *Personnel Review.*

Thomas H. Stone, Department of Management, Spears College of Business, Oklahoma State University. Thomas H. Stone (PhD, University of Minnesota, I/O psychology) has been a Professor of Management at Oklahoma State University since 1989. He has also served on the faculties of the University of Iowa, York and McMaster Universities in Ontario, Canada. Tom has published two HR texts, *Understanding Personnel Management* and *Human Resource Management in Canada* (with Noah Meltz and Lauren Falkenberg). His research spans several areas, including competency modelling, performance appraisal, academic integrity, leadership, decision-making and absenteeism, and has published in the *Journal of Applied Psychology, Academy* *of Management Review*, *Journal of Management*, *Journal of Vocational Behavior*, the *Canadian Journal of Administrative Sciences* and others. Tom has served as Division Chair for both Human Resource Management and Organizational Behavior in the Administrative Sciences Association of Canada and is currently Associate Editor of *Career Development International* and was recently appointed to the editorial board of the *Canadian Journal of Administrative Sciences*.

Donald M. Truxillo, Portland State University, USA. Donald M. Truxillo is a Professor of Psychology at Portland State University in Portland, Oregon. His work examines issues related to older workers, personnel selection, and occupational health and safety. He has published over 70 peer-reviewed journal articles and book chapters. He is currently on the editorial boards of six peer-reviewed journals. He served as Associate Editor for the *Journal of Management* and is currently an Associate Editor at *Work, Aging and Retirement*. He is a fellow of the American Psychological Association, Association for Psychological Science, the International Association for Applied Psychology, and the Society for Industrial and Organizational Psychology (SIOP). His research has been supported by the Society for Human Resource Management (SHRM) Foundation and the National Institute for Occupational Safety and Health (NIOSH).

Monique Valcour, EDHEC Business School, Nice, France. Monique Valcour, PhD, is Professor of Management at EDHEC Business School in France. Her research programme focuses on sustainable careers, work–life integration, and human resource and performance management. Her research has been published in journals including *European Management Journal*, *Human Relations*, *Industrial Relations*, *International Journal of Human Resource Management*, *Journal of Applied Psychology* and *Journal of Vocational Behavior*, and she also blogs for *Harvard Business Review*. Monique Valcour coaches leaders to engage and energize their employees, and she helps individuals align their careers with their strengths and passions. She is a frequent external speaker and workshop leader.

Lou Van Beirendonck, Antwerp Management School, Belgium. Lou Van Beirendonck, PhD, is Academic Director of the Master Class in HRM and Professor in various Masters' and Master classes at Antwerp Management School. He is the pioneer in assessment centres in Belgium and is known for his work in competence and talent management.

Karen Van Dam, Faculty of Psychology and Educational Sciences, Open University of the Netherlands, Heerlen, the Netherlands. Karen Van Dam, PhD, is Full Professor of Work, Organizational and Personnel Psychology at the Faculty of Psychology and Educational Sciences at the Open University of the Netherlands. Her research focuses on how employees adapt to changes in the work situation, including adaptation and emotion regulation, change and learning, and sustainable careers and entrepreneurship. She is currently Chief Editor of *Gedrag & Organisatie*, a Dutch journal of work and organizational psychology, and has published in journals including the *Journal of Applied Psychology*, *Journal of Management*, *Journal of Vocational Behavior*, *Journal of Occupational and Organizational Psychology* and *Personality and Individual Differences*.

Anja Van den Broeck, Human Relations Research Group, KU Leuven, Belgium and Optentia Research Focus Area, North-West University, South Africa. Anja Van den Broeck, PhD, is a work and motivation psychologist. She is Assistant Professor at the faculty of Economics and Business at KU Leuven. Her research goal is to examine how, and under which circumstances, individuals may thrive at work. Her research unravels the interplay between job design and other HR practices, well-being and motivation. She has published her research in journals such as the *Journal of Vocational Behavior*, *Work & Stress* and *Journal of Occupational and Organizational Psychology* and is part of the editorial board of the latter journal.

Beatrice I.J.M. Van der Heijden, Radboud University, Institute for Management Research, Nijmegen and Open University of the Netherlands, Heerlen, the Netherlands. Beatrice I.J.M. Van der Heijden, PhD, is Head of the Department Strategic HRM at the Radboud University, Institute for Management Research, Nijmegen, the Netherlands, and Professor of Strategic HRM at the Open University of the Netherlands. She is Vice-Director of a Dutch Knowledge Centre focusing on sustainable work ability (NKDI; including representatives from the Dutch government, municipalities, unions, large-scale and medium-sized companies, Healthy Ageing Northern Netherlands, temporary agencies, and researchers) which aims to develop evidence-based interventions to facilitate healthy ageing at work. Her main research areas are: career development, employability, and ageing at work. She is Associate Editor of the *European Journal of Work and Organizational Psychology*, and has published in, among others, *Career Development International*, *Human Resource Development Review*, *Human Resource Management*, *Journal of Career Development*, *Journal of Managerial Psychology*, *Journal of Occupational and Organizational Psychology*, *Journal of Vocational Behavior* and *Work & Stress*.

Rolf Van Dick, Institute of Psychology and Center for Leadership and Behavior in Organizations, Goethe University, Frankfurt, Germany. Rolf Van Dick is Professor of Social Psychology in the Department of Psychology at Goethe University. After his PhD in Social Psychology at Philipps-University (Marburg, Germany), he worked at Aston Business School (Birmingham, UK) and was visiting professor in Tuscaloosa (USA, 2001), Rhodes (Greece, 2002) and Kathmandu (Nepal, 2009). He has been Editor-in-Chief of the *British Journal of Management* and is currently Editor-in-Chief of the *Journal of Personnel Psychology*. Rolf's research interests focus on social identity processes in organizations and he has published more than 200 books, chapters and papers in academic journals such as the *Academy of Management Journal*, *Journal of Applied Psychology*, *Journal of Organizational Behavior*, *Journal of Marketing* and *Journal of Personality and Social Psychology*.

Marloes L. Van Engen, HR Studies, Tilburg University, the Netherlands. Marloes L. Van Engen works as Assistant Professor in the Department of Human Resource Studies, and holds a position as gender policy advisor at Tilburg University. Her research focuses on diversity and inclusion in organization, gender and inequality and work–life issues in organizations. She has published in, among others, *Psychological Bulletin*, *Leadership Quarterly*, *Career Development International*, *Organizational Behavior and*

Human Decision Processes, *Journal of Organizational and Occupational Psychology* and *International Journal of Human Research Management*.

Joris Van Ruysseveldt, Open University of the Netherlands, Heerlen, the Netherlands. Joris Van Ruysseveldt, PhD, is Associate Professor of Work and Organizational Psychology at the Faculty of Psychology and Educational Sciences, Open University. He is also a research fellow at the Faculty of Psychology and Educational Sciences, KU Leuven. His focal areas of interest are sustainable employment, proactivity, organizational change, workplace learning and well-being. His work has been published in international peer-reviewed journals including the *Journal of Vocational Behavior*, *Work & Stress*, *European Journal of Work and Organizational Psychology*, *Cognitive, Affective, & Behavioral Neuroscience* and *International Journal of Stress Management*.

Sarah Vansteenkiste, KU Leuven, Belgium. Sarah Vansteenkiste, PhD, is postdoctoral researcher at the Faculty of Economics and Business at KU Leuven. She is also senior researcher at the policy research centre Work and Social Economy, KU Leuven. In her research she mainly focuses on unemployment and job search behaviour, reemployment of older persons and boundaries of boundaryless careers. She has published in international peer-reviewed journals such as the *Journal of Vocational Behavior* as well as in national policy journals.

Annelies E.M. Van Vianen, University of Amsterdam, the Netherlands. Annelies E.M. Van Vianen is Full Professor of Organizational Psychology, and Chair of the Department of Work and Organizational Psychology at the University of Amsterdam. Her research interests are career development, person–environment fit, adaptability, ageing, leadership, and employee well-being. Her work has been published in international peer-reviewed journals including *Personnel Psychology*, *Academy of Management Journal*, *Journal of Organizational Behavior*, *Journal of Vocational Behavior*, *International Journal of Selection and Assessment*, *Leadership Quarterly*, and *Psychological Science*. She serves or has served on several journal review boards, as guest editor, and as Editor of *Behavior & Organization*. She is a member of, among others, the European Society for Vocational Designing and Career Counselling, and the Life Design International Research Group.

Tinka Van Vuuren, Faculty of Management, Science and Technology, Open University of the Netherlands, Heerlen, the Netherlands; Loyalis Consult, Heerlen, the Netherlands. Tinka Van Vuuren holds a chair in Strategic Human Resource Management, i.e. Vitality Management at the Open University of the Netherlands. Since 2002, she has been actively involved in activities for the Dutch Institute of Psychologists (NIP). Since 2006, Tinka Van Vuuren has also worked as senior adviser at APG/Loyalis. Her research concerns sustainable employment, employability, workability, vitality, work and health policies, sickness absence, job insecurity, active ageing, and mobility. She advises and conducts research for all kinds of work organizations, several employers' organizations, the Ministry of Labour and Social Affairs, and the Ministry of Education. She is (co)author of numerous scientific articles.

Marijke Verbruggen, KU Leuven, Belgium. Marijke Verbruggen, PhD, is Associate Professor at the Faculty of Business and Economics, KU Leuven. Her focal areas of interest are career development, work–life issues, person–environment fit, underemployment and unemployment. Her work has been published in international peer-reviewed journals including the *Journal of Vocational Behavior*, *Journal of Career Assessment* and *Gender, Work and Organization*.

Claartje J. Vinkenburg, VU University Amsterdam, the Netherlands. Claartje J. Vinkenburg, PhD, is Associate Professor of Organizational Behavior at VU University Amsterdam and works as an independent consultant. Her research, partly funded by the European Research Council, deals with gender and ethnic diversity in professional and academic careers, critically exploring the impact of implicit bias, normative beliefs, and discursive practices on selection and promotion processes, career patterns and outcomes. Claartje teaches Diversity in Organizations (MSc, HRM) and supervises various PhD candidates. She has written various book chapters and has published in the *Academy of Management Review*, *Journal of Social Issues*, and *Leadership Quarterly*.

Sara Zaniboni, University of Trento, Italy. Sara Zaniboni, PhD, is an Assistant Professor of Work and Organizational Psychology in the Department of Psychology and Cognitive Sciences, University of Trento. Her main research interests include ageing in the workplace, the retirement process, and work integration of people with mental disabilities. She has participated in national and international research on these topics. Dr Zaniboni has published in numerous international academic journals, such as the *European Journal of Work and Organizational Psychology*, *Organizational Psychology Review*, *International Journal of Manpower*, *Journal of Career Assessment*, *Anxiety, Stress & Coping*, *British Journal of Social Psychology*, *Psychiatric Rehabilitation Journal*, and *Journal of Occupational Rehabilitation*. She is a member of the editorial board of *Work, Aging and Retirement*.

Jelena Zikic, School of Human Resource Management, York University, Toronto, Canada. Jelena Zikic is an Associate Professor in the School of Human Resource Management at York University, Toronto. She developed her expertise in the area of career transitions, stress and coping. Her research interests focus on individual and organizational career management issues of diverse populations, migrants most recently. Her work has appeared in journals such as the *Journal of Organizational Behavior*, *Human Relations*, *Journal of Vocational Behavior* and *Journal of Occupational and Organizational Psychology*.

Preface

The origins of this project trace back to AoM Boston 2012 where we (the editors of this *Handbook*) started talking about 'our dream' to edit a *Handbook of Sustainable Careers*. In the same year, Ehnert and Wes came up with a special issue for *Management Revue* entitled 'Recent developments and future prospects on sustainable human resource management'. Over the months to come, through phone calls, Skype appointments, and real-life meetings in the Netherlands and Belgium our ideas became more and more concrete. Our main objective was to focus on a new line of career research, incorporating the perspective of *sustainability*.

Next to coming up with state-of-the-art theorizing and empirical work on sustainable careers, we wanted to operationalize the concept of *sustainable careers*, and, in response to the call by Barbara Lawrence (1984) to put careers in a historical perspective, our four-dimensional conceptualization was 'born'. Over the past year, we have exchanged our ideas about the evolutions in the four dimensions amongst ourselves, as well as with Michael, Barbara and Tim.

In embarking on our work, we decided, sitting together in Antwerp Management School, Belgium, to invite scholars from across the globe, as we wanted to hear the voices of colleagues, and to incorporate data from nations worldwide. To the best of our knowledge, this *Handbook* is the first to add a sustainability perspective to the concept of careers, hereby providing a more nuanced picture of how actors within different contexts (for example, in one's working organization, one's broader life sphere, and in the broader societal context) interact with one another, have their impact on careers and can affect the sustainability of careers over time. The variety of angles from which careers and the sustainability of careers are addressed throughout this *Handbook* responds to the need for a multi-dimensional perspective in the study of careers. Each chapter sheds a different yet complementary light on important elements in the study of sustainable careers. Careers are a complex phenomenon to which simple cause-and-effect models are not applicable. The contributions in this *Handbook* allow for a better understanding of the factors and dynamics that are relevant for understanding how careers can become more sustainable for the whole workforce.

The primary audience for this *Handbook* is advanced undergraduate, graduate, and doctoral students, as well as researchers in both academic and applied settings. In addition, organizational decision makers, HR managers and HR professionals, employee assistance programme representatives, career counsellors and public policy makers will have an interest in this *Handbook*. The disciplines of industrial and organizational psychology, occupational psychology, sociology, economics, management science, Human Resource Management and Human Resource Development studies, serve as the primary audience. Further, given that many chapters reflect on workers' employability, its stimulating and hindering factors throughout one's career, and interesting career outcomes of one's employability, this *Handbook* is useful for employees themselves in order to better understand possible pitfalls and challenges that they may encounter across the life- and career-span, and that may impact their productivity and well-being. As such, our focus was to support employees in finding ways to protect their career sustainability in both paid and volunteer roles, and to encourage all stakeholders involved to optimize their employability regardless of the age of the individual.

We owe particular thanks to a number of people, first of all Michael Arthur, Barbara Lawrence and Tim Hall for helping us to keep believing in our dream and for asking us the right questions to stimulate our thinking. We appreciate their involvement enormously by writing the concluding chapter for this *Handbook*, and by supporting us in our call for a future research agenda on sustainable careers building upon the work in this *Handbook*.

Antwerp Management School, Belgium, and the Radboud University, Institute for Management Research, Nijmegen, the Netherlands, gave us generous trust in our venture. There is a saying that 'luck is what happens when preparation meets opportunity'. Many thanks go to Edward Elgar Publishing, who gave us the opportunity to publish a *Handbook* on sustainable careers exactly when we started talking about our dream for editing such a *Handbook*, and who have supported us along all steps of this project. We would also like to warmly thank our family members for encouraging us as we pursued this challenging task, a task that we performed mainly during the evenings, nights and weekends, and which challenged us to address our personal meaning of a sustainable career. . . We are also very grateful to all of the authors in this *Handbook* for their contributions. As it was no problem eliciting their willingness to embark on this journey with us, we have ample proof that the field of career studies is 'alive and kicking'. We would like to invite scholars across the world to keep 'fastening their seat belts' more often, and to continue crossing our roads of career studies across the globe.

For Luna, Nando, Mona and Carl,
my true north when it comes to navigating my own career.
Ans De Vos, Antwerp, Belgium

I dedicate this book to my dearest mother,
Johanna Isabella Van der Heijden-Van Tuijl,
who is my true example and who always protects my sustainability.
In loving memory of my dearest father.
Beatrice I.J.M. Van der Heijden, Geffen, the Netherlands

1 Sustainable careers: introductory chapter

Beatrice I.J.M. Van der Heijden and Ans De Vos

TOWARDS A CONTEMPORARY CAREER APPROACH

The study of careers became established within the more general field of organization studies in the mid-1970s (see Moore et al., 2007, for an appealing overview of the historical roots of career theory). Since then, to cite Arthur et al. (1989), 'career theory has "gone legitimate". We (people who study careers) have become established. We have become a *field*' (p. xv). 'What was so remarkable about the 1989 *Handbook* was its highly creative approach' (Gunz and Peiperl, 2007, p. 2). Arthur et al. (1989) allowed the structure of the career field to emerge from the 'review chapters with a point of view' (p. xvii, cited in Gunz and Peiperl, 2007, p. 2).

Next, Arthur et al. launched their ground-breaking book *The New Careers: Individual Action & Economic Change* (1999), building upon Karl Weick's work on the *enactment* of careers (1996). From their book you can hear the voices of working people themselves, people from highly different socio-economic backgrounds, with different work histories and employment experiences, and reflecting the uncertainties and hardships in career patterns in the New Economy, which were being reported globally (see the preface of their book). These scholars show that traditional conceptions of careers were rooted in the stable conditions of the Industrial State model which has dominated the twentieth century and that new career models, better attuned to the New Economy of the late twentieth and early twenty-first centuries, are needed. With their work, the idea of careers as actions rather than structures was born, as means of learning rather than means of earning, and as boundaryless entities rather than constrained ones. As such, Arthur et al. (1999) responded to Barbara Lawrence's call for a historical perspective to be used while studying careers by pushing thinking about alternative explanations for phenomena, identifying more or less stable concepts, and expanding research horizons by suggesting new ways of studying old questions (Lawrence, 1984).

In 2007, Inkson's valuable contribution entitled *Understanding Careers: The Metaphors of Working Lives* appeared, and provided us with a unique framework of nine archetypical metaphors (inheritances, cycles, actions, fit, journeys, roles, relationships, resources and stories) to encapsulate the field of career studies, which he illustrated by means of more than 50 career cases. His endeavor stressed the need to study careers in a more complete, balanced and integrated way. Inkson (2007), and in the recently updated version Inkson et al. (2015), advocated the use of these metaphors as they provide a variety of lenses to view the phenomenon of careers and demonstrate the richness of the career concept.

In exactly the same year, and, in a similar vein, supporting the idea that careers should be studied using a wider approach, the *Handbook of Career Studies* by Gunz and Peiperl (2007) appeared, which explicitly focused on the concept as it relates to the world of work. The editors defined work as 'that which one does to make a living' (Gunz and

Peiperl, 2007, p. 4), and explicitly aimed to help reduce the fragmentation of the field's knowledge structure and facilitate scholars working on careers research to move toward a consensus about what really matters. We believe that their endeavor has indeed resulted in what they hoped for: 'greater interdependencies between research streams' (p. 8).

Our own empirical work on careers, their antecedents, both in terms of organizational as well as individual career initiatives, and their outcomes, has inspired us to explore the face validity of focusing on a new line in careers research, incorporating the perspective of *sustainability*. In today's New Economy, wherein uncertainties and hardships in career patterns are highly prevalent worldwide, focusing upon the sustainability of individuals' careers is of utmost importance. As workers have moved from an expectation of lifelong employment towards a focus on the need to protect their employability (Forrier and Sels, 2003; Fugate et al., 2004; Van der Heijden et al., 2009), it is important to increase our knowledge of those elements that contribute to sustainable careers for all workers, and to further our understanding of factors at different levels affecting this sustainability (De Vos and Gielens, 2014a; 2014b).

With this *Handbook*, we therefore intend to help close some knowledge gaps, as highlighted by Schein (2007, p. 576) in his afterword for the *Handbook of Career Studies*, by dealing with contemporary issues and dilemmas, such as the ever-increasing struggle to maintain a work–home balance, the impact of New Ways of Working, and the problems of later career and retirement, to mention but a few. Throughout the book, pertinent questions are addressed with respect to sustainability of contemporary careers, which aim to stimulate thinking and research on this topic.

Next, we will start with the conceptualization of *careers*, followed by an outline of four important elements characterizing the concept that have undergone important changes in recent years. Subsequently, we will go into the concept of *sustainable careers*. Finally, we will outline the *content of this Handbook* by putting the spotlight on every contribution, and by giving an overview of what our colleagues will offer you in the chapters that follow.

THE NEED FOR A NEW CAREER CONCEPT

A career is defined as the sequence of work experiences that evolves over the individual's life course (Arthur et al., 1989; Arthur et al., 1999; Greenhaus et al., 2010; Hall, 1976; 2002). Arthur et al. (1989) pointed out two central elements in this definition, namely 'work' and 'time' (p. 8). Building upon their conceptual work and the work by others on the changing nature of careers (for example, Arthur et al., 1999), we differentiate between four central elements in the definition of careers, namely the elements of *time*, *social space*, *agency* and *meaning*. Over the past decades, substantial evolutions have taken place in the world of work which have important implications for each of these elements, and which call for the reconsideration of the notion of contemporary careers, leading us to introduce the notion of 'sustainable careers'. We thereby aim to continue to respond to the call by Barbara Lawrence (1984) to put careers in a historical perspective in order to better understand what has changed in the time frame of careers, the social space in which careers take place, the agency with regard to careers, and the meaning of a career for the individual employee. Let us continue with an explanation of these four elements:

- *Time*: careers provide a 'moving perspective' (Hughes, 1958) on the unfolding interaction between a person and society (in Arthur et al., 1989, p. 8). That is to say, a career refers to the movement of a person through time, and hence, time is an inherent ingredient of every career. Over the past decades, there have been substantial changes in this element of time. One only has to think about changes in length of different career episodes or sequences, decreasing predictability of what will happen with one's career over time, even changes in the timing of when and where you do your work (cf. New Ways of Working), to understand that careers indeed are to be characterized as 'new' (see also Thijssen et al., 2008 who gave a historical overview and a critical analysis of the concept of employability). In addition, another important change in the time element of careers concerns its length. Especially in Europe, over the past decade there has been a change in mindset that careers should last longer, meaning that individuals face a longer career in terms of expected retirement age. This combination of longer careers with less predictable and, in many cases, shorter-term career sequences calls for a reconsideration of the traditional notion of a career. The disappearance of careers with a predictable length and order of sequences, which was more deterministic for individuals, has made room for more options and opportunities to shape one's career over time. Obviously, more options entail more choices to be made but also more uncertainties and hardships, as career scripts are becoming less clear.
- *Social space*: careers reflect the relationships between people and the providers of official positions, namely organizations or institutions, and how these relationships fluctuate over time (Arthur et al., 1989, p. 8). Careers are at the intersection between both, and as such are influenced by factors that stem from individuals' life spheres (family or one's broader life context) and by factors situated in the organization. Both, in turn, are situated within a broader societal context that is also affecting individuals' career experiences (Greenhaus and Kossek, 2014). That is to say, as a career refers to the movement of a person through social space as well, careers cannot be studied without considering the context with which they are inherently connected. This element of context has also undergone substantial changes over the past decades. Careers have moved from being bounded to being boundaryless (Arthur, 2014; DeFillippi and Arthur, 1994), as both the broader life and organizational context as well as the broader societal context of individuals and organizations have undergone substantial changes (think, for instance, of the increasing globalization, technological evolutions, changes in the nature of work, demographic changes like ageing of the working population, and the growing prevalence of dual career patterns, to give some examples). Obviously, these changes have made careers more complex. As an individual's career is no longer contained within a single or only a few employment settings over time, the 'career playing field' is seemingly endless (boundaryless). That is to say, the amount of choices individuals have to make across life spheres has expanded, yet, at the same time, we perceive an ever-increasing amount of unpredictability of career outcomes, and a decrease in job security (Lee et al., 2011). Otherwise stated, individuals may perceive more career opportunities, which, however, are in many cases at the risk of the sustainability of their careers.
- *Agency*: notwithstanding the many influential (structural) factors on all levels

(personal circumstances, job, organization, profession, society) that shape careers, a career is owned by an individual, and he or she is the one that has to idiosyncratically deal with, and respond to, stability and/or change in the world of work (Briscoe and Hall, 2006). We observe a general tendency to conceive of careers as more independent from organizations than they used to be in times of more predictability, stable growth, and employment contracts with a long-term perspective (for example, Arthur, 2014; Bidwell and Briscoe, 2010; Briscoe et al., 2006; Gubler et al., 2013; Mainiero and Sullivan, 2005). Contrary to the traditional organization-based career, where the organization had primary responsibility for managing individuals' careers, in contemporary careers individual agency is the key to continuous career success. The individual is considered as the primary owner of his or her career and this ownership comes together with an increased responsibility in a world wherein everything seems to be more complex, and with seemingly more choices than ever. All in all, contemporary careers are not easy to handle, and entail the need for individuals to focus on a longer-term approach instead of taking career decisions with a short-term view in mind, the need to integrate career decisions with other life domains instead of a one-sided approach, the need to align individual career norms and objectives with employer norms and objectives, and so on. To conclude, agency requires the development of a set of career competencies (knowing how, knowing why, knowing whom; Arthur et al., 1995). Moreover, individuals are not as rational in their career decisions as an overemphasis on individual agency might suggest (De Vos, 2013). Finally, this individual agency does not imply that other actors in the career field (organizations, institutions) no longer have any responsibility in terms of managing careers (De Vos and Gielens, 2014b).

- *Meaning*: careers are subject to change in terms of what they bring to an individual, not in the least in terms of the value of specific career outcomes, as nicely pointed out by Arthur et al. (1999) when describing the evolution of careers from 'means of earning to means of learning'. In a similar vein, Inkson (2007) reported that individuals can have many different conceptions of careers, as reflected in the different metaphors that people use to describe their careers. The 'new' careers literature stresses that with the gradual displacement of the traditional psychological contract, based upon an exchange of long-term employment for loyalty and upward progress, by a new employability-based psychological contract, the meaning of careers and career success has changed (Dries et al., 2008; Sullivan and Baruch, 2009). Careers are no longer a mere succession of related jobs, arranged in a hierarchy, through which persons move in an ordered sequence. Evolutions in the socio-economic context have diminished the occurrence of traditional, upwardly mobile careers and as such the experience of objective career success reflected in observable attainments such as pay, promotion and occupational status (Dries et al., 2008). With careers being defined as the evolving sequence of a person's work experiences over time (Arthur et al., 1989), subjective career success refers to career satisfaction about all aspects of these career experiences relevant to an individual. This implies that the meaning of career success will be determined by what one is realizing in comparison with one's internal career anchors (Schein, 1985). This makes the *meaning* of a career much more idiosyncratic than it used to be. This is both an opportunity, as career choices can be made in accordance with one's inner life values, but also a challenge, as individuals have to derive satisfaction and fulfillment from their own anchors, rather than from how others evaluate them. In combination with the three elements described above, in an increasingly unpredictable and complex world of work, individuals are viewed as having primary responsibility for their own career and career success, in line with their subjective values. Yet, at the same time, underlying this new view on career success is that employability has become a core element and a critical vehicle for attaining whatever type of subjective success criterion that individuals might strive for.

All in all, we believe that these changes with regard to time, social space, agency and meaning have important implications for careers, the practice of career management, and the field of career studies. Contemporary career research departed from this complex and constantly changing socio-economic environment and has introduced new career concepts, such as the boundaryless career (Arthur, 1994), protean career (Hall, 1976; 2002), kaleidoscope career (Mainiero and Sullivan, 2005), customized career (Valcour et al., 2007), and post-corporate career (Peiperl and Baruch, 1997). These new career concepts respond to changing employment relationships, for example, by stressing boundaryless careers or the importance of individual agency and personal meaning in careers. Over the past decades, the theory building and stream of empirical research in these fields have significantly contributed to our understanding of careers and the factors affecting careers and career outcomes.

However, in this *Handbook*, we go one step further by adding the perspective of 'sustainability', thereby incorporating evolutions in the four dimensions described above. As such, we do not so much aim to replace the contemporary career concepts, we rather advocate a fresh perspective on careers that recognizes the complexity of the career concept, thereby elaborating on these existing career concepts. For instance, whilst individual agency and personal meaning are central to the protean career concept, adding long-term implications of career choices as reflected in the time perspective, and contextual constraints as reflected in the dimension of social space can yield further insights into the sustainability of careers. In a similar vein, the concept of boundaryless careers suggests an independent stance of individuals towards their careers. Adding a sustainability perspective to this would provide a more nuanced picture of how actors within different contexts (for example, in one's working organization, one's broader life sphere, and in the broader societal context) interact with one another, have their impact on careers and can affect the sustainability of careers over time.

A more recent but growing line of careers research addresses the concept of employability as a prerequisite for career success (see, for instance, Van der Heijde and Van der Heijden, 2006). In line with theories on employability, we advocate a broader approach to careers that recognizes the challenges and pitfalls that are inherent in it. Adding the individual's employability (that is, career potential) to the range of interesting career outcomes, in addition to objective and subjective career success indicators that have been prevalent in research up to now, is another example of how the sustainability perspective might be incorporated in careers research. Taken together, career reality is complex and this implies that research questions are complex, and ideally need to address the different dimensions that have been distinguished above. Careers form a complex mosaic of objective experiences and subjective evaluations, unfolding over time and within an increasingly complex environment. The rich variety of possible sequences of experiences making up an individual's career implies that we may encounter examples of both a 'positive spiral', wherein career episodes over time become enriched, and a 'negative spiral', wherein career episodes may be characterized by, for instance, demotivating and/or unrewarding experiences. The complexity of our world today entails many opportunities for individuals to make choices in line with their inner drives, but yet there is also an ample list of factors (as shown by the contributors to this *Handbook*) that might put careers 'at risk' for many individuals in today's society. Moreover, what might appear to be a 'successful' or 'satisfying' career in the short run does not always turn out to remain so in the long run. For instance, an overly ambitious young graduate might face a burnout during his thirties due to constantly running after new challenges, and this might put the long-term success of his career at risk. Or another employee might feel satisfied with a repetitive job without training or development opportunities, which allows her to combine work easily with family life, but then, unfortunately, faces the reality of her skills having become obsolete at a certain point in time, leading to job loss. These are just a few examples demonstrating that a fresh perspective on contemporary careers is urgently needed. First, this perspective needs to be multi-dimensional as this entails opportunities to study contemporary careers using a non-normative, yet rather flexible framework, clearly depicting the increasing variety in careers. Second, to fully understand careers, a long-term perspective is needed.

As mentioned by Arthur et al. (1989) in the preface of their *Handbook*, careers 'have to do with the long-term issues associated with working in organizations' (p. xv). Arthur et al. (1989) posited that career studies might suffer from the fact that many scholars address increasingly narrow and decreasingly innovative questions, and called for 'a good shot in the arm' in order to help rejuvenate career theory and to help us adapt to the dynamic character of modern industrial society (p. 7). Fortunately, a lot has happened over time, and career scholars have dealt with many appealing questions over the past decades. Still we believe that, exactly a quarter of an era later, time has come to give 'another good shot in the arm' responding to the new dynamics of current industrial society. This is why we introduce the concept of 'sustainable careers', yet only after we have briefly summarized some key notions on the concept of 'sustainability'.

SUSTAINABILITY

In Merriam-Webster, 'sustainable' is referred to as things that are 'able to last or continue for a long time' and that are 'able to be used without being depleted or destroyed', as well as 'methods of using resources that support their conservation and renewal' (http://www.merriam-webster.com/dictionary/sustainable). The UN defines 'sustainability' as: 'a general worldview according to which people should strive to fulfill their needs in a manner such that the ability of future generations to fulfill their needs is not endangered' (Docherty et al., 2009, p. 3). In a similar vein, Latzke and colleagues (Chapter 4, this volume) defined sustainability as development that meets the need of the present without compromising the ability of future generations to meet their own needs (WCED,

1987, p. 43; cf. Ehnert and Harry, 2012, p. 223), (see De Lange et al., 2015, for a historical overview of the concept of 'sustainability' and its relevant components).

De Lange et al. (2015) who explicitly aimed to conceptualize 'sustainability at work', signaled the recent addition of the notion of human (also labeled as social) to the sustainability debate (Garavan and McGuire, 2010, p. 491), and cited Pfeffer (2010) who referred to human sustainability as follows: 'Just as physical sustainability considers the consequences of organizational activity for material or physical resources, social sustainability might consider how organizational activities affect people's physical and mental health and well-being – the stress of work practices on the human system' (p. 35). An exemplary definition in this regard was provided by Carl Holling (2001), who defined human sustainability as: 'the capacity to create, test and maintain adaptive capability' (p. 390). Holling's definition is related to the operationalization of the concept of employability by Van der Heijde and Van der Heijden (2006): 'the capacity of continuously fulfilling, acquiring or creating of work through the optimal use of competences' (p. 453). The latter suggests an important responsibility of the individual employee in creating, testing and maintaining his or her own work capacity or ability. In a similar vein, Oldham and Hackman (2010) stressed the increasing importance of personal initiative of workers to successfully progress or adjust one's work capacity or ability across time by shaping or customizing their jobs in order to protect their sustainability at work (for example, via job crafting; Wrzesniewski and Dutton, 2001).

SUSTAINABLE CAREERS

In view of the above, we introduce the concept of *sustainable careers* and define it as *the sequence of an individual's different career experiences, reflected through a variety of patterns of continuity over time, crossing several social spaces, and characterized by individual agency, herewith providing meaning to the individual.*

- Different patterns of *continuity over time* means that in the sequence of different kinds of career experiences, periods of employment can be interchanged by periods of part-time work, volunteering, unemployment, sabbatical leave, care-giving, and so on. In responding to individual aspirations, capabilities, needs and expectations with regard to work and personal life, satisfying, healthy, meaningful and productive career episodes (or experiences) are obtained and may be better protected thanks to career adaptability and employability-enhancing competencies. This continuity is preserved by taking into consideration consequences of career decisions over time. In line with the general notion of sustainability outlined above, continuity implies that present needs are being fulfilled without compromising future needs. A career is, in essence, dynamic. It is a cycle of events and decisions that determine the work people are doing, the changes they make from one job to another (within or across organizations), or transitions between paid work and other statuses (for example, non-paid work, unemployment, temporary leave, and retirement). These events, decisions and their outcomes (that is, subjective and objective career success) are intertwined. Given this dynamism, sustainability might have strategic potential as a concept for careers, and aligning sustainability to careers might allow us to better understand what is sustainability at work, how we can foster sustainability at work, and which determinants play a role in maintaining and further developing sustainable careers.

- *Social space.* It goes without saying that the previously mentioned substantial changes in the career context, that is the economic and broader societal environment and the way organizations operate, do have effects upon the *social space* wherein careers unfold. Careers are enacted within and across different types of contexts (work, home, friends, leisure) (Greenhaus and Kossek, 2014), and they have become more boundaryless (Arthur, 1994; 2014). Continuity here implies that influences of actors and factors in the social space, as well as the choices individuals make regarding (the combination of) the different social spaces they live in, may impact the sustainability of their careers. There is an urgent need to gain more insight into the impact on employees' careers of the growing unpredictability of the economic environment, of New Ways of Working and new types of organizations, dual career couples, and the need to care for elderly parents, to give some examples. How can different stakeholders, residing in the individual's broader social space (such as employers, employees, and one's relatives), help to protect and enhance sustainable careers across the life-span, despite – or maybe thanks to – these evolutions?
- As reflected in the dimension of 'social space' elaborated above, the organizational and broader life context will affect individuals' career choices. By *agency* we mean that how the career develops over time is the result of many choices made by the individual owner of the career, not the mere consequence of external influences and constraints stemming from this social space. Choices are made in line with the individual's career and private needs and aspirations, yet, obviously, these have to be aligned with organizational (employer) objectives and cannot be separated from the individual's broader life context in order to balance or compromise between (opposing) the individual's work, career and private interests, on the one hand, and (opposing) the employer's interests on the other hand (Van der Heijde and Van der Heijden, 2006; Van der Heijden et al., 2009). Sustainability in careers will stem from alignment, from mutual benefits for the individual and organization, as well as mutual benefits for the individual and his or her broader life context. Given that individuals are the primary owners of their careers, they are 'in charge' of expressing their interests and needs to all stakeholders involved. Yet, given the many social spaces in which careers are involved, over time this has not become an easy task. We advocate that sustainable career management is only possible if employers and employees, and all other stakeholders involved, strive for more openness in communication about expectations regarding work and personal development (see also Van der Heijden, 2005). However, given the pluriformity of the workforce and the increasing differentiation in individual aspirations, capabilities, career competencies and employability needs, individuals need to steer their career development by accepting and reflecting agency. Agency is also a timely topic when considering the sustainability of careers for those groups who are more vulnerable on the labor market (for example, young workers without qualifications, unemployed older workers, to name just a few). The latter often experience a lack of agency due to a lack of required (career) competencies, or due to the

negative experiences they encounter when putting this agency into practice without the desired result of obtaining a job.

- *Meaning*. Nowadays, careers entail a continuous need to produce new expertise, while, at the same time, they create new opportunities for development. The qualifications that are required for a job are becoming increasingly complex while, simultaneously, the 'half life' of these qualifications is becoming increasingly shorter (Van der Heijden, 2005). Employees who are able to make their careers sustainable and who are able to survive the current needs are the ones with not only the most up-to-date knowledge and skills, but also the capability to continuously build up the new expertise requirements, whilst at the same time deriving *meaning* from their professional activities. The more pluriform the working population, the increasing importance of other areas of life, such as 'quality time' with family and friends, leisure, differences in coping style, personality, and the increasing individualization, to mention but a few, all urge us to prevent thinking in categories regarding retirement age, career peaks, career success, learning needs and so on. Employees have totally different ideas on and answers to career-related questions like: How long do I have to go on for? How long will I be allowed to? How long do I still have? How long do I want to go on for? That is to say, individual employees attach highly different values (or meaning) to different career sequences and outcomes.

Unarguably, the variety in possible answers to these questions supports the notion to elaborate research on careers incorporating the dimensions of continuity over time, social space, agency and meaning. That is to say, sustainable careers are the ones that respect the pluriformity in the working population. Moreover, while earlier work seems to focus upon professional workers, in our approach we take an 'inclusive' perspective on careers. Careers are not the exclusive domain of professional workers, but instead apply to all individuals as part of the workforce. Challenges with regard to sustainability of careers might differ depending on the segment of the workforce (for example, depending on the individual's education, occupation/profession or position), yet the notion of careers applies to everyone and this also holds when studying sustainable careers.

We would like to emphasize that the focus of our definition lies on the individual, yet, as indicated above, a career that is sustainable implies a balance between individual and organizational needs, and hence should imply continuity not only for the individual but also for the organization. In this sense, we bring the organization back into the definition of careers, albeit while attaching a broader meaning to it than usual. Nowadays, there are many different types of organizations and the range is very broad (from the typical 'GE' type of company, at one end of the continuum, versus an alliance of some freelance persons, at the other end), implying that sustainability of the individual's career is highly dependent upon the ability one has to align individual needs with the needs of the specific type of organization with which one is employed. As such, we turn back to Schein's (1978) conception of careers as a matching process between individual and organizational expectations.

TOWARDS MORE SCHOLARLY WORK ON SUSTAINABLE CAREERS

We believe that, in line with current socio-economic evolutions and the increasing need to better understand factors that might contribute to sustainability at work, the boundaryless career concept defined as 'sequences of job opportunities that go beyond the boundaries of single employment settings' (DeFillippi and Arthur, 1994, p. 307; DeFillippi and Arthur, 1996, p. 116) still forms a rich and relevant framework, allowing sustainability to be studied. This ought to be done by going beyond the study of career sequences from the limited perspective of direct physical mobility (personal conversation with Michael Arthur, 5 July 2014; Arthur, 2014), and taking the previously outlined multi-dimensional perspective incorporating continuity over time, social space, agency and meaning. This also means that we elaborate on ideas from protean career theory (Hall, 2002) by stressing the importance of meaning and individual ownership of careers, while at the same time acknowledging the contextual constraints (as reflected in the other three dimensions of our conceptualization). Obviously, one can come up with similar lines of reasoning building upon the other contemporary career concepts, such as kaleidoscope career, customized career, and post-corporate career.

As such, we advocate the rich approach outlined by Arthur (2014), who described a boundaryless career as typified by the following six characteristics: (a) moves across the boundaries of separate employers; (b) occupational careers drawing validation from outside any single employer; (c) careers sustained by external networks or information; (d) careers where traditional hierarchical reporting relationships were broken; (e) rejection of career opportunities for personal or family reasons; and (f) careers where people 'may perceive a boundaryless future, regardless of structural constraints' (p. 3).

The 'boundaryless career' concept referring to careers as actions rather than structures, as means of learning rather than means of earning, and as boundaryless entities rather than constrained ones (Arthur et al., 1999) forms a sound basis or starting point to help individual employees understand the ample amount of opportunities all parties involved have to shape careers in order to make them sustainable. The notion of a boundaryless career seems to depart from an 'optimistic' or 'positive' perspective, implicitly stating that – whatever conception of 'boundaryless' individuals might enact in their career – the concept is associated with positive career outcomes. However, we believe that the complexity of today's world calls for the need to take a broader and long-term view, incorporating both stimulating and hindering factors in the light of sustainable career outcomes. While aiming to build upon the notion of 'independence from, rather than dependence on, traditional organizational career arrangements' (Arthur and Rousseau, 1996), we have invited the contributing authors to reflect on present-day careers, and their possible influencing factors, while focusing upon their ideas about sustainability at work.

According to Latzke and colleagues (Chapter 4, this volume), a sustainable career is viable (renewable, flexible, integrative), a sound career strategy should be long term, and career investments are based on a holistic foundation, but also dependent on the other agents' strategies and behaviors. They state: 'Even the most viable, holistic and long-term strategy may fail if the significant others' behavior is at odds with a sustainable destiny in the field. On top of this, in contexts where mere survival is the ultimate career goal [. . .], questions of sustainability do not even arise'.

A sustainable career is thus one that endures over time and that is characterized by development, conservation and renewal of the working individual's career-related resources, including human and social capital (for example, skills, credentials, reputation, relationships) as well as personal characteristics such as proactivity and resilience that aid in career self-management (for example, Arthur and Kram, 1989; Granrose and Portwood, 1987; Parker et al., 2010; Pazy, 1988) (Valcour, Chapter 2, this volume).

Building on the general notion of sustainability, sustainability in careers implies protecting and fostering (rather than depleting) human and career development with a focus on balance and renewal (Newman, 2011). Correspondingly, Fleisher et al. (Chapter 6, this volume) stated that 'sustainable career management entails increasing employees' awareness for career capital acquisition, stimulating them in making use of these resources, and having them reflect on how they can benefit from these in their job or future career'.

If we consider the concept of sustainable careers across the life-span, it is obvious that sustainability appears to be increasingly problematic in many key stages of the career life cycle (Greenhaus and Kossek, 2014). For example, more and more career starters are facing serious problems in finding employment in their early career phase, while at the same time endangering their employability by a lack of learning opportunities in the workplace. In addition, older adults, coping with late career issues, are being let go years before they planned to retire as industries are restructured and jobs are changing at an ever-increasing rate. As regards employees facing mid-career issues, parents, caregivers for elders, and many highly-talented individuals (especially women) are finding it increasingly difficult to synthesize family demands with careers and leadership roles (Gautun and Hagen, 2010). Zaniboni et al.'s definition (Chapter 18, this volume) of sustainable careers provides a clear example of incorporating this life-span perspective into conceptualizing the concept: 'a career path that fits with the needs and aspirations of the person, together with the opportunities and constraints of organizations and societies. In particular, regarding older workers, this could mean staying longer in the labor market and staying satisfied, engaged, productive and healthy'.

De Hauw and Greenhaus (Chapter 15, this volume) defined a sustainable career as a career in which employees remain healthy, productive, happy and employable throughout its course and that fits into their broader life context. This definition is based upon the work of Greenhaus and Kossek (2014) and Kossek et al. (2014), who stated that a sustainable career has the following essential characteristics: (a) is successfully integrated into a satisfying personal and family life that fits with one's core and career and life values; (b) provides employees a sense of sufficient security to meet economic needs and well-being; (c) comprises flexibility and capacity to suit one's changing needs and interests; and (d) is characterized by renewability such that an individual has regular opportunities for rejuvenation.

Given the theoretical outline that has been given above, we may conclude that different trends are observable in these reflections. First, the trend of individualism and individual agency. Second, the increasing awareness of the impact of the organizational, broader life context, and societal context when studying and enhancing sustainability in careers. Therefore, we advocate an integrative approach that highlights the role and interconnectedness of multiple actors (that is, individual employees, employers, organizations, and other stakeholders) (see also De Lange et al., 2015). Notwithstanding the individual responsibility for sustainable careers, organizations should also be actively engaged in protecting and enhancing sustainability at work. That is to say, the efforts and activities of both employees and employers should be carefully aligned in order to come up with life-span-aware and diversity-friendly sustainable career management.

Moreover, we would like to call for a non-normative framework aimed at enhancing healthy, prosperous, productive and challenging careers that are beneficial for both parties involved (see the bullet point above on the dimension of Meaning for more specific thoughts in this regard). Sustainable careers are built upon the notion that they should allow individuals to have positive career experiences over the long term in ways that promote organizational and individual effectiveness (Herman and Lewis, 2012; Kossek et al., 2014). Therefore, in our opinion, mutual understanding between employee and employer (in particular direct management parties) is key in order to respond to the above-mentioned pluriformity of the workforce and to align employees' individual aspirations, capabilities and expectations with regard to work and private life with the employer's goals and expectations (see also Van der Heijden, 2005).

The focus of this *Handbook* is on the individual employee's career and its sustainability. Across the different chapters this career concept is considered through different lenses, including meso- and macro-level changes that might influence the micro-level of individual careers. However, the macro- and meso-level in themselves do not form part of this *Handbook*. Particularly, we follow the conceptualization of the career as an individual's construction – through sense-making – of their experiences in their work as well as their broader (private) life. As such, careers comprise a constant interplay of external events and individual actions developing over time (Lee et al., 2011). Similarly, Valcour (Chapter 2, this volume) refers to a so-called struggle 'to find work that fits their skills and interests, to keep learning and developing, to manage both work and personal responsibilities, and to achieve security and stability in the midst of a dynamic and often difficult business and labor market environment' (individual perspective) in combination with the struggle of 'employers [that] need to find ways to attract, retain, motivate, develop and manage employees that are cost-effective and responsive to both the needs of the business and the needs and preferences of employees'.

To conclude, in line with Valcour, we plead for far more attention to the alignment of career-related needs and goals of employees and organizations which come together in the notion of a sustainable career. It goes without saying that the contributing authors to this *Handbook* have truly helped us in shaping our ideas on sustainable careers as well, and, as such, this introductory chapter shows that the concept is under construction.

OUTLINE OF THIS *HANDBOOK*

In this introductory chapter we have dealt with our conceptualization of 'sustainable careers', and advocated an integral perspective wherein both the importance of individual responsibility and (broader) contextual factors are taken into account. Moreover, we have given an overview of different factors and ingredients that ought to form the basis for contemporary approaches both in research and practice aimed at maintaining and enhancing sustainability at work. Valcour's contribution helps us to better understand the concept of sustainable careers, its responsible parties, and possible outcomes. She comes up with an appealing categorization of four primary attributes of sustainable careers: (1) alignment of work with the individual's strengths, interests and values; (2) ongoing learning and renewal; (3) security via employability; and (4) work–life fit over the life course. Next, she moves to a discussion of possible consequences of these attributes, and differentiates between four core objectives of talent management: (1) maximum yield on human capital value; (2) continuous updating of organizational competencies; (3) stability via adaptability; and (4) organizational commitment and retention. Herewith, she explicitly supports our notion that the crafting of sustainable careers within organizations occurs at the *intersection between individuals and organizations*, and that in the case of a collaborative partnership between both parties, advantageous outcomes are attainable.

The chapter by Buyken and colleagues goes into the fostering role that career adaptability of employees can play in the light of constructing sustainable careers. In addition to presenting an interesting *multi-dimensional operationalization of the concept*, their contribution responds to the need for taking up a *life-span perspective* in contemporary career research. Specifically, they discuss career adaptability by dealing with employees in different life transitions and career stages. Moreover, both the individual and (broader) societal perspective are taken into account, herewith complying with our call for this mutual responsibility perspective in research on sustainable careers. Latzke and associates, in their contribution on relational career capital, add the importance of the *relational dimension* to research and practice on sustainable careers. The authors stress that using a *holistic view*, wherein viable investments in building up career capital use a *long-term strategy*, is the key for sustainable career management. Their Bourdieuian-inspired concept of career capital is built upon the idea that, in comparison with traditional views of career capital, the complex interrelation between individual agency and the social structure should be emphasized in order to enhance our understanding of the value of career capital. Specifically, they focus upon empirical work on the value of career capital by studying business school graduates across several career fields. Bozionelos also adds the *relational perspective* to the study of sustainable careers and deals with the value of social capital (that is, resources that become available via relationship ties in the workplace and the society) in the light of individual career prospects, over and above other forms of capital, including human capital. He goes into specific career activities, such as mentoring relationships and network ties, and how these contribute to social capital. Moreover, Bozionelos critically reflects on the tensions that utilization of social capital for career benefit might cause by comparing the interests of individuals or circumscribed groups versus the interests of the wider collective, and cautions for a 'dark side' to it. Fleisher and colleagues proceed with enhancing our insight into the value of the *relational dimension* in sustainable careers research and practice, and advocate that employees' engagement in corporate volunteering initiatives may be beneficial in the light of *career capital building*. Their qualitative case study focuses on the importance of volunteering initiatives for individual workers' psychological, human and social capital, which they may use, in turn, to contribute to organizational culture, capabilities and connections. In addition, in the light of the *balance dimension* to sustainable careers, from their contribution, we may conclude that volunteering experiences might be beneficial for both individual career outcomes as well as for further organizational development. Egold and Van Dick add to the scholarly work regarding the *relational perspective* to the study of sustainable careers and suggest that identification, disidentification, ambivalent identification and neutral identification, on the one hand, with an organization or a professional network, and/or occupational groupings, on the other hand, are important aspects that might explain career outcomes related to sustainability at work (that is, job satisfaction, well-being and work engagement). In their empirical work, they moreover deal with potential antecedents of identification, that is, need for identification, positive and negative affectivity, tenure, intra-role conflict, role ambiguity and individualism. They herewith provide us with empirical proof for the importance of including the relational dimension within future work on sustainable careers. In a different vein, Richardson and Kelliher add a further operationalization of the *relational dimension* of the sustainable career concept. Their large-scale empirical work explores the implications of developments in technology that facilitate remote workers' interaction with colleagues, managers and customers. In addition to meeting formal performance targets, this study found a perceived need to maintain and enhance visibility to ensure career progression and continued employment. Richardson and Kelliher critically reflect on the implications of these outcomes in the light of current HR policies related to sustainable careers. Their contribution is important in the light of the increasing implementation of New Ways of Working across the globe. Vinkenburg and associates come up with a conceptual integrative *framework on sustainability in combining career and care*. They plead for exposing, challenging and changing underlying normative and gendered beliefs about ideal workers and ideal parents or care providers, as the interplay between normative beliefs, behavior or 'choice', and career outcomes has important consequences in the light of possibilities to promote sustainability and true *flexibility* in combining career and care. Semeijn et al. provide a framework for individual (being the micro-level dimension) sustainable labor participation, in terms of its components employability, vitality and workability. However, when discussing the impact of possible determinants of sustainable labor participation, they take *a broader view* building upon the Job Demands–Resources Model, and differentiate between what *employees (micro-level)* and *employers (meso-level)* can do to realize more sustainable organizational practices. De Cuyper and colleagues deal with the relationship between felt job insecurity and perceived employability, both being important characteristics reflecting negative and positive sides of the concept of sustainable careers. They conclude that in order to better understand issues of causality in this relationship, multiple mediators as well as personal and structural factors as potential moderators are to be included. Herewith, they support our view that sustainable careers should be studied at the *intersection between individual employees and organizations*, and that a *mutual responsibility perspective* should be taken. Verbruggen and associates examined antecedents (career competences) and outcomes (perceived employability) of two aspects of job mobility (boundaryless mindset and organizational mobility preference) using a sample of unemployed job seekers. They concluded that the relationship between psychological mobility and career outcomes might be significantly different across different groups in the labor market. Herewith the importance of including the *broader context dimension* in research and practice on sustainable careers is further backed up. It seems that a multidimensional perspective to sustainable careers indeed helps us to better facilitate individual career management. Van Dam and colleagues, in their contribution on the role of employee adaptability, proactivity and goal striving in the light of sustainable careers, first stress the individual responsibility in modern careers. On the other hand, they support our *mutual responsibility perspective* by arguing that career sustainability requires adaptive behavior that is aimed at establishing or restoring the balance between the goals, interests, values and expectations of both the organization and the individual employee. Guest and Rodrigues, in their contribution on the importance of career control, provide further support for our notion on careers being at the *intersection between individuals and organizations, and incorporating a (broader) context.* The authors argue that career preferences and attitude, personality and human capital help to shape career decisions, yet that the latter will be influenced by external factors, such as parents and schooling, employing organizations, work–family issues, legislative factors, as well as macro-contextual factors. It is at this intersection between the individual and the organization where the potential for conflict over career control might evolve. Their empirical work indicates that career control is associated with career sustainability, measured as higher job, career and life satisfaction. Moving to the *life sphere domain,* De Hauw and Greenhaus go into the importance of work–home balance as a driver for career decisions. They come up with an appealing model, illustrated by means of clear examples of career decisions that individual employees may use, such as moving upwards, becoming self-employed, or working part-time, to protect or restore their career sustainability. Herewith, the *diversity dimension* is added to our thinking about contemporary careers in terms of an increased variety in possible career patterns. Mauno et al.'s empirical quantitative work, which also goes into the importance of the *life sphere domain,* indicates that atypical work arrangements, including non-standard working hours and temporary work, do not automatically imply negative family-related outcomes. However, there are certain risk factors (such as night shifts, and small children at home) that are positively associated with negative family-related outcomes (such as work–home conflict, marital instability, and children's socio-emotional or cognitive problems). Obviously, their outcomes are highly relevant as negative family-related outcomes have important implications in the light of career sustainability. Aalbers and De Lange emphasize the importance of *healthy lifestyle and cognitive functioning* in the light of sustainable careers. In addition to describing the most frequently used behavior change theories, the current state of lifestyle intervention research and its many applications, the authors discuss different types of interventions, how they have been developed in practice, and go into appealing examples of eHealth interventions. They conclude with some insightful thoughts on how more *personalized care* may help us in sustainable career management across the life-span. Changing to the *time dimension* of sustainable careers, in this particular case life-stage, the work by Zaniboni and colleagues goes into the influence of job characteristics. They call for more work in the field of sustainable careers by taking a *broader view incorporating the importance of both individual effort, as well as organizational interventions,* in particular focusing on the role of job characteristics in the light of promoting successful ageing at work. Herewith, in addition to taking a *multi-dimensional approach to sustainable careers,* they also stress the *mutual responsibility perspective.* Schalk and colleagues continue to increase our insight into sustainable career management in the second half of the career (herewith touching upon the *diversity dimension* in career research) by focusing on specific issues that are prominent in the second half of the career, such as the difference in motives, career perspectives, the role of stereotypes, and health issues. They stress that career sustainability is only possible in the event of a good fit between work and employee, and requires active efforts from both parties, that is employee and organization (by means of sound HR activities). They highlight particular challenges that women workers have to deal with in order to develop a sustainable career. Bal, in his search for ways to enable older workers to continue working, stresses the importance of *individualization of career arrangements*, and herewith supports our view of using a *non-normative framework in the management of sustainable careers*. Specifically, he goes into the added value of idiosyncratic deals (or I-deals) for retaining older workers' motivation and performance. In addition, his contribution is in line with our plea for incorporating the (broader) context. Supportive climate, psychological processes that occur within the worker, and fairness in the distribution of negotiated deals across the organization are all dealt with. De Prins and colleagues introduce a broader scope by moving from a single career perspective to a more integrated HRM and Corporate Social Responsibility (CSR) perspective. Their contribution definitely adds to the literature on contemporary careers by adopting a *critical reflection on present-day dominant HRM practices, systems and models*. They refer to sustainable career management as a specific domain of HRM that brings Respect, Openness and Continuity into career management by *balancing short- and long-term employee needs*. De Coen and colleagues move to the 'final' stage in sustainable career management and deal with the transition that employees go through when they face retirement. Specifically, they investigate how career competencies (self-awareness and adaptability) influence the intention to retire through their impact on self-directedness, career satisfaction and employability. From their empirical work they have found that self-awareness and adaptability increase self-directedness, which, in turn, relates positively to external employability and career satisfaction. The latter two appear to decrease retirement intention, and herewith are important career indicators in the light of sustainability at *the end of career span*. Adaptability thereby outweighs the impact of self-awareness. Froidevaux and Hirschi add to our understanding of how to ensure a 'smooth' transition to retirement by focusing on the role of meaning in life for retirees and meaningful work for older workers who are close to retirement. Building upon quotations from qualitative research, they describe ways to promote meaningful work for older workers and how to create a new meaning or to pursue a previous meaning as a retiree, and discuss different roles that individuals, organizations and career counselors can play in this regard. In addition to advocating a *multi-actor perspective*, they discuss the importance of the *dimensions of continuity and personal agency* as the building blocks of sustainable careers. Baruch comes up with a novel perspective on internal and external labor markets (within and outside organizations) that supports our notion of the importance of including *the broader labor market context in career research*. He discusses paradoxes, such as the co-existence of stable and dynamic labor markets or the existence of so-called different 'rules of the game' for different labor market segments (across professions, sectors and geographies). Next, he explores the potential of the concept of the ecosystem for understanding and managing sustainable careers. Bernhard-Oettel and Näswall continue to increase our insight into how to protect sustainability in careers across labor market transfers (and add to our understanding of the broader labor market context dimension), by dealing with career continuance and competency transfer in the context of re-employment coaching. Based upon their expertise, they discuss the importance of job context and content similarity for successful competency transfer. In addition, they go into the influence of individuals' competency profile, their willingness to transfer their competencies, as well as factors which either facilitate or hinder competency transfer. Stone and Jawahar's contribution on the significance of task, citizenship and counter-productive performance behaviors for sustainable career development in organizational settings comprises exemplary work that illustrates the need to study careers at the *inter-section between individuals and organizations*. Their fascinating outcomes, which have far-reaching consequences in the light of our specific careers, being academics, is important as it introduces the idea of a possible 'spillover' of the importance of predictors across life and career domains, and calls for more longitudinal research to better understand the impact in the light of sustainability in careers. Briscoe goes into the classroom setting and provides us with very interesting ideas on educational approaches for developing and maintaining careers for student-practitioners in a sustainable fashion. He emphasizes the independent and interactive roles of both the educators and student-practitioners, and he stresses the need to take a long-term view when having a dialogue on career development. He advises that the latter should comprise exchanges on identity, values, skills, experience, history and behaviors when trying to understand one's present and past, and outlines how to respond to the environment in order to create sustainable careers. Obviously, Briscoe touches upon all four elements of our conceptualization (time, social space, ownership and meaning).

To conclude, just as we approached our fellow authors to contribute to this *Handbook*, we also aim to invite scholars to continue working in this niche of career research, and to add new elements (or dimensions) to the definition of sustainable careers. Obviously, only time will tell us how sustainable our current thinking on careers is. We do hope, however, that by sharing our notions on sustainable careers, we will encourage many scholars to continue empirical work in this important knowledge field.

REFERENCES

Arthur, M.B. (1994). The boundaryless career: A new perspective for organizational inquiry. *Journal of Organizational Behavior*, 15(4), 295–306.

Arthur, M.B. (2014). The boundaryless career at 20: Where do we stand and where can we go? *Career Development International*, 19(6).

Arthur, M.B., Claman, P.H. and DeFillippi, R.J. (1995). Intelligent enterprise, intelligent careers. *The Academy of Management Executive*, 9(4), 7–20.

Arthur, M.B., Hall, D.T. and Lawrence, B.S. (1989). Generating new directions in career theory: The case for a transdisciplinary approach. In M.B. Arthur, D.T. Hall and B.S. Lawrence (eds), *Handbook of Career Theory* (pp. 7–25). Cambridge, UK: Cambridge University Press.

Arthur, M.B., Inkson, K. and Pringle, J.K. (eds) (1999). *The New Careers: Individual Action & Economic Change*. London: Sage Publications.

Arthur, M.B. and Kram, K.E. (1989). Reciprocity at work: The separate, yet inseparable possibilities for individual and organizational development. In M.B. Arthur, D.T. Hall and B.S. Lawrence (eds), *Handbook of Career Theory* (pp. 292–312). Cambridge, UK: Cambridge University Press.

Arthur, M.B. and D.M. Rousseau (eds) (1996). *The Boundaryless Career: A New Employment Principle for a New Organizational Era*. New York: Oxford University Press.

Bidwell, M. and Briscoe, F. (2010). The dynamics of interorganizational careers. *Organization Science*, 21(5), 1034–53.

Briscoe, J.P. and Hall, D.T. (2006). The interplay of boundaryless and protean careers: Combinations and implications. *Journal of Vocational Behavior*, 69(1), 4–18.

Briscoe, J.P., Hall, D.T. and Frautschy DeMuth, R.L. (2006). Protean and boundaryless careers: An empirical exploration. *Journal of Vocational Behavior*, 69(1), 30–47.

DeFillippi, R.J. and Arthur, M.B. (1994). The boundaryless career: A competency-based perspective. *Journal of Organizational Behavior*, 15(4), 307–24.
DeFillippi, R.J. and Arthur, M.B. (1996). Boundaryless contexts and careers: A competency-based perspective. In M.B. Arthur and D.M. Rousseau (eds), *The Boundaryless Career: A New Employment Principle for a New Organizational Era* (pp. 116–31). New York: Oxford University Press.
De Lange, A.H., Kooij, D.T.A.M. and Van der Heijden, B.I.J.M. (2015). Human resource management and sustainability at work across the lifespan: An integrative perspective. In L. Finkelstein, D.M. Truxillo, F. Fraccaroli and R. Kanfer (eds), *Facing the Challenges of a Multi-Age Workforce. A Use-Inspired Approach* (pp. 50–79). SIOP Society for Industrial and Organizational Psychology. New York: Routledge.
De Vos, A. (2013). Over de (ir)rationaliteit van het loopbaanbeleid. *Gedrag en Organisatie*, 26(4), 431–48.
De Vos, A. and Gielens, T. (2014a). System level practices to facilitate sustainable careers. *White paper for the European Network on Careers & AGE (Age, Generations, Experience)*. Antwerp: Antwerp Management School.
De Vos, A. and Gielens, T. (2014b). Organizational level practices to facilitate sustainable careers. *White paper for the European Network on Careers & AGE (Age, Generations, Experience)*. Antwerp: Antwerp Management School.
Docherty, P., Kira, M. and Shani, A.B. (2009). What the world needs now is sustainable work systems. In P. Docherty, M. Kira and A.B. Shani (eds), *Creating Sustainable Work Systems* (pp. 1–23). London: Routledge Taylor & Francis Group.
Dries, N., Pepermans, R. and Carlier, O. (2008). Career success: Constructing a multidimensional model. *Journal of Vocational Behavior*, 73(2), 254–67.
Ehnert, I. and Harry, W. (2012). Recent developments and future prospects on sustainable Human Resource Management: Introduction to the Special Issue. *Management Revue*, 23(3), 221–38.
Forrier, A. and Sels, L. (2003). The concept employability: A complex mosaic. *International Journal of Human Resources Development and Management*, 3(2), 102–24.
Fugate, M., Kinicki, A.J. and Ashforth, B.E. (2004). Employability: A psycho-social construct, its dimensions, and applications. *Journal of Vocational Behavior*, 65(1), 14–38.
Garavan, T.N. and McGuire, D. (2010). Human resource development and society: Human resource development's role in embedding corporate social responsibility, sustainability, and ethics in organizations. *Advances in Developing Human Resources*, 12(5), 487–507.
Gautun, H. and Hagen, K. (2010). How do middle-aged employees combine work with caring for elderly parents? *Community, Work & Family*, 13, 393–409.
Granrose, C.S. and Portwood, J.D. (1987). Matching individual career plans and organizational career management. *Academy of Management Journal*, 30(4), 699–720.
Greenhaus, J.H., Callanan, G.A. and Godshalk, V.M. (2010). *Career Management* (4th edn). Thousand Oaks, CA: Sage Publications.
Greenhaus, J.H. and Kossek, E.E. (2014). The contemporary career: A work–home perspective. *Annual Review of Organizational Psychology and Organizational Behavior*, 1(1), 361–88.
Gubler, M., Arnold, J. and Coombs, C. (2013). Reassessing the protean career concept: Empirical findings, conceptual components, and measurement. *Journal of Organizational Behavior*, 35(S1), S23–S40.
Gunz, H. and Peiperl, M. (eds) (2007). *Handbook of Career Studies*. Los Angeles, CA: Sage Publications.
Hall, D.T. (1976). *Careers in Organizations*. Glenview, IL: Scott, Foresman.
Hall, D.T. (2002). *Careers In and Out of Organizations*. Thousand Oaks, CA: Sage Publications.
Herman, C. and Lewis, S. (2012). Entitled to a sustainable career? Motherhood in science, engineering, and technology. *Journal of Social Issues*, 68(4), 767–89.
Holling, C.S. (2001). Understanding the complexity of economic, ecological, and social systems. *Ecosystems*, 4, 390–405.
Hughes, E.C. (1958). *Men and their Work*. Glencoe, IL: Free Press. (Original work published 1928–56).
Inkson, K. (2007). *Understanding Careers: The Metaphors of Working Lives*. London: Sage Publications.
Inkson, K., Dries, N. and Arnold, J. (2015). *Understanding Careers*. London: Sage Publications.
Kossek, E.E., Valcour, M. and Lirio, P. (2014). The sustainable workforce: Organizational strategies for promoting work–life balance and well-being. In P. Chen and C.L. Cooper (eds), *Work and Wellbeing* (pp. 295–318). Oxford and New York: Wiley-Blackwell.
Lawrence, B.S. (1984). Historical perspective: Using the past to study the present. *Academy of Management Review*, 9(2), 307–12.
Lee, M.D., Kossek, E.E., Hall, D.T. and Litrico, J. (2011). Entangled strands: A process perspective on the evolution of careers in the context of personal, family, work, and community life. *Human Relations*, 64(12), 1531–53.
Mainiero, L.A. and Sullivan, S.E. (2005). Kaleidoscope careers: An alternate explanation for the opt-out revolution. *Academy of Management Executive*, 19(1), 106–23.
Moore, C., Gunz, H. and Hall, D.T. (2007). Tracing the historical roots of career theory in management and

organization studies. In H. Gunz and M. Peiperl (eds), *Handbook of Career Studies* (pp. 13–38). Los Angeles, CA: Sage Publications.
Newman, K.L. (2011). Sustainable careers: Lifecycle engagement in work. *Organizational Dynamics*, 40(2), 136–43.
Oldham, G.R. and Hackman, J.R. (2010). Not what it was and not what it will be: The future of job design research. *Journal of Organizational Behavior*, 31(2–3), 463–79.
Parker, S.K., Bindl, U.K. and Strauss, K. (2010). Making things happen: A model of proactive motivation. *Journal of Management*, 36(4), 827–56.
Pazy, A. (1988). Joint responsibility: The relationships between organizational and individual career management and the effectiveness of careers. *Group & Organization Management*, 13(3), 311–31.
Peiperl, M. and Baruch, Y. (1997). Back to square zero: The post-corporate career. *Organizational Dynamics*, 25(4), 7–22.
Pfeffer, J. (2010). Building sustainable organisations: The human factor. *Academy of Management Perspectives*, 24(1), 34–45.
Schein, E.H. (1978). *Career Dynamics: Matching Individual and Organizational Needs*. Reading, MA: Addison-Wesley.
Schein, E.H. (1985). *Career Anchors: Discovering Your Real Values*. San Diego, CA: University Associates.
Schein, E.H. (2007). Afterword. Career research: Some issues and dilemmas. In H. Gunz and M. Peiperl (eds), *Handbook of Career Studies* (pp. 573–6). Los Angeles, CA: Sage Publications.
Sullivan, S.E. and Baruch, Y. (2009). Advances in career theory and research: A critical review and agenda for future exploration. *Journal of Management*, 35(6), 1542–71.
Thijssen, J.G.L., Van der Heijden, B.I.J.M. and Rocco, T. (2008). Toward the employability-link model: Current employment transition to future employment perspectives. *Human Resource Development Review*, 7(2), 165–83.
Valcour, M., Bailyn, L. and Quijada, M.A. (2007). Customized careers. In H.P. Gunz and M.A. Peiperl (eds), *Handbook of Career Studies* (pp. 188–210). Newbury Park, CA: Sage Publications.
Van der Heijde, C.M. and Van der Heijden, B.I.J.M. (2006). A competence-based and multidimensional operationalization and measurement of employability. *Human Resource Management*, 45(3), 449–76.
Van der Heijden, B.I.J.M. (2005). 'No one has ever promised you a rose garden'. On shared responsibility and employability enhancing strategies throughout careers. Inaugural address, Heerlen: Open University of the Netherlands. Assen: Van Gorcum.
Van der Heijden, B.I.J.M., De Lange, A., Demerouti, E. and Van der Heijde, C.M. (2009). Employability and career success across the life-span. Age effects on the employability–career success relationship. *Journal of Vocational Behavior*, 74, 156–64.
WCED (World Commission on Environment and Development) (1987). Our common future: Report of the World Commission on Environment and Development. Brussels.
Weick, K. (1996). Enactment and the boundaryless career: Organizing as we work. In M.B. Arthur and D.M. Rousseau (eds), *The Boundaryless Career: A New Employment Principle for a New Organizational Era* (pp. 40–57). Oxford: Oxford University Press.
Wrzesniewski, A. and Dutton, J.E. (2001). Crafting a job: Revisioning employees as active crafters of their work. *Academy of Management Review*, 26, 179–201.

2 Facilitating the crafting of sustainable careers in organizations

Monique Valcour

Human resource management practices, labor market conditions and career patterns have evolved significantly in recent decades. Scholars have observed a general and ongoing weakening of the employment contract between individuals and the organizations that employ them since the 1980s (Cappelli and Keller, 2013). Companies have embraced both downsizing and hiring from outside for management posts, with the effect that many employees lack job security and the expectation of career growth with their employer. Career progression systems in companies have waned, thereby removing the signposts that previously guided employees on managerial career paths. Decreased standardization of career paths and organizationally directed career development is accompanied by reduced clarity about what constitutes career success and what career strategies one should pursue. Career shifts have increased both in number and magnitude, so that individuals are not only making more changes of job and employer, but also navigating more career changes across industries and occupations. Job and employment security has fallen for many people, even those with strong human capital including university education and extensive work experience (Goodman and Mance, 2011). Occupations have proliferated, leaving many individuals feeling that there must be some job that would be a good fit for their qualifications and interests, but they don't know what it might be, or how to go about identifying it.

A number of macro-level factors account for the aforementioned changes in careers, including an increasingly dynamic and globalized economy and rapid technological innovation, which are reflected in decreased stability of employment and an increase in the pace with which industries expand and contract, as well as a tendency in some Western countries for disappearing high-wage jobs to be replaced by much more precarious low-wage service jobs (Friedman, 2005). Management practices have also exerted a profound impact on career patterns. Most significant among these are organizational delayering (resulting in fewer opportunities for promotion), decreased emphasis on employer-driven career management programs, increased focus on short-term financial results, the widespread use of reductions in force to influence those results, the use of off-shoring to countries with lower labor costs, and externalization of a greater proportion of the workforce into contract positions that do not offer security of employment (Cappelli and Keller, 2014). Cappelli (2010) argued that hiring talent from the external labor market rather than developing employees internally has become so commonplace that it essentially represents a core talent management strategy for many firms, replacing workforce and succession planning, internal development, and even assessment (see also Cappelli and Keller, 2014).

In addition to these macroeconomic shifts and changes in managerial and employment practices, demographic factors are also driving increased career complexity. The documented increase in dual-earner and single-parent households, and in households providing elderly care, translates into a high level of non-work demands for many employees (Cullen et al., 2009). Among working parents, 90 percent of mothers and 95 percent of fathers report experiencing work–life conflict (Williams and Boushey, 2010). The hectic lives of dual-career couples are well-documented (Schulte, 2014). The workforce is aging dramatically in many countries, creating potentially serious challenges for organizations whose success relies on retention of knowledge and competencies (Burke and Ng, 2006). At the same time, the proportion of workers in their fifties, sixties and seventies who plan to continue working past traditional retirement age is increasing for reasons including financial need and preference for a more active lifestyle (Nakai et al., 2011). Research suggests that, while all employees value work–life balance and meaningful work, younger employees place an especially high premium on these aspects of work (PriceWaterhouseCoopers, 2013a; Twenge, 2010). HRM and other organizational leaders are increasingly aware of these employee expectations, but are still struggling to meet them (Brack, 2012).

It is clear that individuals must now assume primary responsibility for managing their own careers in order to achieve career stability (Abele and Wiese, 2008; Sullivan and Baruch, 2009). This holds true even in large organizations with robust career development offerings. Rather than moving employees systematically through a prescribed set of training workshops, work assignments and positions, nowadays large employers are more likely to offer employees a menu of career resources and expect them to avail themselves of offerings related to their career objectives. Many employees face the challenge of maintaining their employability (their ability to gain and maintain suitable employment) without employer support. Voluntary or involuntary job loss can render employees unemployable – even after many years of excellent performance and contributions to a firm – if they lack skills that are marketable to other companies, a strong network and a clever strategy for parlaying these assets into paid employment. The 'career pandemonium' (Brousseau et al., 1996) that characterizes the contemporary labor market creates anxiety and confusion for many people as they try to guide their own careers (De Vos and Soens, 2008).

Individuals are not alone in their efforts to craft stable careers in this new world of work. Employers face complex talent management challenges that result from the same trends that have reshaped individual careers. A recent global survey of 1605 companies found that nearly three in four report difficulties attracting qualified employees, and more than half indicated they are having difficulty retaining them (Towers Watson, 2012). Work–life conflict drives a substantial amount of voluntary turnover, especially among women (Steel et al., 2002). There is strong consensus among CEOs that a lack of key skills among their workforces and in the external labor market poses a primary threat to profitability (PriceWaterhouseCoopers, 2013b). A report on the future of HR found that executives in 27 European countries listed talent management as both their firms' most critical capability – and the one in which they were weakest (Boston Consulting Group, 2010). Many companies' provision of developmental opportunities is limited, whether for lack of budget, creativity, or culturally-embedded learning orientation. Yet evidence indicates that opportunities for learning and career development exert significant influence on job candidates' selection of one employer over another (Uggerslev et al., 2012), as well as on employees' turnover decisions, performance and engagement (Armstrong-Stassen and Ursel, 2009; Spell et al., 2014).

When we consider the challenges that individuals face in managing their careers alongside the major talent management challenges that companies are struggling with at present, we can see that they have been shaped by a common set of changes in economic and labor market conditions, managerial policies and practices, and demographic and attitudinal factors. As they struggle to find work that fits their skills and interests, to keep learning and developing, to manage both work and personal responsibilities, and to achieve security and stability in the midst of a dynamic and often difficult business and labor market environment, today's employees long for careers that feel more sustainable than the ones they currently have. For their part, employers clearly need to find ways to attract, retain, motivate, develop and manage employees that are cost-effective and responsive to both the needs of the business and the needs and preferences of employees. The purpose of this chapter is to argue that the fusion of the career-related needs and goals of individuals and organizations comes together in the notion of a sustainable career. I develop this argument in the following section, followed by a review of practices that support sustainable careers in organizations.

SUSTAINABLE CAREERS INTEGRATE INDIVIDUAL AND ORGANIZATIONAL EMPLOYMENT NEEDS

According to Merriam-Webster, the word 'sustainable' describes things that are 'able to last or continue for a long time' and that are 'able to be used without being depleted or destroyed', as well as 'methods of using resources that support their conservation and renewal' (http://www.merriam-webster.com/dictionary/sustainable). A sustainable career is thus one that endures over time and that is characterized by development, conservation and renewal of the working individual's career-related resources, including human and social capital (for example, skills, credentials, reputation, relationships) as well as personal characteristics such as proactivity and resilience that aid in career self-management.

In view of the trends and career challenges outlined in the introduction, I propose that a sustainable career is characterized by four primary attributes: (1) alignment of work with the individual's strengths, interests and values; (2) ongoing learning and renewal; (3) security via employability; and (4) work–life fit over the life course. In other words, people who enjoy sustainable careers perform work that makes full use of their skills and challenges them to develop new ones. Their work interests and holds meaning for them, thereby boosting their engagement, performance and satisfaction. They enjoy opportunities for learning and development. Learning and development build their skills and competencies, thus enhancing their value and marketability in internal and external labor markets. They build and maintain connections to others who may be sources of career information and opportunity, and also seek to help their connections, both of which enhance their employability and career options (Grant, 2013). In turn, employability provides security. They are able to integrate and manage the demands of both their work and personal lives and maintain a satisfactory degree of engagement in both domains (Friedman, 2008).

A career with these four attributes may sound too good to be true. However, unlike other career concepts that are unbounded from organizational career management systems, such as protean (Hall, 2004a), boundaryless (Arthur and Rousseau, 1996) and customized careers (Valcour et al., 2007), the sustainable career model is specifically intended to jointly serve the concerns of both employees and employers. It addresses the aforementioned contemporary career-related challenges that confront both individuals and employers. From the employer's perspective, the four pillars that characterize sustainable careers for employees map onto four core objectives of talent management: (1) maximum yield on human capital value; (2) continuous updating of organizational competencies; (3) stability via adaptability; and (4) organizational commitment and retention. The following paragraphs discuss how each pair of sustainable career attributes yields advantages for both individuals and employers.

Attribute pair 1: work alignment–human capital yield. When work is aligned with employees' strengths, interests and values, firms stand to yield greater value from their human resources. Research suggests that performing work that aligns with one's strengths, interests and values boosts intrinsic motivation, sense of experienced meaningfulness, job performance, and commitment to the organization (Berg et al., 2013; Kahn, 1990; Rich et al., 2010; Ryan and Deci, 2000). This alignment not only energizes employees and contributes to their satisfaction and well-being, it also pays dividends for firms. Research by the Gallup organization has found that business units where there is an increase in the proportion of employees who report that they are able to use their strengths on a daily basis at work, experience comparable increases in productivity, customer loyalty, and employee retention (Gallup, 2013).

Attribute pairs 2: learning and renewal–updating of organizational competencies and 3: security via employability–stability via adaptability. The knowledge, skills and abilities distributed among members of an organization's workforce are constituent elements of the core competencies that underlie its potential for competitive success in its marketplace. Similarly, the ongoing learning and updating of skills and knowledge that marks each individual sustainable career contributes to the capacity of the employer's competencies to evolve over time to meet market challenges (Arthur et al., 1995). Just as continuous learning and acquisition of new competencies contribute to an individual's employability, continuous organizational learning increases stability by improving the organization's ability to adapt to changing competitive pressures and disruptions in its environment. Employees in learning-rich work environments are more likely than others to be oriented towards learning, to learn more effectively and transfer learning to performance, as well as to have a proactive approach to career development (Brown et al., 2010). Research on high-performance work systems and organizational agility has documented how training and learning practices enhance firms' competitive performance and ability to adapt in dynamic markets (Arthur, 1994; Dyer and Shafer, 2003; Huselid, 1995; Lepak and Snell, 1999; Shafer et al., 2001; Way, 2002).

Attribute pair 4: work–life fit over the life course–retention and commitment. Much of the work–life conflict that disrupts employees' careers – and the resulting turnover that undermines organizational effectiveness – stems from an outdated yet enduring traditional career template featuring an 'ideal worker' who is expected to work long hours, avoid career breaks, and grant priority to work over other life domains (Valcour et al., 2007). In contrast to the rigid traditional career, sustainable careers are dynamic and flexible. They allow individuals to modify their working arrangements and to turn the level of work intensity up and down over the course of their careers in order to achieve a satisfactory integration of work and non-work commitments. Sustainable careers enable longer-term contributions to organizations by avoiding the stress and career withdrawal that often occur when work demands prevent employees from being able to meet non-work responsibilities (Stone, 2007). Research has demonstrated that work and career flexibility is associated with higher levels of organizational commitment and retention (Aryee et al., 1998; Briscoe, 2006; Cabrera, 2009; Casper and Harris, 2008).

EMPLOYEE PROACTIVITY AND ADAPTATION IN THE SUSTAINABLE CAREER

The hallmark of the sustainable career is its dynamic alignment with the evolving strengths, interests, values and preferences of the individual over time. Sustainable careers therefore necessarily demand significant active career self-management on the part of individuals. In particular, self-awareness and proactivity are vital to the realization of a sustainable career. Self-awareness refers to the extent to which people are conscious of the components of their identities and the extent to which their self-perceptions are internally integrated and consistent with the way other people perceive them (Hall, 2004b, p. 154). In the process of career self-management, one's self or identity – whether current or a hoped-for future self that one is moving toward – acts as a cognitive compass that motivates one to actively adapt in order to identify, take advantage of, or create opportunities that are concordant with one's aspirations (Fugate et al., 2004; Strauss et al., 2012). Self-awareness includes understanding one's strengths, weaknesses, values, motives and optimal working conditions. It facilitates career self-management by increasing the individual's ability to identify or create favorable opportunities, persuade career gatekeepers to facilitate opportunities, and make sound career decisions.

Proactivity has a dispositional basis (commonly referred to as proactive personality) and is manifested through behaviors such as identifying new opportunities, taking initiative, seeking feedback, challenging the status quo, issue selling, proactive socialization (Crant, 2000), and creating favorable conditions in which one can perform well. Proactive people feel relatively unconstrained by situational forces; they seek opportunities, take action to make the most of them, and persevere until meaningful change occurs (Bateman and Crant, 1993).

Integrating research on self-awareness and proactivity for career self-management, Fugate and colleagues (Fugate and Kinicki, 2008; Fugate et al., 2004) articulated a comprehensive dispositional construct of employability, specifically linked to the challenges of managing one's career in today's economy. In their definition and measure, employability is a constellation of individual differences that predispose individuals to proactive adaptability specific to work and careers. It comprises the following: (1) openness to changes at work; (2) work and career resilience; (3) work and career proactivity; (4) career motivation; and (5) work identity. People with dispositional employability have a strong sense of self, a sense of 'who I am' within the work context. In the absence of clear organizationally-defined career structures to give meaning to employees' career experiences and shape their career expectations, a strong individual psychological structure is a critical resource for identifying desired career direction and directing effort toward the achievement of career goals (Fugate and Kinicki, 2008). In addition to facilitating the identification of career goals and opportunities, dispositional employability is reflected in a proactive orientation towards adaptability, to undertaking self-directed learning and personal change necessary to attain career goals (Van Veldhoven and Dorenbosch, 2008). Career adaptation involves activity directed both inward and outward. In other words, individuals high on dispositional employability 'actively engage the situation, learning and asserting whatever influence is possible to change the situation to fit their own needs and desires; at the same time, they alter their own cognitions and behaviors to optimize the situation' (Fugate et al., 2004, p. 17).

Self-awareness and dispositional proactivity/employability function as powerful resources that enable employees to navigate a variety of external circumstances effectively. Research has linked proactivity to job performance and to objective and subjective measures of career success (Greguras and Diefendorff, 2010; Seibert et al., 1999; Seibert et al., 2001). Furthermore, proactive employees engage in more job crafting and, in turn, experience greater work engagement and increased job performance (Bakker et al., 2012). Job crafting is an employee-directed process of changing one's current job and work environment in order to make them more favorable to one's performance and well-being (Lyons, 2008; Wrzesniewski and Dutton, 2001). As operationalized by Bakker et al., (2012), job crafting entails increasing one's structural and social job resources (for example, trying to develop oneself professionally, trying to use one's capacities to the fullest, asking for feedback and coaching), decreasing hindrance demands in the job (for example, organizing one's work so as to minimize contact with people whose expectations are unrealistic and with people whose problems affect one emotionally) and increasing job challenges (for example, volunteering for interesting projects, proactively learning about new developments).

Raising Employees' Self-awareness

There are a number of actions that HR and line managers can take to help raise employees' self-awareness. Making a variety of inventories (for example, personality, leadership style, career values, career interests) available to employees online is a first step that can help build self-awareness in those employees proactive enough to make use of them (Hall and Moss, 1998). Administering and debriefing inventories in workshops that employees are expected to attend may be a more powerful approach that reaches more employees and sends a signal that the organization values and supports the development of self-awareness, though it is possible that attempts to 'force' self-awareness may be viewed negatively by some employees. Following administration of inventories with either facilitated group discussion or one-on-one sessions with a coach or trained facilitator offers the additional benefit of helping employees to understand how the information gleaned from the inventory yields actionable implications for their own work performance and career direction (Chandler et al., 2010). Self-awareness can be increased through 360-degree feedback, and for this reason it is a common feature of leadership development initiatives (Ely et al., 2011).

Mindfulness

In a more holistic vein, mindfulness shows great potential as a tool for developing the self-awareness needed to craft and thrive in a sustainable career. Mindfulness training and practice is catching on in many organizations due to its established relationships with increased psychological well-being and ability to focus. Mindfulness can be defined as a receptive, non-judgmental attention to and awareness of external (for example, sounds) and internal (for example, emotions) present-moment states, events and experiences (Brown and Ryan, 2003; Dane, 2011). Drawing on a large body of literature, Jordan et al. (2009) noted that mindfulness has been widely characterized as an individual learning process. Research has shown that mindfulness training is associated with increased self-awareness (Brown and Ryan, 2003) and effective coping with unemployment uncertainty (Jacobs and Blustein, 2008), as well as with increased job performance and decreased turnover intentions (Dane and Brummel, 2014). The self-awareness and capacity for reflection that mindfulness fosters are integral to crafting a career that is aligned with one's values, that generates positive emotions, and that is well integrated with one's life outside of work (Kopelman et al., 2012). Recent research has shown that mindfulness training is associated with increases in authentic functioning, that is, being aware of one's self, values, emotions, reactions, and managing oneself accordingly, and with work engagement (Leroy et al., 2013). Thus, mindfulness helps people attain greater knowledge of what it is they value most, greater openness and receptivity, greater awareness of their emotions and behaviors in interactions with others and greater ability to focus on and derive enjoyment from the work that they value.

INTERPERSONAL SUPPORT FOR SUSTAINABLE CAREERS

Crafting a sustainable career is an interactive process that relies on facilitative interactions between the individual employee and others in the organization, including managers and HR professionals. Research suggests that proactivity and interpersonal support form a mutually-reinforcing virtuous cycle that drives sustainable career success. Proactive personality exerts beneficial lagged effects on increases in job demands, job control, and supervisor support, and on decreases in organizational constraints (Li et al., 2014). The more that people possess the career self-management-boosting resources that comprise dispositional employability, the more likely they are to both be offered and make use of various forms of career support (De Vos et al., 2009; Lips-Wiersma and Hall, 2007; London, 1993). This career support includes training and development programs and informal interpersonal support such as developmental feedback, invitations to join social groups or work on important projects, mentoring or career sponsorship. Supervisor career support is associated with greater employee career self-management and adaptability (Ito and Brotheridge, 2005). Van Veldhoven and Dorenbosch (2008) found that HR practices for career development were associated with greater employee proactivity, both on the job and in terms of their own career development.

Self-determination theory (Ryan and Deci, 2000) posits that employees are more likely to experience motivation to perform tasks and activities that are valuable to the organization when they feel competent performing the activities and when performance of the activities is valued and recognized by people to whom the employee values connection. Thus, supervisors and others in leadership roles in organizations can support employees' performance of organizationally-valuable work by recognizing it, and also by providing support and resources to increase employees' competence (for example, training, time, membership in and attendance at professional meetings of relevant experts and practitioners, mentoring by and connection to others inside and outside of the organization who have already mastered the skills needed to perform the work). Research has found that participation in developmental activities is positively related to employees' perceptions of organizational support for development (Kraimer et al., 2011). Contrary to some managers' concerns that supporting employability may hurt businesses by helping their best employees find jobs elsewhere, employers may be able to strengthen organizational commitment and to reduce turnover by actively supporting their career development, even if it isn't done specifically to meet organizational needs (Benson, 2006; De Cuyper and De Witte, 2011).

Coaching

Career coaching helps individuals to clarify their career strengths and interests, make informed decisions about their career development and trajectory, and develop strategies for pursuing career goals (Coutu and Kauffman, 2009). It is therefore a valuable tool for facilitating career self-management. Coaching can also be used to help employees think creatively about ways in which they can better use their strengths to support key organizational objectives, thereby increasing employee–organization alignment. From the employee perspective, career coaching can be a way to improve performance, brighten their career outlook, and enhance job and career satisfaction (Feldman, 2001). To maximize the effectiveness of career coaching initiatives for facilitating sustainable careers, it is desirable that corporations make the investment in either providing internal specialists with the training and clinical supervision needed to develop expertise and effectiveness as a coach or in contracting with professional coaches for the delivery of career coaching.

I-deals

In recent years, research on job crafting and 'i-deals' (idiosyncratic work arrangements) has examined approaches to customizing the content of jobs and the way in which they are performed in order to better align with the strengths, motives, needs and preferences of employees. An excellent model of sustainable career crafting, idiosyncratic deals are non-standard, personalized work arrangements negotiated between individual employers and their employees that benefit each party (Rousseau, 2005). Like job crafting, i-deals are typically initiated by the employee and therefore depend on employee proactivity; unlike job crafting, i-deals necessarily involve negotiation with one's manager and are intended to deliver benefits to the organization as well as to the individual (Hornung et al., 2010). I-deals can take many different forms, including customized learning or career development opportunities, changes to job content, special compensation arrangements, and flexibility in the amount, time and/or place of work (Rosen et al., 2013). Research has shown that i-deals are associated with increased performance, organizational commitment, organizational citizenship behavior, and work–life balance, as well as with more positive employee assessments of work characteristics (Anand et al., 2010; Hornung et al., 2008; Hornung et al., 2010; McInnis et al., 2009; Ng and Feldman, 2010).

HR APPROACHES TO FACILITATING SUSTAINABLE CAREERS

Just as career and workforce realities have changed, so too does HRM need to change – from a standardized approach to one that enables customization. This means understanding each employee's strengths, interests and motives; being aware of and helping to build their human and social capital, as well as to apply them to organizational problems; encouraging the articulation, expression and pursuit of career goals that are both personally meaningful and valuable for the company; and freeing employees and managers to find work arrangements that support employees' productivity, well-being and work–life integration. HRM needs to build flexibility into HR policy and people management practices in order to maximally engage each individual employee. Cantrell and Smith (2010) call this the 'workforce of one' approach. In addition to supporting sustainable careers, this evolution holds the promise of transforming the HR function from one that is viewed as ancillary in many companies to one that is much more vital and directly engaged in strategy implementation.

Cantrell and Smith (2010) outline four major strategies for personalizing the employment relationship with each employee in a scalable and reliable way that helps organizations capture greater value from employees, supports sustainable careers, and boosts employee outcomes. The first step toward the full customization that provides ideal support for sustainable careers is *segmentation*, that is, making customized HR choices available to employees based upon their characteristics and preferences. The second strategy involves providing *modular choices* to employees. Like the segmentation strategy, this approach is an introductory step towards embracing customization. Whereas customization involves applying sets of HR practices to groups that have been identified as having a unique set of preferences, the modular choice approach implies giving all employees the same menu of HR programs and benefits, from which they can choose the ones that they care about most. One of the most well known and well-documented sustainable career programs that relies heavily on modular choices is Deloitte's Mass Career Customization (MCC) program (Benko and Weisberg, 2007), an adaptive career progress model that enables employees to customize their career development and advancement pathways. As a part of the regular performance appraisal, the MCC process guides employees and their managers to make choices around four major dimensions of career progression: role (leader or individual contributor), pace, location/schedule and workload, calibrating each based on the employee's current career aspirations and life circumstances. Since the system is modular, with the ability to personalize each arrangement at any point in time, the MCC creates a template for managing new trends that may emerge in the future by avoiding an overly specific focus on any one group. Since initial implementation in 2008, the MCC program has produced impressive results including increased satisfaction and commitment from employees, decreased turnover and increased productivity (Galinsky and Matos, 2011).

The third strategy involves defining *broad and simple rules* that provide general guidance and define boundaries within which employees and their managers can operate autonomously. For instance, strategic boundaries describe the organization's broad mission and direction to provide guidance with respect to how employees should conduct themselves and contribute to the success of the organization. Results or outcome boundaries define expected performance results and grant employees independence with respect to the methods they use to achieve them.

The fourth strategy is *fostering employee-defined personalization.* In this approach, HR supports individuals in defining their own personalized practices. Employee-defined personalization enables employees to customize such elements as the content and title of their job, their career pathway, the potential composition of the workforce (for example, by referring acquaintances as candidates for recruiting), their development (for example, by deciding how and when to learn from one another), and the timing and content of their work (for example, by trading work shifts and projects with other employees). Cantrell and Smith (2010) report that of the four 'workforce of one' strategies, employee-defined personalization has yielded the most innovation in HRM in recent years. For example, The Container Store, the Dallas-based retail chain specializing in products for household storage, relies heavily on its current employees for recruitment. Associates have their employment referral forms that they can give to customers or acquaintances who they identify as fitting the profile of a successful retail employee. They receive bonuses for successful hires. This practice is part of a system of staffing practices that have made The Container Store a retail leader as well as an award-winning 'Best Places to Work' employer, with an annual employee turnover level of 10–12 percent, which is virtually unheard of in retail.

Additional actions that HR can take to foster sustainable careers include the following: (1) share information with employees about the strategic direction of the business as well as about ongoing organizational activities and results; (2) encourage employee social networks that span functions and divisions in order to give employees broader understanding of the organization and to promote learning; (3) train and support managers in having frequent career conversations with all of their direct reports; (4) support work–life fit for employees by specifically looking for ways to meet both employee and organizational needs in the design of work; (5) develop and legitimate alternative career pathways that enable employees to modify the pace and scheduling of work as well as the trajectory and pace of career advancement; and (6) facilitate future re-entry for departing employees with a robust alumni network that keeps previous employees connected to the firm.

CONCLUSION AND IMPLICATIONS FOR PRACTICE AND RESEARCH

Harmonizing employee preferences and employer needs is easier to talk about than to execute. Employees present an increasingly diverse profile of needs and expectations. Some don't seem to respond to the programs and practices that have worked for a firm for years. Still others present needs and expectations that the firm has no experience in responding to. So the partnership between employee and organization must be flexible, dynamic and customizable. It needs to be updated over time to accommodate changing circumstances and demands on both sides of the table – and to make sure that it continues to work for both employer and employee. Longitudinal research tracking the interplay of employee career preferences and strategies with HR and managerial initiatives over time would be very useful in illuminating the dynamics of how sustainable careers unfold over time, what conditions facilitate them, and how they impact individuals and organizations.

The conceptualization of employee alignment with organizational strategic objectives is unique to the concept of sustainable careers. To facilitate sustainable careers in organizations, employees, their managers and HR professionals need to have a clear understanding of the organization's strategic objectives and be able to see how individual employees' work and growth objectives connect to the larger strategy. In order to manage their own sustainable careers, employees need to understand what value they can provide to the organization, especially with respect to the firm's strategic direction. Just as HR directors need to pay attention to business and employment trends internal and external to their employer in order to be able to add value to the business, so do employees need to do so in order to manage their value and marketability. This is a linchpin of the sustainable career, and it requires a key managerial and HR competency: helping employees to explore and identify the overlap between the firm's strategic imperatives and their own skills, interests and values. Research in this area is sorely needed, particularly with regard to the following questions: Does lack of clarity in the articulation of strategic objectives limit the ability of HR and managers to facilitate sustainable careers? What mechanisms are most effective in aligning organizational strategy with individual jobs? How does understanding of organizational strategy and its linkage to one's own work affect employees' job attitudes and work performance? How and to what extent does organizational–individual alignment increase the performance and effectiveness of organizations?

One of the obvious limitations to the full implementation of sustainable careers in organizations is the need for self-awareness and proactivity, both among employees and their supervisors. Some people are low on dispositional proactivity, and there are limitations to the extent to which organizations can catalyze significant increases in self-awareness in some people, as coaches and leadership development experts have long known. For example, research has shown that people with the highest levels of self-awareness are most open to feedback and to making efforts at self-improvement, while those with low levels of self-awareness are both resistant to feedback about their deficit and also uninterested in working to improve it (Sheldon et al., 2014). A study that tested the effects of a three-day career self-management training program found that the initiative was unsuccessful in resocializing employees of a major US transportation company to engage in career self-management (Kossek et al., 1998). Furthermore, the researchers found that, when carried out as an isolated HR initiative, the training actually decreased trainees' likelihood of engaging in career self-management behaviors. These results suggest that efforts to encourage employees to take ownership of their career development should be integrated systematically into organizations' talent management activities. There may also be value in incorporating a self-awareness inventory into selection testing (Thompson, 2014) and in communicating the importance of career self-management in recruitment communication, especially in companies with a clearly articulated expectation of employee career self-management. Companies that are not clear about their expectations that employees will manage their own careers are likely to depress employee morale and increase turnover intentions rather than motivate sustainable career crafting. Research is needed to examine the malleability of self-awareness and proactivity. In particular, studies that identify what types of initiatives are most effective at building these critical career resources would be helpful.

REFERENCES

Abele, A.E. and B.S. Wiese (2008), 'The nomological network of self-management strategies and career success'. *Journal of Occupational and Organizational Psychology*, 81(4), 733–49.

Anand, S., P.R. Vidyarthi, R.C. Liden and D.M. Rousseau (2010), 'Good citizens in poor-quality relationships: Idiosyncratic deals as a substitute for relationship quality'. *Academy of Management Journal*, 53(5), 970–88.

Armstrong-Stassen, M. and N.D. Ursel (2009), 'Perceived organizational support, career satisfaction, and the retention of older workers'. *Journal of Occupational and Organizational Psychology*, 82(1), 201–20.

Arthur, J.B. (1994), 'Effects of human resource systems on manufacturing performance and turnover'. *Academy of Management Journal*, 37(3), 670–87.

Arthur, M.B. and D.M. Rousseau (eds) (1996), *The Boundaryless Career: A New Employment Principle for a New Organizational Era*, New York: Oxford University Press.

Arthur, M.B., P.H. Claman and R.J. DeFillippi (1995), 'Intelligent enterprise, intelligent careers'. *Academy of Management Executive*, 9(4), 7–20.

Aryee, S., V. Luk and R. Stone (1998), 'Family responsive variables and retention-relevant outcomes among employed parents'. *Human Relations*, 51(1), 73–87.

Bakker, A.B., M. Tims and D. Derks (2012), 'Proactive personality and job performance: The role of job crafting and work engagement'. *Human Relations*, 65(10), 1359–78.

Bateman, T.S. and J.M. Crant (1993), 'The proactive component of organizational behavior'. *Journal of Organizational Behavior*, 14, 103–18.

Benko, C. and A. Weisberg (2007), *Mass Career Customization: Aligning the Workplace with Today's Nontraditional Workforce*, Boston, MA: Harvard Business School Press.

Benson, G.S. (2006), 'Employee development, commitment and intention to turnover: A test of "employability" policies in action'. *Human Resource Management Journal*, 16(2), 173–92.

Berg, J.M., J.E. Dutton and A. Wrzesniewski (2013), 'Job crafting and meaningful work', in B.J. Dik, Z.S. Byrne and M.F. Steger (eds), *Purpose and Meaning in the Workplace* (pp. 81–104), Washington, DC: American Psychological Association.

Boston Consulting Group (2010), 'The future of HR in Europe'. Paris: Boston Consulting Group.

Brack, J. (2012), 'Maximizing millennials in the workplace'. Chapel Hill, NC: University of North Carolina, Keenan-Flagler Business School, UNC Executive Development.

Briscoe, F. (2006), 'Temporal flexibility and careers: The role of large-scale organizations for physicians'. *Industrial & Labor Relations Review*, 60(1), 88–104.

Brousseau, K.R., M.J. Driver, K. Eneroth and R. Larsson (1996), 'Career pandemonium: Realigning individuals and organizations'. *Academy of Management Executive*, 10(4), 52–66.

Brown, A., J. Bimrose, S.-A. Barnes, S. Kirpal, T. Grønning and M. Dæhlen (2010), 'Changing patterns of working, learning and career development across Europe'. Warwick, UK: Institute for Employment Research of the University of Warwick.

Brown, K.W. and R.M. Ryan (2003), 'The benefits of being present: Mindfulness and its role in psychological well-being'. *Journal of Personality and Social Psychology*, 84(4), 822–48.

Burke, J.R. and J.E. Ng (2006), 'The changing nature of work and organizations: Implications for human resource management'. *Human Resource Management Review*, 16(2), 86–94.

Cabrera, E.F. (2009), 'Protean organizations: Reshaping work and careers to retain female talent'. *Career Development International*, 14(2), 186–201.

Cantrell, S.M. and D. Smith (2010), *Workforce of One: Revolutionizing Talent Management Through Customization*, Boston, MA: Harvard Business Press.

Cappelli, P. (2010), 'The rise and decline of managerial development'. *Industrial and Corporate Change*, 19(2), 509–48.

Cappelli, P. and J.R. Keller (2013), 'Classifying work in the new economy'. *Academy of Management Review*, 38(4), 575–96.
Cappelli, P. and J.R. Keller (2014), 'Talent management: Conceptual approaches and practical challenges'. *Annual Review of Organizational Psychology and Organizational Behavior*, 1, 305–31.
Casper, W.J. and C.M. Harris (2008), 'Work–life benefits and organizational attachment: Self-interest utility and signaling theory models'. *Journal of Vocational Behavior*, 72(1), 95–109.
Chandler, D.E., D.T. Hall and K.E. Kram (2010), 'A developmental network & relational savvy approach to talent development: A low-cost alternative'. *Organizational Dynamics*, 39(1), 48–56.
Coutu, D. and C. Kauffman (2009), 'What can coaches do for you?'. *Harvard Business Review*, 87(1), 91–7.
Crant, J.M. (2000), 'Proactive behavior in organizations'. *Journal of Management*, 26(3), 435–62.
Cullen, J.C., L.B. Hammer, M.B. Neal and R.R. Sinclair (2009), 'Development of a typology of dual-earner couples caring for children and aging parents'. *Journal of Family Issues*, 30(4), 458–83.
Dane, E. (2011), 'Paying attention to mindfulness and its effects on task performance in the workplace'. *Journal of Management*, 37(4), 997–1018.
Dane, E. and B.J. Brummel (2014), 'Examining workplace mindfulness and its relations to job performance and turnover intention'. *Human Relations*, 67(1), 105–28.
De Cuyper, N. and H. De Witte (2011), 'The management paradox: Self-rated employability and organizational commitment and performance'. *Personnel Review*, 40(2), 152–72.
De Vos, A. and N. Soens (2008), 'Protean attitude and career success: The mediating role of self-management'. *Journal of Vocational Behavior*, 73(3), 449–56.
De Vos, A., K. Dewettinck and D. Buyens (2009), 'The professional career on the right track: A study on the interaction between career self-management and organizational career management in explaining employee outcomes'. *European Journal of Work & Organizational Psychology*, 18(1), 55–80.
Dyer, L. and R.A. Shafer (2003), 'Dynamic organizations: Achieving marketplace and organizational agility with people', in R.D. Day, R.S. Peterson and E.A. Mannix (eds), *Leading and Managing People in the Dynamic Organization* (pp. 7–40), Mahwah, NJ: Lawrence Erlbaum Associates.
Ely, R.J., H. Ibarra and D.M. Kolb (2011), 'Taking gender into account: Theory and design for women's leadership development programs'. *Academy of Management Learning & Education*, 10(3), 474–93.
Feldman, D.C. (2001), 'Career coaching: What HR professionals and managers need to know'. *Human Resource Planning*, 24(2), 26–35.
Friedman, S.D. (2008), *Total Leadership: Be a Better Leader, Have a Richer Life*, Boston, MA: Harvard Business Press.
Friedman, T.L. (2005), *The World is Flat: A Brief History of the Twenty-first Century*, New York: Farrar, Straus and Giroux.
Fugate, M. and A.J. Kinicki (2008), 'A dispositional approach to employability: Development of a measure and test of implications for employee reactions to organizational change'. *Journal of Occupational and Organizational Psychology*, 81(3), 503–27.
Fugate, M., A.J. Kinicki and B.E. Ashforth (2004), 'Employability: A psycho-social construct, its dimensions, and applications'. *Journal of Vocational Behavior*, 65(1), 14–38.
Galinsky, E. and K. Matos (2011), 'The future of work–life fit'. *Organizational Dynamics*, 40(4), 267–80.
Gallup (2013), 'State of the American workplace: Employee engagement insights for US business leaders'. Washington, DC: Gallup.
Goodman, C.J. and S.M. Mance (2011), 'Employment loss and the 2007–09 recession: An overview'. *Monthly Labor Review*, 134(4), 3–12.
Grant, A.M. (2013), *Give and Take: A Revolutionary Approach to Success*, New York: Viking.
Greguras, G.J. and J.M. Diefendorff (2010), 'Why does proactive personality predict employee life satisfaction and work behaviors? A field investigation of the mediating role of the self-concordance model'. *Personnel Psychology*, 63(3), 539–60.
Hall, D.T. (2004a), 'The protean career: A quarter-century journey'. *Journal of Vocational Behavior*, 65(1), 1–13.
Hall, D.T. (2004b), 'Self-awareness, identity, and leader development', in D.V. Day, S.J. Zaccaro and S.M. Halpin (eds), *Leader Development for Transforming Organizations: Growing Leaders for Tomorrow* (pp. 153–76), Mahwah, NJ: Lawrence Erlbaum Associates.
Hall, D.T. and J.E. Moss (1998), 'The new protean career contract: Helping organizations and employees adapt'. *Organizational Dynamics*, 26(3), 22–37.
Hornung, S., D.M. Rousseau and J. Glaser (2008), 'Creating flexible work arrangements through idiosyncratic deals'. *Journal of Applied Psychology*, 93(3), 655–64.
Hornung, S., D.M. Rousseau, J. Glaser, P. Angerer and M. Weigl (2010), 'Beyond top-down and bottom-up work redesign: Customizing job content through idiosyncratic deals'. *Journal of Organizational Behavior*, 31(2–3), 187–215.
Huselid, M.A. (1995), 'The impact of human resource management practices on turnover, productivity and corporate financial performance'. *Academy of Management Journal*, 38(3), 635–72.

Ito, J.K. and C.M. Brotheridge (2005), 'Does supporting employees' career adaptability lead to commitment, turnover, or both?'. *Human Resource Management*, 44(1), 5–19.
Jacobs, S.J. and D.L. Blustein (2008), 'Mindfulness as a coping mechanism for employment uncertainty'. *Career Development Quarterly*, 57(2), 174–80.
Jordan, S., M. Messner and A. Becker (2009), 'Reflection and mindfulness in organizations: Rationales and possibilities for integration'. *Management Learning*, 40(4), 465–73.
Kahn, W.A. (1990), 'Psychological conditions of personal engagement and disengagement at work'. *Academy of Management Journal*, 33(4), 692–724.
Kopelman, S., E.R. Feldman, D.M. McDaniel and D.T. Hall (2012), 'Mindfully negotiating a career with a heart'. *Organizational Dynamics*, 41(2), 163–71.
Kossek, E.E., K. Roberts, S. Fisher and B. DeMarr (1998), 'Career self-management: A quasi-experimental assessment of the effects of a training intervention'. *Personnel Psychology*, 51(4), 935–62.
Kraimer, M.L., S.E. Seibert, S.J. Wayne, R.C. Liden and J. Bravo (2011), 'Antecedents and outcomes of organizational support for development: The critical role of career opportunities'. *Journal of Applied Psychology*, 96(3), 485–500.
Lepak, D.P. and S.A. Snell (1999), 'The human resource architecture: Toward a theory of human capital allocation and development'. *Academy of Management Review*, 24(1), 31–48.
Leroy, H., F. Anseel, N.G. Dimitrova and L. Sels (2013), 'Mindfulness, authentic functioning, and work engagement: A growth modeling approach'. *Journal of Vocational Behavior*, 82(3), 238–47.
Li, W.-D., D. Fay, M. Frese, P.D. Harms and X.Y. Gao (2014), 'Reciprocal relationship between proactive personality and work characteristics: A latent change score approach'. *Journal of Applied Psychology*, 99(5), 948–65.
Lips-Wiersma, M. and D.T. Hall (2007), 'Organizational career development is *not* dead: A case study on managing the new career during organizational change'. *Journal of Organizational Behavior*, 28(6), 771–92.
London, M. (1993), 'Relationships between career motivation, empowerment and support for career development'. *Journal of Occupational & Organizational Psychology*, 66(1), 55–69.
Lyons, P. (2008), 'The crafting of jobs and individual differences'. *Journal of Business & Psychology*, 23(1/2), 25–36.
McInnis, K.J., J.P. Meyer and S. Feldman (2009), 'Psychological contracts and their implications for commitment: A feature-based approach'. *Journal of Vocational Behavior*, 74(2), 165–80.
Nakai, Y., B. Chang, A.F. Snell and C.D. Fluckinger (2011), 'Profiles of mature job seekers: Connecting needs and desires to work characteristics'. *Journal of Organizational Behavior*, 32(2), 155–72.
Ng, T.W.H. and D.C. Feldman (2010), 'Idiosyncratic deals and organizational commitment'. *Journal of Vocational Behavior*, 76(3), 419–27.
PriceWaterhouseCoopers (2013a), 'PwC's NextGen: A global generational study'. New York: PriceWaterhouseCoopers.
PriceWaterhouseCoopers (2013b), '16th Annual Global CEO Survey'. London: PriceWaterhouseCoopers.
Rich, B.L., J.A. Lepine and E.R. Crawford (2010), 'Job engagement: Antecedents and effects on job performance'. *Academy of Management Journal*, 53(3), 617–35.
Rosen, C.C., D.J. Slater, C.-H. Chang and R.E. Johnson (2013), 'Let's make a deal: Development and validation of the ex post i-deals scale'. *Journal of Management*, 39(3), 709–42.
Rousseau, D.M. (2005), *I-deals: Idiosyncratic Deals Employees Bargain for Themselves*, New York: M.E. Sharpe.
Ryan, R.M. and E.L. Deci (2000), 'Self-determination theory and the facilitation of intrinsic motivation, social development, and well-being'. *American Psychologist*, 55(1), 68–78.
Schulte, B. (2014), *Overwhelmed: Work, Love and Play When No One Has the Time*, New York: Sarah Crichton Books.
Seibert, S.E., J.M. Crant and M.L. Kraimer (1999), 'Proactive personality and career success'. *Journal of Applied Psychology*, 84(3), 416–27.
Seibert, S.E., M.L. Kraimer and J.M. Crant (2001), 'What do proactive people do? A longitudinal model linking proactive personality and career success'. *Personnel Psychology*, 54(4), 845–74.
Shafer, R.A., L. Dyer, J. Kilty, J. Amos and J. Ericksen (2001), 'Crafting a human resource strategy to foster organizational agility: A case study'. *Human Resource Management*, 40(3), 197–211.
Sheldon, O.J., D. Dunning and D.R. Ames (2014), 'Emotionally unskilled, unaware, and uninterested in learning more: Reactions to feedback about deficits in emotional intelligence'. *Journal of Applied Psychology*, 99(1), 125–37.
Spell, H.B., L.T. Eby and R.J. Vandenberg (2014), 'Developmental climate: A cross-level analysis of voluntary turnover and job performance'. *Journal of Vocational Behavior*, 84(3), 283–92.
Steel, R.P., R.W. Griffeth and P.W. Hom (2002), 'Practical retention policy for the practical manager'. *Academy of Management Executive*, 16(2), 149–62.

Stone, P. (2007), *Opting Out? Why Women Really Quit Careers and Head Home*, Berkeley, CA: University of California Press.
Strauss, K., M.A. Griffin and S.K. Parker (2012), 'Future work selves: How salient hoped-for identities motivate proactive career behaviors'. *Journal of Applied Psychology*, 97(3), 580–98.
Sullivan, S.E. and Y. Baruch (2009), 'Advances in career theory and research: A critical review and agenda for future exploration'. *Journal of Management*, 35(6), 1542–71.
Thompson, R. (2014), 'For a more flexible workforce, hire self-aware people', available at http://blogs.hbr.org/2014/01/for-a-more-flexible-workforce-hire-self-aware-people/.
Towers Watson (2012), '2012–13 Towers Watson global talent management and rewards study'. New York: Towers Watson.
Twenge, J. (2010), 'A review of the empirical evidence on generational differences in work attitudes'. *Journal of Business & Psychology*, 25(2), 201–10.
Uggerslev, K.L., N.E. Fassina and D. Kraichy (2012), 'Recruiting through the stages: A meta-analytic test of predictors of applicant attraction at different stages of the recruiting process'. *Personnel Psychology*, 65(3), 597–660.
Valcour, M., L. Bailyn and M.A. Quijada (2007), 'Customized careers', in H.P. Gunz and M.A. Peiperl (eds), *Handbook of Career Studies* (pp. 188–210), Newbury Park, CA: Sage.
Van Veldhoven, M. and L. Dorenbosch (2008), 'Age, proactivity and career development'. *Career Development International*, 13(2), 112–31.
Way, S.A. (2002), 'High performance work systems and intermediate indicators of firm performance within the US small business sector'. *Journal of Management*, 28(6), 765–86.
Williams, J.C. and H. Boushey (2010), 'The three faces of work–family conflict: The poor, the professionals, and the missing middle'. San Francisco, CA: Center for WorkLife Law, University of California, Hastings College of the Law.
Wrzesniewski, A. and J.E. Dutton (2001), 'Crafting a job: Revisioning employees as active crafters of their work'. *Academy of Management Review*, 26(2), 179–201.

3 Merits and challenges of career adaptability as a tool towards sustainable careers

Maximilian B.W. Buyken, Ute-Christine Klehe, Jelena Zikic and Annelies E.M. Van Vianen

Career adaptability, 'the readiness to cope with the predictable tasks of preparing for and participating in the work role and with the unpredictable adjustments prompted by changes in work and working conditions' (Savickas, 1997, p.254), is an essential concept in career research and counseling. Career adaptability has been described (Savickas and Porfeli, 2012; Super and Knasel, 1981), studied (Klehe et al., 2011; Noe and Steffy, 1987) and recommended (Brown and Lent, 2005; Spokane, 1991) by practitioners and scientists alike for managing sustainable careers of both adolescents and adults. In particular today's adults, who face a continuously changing and insecure world of work (see Gowing et al., 1998; Howard, 1995) are in dire need of the proposed benefits of career adaptability in order to ensure truly sustainable careers (Probst, 2005). Yet, while career adaptability fosters career development under many conditions, there is also a certain disparity between the universal usefulness propagated and the empirical findings on which to base such claims (for example, Luyckx et al., 2008; Zikic and Klehe, 2006).

This chapter will focus on understanding career adaptability and its application to adults in various contexts, in consideration of their specific situations and needs. For this purpose, we first give a short summary of research on career adaptability. Second, we review how current conceptualizations of career adaptability may be responsible for some of the inconclusive results on career development. Third, we try to uncover 'blind spots' in recent conceptualizations of career adaptability and offer recommendations for constructs that are potentially relevant for career development in the context of our modern world of work. With these considerations, we aim to indicate areas of further conceptual development and empirical testing, and to provide promising avenues for future research and practice.

CURRENT RESEARCH ON CAREER ADAPTABILITY

The concept of career adaptability builds on Super's work (1955) on vocational maturity, that is, an individual's vocational development and readiness to make career decisions during the school-to-work transition. Super et al. (1988) introduced the term 'career adaptability' to reflect the fact that not only teenagers, but working adults, too, need a 'readiness to cope with changing work and working conditions' (p. 83) as they face challenges and opportunities, including 'novel, non-maturational problems' (Super and Knasel, 1981, p.199) that force and/or allow them to make career decisions throughout their working lives. Therefore, career adaptability is geared towards the construction of sustainable careers across the life-span.

More recently, Savickas (2005, p. 51) refined career adaptability as 'an individual's readiness and resources for coping with current and imminent vocational development tasks, occupational transitions, and personal traumas'. Inherent in this notion are (a) a person-centered perspective, and (b) a positive and proactive outlook into the future, even in the face of traumas. Thus, career adaptability implies the aim to adapt oneself to one's (work) environment as well as trying to change the environment in order to create a good person–environment fit.

Past research has operationalized career adaptability via different concepts, such as career planning, exploring and deciding (Phillips and Blustein, 1994), career planning, decidedness and confidence (Skorikov, 2007), or as a boundaryless mindset (McArdle et al., 2007).

Savickas (2005, p. 52) presented an overall framework that describes career adaptability by means of four components: concern, control, curiosity and confidence, each reflecting different 'attitudes, competencies, and behaviors that individuals use in fitting themselves to work that suits them' (Savickas, 2005, p. 45). Hence, career adaptability implies looking ahead to one's future career (*concern* or *planning*), knowing what career to pursue (*control* or *decision-making*), looking around at various career options (*curiosity* or *exploration*), and having a feeling of self-efficacy to successfully execute the activities needed to achieve one's career goals (*confidence*).

Positive Effects of Career Adaptability

Empirical research supports the usefulness of most of the aforementioned components. First, career planning (see Gould, 1979) has been linked to both subjective career success (career satisfaction) and objective career success (salary; Ng et al., 2005). Particularly among job seekers, career planning has proven to be a useful longitudinal predictor of later employment quality (Koen et al., 2010; Zikic and Klehe, 2006).

Secondly, career exploration implies the collection of information relevant to the progress of one's career (Jordaan, 1963; Stumpf et al., 1983) with the goal of reaching the knowledge, understanding and reasoning needed for wise career decisions. For this purpose, exploration can focus on the self by exploring one's own needs and values, interests and goals, skills and experiences, and/or can focus on the environment, thus exploring occupations, jobs, and organizations to gain a better understanding of available job options (Stumpf et al., 1983; Werbel, 2000). Self and environmental exploration should therefore help people develop a 'personal compass' to give (new) direction to their life (Hall, 1986), and to (re-)build their career identity; that means the way in which they define themselves in the context of their careers (Fugate et al., 2004).

Finally, self-efficacy – one's judgment of 'how well one can execute courses of action required to deal with prospective situations' (Bandura, 1982, p. 122) – motivates people to set higher goals for themselves and to invest more effort, and also makes them persist longer in the face of difficulties and setbacks (Bandura, 1997). Occupational or career-related self-efficacy serves well in fostering both subjective (Koen et al., 2010; Zikic and Klehe, 2006) and objective career success (for example, Abele and Spurk, 2009 in the form of salary and status; Day and Allen, 2004).

Adverse Findings for Career Adaptability

These positive findings generally support the usefulness of career adaptability. However, other findings suggest a more cautious view. From an organization's perspective, Klehe et al. (2011) found that in the context of organizational downsizing, career exploration was negatively related to loyalty and positively related to employees' subsequent turnover intentions (see also Ito and Brotheridge, 2005), job search and actual turnover.

For individuals, current results are unanimously positive about planning, confidence and decision-making (Koen et al., 2010), yet are far more contradictory regarding career exploration. For example, Koen et al. (2010) failed to find the proposed positive effects on re-employment outcomes such as job satisfaction or needs–supply fit. Werbel (2000) found self-exploration to be unrelated to both initial compensation after job search and to job satisfaction, and environmental exploration was only related to compensation, but not to job satisfaction (see also Stumpf and Hartman, 1984; Zikic and Klehe, 2006). Additionally, Luyckx et al. (2008) found that different forms of exploration, namely in-depth and in-breadth exploration as well as ruminative exploration, correlated with anxiety and depressive symptoms. Similarly, self-exploration and/or environmental exploration are sometimes connected to explorational and decisional stress (Reed et al., 2004; Rowold, 2007).

At first sight, these findings suggest that some parts of career adaptability are useful, while others may be less so. The following section of this chapter addresses possible conceptual and methodological reasons for these ambiguous results.

MISSING LINKS IN THE CONCEPTUALIZATION OF CAREER ADAPTABILITY

When searching for conceptual and methodological reasons for divergent findings on career adaptability as well as potential remedies, we discuss the role of career adaptability as a composite construct and career exploration as a separate composite construct. Further, we address possible boundary or beneficial conditions such as career phases, life goals (also outside the work domain), social context, and chance events. Finally, we discuss cognition (awareness) and behavior (exploration).

Career Adaptability as a Composite Construct?

We usually do not assess career adaptability directly, but rather combine some of its associated constructs such as career exploration (Stumpf et al., 1983), career planning (Gould, 1979), career self-efficacy (Kossek et al., 1998), and career decidedness (Callanan and Greenhaus, 1990; for an overview see Gordon, 1998). This is often done conceptually, for example, by assuming uniform relationships between the sub-dimensions of career-adaptability and its proposed outcomes, but also empirically, for example, by creating a single factor of the sub-dimensions via principal component analysis (Hirschi, 2009). By doing so, researchers implicitly assume that all sub-dimensions simultaneously influence outcomes in a similar manner and that they are equally important at any given time during the career decision-making process.

This is debatable on conceptual and empirical grounds. On the one hand, Marcia's theory of identity development (Marcia, 1966) and empirical findings (Hirschi, 2012; Porfeli et al., 2011) suggest that some people concurrently show high exploration and high commitment to a vocational identity.

On the other hand, how can someone who explores intensely also be very decided? And, why should someone who is decided still explore? An answer to these questions may lie in the distinction between exploration in breadth ('prescreening the potential set of alternatives'; Gati and Asher, 2001, p. 18) and in depth ('exploration of the promising alternatives . . ., resulting in a few *suitable alternatives*'; Gati and Asher, 2001, p. 18, emphasis in the original). Thus, exploration in depth aims at making a specific decision or choice, whereas exploration in breadth may help to reach such a decision in the first place. Accordingly, in-depth exploration was positively related to commitment-making, while in-breadth exploration was positively related to commitment-flexibility in a university sample (Porfeli et al., 2011).

This view is compatible with sequential models of decision-making (Gati and Asher, 2001). Harren (1979) proposed that a stage of awareness about the current situation is followed by a stage of exploration and planning, which then eventually leads to crystallization and ultimately to committing to a clear vocational identity (see also Super and Hall, 1978).

If we follow this approach, it would be unreasonable to call for all sub-dimensions of career adaptability to be equally pronounced at all times. Some might be generally useful (career self-efficacy, or low general indecisiveness; Osipow, 1999), while others may be bound to certain stages of the career decision-making process (for example, exploration in breadth, or decidedness; Callanan and Greenhaus, 1990). In particular career exploration may be a more complex construct than is often assumed, which is why we will examine career exploration and its operationalization in more detail.

A Critical Look at Career Exploration

As career adaptability, career exploration has been conceptualized and operationalized quite differently. Most research focuses on self- and environmental exploration (for example, Hirschi, 2012; Klehe et al., 2011), while some research (for example, Dietrich et al., 2011; Klimstra et al., 2012) differentiates between broad and in-depth exploration.

One of the most widely used scales to assess career exploration is the Career Exploration Survey (CES; Stumpf et al., 1983). Yet, while ample research uses the CES-dimensions of self- and environmental exploration, the original CES includes further scales on potentially useful constructs such as intended-systematic exploration, amount of information obtained, explorational stress, and decisional stress (Stumpf et al., 1983). One may argue that the amount of information obtained is rather an outcome than part of exploration itself. Information obtained may, however, serve as an indicator of the exploration's actual usefulness. Ignoring this factor essentially signifies the assumption that more exploration is always better than less exploration, irrespective of its context, type, or effectiveness. But not all 'explorers' may explore equally effectively, for example, due to access to suboptimal informants unwilling or unable to provide unbiased and complete information.

One might wonder whether the CES subscales add any value above and beyond self- and environmental exploration. However, Stumpf and Hartman (1984) found that the amount of information obtained was positively related to realistic expectations, person–job congruence and later work motivation, whereas environmental exploration itself was unrelated to any of these variables (see also Rowold, 2007).

The more recent distinction between exploration in breadth and in depth (Germeijs and Verschueren, 2006a) seems important because it signifies different goals, which may, in turn, cause different outcomes in terms of employment status and quality. For example, if adult workers experience job insecurity (see Probst, 2005) or know that they will lose their jobs, they may explore in preparation for a new occupation elsewhere (Klehe et al., 2011). If they seek a job similar to their current or last one, they can directly begin exploring their options in depth by enquiring about vacancies that match their needs and experiences. If, however, they are forced or willing to choose an unrelated line of work, these adults face a more open problem. Instead of 'just' deciding *where* to work, they first have to decide *what* to do, and how well this fits their characteristics (see Kristof-Brown et al., 2005), their personal and financial needs, and their wishes for vocational development. This seems like a difficult task whereby broad exploration may not lead to the same desirable outcomes as in-depth exploration (see Porfeli et al., 2011).

Luyckx et al. (2008, p. 61) additionally introduced ruminative exploration – a dysfunctional type of exploration 'characterized by a repetitive and passive focus' – in order to better explain the seemingly controversial findings that exploration has both adaptive (commitment-making) and maladaptive (depression, anxiety) outcomes. They showed that ruminative exploration exhibited considerably higher correlations with depression and anxiety than exploration in breadth and in depth. Also, ruminative exploration correlated strongly and negatively with commitment-making and identification.

In conclusion, it seems useful to revise and extend our view on career exploration as a valuable part of career adaptability.

'The Missing Links' – Missing Dimensions

The current conceptualization of career adaptability is individualistic and agentic. Even though this is a strength of the concept, it neglects important aspects outside people's immediate influence such as their career phase, investments, transitional goals, social context, and chance events. In the following, we will consider how these aspects may influence people's career decision-making and development, over and above individual career adaptability.

Career phases and investments

To date, researchers have adapted models designed for students during the school-to-work transition to the context of adult workers, essentially re-labeling career maturity (Super, 1977) as career adaptability. However, we cannot automatically assume that career transitions of adult employees and job-seekers are comparable to those of adolescents, who are at different stages of their careers (Super, 1980), accompanied by different experiences, entrenchment, expectations and needs. Adults in need of adaptation have already made and invested in some career choice. Consequently, they may find themselves deeply entrenched in their careers, being aware of high occupational investments undertaken, of the high emotional costs of changing these occupations, and also of their limited occupational alternatives (Carson and Carson, 1997).

The model of career entrenchment (Carson and Carson, 1997) suggests that people may well start out in their career based on interests, preferences and available opportunities, followed by investments of time, effort, and money in order to 'make it' in their chosen vocation. People will continue investing if they think that the rewards gained are worth it. If not, however, things become more difficult. Most models on person–environment fit (for example, Dawis, 2005) assume that after a certain flexibility is overstretched, people will start some adjustment behavior or ultimately exit the situation. What most of these theories do not consider, however, are sunk costs and the human propensity to 'throw good money after bad' (Kahneman and Tversky, 1979), which means that the investments made are rationalized in order to achieve psychological preservation. This suggests that careers with high prior investments may be particularly difficult to drop, also making it difficult to distinguish between career identity and career entrenchment.

Despite such entrenchment, people may move into a different vocational field if attractive opportunities arise (Carson and Carson, 1997). However, such opportunities often diminish over time and may come at greater financial costs: for example, no commercial airline would invest in training someone over 40 years old to become a professional pilot. Results among displaced workers consistently show significant earnings reductions upon re-employment, particularly for older job-seekers (Koeber and Wright, 2001; Stevens, 1997), with each year of job tenure in the old job being associated with additional re-employment wage losses (Munnell et al., 2006), particularly when workers gain re-employment outside of their prior career jobs or industry (Couch et al., 2009). These workers are unable to capitalize on their human and social capital established during earlier career stages.

Altogether, exploration and an ensuing change in direction of one's career may come at greater costs for adult workers than for career starters. Consequently, researchers and counselors should study the benefits and pitfalls of career adaptability in general, and career exploration in particular, while paying attention to the context, life stage, experiences, sunk costs, and reduced alternatives that adults may face.

Role of career adaptability in other life transitions

While career exploration has been examined in the context of finding re-employment, its role could be studied more broadly as it may allow individuals to explore other types of outcomes and/or domains of life (family, social and caring needs, hobbies). Namely, career transitions usually encompass a conglomerate of needs and goals not necessarily tied to the type or field of work, or job quality (see Plimmer and Schmidt, 2007). Job-seekers are often concerned with issues related to balancing work and non-work tasks, or with finding employment that allows for flexibility outside of the work setting.

These other types of goals must be included in the exploration, planning and decision-making in the course of a transition. Thus, while we know of the positive spillover between work and non-work domains (Greenhaus and Powell, 2006) we have yet to expand our understanding on the role of career adaptability in managing transitions in the context of the numerous roles that people enact in their lives. For example, a dual career couple with young children may explore towards finding a better integration of family commitments and work roles. Thus, a more detailed understanding of specific context and goals of the job-seeker may allow us to grasp the limits, type, and optimal quantity and/or quality of exploration.

Exploration and adaptability may further come into question during major career transitions, such as challenges of diverse job-seekers (such as migrant workers), who often experience major structural barriers like strong regulatory mechanisms and organizational gatekeepers (Zikic et al., 2010). Given these strong external barriers, the initial exploration of migrant workers may be geared towards finding a survival job as a way of supporting their family and settling down. Later, these individuals may enter another career transition with the ultimate goal of finding a better-quality job more fitting with their training and experience – requiring a broader and more holistic type of career adaptability. Thus, saying that finding a survival job is a rather unsuccessful outcome of career adaptability in terms of re-employment quality may only be correct within a rather narrow focus. Conversely, if a survival job is a necessary stepping-stone towards finding high-quality employment (for example, in order to ensure financial stability), we have to broaden our scope of the entire process in order to correctly judge the usefulness of career adaptability. This is, of course, not to make the mistake of glorifying survival jobs (see McCoy and Masuch, 2007).

In conclusion, we need research that focuses on understanding initial goals of transitioning actors and their needs in the broader context of life. Also, while we have only started to understand the variety of contextual domains where career adaptability may play a key role (for example, during downsizing, Klehe et al., 2011),there is still a need to examine the role of career adaptability in transitions such as retirement (Sargent et al., 2013) or migration (Zikic et al., 2010). Depending on the magnitude of the transition and the characteristics of the actor, we may see differential emphasis on each of the four domains of concern, control, confidence, and curiosity. For example, potential retirees may have different concerns typical of 'second careers', whereas immigrants may face uncertainty and may need reassurance, with social support and career confidence being key aspects of their adaptability and ways to control their destiny. We turn to the role of social context, because the role of 'others' has not been considered much as a key to career adaptability (for an exception see Zikic and Hall, 2009).

Social context

Careers research has already been concerned with the importance of social context for quite some time (Lent et al., 1994), without, however, regarding it as a part of career adaptability, as adaptability is focused on the individual person and an agentic perspective. Therefore, we want to stress that considering the social context of a person in a career transition might provide a broad and useful perspective that career adaptability alone may not be able to deliver.

In the realm of careers, a specific and crucial part of the social context has often been referred to as *social capital* (or social barriers as a counterpart; see Lent et al., 1994); that means individuals' social skills, network, and support, which are all important sources for career behaviors. Social capital is – besides adaptability, human capital, and career identity – one of the pillars of employability which is 'a form of work specific active adaptability that enables workers to identify and realize career opportunities' (Fugate et al., 2004, p. 16). People who are employable are able to hold a job, develop a career, and find a job when unemployed.

Social capital affects people's career behaviors in several ways. First, social support and networks positively influence the intensity of job search during unemployment (Boswell et al., 2011) and, second, they provide access to potential employers and thus enhance one's chance of finding a job (McKee-Ryan et al., 2005; Wanberg et al., 1999). In a recent study among long-term unemployed people, Koen et al. (2013a) found that adaptability and social capital affected the re-employment process differently: adaptability (career exploration and planning) was primarily important for persisting in job search, whereas social capital helped to find re-employment. In other words, adaptability taps into motivational processes while social capital opens (employment) doors. Third, salient role models in one's social context can prompt the development of a career identity. Koen et al. (2013b) showed that disadvantaged young adults who participated in an internship program developed a career identity when they actively distinguished themselves from their former social identity of disadvantaged youth, or when they identified themselves with group members in the program who had a positive stance towards employment.

Making use of the unknown

The personal circumstances of working adults and their social context contain many uncontrollable factors. While we agree with other career development theories (for example, Lent et al., 1994; Savickas, 2013) that an agentic perspective of deliberate career construction is necessary for satisfactory vocational development, most theories ignore the element of chance and unpredictability. As a matter of fact, most theories and counselors act as if career development had nothing to do with chance or try to minimize its impact (Mitchell et al., 1999). This is where theories like the chaos theory of careers (Pryor and Bright, 2003) or the theory of planned happenstance (Mitchell et al., 1999) can be helpful, because they incorporate aspects like chance, chaos and non-linearity into career development.

Still, previous scholarly work has not systematically picked up this notion (see Betsworth and Hansen, 1996). On the one hand, this is understandable, as it is probably difficult to methodically incorporate chance into empirical investigations. As one of a few exceptions, Betsworth and Hansen (1996, p.91) dealt with 'the categorization of serendipitous career development events', without, however, directly linking them to outcomes. On the other hand, chance events and the way people make use of them may account for a substantial amount of variance in positive or negative outcomes of career transitions. Even more so, an individual's past or characteristics may influence the occurrence of chance events (Mitchell et al., 1999). Consequently, it is possible that people high on career adaptability raise the probability of beneficial chance events happening to them. As an example: if people explore and talk to job-holders in the vocational area they would like to work in, those job-holders might not only give them the requested information, but might also notify them of emerging employment opportunities. This way, being highly adaptable might cause some sort of a Matthew Effect ('for to everyone who has will more be given'; Matthew 25:29, English Standard Version).

Awareness instead of deliberate exploration

Considering the amount of unpredictable and uncontrollable influences on career development, people need a strategy that matches the challenges associated with these influences. For example, non-traditional careers require that employees make periodic career decisions throughout their working lives (Savickas et al., 2009). Career decision-making is effective when people find work (environments) compatible with their preferences, aptitudes, needs, and goals (see Kristof-Brown et al., 2005). Hence, effective decision-making may involve the weighing of possible job options as nourished by reflections on one's own characteristics and those of (possible) work and non-work activities and environments. The more aware employees are of themselves and their environment, the better they will be able to anticipate career transitions and to actually make these transitions.

First, self-awareness and environment-awareness are necessary for the setting and planning of career goals (concern), getting personal control, prompting exploratory behaviors (curiosity), and strengthening one's confidence in goal attainment. In other words, self-awareness and environment-awareness are the primary basis of career adaptability: it is very difficult to imagine adaptability without awareness (see Harren, 1979).

Second, self-awareness and environment-awareness are the mechanisms through which rational and intuitive decision-making strategies increase the chance of finding a fitting job (Singh and Greenhaus, 2004). Rational decision-making is based on the systematic gathering and contemplation of external and internal information and the use of decision rules. In addition, Singh and Greenhaus (2004) found that decision-making was most effective (in fostering a higher person–job fit) when employees combined a rational strategy with a more intuitive one. The complementary use of both head and heart went together with higher self-awareness and environment-awareness. People's intuitions or gut feelings are likely to be the result of (unconscious) information (prior experiences) as stored in the brain. Reflections on the self and the environment activate this information and its associated emotions, which evoke an intuitive sense of direction when making decisions (Nordgren et al., 2011). All in all, rational decision-making triggers self-awareness and environmental awareness which, in turn, support the use of a more intuitive strategy.

The concept of awareness complements intentional and deliberate career exploration and focuses on a sensitivity and openness to resources already available to the person. In contrast to the traditional definition of exploration (Stumpf et al., 1983, p. 192) as a 'purposive behavior and cognitions that afford access to information about occupations, jobs, or organizations that was not previously in the stimulus field', the resources and opportunities to be discovered via awareness are technically already in the stimulus field. The task of the person switches from intentional information gathering to signal detection and thereby reflects a more chaotic and unpredictable notion of career development.

A blessing in disguise – strengthening the notion

The recent conceptualization or understanding of career adaptability as a way of proactive coping (Klehe et al., 2012) stresses its importance for people's career development. Changes in the way we work may be associated with 'personal traumas' (Savickas, 2005, p. 51) such as job insecurity, job loss, or unemployment, which are generally viewed as causing a strain on physical and mental health (Paul and Moser, 2009; Sverke et al., 2002). So when we define career adaptability as a form of coping, we treat it as a set of behaviors and attitudes that help deal with or end unwanted and aversive states. The notion that stressful events like job loss can also be helpful for people's careers and thus may act as a 'blessing in disguise' (Zikic and Klehe, 2006, p. 391) opposes the view that all such career transitions are necessarily bad. But what if the blessing is not that disguised after all? What if, for example, a person intentionally takes a job that offers less employment security, but that compensates this disadvantage with features such as adventure and excitement or great learning opportunities? In such a situation, ending the state of job insecurity would not be the desired course of action. On the contrary, the advantages of the insecure job may actually foster the person's career development, for example, by further increasing his or her human capital. People could then use their adaptability, for example their career self-efficacy to cope with the – otherwise existing – negative effects of job insecurity.

Due to changes in the labor market and especially the way these changes are perceived, job security and lifelong employment may lose their centrality to people (see Arthur and Rousseau, 1996). Actually, we seem to lack straightforward evidence that proves the popular assumption that employment stability is decreasing (Auer and Cazes, 2000; Doogan, 2001). Thus, regardless of whether 'longer-term full-time employment relationships belong to the past' (see Auer and Cazes, 2003, p. 2), people nowadays may be socialized into a labor market in which job security and stable employment may not even be something that they aspire to any more (Lippmann, 2008). This would also impact the domain of career counseling. Under this assumption, counselors could adapt their services to the type of career adaptability of their clients. Other characteristics to look out for, which are missing in current conceptualizations, could be the appraisal of the employment situation (challenge versus threat or hindrance; see Webster et al., 2011) and tolerance of uncertainty or ambiguity (see Furnham, 1994).

THE FUTURE OF CAREER ADAPTABILITY – IMPLICATIONS

Analogous to changes in the world of work and of career construction, career adaptability has undergone changes over the years and decades. Therefore, just as the notion of 'career maturity' may not fit modern careers any more, the concept of career adaptability is also bound to evolve further. With this chapter, we want to contribute to this evolution.

Before we turn to the implications for practice and research, we want to stress that career adaptability describes a very useful set of behaviors, attitudes and competencies for both adolescents' and adults' career decision-making and career development. Therefore, we intend to give suggestions on how to further improve the concept, with implications for career counseling and research. While we therefore scrutinized career adaptability in this chapter, our goal was to explore avenues for further applications of career adaptability beyond the agentic perspective.

Implications for Research

First and foremost, research needs to consider that adults face a different contextual milieu than adolescents. Hence, we need to adapt our understanding of career adaptability and of the challenges associated with adulthood and adult transitions (see also Conroy and O'Leary-Kelly, 2013) and – in order to examine these differences in more detail – we need more research on the career adaptability of adults. For instance, how open and free are they in their exploration and what costs, but also what benefits, are associated with considering a total change in their career paths, considering previous investments? If research and ultimately practice want to understand, predict, and foster the construction of sustainable careers and to give recommendations to people in transition, we need to consider the entire life-span and not just the school-to-work-transition. Research on exploration in breadth and in depth so far mainly focuses on adolescents or young adults just prior to or in the process of entering their first vocation (for example, Germeijs and Verschueren, 2006b; Porfeli and Skorikov, 2010), whereas we are not aware of such research among adults who can already look back over a certain career trajectory and face a work-to-work or the unemployment-to-work-transition. Porfeli and Lee (2012, p. 13) argued that 'both forms of exploration likely operate across the life span', whereas others have argued that exploration in breadth is less relevant for adults than for (late) adolescents (see Klimstra et al., 2012). These contradictory arguments have yet to be tested empirically.

Secondly, we need to understand how mechanisms of career adaptation actually work in the context of multiple life transitions, which may be more complex than previously assumed. In order to achieve this, more research should reflect the process perspectives that career theories often encompass (see Savickas, 2002), rather than relying on cross-sectional or at most single repeated measurements. Additionally, research could – while still maintaining a positive view on career adaptability as an agentic concept – consider more aspects and influences not entirely controllable by people in transition, such as chance and the social context. A strengthened focus on concepts like awareness could help in terms of utilizing these harder-to-capture influences on career development. What stands out from our thoughts and considerations on career adaptability, though, is that career exploration seems to be much more complicated and even potentially 'problematic' in terms of functioning and outcomes than other aspects of career adaptability. Therefore, it would be appropriate to examine the correlates and effects of career exploration more thoroughly.

Catering to the changing world of work and a more holistic view of the adult career, research could investigate the characteristics of people who are well-adapted to more and more common aspects of such changes, like (perceived) job insecurity. Who does deliberately choose insecure jobs and what makes these people successful despite such economic stressors? This knowledge will be vital if we assume that insecure conditions are not going to change (for the 'better') again in the future, in order to determine how people can nonetheless construct sustainable careers.

Implications for Practice

A first implication for practice may be a somewhat more critical stance towards career exploration. We do not argue that exploration is generally harmful to clients, but rather say that exploration may be far from the 'cure-it-all' often implied in counseling. Exploration often incurs considerable stress and anxiety, with the long-term benefits being less certain. Here, career interventions that help clients translate exploratory results into a sense of decidedness, planfulness and self-efficacy may be more suitable. Practitioners, like their scientist colleagues, should consider the sequential nature of career decision-making by adapting their counseling activities to each specific stage and its associated requirements (for example, administering interest inventories and encouraging in-breadth exploration in earlier stages, and promoting in-depth exploration and rendering assistance with regard to job search in later stages).

Taking this a step further, the view that counselors may have on the goals of career adaptation and the desired outcomes might be bound to change. Counselors could be less prescriptive and normative about what is considered a desirable employment outcome and instead turn to a more flexible goal-outcome match. This may heighten their and their clients' awareness of possible job opportunities. In doing so, career adaptability may help achieve what the concept of the protean career calls for in terms of subjective success criteria (Hall, 2004).

To conclude, we are convinced that researchers and practitioners will benefit from those aspects of career adaptability that have proven useful. At the same time they should extend the adaptability concept in order to fit the needs of adults in career transitions.

ACKNOWLEDGEMENT

This chapter was funded by a grant from the German Research Foundation (ORA-plus project KL 2366/2-1).

REFERENCES

Abele, A.E. and Spurk, D. (2009). The longitudinal impact of self-efficacy and career goals on objective and subjective career success. *Journal of Vocational Behavior*, 74, 53–62.

Arthur, M.B. and Rousseau, D.M. (eds) (1996). *The Boundaryless Career: A New Employment Principle for a New Organizational Era*. New York: Oxford University Press.

Auer, P. and Cazes, S. (2000). The resilience of the long-term employment relationship: Evidence from the industrialized countries. *International Labour Review*, 139, 379–408.

Auer, P. and Cazes, S. (eds) (2003). *Employment Stability in an Age of Flexibility: Evidence from the Industrialized Countries*. Geneva: International Labour Office.

Bandura, A. (1982). Self-efficacy mechanism in human agency. *American Psychologist*, 37, 122–47.

Bandura, A. (1997). *Self-efficacy: The Exercise of Control*. New York: Freeman.

Betsworth, D.G. and Hansen, J.-I.C. (1996). The categorization of serendipitous career development events. *Journal of Career Assessment*, 4, 91–8.

Boswell, W.R., Zimmerman, R.D. and Swider, B.W. (2011). Employee job search: Toward an understanding of search context and search objectives. *Journal of Management*, 38, 129–63.

Brown, S.D. and Lent, R.W. (eds) (2005). *Career Development and Counseling: Putting Theory and Research to Work*. Hoboken, NJ: Wiley.

Callanan, G.A. and Greenhaus, J.H. (1990). The career indecision of managers and professionals: Development of a scale and test of a model. *Journal of Vocational Behavior*, 37, 79–103.

Carson, K.D. and Carson, P.P. (1997). Career entrenchment: A quiet march toward occupational death? *Academy of Management Perspectives*, 11, 62–75.

Conroy, S.A. and O'Leary-Kelly, A.M. (2013). Letting go and moving on: Work-related identity loss and recovery. *Academy of Management Review*, 39, 67–87.

Couch, K.A., Jolly, N.A. and Placzek, D.W. (2009). Earnings losses of older displaced workers: A detailed analysis with administrative data. *Research on Aging*, 31, 17–40.

Dawis, R.V. (2005). The Minnesota theory of work adjustment. In S.D. Brown and R.W. Lent (eds), *Career Development and Counseling. Putting Theory and Research to Work* (pp. 3–23). Hoboken, NJ: Wiley.

Day, R. and Allen, T.D. (2004). The relationship between career motivation and self-efficacy with protégé career success. *Journal of Vocational Behavior*, 64, 72–91.

Dietrich, J., Kracke, B. and Nurmi, J.-E. (2011). Parents' role in adolescents' decision on a college major: A weekly diary study. *Journal of Vocational Behavior*, 79, 134–44.
Doogan, K. (2001). Insecurity and long-term employment. *Work, Employment & Society*, 15, 419–41.
Fugate, M., Kinicki, A.J. and Ashforth, B.E. (2004). Employability: A psycho-social construct, its dimensions, and applications. *Journal of Vocational Behavior*, 65, 14–38.
Furnham, A. (1994). A content, correlational and factor analytic study of four tolerance of ambiguity questionnaires. *Personality and Individual Differences*, 16, 403–10.
Gati, I. and Asher, I. (2001). The PIC model for career decision making: Prescreening, in-depth exploration, and choice. In F.T.L. Leong and A. Barak (eds), *Contemporary Models in Vocational Psychology. A Volume in Honor of Samuel H. Osipow* (pp. 7–54). Mahwah, NJ: Lawrence Erlbaum.
Germeijs, V. and Verschueren, K. (2006a). High school students' career decision-making process: Development and validation of the Study Choice Task Inventory. *Journal of Career Assessment*, 14, 449–71.
Germeijs, V. and Verschueren, K. (2006b). High school students' career decision-making process: A longitudinal study of one choice. *Journal of Vocational Behavior*, 68, 189–204.
Gordon, V.N. (1998). Career decidedness types: A literature review. *The Career Development Quarterly*, 46, 386–403.
Gould, S. (1979). Characteristics of career planners in upwardly mobile occupations. *Academy of Management Journal*, 22, 539–50.
Gowing, M.K., Kraft, J.D. and Campbell Quick, J. (eds) (1998). *The New Organizational Reality: Downsizing, Restructuring, and Revitalization*. Washington, DC: American Psychological Association.
Greenhaus, J.H. and Powell, G.N. (2006). When work and family are allies: A theory of work–family enrichment. *Academy of Management Review*, 31, 72–92.
Hall, D.T. (1986). *Breaking Career Routines: Midcareer Choice and Identity Development*. San Francisco, CA: Jossey-Bass.
Hall, D.T. (2004). The protean career: A quarter-century journey. *Journal of Vocational Behavior*, 65, 1–13.
Harren, V.A. (1979). A model of career decision making for college students. *Journal of Vocational Behavior*, 14, 119–33.
Hirschi, A. (2009). Career adaptability development in adolescence: Multiple predictors and effect on sense of power and life satisfaction. *Journal of Vocational Behavior*, 74, 145–55.
Hirschi, A. (2012). Vocational identity trajectories: Differences in personality and development of well-being. *European Journal of Personality*, 26, 2–12.
Howard, A. (1995). *The Changing Nature of Work*. San Francisco, CA: Jossey-Bass.
Ito, J.K. and Brotheridge, C.M. (2005). Does supporting employees' career adaptability lead to commitment, turnover, or both? *Human Resource Management*, 44, 5–19.
Jordaan, J.P. (1963). Exploratory behavior: The formation of self and occupational concept. In D.E. Super, R. Starishevsky, N. Matlin and J.P. Jordaan (eds), *Career Development: Self-concept Theory* (pp. 42–78). New York: College Entrance Examination Board.
Kahneman, D. and Tversky, A. (1979). Prospect theory: An analysis of decision under risk. *Econometrica*, 47, 263–91.
Klehe, U.-C., Zikic, J., Van Vianen, A.E.M. and De Pater, I.E. (2011). Career adaptability, turnover and loyalty during organizational downsizing. *Journal of Vocational Behavior*, 79, 217–29.
Klehe, U.-C., Zikic, J., Van Vianen, A.E.M., Koen, J. and Buyken, M. (2012). Coping proactively with economic stress: Career adaptability in the face of job insecurity, job loss, unemployment, and underemployment. In P.L. Perrewé, J.R.B. Halbesleben and C.C. Rosen (eds), *Research in Occupational Stress and Well-being: Vol. 10. The Role of the Economic Crisis on Occupational Stress and Well Being* (pp. 131–76). Bingley: Emerald.
Klimstra, T.A., Luyckx, K., Germeijs, V., Meeus, W.H.J. and Goossens, L. (2012). Personality traits and educational identity formation in late adolescents: Longitudinal associations and academic progress. *Journal of Youth and Adolescence*, 41, 346–61.
Koeber, C. and Wright, D.W. (2001). W/age bias in worker displacement: How industrial structure shapes the job loss and earnings decline of older American workers. *The Journal of Socio-Economics*, 30, 343–52.
Koen, J., Klehe, U.-C. and Van Vianen, A.E.M. (2013). Employability among the long-term unemployed: A futile quest or worth the effort? *Journal of Vocational Behavior*, 82, 37–48.
Koen, J., Zikic, J., Klehe, U.-C. and Van Vianen, A.E.M. (2013). Constructing career identity. Paper presented at the 16th congress of the European Association of Work and Organizational Psychology, Münster, Germany, May.
Koen, J., Klehe, U.-C., Van Vianen, A.E.M., Zikic, J. and Nauta, A. (2010). Job-search strategies and reemployment quality: The impact of career adaptability. *Journal of Vocational Behavior*, 77, 126–39.
Kossek, E.E., Roberts, K., Fisher, S. and Demarr, B. (1998). Career self-management: A quasi-experimental assessment of the effects of a training intervention. *Personnel Psychology*, 51, 935–60.
Kristof-Brown, A.L., Zimmerman, R.D. and Johnson, E.C. (2005). Consequences of individuals' fit at work:

A meta-analysis of person–job, person–organization, person–group, and person–supervisor fit. *Personnel Psychology*, 58, 281–342.
Lent, R.W., Brown, S.D. and Hackett, G. (1994). Toward a unifying social cognitive theory of career and academic interest, choice, and performance. *Journal of Vocational Behavior*, 45, 79–122.
Lippmann, S. (2008). Rethinking risk in the new economy: Age and cohort effects on unemployment and re-employment. *Human Relations*, 61, 1259–92.
Luyckx, K., Schwartz, S.J., Berzonsky, M.D., Soenens, B., Vansteenkiste, M., Smits, I. and Goossens, L. (2008). Capturing ruminative exploration: Extending the four-dimensional model of identity formation in late adolescence. *Journal of Research in Personality*, 42, 58–82.
Marcia, J.E. (1966). Development and validation of ego-identity status. *Journal of Personality and Social Psychology*, 3, 551–8.
McArdle, S., Waters, L., Briscoe, J.P. and Hall, D.T. (2007). Employability during unemployment: Adaptability, career identity and human and social capital. *Journal of Vocational Behavior*, 71, 247–64.
McCoy, L. and Masuch, C. (2007). Beyond 'entry-level' jobs: Immigrant women and non-regulated professional occupations. *Journal of International Migration and Integration/Revue de l'integration et de la Migration Internationale*, 8, 185–206.
McKee-Ryan, F., Song, Z., Wanberg, C.R. and Kinicki, A.J. (2005). Psychological and physical well-being during unemployment: A meta-analytic study. *Journal of Applied Psychology*, 90, 53–76.
Mitchell, K.E., Al Levin, S. and Krumboltz, J.D. (1999). Planned happenstance: Constructing unexpected career opportunities. *Journal of Counseling & Development*, 77, 115–24.
Munnell, A.H., Sass, S., Soto, M. and Zhivan, N. (2006). *Has the Displacement of Older Workers Increased?* Chestnut Hill, MA: Center for Retirement Research at Boston College.
Ng, T.W.H., Eby, L.T., Sorensen, K.L. and Feldman, D.C. (2005). Predictors of objective and subjective career success: A meta-analysis. *Personnel Psychology*, 58, 367–408.
Noe, R.A. and Steffy, B.D. (1987). The influence of individual characteristics and assessment center evaluation on career exploration behavior and job involvement. *Journal of Vocational Behavior*, 30, 187–202.
Nordgren, L.F., Bos, M.W. and Dijksterhuis, A. (2011). The best of both worlds: Integrating conscious and unconscious thought best solves complex decisions. *Journal of Experimental Social Psychology*, 47, 509–11.
Osipow, S.H. (1999). Assessing career indecision. *Journal of Vocational Behavior*, 55, 147–54.
Paul, K.I. and Moser, K. (2009). Unemployment impairs mental health: Meta-analyses. *Journal of Vocational Behavior*, 74, 264–82.
Phillips, S.D. and Blustein, D.L. (1994). Readiness for career choices: Planning, exploring, and deciding. *The Career Development Quarterly*, 43, 63–73.
Plimmer, G. and Schmidt, A. (2007). Possible selves and career transition: It's who you want to be, not what you want to do. *New Directions for Adult and Continuing Education*, 2007, 61–74.
Porfeli, E.J. and Lee, B. (2012). Career development during childhood and adolescence. *New Directions for Youth Development*, 134, 11–22.
Porfeli, E.J. and Skorikov, V.B. (2010). Specific and diversive career exploration during late adolescence. *Journal of Career Assessment*, 18, 46–58.
Porfeli, E.J., Lee, B., Vondracek, F.W. and Weigold, I.K. (2011). A multi-dimensional measure of vocational identity status. *Journal of Adolescence*, 34, 853–71.
Probst, T.M. (2005). Economic stressors. In J. Barling, E.K. Kelloway and M.R. Frone (eds), *Handbook of Work Stress* (pp. 267–97). Thousand Oaks, CA: Sage.
Pryor, R.G.L. and Bright, J. (2003). The chaos theory of careers. *Australian Journal of Career Development*, 12, 12–20.
Reed, M.B., Bruch, M.A. and Haase, R.F. (2004). Five-factor model of personality and career exploration. *Journal of Career Assessment*, 12, 223–38.
Rowold, J. (2007). The effect of career exploration on subsequent training performance. *Human Resource Development International*, 10, 43–58.
Sargent, L.D., Lee, M.D., Martin, B. and Zikic, J. (2013). Reinventing retirement: New pathways, new arrangements, new meanings. *Human Relations*, 66, 3–21.
Savickas, M.L. (1997). Career adaptability: An integrative construct for life-span, life-space theory. *Career Development Quarterly*, 45, 247–59.
Savickas, M.L. (2002). Reinvigorating the study of careers. *Journal of Vocational Behavior*, 61, 381–5.
Savickas, M.L. (2005). The theory and practice of career construction. In S.D. Brown and R.W. Lent (eds), *Career Development and Counseling. Putting Theory and Research to Work* (pp. 42–70). Hoboken, NJ: Wiley.
Savickas, M.L. (2013). Career construction theory and practice. In S.D. Brown and R.W. Lent (eds), *Career Development and Counseling. Putting Theory and Research to Work* (2nd edn, pp. 147–83). Hoboken, NJ: Wiley.
Savickas, M.L. and Porfeli, E.J. (2012). Career adapt-abilities scale: Construction, reliability, and measurement equivalence across 13 countries. *Journal of Vocational Behavior*, 80, 661–73.

Savickas, M.L., Nota, L., Rossier, J., Dauwalder, J.-P., Duarte, M.E., Guichard, J., Soresi, S., Van Esbroek, R. and Van Vianen, A.E.M. (2009). Life designing: A paradigm for career construction in the 21st century. *Journal of Vocational Behavior*, 75, 239–50.
Singh, R. and Greenhaus, J.H. (2004). The relation between career decision-making strategies and person–job fit: A study of job changers. *Journal of Vocational Behavior*, 64, 198–221.
Skorikov, V. (2007). Continuity in adolescent career preparation and its effects on adjustment. *Journal of Vocational Behavior*, 70, 8–24.
Spokane, A.R. (1991). *Career Intervention*. Englewood Cliffs, NJ: Prentice-Hall.
Stevens, A.H. (1997). Persistent effects of job displacement: The importance of multiple job losses. *Journal of Labor Economics*, 15, 165–88.
Stumpf, S.A. and Hartman, K. (1984). Individual exploration to organizational commitment or withdrawal. *Academy of Management Journal*, 27, 308–29.
Stumpf, S.A., Colarelli, S.M. and Hartman, K. (1983). Development of the Career Exploration Survey (CES). *Journal of Vocational Behavior*, 22, 191–226.
Super, D.E. (1955). Dimensions and measurements of vocational maturity. *Teachers College Record*, 57, 151–63.
Super, D.E. (1977). Vocational maturity in mid-career. *Vocational Guidance Quarterly*, 25, 294–302.
Super, D.E. (1980). A life-span, life-space approach to career development. *Journal of Vocational Behavior*, 16, 282–98.
Super, D.E. and Hall, D.T. (1978). Career development: Exploration and planning. *Annual Review of Psychology*, 29, 333–72.
Super, D.E. and Knasel, E.G. (1981). Career development in adulthood: Some theoretical problems and a possible solution. *British Journal of Guidance & Counselling*, 9, 194–201.
Super, D.E., Thomson, A.S. and Lindeman, R.H. (1988). *Adult Career Concerns Inventory: Manual for Research and Exploratory Use in Counseling*. Palo Alto, CA: Consulting Psychologists Press.
Sverke, M., Hellgren, J. and Näswall, K. (2002). No security: A meta-analysis and review of job insecurity and its consequences. *Journal of Occupational Health Psychology*, 7, 242–64.
Wanberg, C.R., Kanfer, R. and Rotundo, M. (1999). Unemployed individuals: Motives, job-search competencies, and job-search constraints as predictors of job seeking and reemployment. *Journal of Applied Psychology*, 84, 897–910.
Webster, J.R., Beehr, T.A. and Love, K. (2011). Extending the challenge–hindrance model of occupational stress: The role of appraisal. *Journal of Vocational Behavior*, 79, 505–16.
Werbel, J.D. (2000). Relationships among career exploration, job search intensity, and job search effectiveness in graduating college students. *Journal of Vocational Behavior*, 57, 379–94.
Zikic, J. and Hall, D.T. (2009). Toward a more complex view of career exploration. *The Career Development Quarterly*, 58, 181–91.
Zikic, J. and Klehe, U.-C. (2006). Job loss as a blessing in disguise: The role of career exploration and career planning in predicting reemployment quality. *Journal of Vocational Behavior*, 69, 391–409.
Zikic, J., Bonache, J. and Cerdin, J.-L. (2010). Crossing national boundaries: A typology of qualified immigrants' career orientations. *Journal of Organizational Behavior*, 31, 667–86.

4 Relational career capital: towards a sustainable perspective

Markus Latzke, Thomas M. Schneidhofer, Katharina Pernkopf, Carina Rohr and Wolfgang Mayrhofer

INTRODUCTION

The very term 'capital' is relational by definition. 'Capital is not a thing, but a social relation between persons which is mediated through things' (Marx 1977 [1867], p. 932). With reference to careers, capital may be perceived as core competencies possessed by the individual in a given social space for pursuing a career (DeFillippi and Arthur, 1994). For researchers, developments of the concept have become a helpful tool for gaining insights into success factors and career-related investments accounting for both structure and agency (Duberley et al., 2006). Agency concerns the career-related opening of possibilities: if I know how, why and with whom I have to work, I will most probably experience fewer obstacles in the course of my career. For structure, one addresses the question of acknowledging this corridor: to what extent do my supervisors, colleagues and significant others agree on the value of my capital portfolio?

This chapter develops this idea and conceptualizes careers as 'serious games' (Ortner, 2006) for which capital operates as chips subject to career-related investment, conversion and levy. Since individuals dispose of different guises of capital, they may invest it strategically, exchange one guise for another, or yield the profits of their investments. Of course, these actions are also dependent on the way others play the game, the implicit or explicit rules, and the conversion rates prevalent in a specific field. In contrast to simple games of chance offering the possibility of a miracle at any moment, the career game is the result of accumulated individual and social history, and is as such dependent on the prior decisions of the agent in focus, other agents' behavior, or future-oriented strategies of both (Bourdieu, 1986). These serious games have nothing to do with formalistic game theory, however. Rather we assume contextually variable and subjectively complex agents making a career ontologically based on the idea of relationality (Emirbayer, 1997). Moreover, this game is not the sole product of a deliberate act of creation. It merely follows regularities that are neither fully explicit nor codified (Bourdieu and Wacquant, 1992, p. 98). The resulting practice is called a career, understood as movement through a space (social, occupational or organizational) within time (Gunz and Mayrhofer, 2011), such that the 'movement is contextualized, anchored in a specific social space' (Collin, 2006). Hence we build on practice theories (for example Bourdieu, 1977; Ortner, 2006; Schatzki et al., 2001) but also move beyond them.

We will argue that these games may be played sustainably as well, if three conditions are considered: (a) my investments are *viable*, that is, they fit a field and enable agency which does not overstretch individual, organizational or societal resources while realizing the potential of a relation between an individual and his/her context; (b) my strategy is *long term*, that is, it includes a process perspective and may fit my values and beliefs even at the end of my career; and (c) the investments are based on a *holistic* foundation, including other relevant fields within which an actor is embedded (for example family, friends), and combines perceptual, cognitive and emotional facets.

We will first illustrate how career capital can be conceptualized in a way that focuses simultaneously on agency and structure. We will then provide some empirical evidence showing the value of the context for studying careers. Finally, we will link the discourse on sustainability and sustainable careers to a relational concept of career capital and argue that a career can only be regarded as sustainable if capital is invested in a way that allows for returns in the long run.

CURRENT CAREER CAPITAL CONCEPTS AND THEIR APPLICATION

The mainstream concept of career capital in career research – 'the three ways of knowing' (DeFillippi and Arthur, 1994) – fits the concept of 'boundaryless careers', emerging in the 1990s (Arthur, 1994). Furthermore the definition of careers as repositories of knowledge is related hereto: 'accumulations of information and knowledge embodied in skills, expertise, and relationship networks acquired through an evolving sequence of work experiences over time' (Bird, 1994, p. 326). Acquiring career competencies should help to respond to changing contextual demands and is claimed to have mutual advantages for both the individual and organizations (Arthur et al., 1995).

What are 'the three ways of knowing?' Knowing why relates to career motivation, personal meaning, identification and self-concept. Beyond identification with the firm, it increasingly becomes a task for the individual to engage in the sense-making process itself (for example Ibarra and Barbulescu, 2010) and to decouple one's identity from the current employer (DeFillippi and Arthur, 1994, p. 308). The protean career concept is closely related to this aspect of career capital as it focuses on individual motives to follow a particular career path and search for self-fulfillment (Gubler et al., 2013; Hall, 1996). Knowing how encompasses job-related knowledge and career-relevant skills acquired in formal education, on-the-job training and informal learning activities (see the concept of human capital: Becker, 1962). These competencies embrace both tacit and explicit knowledge (Nonaka, 1994) and can be differentiated insofar as they are firm-specific, task-specific, employment-specific, or context-transferable (Arthur, 1994, p. 319). Knowing whom relates to career-relevant social networks. Besides inter-firm communication, relationships with key customers and suppliers, contacts drawn from personal interaction with family, friends and colleagues comprise a network that helps to gather career-relevant information and new contacts. Social capital as 'the advantage created by a person's location in a structure of relationships' (Burt, 2005, p. 4) serves as a core factor in the mainstream concept (for an overview see Adler and Kwon, 2002).

In empirical studies the concept is either regarded as a predictor of career success or as an outcome of various career investments. Concerning the former, researchers investigate the effects of mentoring compared to other forms of career capital on career success

(Singh et al., 2009) or the moderating role of career autonomy and career insecurity in this relation (Colakoglu, 2011). Eby et al. (2003) apply the three ways of knowing to explore their relation with career success and the perceived internal and external marketability among a large sample of university alumni. Concerning the latter, Sturges et al. (2003) study the effects of an MBA on developing career competencies. However, it is particularly research on global careers and expatriate assignments that makes the most use of the concept.

While studies on global careers (Jokinen, 2010; Suutari and Mäkelä, 2007) suggest that successive assignments and multiple international relocations generally lead to an increase in all career capital dimensions, those on expatriate assignments nevertheless indicate a certain context dependency. In a study with 200 Finnish expatriates, Jokinen et al. (2008) reveal that all forms of career capital have developed because of their work experience abroad. Focusing primarily on the individual, the role of context was omitted in this study. Dickmann and Doherty (2008) point to the relevance of the organizational context when studying the effects of international assignments on career capital in two UK-based companies. In particular the development of the knowing-whom dimension varies remarkably due to the degree of networking support policies. Moreover, not all research results indicate an increase in career capital for self-initiated expatriates, but rather urge one to include contextual considerations. A study on the career development of expatriates in Qatar (Rodriguez and Scurry, 2014), for instance, shows that individual career capital can also be affected negatively in self-initiated international work.

A related capital concept was established in career studies as part of a theoretical model of career mobility that considers structure and agency. Forrier et al. (2009) introduce the notion of 'movement capital' and assign it explicitly to the agency perspective as it 'encompasses the individual skills, knowledge, competencies, and attitudes' (p. 742). They identify four dimensions, with the first three being directly aligned with the three ways of knowing and an additional one called adaptability, which means the ability and willingness to change. Earlier publications on the three ways of knowing primarily addressed the individual, since careers have been regarded as 'personal property' and 'each of us is a knowledge capitalist' (Inkson and Arthur 2001, p. 51).

The importance of different aspects of the context for analyzing the role of career capital is revealed when taking a look at success factors for employees, self-employed and professionals. Conscientiousness is relevant for employees (Ng et al., 2005) and self-employed (Zhao et al., 2010), whereas the latter also benefit from openness, need for autonomy and need for achievement (Rauch and Frese, 2007). Besides factors like hours worked, organization tenure, education, political knowledge and skills, socio-economic considerations such as being male, married and older affect the income of employees positively (Ng et al., 2005). In addition, networking influences the success of employees (Wolff and Moser, 2009) and the self-employed (Davidsson and Honig, 2003), whereas the latter draw on different sources of social capital for business creation (parents and friends owning a business or supporting the idea) and business success (being a member of a business network). Professionals working in areas characterized by production at short notice, flexibility, limited budget and a high level of interdependency, stress the predominant role of social capital to get new contracts (for the UK TV industry, see Grugulis and Stoyanova, 2012; for German theaters, Eikhof and Haunschild, 2006).

Intense working patterns and a clear subordination of private life to their artistic work are reflected in their networks, which consist mainly of other professionals. For knowledge workers in IT, their history with the recruitment agency is the most important factor for access to job vacancies (King et al., 2005). Rules which were only crucial for professionals a few years ago have now become important for all employees due to contextual changes. Enhancing one's employability via identity work, training, networking and volunteering is regarded as increasingly relevant (Smith, 2010) in times of a turbulent economy, large-scale job reallocation, delayering, outsourcing and an extensive reliance on temporary and contract employees (DiRenzo and Greenhaus, 2011).

Consequently the context has to be remembered when analyzing capital, because the value of the various forms might vary with contextual changes. In a conceptual article, Parker et al. (2009) show potential connections between the three ways of knowing and acknowledge that the links between knowing whom and knowing why involve relations between the individual and the social arena. Thus they shift the focus slightly away from just the individual. Although the important role of occupational learning versus job-related learning has been noted before (DeFillippi and Arthur, 1996), we agree with Duberley and Cohen (2010), who criticize the overemphasis on agency in the career capital concept.

After outlining the traditional view of career capital, its use in empirical research and indicating some of the potential limitations, we will now delineate an alternative concept of career capital, putting more emphasis on the complex relationship between the social structure and individual agency.

CAPITAL IN CAREER FIELDS

Our understanding of capital in and across fields is different from the three ways of knowing and movement capital in at least two ways. First, we do not conceptualize guises of capital as characteristics of individuals. Rather, we view them as dynamic relational qualities at stake and in use for enabling career-related strategies and investments in a certain context. 'The real is the relational' (Bourdieu and Wacquant, 1992), and what we call individuals arises from the net of configurations between agents within a field. Hence, in contrast to, for example, psychological contract theory (Rousseau, 1995) using the same word for describing the quality of a relationship, we view 'relational' as a dynamic process between terms or units (regardless of its quality) (Emirbayer 1997, p. 289). Moreover, it assumes that what we call substance (individual, structure) is inextricably interwoven with the structures both emerging from them and representing their condition. Consequently, the 'relational' is 'transactional' in that it points beyond a single actor as the unit of analysis. 'Previously constituted actors enter [transactions] but have no ability to traverse [them] inviolable [*sic*!]. They ford [them] with difficulty and in [them] many disappear. What comes out are new actors, new entities, new relations among old parts' (Abbott, 1995, p. 863). That is the reason why we will speak of agents (instead of individuals), who are equipped with (or dispose of, instead of having, or possessing) capital in a specific field.

Second, and linked with this, 'capital' does not exist and function independently of, but only in relation to, a specific field. Hence we do not imply universality to a capital portfolio, but acknowledge that 'what is perceived as capital in one field may have little value in another' (Duberley and Cohen, 2010, p. 196), and what once used to be an advantage may lose its importance in the course of time (Bourdieu and Wacquant, 1992, p. 101).

Agents, equipped with a certain volume and structure of capital as a result of socialization and education, continue accumulating various guises of capital and investing them in return. Three basic forms of capital exist (Bourdieu, 1986). *Economic* capital is only the most obvious manifestation. Income is a particularly important facet of this guise of capital, but any property right (shares) might be included as objectified economic capital as well. Both may be converted into *cultural* capital, like titles and degrees (institutionalized cultural capital), a flashy website (objectified cultural capital), or abilities and competencies (embodied cultural capital), which require time and effort. Correspondingly, cultural capital may serve as the basis for economic capital in return. In this respect, constructs like the educational system, which decides which titles count (and which don't), or the social origin, which determines the socio-economic status and hence the access to educational institutions or the sustainability of an educational career, are important determinants for a career. Both basic guises of capital – economic and cultural – serve as a basis, and a consequence, of *social* capital, which refers to access to networks, group membership, or the possession of titles of nobility. It may leverage other species of capital.

Career fields constitute the social context within which career-related capital is accumulated and invested (Iellatchitch et al., 2003). They are semi-autonomous, meaning that no universal law connects fields with one another or with the social space. On the contrary, each field follows specific rules and logic. Within these arenas, careers are not solely the result of individual efforts, let alone structural determinants. Through the notion of agents equipped with a particular capital portfolio heading for advancement in the form of improved position-takings within the field, the interplay of structure (field) and agency (capital) comes into focus (Schneidhofer, 2013). The essential contextualization of career capital can be conceptualized in various ways. Below we offer one approach.

Drawing on ideas of Orton and Weick (1990), on the one hand, and Elias (1970), on the other, four different managerial career fields can be identified (Iellatchitch et al., 2003) (see Figure 4.1). The Company World (CW) career field relates to traditional organizational careers, with few changes in the configuration of relationships between the focal agent and other relevant agents (stable configuration) and with closely intertwined agents influencing each other (tight coupling). In the career field of Free Floating Professionalism (FFP) the agents – mainly specialists – also have a close relationship with one customer at a time, but in contrast to the Company World field it is a short-term relationship and customers change fast (variable configuration). Individuals that work outside organizations are located in the field of Self-Employment (SE). They are loosely coupled with other actors in the field but do face a comparatively stable mix of agents, that is, typically they have several customers simultaneously who do not change rapidly. The fourth career field is characterized by frequent job changes, radical professional transitions and a great diversity of tasks – it is therefore labeled as the field of Chronic Flexibility (CF).

Based on this understanding of career capital as having a dynamic relational quality

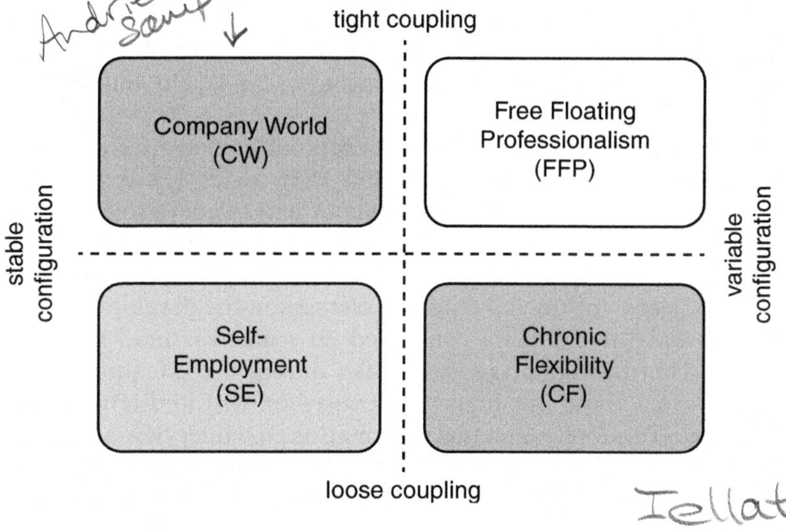

Figure 4.1 Four managerial career fields

and being tied to specific fields, we will now illustrate the fruitfulness of such a view by examining different kinds of career transitions within and between fields.

RELATIONAL CAREER CAPITAL APPLIED: THE TEST BED OF TRANSITIONS

Following Nicholson and West (1989, p. 195), transitions can be interpreted as 'critical incidents in the nexus between self-consciousness and social structure'. Whenever an individual seeks a change of job, it is an opportunity to learn not just about the individual but also about the context in which this transition occurs. A PhD, for example, might be evaluated very differently depending on the field of work; it might enhance or reduce the possibility of successful career transitions, depending on the area where the desired job is found. In other words, individual career transitions are also able to elucidate the relationship of the individual and the social order, as Duberley et al. (2006) stated in their qualitative study of structure and agency in careers.

To map out the objectified structure of the relations between the positions occupied by the agents within each field we will take an empirical look at the transitions within and across these fields. A transition is characterized by the source and target field as well as the capital relevant for the transition process. These characteristics are especially salient in transitions between different fields, emphasizing the importance of the context.

Transitions within a career field require reputation or prestige acquired within the field. This becomes visible when an agent who makes a career investment yields a return on investment for the capital employed, but this return is only restricted to the advancement within that particular field. In transitions between fields it is important to reveal the more general applicability of relational career capital (and recognition of one's capital portfolio). Of course, a career within a field can subsequently allow a smooth transition to another field, but this does not have to be the case (as shown by Huppatz, 2009 in the field of paid caring work). A career in one field may be restricted to that field; nevertheless agents may encounter difficulties in advancing within a field, but succeed in crossing field boundaries.

To illustrate some particularities of our conceptual framework for transitions within and across career fields, we draw illustrations from an explorative qualitative study, mainly from interviews conducted in the Vienna Career Panel Project (ViCaPP) (www.wu.ac.at/vicapp). This longitudinal project follows the careers of four cohorts (business school graduates from 1970, 1990, 2000 and 2010) both quantitatively and qualitatively with the objective of tracing potential changes in the development of managerial careers. In the study at hand, we conducted 30 semi-structured in-depth interviews with graduates from two cohorts (1990, 2000) during the last three years (2011–13). The interviews lasted about one hour and focused on why and how career transitions were undertaken. For more contextual information, the interview also covered various aspects of personal and educational background, career motives as well as critical success factors. Appendix Table 4A.1 contains more detailed information about the interviewees.

The following paragraphs illustrate some aspects of capital relevant for interviewees making transitions within a field. Since transitions within, from or to the field of CF were not included in the sample, this field was excluded in the subsequent analysis.

Economic Capital: Risk-taking Versus Stability

For the self-employed, economic capital is of central importance for survival and advancement within the SE field, because self-employment is directly linked to economic capital continuously accumulated over time and ceases with the lack of it (that is, too little economic capital leads to instability and greater financial risk). It also provides stability as a source of income (the objectivized and comparable result of individual performance) and motivates individuals to make a transition to or within CW. Among free-floating professionals, economic capital is regarded as an adequate, taken-for-granted remuneration for professional service. However, it seems to be an insufficient incentive for transitions within the FFP field.

Social Capital: From Lateral Networks, Headhunters and Family

Social capital in the CW varies. Its relevance results from its linkage to other guises of capital such as cultural capital (that is, professional merits, information about career opportunities and access to central decision makers). Within one company, the direct superior is considered the most relevant social capital providing references and supporting further advancement. For transitions within the CW and FFP fields, headhunters and informal lateral networks are considered important. They act as labor market intermediaries between the individual and the respective field. In the SE field, however, social capital relates to customers and one's private background, the former being the most relevant both in terms of economic and social capital (that is, attracting new customers), and the latter helping out when times get rough.

Cultural Capital – and How to Make it Visible

Cultural capital, that is, occupational knowledge and job-related skills, is acknowledged within all three career fields – albeit in differing degrees. While in the CW organizational knowledge and social webs inside the company are highly valued (sometimes in contrast to the actual performance), individuals in the SE field rely on their performance assessed by customers to enhance their credibility and trustworthiness in the field. In the CW and FFP fields, the emphasis is on making the performance and respective skills visible to relevant position holders. Competencies such as self-presentation and proactivity are recognized in all three career fields, although their importance varies. One may conclude that in the SE field, proactivity combined with risk-taking are applied to transitions more intensively than in other fields. Within the CW and FFP fields, self-presentation and visibility of performance are necessary for transitions within the fields.

A very frequent variant of transitions within a field is the transition from one company to another within the CW. To it we turn next.

From CW to CW: Social Capital Providing Access to Cultural Capital

Economic capital is not applied by the individual when making a transition within the CW, but is offered by the company as a yield. Social capital recognized for transitions within the CW differs along organizational lines, which points towards the relevance of organizations as fields within the field of the CW. Boundaries can be explained by the internal network and the easier visibility of the individual's performance. A hierarchical network is more important for transitions within one company, while a lateral network is more useful for transitions undertaken in the CW in general. The empirical material from ViCaPP also indicates that not only can the transitioning individual's social capital be applied to facilitate a transition between companies, the social capital of a superior can also be utilized. For a transition within the CW, information about job opportunities – cultural capital – is recognized by the field, which links back to social capital as the information source. With the increasing number of transitions to other industries, adaptability and flexibility in handling new situations are becoming increasingly relevant types of cultural capital. Also valued are industry and organizational knowledge, including reporting structures. However, because there are transitions in the CW which cross industry boundaries but not occupational boundaries, occupational knowledge can be interpreted as the more valued cultural capital within the CW.

Besides transitions within a field, many transitions also occur between fields. We highlight three kinds of such transitions.

From CW to SE: Social and Cultural Capital Used to Gain Access to More Economic Capital

Economic capital provides access to the SE field. The economic capital is differentiated based on the source from which the capital is derived, which is either net equity or credit capital. The sources of economic capital range from equity capital accessed via the family background, obtained from banks or investors, or acquired in positions formerly held in the CW field – converting former income as a symbol of stability into a generalized capital for taking risks. The former employer or one's social origin, however, serve not only as sources of economic capital. They are also social capital establishing relations to potential customers. For instance, the current company as the employer is the future customer of the self-employed and the former superior could become the new business partner. Concerning cultural capital, knowledge and skills are institutionalized and objectivized in trade licenses which establish and secure the boundaries of the SE field. Proactivity, risk-taking, tolerance for insecurity and self-reflectivity are valuable capital in the transition process.

From SE to CW via FFP: Social Capital Standing Alone or in Combination with Cultural capital

Our data suggest that a transition from the SE to the CW needs either a strong lateral social network or a transition through the FFP field as an intermediary step. Social capital such as friends or former university colleagues is relevant for transitions from the SE field, because self-employed individuals are not targeted by institutional forms of social capital such as headhunters. Social capital is only acknowledged in connection with job-related knowledge as a form of cultural capital. However, in transitions to the CW from the field of FFP, headhunters or former customers are mentioned as social capital.

From FFP to CW: Social Capital Used to Show Off Cultural Capital

When transitioning from FFP to the CW, the social capital cultivated during work relations with customers paves the way to the company in question and its managers. Strong ties to customers, often gained through project work at the customer's company, are mobilized in the FFP field as social career capital. Hence, the present customer acts as social capital and becomes the individual's future employer. Moreover, knowledge about the industry and/or its competitors is considered as generalized capital.

Summary of Empirical Findings

In contrast to traditional career capital studies, the illustrations above show that the question 'what counts?' depends on the interplay of the individual agent and the respective field, without emphasizing one or the other. Although our data suggest some overlap between capital relevant in transitions within and across fields, some context-specific differences emerge. The three guises of capital are recognized in the fields of the CW, FFP and SE, but upon closer examination of the data, the application and interplay of capital provide some interesting insights. Economic capital, for instance, can either be an undisputed entrance requirement (into the SE field) or a motivator for a transition (to the CW field) that suggests stability and regular income.

Thus far, the traditional conceptualization of career capital has been regarded as a 'trait-like characteristic' of the individual. Now we have developed an alternative conceptualization focusing on the relational and field-specific qualities of career capital, and have given some empirical examples illustrating these qualities. In a final step we will discuss the implications of our approach for examining sustainable careers.

ONE STEP FURTHER: SUSTAINABLE CAREERS WITH A RELATIONAL CAREER CAPITAL CONCEPT

It is certainly not enough to just contextualize capital in order to ensure career sustainability. Consider the paradigmatic case where agents are only equipped with abundant social capital, which is nevertheless highly appreciated in a specific field. If they continue investing this capital to advance in the career field without, for example, reciprocating in the long run, or if they neglect acquiring other guises of capital (for example an adequate amount of cultural capital, like expertise or know-how) and fail to coordinate a viable structure of the different guises of capital, their success will probably not reach its full potential. Similarly, if they neglect the bigger picture of their career context, such as family responsibilities, or work–non-work balance, their career will be unsustainable. Hence, our delineated method is merely the first step, but not the giant leap for understanding sustainable careers. From a relational viewpoint, a career can only be considered sustainable if agents play the serious game called career in a viable, long-term and holistic manner. We will now outline how we may spot a sustainable career with a relational career capital framework.

Sustainability, in general, is defined as development that meets the needs of the present without compromising the ability of future generations to meet their own needs (WCED, 1987, p. 43, cf. Ehnert and Harry, 2012, p. 223). Van der Heijden and De Vos translate this to a sustainable career being characterized by continuity for the individual (see Chapter 1 in this volume). As such, it is the result of choices, not the mere consequence of external influences and constraints.

> A sustainable career is dynamic and flexible; it features continuous learning, periodic renewal, the security that comes from employability, and a harmonious fit with your skills, interests, and values [. . .] A sustainable career is built upon the ability to show that you can fill a need that someone is willing to pay for. (Valcour, 2013)

With a relational perspective, we may also explain where this ability to show and willingness to pay for it comes from. To this end we have to take two different levels of analysis into account: the 'minds' and the 'things'.

Beginning with 'minds', to play the career game sustainably, it has to encompass three criteria: first, investments should be (a) *viable*, that is, fit to a field and enable agency which does not overstretch individual, organizational, or societal resources but at the same time realizing the potential embedded in a relation between an individual and his/her context. Newman (2011) already suggested three dimensions of this criterion: renewability, referring to the ability to refresh and consolidate. Hence, my capital acquisition strategy should consider preventing burnout and ensuring resilience. Next, flexibility, that is, enabling continuous learning and guaranteeing bending without breaking. Both in response to and in anticipation of change, the needs of the career stakeholders (prototypically the employer and employee) should be balanced. Finally, drawing on Erikson's stage of adult development (Erikson, 1980) Newman argues for an integrative dimension, implying completeness and consistency between values and behaviors. Here the point is not only seeing the big picture for the individual, but also retaining the acquired knowledge in the company.

The latter directly leads to the second criterion of the 'mind', that is, the career strategy should be (b) *long-term*, that is, it includes a process perspective and may fit my values and beliefs even at the end of my career. In other words, thinking careers 'from the end' ensures that nothing has to be regretted when the final curtain falls. This implies a time horizon beyond the focused point in time. Whereas viability always focuses on specific points in time (renewability points to the present; flexibility to a future point; integration to a point in the past), the long-term orientation offers a perspective which emphasizes the process relevant to sustainable careers through a longer period. In addition to a viable capital portfolio (volume, structure), the viability is based on a history of capital accumulation, and both the present investment strategy and future investment behavior should be in line with this history, thus fulfilling the 'long-term' criterion.

The last criterion of the mind is that the investments are based on a (c) *holistic* foundation, including other relevant fields within which an actor is embedded (for example family, friends). It combines perceptual, cognitive and emotional facets. The former refers to other agents relevant to the agent in focus. Each of us is a player in several fields, and we have to find a balance between the needs of succeeding in each of them. Prioritizing the needs of the career field each and every time affects the possibilities in other fields, which leads directly to the second facet of the holistic criterion, referring to the wholeness of identity: perception, cognition and emotions. Accumulating economic capital (for example, earning a lot of money) in the career field without the possibility of transferring the profit into, for example, satisfaction (a guise of capital appreciated in the field of family) will not lead to a sustainable career. Figure 4.2 illustrates this.

At this point, it must be noted that O'Neil and her colleagues (2010) also offered a similar framework of sustainable career development, based on three elements: (a) the interdependent relationships of individual careerists and their ecosystems; (b) the focus on both short- and long-term career development strategies; and (c) a balanced perspective between economic, environmental and social concerns. A full outline of the differences to the practice theories offered here is beyond the scope of this chapter. But we would like at least to touch upon the last point mentioned, 'the career triple bottom line' (c). Since the notion of the field excludes functionalism and organicism in contrast to a 'system' theorized by Luhmann and others (Bourdieu and Wacquant, 1992, p. 103), it is yet open to debate if a sustainable career from a relational perspective necessarily has to be 'sustainable' in the original sense of the word, referring to products outside of the field in focus. While it is clear that other fields in the social space influence the focused agent's behavior (see the holistic dimension explained above), this is less apparent for the consequences of these practices in other spheres of the social world (for example, the environment). Bluntly stated: a career might be perfectly sustainable even if it depletes natural resources, as long as this depletion does not influence the field's social structure. It is a philosophical question if this can ever meet the criterion of viability, which we cannot answer here. For the time being we argue that this does not necessarily have to be the case.

However our three dimensions of the 'mind' – viability, long-term orientation, holistic identity – are not only the condition to, but also the consequence of the structure of the field ('things'). In other words, stopping at this point would make the career game rational. Owing to effort, circumspection or shrewdness, everyone would have the same opportunity for pursuing a career sustainably. Yet we know that the chances are unevenly distributed from the start, and – to quote the famous dictum attributed

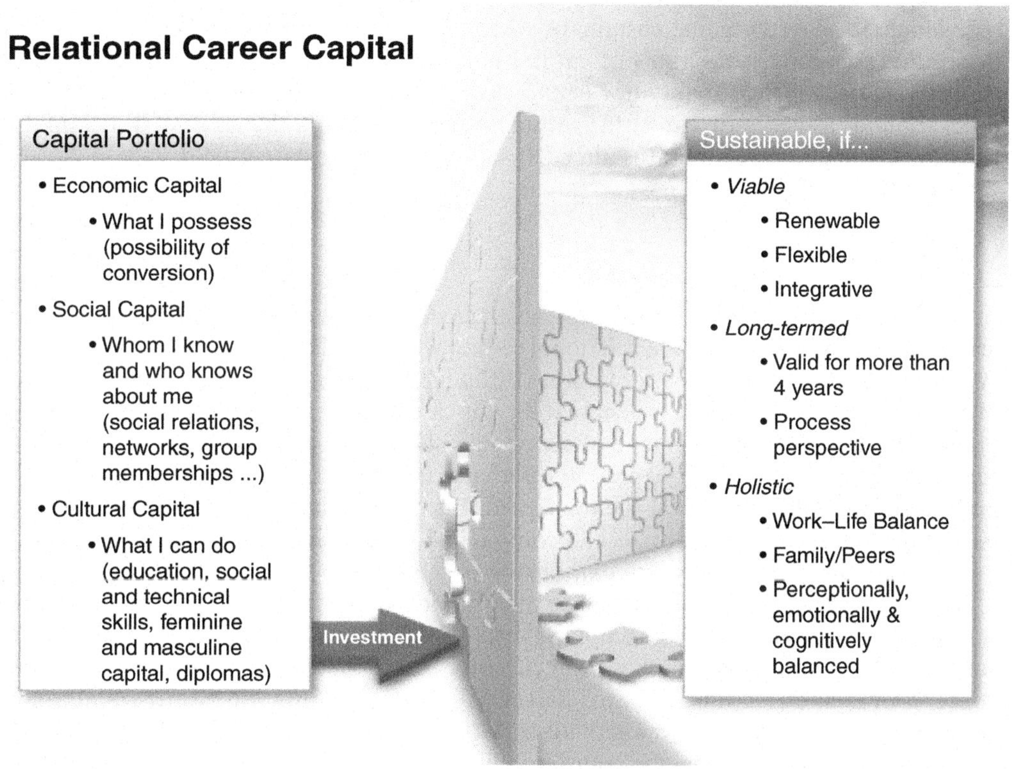

Figure 4.2 Relational career capital and sustainable investment criteria

to Napoleon – not 'every soldier has a marshal's baton in his knapsack' (Bourdieu, 1986, p. 46). Moreover space in a field is limited; this is why the serious game career is also dependent on the other agents' strategies and behaviors. Even the most viable, holistic and long-term strategy may fail if the significant others' behavior is at odds with a sustainable destiny in the field. On top of this, in contexts where mere survival is the ultimate career goal (for example, low-scaled workers in developing countries), questions of sustainability do not even arise.

Since agents are always involved in, and can never act outside of, the multiplicity of relations in which they are enmeshed (Ortner, 2006), a framework for sustainable careers has to include a link between structure and agency. This often forgotten link is called habitus (Lahire, 2003). It refers to the 'system of lasting and transposable dispositions which, integrating past experiences, functions at every moment as a matrix of perceptions, appreciations and actions and makes possible the achievement of infinitely diversified tasks' (Bourdieu, 1968, p. 95). Habitus represents the sense for the career game (Schneidhofer, 2013) and in order to play this game sustainably, the structures of the field must have made the idea of sustainable careers at least possible. If many others in the field play the game sustainably (even without knowing it), these practice structures become incorporated in habitus. Conversely, if the majority in the field plays its capital short-handedly, short-termed and with focus on immediate return, it will be difficult for individuals to play the game sustainably. Moreover, due to the fact that the majority determines the conversion rates of capital guises, a hoped-for sustainable investment is, in that case, most probably not acknowledged. In other words: if burnout was the decoration for a successful career (a symbol for hard working), the value of a sustainable career will not fit a career habitus aimed at succeeding in the career field.

CONCLUSION

In this chapter we have explained how a career develops with the accumulation of (at least) three forms of capital in a relational setting within and across distinct career fields. We have suggested that transitions across different career fields are especially suited for investigating and assessing the sustainability of careers as they provide visibility for the application and acknowledgment of economic, social and cultural capital. In contextualizing the forms of career capital in different kinds of transitions, the transferability and transformability of capital is emphasized. Further, we have developed a theoretical perspective of a sustainable career encompassing three dimensions, namely viability, long-term orientation and holisticity/holism.

Building on this perspective, we pose the question of whether sustainable careers are thus moving closer to the life concept (Savickas, 1997; Super, 1990). The holistic dimension of a sustainable career implies the inclusion of other fields such as family. Moreover, concepts of lifelong learning or individual endeavor in accumulating more capital can be connected to and seen as one individual strategy to attain a sustainable career. However, we emphasize that ensuring the transferability of the capital across different kinds of transition is of utmost importance. We reach this conclusion as a result of different career fields recognizing different forms of capital. Thus, the challenges for the individual are to ensure employability via the visibility of individual performance to central position holders in the field. In these terms, sustainable careers are a result of balanced interests between the individual agent, the other agents (including the organization), the career field itself, and other stakeholders outside the field. This, however, leads to the question: where does career end and life begin?

We started our journey with a quote of one of the big minds of contemporary time. Let us conclude with Kierkegaard (1843, p. 306):

> It is really true what philosophy tells us, that life must be understood backwards. But with this, one forgets the second proposition, that it must be lived forwards. A proposition which, the more it is subjected to careful thought, the more it ends up concluding precisely that life at any given moment cannot really ever be fully understood; exactly because there is no single moment where time stops completely in order for me to take position [to do this]: going backward.

But considering a viable, long-term oriented and holistic game is at least worth a try – even if only tentatively.

REFERENCES

Abbott, A. (1995), 'Things of boundaries', *Social Research*, **62** (4), 857–82.

Adler, P.S. and S.W. Kwon (2002), 'Social capital: Prospects for a new concept', *Academy of Management Review*, **27** (1), 17–40.

Arthur, M.B. (1994), 'The boundaryless career: A new perspective for organizational inquiry', *Journal of Organizational Behaviour*, **15** (4), 295–306.

Arthur, M.B., P.H. Claman and R.J. DeFillippi (1995), 'Intelligent enterprise, intelligent careers', *The Academy of Management Executive*, **9** (4), 7–20.

Becker, G.S. (1962), 'Investment in human capital: A theoretical analysis', *Journal of Political Economy*, **70** (5), 9–49.

Bird, A. (1994), 'Careers as repositories of knowledge: A new perspective on boundaryless careers', *Journal of Organizational Behaviour*, **15** (4), 325–44.

Bourdieu, Pierre (1968), 'Intellectual field and creative project', *Social Science Information*, **8**, 89–119.

Bourdieu, Pierre (1977), *Outline of a Theory of Practice*, Cambridge: Cambridge University Press.

Bourdieu, Pierre (1986), 'The forms of capital', in John G. Richardson (ed.), *Handbook of Theory and Research for the Sociology of Education*, Westport, CT: Greenwood Publishing, pp. 241–58.

Bourdieu, Pierre and Loic J.D. Wacquant (1992), *An Invitation to Reflexive Sociology*, Chicago, IL: University of Chicago Press.

Burt, Ronald S. (2005), *Brokerage and Closure: An Introduction to Social Capital*, Oxford, and New York: Oxford University Press.

Colakoglu, S.N. (2011), 'The impact of career boundarylessness on subjective career success: The role of career competencies, career autonomy, and career insecurity', *Journal of Vocational Behavior*, **79** (1), 47–59.

Collin, Audrey (2006), 'Career', in Jeffrey H. Greenhaus and Gerard A. Callanan (eds), *Encyclopedia of Career Development*, Thousand Oaks, CA: Sage, pp. 61–4.

Davidsson, P. and B. Honig (2003), 'The role of social and human capital among nascent entrepreneurs', *Journal of Business Venturing*, **18** (3), 301–31.

DeFillippi, R.J. and M.B. Arthur (1994), 'The boundaryless career: A competency-based perspective', *Journal of Organizational Behaviour*, **15** (4), 307–24.

DeFillippi, R.J. and M.B. Arthur (1996), 'Boundaryless contexts and careers: A competency-based perspective', in M.B. Arthur and D. Rousseau (eds), *The Boundaryless Career*, Oxford: Oxford University Press, pp. 116–31.

Dickmann, M. and N. Doherty (2008), 'Exploring the career capital impact of international assignments within distinct organizational contexts', *British Journal of Management*, **19** (2), 145–61.

DiRenzo, M.S. and J.H. Greenhaus (2011), 'Job search and voluntary turnover in a boundaryless world: A control theory perspective', *Academy of Management Review*, **36** (3), 567–89.

Duberley, J. and L. Cohen (2010), 'Gendering career capital: An investigation of scientific careers', *Journal of Vocational Behavior*, **76** (2), 187–97.

Duberley, J., M. Mallon and L. Cohen (2006), 'Exploring career transitions: Accounting for structure and agency', *Personnel Review*, **35** (3), 281–96.

Eby, L.T., M. Butts and A. Lockwood (2003), 'Predictors of success in the era of the boundaryless career', *Journal of Organizational Behavior*, **24** (6), 689–708.

Ehnert, I. and W. Harry (2012), 'Recent developments and future prospects on sustainable human resource management: Introduction to the special issue', *Management Revue*, **23** (3), 221–38.

Eikhof, D.R. and A. Haunschild (2006), 'Lifestyle meets market: Bohemian entrepreneurs in creative industries', *Creativity and Innovation Management*, **15** (3), 234–41.

Elias, Norbert (1970), *Was ist Soziologie?*, Munich: Juventa.

Emirbayer, M. (1997), 'Manifesto for a relational sociology', *American Journal of Sociology*, **103** (2), 281–317.

Erikson, Erik H. (1980), *Identity and the Life Cycle*, New York: WW Norton & Company.

Forrier, A., L. Sels and D. Stynen (2009), 'Career mobility at the intersection between agent and structure: A conceptual model', *Journal of Occupational and Organizational Psychology*, **82** (4), 739–59.

Grugulis, I. and D. Stoyanova (2012), 'Social capital and networks in film and TV: Jobs for the boys?', *Organization Studies*, **33** (10), 1311–31.

Gubler, M., J. Arnold and C. Coombs (2013), 'Reassessing the protean career concept: Empirical findings, conceptual components, and measurement', *Journal of Organizational Behavior*, **35** (S1), S23–S40.

Gunz, H. and W. Mayrhofer (2011), 'Re-conceptualizing career success: A contextual approach', *Zeitschrift für ArbeitsmarktForschung*, **43** (3), 251–60.

Hall, D.T. (1996), 'Protean careers of the 21st century', *Academy of Management Executive*, **10** (4), 8–16.

Huppatz, K. (2009), 'Reworking Bourdieu's capital: Feminine and female capitals in the field of paid caring work', *Sociology*, **43** (1), 45–66.

Ibarra, H. and R. Barbulescu (2010), 'Identity as narrative: Prevalence, effectiveness, and consequences of narrative identity work in macro work role transitions', *Academy of Management Review*, **35** (1), 135–54.
Iellatchitch, A., W. Mayrhofer and M. Meyer (2003), 'Career fields: A small step towards a grand career theory?', *International Journal of Human Resource Management*, **14** (5), 728–50.
Inkson, K. and M.B. Arthur (2001), 'How to be a successful career capitalist', *Organizational Dynamics*, **30** (1), 48–61.
Jokinen, T. (2010), 'Development of career capital through international assignments and its transferability to new contexts', *Thunderbird International Business Review*, **52** (4), 325–36.
Jokinen, T., C. Brewster and V. Suutari (2008), 'Career capital during international work experiences: Contrasting self-initiated expatriate experiences and assigned expatriation', *The International Journal of Human Resource Management*, **19** (6), 979–98.
Kierkegaard, Søren (1843), *Journalen JJ:167*, reprinted in Søren Kierkegaard Research Center (1997) *Søren Kierkegaards Skrifter*, Vol. 18, Copenhagen.
King, Z., S. Burke and J. Pemberton (2005), 'The "bounded" career: An empirical study of human capital, career mobility and employment outcomes in a mediated labour market', *Human Relations*, **58** (8), 981–1007.
Lahire, B. (2003), 'From the habitus to an individual heritage of dispositions. Towards a sociology at the level of the individual', *Poetics*, **31** (5), 329–55.
Marx, Karl (1977) [1867], *Capital Volume 1: A Critique of Political Economy*, New York: Vintage Books.
Newman, K.L. (2011), 'Sustainable careers: Lifecycle engagement in work', *Organizational Dynamics*, **40** (2), 136–43.
Ng, T., L. Eby, K. Sorensen and D. Feldman (2005), 'Predictors of objective and subjective career success: A meta-analysis', *Personnel Psychology*, **58** (2), 367–408.
Nicholson, Nigel and Michael West (1989), 'Transitions, work histories and careers', in Michael B. Arthur, Douglas T. Hall and Barbara S. Lawrence (eds), *The Handbook of Career Theory*, Cambridge: Cambridge University Press, pp. 181–201.
Nonaka, I. (1994), 'A dynamic theory of organizational knowledge creation', *Organization Science*, **5** (1), 14–37.
O'Neil, D.A., M.M. Hopkins, D. Bilimoria and J. Schalk (2010), 'A framework of sustainable career development: The career triple bottom line', *Academy of Management Annual Meeting*, Montreal, 6–10 August.
Ortner, Sherry B. (2006), *Anthropology and Social Theory: Culture, Power, and the Acting Subject*, Durham, NC: Duke University Press.
Orton, J.D. and K.E. Weick (1990), 'Loosely coupled systems: A reconceptualisation', *Academy of Management Review*, **15** (2), 203–23.
Parker, P., S.N. Khapova and M.B. Arthur (2009), 'The intelligent career framework as a basis for interdisciplinary inquiry', *Journal of Vocational Behavior*, **75** (3), 291–302.
Rauch, A. and M. Frese (2007), 'Let's put the person back into entrepreneurship research: A meta-analysis on the relationship between business owners' personality traits, business creation, and success', *European Journal of Work and Organizational Psychology*, **16** (4), 353–85.
Rodriguez, J.K. and T. Scurry (2014), 'Career capital development of self-initiated expatriates in Qatar: Cosmopolitan globetrotters, experts and outsiders', *The International Journal of Human Resource Management*, **25** (7), 1046–67.
Rousseau, Denis (1995), *Psychological Contracts in Organizations: Understanding Written and Unwritten Agreements*, Thousand Oaks, CA: Sage.
Savickas, M.L. (1997), 'Career adaptability: An integrative construct for life-span, life-space theory', *Career Development Quarterly*, **45** (3), 247–59.
Schatzki, Theodore R., Karin Knorr-Cetina and Eike von Savigny (2001), *The Practice Turn in Contemporary Theory*, London: Routledge.
Schneidhofer, T.M. (2013), 'Bridging (at least?) sociology and psychology? A relational view on career boundaries at the nexus of structure and agency', *EGOS Colloquium*, Montreal, 4–6 July.
Singh, R., B.R. Ragins and P. Tharenou (2009), 'What matters most? The relative role of mentoring and career capital in career success', *Journal of Vocational Behavior*, **75** (1), 56–67.
Smith, V. (2010), 'Review article: Enhancing employability: Human, cultural, and social capital in an era of turbulent unpredictability', *Human Relations*, **63** (2), 279–303.
Sturges, J., R. Simpson and Y. Altman (2003), 'Capitalising on learning: An exploration of the MBA as a vehicle for developing career competencies', *International Journal of Training and Development*, **7** (1), 53–66.
Super, Donald E. (1990), 'A life-span, life-space approach to career development', in Duane Brown and Linda Brooks (eds), *Career Choice and Development: Applying Contemporary Theory to Practice*, San Francisco, CA: Jossey-Bass, pp. 197–261.
Suutari, V. and K. Mäkelä (2007), 'The career capital of managers with global careers', *Journal of Managerial Psychology*, **22** (7), 628–48.

Valcour, M. (2013), 'Craft a sustainable career', available at http://blogs.hbr.org/2013/07/craft-a-sustainable-career/ (accessed 2 November 2013).
Wolff, H.G. and K. Moser (2009), 'Effects of networking on career success: A longitudinal study', *Journal of Applied Psychology*, **94** (1), 196–206.
WCED (World Commission on Environment and Development) (1987), *Our Common Future: Report of the World Commission on Environment and Development*, Brussels.
Zhao, H., S.E. Seibert and G.T. Lumpkin (2010), 'The relationship of personality to entrepreneurial intentions and performance: A meta-analytic review', *Journal of Management*, **36** (2), 381–404.

APPENDIX

Table 4A.1 Interviewees' gender, work experience and number of transitions

	Interviewees	Across field transitions	Within field transitions
Female	*10*	*16*	*20*
20 years' work experience	5	8	13
10 years' work experience	5	8	7
Male	*20*	*30*	*27*
20 years' work experience	13	17	20
10 years' work experience	7	13	7
Total	*30*	*46*	*47*

5 Social capital and careers: indisputable evidence and note for caution

Nikos Bozionelos

INTRODUCTION

This chapter discusses the link between careers and social capital, which is a form of capital that individuals possess through their connections with others or their membership to particular groups. The idea that social capital is connected with career outcomes has been formalized relatively recently (Seibert et al., 2001) though, as to be seen, it has been present within career theory for longer. The link of social capital with career progression is also strongly embedded in the popular wisdom as epitomized in the motto: 'It does not matter what you know, what matters is whom you know', which is found in a pretty invariant form across cultures.

The construct of social capital was introduced by the French sociologist Bourdieu (1980, 1986) and represented an addition to the eternal construct of economic capital, and to human capital that had been introduced in the 1960s (Becker, 1964). Economic capital reflects financial resources, while human capital reflects knowledge, skills and abilities that individuals may innately possess (for example, personality, some physical traits) or accumulate via various means (for example, education, training, work experience and experience in life in general), which allow them to add value to their work output. Human capital along with structural factors (for example, the state of the economy, the conditions in a particular industry or a particular profession) indisputably influence career outcomes (Baruch and Bozionelos, 2010, for a review). The core idea behind the social capital view of careers is that social ties, and the resources these may bring or deprive the individual of, provide explanations for career outcomes that go beyond structural and human capital factors.

Below, we are going to define social capital, review the evidence for its link with career outcomes, and then develop an account of its antecedents and ways of creation. The next step will involve an attempt to identify the mechanism via which social capital influences careers, and we will be concerned with the issue of actual output versus political processes. That last part will inevitably bring us before the 'dark side' of social capital, an issue that has been largely neglected so far. The 'dark side' view suggests that though social capital may bring career advantages to individuals or particular groups, the way these advantages are realized may be to the eventual detriment of the greater collective. This is directly connected to the issue of sustainability in careers with two major questions to answer: first, whether social capital is a resource that individuals can rely upon on a consistent basis for a successful career trajectory; and second, whether a collective where social capital is the dominant career resource can itself endure in the long term.

WHAT IS SOCIAL CAPITAL?

Social capital refers to resources that a person has at one's disposal by means of his/her relationship ties with other individuals within a particular social entity (Bourdieu, 1986; Portes, 1998). Examples of social entities include organizational functions, firms, professions, alumni, or even political parties. These entities may themselves be connected with each other by means of social ties between their members or overlapping memberships.

The resources that social capital provides include information, influence and solidarity (Adler and Kwon, 2002; Bourdieu, 1986). With respect to information, social ties (for example, friends, acquaintances) can provide access to facts, opinions or attitudes of others that otherwise the individual may not have been aware of (for example, a job opening, particular likes and dislikes of a potential customer). Regarding influence, relationships ties can enable someone to impact and control events and outcomes that they would not be able to do otherwise. For instance, an acquaintance may bring us into contact with a key decision-maker he/she has access to or may expose him/her to our views. Solidarity means that people who are linked with social ties may provide mutual support to each other in the face of a common cause or threat. This support can be emotional, instrumental or both. It should be kept in mind that social capital encompasses the resources that ties (direct or indirect) with others bring, and it does not just refer to the ties themselves. In addition, many benefits of social capital may not be realized unless the individual is proactive in the mobilization of these resources (Obukhova and Lan, 2013).

Social capital can also be viewed from a macro-level perspective (Glanville and Bienenstock, 2009). In that case it denotes the ties and their attached resources within a whole social entity as well as between that entity and outsiders (other social entities or individuals). The former can be described as bonding social capital whilst the latter can be described as bridging social capital (Putman, 2000). The macro-level perspective is not visited in the present work because careers are mostly seen from the viewpoint of individual career actors. However, the macro-perspective becomes relevant when individual career interests are considered against the sustainability of the interests of the collective.

SOCIAL CAPITAL AND SOCIAL OUTCOMES

Social capital is able to influence social outcomes, such as career success, via its properties of substitutability and appropriability (Adler and Kwon, 2002; Kim, 2013). Substitutability means that social capital can replace or complement qualities that an individual lacks. Such qualities may include anything that is valued within a social system, such as abilities, skills, credentials, information, position power, or actual output. Information about the needs of a potential client given by a friend, meeting a senior officer via a common acquaintance, or preference for a job candidate who lags behind in key skills because that candidate is acquainted with a member of a selection panel are examples of substitutability. Appropriability means that relationship ties of a particular type can serve multiple functions. For example, a friend who works for another employer may offer emotional support in a variety of domains, but also information on a job opening at that employer. It is via these properties that, as Coleman

(1988, p. S98) worded it, '[social capital makes] possible the achievement of certain ends that in its absence would not be possible.'

The idea that social capital plays a role in careers has been in existence before the advent of relevant theory that appeared at the beginning of this century (Seibert et al., 2001). To illustrate, the notion of social capital was incorporated in the 'knowing-whom' dimension of the intelligent careers framework (Arthur et al., 1995). Knowing-whom reflects any relationship ties the individual has and can assist in one's career progression. Arthur et al. (1995) employed the paradigm of using one's contacts to add value to one's current job and employer, though later the framework became more general (Parker et al., 2009). However, as we will see, this is not the only way social capital enhances careers prospects. Furthermore, the instrumental value of relationship ties in career progression has been highlighted in early practitioner accounts on mentoring (Collins and Scott, 1978) that led to the development of systematic mentoring theory and research (exemplified by the work of Kram, 1983; 1985), as well as in literature that attested to the link between network ties and career development (for example, Lincoln and Miller, 1979).

Social Capital and Career Success: The Evidence

There is substantial empirical support for the link between social capital and career success, especially objective or extrinsic career success that means externally verifiable career accomplishments. These include easiness of entering the labor force, as well as early and later career progression (promotions, favorable moves, status and financial attainment). In the contemporary environment of uncertainty and fast tumultuous change, career success partly overlaps with employability (De Vos et al., 2011), that is the individual's ability to consistently maintain their employment (Van der Heijde and Van der Heijden, 2006). To illustrate, social capital predicts whether graduates are able to find employment commensurate with their credentials (Jokisaari and Nurmi, 2005), while a recent study with a similar population suggested that utilization of social capital in job search yields better outcomes than other methods, including responding to advertisements and using formal career services (Obukhova and Lan, 2013). And in a long-term retrospective alumni study, Seibert et al. (2001) found that social capital was related to the total number of promotions during the entire career and to current salary. As further illustration, in line with its substitutability property, social capital has been found to compensate for serious deficiencies in one's publication record at the hiring stage of academia (Combes et al., 2008), while Cocchiara et al. (2010) found that graduate school alumni perceived that it was only the social capital but not the human capital they had acquired during graduate work that was related to their subsequent career success (salary gains and hierarchical status).

Finally, social capital also relates to subjective career success (Jokissari and Nurmi, 2005; Seibert et al., 2001), though the relationship is not as consistent as with objective success. Subjective career success reflects one's own private evaluations of one's up-to-date and prospective accomplishments (Gattiker and Larwood, 1986; and also Dries, 2011), and in cases is as important as extrinsic success because they are perceptions rather than objective facts that mostly dictate outcomes such as employee loyalty and effort expenditure (Baruch and Bozionelos, 2010).

Social capital as mentoring and network resources

A comprehensive conceptualization of social capital is in terms of mentoring relationships and network resources (for example, Baruch and Bozionelos, 2010; Bozionelos, 1997; 2003; Seibert et al., 2001). Mentoring in its traditional genre means an intensive developmental relationship between two persons with different seniority, the mentor and the protégé, in which the latter receives a variety of career instrumental (for example, challenging assignments, exposure and visibility) and socio-emotional (for example, acceptance and confirmation) functions from the former (for example, Kram, 1985). The mentoring relationship develops over a long period of time, goes through various stages (from initiation to separation and redefinition; Kram, 1983), and may transcend organizational boundaries (Baugh and Fagenson-Eland, 2005). As expected, individuals differ widely in their involvement in such relationships (for example, Bozionelos, 2006), while there is extensive variation in the number and quality of functions provided within them (Fletcher and Ragins, 2007).

Network ties signify all interpersonal links of the individual, excluding those that fall within traditional mentoring. Network ties have a number of properties including strength, range (the social distance the tie can reach), direction (whether the power differential is upwards or downwards) and diversity (the multiplicity of social settings ties originate from), while a person's social network has density (the proportion of ties it occupies within all potential ties in a particular social system). Peer or lateral mentoring (McManus and Russell, 2007) can be seen within the framework of network ties. Network resources are the resources individuals have at their disposal by means of their network ties. In a way analogous to mentoring, network ties, and their consequent resources, can also be characterized as career-instrumental and socio-emotional (for example, Fombrun, 1982; Saint-Charles and Mongeau, 2009) with most of these falling in-between depending on the degree of instrumental and socio-emotional qualities they contain (Brass, 1992).

Empirical evidence on mentoring and networking Much of the voluminous empirical research on mentoring has focused on its relationship with career outcomes, and meta-analyses of that work generally attest to its career-enhancing properties (Allen et al., 2004; Kammeyer-Mueller and Judge, 2008; Underhill, 2006). For example, a recent study found that presence of a strong mentor was one of the most powerful predictors of gaining a professorship in the highly competitive German academic labor market (Jungbauer-Gans and Gross, 2013). Furthermore, there is evidence for the benefits of mentoring for mentors' careers (Bozionelos et al., 2011; Gentry et al., 2008). As a result of such empirical findings, firms have long been investing in formal mentoring systems (that is, mentoring arrangements that are officially sponsored and recognized by the organization). Such systems, however, take a long time to take off (Weinberg and Lankau, 2011), their benefits lag behind those of informal mentoring (Baugh and Fagenson-Eland, 2007; Underhill, 2006), and when these benefits are realized they are mostly of a subjective rather than an objective nature (Baugh and Fagenson-Eland, 2007) – though this is still a benefit given the importance of perceptions in organizational life. This essentially means that formal structures cannot fully replace naturally occurring social interaction or personal 'chemistry' in the development of social relationships.

A smaller volume of systematic empirical research has focused exclusively (that is, was designed especially for that reason) on the link of network resources with career outcomes. Nonetheless, in a rigorous longitudinal study Wolff and Moser (2009) found that certain networking behaviors, such as maintaining and using internal-to-the-employer ties, predicted financial attainment over a two-year period. And in another in-depth study, Higgins (2005) concluded that executives of a particular firm utilized the flow of information and solidarity among them to gain CEO positions in start-up firms within the industry.

Given the considerable empirical evidence, the ensuing suggestion is that the building of social capital must be a core priority for career actors. However, building and maintaining social capital requires investment of both energy and time. As these resources are finite, a question that naturally arises is what is preferable: few intense relationships, like those with mentors or very strong ties, or large numbers of weak ties?

Mentoring or network ties? The above dilemma is partly reduced to whether mentoring relationships and network ties are substitutable. Pertinent research provides a mixed picture (Baruch and Bozionelos, 2010), which is further complicated by issues such as the type of mentoring or network ties (instrumental or socio-emotional), the career stage, and the form of outcome (objective or subjective).

Nonetheless, the following general patterns appear to hold:

1. Mentors and network ties mutually reinforce each other (for example, a mentor can assist in the development of a network: Blickle et al., 2009).
2. The mentoring relationship is based on mutuality and involves two parties (for example, Fletcher and Ragins, 2007), while learning from less senior organizational members is often a contemporary imperative (see also Murphy, 2012). This means that seeking intense developmental relationships (as mentor or protégé) should be on one's agenda even after having achieved substantial seniority.
3. Generally networks that involve weak – usually instrumental – ties with others who are not connected with each other (that is, structural holes) are beneficial for both employability and career progression. This is because they provide access to non-redundant resources (that is, multiple sources of differential information and influence) that are helpful in the career entry stage (in other words, finding the first job) and in career transitions (moving across employers for career enhancement or finding work after redundancy) (for example, Brandt, 2006; Demchenko, 2011; Seibert et al., 2001; Zenou, 2013).
4. Career instrumental mentoring functions and network resources offer more objective career benefits than their socio-emotional and expressive counterparts (for example, Allen et al., 2004; Bozionelos, 2003).
5. Contemporary careers involve considerable movement, uncertainty and challenge, and are unsuitable for being served solely by long-term intense relationships with traditional mentors (as in the era of the 'traditional linear career' archetype). This means that multiple ties, along with regular reconfigurations of our relationships constellations, may be the optimal long-term career development strategy (Crocitto et al., 2005; DeCastro et al., 2013; Dobrow et al., 2012; Higgins and Kram, 2001). To illustrate, Higgins and Thomas (2001) concluded that career benefits of network ties

are realized at later career stages, hence, they may be more beneficial in the longer term than mentoring relationships and vice versa.

THE ACQUISITION OF SOCIAL CAPITAL

Building Social Capital

Social capital through behaviors

Regardless of its optimal configuration, the next question that arises is how social capital can be built. One way to pose that query is what kinds of behaviors increase the likelihood of building relationships with mentors or other types of ties? Research that informs us on that issue includes studies on the link between personality and social capital because personality is manifested through behaviors and behavioral tendencies. Though changing one's personality is very difficult, adoption of particular behaviors may be feasible. Social capital-enhancing behaviors include proactively seeking advice, genuinely demanding performance feedback, demonstrating motivation in improving current affairs, displaying confidence in oneself, attending professional and social functions, showing interest in novelty and in disparate points of view, and being cooperative and helpful (Bozionelos and Bozionelos, 2010; Forret and Dougherty, 2001; Liang and Gong, 2013; Thomas et al., 2010; Wolff and Kim, 2012). These behaviors must be displayed consistently and in concert.

There are, however, two caveats that need attention. First, the effects of particular behavioral patterns may differ according to the form of social capital. For example, meticulous attention to one's work duties may be instrumental in initiating a relationship with a mentor (because mentors tend to be attracted to promising and hard-working employees, Singh et al., 2009), but detrimental in building ties with peers or outsiders. This is because the individual may not have time and energy to invest in building such relationships, or may not be seen by colleagues or external others as an attractive person to associate with (Bozionelos, 2003). Second, there is some evidence that the benefits of certain behaviors do not follow a linear pattern, but rather an inverted-U one. This means that engagement in particular tactics beyond a certain limit may in fact be harmful for acquisition of social capital. For example, at very strong levels, inquisitiveness, novelty in thinking, and display of variety of interests may turn from beneficial to detrimental for mentoring receipt, because they may make the individual appear unfocused, lacking perseverance and unreliable (Bozionelos et al., 2014a).

Creating social capital from other forms of capital

The previous section assumes that individuals are pretty much similar in other forms of capital, such as human capital and socioeconomic background. However, various forms of capital are exchangeable, and one form can, with appropriate investment, produce another form (Adler and Kwon, 2002; Bourdieu, 1986). Hence, economic and human capital can produce social capital. This means that initial inequalities in other forms of capital can lead to subsequent inequalities in social capital. One route – to be presented here – is the conversion of economic capital, first, into human capital by means of schooling, and subsequently into social capital by means of alumni membership.

It is a fact that possession of financial means (that is, economic capital) facilitates acquisition of culture and education. For example, affluence in a family can allow private tuition for children, living in 'catchment areas' for prestigious schools, or affordance of fees for such private schools. Furthermore, affluence provides resources such as equipment, space and peace of mind that facilitate assimilation of schooling. This, in turn, increases the prospects of entering into highly ranked higher education institutions but also of staying in education for longer (see Bourdieu, 1986). Attending and graduating from a prestigious secondary school or university provides automatic entry to its network of alumni, which is a concentrate of social capital, a circumscribed set of endurable social ties where there is flow of information, solidarity and reaches of influence. The primary purpose of the alumni association is to promote the institution, and one of the main ways of achieving that is by facilitating career progression of its members. Indeed, the most well-paid first jobs for graduates of elite universities are found via ties with various types of alumni (Marmaros and Sacerdote, 2002), while nearly 40 percent of all Fortune 500 CEOs are alumni of only ten prestigious private universities (Wecker, 2012). Furthermore, when attendance of higher education incurs substantial fees, financial capital delivers the ability to attend a prestigious institution regardless of previous achievements or abilities, and it is attendance of universities with high fees rather than universities with tough selection criteria that leads to subsequent career success (Dale and Krueger, 2002), presumably because of stronger alumni networks. The above creates a self-perpetuating cycle.

What was described above was of course only one of the many possible routes. Economic capital of the family may also directly create social capital for the offspring, for example, by allowing the offspring to attend activities and social clubs that can be afforded only by affluent individuals. Because affluence is largely associated with influence (for example, Cousin and Chauvin, 2012; Gilens, 2005), ties with affluent others are likely to facilitate access to better entry-level positions, and hence, to better long-term career prospects.

Ascriptive characteristics and a priori social capital

However (and unfortunately), social capital is also conferred by ascribed characteristics. Such characteristics include overtly identifiable features that are often genetically rooted, such as racial background and gender (Tsui et al., 1992). Generally, people prefer to associate with others whom they perceive as belonging to groups that are similar to the group they categorize themselves in (Byrne, 1971; Tajfel and Turner, 1986), and ascribed characteristics (or surface level diversity, Harrison et al., 1998) evoke perceptions of similarity. This tends to create homophily in social networks; that is, people tend to develop ties with others whom they see as similar to themselves (for example, women integrate into work and professional networks that include mostly other women) (Morrison and Von Glinow, 1990). Furthermore, for a number of reasons, within most societies, particular groups have been established as dominant and are associated with power and success. Therefore, ties with members of such dominant or privileged groups may carry (or be perceived to carry) more value than ties with members of less privileged groups (Ibarra, 1993; Ragins and Sundstrom, 1989).

This means that many people may in fact be endowed with, or deprived of, social capital simply because of ascribed features they have no control over, which nevertheless 'stream' them towards integrating into networks or developing relationships with mentors that represent particular (privileged or underprivileged) social groups. This also means that opportunities of many people to benefit from social capital are partly a priori determined. Indeed, a recent study in a representative sample of the US population (McDonald, 2011) found clear evidence for gender and race segregation in occupational social networks, and a clear career-enhancing social capital effect (for example, access to more powerful individuals or information that can lead to a job) that arose from affiliation with white male networks only (McDonald, 2011).

THE MECHANISM OF THE SOCIAL CAPITAL EFFECT: POLITICS OR ACTUAL PERFORMANCE OUTPUT?

As seen, social capital indisputably aids career progression. The way – that is, the mechanism with which – it does so, however, is not exactly clear as yet. The alternative routes are either through job performance or via political processes. The performance route attests that social capital helps those who possess it to achieve better work output (for example, more efficient performance of tasks, greater reliability in output, greater customer satisfaction, and more timely identification of opportunities or threats), which is then translated into career success. To illustrate, two functions of mentoring, challenging assignments and role modeling, are intuitively linked with increases in protégé job proficiency. This should reflect on job performance that in turn should presumably be rewarded by employers. The political route, on the other hand, suggests that there are political processes that account for career benefits of social capital. To illustrate again, via visibility and direct forms of sponsorship, also functions of mentoring and networking, a mentor or a powerful tie, may influence, directly or indirectly, a promotion, a favorable transfer, or a hiring decision in favor of a particular individual. This is in line with the view that career outcomes are largely the result of political processes rather than transparent procedures that rely on merit and actual output (for example, Tharenou, 1997). Empirical evidence is available in support of both accounts, although – maybe to the surprise of some – most of it leans towards the political explanation.

There are certainly findings that signal a positive effect of social capital on work performance. For example, Thompson (2005) found a relationship between network-building behaviors and supervisory performance ratings. More recently Reiche (2012) found that social capital of inpatriates (that is, subsidiary countries' nationals who have moved to the headquarters of a multinational corporation) was related to the continuity of knowledge transfer from the headquarters towards the subsidiary after they had returned to the subsidiary, while Bozionelos et al. (2014b) found that the amount of mentoring software engineers had received was related to their job performance as rated by their line managers.

On the other hand, however, work that is directed towards the political route is rather more voluminous. Studies in academia are especially helpful in this quest because academic work includes performance criteria that can be measured reasonably objectively, such as volume and quality of research output. In a recent study, Hadani et al. (2012)

found that social capital of PhD graduates, as indicated by network centrality of the attended institution, was able to predict the prestige of their first academic post (an index of career success), but not the quality of their publications (an index of job performance) during early career stages. This renders social capital instrumental for early success outcomes but not for actual output. And in yet another study within academia, Kirchmeyer (2005) found more evidence for the political rather than the performance-enhancing route of mentoring towards career outcomes. In addition, recent research in the commercial corporate environment (Wei et al., 2012) suggested that network ties enhance supervisor ratings of job performance and career potential, but only for those employees who have good political skills, also indicating a pivotal role of politics in the realization of career benefits from social capital. Finally, other recent empirical work indicates that within meritocracies (systems where criteria and assessments are unambiguous, objective and detached) social capital brings no distinct advantages and it is only human capital that determines hiring outcomes (Chua, 2011). This also stands against the output route.

The issue of the mechanism that links social capital with career outcomes is critical from a number of perspectives, and certainly from a sustainability point of view. Given that it is actual output that keeps firms in business and societies progressing, having politics instead of actual output determining career rewards may not be sustainable in the long term. This issue is visited in the following section.

THE DELETERIOUS OR 'DARK SIDE' OF SOCIAL CAPITAL

Most work, starting from early seminal studies (for example, Granovetter, 1973) and other influential scholarship (Coleman, 1988), has been interpreted from the point of view of those who benefit from social capital (for example, individuals who use their ties in order to maintain their employability). As a result, social capital has been overwhelmingly embraced as a beneficial resource, and the literature is replete with recommendations and prescriptive advice to individual career actors and managers about developing, nourishing and utilizing their own and their group's social capital (for example, Hannon, 2011; Misner, 2011; Prusak and Cohen, 2001). The numerous web-based professional and social networking sites rely on this premise too. Though lines for caution did exist (for example, Portes, 1998, pp. 15–18) these were thin, few and drifted away in the stream of enthusiasm.

However, a legitimate question can be the following: what happens to those who do not have or do not wish to use their social ties to help themselves into a job or to a better position? These people may be equally as or better qualified than those who utilize their connections to enhance their careers and employability. And a consequent question concerns the fate of employers where those who are hired or promoted are the ones who are better connected and willing to use their connections to gain advantage. These employers are likely to have in their ranks mostly people who prioritize their own interests, including helping their own people within the organization, over the interests of their employer. When the situation is viewed from the reverse point of view, what has been labeled as the 'dark side' of social capital makes its appearance.

Some Early Systematic Evidence on the 'Dark Side'

It is only recently that scholarly work has devoted some systematic attention at the 'dark side' of social capital (Bizzi, 2013; Teagarden and Schotter, 2013; Van Deth and Zmerli, 2010). Though still scarce, that research is illustrative. For example, looking at sport governance in Italy and Czech Republic, Numerato and Baglioni (2012) observed that social capital may indeed benefit particular individuals and groups who share and utilize it to advance their own career-related interests (that is, advancement into positions of power and acquisition of material resources). However, this runs against the interests of the sector or the whole society, which are eventually harmed because inappropriate individuals advance into positions of responsibility and leadership, and because resources and prizes are not awarded or won on merit (Numerato and Baglioni).

The case of Greek academia: an illustration of the 'dark side' mechanism and effect

Bozionelos (2014), using a mix of methods including ethnography, developed a historical account of how an 'in-group' of individuals who are connected by means of blood, family friendship, political and business ties fully control the sizable academic labor market in a whole country: Greece. Those individuals, and the families they represent, form a web that extends over virtually the whole of the country's academia, being especially dense in upper academic ranks. The links extend into political parties and part of the rest of the country's aristocracy (that is, influential and wealthy families). The creation and establishment of that 'in-group' has evolved over many decades, and is attributed to an interplay of historical events (the civil war in the country that took place in the middle of the twentieth century) and cultural characteristics (the country profile in the cultural dimensions of institutional and in-group collectivism, the profound in-group–out-group polarization, the standing of academics, and the key role of political ideology and political party affiliation in Greek society).

That 'in-group' is held together by strong bonding social capital that generates a constant flow of solidarity and information among its members. Holding virtually all positions of power within academia itself and having influence on most key public office positions (that is, within ministries or other offices of importance) that 'in-group' is able to control in its favor hiring, promotion and disciplinary processes and decisions across academic institutions, which is in essence the whole academic labor market within the country. This allows their offspring or other 'in-group' members to enter academia regardless of their abilities, potential and credentials, to advance safely through the ranks, and establish themselves in leadership and other positions of power and influence; hence, perpetuating what is to some extent an 'inheritance' system. Social capital substitutes for lack of other qualities and provides the resources that keep the 'in-group' together. 'Outsiders' (individuals without the same aristocratic roots or without family, business or political party affiliations to that 'in group') are either denied entry, or when they enter (normally having been 'allowed to' in order to carry out tasks, such as teaching and 'window-dressing' research, on behalf of 'in-group' members, also Bozionelos, in press) they can follow only certain paths according to the attitude they demonstrate towards the 'in-group'.

In this particular case, social capital is indeed instrumental in career progression and success, and careers within a whole sector are nearly entirely determined by it. On the other hand, human capital (academic credentials, output and ability) plays a minor role (Bozionelos, 2014). It is exactly for that reason that the case is demonstrative of the deleterious aspects of social capital. Because the consequence – apart of course from lack of fairness and other ethical concerns – is the handicapping of the whole of academia within the country. Indeed, as Bozionelos (2014) demonstrates, Greek academia, as represented by the country's state higher education institutions, has been substantially underperforming. This is the natural outcome of two facts: first, hiring, promotions and ascendance into leadership are not based on merit; and second, those within the system are either unable or demotivated to focus on core academic activities but instead they engage in political ventures because it is these that confer career benefits (Bozionelos, 2014). And a crippled academia probably has negative repercussions on the competitiveness of the whole country.

THE SUSTAINABILITY OF CAREERS THAT ARE SOCIAL CAPITAL DEPENDENT

Returning to the questions on sustainability, the first of them pertains to whether careers that are based on social capital are sustainable, that is whether career actors can engage in successful career trajectories by relying on their social ties and the resources these bring to them. The response to this is probably positive, provided, however, that the system within which careers are pursued is receptive and remains stable in this respect. The answer to the second question, which is whether a social entity (for example, a firm, an industry within a country, or even a whole country) can sustain itself when careers within it are mostly determined by social capital is more complicated, but it is probably negative. This is because social entities within which social capital eclipses merit cannot remain antagonistic within competitive environments. Survival within such environments necessitates certain output, which means that most individuals within must add value. Otherwise, there cannot be sustainability in the long term (firms will decline and disappear, industries will fall, while countries will get into debt or see their standards of living drop substantially).

It should be kept in mind that it is the way in which social capital may benefit individual careers rather than its beneficial career effects per se that can be problematic. For example, finding out from an acquaintance about a job opening or being invited to apply for a position by someone who appreciates us as people may not cause harm. What is harmful is when others are excluded from competition because the formal communication channel is not properly utilized, or when the hiring decision is not based on merit or the needs of the position but on social capital instead. This concurs with suggestions that whether social capital has benign or harmful effects depends on the broader cultural context (Van Deth and Zmerli, 2010; Lin and Si, 2010). Culture means collective tuning to a particular way of thinking, such as whether it is acceptable to utilize our social resources to advance what we perceive as our own personal interests instead of advancing the interests of the whole collective (for example, Jones, 2005). Indeed, Bozionelos' work highlighted uniquely configured cultural characteristics (such as the profound in-group–out-group polarization, and the profile of strong in-group and weak institutional collectivism of the country) that gave rise to and sustain the 'in-group' ruling of academia in Greece. A different cultural configuration may not have been conducive to such a situation, at least not in that form (Bozionelos, 2013, in press; see also Gu et al., 2008; Numerato and Baglioni, 2012).

IMPLICATIONS FOR PRACTICE AND DIRECTIONS FOR FUTURE RESEARCH

Considering that a perfectly meritocratic world is yet very much into the future, we must be aware of the importance of cultivating social capital for the sake of our employability and career progression. Though creation of social capital is not entirely under one's personal control – due to the role of personality and other forms of capital – strategies and behavioral patterns that nearly everyone can implement do exist. A balance of strong developmental relationships and weak ties appears the optimal configuration, considering the uncertainty inherent in today's careers. In addition, it is important to constantly nourish, update and refresh our ties and their configuration. On the other hand, we must be aware of the fact that blunt utilization of social capital in order to get ahead may in the long term harm our own interests through harming the larger collective in which we operate and live. Therefore, when we find ourselves in influential positions we should prioritize merit and value-adding potential over personal acquaintance or other pressures associated with social capital, however difficult this may seem at the time.

From the viewpoint of firms, institutions and governments, what is certain is that simple legislation (for example, all vacancies are externally advertised by law) cannot effectively inoculate against the deleterious effects of social capital. This is because structures and regulations cannot eliminate social interaction (Luthans, 2011) while cultures are often superimposed upon structures, formal rules and legislation (for example, Bozionelos, 2014, in press; Galbraith, 1973; Luthans, 2011). In addition, regulations and formal rules may suppress positive effects of social capital, such as enhanced synergy, information and knowledge sharing (Kostopoulos et al., in press; Xiang et al., 2013) that promote innovation and output. The way forward, therefore, is much more difficult and painful, and pertains to systematic effort to change perceptions of individuals, groups and whole societies about principles of engagement into career-related activities and socially responsible use of the resources that interpersonal ties offer.

Future research should focus further on the development of a more nuanced idea about optimal social capital configurations according to career stage, environmental characteristics (for example, type of industry, conditions of the economy) and career type (for example, domestic vs. international). Moreover, the relative contribution of social capital in comparison with other types of capital and the dynamics of their interactions in the generation of career success must be further looked at. In addition, scholars should work towards comprehensive models of social capital creation that incorporate other forms of capital, but also individual dispositional characteristics (that is, personality and mental ability) and contextual factors (such as societal and cultural features). Furthermore, it appears that acquisition of social capital is partly determined by ascribed attributes, such as ethnic/racial origin. Future studies should investigate whether the increasingly multicultural nature of societies (as a consequence of ongoing globalization) is limiting the extent of that phenomenon, and should identify factors that facilitate or hinder that process. Finally, the inquiry on the 'dark side' of social capital must continue. Apart from seeking to further consolidate evidence on the deleterious effects, future research should also identify the conditions (for example, particular cultural features and their configurations) that turn social capital into malignant or benevolent. This is a very important issue into which future research ought to delve.

REFERENCES

Adler, P.S. and Kwon, S.-W. (2002). Social capital: Prospects for a new concept. *Academy of Management Review*, 27, 17–40.

Allen, T.D., Eby, L.T., Poteet, M.L., Lentz, E. and Lima, L. (2004). Career benefits associated with mentoring for protégés: A meta-analysis. *Journal of Applied Psychology*, 89, 127–36.

Arthur, M.B., Claman, P.H. and DeFillippi, R.J. (1995). Intelligent enterprise, intelligent careers. *Academy of Management Executive*, 9(4), 7–20.

Baruch, Y. and Bozionelos, N. (2010). Career issues. In S. Zedeck (ed.), *APA Handbook of Industrial and Organizational Psychology, Volume 2: Selecting & Developing Members of the Organization* (pp. 67–113). Washington, DC: American Psychological Association.

Baugh, S.G. and Fagenson-Eland, E.A. (2005). Boundaryless mentoring: An exploratory study of the functions provided by internal versus external organizational mentors. *Journal of Applied Social Psychology*, 35, 939–55.

Baugh, S.G. and Fagenson-Eland, E.A. (2007). Formal mentoring programs: A 'poor cousin' to informal relationships? In B.R. Ragins and K.E. Kram (eds), *Handbook of Mentoring at Work* (pp. 249–71). Thousand Oaks, CA: Sage.

Becker, G.S. (1964). *Human Capital*. New York: National Bureau of Economic Research.

Bizzi, L. (2013). The dark side of structural holes: A multilevel investigation. *Journal of Management*, 39, 1554–78.

Blickle, G., Witzki, A.H. and Schneider, P.B. (2009). Mentoring support and power: A three year predictive field study on protégé networking and career success. *Journal of Vocational Behavior*, 74, 181–9.

Bourdieu, P. (1980). Le capital social: Notes provisoires [Social capital: Provisional notes]. *Actes de la Recherche en Sciences Sociales*, 31, 2–3.

Bourdieu, P. (1986). The forms of capital. In J.E. Richardson (ed.), *Handbook of Theory for Research in the Sociology of Education* (pp. 241–58). New York: Greenwood Press.

Bozionelos, N. (1997). Modeling career success: The influence of personality and interpersonal variables (Unpublished doctoral dissertation). University of Strathclyde, Glasgow.

Bozionelos, N. (2003). Intra-organizational network resources: Relation to career success and personality. *International Journal of Organizational Analysis*, 11, 41–66.

Bozionelos, N. (2006). Mentoring and expressive network resources: Their relationship with career success and emotional exhaustion among Hellenes employees involved in emotion work. *International Journal of Human Resource Management*, 17, 362–78.

Bozionelos, N. (2013). Response letter to reviewers #1 and #3, Revision 1: Career patterns in Greek academia: Social capital and intelligent careers, but for whom? *Career Development International*.

Bozionelos, N. (2014). Career patterns in Greek academia: Social capital and intelligent careers, but for whom? *Career Development International*, 19, 264–94.

Bozionelos, N. (in press). Greece: Incivility, bullying and forcing in the land of bullying Gods and lesser mortals. In M. Omari and M. Paull (eds), *Workplace Abuse, Incivility and Bullying: Methodological and Cultural Perspectives*. Melbourne: Taylor & Francis.

Bozionelos, N. and Bozionelos, G. (2010). Mentoring received by protégés: Its relation to personality and mental ability in the Anglo-Saxon organizational environment. *International Journal of Human Resource Management*, 21, 509–29.

Bozionelos, N., Bozionelos, G., Kostopoulos, K. and Polychroniou, P. (2011). How providing mentoring relates to career success and organizational commitment: A study in the general managerial population. *Career Development International*, 16, 446–68.

Bozionelos, N., Bozionelos, G., Polychroniou, P. and Kostopoulos, K. (2014a). Mentoring receipt and personality: Evidence for non-linear relationships. *Journal of Business Research*, 67, 171–81.

Bozionelos, N., Kostopoulos, K., Van der Heijden, B., Rousseau, D.M., Bozionelos, G., Hoyland, T., Van der Heijde, C. et al. (2014b). Employability and job performance as links in the relationship of mentoring receipt with career success. Manuscript submitted for publication.

Brandt, M. (2006). Soziale Kontakte als weg aus der erwerbslosigkeit [Finding a job via social contacts]. *Kölner Zeitschrift für Soziologie und Sozialpsychologie*, 58, 468–588.
Brass, D.J. (1992). Power in organizations: A social network perspective. In G. Moore and J. A. Whitt (eds), *Research in Politics and Society: The Political Consequences of Social Networks* (Vol. 4, pp.295–323). Greenwich, CT: JAI Press.
Byrne, D.E. (1971). *The Attraction Paradigm*. New York: Academic Press.
Chua, V. (2011). Social networks and labour market outcomes in a meritocracy. *Social Networks*, 33, 1–11.
Cocchiara, F.K., Kwesiga, E., Bell, M.P. and Baruch, Y. (2010). Influences on perceived career success: Findings from US graduate business degree alumni. *Career Development International*, 15, 39–58.
Coleman, J.S. (1988). Social capital in the creation of human capital. *American Journal of Sociology*, 94, S95–S120.
Collins, E.G.C. and Scott, P. (1978). Everyone who makes it has a mentor. *Harvard Business Review*, 56(4), 89–110.
Combes, P.-P., Linnemer, L. and Visser, M. (2008). Publish or peer-ish? The role of skills and networks in hiring economics professors. *Labour Economics*, 15, 423–41.
Cousin, B. and Chauvin, S. (2012). L'économie symbolique du capital social. *Actes de la Recherche en Sciences Sociales*, 193, 96.
Crocitto, M.M., Sullivan, S.E. and Carraher, S.M. (2005). Global mentoring as a means of career development and knowledge creation: A learning-based framework and agenda for future research. *Career Development International*, 10, 522–35.
Dale, S.B. and Krueger, A.B. (2002). Estimating the payoff to attending a more selective college: An application of selection on observables and unobservables. *Quarterly Journal of Economics*, 117, 1491–526.
De Vos, A., De Hauw, S. and Van der Heijden, B.I.J.M. (2011). Competence development and career success: The mediating role of employability. *Journal of Vocational Behavior*, 79, 438–47.
DeCastro, R., Sambuco, D., Ubel, P.A., Stewart, A. and Jagsi, R. (2013). Mentor networks in academic medicine: Moving beyond a dyadic conception of mentoring for junior faculty researchers. *Academic Medicine*, 88, 488–96.
Demchenko, O. (2011). Social network and occupational mobility: A mathematical model. *Social Science Quarterly*, 92, 1118–32.
Dobrow, S.R., Chandler, D.E., Murphy, W.M. and Kram, K.E. (2012). A review on developmental networks: Incorporating a mutuality perspective. *Journal of Management*, 38, 210–42.
Dries, N. (2011). The meaning of career success: Avoiding reification through a closer inspection of historical, cultural, and ideological contexts. *Career Development International*, 16, 364–84.
Fletcher, J.K. and Ragins, B.R. (2007). Stone Center relational cultural theory: A window on relational mentoring. In B.R. Ragins and K.E. Kram (eds), *Handbook of Mentoring at Work* (pp. 373–99). Thousand Oaks, CA: Sage.
Fombrun, C.J. (1982). Strategies for network research in organizations. *Academy of Management Review*, 7, 280–91.
Forret, M.L. and Dougherty, T.W. (2001). Correlates of networking behavior for managerial and professional employees. *Group and Organization Management*, 26, 283–311.
Galbraith, J.R. (1973). *Designing Complex Organizations*. Reading, MA: Addison-Wesley.
Gattiker, U.E. and Larwood, L. (1986). Subjective career success: A study of managers and support personnel. *Journal of Business and Psychology*, 1, 78–94.
Gentry, W.A., Weber, T.J. and Sadri, G. (2008). Examining career-related mentoring and managerial performance across cultures: A multilevel analysis. *Journal of Vocational Behavior*, 72, 241–53.
Gilens, M. (2005). Inequality and democratic responsiveness. *Public Opinion Quarterly*, 69, 778–96.
Glanville, J.L. and Bienenstock, E.J. (2009). A typology for understanding the connections among different forms of social capital. *American Behavioral Scientist*, 52, 1507–30.
Granovetter, M. (1973). The strength of weak ties. *American Journal of Sociology*, 78, 1360–80.
Gu, F.F., Hung, K. and Tse, D.K. (2008). When does guanxi matter? Issues of capitalization and its dark sides. *Journal of Marketing*, 72, 12–28.
Hadani, M., Coombes, S., Das, D. and Jalajas, D. (2012). Finding a good job: Academic network centrality and early occupational outcomes in management academia. *Journal of Organizational Behavior*, 33, 723–39.
Hannon, K. (2011). How to find a mentor. Forbes.com. 31 October. Available at http://www.forbes.com/sites/kerryhannon/2011/10/31/how-to-find-a-mentor/.
Harrison, D.A., Price, K.H. and Bell, M.P. (1998). Beyond relational demography: Time and the effects of surface- and deep-level diversity on work group cohesion. *Academy of Management Journal*, 41, 96–107.
Higgins, M. (2005). *Career Imprints: Creating Leaders Across an Industry*. San Francisco, CA: Jossey-Bass.
Higgins, M.C. and Kram, K.E. (2001). Reconceptualizing mentoring at work: A developmental network perspective. *Academy of Management Review*, 26, 264–88.

Higgins, M.C. and Thomas, D.A. (2001). Constellations and careers: Toward understanding the effects of multiple developmental relationships. *Journal of Organizational Behavior*, 22, 223–47.
Ibarra, H. (1993). Personal networks of women and minorities in management: A conceptual framework. *Academy of Management Review*, 18, 56–87.
Jokisaari, M. and Nurmi, J.-E. (2005). Company matters: Goal-related social capital in the transition to working life. *Journal of Vocational Behavior*, 67, 413–28.
Jones, O. (2005). Manufacturing regeneration through corporate entrepreneurship: Middle managers and organizational innovation. *International Journal of Operations and Production Management*, 25, 491–511.
Jungbauer-Gans, M. and Gross, C. (2013). Determinants of success in university careers: Findings from the German academic labor market. *Zeitschrift für Soziologie*, 42, 74–92.
Kammeyer-Mueller, J.D. and Judge, T.A. (2008). A quantitative review of mentoring research: Test of a model. *Journal of Vocational Behavior*, 72, 269–83.
Kim, S. (2013). Networking enablers, constraints and dynamics: A qualitative analysis. *Career Development International*, 18, 120–38.
Kirchmeyer, C. (2005). The effects of mentoring on academic careers over time: Testing performance and political perspectives. *Human Relations*, 58, 637–69.
Kostopoulos, K., Bozionelos, N. and Syrigos, E. (in press). Ambidexterity and unit performance: Intellectual capital antecedents and cross-level moderating effects of human resource practices. *Human Resource Management*.
Kram, K. (1983). Phases of the mentor relationship. *Academy of Management Journal*, 26, 608–25.
Kram, K.E. (1985). *Mentoring in the Workplace: Development Relationships in Organizational Life*. Glenview, IL: Scott Foresman.
Liang, J. and Gong, Y.P. (2013). Capitalizing on proactivity for informal mentoring received during early career: The moderating role of core self-evaluations. *Journal of Organizational Behavior*, 34, 1182–201.
Lin, J. and Si, S.X. (2010). Can guanxi be a problem? Contexts, ties, and some unfavorable consequences of social capital in China. *Asia Pacific Journal of Management*, 27, 561–81.
Lincoln, J.R. and Miller, J. (1979). Work and friendship ties in organisations: A comparative analysis of relational networks. *Administrative Science Quarterly*, 24, 181–99.
Luthans, F. (2011). *Organizational Behavior* (12th edn). Boston, MA: McGraw-Hill.
Marmaros, D. and Sacerdote, B. (2002). Peer and social networks in job search. *European Economic Review*, 46, 870–79.
McDonald, S. (2011). What's in the 'old boys' network? Accessing social capital in gendered and racialized networks. *Social Networks*, 33, 317–30.
McManus, S.E. and Russell, J.E.A. (2007). Peer mentoring relationships. In B.R. Ragins and K.E. Kram (eds), *Handbook of Mentoring at Work* (pp. 273–97). Thousand Oaks, CA: Sage.
Misner, I. (2011). Four steps to building social capital. Entrepreneur. 9 May. Available at http://www.entrepreneur.com/article/219590.
Morrison, A.M. and Von Glinow, M.A. (1990). Women and minorities in management. *American Psychologist*, 45, 200–208.
Murphy, W.M. (2012). Reverse mentoring at work: Fostering cross-generational learning and developing millennial leaders. *Human Resource Management*, 51, 549–73.
Numerato, D. and Baglioni, S. (2012). The dark side of social capital: Ethnography of sport governance. *International Review for the Sociology of Sport*, 47, 594–611.
Obukhova, E. and Lan, G. (2013). Do job seekers benefit from contacts? A direct test with contemporaneous searches. *Management Science*, 59, 2204–16.
Parker, P., Khapova, S.N. and Arthur, M.B. (2009). The intelligent career framework as a basis of interdisciplinary inquiry. *Journal of Vocational Behavior*, 75, 291–302.
Portes, A. (1998). Social capital: Its origins and applications in modern sociology. *Annual Review of Sociology*, 24, 1–24.
Prusak, L. and Cohen, D. (2001). How to invest in social capital. *Harvard Business Review*, 79(6), 86–93.
Putman, R.D. (2000). *Bowling Alone: The Collapse and Revival of American Community*. New York: Simon & Schuster.
Ragins, B.R. and Sundstrom, E. (1989). Gender and power in organizations. *Psychological Bulletin*, 105, 51–88.
Reiche, B.S. (2012). Knowledge benefits of social capital upon repatriation: A longitudinal study of international assignees. *Journal of Management Studies*, 49, 1052–77.
Saint-Charles, J. and Mongeau, P. (2009). Different relationships for coping with ambiguity and uncertainty in organizations. *Social Networks*, 31, 33–9.
Seibert, S.E., Kraimer, M.L. and Liden, R.C. (2001). A social capital theory of career success. *Academy of Management Journal*, 44, 219–37.

Singh, R., Ragins, B.R. and Tharenou, P. (2009). Who gets a mentor? A longitudinal assessment of the rising star hypothesis. *Journal of Vocational Behavior*, 74, 11–17.
Tajfel, H. and Turner, J.C. (1986). The social identity theory of intergroup behavior. In S. Worchel and W.G. Austin (eds), *Psychology of Intergroup Relations* (pp. 7–24). Chicago,IL: Nelson-Hall.
Teagarden, M.B. and Schotter, A. (2013). Favor prevalence in emerging markets: A multi-level analysis. *Asia Pacific Journal of Management*, 30, 447–60.
Tharenou, P. (1997). Managerial career advancement. In C.L. Cooper and I.T. Robertson (eds), *International Review of Industrial and Organizational Psychology* (Vol. 12, pp. 39–93). New York: Wiley.
Thomas, J.P., Whitman, D.S. and Viswesvaran, C. (2010). Employee proactivity in organizations: A comparative meta-analysis of emergent proactive constructs. *Journal of Occupational and Organizational Psychology*, 83, 275–300.
Thompson, J.A. (2005). Proactive personality and job performance: A social capital perspective. *Journal of Applied Psychology*, 90, 1011–17.
Tsui, A.S., Egan, T.D. and O'Reilly III, C.A. (1992). Being different: Relational demography and organizational attachment. *Administrative Science Quarterly*, 37, 549–79.
Underhill, C.M. (2006). The effectiveness of mentoring programs in corporate settings: A meta-analytical review of the literature. *Journal of Vocational Behavior*, 68, 292–307.
Van der Heijde, C.M. and Van der Heijden, B.I.J.M. (2006). A competence-based and multidimensional operationalization and measurement of employability. *Human Resource Management*, 45, 449–76.
Van Deth, J.W. and Zmerli, S. (2010). Introduction: Civicness, equality, and democracy – a 'dark side' of social capital? *American Behavioral Scientist*, 53, 631–9.
Wecker, M. (2012). Where the Fortune 500 CEOs went to school. US News. 14 May. Available at http://www.usnews.com/education/best-graduate-schools/top-business-schools/articles/2012/05/14/where-the-fortune-500-ceos-went-to-school.
Wei, L.Q., Chiang, F.F.T. and Wu, L.Z. (2012). Developing and utilizing network resources: Roles of political skill. *Journal of Management Studies*, 49, 381–402.
Weinberg, F.J. and Lankau, M.J. (2011). Formal mentoring programs: A mentor-centric and longitudinal analysis. *Journal of Management*, 37, 1527–57.
Wolff, H.-G. and Kim, S. (2012). The relationship between networking behaviors and the big five personality dimensions. *Career Development International*, 17, 43–66.
Wolff, H.-G. and Moser, K. (2009). Effects of networking on career success: A longitudinal study. *Journal of Applied Psychology*, 94, 196–206.
Xiang, C.J., Lu, Y.B. and Gupta, S. (2013). Knowledge sharing in information system development teams: Examining the impact of shared mental model from a social capital theory perspective. *Behaviour and Information Technology*, 32, 1024–40.
Zenou, Y. (2013). Social interactions and the labor market. *Revue D'Economie Politique*, 123, 307–31.

6 Career capital acquisition through corporate volunteering

Chen Fleisher, Svetlana N. Khapova and Mette M. Schipper

Along with the increase in the number of companies engaging in corporate volunteering programs, volunteer experiences are becoming a common category on employee résumés (Boccalandro, 2009). Corporate volunteering refers to 'giving one's time, knowledge, or skills as part of a community service, outreach, or social responsibility activity during company time without additional compensation or direct personal remuneration' (Grant, 2012, p. 592). Several recent studies have demonstrated that participation in volunteering makes employees feel more engaged at work and more committed to their company (Caligiuri et al., 2013; Jones, 2010).

While employees' engagement and commitment have been always highly useful concepts in the context of a healthy economy, few organizations can currently offer stable employment to their employees (DiRenzo and Greenhaus, 2011). Increasingly, the contemporary career discourse is shifting from employees' satisfaction with their work to employees' satisfaction with their perceived employability or, in other words, 'the continuous fulfilling, acquiring or creating of work through the optimal use of [transferable] *competencies*' (Van der Heijde and Van der Heijden, 2006, p. 453, emphasis added). Indeed, the contemporary perspective on volunteering suggests that in the absence of work experiences, more and more professionals engage in volunteer experiences to accumulate new career capital, which is assumed to improve their employability (for example, Grant, 2012). However, in this chapter, we posit that researchers and practitioners do not need to stress one set of benefits over another. As Arlington (2013) notes, corporate volunteering can be good for both employees and their organizations: '[Volunteering] makes work more meaningful to them and at the end of the day, they're happier at work. It is a win–win–win situation – it's good for the community, good for the employers . . . [and] good for the employee'.

Based on a study of one large financial service organization in the Netherlands, we attempt to bring these two perspectives together. First, we seek to answer the question: How does corporate volunteering contribute to employees' career capital development? To organize our findings concerning career capital acquisition, we draw on Luthans et al.'s (2004) framework, which suggests that human behavior and motivation in modern organizations can be viewed as three non-financial forms of capital: psychological ('who you are' and, more importantly, 'who you are becoming'), human ('what you know') and social capital ('who you know'). By doing so, we can better understand the potential value of volunteering as a career experience to enhance one's employability. Next, drawing on the suggestion of Luthans and his colleagues (Luthans et al., 2004) that the capital employees possess is a critical resource for the sustainable competitive advantage of organizations in the global economy, we seek to answer the question: How and for what purposes do employees apply their accumulated career capital upon returning from volunteering?

Answering these two questions in conjunction with one another, this chapter aims to make several important theoretical and practical contributions. First, it extends the strategic management and organizational behavior literature by offering a renewed look at the link between sustainable careers and sustainable organizations. From the perspective of our study, corporate volunteering is not only a source for organizations to give back to society but also an opportunity to provide employees with fresh work and learning experiences, helping them make their own careers more sustainable (Grant, 2012).

Second, by delineating the relationship between the volunteering and workplace context, this chapter further contributes to the multiple-domains perspective (Rodell, 2013). While the extant literature provides ample evidence of career capital accumulation by individuals, how this accumulated capital can be brought back from volunteer experiences and be of value to the employing organization is less observable. This is particularly important if we recognize that a career is 'an individual's work-related and other relevant experiences, both inside and outside of organizations, that form a unique pattern over the individual's life span' (Sullivan and Baruch, 2009, p. 1543). However, most of the extant research on corporate volunteering has focused on how to attract and manage volunteers, mainly capturing the 'marketing' and strategic sides of corporate volunteering (De Gilder et al., 2005; Van Schie et al., 2011). In line with the organizational learning literature (Crossan et al., 1999), this chapter suggests that learning stemming from individuals' volunteer experiences transforms into learning on the organizational level over time and can contribute to sustaining business for these organizations.

Finally, by focusing on one specific and under-researched type of career experience, we aim to contribute to generating evidence of the effects of volunteer experiences on employees' employability. Earlier in this book, De Vos and Van der Heijden have noted that it is not always easy to see the link between one's daily tasks and sustainable employability. People continue engaging in employability-enhancing activities with the hope (although not always directed towards this goal) that it will pay off at some point in the future (Smith, 2010). We extend this notion by exploring the importance of corporate volunteering as a source of career capital acquisition. In the following sections, we will present our study and its findings, addressing the two main research questions discussed above.

THE STUDY

Corporate Volunteering in the Netherlands

Volunteering is highly popular in the Netherlands, which makes it an interesting context for studying corporate volunteering. According to the Organization for Economic Co-operation and Development's (OECD) Better Life Index, almost 60 percent of the Dutch population reports having helped a stranger (OECD, 2013). In fact, Dutch people spend on average about five minutes per day in volunteering activities. For a matter of comparison, the OECD average is four minutes per day (OECD, 2013). This and other indices that examine the giving behavior trends around the world have continuously placed the Netherlands in one of the top ten countries (CAF, 2011). These numbers, which are growing, serve as an example of how the sense of social and community responsibility is instilled in the Dutch society. It is not surprising then that many people in the Netherlands are willing to take part in volunteering programs through their employers. Finally, the context in which marketing and corporate philanthropy visibility are not the primary triggers for Dutch management (Meijer et al., 2006) revitalizes the 'pure' focus and understanding of corporate volunteering as an experience and the effects it may have on the organization (De Gilder et al., 2005; Meijs, 2003). Within the service sector, which accounts for over 50 percent of Dutch GDP, banking and consultancy organizations have been most involved in corporate volunteering (Meijs and Van der Voort, 2004).

Research Context and Sample

The current chapter reports on a study conducted in a multinational organization in the financial services sector. This global organization has 84000 employees worldwide and is present in more than forty countries. The organization's sustainable objective is to make a positive contribution to the many communities in which it operates around the world. This is derived from the idea that a strong and healthy community has far-reaching benefits for its businesses, inhabitants and future generations. The company's activities in the field of sustainability are led and coordinated by a dedicated functional department, which is based at its headquarters in the Netherlands. Their main task is to facilitate and promote volunteering within the organization as well as to monitor and evaluate different volunteering projects. The department has measured the firm's performance in the ethical, social and environmental fields since 1995. In 2012, more than 15000 employees, or almost 26 percent of its total staff worldwide, participated in various volunteering initiatives. These projects, which take place mostly during work hours, can be grouped into two main categories of community work: Children and Education, and Financial and Business Literacy. The employees have the opportunity to choose when and in which volunteering projects they would like to participate. To explore the benefits of the accumulated career capital during corporate volunteer experiences for both the employees and their organization, we interviewed 22 employees who participated in one or more volunteering projects.

Data Collection

Initial meetings and interviews with three managers were held to gain more insight about the organization, its approach to corporate volunteering projects, and its activities. Given our interest in exploring volunteer experiences as a source of career capital, we purposefully focused only on knowledge-intensive volunteering projects. These types of projects focus on leveraging employees' learning and experience and links them with the community and service programs (Bell, 2007; Corporation for National and Community Service, 2013; Deloitte, 2009). To increase the validity of our findings, several projects that satisfied these criteria were selected, ensuring that the results were generic and not project-based. In our case, these projects mainly included activities of the teaching and coaching of students or nascent entrepreneurs (Table 6.1).

We arranged and conducted semi-structured interviews with employees who

Table 6.1 Overview of volunteering projects in this study

Project	Main tasks	Total duration	Intensity
Project 1	Teaching high school students about financial topics focusing on their personal situations; how to deal with money and having a bank account	One month	Four half-days
Project 2	Teaching and mentoring high school students about their future careers	One month	Four half-days
Project 3	Coaching high school students about setting up their own business	Three months	Seven training sessions
Project 4	Virtual coaching of entrepreneurs in Asia, Africa and South America by helping to develop a business proposal	Three months	Once a week
Project 5	One-on-one coaching of a student who is facing difficulties at school	18 months	Once a week
Project 6	Virtual teaching project with high school students abroad to improve their English	10 weeks	Once a week
Project 7	Teaching English to high school students	Three months	Seven training sessions
Project 8	Coaching high school students about applying for a job and doing presentations	Three months	Seven training sessions

participated in one or more of the chosen volunteering projects. The interview protocol involved three main parts and covered various themes. First, participants were invited to share their motivations to volunteer, as well as previous career and volunteer experiences. Then, participants were asked to reflect both on their volunteering work as well as on their work environment with an emphasis on learning opportunities, work dynamics, social relations and meaningful related events. During the final portion of the interview, participants were asked to express their individual perspectives on the meaning of (corporate) volunteering in relation to their professional and personal development, colleagues and work, and society. The flexible nature of the questions allowed us to explore both the individual and organizational consequences of corporate volunteering that would not otherwise be visible through a survey (Baxter and Jack, 2008; Legard et al., 2003).

All in all, we solicited information from 15 male and 7 female volunteers participating in 8 different volunteering projects. We interviewed 6 (senior) managers and 16 professionals, with an average age of 39. The raw material generated through the 22 interviews was sufficient enough to achieve data saturation (Guest et al., 2006), on which we will base the arguments presented in the remainder of this chapter.

Data Analysis

We analyzed our empirical data following a thematic content analysis, which involves the iterative steps of going back and forth between the data and emerging theoretical arguments (Locke, 2001; Pratt, 2009). Through this analysis, we revealed two main groups

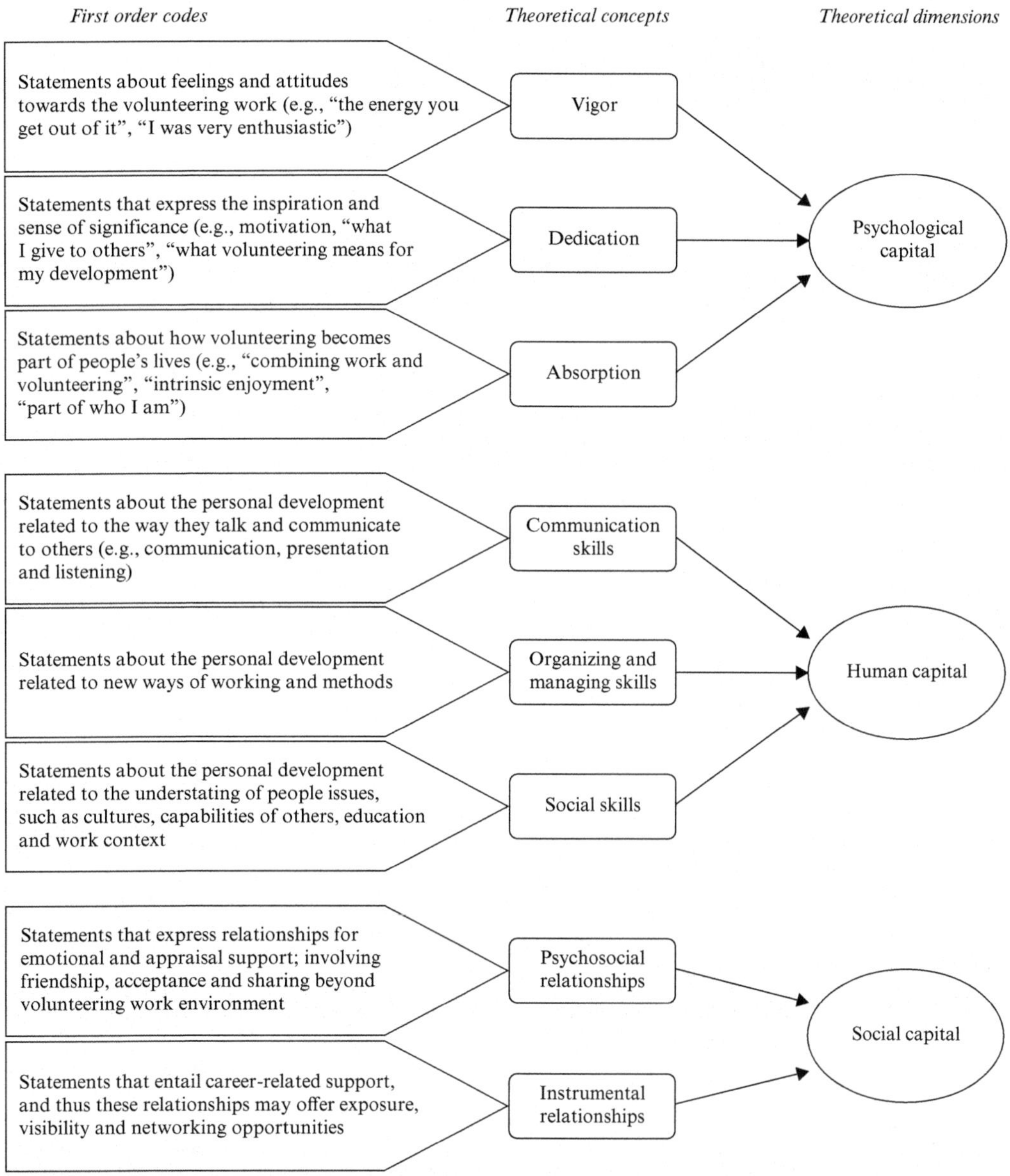

Figure 6.1 Overview of data analysis process – career capital acquisition

of statements: on the individual and organizational levels. By collaboratively discussing and reflecting the statements between the authors, they materialized into theoretical categories, which we explicate below. Figures 6.1 and 6.2 summarize this inductive process and show in particular the aggregated theoretical dimensions we identified, which, to our knowledge, best related to the theoretical concepts we are familiar with from the career and organizational behavior literature.

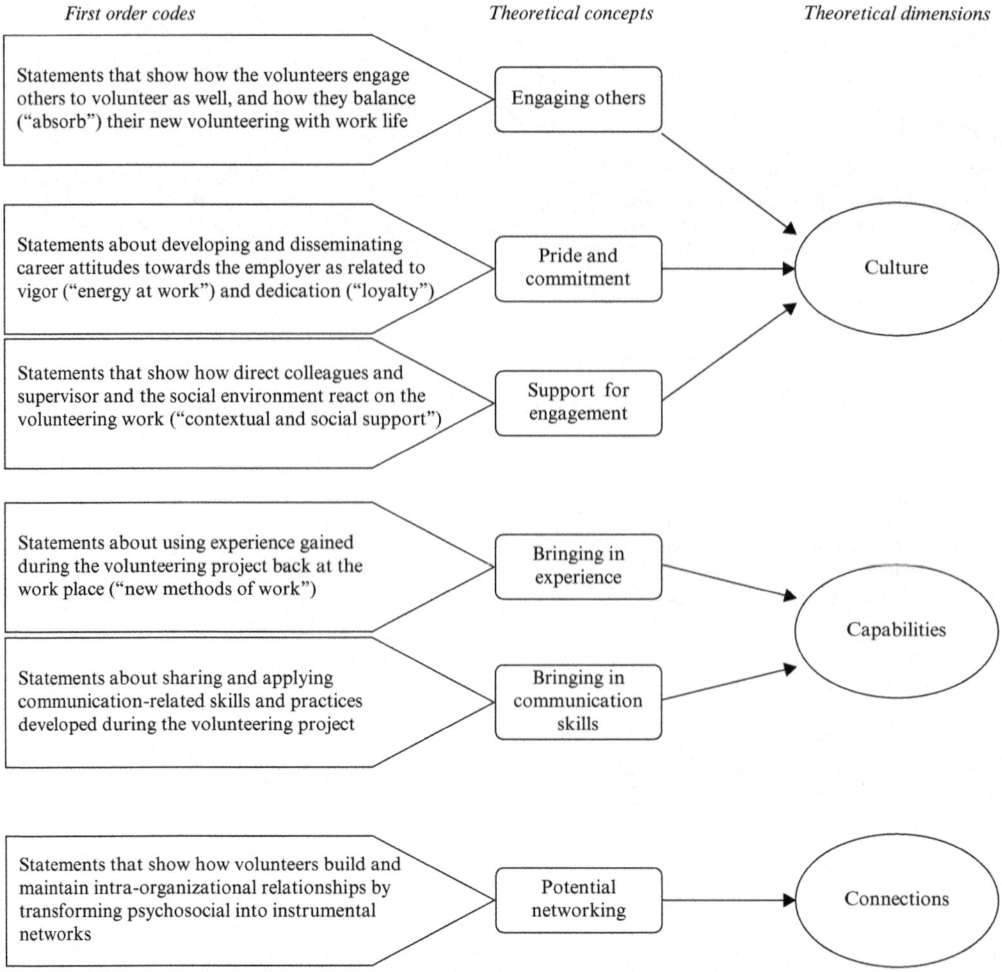

Figure 6.2 Overview of data analysis process – individual contributions to organizational core competencies

FINDINGS

In our analysis, we searched for relevant text excerpts and explored the links between the categorizations. The causal links that became apparent from the participants' answers helped us develop the argument that volunteer experiences facilitate employees' career capital acquisition and their consequent contributions to organizational development. We will discuss these links below.

Corporate Volunteering and Career Capital Acquisition

Psychological capital

One of the prominent factors emerging from the data comprises the attitudes that participants have developed through participation in corporate volunteering. Particularly, the interviewees spoke about their motivations and psychological involvement, which changed their perceptions not only of themselves, but also of their profession and work. Our data showed that the volunteers described this renewed engagement through the development of three distinct psychological elements. As reflected in one of the interview excerpts, the first psychological element the volunteering employees developed is energy and vigor:

> You are getting so much back from [the volunteering] (. . .) you get a lot of energy out of it. It gives you energy to do something for other people. [Whether] in the company or at the project, it gives you more value. [2]

Furthermore, the data revealed that by dedicating themselves to a meaningful cause through volunteering, participants experienced a greater sense of significance and inspiration in both their personal and professional lives. As one interviewee explained, this concerns the development of psychological dedication.

> You are changing the world for the better. [Volunteering as part of a project] is more than about one specific person or topic, it's really a small contribution, but it is still very significant to do. So, the idea is that you are changing the world by changing one specific person. If we all try to adopt this perspective, we will build a better world. [10]

Finally, our interviewees further described how captivating the volunteer experience was to them. As shown in the following interview excerpt, through the development of psychological absorption, participants became so immersed in being a volunteer that the majority were willing to stay involved in the same or in other projects past the official end date:

> When I have more spare time after this summer, I will reinvest in the [volunteering] organization again to see if they have improved. I will, in the same way as I do now, try to help them get better organized. Something is missing, and that can put the whole concept in danger. This would be a shame because I think it is a very good concept. [6]

Human capital

We identified three main sets of skills and competencies, which employees mentioned they acquired and improved while volunteering. First, as illustrated by the following interviewee, working with people in a volunteering project facilitated the development of generic management and organizing skills:

> [At work] I'm used to people doing things by themselves. What you learn from [this volunteering] experience is that you have to be much more directive and clear about your expectations and what's going to happen. [8]

Next, volunteers clearly referred to the acquisition of communication skills. These skills appear to be an imperative component of volunteer work. As illustrated in the following example, it involved presentation and listening skills that participants would not otherwise have the opportunity to develop in their work environment:

> I learned a lot from it because when you're giving a presentation, you're explaining things on a completely different level than you're used to in your general work. The most important example is how to explain things in a very different, simple and clear way, than you are used to within your job. Because you have to explain what you are doing in a daily job to someone who is not completely familiar with it. [9]

Thirdly, participants spoke about acquiring distinct social skills. The interviews offered evidence that developing social skills was facilitated through the unique social context provided by the volunteering projects. Our data showed that through social interactions with people in the community, participants developed (a) social and cultural awareness, (b) an understanding of others' capabilities and socio-economic background, and (c) patience. As one example portrayed:

> It gives more insight into people of other cultures, how to deal with them, and how they respond to you [. . .]. You learn about the things they are confronted with as foreigners, the barriers they are confronted with. [15]

Social capital

Finally, the data revealed the way in which employees built and maintained their social capital. Our analysis showed that the new relations provided a different source of support. As one interviewee noted, some of the new relationships involved friendships, acceptance and sharing experiences beyond the volunteering work environment, thus offering 'emotional' (that is, psychosocial) support:

> I met some co-coaches, and there were a few people I knew from the company. And because we met at this coaching project, we went for a drink together where we actually got to know each other better. [11]

Other relationships, on the other hand, entailed career support networks and thus had a potential to offer instrumental assistance, such as exposure, visibility and networking opportunities. As explained by another interviewee, although these relations were not necessarily utilized right away, they could potentially become useful in the future:

> The best relationships are still with the people I coached; I have regular contact with three of them to see how they are doing. I don't see it [the potential for career benefits] now, but that is always the case with a network. It is very important to keep in touch with each other, you never know if you can help each other [in the future]. [6]

Corporate Volunteering and the Organizational Benefits of Acquired Career Capital

With respect to the organizational benefits of corporate volunteer experiences, the data analysis further revealed that upon their return, participants brought back and disseminated their acquired career capital. It therefore supports the existing literature showing that by enacting their career capital, individuals engage in shaping their work environment (Weick, 1996). In the following, we will provide support for our earlier assertions that corporate volunteering in turn facilitates individuals' contributions to their employing organizations. Particularly, we identified Quinn's (1992) organizational core competencies model to constructively frame our findings. As we will argue below, these core competencies can be recognized in terms of culture (organizational purpose, mission and core values), capabilities (knowledge and skills embodied in organizational activities), and connections (organizational, internal and external social capital, such as suppliers, customers and alliance partners) (DeFillippi et al., 2006; Quinn, 1992).

Culture

Our data illustrated how the participants specifically utilized their newly developed psychological capital (that is, engagement, pride and commitment) to: (a) engage others in volunteering work, and (b) disseminate positive perceptions (that is, pride and commitment) toward their employer:

> I got a lot of energy from those trainings, and I feel that when I talk about it to my colleagues, for example, they are really enthusiastic – 'oh this is great doing this [volunteering project], can I also join? I also would like to do something like that'. [. . .] I think it also helps a lot of people become enthusiastic about volunteering. [9]

Our data analysis also confirmed that by engaging colleagues and disseminating positive perceptions, the participants developed what other scholars have described (Wenger, 1998) as a deeper sense of shared commitment and identification among organizational members. Thus, they contributed to the organizational culture. Indeed, interviewees raised the point that sharing their volunteer experiences allowed them to show their pride and identify with their employer in a way that is visible to others:

> [I feel] a little bit more proud [. . .] I think if you have a nice challenging job and nice colleagues and your company is socially responsible, it's a very nice extra. And gives you pride – yes. It has a higher impact on job stickiness, so you are more loyal to a company like that. In my case, it makes me more loyal to my employer, it makes me more proud. [11]

Although participants were proud and eager to apply their psychological capital upon their return from volunteering, evidence suggested that shaping organizational culture through engaging, motivating and sharing may be contingent on employees' perceptions of contextual and social support (Caligiuri et al., 2013). The empirical analysis showed that both work and non-work contexts played an important role in facilitating the individual contribution of psychological capital to organizational culture, as one of the interviewees explained:

> They [my colleagues] were happy that I did it and they were supportive! So I tried to bring other people in [. . .] I told him it's really fun to do, and he should join. And he picked it up and for the first time, we did together the training on how to apply for a job, and it was really fun to do because you are with each other in the classroom. He continued doing it. [21]

Furthermore, this contextual and social support appeared to have an even stronger effect on participants' contributions to organizational culture when it directly involved senior managers, such as CEOs. As one of the participants described:

> Twice, I sat in class with someone from the Board, and I felt proud of the company, that they have people and other colleagues from all levels and corners of the bank to join in the [volunteering] project. [13]

Capabilities

Research has suggested that sharing knowledge (tacit or explicit) and practices from personal experience can create a collective understanding regarding new ways of working. This may evolve into routines and coherent actions, especially if the human capital that individuals bring can be applied to the work environment (Geroy et al., 2000). However, our data analysis showed that generic skills such as leadership and communication skills could also be employed at work and potentially translated into organizational capabilities. As one of the interviewees explained:

> I think I developed more in teaching [. . .] And that of course helps in my work, when you are, for example, in a meeting and you try to relay a message to the team that sometimes requires you to go into detail [. . .] These aspects of communication that you get from the volunteering work help you deal with daily work. [14]

Furthermore, the data showed that in some cases, the newly acquired human capital allowed participants to discover and experiment with new ideas and working methods. The wide acceptance of these new activities by other colleagues could lead to them being further developed and institutionalized. For example, upon his return, one interviewee applied the skills he developed during volunteering by self-initiating a coaching practice for colleagues regarding working at the company. He described how this initiative was widely accepted by others:

> I use it [coaching] in my daily work. I coach one of the employees at the bank, and that is one of the things. Actually, that's expanding a little bit. I also give some people advice on how things work in the company. I didn't do it before, and if somebody asks me – 'can you help me?' – for example, I'll make the time to help him or her. [2]

Connections

As we found earlier with regard to social capital development, volunteer experiences provided employees with opportunities to develop networks, which could potentially support their career and work. At first glance, the psychosocial-friendly relationships, contrary to the instrumental relations, may be less useful for organizational connections, as the first focuses on the personal psychological and emotional levels. Consequently, as the analysis suggested, most of these relationships did not appear to evolve beyond the friendship level. However, in some cases, what started as a 'casual' friendship in which to exchange thoughts and ideas transformed into a more instrumental relationship. This could be useful in connecting departments and business units and could thus contribute to organizational connections, as one interviewee described:

> We [participants in the tutors' project] are in touch, and sometimes, when we need something from the related department, I email them and ask them – 'can you help me out?' – Because this is a very big organization, so when you need something done, it's often very complicated to get it done or get the right person. So that really helps, because we are people with very different backgrounds and different departments. It's a good opportunity to widen your network and get to know other people [within the company]. [16]

Nevertheless, our data analysis showed that examples such as the one described above are scarce. Our findings illustrated that corporate volunteering provided opportunities for employees to develop networks on the intra-organizational level (for example, across business units). However, these results are very limited and, thus, it appeared that none of the acquired social capital was applied to contribute to organizational connections.

DISCUSSION

The aim of this study was to explore the effects of corporate volunteering on both individuals and organizations. Based on qualitative data gathered from 22 employees from a large financial service firm that participated in a corporate volunteering program, we identified that through participation in volunteer experiences, employees acquired career capital (psychological, human and social) and applied it in the workplace upon their return. The volunteer experience was a vehicle through which employees explored opportunities to manifest and prioritize their career meanings and interests (Brown, 2002; Schein, 1996). Expanding on previous work on the link between individual and organizational resources (for example, DeFillippi and Arthur, 1994; Ichijo and Nonaka, 2006; Nahapiet and Ghoshal, 1998), we further found that by employing a range of social-cognitive behavior and tactics, employees contributed to the organization's culture, capabilities and connections. Below, we will reflect on our findings to elucidate how our study makes important theoretical contributions.

First and foremost, our findings contribute to the research on career capital acquisition (Inkson and Arthur, 2001). Career capital, which draws on the 'intelligent career' framework (Arthur et al., 1995), is accumulated through career and other experiences and has been found to be broadly related to the accumulation of motivation, professional identity, skills and expertise, and networks (Parker et al., 2009). Scholars in this area have been persistently engaged in efforts to understand how career capital relates to career development but less on what it entails (Kuijpers and Scheerens, 2006; Parker, 2006). We addressed this gap by identifying and further refining the components of career capital in the context of career experiences across organizational boundaries (Lamb and Sutherland, 2010). More specifically, our findings showed that corporate volunteers in the Netherlands developed important intangible career capital, which broadly comprises three distinct categories, namely psychological, human and social. As our data revealed, psychological capital involves the vigor, dedication and absorption that participants developed through their engagement in volunteer experiences (Bakker and Schaufeli, 2008). The data further showed that human capital entails the development of three main sets of skills and competencies (including generic and volunteering-specific): communication, organizing and managing, and social skills. Finally, we found that social capital involved the development and maintenance of relationships, which provided psychosocial and instrumental support for the participants (Chandler and Kram, 2007).

These findings further relate to the second contribution of this chapter concerning the notion of sustainable careers. Our findings confirmed that career capital appears to be an essential source not only for individuals' careers but also for the organization. As such, our study contributes to the existing ideas about the link between individual and organizational development (for example, Nonaka and Toyama, 2005). The data analysis showed how each core organizational competence emulates a distinct area of individual career capital (DeFillippi et al., 2006). By taking a broader view on careers to include non-work experiences, we were able to identify distinct social-cognitive behaviors and tactics that employees use to apply their acquired career capital at their workplace. Although these actions are not considered from that perspective at the moment they occur, employees appeared to engage and disseminate positive attitudes at work, apply newly acquired skills and methods of work, and build inter-organizational relationships. This is in line with recent evidence found by both strategic and management scholars, who have elucidated the link between individuals' career behavior and contribution to organizations (for example, Inkpen and Tsang, 2005; Kang et al., 2007). Nevertheless, as the findings suggested, recognizing the value of individuals' career capital does not always take place immediately. Future research therefore needs to take a closer look at the long-term consequences of how and when career capital developed through non-work experiences benefits organizations.

Additionally, this study contributes to the research on the consequences of the context in career development (Savickas, 2005). While this line of research is interested in the careers of different cultural and environmental settings (Khapova et al., 2009), it has predominantly emphasized the impact on the conceptualization and operationalization of careers in these contexts (Khapova and Korotov, 2007). The findings of this study suggested that the particular context in which the career experience is embedded might affect which components and content of career capital will change (cf. Cappellen and Janssens, 2008; Lamb and Sutherland, 2010; Rodriguez and Scurry, 2014). However, contrary to expatriation or global careers (for example, Jokinen et al., 2008; Suutari and Mäkelä, 2007), corporate volunteering takes place beyond one's direct professional work environment, and thus creates new ways in which to engage in sustainable careers. In that respect, it seems that although corporate volunteering is a short-term activity with somewhat limited leverage on work experience, it provides unique opportunities for personal career development. This is in line with previous research that has recognized the value of non-work-related experience not only for individuals but also for their employers (Hudson and Inkson, 2006; Inkson and Myers, 2003; Lee and Higgins, 2001). As shown, participation in corporate volunteering provided a range of developmental opportunities, which employees, most likely, would not have experienced in a business setting and which may be further useful in the workplace. This finding opens a new window of opportunities for research about the impact of context on opportunities for sustainable career development and organizations.

Finally, seeing careers as a 'matching process' (Baruch, 2006), the findings suggested that Corporate Social Responsibility (CSR) can be a potential starting point for aligning current individual and organizational needs. Thus, this study emphasizes the attention scholars and managers should give to sustainable career management in the knowledge economy (see Chapter 21, this volume). The employees' volunteer experiences inspired them to become involved in self-initiated change behaviors at work, suggesting that CSR activities such as corporate volunteering could be used to engage and motivate employees' contributions to organizational development. This, as shown, might be related to the relatively strong contextual and social support perceived by the participants. Indeed, the data showed that individuals' attitudes towards the employer (that is, pride and commitment) have been positive, particularly when management was directly involved in the volunteering activities. This is in line with previous studies, which have suggested that management involvement sets an example for others and provides legitimation for the employees (for example, Carroll, 1990). Furthermore, the supportive attitude of managers and colleagues towards volunteering facilitates a safe environment in which employees can engage and share their learning (Caligiuri et al., 2013). This is further supported by the fact that employees shared their engagement and pride with other people in their environment upon return from volunteering. Thus, sustainable career management entails increasing employees' awareness for career capital acquisition, stimulating them in making use of these resources, and having them reflect on how they can benefit from these experiences in their job or future career. This holds true particularly in the nexus between the work and non-work environment. We hope that the results of this study will encourage others to further investigate the ways in which management could employ CSR to facilitate related change behavior, such as job crafting (Tims et al., 2012) and work engagement (Xanthopoulou et al., 2009).

LIMITATIONS

As with any empirical study, caution should be exercised when generalizing these findings to other settings. In particular, this study focused on professional employees in a Dutch financial firm and thus limits the applicability of the findings to other types of organizations, industries and cultures. While the financial sector may be an interesting context for studying employees' participation in volunteering in light of social responsibility (see, for example, Brewis, 2004; De Gilder et al., 2005), we see potential in future studies exploring corporate volunteering in other sectors. Furthermore, opportunities to extend the theory lie in conducting similar research in other national settings. These comparative endeavors could provide insights on whether our findings are applicable in other countries.

Another limitation concerns the focus on the employee perspective. While corporate volunteers provided important information on how the acquired career capital is important for their career and work, they might not always be conscious about how and in what way it has relevance for the organization itself. Furthermore, due to the limited perspective we had on the societal context, we were unable to shed light on the effects on the community and the non-governmental agencies involved. Recent studies have suggested that giving attention to a particular target group (for example, NGOs and the community) may limit our efforts to advance theory (Caligiuri et al., 2013). To gain a more comprehensive picture of the story, future research would benefit from including various stakeholders when studying corporate volunteering and career development.

REFERENCES

Arlington, K. (2013, 9 November). Employees who volunteer are more fulfilled. *The Sydney Morning Herald*. Retrieved 29 March, 2014, from http://www.smh.com.au/nsw/employees-who-volunteer-are-more-fulfilled-20131108-2x6tt.html.

Arthur, M.B., Claman, P.H. and DeFillippi, R.J. (1995). Intelligent enterprise, intelligent careers. *Academy of Management Executive*, 9(4), 7–20.

Bakker, A.B. and Schaufeli, W.B. (2008). Positive organizational behavior: Engaged employees in flourishing organizations. *Journal of Organizational Behavior*, 29(2), 147–54.
Baruch, Y. (2006). Career development in organizations and beyond: Balancing traditional and contemporary viewpoints. *Human Resource Management Review*, 16(2), 125–38.
Baxter, P. and Jack, S. (2008). Qualitative case study methodology: Study design and implementation for novice researchers. *The Qualitative Report*, 13(4), 544–59.
Bell, C. (2007). Using employee volunteering programs to develop leadership skills. *Development and Learning in Organizations*, 21(1), 6–8.
Boccalandro, B. (2009). Mapping success in employee volunteering: The drivers of effectiveness for employee volunteering and giving programs and Fortune 500 performance. Boston College Center for Corporate Citizenship.
Brewis, G. (2004). Beyond banking: Lessons from an impact evaluation of employee volunteering at Barclays Bank. *Voluntary Action*, 6(3), 13–25.
Brown, D. (2002). The role of work and cultural values in occupational choice, satisfaction, and success: A theoretical statement. *Journal of Counseling & Development*, 80(1), 48–56.
CAF (2011). Charities and Aid Foundations World Giving Index 2011. Retrieved from https://www.cafonline.org/pdf/world_giving_index_2011_191211.pdf.
Caligiuri, P.M., Mencin, A. and Jiang, K. (2013). Win–Win–Win: The influence of company-sponsored volunteerism programs on employees, NGOs, and business units. *Personnel Psychology*, 1–36.
Cappellen, T. and Janssens, M. (2008). Global managers' career competencies. *Career Development International*, 13(6), 514–37.
Carroll, P.B. (1990). Chivas Regal report on working Americans: Emerging values for the 1990s. *Wall Street Journal, 10*, B6.
Chandler, D.E. and Kram, K.E. (2007). Mentoring and developmental networks in the new career context. In H.P. Gunz and M.A. Peiperl (eds), *Handbook of Career Studies* (pp. 241–67). Thousand Oaks, CA: Sage.
Corporation for National and Community Service (2013). Skill-based volunteering. Retrieved 24 July, 2013, from https://www.nationalserviceresources.org/sbv.
Crossan, M.M., Lane, H.W. and White, R.E. (1999). An organizational learning framework: From intuition to institution. *The Academy of Management Review*, 24(3), 522–37.
De Gilder, D., Schuyt, T.N.M. and Breedijk, M. (2005). Effects of an employee volunteering program on the work force: the ABN-AMRO case. *Journal of Business Ethics*, 61(2), 143–52.
DeFillippi, R.J. and Arthur, M.B. (1994). The boundaryless career: A competency-based perspective. *Journal of Organizational Behavior*, 15(4), 307–24.
DeFillippi, R.J., Arthur, M.B. and Lindsay, V.J. (2006). *Knowledge at Work: Creative Collaboration in the Global Economy*. Oxford: Blackwell Publishing.
Deloitte (2009). Key considerations for launching a skills-based volunteer program. Retrieved 24 July, 2013, from http://www.deloitte.com/view/en_us/us/b2d4344d9a0fb110VgnVCM100000ba42f00aRCRD.htm.
DiRenzo, M.S. and Greenhaus, J.H. (2011). Job search and voluntary turnover in a boundaryless world: A control theory perspective. *Academy of Management Review*, 36(3), 567–89.
Geroy, G.D., Wright, P.C. and Jacoby, L. (2000). Toward a conceptual framework of employee volunteerism: An aid for the human resource manager. *Management Decision*, 38(4), 280–87.
Grant, A.M. (2012). Giving time, time after time: Work design and sustained employee participation in corporate volunteering. *Academy of Management Review*, 37(4), 589–615.
Guest, G., Bunce, A. and Johnson, L. (2006). How many interviews are enough? An experiment with data saturation and variability. *Field Methods*, 18(1), 59–82.
Hudson, S. and Inkson, K. (2006). Volunteer overseas development workers: The hero's adventure and personal transformation. *Career Development International*, 11(4), 304–20.
Ichijo, K. and Nonaka, I. (eds) (2006). *Knowledge Creation and Management: New Challenges for Managers*. New York: Oxford University Press.
Inkpen, A.C. and Tsang, E.W.K. (2005). Social capital, networks, and knowledge transfer. *Academy of Management Review*, 30(1), 146–65.
Inkson, K. and Arthur, M.B. (2001). How to be a successful career capitalist. *Organizational Dynamics*, 30(1), 48–61.
Inkson, K. and Myers, B.A. (2003). 'The big OE': Self-directed travel and career development. *Career Development International*, 8(4), 170–81.
Jokinen, T., Brewster, C. and Suutari, V. (2008). Career capital during international work experiences: Contrasting self-initiated expatriate experiences and assigned expatriation. *The International Journal of Human Resource Management*, 19(6), 979–98.
Jones, D.A. (2010). Does serving the community also serve the company? Using organizational identification and social exchange theories to understand employee responses to a volunteerism programme. *Journal of Occupational & Organizational Psychology*, 83(4), 857–78.

Kang, S.C., Morris, S. and Snell, S. (2007). Relational archetypes, organizational learning, and value creation: Extending the human resource architecture. *The Academy of Management Review*, 32(1), 236–56.

Khapova, S.N. and Korotov, K. (2007). Dynamics of western career attributes in the Russian context. *Career Development International*, 12(1), 68–85.

Khapova, S.N., Vinkenburg, C.J. and Arnold, J. (2009). Careers research in Europe: Identity and contribution. *Journal of Occupational & Organizational Psychology*, 82, 709–19.

Kuijpers, M.A.C.T. and Scheerens, J. (2006). Career competencies for the modern career. *Journal of Career Development*, 32(4), 303–19.

Lamb, M. and Sutherland, M. (2010). The components of career capital for knowledge workers in the global economy. *The International Journal of Human Resource Management*, 21(3), 295–312.

Lee, L. and Higgins, C. (2001). Corporate volunteering: Ad-hoc interaction or route to dialogue and partnership? *Journal of Corporate Citizenship*, 2001(4), 79–90.

Legard, R., Keegan, J. and Ward, K. (2003). In-depth interviews. In J. Ritchie and J. Lewis (eds), *Qualitative Research Practice: A Guide for Social Science Students and Researchers* (pp. 138–69). London: Sage.

Locke, K.D. (2001). *Grounded Theory in Management Research*. London: Sage.

Luthans, F., Luthans, K.W. and Luthans, B.C. (2004). Positive psychological capital: Beyond human and social capital. *Business Horizons*, 47(1), 45–50.

Meijer, M.M., De Bakker, F.G.A., Smit, J.H. and Schuyt, T. (2006). Corporate giving in the Netherlands 1995–2003: Exploring the amounts involved and the motivations for donating. *International Journal of Nonprofit and Voluntary Sector Marketing*, 11(1), 13–28.

Meijs, L.C.P.M. (2003). Book review, For your bookshelf: Making money while making a difference: how to profit with a non-profit partner. *Corporate Reputation Review*, 6(3), 291–5.

Meijs, L.C.P.M. and Van der Voort, J.M. (2004). Corporate volunteering: From charity to profit–non-profit partnerships. *Australian Journal on Volunteering*, 9(1), 22.

Nahapiet, J. and Ghoshal, S. (1998). Social capital, intellectual capital, and the organizational advantage. *The Academy of Management Review*, 23(2), 242–66.

Nonaka, I. and Toyama, R. (2005). The theory of the knowledge-creating firm: Subjectivity, objectivity and synthesis. *Industrial and Corporate Change*, 14(3), 419–36.

OECD (2013). OECD Better Life Index. Retrieved 19 July, 2013, from http://www.oecdbetterlifeindex.org/countries/netherlands/.

Parker, P. (2006). Card sorts: Constructivist assessment tools. In M. McMahon and W. Patton (eds), *Career Counseling: Constructivist Approaches* (pp. 176–86). Abingdon: Routledge.

Parker, P., Khapova, S.N. and Arthur, M.B. (2009). The intelligent career framework as a basis for interdisciplinary inquiry. *Journal of Vocational Behavior*, 75(3), 291–302.

Pratt, M.G. (2009). For the lack of a boilerplate: Tips on writing up (and reviewing) qualitative research. *The Academy of Management Journal*, 52(5), 856–62.

Quinn, J.B. (1992). The intelligent enterprise a new paradigm. *Academy of Management Executive*, 6(4), 48–63.

Rodell, J. (2013). Finding meaning through volunteering: Why do employees volunteer and what does it mean for their jobs? *Academy of Management Journal*, 56(5), 1274–94.

Rodriguez, J.K. and Scurry, T. (2014). Career capital development of self-initiated expatriates in Qatar: Cosmopolitan globetrotters, experts and outsiders. *The International Journal of Human Resource Management*, 25(7), 1046–67.

Savickas, M.L. (2005). The theory and practice of career construction. In S.D. Brown and R.W. Lent (eds), *Career Development and Counseling: Putting Theory and Research to Work* (pp. 42–70). Hoboken, NJ: John Wiley & Sons.

Schein, E.H. (1996). Career anchors revisited: Implications for career development in the twenty-first century. *Academy of Management Executive*, 10(4), 80–88.

Smith, V. (2010). Review article: Enhancing employability: Human, cultural, and social capital in an era of turbulent unpredictability. *Human Relations*, 63(2), 279–300.

Sullivan, S.E. and Baruch, Y. (2009). Advances in career theory and research: A critical review and agenda for future exploration. *Journal of Management*, 35(6), 1542–71.

Suutari, V. and Mäkelä, K. (2007). The career capital of managers with global careers. *Journal of Managerial Psychology*, 22(7), 628–48.

Tims, M., Bakker, A.B. and Derks, D. (2012). Development and validation of the job crafting scale. *Journal of Vocational Behavior*, 80(1), 173–86.

Van der Heijde, C.M. and Van der Heijden, B.I.J.M. (2006). A competence-based and multidimensional operationalization and measurement of employability. *Human Resource Management*, 45(3), 449–76.

Van Schie, S., Guentert, S.T. and Wehner, T. (2011). No corporate volunteering without volunteers. *International Journal of Business Environment*, 4(2), 121–32.

Weick, K. (1996). Enactment and the boundaryless career: Organizing as we work. In M.B. Arthur and

D.M. Rousseau (eds), *The Boundaryless Career: A New Employment Principle for a New Organizational Era* (pp. 40–57). Oxford: Oxford University Press.
Wenger, E. (1998). *Communities of Practice: Learning, Meaning, and Identity*. New York: Cambridge University Press.
Xanthopoulou, D., Bakker, A.B., Demerouti, E. and Schaufeli, W.B. (2009). Work engagement and financial returns: A diary study on the role of job and personal resources. *Journal of Occupational and Organizational Psychology*, 82(1), 183–200.

7 Career and organizational identification: extending the expanded model of identification

Nikolai Egold and Rolf Van Dick

INTRODUCTION

Individuals have needs for positive self-esteem and for belongingness which can be satisfied by membership in social groups (Tajfel and Turner, 1986). Employees are members of a variety of such social groupings, for instance, their organization, but also smaller entities such as their teams or departments or larger groups such as organizational networks or their professional group (Riketta and Van Dick, 2005). Identification with the organization or with other work-related social groups has been shown to be important for individual performance, well-being, absenteeism, job satisfaction (Riketta and Van Dick, 2005), job involvement and job motivation (Van Knippenberg and Van Schie, 2000). Employees identifying with a work-related group also tend to act on behalf of that group and spend more effort in doing so than others (Riketta, 2005; Van Dick, 2004). Therefore, a sense of identification plays an important role in organizational success. In this chapter, we will consider employees' identification with both their career and their organization. We will show that both are important foci of employees' self-concepts and we will explore their antecedents and consequences.

However, the sheer fact of being a member of a specific organization does not automatically lead to strong organizational identification (OI). Rather, establishing one's own identity – including both personal and social aspects – is an active process and it is also possible that one develops an identity by actively distinguishing oneself from certain aspects of the organization or by having ambivalent feelings towards it (Kreiner and Ashforth, 2004).

In the following section, we will define identification in the workplace, provide evidence for its (mostly positive) effects and discuss their forms and foci.

Identification in the Workplace: Defining Organizational Identification

Bergami and Bagozzi (2000) argued that groups related to work and organizations are among the most important social groups for an individual (see also Hogg and Terry, 2000). Identification is a positive self-description in which an individual experiences him- or herself as being part of a group, which results in shared norms, values and behaviours. It is the feeling of belongingness or oneness that makes identification different from commitment (Ashforth and Mael, 1989). Research on identification has focused mainly on the organization as a target (Reade, 2001). We follow the idea, first proposed by Van Knippenberg and Van Schie (2000) and Van Dick and Wagner (2002), of different foci of identification that can be present at the same time in the workplace. We will focus on organizational and career identification in our research, and we will demonstrate that the antecedents and consequences of organizational and career identification relate differentially with these foci.

Identification in the Workplace: Defining Career Identification

Social categorization theory proposes three different levels of self-categorization: the human level, the group level in which individuals categorize themselves as a part of a group, and the individual level in which one's unique characteristics are emphasized (Turner et al., 1987). Employees are members of different groups related to their organization or profession, and they have the opportunity to identify with each of these groups. One can, for instance, be an employee of a university, a team member of a department of psychology or one can see oneself as a member of the occupational group of psychologists. Therefore, there are multiple foci of identification present at the same time (Van Knippenberg and Van Schie, 2000; Van Dick et al., 2004). At least three different foci of identification in the workplace can be differentiated: (a) identification with the occupational group, that is, one's career; (b) identification with the organization as a whole; and (c) identification with the team (Snape et al., 2000; Van Dick and Wagner, 2002).

Individuals not only gain self-esteem and positive identity via organizational identification or identification with a team in the organization: before entering an organization and being bound by a work contract, individuals are socialized by professional education and training. As a result, individuals can also identify with their professional group and career, for example, being a psychologist or being a scientist. Van Dick et al. (2004) have shown that the different foci of identification are differentially related to work-related attitudes and behaviours in a way that the more the variables correspond at the same level (that is, individual, team, organization, career), the more they are related. Career identification, for instance, appeared to be related to citizenship behaviour towards the employees' career (Christ et al., 2003) and less to citizenship behaviour towards one's colleagues. Van Knippenberg and Van Schie (2000) argued that identification with a smaller group, such as a team, should be stronger than identification with large groups such as the organization as a whole. This could be transferred to the occupational group, which is more abstract and comprises many more individuals than a typical organization.

Following the arguments of Brewer (1991; 1993) group size matters, because people have a need for belongingness, on the one hand, but a need for distinctiveness on the other, simultaneously. Identifying with a larger group means being similar to or the 'same' as many other group members, which threatens feelings of distinctiveness. Smaller groups are closer to the ideal of fulfilling the needs of distinctiveness and belongingness at the same time (Van Knippenberg and Van Schie, 2000). Another important variable influencing successful identification discussed by Ellemers (1993) is the status of a social group. People tend to identify with high status groups, because they want to maintain a positive self-image (Ellemers, 1993; Tajfel, 1978). This can mean, for instance, that an employee identifies more strongly with his or her team that has a high status within the organization (for example, a strategy group running a money-earning MBA program) rather than with an organization that is not in the top ranks in their industry (for example, a business school that is not in the top of the global league tables); this can be just the opposite when someone belongs to a top-ranked university with which this employee might identify much more strongly than with a less well respected team within that university.

Next, we will describe alternative forms of social identification and will combine them with the foci of organizational and career identification.

Forms of Identification

Disidentification

Being a member of an organization does not automatically lead to identification. When an individual learns about aspects of an organization opposing his or her own values and norms, there is the possibility that they will gain identity by separating from that organization, especially from its negative aspects (Elsbach, 1999; Kreiner and Ashforth, 2004; Pratt, 2000). As Elsbach (1999) and Kreiner and Ashforth (2004) noted, disidentification means an active separation and is not just the opposite of identification. A mere absence of identification with the organization may result in behaviours harmful to it, such as absenteeism and turnover intentions (Kreiner and Ashforth, 2004). Behaviours of disidentified employees, however, may involve whistle-blowing or other active forms of dispute (Kreiner and Ashforth, 2004). In a way, disidentification is a more unpleasant state which results in activities to alter this unpleasantness, while the absence of identification is accompanied by avoidance (for example, absence from the organization or turnover) and not caring about the organization.

Ambivalent identification

When employees perceive certain aspects of their organization as not desirable, or in contrast to their own norms and values, this must not automatically result in disidentification. It is also possible that individuals are conscious of both negative and positive aspects of their groups (Elsbach, 1999). This will lead to ambivalent feelings towards an employer, where an individual can identify with some and disidentify with other aspects of an organization (Kreiner and Ashforth, 2004). This will lead to an uncomfortable state as individuals, on the one hand, want to act on behalf of the organization and, on the other hand, they do not want to support the organization or parts of it.

Neutral identification

Kreiner and Asforth (2004) and Elsbach (1999) argued that an employee can feel neither attachment to nor separation from the organization at the same time. Being in such a state means, that, on the one hand, an individual avoids behaviours that could build up commitment (for example, organizational citizenship behaviour) but, on the other hand, has no tendency to leave the organization or talk negatively about it. Neutral identification, therefore, is an explicit lack of identification and disidentification. From the view of the organization, neutral identification is undesirable as employees who are high on neutral identification are less likely to be 'good soldiers' (Elsbach, 1999; Kreiner and Ashforth, 2004).

Consequences of Identification

Mael and Ashforth (1992) reasoned that identification serves as a basis for many attitudes and behaviours of an individual in the workplace. Research on identification suggests that OI leads employees to act on behalf of the organization (Van Knippenberg, 2000). In a meta-analysis, Riketta (2005) has demonstrated that OI is positively related to a broad range of work-related attitudes and behaviours such as job involvement, job satisfaction, in-role and extra-role behaviour, and negatively related to absenteeism and turnover intentions (Bartel, 2001; Bhattacharya et al., 1995; Haslam, 2001; Mael and Ashforth, 1992; Tyler, 1999; Van Knippenberg, 2000).

Individuals, by identifying with a group they belong to, derive part of their self-concept from membership in this group (Van Knippenberg, 2000). Following this idea, the individual will act on behalf of his/her group to maintain a positive self-evaluation and to gain pride and satisfaction from the group's success (Tyler and Blader, 2000). Employees with high OI should engage more in in-role and extra-role activities (Van Dick et al., 2006). Work engagement is the extent to which employees experience vigour, dedication and absorption at work (Bakker et al., 2011). The concepts of OI and work engagement overlap in so far as both are psychological states in which an individual feels positive towards the organization or their work (Schaufeli and Bakker, 2010). Work engagement is also characterized by high identification with one's own work. Therefore, we propose:

Hypothesis 1: Work engagement will be positively related to employees' identification with (a) their organization and (b) their career.

When individuals identify with the organization they are working for, work itself will become an important aspect of the self. Tajfel and Turner (1986) have postulated that people want to evaluate themselves positively. If work as an important part of the self, is evaluated positively, this should also lead, for example, to higher job satisfaction as the result of a positive evaluation of one's own work. Van Dick et al. (2004) demonstrated that identification is positively related to job satisfaction. In studies with teachers, call-centre agents and bank clerks, they have shown that organizational identification is consistently related to job satisfaction with correlations between $r = .36$ and $r = .50$. The importance of identification is strengthened by the fact that general job satisfaction is better predicted by identification than by satisfaction with one's salary (Van Dick, 2004).

As explained before, the relationship between forms of identification and work-related attitudes and behaviours should be higher for more proximal social groups (Van Dick, 2004), for example, the work group, and lower for more distal groups or entities, for example, the organization or the occupational group (Van Dick and Wagner, 2002). Therefore, OI should be predicting job satisfaction better than career identification. We therefore propose:

Hypothesis 2: Job satisfaction is positively related to employees' identification with (a) their organization and (b) their career.

Van Dick (2004) stated that job satisfaction is an aspect of general well-being. Referring to Haslam et al. (2009), it could easily be argued that people who identify highly with their organization gain positive self-esteem and will have greater well-being than people lower in identification. They also reasoned that identification may buffer the negative effects of stress. Therefore, belonging helps us feel better, gives us social support, helps us cope with stress and is a determinant of health-related behaviour (see Haslam and Van Dick, 2011; Van Dick and Haslam, 2012). Identification with the organization should motivate healthy behaviour because group membership can only be maintained if one is healthy. Following the arguments, we propose:

Hypothesis 3: Well-being is positively related to employees' identification with (a) the organization and (b) the career.

In the following, we will discuss factors that contribute to the emergence of identification.

Antecedents of Forms and Foci of Identification

Antecedents of identification and disidentification

When do individuals identify and what are the variables influencing identification with a group? The need for belongingness stated by Tajfel and Turner (1986) could vary considerably between individuals, which means that some individuals have a stronger desire to belong to a group than others (Glynn, 1998; Kreiner and Ashforth, 2004). Therefore, we propose:

Hypothesis 4: The need for identification is positively related to employees' identification with (a) the organization and (b) the career.

Hypothesis 5: Need for identification is negatively related to employees' disidentification with (a) the organization and (b) the career.

Another variable which may be associated with identification is positive affectivity, which is described as the tendency to experience situations as enjoyable and pleasurable (George, 1992). Negative affectivity, in contrast, means experiencing situations negatively or as unpleasant. As described before, individuals identifying with their organization or career perceive aspects relating to their group positively. Therefore, positive affectivity should make it easier to perceive positive aspects of the organization. Naturally, negative affectivity makes it more difficult to recognize positive organizational aspects and will then result in separating behaviour, that is, disidentification (Kreiner and Ashforth, 2004). We therefore propose:

Hypothesis 6: Positive affectivity is positively related to employees' identification with (a) the organization and (b) the career.

Hypothesis 7: Negative affectivity is positively related to employees' disidentification with (a) the organization and (b) the career.

Identification is a process and therefore needs time to develop. Individuals will evaluate the group and their group membership, and need to differentiate their group from relevant out-groups and their own self in relation to other group members (cf. Van Dick, 2004; Tajfel and Turner, 1986). Thinking about the organization's characteristics involves getting to know the organization and its members, and is dependent on the experience of a variety of situations. Therefore, we propose that tenure is associated with OI. Career identification should not be related to tenure, because simply time spent with the organization does not add to one's career identity. Therefore we propose:

Hypothesis 8: Tenure is (a) positively related to employees' identification with the organization but (b) unrelated to their career identification.

Antecedents of ambivalent identification

Ambivalent identification represents a type of conflict between two opposing attitudes towards the organization, which can be both negative and positive (Kreiner and Ashforth, 2004). Kreiner and Ashforth (2004) argued that organizational conflicts, like intra-role conflicts, are the main reason for ambivalent identification. Intra-role conflicts are correlated positively with stress, burnout, turnover and absenteeism and negatively with job satisfaction (Fisher and Gitelson, 1983; Jackson and Schuler, 1985). Roles and identity have much in common and both involve, for instance, behaviour in line with norms and standards (Ashforth, 2001; Kreiner and Ashforth, 2004).

However, roles can not only help to act correctly but they can also be a source of conflict. Following Katz and Kahn (1978), role conflicts occur when individuals receive conflicting instructions or when their role requirements clash with norms of other roles. For example, a financial consultant could be told to serve customers as well as possible but at the same time is asked to sell as much as possible – whether the customer needs it or not. Rizzo et al. (1970) discuss several aspects of role conflicts and define intra-role conflicts as incongruity of requirements of the role, which can result from incompatible characteristics of work, person or organization (see also Sluss et al., 2011). Hence, we propose:

Hypothesis 9: Intra-role conflict is positively related to employees' ambivalent identification with (a) the organization and (b) the career.

Role ambiguity is defined as the amount of clarity of the requirements of the task (Rizzo et al., 1970). Role ambiguity is said to have negative and undesirable effects for the individual, like anxiety, fear, lower satisfaction and self-confidence (Rizzo et al., 1970). Role ambiguity results from organizational change, size, complexity and other aspects (Kahn et al., 1964), which also would make it difficult for individuals to identify with. Ellemers (2003), for example, has shown that individuals tend to view organizational change as a threat, especially when they do identify with the organization. One could argue that the organizational aspects discussed above can result in role ambiguity, which in turn will relate to employees seeing the negative aspects of the organization more clearly, which leads to developing ambivalent identification. Therefore, we propose:

Hypothesis 10: Role ambiguity is positively related to employees' ambivalent identification with (a) the organization and (b) the career.

Antecedents of neutral identification

Finally, neutral identification is based on the idea that some individuals may neither identify nor disidentify with a group (Kreiner and Ashforth, 2004). This is not just the

Table 7.1 Summary of the hypotheses

Hypothesis	Antecedents	Outcome	Relationship
1	Organizational identification	Work engagement	+
	Career identification	Work engagement	+
2	Organizational identification	Job satisfaction	+
	Career identification	Job satisfaction	+
3	Organizational identification	Well-being	+
	Career identification	Well-being	+
4	Need for identification	Organizational identification	+
	Need for identification	Career identification	+
5	Need for identification	Organizational disidentification	−
	Need for identification	Career disidentification	−
6	Positive affectivity	Organizational identification	+
	Positive affectivity	Career identification	+
7	Negative affectivity	Organizational disidentification	+
	Negative affectivity	Career disidentification	+
8	Tenure	Organizational identification	+
	Tenure	Career identification	0
9	Intra-role conflict	Ambivalent organizational ident.	+
	Intra-role conflict	Ambivalent career ident.	+
10	Role ambiguity	Ambivalent organizational ident.	+
	Role ambiguity	Ambivalent career ident.	+
11	Individualism	Neutral organizational identification	+
	Individualism	Neutral career identification	+

absence of identification or disidentification, but comprises a situation wherein an individual does not think negatively or positively about an organization but gains identity by maintaining neutrality towards the organization (Elsbach, 1999). Being neutral towards groups could be driven by traits like individualism (Earley and Gibson, 1998), whereas collectivists who act on behalf of their groups show solidarity and go the extra mile to help their colleagues (Earley and Gibson, 1998). We propose:

Hypothesis 11: Individualism is positively related to employees' identification with (a) the organization and (b) the career.

Table 7.1 provides an overview of the hypotheses.

METHOD

First, we distributed 120 paper-and-pencil questionnaires in 17 establishments of occupational therapists and clinics that employed occupational therapists. Next, we sent a link to an identical online survey to 250 clinics with departments of occupational therapy. Overall response rate was 71 per cent. We tested our hypotheses in a sample of 246 participants, of whom 224 were female, which represents the gender ratio among occupational therapists. Of all participants, 21 per cent were under 26 years old, 49 per cent were between 26 and 35, and 28 per cent between 36 and 65 years old; 187 participants were married or in stable relationships. Of all participants, 169 had a full-time job and 192 had a permanent contract; 49 participants had worked in their job for less than two years, 121 had worked between 2 and 10 years, and 42 more than 10 years; 109 had been working for their current employers for between 1 and 5 years, 48 between 5 and 10 years and 27 more than 10 years. We used SPSS to test the hypotheses.

Measures

All items were formulated in a Likert format five-point response scale with endpoints 1 = 'strongly disagree', and 5 = 'strongly agree'. We adapted all scales so that they matched one of the foci of identification, that is, career and organization. To measure identification, we used the 6-item scale of Mael and Ashforth (1992) with an internal consistency of Cronbach's $\alpha = .85$. A sample item was: 'When someone praises this organization, it feels like a personal compliment'. To assess the other forms of identification we used the scales by Kreiner and Ashforth (2004). Disidentification consisted of four items and showed an internal consistency of $\alpha = .86$. A sample item was 'I have tried to keep the organization I work for a secret from people I meet'. Ambivalent identification was measured using a three-item scale. It had a Cronbach's $\alpha = .91$. A sample item was: 'I'm torn between loving and hating this organization'. Neutral identification was assessed with three items such as: 'It really doesn't matter to me what happens to this organization'. Internal consistency was $\alpha = .68$.

We assessed the need for organizational identification with a scale from Kreiner and Ashforth (2004). Sample items of this seven-item scale were: 'Without an organization to work for, I would feel incomplete' or 'An important part of who I am would be missing if I didn't belong to a work organization', Cronbach's α was =.74.

We used the German version of the Positive and Negative Affect Schedule (PANAS) (Watson et al., 1988) by Krohne et al. (1996) to measure positive and negative affectivity. The scale consists of 20 items, which are adjectives such as interested, strong, nervous or anxious, 10 for each form of affectivity. Participants were asked how they had felt at work during the past 12 months. Positive affectivity had a Cronbach's $\alpha = .88$ and negative affectivity a Cronbach's $\alpha = .87$.

Intra-role conflict was assessed using a nine-item scale from Rizzo et al. (1970) (sample item: 'I have to do things that should be done differently.'). Internal consistency was $\alpha = .76$.

To measure role ambiguity we used a scale from Rizzo et al. (1970) (sample item: 'I know exactly what is expected from me'), of which six items were used in our questionnaire. Cronbach's α for both scales was .76.

Individualism was measured using an eight-item scale from Triandis and Gelfand (1998). A sample item was: 'One performs better alone than in a group'. Internal consistency was $\alpha = .73$.

To measure job satisfaction, we used a translation of a three-item scale based on Morgeson and Humphrey's (2006) Work Design Questionnaire (WDQ) by Stegmann et al. (2010); sample item: 'All in all I am very happy with my job'. Internal consistency was $\alpha = .55$.

Well-being was measured using three items based on Warr (1990). We used a short scale translated by Bullinger and Kirchberger (1998), which showed an internal consistency coefficient of $\alpha = .79$. A sample item was: 'My health is excellent'.

Work engagement was assessed using a six-item short scale based on the Utrecht Work Engagement Scale (UWES) (Schaufeli and Bakker, 2004), which showed an internal consistency of $\alpha = .77$.

RESULTS

Table 7.2 shows the means, standard deviations and correlations between the four different forms of identification of the two foci, organizational and career identification, and their consequences.

Our first three hypotheses propose that organizational and career identification relate positively to work engagement, job satisfaction and well-being. Results show positive relationships of organizational identification and work engagement ($r = .31$), job satisfaction ($r = .32$) and well-being ($r = .18$). The correlation coefficients are not significant for the relations between career identification and the consequences, as predicted. Therefore Hypotheses 1, 2 and 3 are confirmed for organizational identification, but not for career identification. All three forms of identification with the organization of the expanded model correlate negatively with work engagement, job satisfaction and well-being. This is also the case for disidentification, ambivalent identification and neutral identification with one's career.

Table 7.3 provides correlations between the antecedents and different forms of organizational and career identification.

In addition to the correlations, we also conducted separate regression analyses controlling for age and sex. The betas for the respective antecedents are reported following each correlation.

We proposed that the need for identification and positive affectivity would relate positively to organizational and career identification. Results show a significant correlation of need for identification and organizational ($r = .72$; $\beta = .72$) and career identification ($r = .20$; $\beta = .23$). We also found positive affectivity positively related to organizational ($r = .43$; $\beta = .43$) and career identification ($r = .14$; $\beta = .16$). This provides support for Hypotheses 4 and 6. We predicted a positive correlation for tenure and organizational identification and a negative correlation with career identification (Hypothesis 8). Table 7.3 shows that tenure relates positively to identification with the organization ($r = .14$; $\beta = .14$). The coefficient for the correlation of tenure and career identification is negative ($r = -.11$; $\beta = -.02$) but not significant. Thus, Hypothesis 8 is supported.

Hypotheses 9 and 10 predicted that ambivalent identification with organization and career would be positively related to intra-role conflict and role ambiguity. Results show that ambivalent organizational identification correlates positively with intra-role conflict, with $r = .57$ ($\beta = .57$) and also ambivalent career identification ($r = .23$; $\beta = .24$). We also found evidence for the relation between role ambiguity and the foci of ambivalent identification with $r = -.28$ ($\beta = -.27$) for ambivalent organizational and $r = -.22$ ($\beta = -.22$) for ambivalent career identification. Hypotheses 9 and 10 are thus supported.

Table 7.2 Inter-correlation matrix of study variables: consequences and forms of identification

Variables	M	SD	1	2	3	4	5	6	7	8	9	10	11	12	13	14	15
1. Age	/	/															
2. Sex	/	/	.37**														
3. Family status	/	/	−.42**	−.14*													
4. Contract – short/long	/	/	−.28**	−.10													
Forms of OI																	
5. Identification	3.52	.77	.10	.01	−.17*	−.16*	(.85)										
6. Disidentification	1.55	.76	−.15*	−.02	.03	.04	−.35**	(.86)									
7. Ambivalent identification	1.70	.92	−.14*	−.04	.04	.09	−.37**	.82**	(.91)								
8. Neutral identification	1.56	.74	−.12	−.02	.06	.09	−.47**	.71**	.63	(.68)							
Forms of CI																	
9. Identification	3.57	.76	−.18**	−.12	.04	−.06	.37**	.07	.07	.04	(.84)						
10. Disidentification	1.41	.62	−.03	−.08	−.05	.03	−.01	.16*	.16*	.15*	−.07	(.81)					
11. Ambivalent identification	1.45	.76	−.09	−.09	.02	.07	−.06	.17*	.19*	.19*	−0.8	.81**	(.93)				
12. Neutral identification	1.34	.58	.12	.01	−.08	−.05	−.03	.10	.10	.19*	−.30**	.57**	.64**	(.68)			
Consequences																	
13. Job satisfaction	4.16	.64	.00	−.05	.00	−.03	.32**	−.46**	−.52**	−.52**	.04	−.20**	−.22**	−.13*	(.55)		
14. Well-being	3.80	.80	−.12	−.03	.05	.09	.18**	−.19*	−.28**	−.26**	.04	−.21*	−.21**	−.19*	.46**	(.79)	
15. Work engagement	3.80	.54	.10	.00	−.09	−.04	.31**	−.33**	−.37**	−.37**	−.01	−.15*	−.23**	−.09	.61**	50**	(.77)

Notes: $n = 246$; * $p \leq 0.05$; ** $p \leq 0.01$. Cronbach's alpha coefficients are on the diagonal. OI = organizational identification, CI = career identification.

Table 7.3 Inter-correlation matrix of study variables: controls, antecedents and forms of identification

Variables	1	2	3	4	5	6	7	8	9	10	11	12	13	14	15	16	17	18
Control variables																		
1. Age																		
2. Sex	.37**																	
3. Family status	−.42**	−.14*																
4. Contract – short/ long	−.28**	−.06	.17**															
Antecedents of OI and CI																		
5. Tenure	.57**	.17**	−.29**	−.43**														
6. Need for identification	.10	.06	−.17**	−.14*	.12	(.74)												
7. Pos aff	.05	.08	−.02	−.06	.03	.40**	(.88)											
8. Neg aff	−.17*	−.03	−.01	.01	−.15*	−.17*	−.32**	(.87)										
9. Intrarole conf	−.11	.04	.04	−.01	−.11	−.39**	−.47**	.44**	(.76)									
10. Role ambiguity	.20**	.12	−.04	−.19**	.28**	.27**	.47**	−.40**	−.47**	(.76)								
11. Individualism	.06	.02	−.10	.09	−.02	.24**	.07	.18*	−.02	.00	(.73)							
Forms of OI																		
12. OI	.10	.01	−.17*	−.16*	.14*	.72**	.43**	−.10	−.30**	.20**	.20**	(.85)						
13. OI dis-I	−.15*	−.02	.03	.04	−.09	−.33**	−.36**	.35**	.49**	−.25**	.30**	−.35**	(.86)					
14. OI ambiv	−.14*	−.04	.04	.09	−.09	−.34**	−.39**	.37**	.57**	−.28**	.26**	−.37**	.82**	(.91)				
15. OI neutral	−.12	−.02	.06	.09	−.11	−.46**	−.40**	.33**	.49**	−.24**	.07	−.47**	.71**	.69**	(.68)			
Forms of CI																		
16. CI	−.18**	−.12	.04	−.06	−.11	.20**	.14**	−.15*	.07	−.01	.09	.37**	.07	.08	.04	(.84)		
17. CI dis-I	−.03	−.08	−.05	.03	−.05	−.03	−.12	.30**	.19**	−.20**	.30**	−.01	.16*	.06*	.15*	−.07	(.81)	
18. CI amb	−.09	−.09	.02	.07	−.06	−.07	−.20**	.34**	.23**	−.22**	.26**	−.06	.17**	.19**	.19**	−.08	.81**	(.93)
19. CI neutral	.12	.01	−.08	−.05	.09	−.11	−.09	.21**	.14*	−.10	.14*	−.03	.10	.10	.19**	−.30**	.57**	.64**

Notes: $n = 246$; * $p \leq 0.05$; ** $p \leq 0.01$. Cronbach's alpha coefficients are on the diagonal. OI = organizational identification, CI = career identification.

Hypothesis 11 predicted a relation between neutral organizational and neutral career identification and individualism. The correlation of neutral organizational identification and individualism was not significant (r = .07; β = .06) while the correlation of career identification and individualism was (r = .14; β = .14). Therefore Hypothesis 11 is partly supported.

To test the influence of the forms and foci of organizational and career identification on outcome variables, we conducted hierarchical regression analyses predicting job satisfaction, work engagement and well-being. We entered the control variables 'age' and 'sex' in the first step, and the two foci of identification in the next step, calculating the hierarchical analysis for each of the four forms of identification separately. The results are shown in Table 7.4.

First, the demographic variables accounted for only negligible amounts of variation. As we have shown before, the negative forms of career identification do relate negatively to job satisfaction, work engagement and well-being. Organizational identification predicts satisfaction, engagement and well-being as predicted in Hypotheses 1, 2 and 3, whereas career identification is not related to any of these outcomes. Table 7.4 shows that career identification as well as neutral career identification do not explain variance. Hence, we will focus on the two other forms of organizational and career identification. For job satisfaction, organizational and career disidentification account for 22 per cent of explained variance. Career disidentification has a smaller relation (β = −.14) than organizational disidentification (β = −.45). Regarding well-being as the dependent variable, disidentification with the career was β =−.19 and is almost identical to β = −.20 for organizational disidentification (ΔR^2=.12). Ambivalent career identification is significantly related to job satisfaction, work engagement and well-being, as shown in Table 7.3, and this is supported by the regression analyses with β = −.52 for ambivalent organizational identification and β = −.13 for career identification and the largest amount of explained variance (ΔR^2=.28).

Ambivalent career identification also explains variance in job satisfaction (β = −.16), while the coefficient for organizational ambivalent identification is β = −.35. The effect of both foci of ambivalent identification on well-being also explains a significant amount of variance (ΔR^2=.28). This is interesting because of the relatively smaller size of the regression coefficients, with β = −.28 for organizational and β = −.18 for career identification.

DISCUSSION

The present study gives insight into forms and foci of identification in work-related contexts. We transferred the expanded model of identification proposed by Kreiner and Ashforth (2004) onto the foci of identification with one's career in addition to the focus of the organization as in Kreiner and Ashforth's seminal paper. We expected that identification with both career and organization would relate positively to job satisfaction, work engagement and well-being, while disidentification, ambivalent and neutral identification were expected to correlate negatively with these consequences. Identification with the organization was expected to be positively related to tenure, need for identification and positive affectivity. Disidentification was expected to correlate with negative

Table 7.4 Hierarchical regression analysis for predicting job satisfaction, work engagement and well-being

Step variables	Job satisfaction			Work engagement			Well-being		
	β	ΔR²	ΔF	β	ΔR²	ΔF	β	ΔR²	ΔF
Step 1:		−.01	.14		−.00	.89		.02	3.04
Age	.00			.04			−.21**		
Sex	−.04			−.02			.04		
Step 2:		.09	6.65**		.10	7.20**		.05	3.87**
Organizational identification	.35**			.36**			.21*		
Career identification	−.09			−.12			−.05		
Total R²		.08			.10			.07	
Step 1:		−.01	.14		−.00	.89		.02	3.04
Age	−.08			.04			−.21**		
Sex	−.03			−.02			.03		
Step 2:		.23	17.73**		.11	7.70**		.10	7.05**
Organizational disidentification	−.45**			−.31**			−.20**		
Career disidentification	−.14*			−.10			−.19**		
Total R²		.22			.11			.12	
Step 1:		−.01	.14		−.00	.89		.02	3.04
Age	−.09			.03			−.23**		
Sex	−.03			−.03			.03		
Step 2:		.29	24.17**		.16	11.55**		.14	10.00**
Ambivalent organizational identification	−.52**			−.35**			−.28**		
Ambivalent career identification	−.13*			−.16**			−.18**		
Total R²		.28			.16			.16	
Step 1:		−.01	.14		−.00	.89		.02	3.04
Age	−.07			.05			−.20**		
Sex	−.02			−.01			.04		
Step 2:		.27	21.77**		.13	9.15**		.10	7.58**
Neutral organizational identification	−.53**			−.37**			−.26**		
Neutral career identification	−.02			−.03			−.12		
Total R²		.26			.13			.12	

Notes: $n = 246$; * $p \leq 0.05$; ** $p \leq 0.01$. Cronbach's alpha coefficients are on the diagonal.
OI = organizational identification, CI = career identification.

affectivity, intra-role conflict and role ambiguity with ambivalent identification, and neutral identification with individualism.

First, the correlations of the antecedents and consequences for all four different forms of identification with the career were not as strong as for identification with the organization. This is not surprising because groups that are smaller and more proximal to the individual are more likely to become a target for identification (Riketta and Van Dick, 2005; Van Knippenberg and Van Schie, 2000). The occupational group is also more abstract than the organization. Employees spend more time with colleagues who are also members of an organization and become more familiar with the habits and norms of these members who may not be part of their own occupational group. As a result of this socialization process, colleagues in the same team or the organization are more important than those of one's occupational group, and membership in the organization may be more salient than membership in an occupational group. Another reason for lower correlations of career identification could be the relatively lower status of this group. As Ellemers (1993) stated, people could identify more easily with high status groups to keep a positive self-image (Tajfel, 1978). The status of occupational therapists in our sample is generally not particularly high as they are often considered to serve as assistants to the high status general practitioners (at least in Germany).

When discussing the foci of identification, we argued that a greater fit of the measures of consequences and forms of identification (related to the organizational level or to the occupational group level) should lead to stronger relations (Van Dick et al., 2004), and this pattern found support in our analyses. Disidentification and ambivalent career identification do have negative effects in the same way that organizational disidentification and ambivalent organizational identification have. Disidentifying or experiencing ambivalence toward one's own occupational group leads to lower job satisfaction, less work engagement and also to lower well-being. This is important theoretically but also for practitioners, because job satisfaction, work engagement and well-being could be improved by focusing on the organizational level, for example, by improving working conditions. The occupational group, however, also plays its role when employees feel negative about their career. Therefore, it is necessary to help people to identify with the organization while keeping an eye on what they think about their occupational group. It seems, for instance, that employees' job satisfaction is positively influenced by identification with the organization but negatively by career disidentification, which would reduce the efforts of the organization to strengthen organizational identification.

The correlations of the forms of identification are also interesting, because identification with the organization and with the career correlate positively with each other. Organizational identification does not relate to the negative forms of career identification as does career identification. The only exception is neutral career identification, which is significantly and negatively related to career identification. The negative forms of organizational identification, as well as the negative forms of career identification, are also related to each other. We argue, following Kreiner and Ashforth (2004), that the forms of identification are related but distinct. For example, the negative forms of career identification correlate negatively with the outcomes (job satisfaction, work engagement and well-being), while career identification does not correlate with these variables. The results for organizational identification nicely match the findings of Kreiner and Ashforth (2004). The fact that career identification does not relate to the two negative forms of career identification supports the idea that identification, disidentification and ambivalent identification are separate constructs. It may be that this is even more the case for foci other than the organization.

Limitations and Suggestions for Future Research

Several limitations of this study should be acknowledged. First, we collected data from only one occupational group. The advantage is that our participants shared very similar working conditions. The health care system in Germany is a highly regulated system, in which patients are sent from general practitioners to 'assisting' therapist or specialists. Occupational therapists play their part in restoring health without much variability in how to do so. The downside of our sampling strategy is the lack of generalizability. More research in other groups is thus needed, for instance, in different service sectors and by comparing profit and non-profit organizations. As the health care system is highly regulated, opportunities for advancing in their careers are also limited for specialists or 'assisting' professions. Therefore, the relations of career identification with antecedents and consequences could be stronger in other organizational contexts.

We would also like to suggest the use of objective measures for the consequences of the forms and foci of identification. We replicated and extended the study of Kreiner and Ashforth (2004) using a survey method. This use of same source self-report measures might cause inflation in common-method variance. It would be interesting to see whether the different forms of identification result in different consequences, for instance, if disidentification of the employee is correlated with data of employee absence or performance reported by supervisors or peers.

Practical Implications

Our research suggests that practitioners should not only focus on identification with the organization but also on other forms of identification in combination with other foci of identification. Employees do not only reflect their organizational memberships but also their careers. As we have shown, it is particularly the negative forms of identification with one's career that have an impact on job satisfaction, well-being and work engagement. It is therefore important to get to know employees' feelings about their occupational groups if one wants to contribute to an engaged and happy workforce. Employees are always members of both their organization and their profession and only when the identities of these two foci are in congruence will employees be happy and motivated in the long run.

REFERENCES

Ashforth, B.E. (2001), *Role Transitions in Organizational Life: An Identity-Based Perspective*, Mahwah, NJ: Erlbaum.

Ashforth, B.E. and F. Mael (1989), 'Social identity and the organization', *Academy of Management Review*, 14, 20–39.

Bakker, A.B., S.L. Albrecht and M.P. Leiter (2011), 'Key questions regarding work engagement', *European Journal of Work and Organizational Psychology*, 20 (1), 4–28.

Bartel, C.A. (2001), 'Social comparisons in boundary-spanning work: effects of community outreach on members' organizational identity and identification', *Administrative Science Quarterly*, 46, 379–413.
Bergami, M. and R.P. Bagozzi (2000), 'Self-categorization, affective commitment and group self-esteem as distinct aspects of social identity in the organization', *British Journal of Social Psychology*, 39, 555–77.
Bhattacharya, C.B., H. Rao and M.A. Glynn (1995), 'Understanding the bond of identification: an investigation of its correlates among art museum members', *Journal of Marketing*, 59(4), 46–57.
Brewer, M.B. (1991), 'The social self: on being the same and different at the same time', *Personality and Social Psychology Bulletin*, 17, 475–82.
Brewer, M.B. (1993), 'The role of distinctiveness in social identity and group behavior', in Michael A. Hogg and D. Abrams (eds), *Group Motivation: Social Psychological Perspectives*, New York: Harvester Wheatsheaf, pp. 1–16.
Bullinger, M. and I. Kirchberger (1998), *SF-36. Fragebogen zum Gesundheitszustand*, Göttingen: Hogrefe.
Christ, O., R. Van Dick, U. Wagner and J. Stellmacher (2003), 'When teachers go the extra-mile: foci of organizational identification as determinants of different forms of organizational citizenship behavior among schoolteachers', *British Journal of Educational Psychology*, 73, 329–41.
Earley, P.C. and C.B. Gibson (1998), 'Taking stock in our progress on individualism-collectivism: 100 years of solidarity and community', *Journal of Management*, 24(1998), 265–304.
Ellemers, N. (1993), 'The influence of socio-structural variables on identity enhancement strategies', *European Review of Social Psychology*, 4, 27–57.
Ellemers, N. (2003), 'Identity, culture, and change in organizations: a social identity analysis and three illustrative cases', in S. Alexander Haslam, Michael J. Platow and Dan Van Knippenberg (eds), *Social Identity at Work: Developing Theory for Organizational Practice*, New York: Taylor and Francis, pp. 191–204.
Elsbach, K.D. (1999), 'An expanded model of organizational identification', *Research in Organizational Behavior*, 21, 163–200.
Fisher, C.D. and R. Gitelson (1983), 'A meta-analysis of the correlates of role conflict and ambiguity', *Journal of Applied Psychology*, 68, 320–33.
George, J.M. (1992), 'The role of personality in organizational life: issues and evidence', *Journal of Management*, 18, 185–213.
Glynn, M.A. (1998), 'Individuals' need for organizational identification (nOID): speculations on individual differences in the propensity to identify', in David A. Whetten and Paul C. Godfrey (eds), *Identity in Organizations: Building Theory Through Conversations*, Thousand Oaks, CA: Sage, pp. 238–44.
Haslam, S.A. (2001), *Psychology in Organizations: The Social Identity Approach*, London: Sage.
Haslam, S.A. and Rolf Van Dick (2011), 'A social identity analysis of organizational well-being', in David De Cremer, Rolf Van Dick and Keith Murnighan (eds), *Social Psychology and Organizations*, New York: Taylor and Francis, pp. 325–52.
Haslam, S.A., J. Jetten, T. Postmes and C. Haslam (2009), 'Social identity, health and well-being: an emerging agenda for applied psychology', *Applied Psychology: An International Review*, 58, 1–23 (special issue on 'Social Identity, Health and Well-being').
Hogg, M.A. and D.J. Terry (2000), 'Social identity and self-categorization processes in organizational contexts', *Academy of Management Review*, 25, 121–40.
Jackson, S.E. and R.S. Schuler (1985), 'A meta-analysis and conceptual critique of research on role ambiguity and role conflict in work settings', *Organizational Behavior and Human Decision Processes*, 36, 16–78.
Kahn, R.L., D.M. Wolfe, R.P. Quinn, J.D. Snoek and R.A. Rosenthal (1964), *Organizational Stress*, New York: Wiley.
Katz, D. and R.L. Kahn (1978), *The Social Psychology of Organizations*, New York: Wiley.
Kreiner, G.E. and B.E. Ashforth (2004), 'Evidence toward an expanded model of organizational identification', *Journal of Organizational Behavior*, 25, 1–27.
Krohne, H.W., B. Egloff, C.W. Kohlmann and A. Tausch (1996), 'Untersuchungen mit einer deutschen Form der "Positive and Negative Affect Schedule" (PANAS)', *Diagnostica*, 42, 139–56.
Mael, F.A. and B.E. Ashforth (1992), 'Loyal from day one: biodata, organizational identification, and turnover among newcomers', *Personnel Psychology*, 48, 309–33.
Morgeson, F.P. and S.E. Humphrey (2006), 'The Work Design Questionnaire (WDQ): developing and validating a comprehensive measure for assessing job design and the nature of work', *Journal of Applied Psychology*, 91(6), 1321–39.
Pratt, M.G. (2000), 'The good, the bad, and the ambivalent: managing identification among Amway distributors', *Administrative Science Quarterly*, 45, 456–93.
Reade, C. (2001), 'Dual identification in multinational corporations: local managers and their psychological attachment to the subsidiary versus the global organization', International *Journal of Human Resource Management*, 12, 405–24.

Riketta, M. (2005), 'Organizational identification: a meta-analysis', *Journal of Vocational Behavior*, 66(2005), 358–84.

Riketta, M. and R. Van Dick (2005), 'Foci of attachment in organizations: a meta-analysis comparison of the strength and correlates of work-group versus organizational commitment and identification', *Journal of Vocational Behavior*, 67(2005), 490–510.

Rizzo, J.R., R.J. House and S.I. Lirtzman (1970), 'Role conflict and ambiguity in complex organizations', *Administrative Science Quarterly*, 15(2), 150–63.

Schaufeli, W.B. and A.B. Bakker (2004), 'UWES: Utrecht Work Engagement Scale', Preliminary Manual, Occupational Health Psychology Unit, Utrecht University.

Schaufeli, W.B. and A.B. Bakker (2010), 'Defining and measuring work engagement: bringing clarity to the concept', in Arnold B. Bakker and Michael P. Leiter (eds), *Work Engagement: A Handbook of Essential Theory and Research*, New York: Psychology Press, pp. 10–24.

Sluss, D., R. Van Dick and B. Thompson (2011), 'Role theory in organizations: a relational perspective', in Sheldon Zedeck (ed.), *Handbook of I/O Psychology*, Vol. 1, Washington, DC: American Psychological Association, pp. 505–34.

Snape, E., T. Redman and A.W. Chan (2000), 'Commitment to the union: a survey of research and the implications for industrial relations and trade unions', *International Journal of Management Reviews*, 2(2000), 205–30.

Stegmann, S., R. Van Dick, J. Ullrich, J. Charalambous, B. Menzel, N. Egold and T. Wu (2010), 'Der Work Design Questionnaire – Vorstellung und erste Validierung einer deutschen Version' ['The work design questionnaire: introduction and first validation of a German version'], *Zeitschrift für Arbeits- und Organisationspsychologie*, 54, 1–28.

Tajfel, H. (1978), *Differentiation between Social Groups: Studies in the Social Psychology of Intergroup Relations*, London: Academic Press.

Tajfel, H. and J.C. Turner (1986), 'The social identity theory of intergroup behaviour', in Stephen Worchel and William G. Austin (eds), *Psychology of Intergroup Relations*, 2nd edn, Chicago: Nelson-Hall, pp. 7–24.

Triandis, H.C. and M.J. Gelfand (1998), 'Converging measurement of horizontal and vertical individualism and collectivism', *Journal of Personality and Social Psychology*, 1(74), 118–28.

Turner, J.C., M.A. Hogg, P.J. Oakes, S.D. Reicher and M.S. Wetherell (1987), *Rediscovering the Social Group*, Oxford: Blackwell.

Tyler, T.R. (1999), 'Why people cooperate with organizations: an identity-based perspective', *Research in Organizational Behavior*, 21, 201–46.

Tyler, T.R, and S.L. Blader (2000), *Cooperation in Groups*, Philadelphia, PA: Psychology Press.

Van Dick, Rolf (2004), *Commitment und Identifikation mit Organisationen*, Göttingen: Hogrefe.

Van Dick, R. and S.A. Haslam (2012), 'Stress and well-being in the workplace: support for key propositions from the social identity approach', in J. Jetten, C. Haslam and S. Alexander Haslam (eds), *The Social Cure: Identity, Health, and Well-Being*, Hove and New York: Psychology Press, pp. 175–94.

Van Dick, R. and U. Wagner (2002), 'Social identification among school teachers: dimensions, foci, and correlates', *European Journal of Work and Organizational Psychology*, 11, 129–49.

Van Dick, R., M.W. Grojean, O. Christ and J. Wieseke (2006), 'Identity and the extra mile: relationships between organizational identification and organizational citizenship behaviour', *British Journal of Management*, 17, 283–301.

Van Dick, R., U. Wagner, J. Stellmacher and O. Christ (2005), 'Category salience and organisational identification', *Journal of Occupational and Organizational Psychology*, 78, 273–85.

Van Dick, R., O. Christ, J. Stellmacher, U. Wagner, O. Ahlswede, C. Grubba, M. Hauptmeier, C. Höhfeld, K. Moltzen and P.A. Tissington (2004), 'Should I stay or should I go? Explaining turnover intentions with organizational identification and job satisfaction', *British Journal of Management*, 15 (2004), 351–60.

Van Knippenberg, D. (2000), 'Work motivation and performance: a social identity perspective', *Applied Psychology: An International Review*, 49, 357–71.

Van Knippenberg, D. and E.C.M. Van Schie (2000), 'Foci and correlates of organizational identification', *Journal of Occupational and Organizational Psychology*, 73, 137–47.

Warr, P. (1990), 'The measurement of well-being and other aspects of mental health', *Journal of Occupational Psychology*, 63, 193–210.

Watson, D., L.A. Clark and A. Tellegen (1998), 'Development and validation of brief measures of positive and negative affect: the PANAS scales', *Journal of Personality and Social Psychology*, 54, 1063–70.

8 Managing visibility for career sustainability: a study of remote workers

Julia Richardson and Clare Kelliher

INTRODUCTION

Background

The past few decades have seen changes which have challenged traditional notions of what work involves, how and where it is done and the relationship between employees and their employers. These changes have stemmed from a number of broader trends, such as increased competitive pressures, demands for greater global integration and advances in information and communication technologies (ICT) (Kelliher and Anderson, 2010; Kelliher and Richardson, 2012). In the context of managing labour, this has often meant increased flexibility in the way in which labour is utilized, for example, by increased use of temporary or fixed term contract arrangements (Coe et al., 2007; Van Dyne et al., 2007; Kossek and Van Dyne, 2008). Likewise some organizations have sought to reduce property costs by encouraging employees to work away from the office for some or all of their working time. Globalization, in addition to contributing to increased competition, has resulted in the delocalization of some types of work, resulting in it being carried out across geographical boundaries and in different time zones (Taylor and Bain, 2005; Urry, 2007). Geographically distributed teams, for example, may need to use different means of communication and coordination in order to accommodate the lack of shared 'real-time' working (Collins and Kolb, 2012). Similarly, working with clients in different times zones may require changes in work schedules. Developments in ICT have allowed for more dynamic work scheduling, allowing employees and management to communicate and access resources from remote locations (Castells et al., 2007).

Demographic and social changes, such as increasing levels of immigration and changing family structures, have also impacted on how both employers and employees approach the employment relationship (Eurofound, 2012) and consequently how careers evolve. For example, in some societies employers may now need to consider how to retain older employees in the workforce and how to cater to employees' caring commitments (Porter and Ayman, 2010). In addition, some employees are increasingly concerned about achieving a more satisfactory work–life balance and as a result seek opportunities to adjust their working arrangements to accommodate the non-work aspects of their lives (Bloom and Van Reenen, 2006; Hooker et al., 2007; Yanadori and Kato, 2009). Furthermore, the so-called generation Y are reported to have different expectations of work, including a desire to work more flexibly, which has a related impact on their career aspirations (Gerdes, 2009; Svyantek et al., 2012).

As noted above, these changes have important implications for careers, impacting both on how organizations design and develop career opportunities and on how employees are able to shape their careers and what they expect from employers (Baruch, 2006). In many respects, moves towards increased remote working imply that employees are being given greater control over their career experiences, such as how and when they work (Tietze et al., 2009). Indeed, if remote is understood as connoting decentralization of work and work monitoring processes, it also suggests a requirement for employees to assume greater responsibility for their own performance and career development.

In this regard, careers characterized by remote working have a strong synergy with contemporary notions of the 'boundaryless career' (Arthur and Rousseau, 1996; Arthur et al., 2005), where individuals are understood to be more proactive, taking greater responsibility for their own career experiences, achievements and trajectories, rather than ceding that responsibility to their employer. This also reflects opportunities for individual 'career capitalism' (Inkson and Arthur, 2001) where the career actor him/herself proactively steers their career and work opportunities according to their own aspirations, rather than simply reacting to employer-led initiatives and opportunities.

Working remotely also changes the social dynamic of careers, in the sense that rather than working in an organizational environment (for example, office, store, unit), surrounded by, or at least in close proximity to, colleagues or clients, the remote worker normally carries out their work away from the physical locale of their employer and hence their work colleagues/clients as well. The potential of this remoteness to cause feelings of isolation and the implications for career identity have been the subject of growing research interest (for example, Crandall and Gao, 2005; Grote and Raeder, 2009; Richardson, 2010). However, the extent to which this impacts on how remote workers manage their careers is, as yet, not fully understood. In particular, whereas there has been extensive research on how remote workers might achieve 'life balance' (Tremblay et al., 2006; Korabik et al., 2008; Kossek and Van Dyne, 2008; Kossek et al., 2010) and how they might maintain and even enhance their performance (for example, Whitehouse et al., 2002; Golden, 2007; Martinez-Sanchez et al., 2007a; 2007b; Lero et al., 2009), how they manage relationships with colleagues, managers and clients is less well understood. Given widespread assumptions about the impact of social networks and relationships on career experiences and opportunities, alongside broader conceptions of careers as being essentially relational (for example, Higgins and Thomas, 2001; Chandler and Kram, 2007; Cotton et al., 2011; O'Neill et al., 2011), working remotely may well have a negative impact on career sustainability. Therefore, in line with the focus of this book, and focusing specifically on the theme of 'visibility', we draw on a large study of remote workers in Canada to explore how they managed their relationships with colleagues and clients in order to enhance their career sustainability.

Before introducing the study, however, we make two points of clarification. First, for the purposes of this chapter, career sustainability is understood as conferring a sense of not just being employed, but also maintaining employability by accessing opportunities for career and personal development. Second, we focus on visibility because this was a dominant theme which emerged in interviewees' accounts of how they managed their relationships with others and how they maintained/enhanced their career opportunities and experiences.

Next, we will explore the current literature on remote working, pointing to some of the key dimensions of what it means to work remotely and identifying factors which have been found to impact on work experiences and, ultimately, on an individual's career experiences.

Remote Working

We take remote working here to mean where an employee works away from their employing organization's premises for some or all of their working time (elsewhere also termed 'flexwork' or 'flexible work'). By its very nature, employees are either absent or have a reduced physical presence in the workplace, which has been found to influence the perceptions of co-workers and managers about how the employee performs their work (Harris, 2003; Golden, 2007; Lautsch et al., 2009; Richardson, 2010). For example, Golden (2007) reported that non-remote co-workers often feel a sense of injustice where they have to 'pick up the slack' for their teleworking counterparts, which may, in turn, have a negative impact on perceptions of procedural, distributive and interactional justice. The same study also showed that non-remote workers experienced large reductions in co-worker satisfaction and felt that they had a heavier workload, which further reduced their satisfaction with their teleworking colleagues. It is also notable that recently some companies such as Yahoo and Hewlett Packard have changed their approach to remote working. Whereas they had previously actively encouraged such practices, reports in the media indicate they are now reducing opportunities for remote working, due to concerns about the potential impact on collaboration, knowledge transfer and employee performance (Matos, 2013).

These changes at Yahoo and Hewlett Packard notwithstanding, recent years have seen significant growth in the number of remote workers in many parts of the world (WorldatWork, 2012). For example, according to the Fourth Work–Life Balance Employee Survey in the UK, 30 per cent of employees perceive working from home to be available in their workplace and 44 per cent of these reported that they had taken up this opportunity (Tipping et al., 2012). The report also shows, though, that take-up was more common amongst parents, older employees and those with higher professional and educational qualifications, income and managerial responsibilities. Similarly, across the EU, significant numbers of employees chose to work remotely for some of their working time, although there are considerable variations between individual countries (Eurofound, 2012). Looking specifically at Canada, where the study reported in this chapter was conducted; recent figures from Stats Canada show that in 2008, 11.2 per cent of employees worked at home, a 1 per cent increase since 2000. However, by comparison, self-employed workers are more likely to work remotely and their participation rate climbed from 54 per cent to 60 per cent between 2006 and 2008, meaning that in 2008, 1 842 000 self-employed persons were working at home compared to 1 748 600 employees (StatsCanada, 2013). The combined effect of the slight increase for employees and the more substantial increase for the self-employed pushed the overall proportion of people working at home up about 2 percentage points between 2000 and 2008 (from 17 per cent to 19 per cent). Opportunities to work remotely in Canada tend to be concentrated in larger organizations and around major metropolitan areas such as Vancouver, British Columbia; Alberta and Calgary, Edmonton; Montreal, Quebec; Ottawa and Toronto, Ontario; and Nova Scotia. They are also more likely to be found in finance, engineering, environment, arts and entertainment, sales, computing and IT, web and software, medical and health, customer services, telecommunications, business development, and travel and tourism industries.

The growth in remote working has been enabled by developments in ICT which allow employees to access the same resources as when physically present in the workplace. Remote working, like many other flexible working arrangements, is generally seen to be 'employee friendly' and some governments have encouraged employers to provide greater flexibility to employees with caring commitments (Haddon and Brynin, 2005; Towers et al., 2006; Martinez-Sanchez et al., 2007b; Lero et al., 2009). There is also evidence that such working arrangements are popular with all employees and are often seen as a highly regarded benefit (Bloom and Van Reenen, 2006). Working remotely may be attractive because it allows employees to balance their lives more effectively, echoing contemporary notions of the 'boundaryless career' where individuals are understood to seek out greater integration between their work and non-work lives (Briscoe and Hall, 2006; Sullivan and Arthur, 2006). Additionally, avoiding a long or difficult commute to the workplace may be a means of alleviating stress and fatigue for employees. There are also advantages for employers (Manoocherhri and Pinkerton, 2003), since allowing employees some degree of choice over where, when and how much they work has been shown to result in a range of business benefits.

A recent cost–benefit analysis of family-friendly work practices (Lero et al., 2009) found remote working to be positively associated with profit, and a number of studies have found a positive link between remote working and organizational performance (Martinez-Sanchez et al., 2007a; 2007b) and other measures such as reduced costs (Bailey and Kurland, 2002). In a meta-analysis, Gajendran and Harrison (2007) concluded that remote working is associated with reduced turnover intent. At an individual level, there is also evidence of a positive association between remote working and individual performance, although most studies have relied on self-reported performance measures (Bailey and Kurland, 2002; Gajendran and Harrison, 2007). In addition to direct links with performance, some studies have also looked at employee attitudes demonstrated more generally to be linked to performance. For example, Gajendran and Harrison (2007) found a link with job satisfaction, and Kelliher and Anderson (2010) found an association with organizational commitment.

Having explored some of the key themes in the contemporary literature on remote working, we now turn to the study upon which this chapter is based.

ORGANIZATIONAL CONTEXT

This study was carried out in the Canadian subsidiary of a multinational company in the high-tech industry. It began with discussions with the VP and Assistant VP of HR exploring organizational policies on remote working and the perceived implications for organizational and individual performance, including career development. Although sales staff had always had access to remote working practices, opportunities had been expanded to employees in other departments with the primary aim of making remote working available to all employees, subject to their manager's approval and in accordance with the nature of their jobs.

DATA COLLECTION

Although this chapter focuses solely on remote workers' approaches to managing social relationships, in order to support the future sustainability of their careers, the broader study explored more general themes including productivity, organizational commitment and life balance. In addition to the interview data, demographic data were collected, including age, marital status, number and ages of any children, tenure, management responsibility, area of employment (for example, sales, operations, marketing), and time on a remote working arrangement. Focusing on the objectives of this chapter, an agenda of themes with related open-ended questions supported in-depth exploration of interviewees' perceptions of the impact of remote working on their relationships with their remote and non-remote working counterparts. These themes can be loosely divided into two groups. The first was concerned with their perceptions of how remote working impacted on their relationships with co-workers, managers and clients and the impact of those relationships on opportunities for promotion, access to developmental activities, and activities not directly work-related, but that might, nonetheless, impact on career opportunities, such as extra-organizational social events. The second group focused on how they managed those relationships, including questions about any steps they took to improve, consolidate or 'make up for' the fact that they were working at a distance. Interviewees were also encouraged to introduce further themes that they felt were important but which had not been covered elsewhere in the interview.

Sampling

A total of 76 remote workers were interviewed. They all had access to technology which enabled them to work from home or elsewhere and to communicate with their manager, colleagues and clients as required. The sample was self-selected in response to an invitation to participate in the study circulated by the HRM department: 138 employees volunteered to take part; however, due to time and financial restrictions, only 76 interviews were conducted. Each interview was recorded and transcribed verbatim. Interviews lasted approximately 45–60 minutes.

Interviewees were distributed across different departments in the organization ranging from sales, to accounting and legal services. Fifty interviewees did not have a designated desk space in the home office, although they did have access to a 'hot desk'. Length of service ranged from less than one year through to over 10 years, which allowed for a robust understanding of those with extensive corporate memory versus more recent employees. Twenty-seven interviewees were middle-level management with responsibility for managing teams of other remote workers in their department. These interviewees provided information about managing remote workers as well as about being remote workers themselves. Participants were spread across age groups ranging from 20–25 to 56+, with the majority in the 36–50 age range. The majority had one or more children currently living at home.

Data Analysis

Interview transcripts were 'coded' using Nvivo9 (and later 10), a computer assisted qualitative data analysis software programme. Template analysis (King, 2004) was used to create lists of 'themes' contained in the data that responded to the research questions. Some themes, such as feeling isolated from colleagues and mechanisms to deal with that isolation, were created a priori, based on an initial review of the literature on remote working. While these initial themes presented a useful starting-point, further themes were added as the analysis evolved and dominant and subsidiary themes were identified. For example, whereas feeling 'isolated' and remote working having a detrimental impact on relationships with colleagues was identified through the literature review, the theme of 'visibility' specifically emerged in the data. This theme was mentioned extensively by all participants and, as a result, is the primary focus for this chapter. It is also notable that it could be broken down into further subsidiary themes, such as 'mechanisms for maintaining visibility' and the perceived implications of 'becoming invisible' for career opportunities.

LIMITATIONS

The decision to focus on one particular company facilitated an in-depth case study, which was further supported by having access to the VP and AVP of HR, in terms of understanding the overall organizational policy and practice regarding remote working. It is acknowledged, however, that companies will have their own specific practices for managing remote workers and the remote workers themselves are likely to operate according to the specific organizational and business field. Moreover, because this company was in the IT industry, its employees had access to technologies which may not be available in other organizations. Indeed, according to Tremblay (2003), Canadian companies use their own individualized approaches to remote working depending on their respective industry and access to technology, which suggests that the findings may not be transferable (Merriam, 2009) to other organizations, especially those with only limited access to technology. Moreover, as this is a very large multinational organization, the findings may not apply to smaller organizations or organizations in other countries, particularly given that experiences of remote working and management of remote workers have been shown to differ across countries and cultural contexts (Peters and Heusinkveld, 2010).

FINDINGS

Visibility, Fears of Becoming 'Invisible' and the Impact on Relationships with Colleagues and the Employer

Although the majority of interviewees felt that remote working had had a positive impact on their overall work performance, as well as on their ability to achieve a sense of life balance, they invariably cited the problem of visibility, or what some euphemistically referred to as 'managing the optics' of their performance and specifically their relationships with colleagues, managers and clients/customers. There was widespread concern about the risk of becoming invisible and the potential impact of invisibility on their relationships with senior management and colleagues. In this respect, despite reporting that working remotely had enabled them to enhance their productivity, which they felt would also enhance their career opportunities, they worried that they could easily become invisible, simply because they had little physical interaction with colleagues, managers and clients, as suggested by two interviewees below:

> You're at home . . . you become more invisible so you don't have that group support, that cohesion. It would perhaps be a foolish person who would focus too much on the fact that they're working from home. So, you've got to face the issue about needing to show up to work . . . you gotta have some face time! (Michael, manager)

> I think it impresses a lot of managers if you can run with things on your own and handle things remotely by yourself. But my boss always tells me I should go to the office sometimes, that I should make myself more visible because of [the need to maintain] internal visibility. (Pilar, non-management)

Whereas interviewees emphasized that their objective performance was important for sustaining and developing their careers, they also felt that it could easily be overlooked unless they were also visible. They needed to be not just high performers, but also what several interviewees described as 'fully fledged' organizational citizens. The vast majority of interviewees felt that working from home enabled them to focus more clearly on their work because they were less likely to be distracted compared to their office-based counterparts. Yet, many interviewees also felt that even while they were high performers 'on paper' they also had some concerns about how working remotely impacted on career opportunities, as suggested by Anum, below:

> Career wise, you have to be visible, you need for senior management to see you every once in a while. You need them seeing you beyond on paper, because they can obviously see you on paper in terms of what you're bringing in. I'm doing my job, we meet our quota but there's still that, you know, the elevator conversation, or you see them in the hall or they ask you about the deal you're working on or whatever. It's that informal stuff, so you definitely need to be visible (Anum, non-management)

Over half of the interviewees juxtaposed the organizational objective performance measures with the more subjective need to maintain visibility. Both managers and non-managers also emphasized that whereas maintaining objective performance was important, the wider organizational culture was that being visible was essential for securing career development opportunities, and in particular hierarchical promotion. For example, Cristobal (non-manager) described what he saw as a contradiction between organizational policy and what happened in practice:

> If you've been exceptionally productive on paper and you met all your targets or whatever, or however else you're officially evaluated, that lack of social connectivity and visibility might work against you. Corporate policy is just the contrary, 'as long as you are meeting your targets, you shouldn't have any handicap'. My personal take on it is that career advancement requires some sort of social interaction and if you don't display that social interaction and are seen to do it then you may have difficulties ascending here. (Cristobal, non-management)

Many other interviewees echoed this sentiment – including managers who explicitly stated that 'paper performance' (Charles) would not guarantee career advancement and/or career development opportunities. Indeed all managers indicated that being 'visible' was one way of protecting oneself in times of organizational restructuring, and half said that remote workers who were not known beyond paper performance were more likely to be 'let go' than their more visible counterparts. This finding is important in that it suggests that whereas objective performance measures were understood to impact on career opportunities, more informal, relational themes were also an important influence. Lillian, a senior manager with extensive experience in this particular company, captured the impact of visibility on career opportunities and experiences and specifically on the 'social aspect' of work:

> This is how I envision career growth: I believe that your output and performance is definitely a contributor but that other social aspect that people need to know you, feel comfortable with you and have confidence in your personal style and that kind of stuff which is not very visible if you are remote. I do feel that from a career growth opportunity that's why I still go into the office once or twice a week and maintain that face-to-face . . . it is definitely a requirement to pursue your career growth. You've got to be seen. (Lillian, manager)

For Felicia, below, as with other managers and non-managers, there was a particular concern that being invisible would result in being left out of what they called 'decision-making interactions', again drawing attention to the relational dimensions of careers, which might have a negative impact on her career opportunities.

> I think that your career is determined by discussions you have with others, so that requires you to be part of the interaction and visible. If you are working remotely all the time you could very easily get left out and then you find yourself pursuing something only to find out a little bit later that that decision was already made or that project was already put on the back-burner but they never thought to include you in the discussions even though you are impacted. (Felicia)

Put another way, it wasn't the visibility in and of itself that seemed to be a matter of concern, but rather what that visibility, or lack of visibility might create – in Felicia's case, creating a situation where she might be left out of decision-making processes. Where career opportunities and experiences were concerned, interviewees were particularly apprehensive that lack of visibility might result in their being overlooked, or that their achievements might be disregarded precisely because they did not have strong connections with others.

Managing Visibility

Maintaining connections with colleagues and clients

All interviewees expressed concerns about becoming invisible and described taking specific action in order to enhance their visibility. This action invariably involved instigating some form of face-to-face contact with those whom they felt were key stakeholders in their careers, predominantly colleagues and managers, but also for those in sales, with clients and customers. Indeed, whereas all interviewees had access to technology such as Skype, instant messaging and others forms of ICT, there was a dominant feeling that there was no substitute for physical presence. Suzie (non-management) and Bella (management) provide good examples of this finding:

> You could do a conference call but the trade-off then is that you're not visible. It's only when you are in there and you see other sales people, they'll say 'gee I'm glad that I caught you. . .. I want to chat with you about this customer'. Whereas if they have to email you or give me a call, it's a trade-off you might actually lose out on some opportunities if you're not physically visible on somewhat of a regular basis. (Suzie, non-management)

> At least 75 per cent of my time right now is spent online but that's not enough for relationship building with people around me. Physical contact has been critical. One of my managers I work with, he works from a different location but he was driving down today and came to have coffee, he wanted to meet me, so that's critical, face-to-face relations are very very important. You can't do that all online, no matter if we are a high-tech company; I still know that it's not enough (Bella, management)

Another theme which emerged from the data was a belief that overuse or reliance on ICTs would have a deleterious effect on visibility by inhibiting relationships with colleagues, individual performance and, ultimately, their career opportunities and experiences, as suggested by Leora and Petros:

> Oh, sure, we've got electronic online tools for like messaging, if someone's working from home, you can easily send a query 'What about this?' people are used to that but it doesn't always work, even today. People tend to put things off, wait for the other person to come back into the office. Same as if you are presenting in person versus on the phone, the body language is missing . . . suddenly [on the phone] it's just silence but you don't know if they agree with you or not . . . you end up assuming that the person was multi-tasking. No, it's not a good thing to rely on technology. (Petros, manager)

> I think that people want the human touch. I couldn't get used to the conference call thing. I'd prefer to be there face to face, I do think that you get more out of it. I think body language. Besides, with electronic means, it's the simplest thing to do if you don't want to deal with somebody you just don't answer their calls or messages. You can't do that when you are right there with them or they know you are around. (Leora, non-management)

The nature of what they did to enhance their visibility varied between interviewees. Some, for example, specifically arranged office-based meetings to discuss on-going business projects, rather than conducting discussions via phone or email. Others arranged meetings specifically to talk about career opportunities, or to get direct feedback about their performance, alongside paper-based performance reviews. The majority also reported that they would instigate some form of face-to-face interaction with colleagues, not necessarily for the purpose of discussing work or professional issues, but also to simply 'connect' on a social level. These interactions were usually described as more informal catch-ups, getting to know what was going on in the respective person's life outside of work, in order to establish or reaffirm friendships. While they acknowledged that such interactions regularly turned to work issues, they emphasized the importance of keeping in touch with each other's non-work lives and how it could not be done by relying on ICTs.

Being seen

In addition to arranging meetings and connecting with others, over half of the interviewees (managers and non-managers) also reported coming into the office specifically in order to be seen by others – be it colleagues, managers or clients. For example, several explicitly stated that they often returned to the main office, not because they had to meet anyone, but simply because they wanted to 'show their face'. Sean provides a good example of this form of behaviour:

> You need to come in; you have a local office where some of your peers or your customers are. I think; if you have that, it's important that you come into the office once in a while, once or twice a week, or every two weeks, couple of days even. I think if you stay at home you sometimes get forgotten, you are doing your work. They know me, they know me as this but they don't see me there. (Sean, non-manager)

Data analysis suggested a strong connection between 'being seen' and maintaining interaction/relationships with key stakeholders in the home organization, and that in order to facilitate that interaction interviewees felt that they had to be 'known' and/or 'seen' on a fairly regular basis. There was a fairly consistent concern about colleagues, managers and clients perceiving them as 'remote' remote workers rather than physically remote, but relationally and professionally connected. Many described wanting to establish a professional image of being available, despite not working in the office on a regular basis.

Management Support to Create and Maintain Visibility

In addition to exploring how interviewees proactively managed their own visibility, we also explored whether or not managers used specific strategies to ensure the visibility of their subordinates as a means of ensuring stronger working relationships. In this regard, we heard widespread accounts of managers taking multiple initiatives in order to achieve three main objectives: first, to facilitate greater interaction and hence enhance both individual and team level performance. The primary intention here was to facilitate stronger relationships as a means of encouraging knowledge transfer between subordinates as well as between themselves and their subordinates, as suggested by Tom, below:

> I tell my Northern guys that there's a 'radar' in the back of my head. If one of them is becoming invisible, it goes up and then I make an effort to make contact, not that you're checking up on people but you've got to make sure that they are visible.. . . The human interaction is essential for knowledge movement and the challenge is to make that happen so that you don't feel that you are remote from people. (Tom, manager)

It is notable that Tom, like most other managers, specifically emphasized that these initiatives were less about monitoring what employees were doing, than about facilitating knowledge transfer and interaction. Thus, the theme of visibility in this instance relates not to making employees more visible in order to monitor their performance, but rather about making them more visible to augment interaction, relationships and 'knowledge movement' or transfer.

The second objective was to avoid over-dependency on ICTs because, as noted above, even while they were a hi-tech company, all managers and employees felt that ICTs were not a substitute for 'face-to-face' interaction:

> There is no end to what a team can accomplish face-to-face, meaning that it's amazing when you are running a team with 20 people and the kind of dialogue that goes on. You know how you sound when you're on a call, you and I can only talk, and we can only have one conversation. But I tell my team when we are together they can all jump in and ideas get generated, whatever, that cannot happen on the phone because my team stop talking. Technology overrides them. (Charles, management)

Exploring this theme further, many of the managers interviewed said that whereas they were aware of the advantages of ICTs for supporting remote working, they also believed that over-dependency on technology would ultimately inhibit both individual and group performance, and hence the individual's career opportunities. What is interesting here, in particular, is how these managers felt some level of responsibility for enhancing their subordinates' careers. Thus, although they were encouraging autonomy and independence, they still felt a need to guide their subordinates as managers.

The third objective was also connected to managing subordinates' careers, but predominantly because of the potential knock-on effect on their own visibility in the organization and, ultimately, for their own career sustainability. Conversely, they also felt that if their team members were invisible they ran the risk of becoming invisible too. The specific concern was that having an 'invisible team' might also have a negative impact on their own career experiences and opportunities, as suggested by Rupert below:

> Well, it's not just about them though – I have to take into consideration my image and visibility. If my team aren't known then I'm not known either. On the other hand, if they are known then so am I – senior management need to see my team to know me. (Rupert, manager)

However, several managers also raised a caveat suggesting that they had to be cautious not to be seen as someone who was micro-managing remote workers – requiring team members to spend 'too much' time in the office. Indeed being seen as a 'micro-manager' was widely understood as having a negative impact on career sustainability. Several managers described counterparts who they felt were bringing their team members into the home office too regularly, which rendered them 'too visible'. They also suggested that micro-managers were unlikely to be selected for more senior positions precisely because they were unable to delegate and/or 'keep up' with changing working arrangements. This finding points to a potential need for both managers and employees to maintain what appears to be a fine balance between ensuring sufficient visibility to facilitate interaction and recognition, but on the other hand not so much as to undermine their status as remote workers.

DISCUSSION

In the context of significant changes in the business environment, including increased competitive pressures, greater global integration and advances in ICT, alongside changing demographics and attitudes to work, we have seen changes taking place to the way in which work is carried out and the nature of the relationship between employees and their employing organization. One such change has been the growth in remote working in many countries across the world.

There is much evidence to show that there are many benefits associated with remote working, such as enhanced organizational performance, reduced turnover intent and organizational commitment (Lero et al., 2009; Martinez-Sanchez et al., 2007a; Kelliher and Anderson, 2010). This study of 76 remote workers, including both managers and non-managerial employees in Canada, also found evidence of a positive impact on performance, or at least performance as measured by the organization, the so-called 'paper performance'. Yet the findings also highlighted a number of less obvious and, to date, less explored outcomes. Although 'paper performance' was the overt, official measure for career advancement, there was a widespread belief amongst interviewees that there were other, less explicit contributory factors. There was a widespread belief that being visible – being seen and known in the organization – was an important factor and many respondents expressed concerns that working remotely, almost by definition, could impede visibility and as a result their career opportunities, including their continuity of employment. This finding suggests an understanding that career opportunities are often impacted by social relationships and signals that having a reduced physical presence in the workplace may impact career advancement and opportunities for development and consequently career sustainability.

Whether or not this was borne out in practice was not the specific focus of this study and no attempt was made to explore whether or not remote workers were likely to experience greater barriers to career advancement and opportunities than their office-based counterparts. Yet, it is notable that all the managers in the study indicated that employees who did not maintain positive relationships with managers, colleagues and clients, and who become 'remote' remote workers with low visibility, could be overlooked for promotion and were also more likely to be 'let go' during times of downsizing, even if they had high levels of 'paper performance'. Thus from the managers' perspective, even while remote workers may be physically remote, they remain very much reliant on organizational networks and relationships. This finding echoes the work of other scholars who have identified the value of not just networks, but also the essentially relational and informal aspects of contemporary careers (Parker et al. 2004; Parker et al., 2008) and the concomitant influence on opportunities for development and, we argue, career sustainability. This case shows how relationships with others are perceived to have a strong impact on remote workers' careers, even while they are working at a distance from their colleagues, managers and clients.

At the outset, we argued that enabling and allowing employees to work remotely in some senses also implies greater control over when and how to work (Tietze et al., 2009). This has implications for how they then manage their relationships with other organizational members, particularly when they are not physically present. Further, we argue that this increased control has a strong synergy with contemporary career theory, suggesting that in order to ensure continued employability, career actors are now expected to be more proactive and 'assume greater personal responsibility for understanding their own needs, determining their own goals, and managing their own careers' (Parker et al., 2004, p. 490). The remote workers at the centre of this study echo this theme, pointing to how they strategically sought to enhance their visibility and maintain positive relationships with organizational members in order to ensure that their performance was recognized and rewarded and, ultimately, to ensure continued employment. This included scheduling meetings with colleagues, both to discuss ongoing work projects and also specifically to seek feedback. In addition, some reported deliberately coming into the workplace with the specific aim of seeing and being seen. Notably, respondents who were also managers of remote workers reported that they too were keen to increase the visibility of their team members. Their concerns related to the limitations of various ICT mechanisms for communication. Whilst aware of the possible implications for the careers of their team members and for themselves, they also argued that face-to-face meetings were important to facilitate knowledge transfer amongst employees. Thus, in addition to individual proactivity, this research shows how managers continue to take responsibility for, and exhibit a strong interest in, the careers of their subordinates – in this case actively encouraging positive working relationships among remote workers and between remote workers and their non-remote peers. While this interest was closely connected with their own professional status, (for example, being seen as managers with high-functioning teams), it is notable that effectively managing the careers of others emerged as a vehicle through which they also managed their own careers and hence their career sustainability.

Taken together, these findings present an important insight into how remote working was enacted and experienced in one organization. Although remote working may have been seen to be beneficial in terms of employee performance, there seemed to be a fear that reduced physical presence would impact negatively on career trajectories. In this regard, the remote workers in this study seem to have taken on greater responsibility for the management of their own careers, especially with regard to maintaining visibility and maintaining positive social relationships with colleagues, albeit sometimes with the encouragement of their managers.

What is interesting here is that employees and their managers did not challenge this tacit acceptance that visibility was an important element in career advancement and access to development opportunities, although it was acknowledged that the formal system was performance-based, which could be demonstrated by reference to data. Rather than attempting to ensure that the formal system was adhered to as the basis for advancement decisions, they sought ways to address what they saw as impediments presented by remote working to the informal elements of these processes.

More generally, this implies that when different modes of working are adopted, existing organizational systems and practices, designed to manage employees based on a model of traditional, standard working arrangements, may no longer be suitable. In particular where informal, tacit elements have grown up alongside formal policy and practice, they may, albeit inadvertently, discriminate against career actors with non-standard working arrangements. In the case of remote working, practices which are implicitly based on the type of visibility enabled by physical presence in the workplace are likely to disadvantage remote workers, who by the very nature of their working arrangement have a lower degree of physical presence. Organizations committed to developing flexible working arrangements and who wish to gain the benefits of increased employee choice need to carefully examine existing policies to ensure that these are appropriate to accommodate a more diverse range of working patterns. Not doing so potentially puts at risk the benefits, such as improved performance and enhanced commitment, which can accrue from allowing employees flexibility over their working arrangements. Furthermore, if employees believe that they may be subject to disadvantage in their career experiences and opportunities, they may be less likely to adopt alternative working patterns.

REFERENCES

Arthur, M.B. and D.M. Rousseau (eds) (1996). *The Boundaryless Career: A New Employment Principle for a New Organizational Era*. New York, Oxford University Press.

Arthur, M.B., S.N. Khapova and C.P.M. Wilderom (2005). 'Career success in a boundaryless career world'. *Journal of Organizational Behavior* 26(2): 177–202.

Bailey, D.E. and N.B. Kurland (2002). 'A review of telework research: findings, new directions, and lessons for the study of modern work'. *Journal of Organizational Behaviour* 23: 383–400.

Baruch, Y. (2006). 'Career development in organizations and beyond: Balancing traditional and contemporary viewpoints'. *Human Resource Management Review* 16: 125–38.

Bloom, N. and J. Van Reenen (2006). 'Management practices, work–life balance and productivity: A review of some recent evidence'. *Oxford Review of Economic Policy* 22: 457–82.

Briscoe, J.P. and D.T. Hall (2006). 'The interplay of boundaryless and protean careers: Combinations and implications'. *Journal of Vocational Behaviour* 69(1): 4–18.

Castells, M., M. Fernandez-Ardevol, J.L. Qiu and A. Sey (2007). *Mobile Communication and Society*. Cambridge, MA, MIT Press.

Chandler, D.E. and K.E. Kram (2007). 'Mentoring and developmental networks in the new career context'. In H.P. Gunz and M. Peiperl (eds) *Handbook of Career Studies*, Thousand Oaks, CA, Sage, pp. 241–67.

Coe, N.M., J.L. Johns and K. Ward (2007). 'Mapping the globalization of the temporary staffing industry'. *Professional Geographer* 59(4): 503–20.

Collins, P. and D.A. Kolb (2012). 'Innovation in distributed teams: The duality of connectivity norms and human agency'. In C. Kelliher and J. Richardson (eds) *New Ways of Organizing Work: Developments, Perspectives and Experiences*. New York, Routledge, pp. 140–59.

Cotton, R., Y. Shen and R. Livne-Tarandach (2011). 'On becoming extraordinary: The content and structure of the developmental networks of major league baseball hall of famers'. *Academy of Management Journal* 54(1): 15–46.

Crandall, W.R. and L. Gao (2005). 'An update on telecommuting: Review and prospects for emerging issues'. *SAM Advanced Management Journal* Summer: 30–37.

Eurofound (2012). 'Fifth European Working Conditions Survey'. Luxembourg, Publications Office of the European Union.

Gajendran, R.S. and D.A. Harrison (2007). 'The good, the bad, and the unknown about telecommuting: Meta-analysis of psychological mediators and individual consequences'. *Journal of Applied Psychology* 19: 197–220.

Gerdes, L. (2009). 'Bad economy hasn't changed Gen Y's desire for work/life balance'. *Bloomberg Business Week*, 3 September.

Golden, T. (2007). 'Co-workers who telework and the impact on those in the office: Understanding the implications of virtual work for co-worker satisfaction and turnover intentions'. *Human Relations* 60: 1641–67.

Grote, G. and S. Raeder (2009). 'Careers and identity in flexible working: Do flexible identities fare better?' *Human Relations* 62(2): 219–44.

Haddon, L. and M. Brynin (2005). 'The character of telework and the characteristics of teleworkers'. *New Technology, Work and Employment* 20(1): 34–46.

Harris, L. (2003). 'Home-based teleworking and the employment relationship'. *Personnel Review* 32(4): 422–37.

Higgins, M.C. and D. Thomas (2001). 'Constellations and careers: Toward understanding the effects of multiple developmental relationships'. *Journal of Organizational Behaviour* 22: 223–47.

Hooker, H., F. Neathey, J. Casebourne and M. Munro (2007). 'The third work–life balance employee survey: Main findings'. Brighton, Institute for Employment Studies.

Inkson, K. and M.B. Arthur (2001). 'How to be a successful career capitalist'. *Organizational Dynamics* 30(1): 48–61.

Kelliher, C. and D.A. Anderson (2010). 'Doing more with less? Flexible working practices and the intensification of work'. *Human Relations* 63(1): 83–106.

Kelliher, C. and J. Richardson (eds) (2012). *New Ways of Organizing Work: Developments, Perspectives and Experiences*. New York, Routledge.

King, N. (2004). 'Using templates in the thematic analysis of text'. In C. Cassell and G. Symon (eds) *Essential Guide to Qualitative Methods in Organizational Research*. London, Sage, pp. 256–70.

Korabik, K., D.S. Lero and D.L. Whitehead (eds) (2008). *The Handbook of Work–Family Integration: Research, Theory, and Best Practices*. San Diego, Elsevier.

Kossek, E.E. and L. Van Dyne (2008). 'Face-time matters: A cross level model of how work–life flexibility influences work performance of groups and individuals'. In K. Korabik, D.S. Lero and D.L. Whitehead (eds) *Handbook of Work–Family Integration: Research, Theory and Best Practices*. New York, Academic Press, pp. 305–30.

Kossek, E.E., S. Lewis and L.B. Hammer (2010). 'Work–life initiatives and organizational change: Overcoming mixed messages to move from the margin to the mainstream'. *Human Relations* 63(1): 3–19.

Lautsch, B.A., E.E. Kossek and S.C. Eaton (2009). 'Supervisory approaches and paradoxes in managing telecommuting implementation'. *Human Relations* 62(6): 795–827.

Lero, D.S., J. Richardson and K.Korabik (2009). *Cost–Benefit Review of Work–Life Balance Practices – 2009*, Canadian Association of Administrators of Labour Legislation.

Manoocherhri, G. and T. Pinkerton (2003). 'Managing telecommuters: Opportunities and challenges'. *American Business Review* 21(1): 9–16.

Martinez-Sanchez, A., M. Perez, P. De-Luis Carnicer and M.J. Vela-Jimenez (2007a). 'Telework, human resource flexibility and firm performance'. *New Technology, Work and Employment* 22(3): 208–23.

Martinez-Sanchez, A., M.P. Perez, P. De-Luis Carnicer and M.J. Vela-Jimenez (2007b). 'Teleworking and workplace flexibility: A study of impact on firm performance'. *Personnel Review* 36(1): 42–64.

Matos, K. (2013). 'HP & Yahoo's telecommuting breakup: It's not you, it's me!' *Huffington Post Business*, 23 October.

Merriam, S.B. (2009). *Qualitative Research: A Guide to Design and Implementation*. San Francisco, Jossey-Bass.

O'Neill, D.A., M.M. Hopkins and S.E. Sullivan (2011). 'Do women's networks help advance women's careers? Differences in perceptions of female workers and top leadership'. *Career Development International* 16(7): 733–54.

Parker, P., M.B. Arthur and K. Inkson (2004). 'Career communities: A preliminary exploration of member-defined career support structures'. *Journal of Organizational Behavior* 25: 489–514.

Parker, P., D.T. Hall and K.E. Kram (2008). 'Peer coaching: A relational process for accelerating career learning'. *Academy of Management Learning and Education* 7(4): 487–503.

Peters, P. and S. Heusinkveld (2010). 'Institutional explanations for managers' attitudes towards telehomeworking'. *Human Relations* 63(1): 107–35.

Porter, S. and R. Ayman (2010). 'Work flexibility as a mediator of the relationship between work–family conflict and intention to quit'. *Journal of Management and Organization* 16: 411–24.

Richardson, J. (2010). 'Managing flexworkers: The fine art of holding on and letting go'. *Journal of Management Development* 29(2): 137–47.

StatsCanada (2013). Working at home: An update. Available at: www.statcan.gc.ca.

Sullivan, S.E. and M.B. Arthur (2006). 'The evolution of the boundaryless career concept: Examining physical and psychological mobility'. *Journal of Vocational Behaviour* 69(1): 19–29.

Svyantek, D.J., K.L. Cullen and F.L.H. Svyantek (2012). 'Millennial work expectations and organizational incentive systems: "Carrotts" for the new millennium'. In W.I. Sauser and R.R. Sims (eds) *Managing Human Resources for the Millennial Generation*. Charlotte, NC, Information Age Publishing, pp. 53–76.

Taylor, P. and P. Bain (2005). 'India calling to the far away towns: The call centre labour process and globalization'. *Work, Employment and Society* 19(2): 261–82.

Tietze, S., G. Musson and T. Scurry (2009). 'Homebased work: A review of research into themes, directions and implications'. *Personnel Review* 38(6): 585–604.

Tipping, S., J. Chanfreau, J. Perry and C. Tait (2012). 'The Fourth Work–Life Balance Employee Survey', Department for Business Innovation and Skills. URN12/P151.

Towers, I., L. Duxbury, C. Higgins and J. Thomas (2006). 'Time thieves and space invaders: Technology, work and the organization'. *Journal of Organizational Change* 19(5): 593–618.

Tremblay, D.G. (2003). 'Telework: A new mode of gendered segmentation? Results from a study in Canada'. *Canadian Journal of Communication* 28(4): 461–76.

Tremblay, D.G., R. Paquet and E. Najem (2006). 'Telework: A way to balance work and family or an increase in work–family conflict?' *Canadian Journal of Communication* 31(3): 715–31.

Urry, J. (2007). *Mobilities*. Cambridge, Polity Press.

Van Dyne, L., E.E. Kossek and S. Lobel (2007). 'Less need to be there: Cross-level effects of work practices that support work–life flexibility and enhance group processes and group-level OCB'. *Human Relations* 60(8): 1123–54.

Whitehouse, G., C. Diamond and G. Lafferty (2002). 'Assessing the benefits of telework: Australian case study evidence'. *New Zealand Journal of Industrial Relations* 27(3): 257–68.

WorldatWork (2012). *Survey on Workplace Flexibility*. Scottsdale, AZ.

Yanadori, Y. and T. Kato (2009). 'Work and family practices in Japanese firms: Their scope, nature and impact on employee turnover'. *The International Journal of Human Resource Management* 20(2): 439–56.

9 Promoting new norms and true flexibility: sustainability in combining career and care

Claartje J. Vinkenburg, Marloes L. Van Engen and Pascale Peters

INTRODUCTION

In light of current demographic developments and recent technological innovations common to industrialized nations, how to create and promote sustainability in combining career and care is an increasingly important social issue. In this contribution, we focus on the role of societal norms about career and care, rethinking the rhetoric of 'choice' and 'balance' in career decision making (see De Hauw and Greenhaus, Chapter 15, this volume). By exposing, challenging and bending normative beliefs, and by promoting 'true' flexibility, we argue that subjective and objective consequences for individual careers can be optimized, simultaneously improving conditions for giving and receiving care. In this sense, a sustainable combination of care and career requires turning either/or into and/and. And/and is only possible under conditions of 'true flexibility', meaning that flexibilization and customization of work and 'unconventional' choices regarding career and care are not penalized in terms of career outcomes (Leslie et al., 2012).

We start our contribution by conceptualizing sustainability in career and care, by extending an integrative framework that was developed in the editorial of a special issue on 'Sustainability in combining career and care' in the *Journal of Social Issues* (Van Engen et al., 2012; see Figure 9.1). Our premise is that 'choices' of individuals, couples, organizations and policy makers regarding the (facilitation of the) combination of career and care responsibilities are strongly rooted in gendered yet contextualized norms about the roles of men and women in work and care. Following the integrative framework, we show how the reciprocal relationships between beliefs, behaviours and outcomes regarding the work–family interface play out at the societal, organizational and individual level. We illustrate the notions underlying this integrative framework (Van Engen et al., 2012), by focusing on two particular phenomena that have received ample attention, both in the popular press and in academic literature: (a) the phenomenon of part-time work; and (b) flexibility in time and space for work. Taking the Netherlands as a critical case study (Peters, 2011), we argue that policy making on these phenomena might be viewed a blessing for individuals, couples, households, organizations and societies to combine career and care, yet that without exposing and challenging normative gendered beliefs, both part-time work and flexibility pose a threat to sustainability in career and care.

We conclude this chapter by proposing different ways of bending normative beliefs to enhance sustainable careers, and suggesting concrete levers for change for employees, employers and policy makers to promote true flexibility without penalties for those making use of it.

SUSTAINABILITY IN COMBINING CAREER AND CARE

Sustainability or sustainable development refers to meeting present or current needs without compromising the ability to meet future needs (McKenzie-Mohr and Oskamp, 1995; Oskamp, 2000). This responsibility has environmental, economic and social dimensions, linking planet, profit and people (Van Marrewijk and Werre, 2003), as argued elsewhere in this volume (Chapters 10, 21 and 24). While the goal of sustainability is not yet commonly applied to Human Resources Management (Ehnert, 2009), this would imply that employers take the present and future well-being and performance of their employees and their dependents into account. While short-term solutions (using family-friendly arrangements such as taking up care leave, working part-time and teleworking) may sometimes be effective in lessening frictions in combining the daily demands of work and care, potential negative career consequences of using such arrangements require that we take a long-term perspective. Blurring boundaries between work and home on account of technological innovation, in addition to pressing demographic changes, demand a perspective beyond idiosyncratic solutions. We argue that employers need to take up responsibility for creating sustainable employment relationships offering men and women workers room to enhance their employability, their care-giving potential, and consequently their subjective and objective success in both career and care (cf. SER, 2009).

The work–family interface lies at the core of the integrative framework developed by Van Engen et al. (2012), visualizing the interplay of beliefs, behaviours and outcomes at the individual, organizational and societal layers (Figure 9.1), which we will address in more detail below. The work–family interface comprises all (positive and negative) bi-directional influences between the two domains that we label 'career' and 'care'. In our conceptualization, we take a life course and human ecology perspective (cf. Van Engen et al., 2012), moving away from a short-term and individual view on the work–family interface. In this chapter, we will work from the outside in, going from the societal, via the organizational to the individual layer. As normative and gendered beliefs about work, care and flexibility underlie the 'choices' that *all* stakeholders in the labour market make, sustainable careers for men and women alike can only be achieved by critically examining, challenging and changing such beliefs and their impact on decision making and career outcomes.

NORMATIVE BELIEFS ABOUT CAREER AND CARE

In society, individuals share common notions of what attitudes, behaviours and ways of organizing are socially acceptable. These attitudes, behaviours and organizing mechanisms are often guided by normative beliefs (Feldman, 1984). Normative beliefs are influenced by the judgement of important others (for example, parents, spouse, friends, teachers and media) (Ajzen, 1985). In other words, social normative pressures become internalized and guide feelings, actions and behaviours.

Individual decisions about whether or not to use family-friendly arrangements are likely to be influenced by normative beliefs about parenting and gender roles (Cuddy et al., 2004; Fuegen et al., 2004; Marks and Houston, 2002). While being a good father

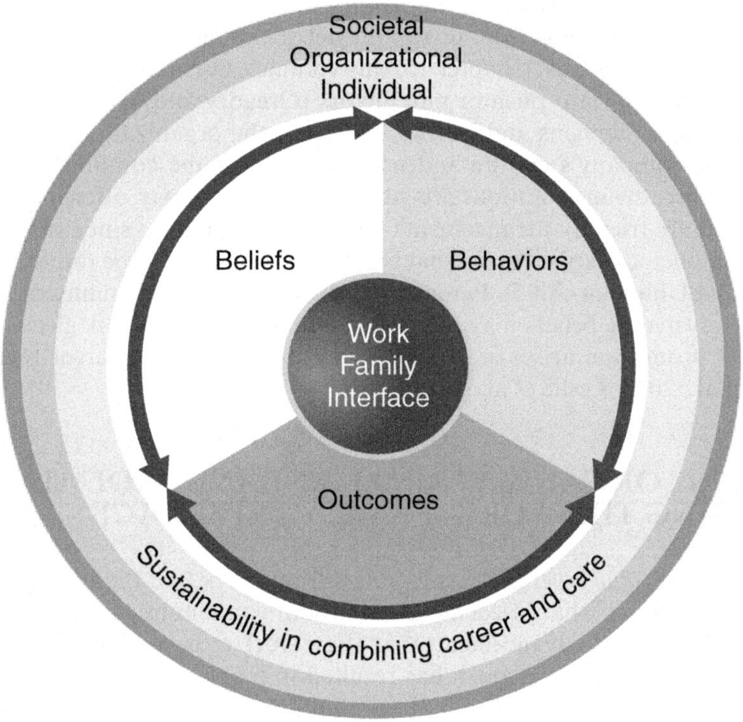

Source: Van Engen et al. (2012), reprinted with permission.

Figure 9.1 Conceptual framework on 'sustainability in combining career and care'

is generally not perceived as incompatible with paid work or a career, earlier research clearly demonstrates ambivalence towards working mothers (for example, Greenberger et al., 1988), the 'maternal wall' (Crosby et al., 2004), and motherhood bias (Heilman and Okimoto, 2008; King, 2008). Motherhood, by its implied communality, results in more incongruence between the female gender role and the work role (Eagly and Karau, 2002; Heilman and Okimoto, 2008), and, consequently, in more negative performance evaluations and lower compensation at work (Crosby et al., 2004; King, 2008). Normative beliefs about care not only describe the ideal mother or father, but also translate into what it means to be a good child, neighbour, or partner, and prescribe how all our caregiving roles shape individual behaviour, attitudes, relationships and identity (Bassin et al., 1994; Van Engen et al., 2009). At the same time, normative beliefs about work and visibility translate into the ideal worker norm (for example, Acker, 1990). The prototypical ideal worker is engaged in full-time paid employment, while unencumbered by family demands or other commitments outside the workplace. This ideal worker norm similarly affects the presence and utilization of family-friendly arrangements (Özbilgin et al., 2011). Furthermore, when we talk about normative beliefs about work and care, we not only refer to the views held by individuals themselves, but also to those expressed by others, such as supervisors, peers or team members, subordinates, family and friends. While the rhetoric of 'choice' dominates the debate about work–family decision-making (De Hauw and Greenhaus, Chapter 15, this volume), normative beliefs about work and care constitute important push or pull factors (Gregory and Milner, 2009; Kossek and Van Dyne, 2008; Stephens and Levine, 2011). At the organizational level, such beliefs may feed the company's culture and norms regarding the combination of career and care. Where breadwinner notions are strong, supervisors may offer mothers more (and different) family-friendly arrangements compared to fathers, since this is more in line with their implicit or explicit belief that mothers are and should be the primary caregivers (Brescoll and Uhlmann, 2005). Parents who disregard such (often unwritten) rules based on others' normative beliefs may risk being 'penalized' by being neglected when opportunities for promotion arise, or as reflected in other negative career-related outcomes (Kossek et al., 2010; Leslie et al., 2012).

SOCIETAL, ORGANIZATIONAL AND INDIVIDUAL LAYERS IN MANAGING THE WORK–FAMILY INTERFACE

Starting at the *societal* layer of the integrative framework (see Figure 9.1), we distinguish two important trends that affect sustainability in combining career and care. The first refers to technological advancements that allow work to be performed more flexibly and across different time zones, which has resulted in more blurry boundaries between the work and the private sphere. Globalization and technological developments have had tremendous impacts on national economies, on how organizations operate, and how work is being organized, with also major implications for employees and their households. Both enhanced global competitiveness and expanding global operations across geographical borders and time zones have not only enabled, but also pressured employees to work anytime, anywhere. Due to the omnipresence of information and the acceleration of business life, telework has become a necessary and unavoidable practice to respond swiftly to market needs and to build an international work community (Kelliher and Richardson, 2012; Peters et al., 2009).

The second trend refers to several important and interconnected demographic developments. First, over the last few decades, female labour force participation has increased strongly in most industrialized countries, despite large cross-country differences in the timing of the increase and level of female participation (Jaumotte, 2003a). As a consequence, the number of dual-earner couples and families has also grown considerably, resulting in new challenges in combining the demands of work and family uncommon to the male breadwinner model (Lewis, 2001). This has led to couples postponing or (unwillingly) declining having children. Fertility rates among OECD countries have declined dramatically over the past few decades, falling from an average of 2.7 children per woman in 1970 to just over 1.7 in 2009 (OECD, 2011), which is well below the replacement level. In combination with low fertility, low mortality rates are leading to ageing populations in most developed countries (Christensen et al., 2009), which implies several challenges for society in terms of not only paying for, but also physically providing care for an increasingly larger part of the population. While many people who live longer are also expected, or even forced, to work longer (OECD, 2006), the main burden of these increasing financial and care responsibilities will lie primarily with younger generations. These demographic developments, common to most industrialized nations, raise the social issue of creating and supporting sustainability in combining demands of career and care. Specifically, whether and how social policies can help improve fertility levels and reduce postponement of childbearing has been the subject of much policy debate at the (inter) national level (Bongaarts, 1998). To help resolve the debate, Ellingsæter (2009) called for comparative studies of the interplay of family-friendly policies with other processes of social change, such as changes on the labour market and changes in gender norms. Clearly, national differences exist in gender roles and government support, laws and policies for combining work and family (Lewis et al., 2008). Several studies have been done that take a cross-national comparative perspective in looking at societal norms, behaviours in terms of using different arrangements, and policies (Lück, 2006; Ray et al., 2010; Sjöberg, 2004; Crompton and Lyonette, 2006) and how these may be related over time. A recent comparison by Daly (2011) of social policy reform across several European countries showed that when norms about work and care remain uncontested, reforms typically promote dual-earner, *gender-specialized* family arrangements, resulting in more rather than less complexity and ambiguity for employers and employees. Paradoxically, social policies supporting a true *individual* adult worker model and work–home arrangements that allow customization depending on individual needs are more likely to generate positive outcomes not only for individual careers but also for dependents.

Although policies and behaviours are embedded in the normative beliefs within countries, showing significant differences in career and care patterns between countries and within countries, the causal direction is clearly bi-directional in the sense that beliefs often follow changes in policies and behaviours (Sjöberg, 2004). This implies that beliefs are not set in stone, and that policy changes can result in sustainable societal outcomes such as higher participation and better representation of women, less poverty, higher fertility, and improved wellbeing of all who work and all who need care.

Looking at the *organizational* layer of the integrative framework (see Figure 9.1), we see that many employers in industrialized nations have adopted family-friendly arrangements (including policies, programmes and benefits), often above and beyond what is legally required by social policies. Many organizations offer a host of different options for parents to choose from, separately or in combination, as an individual, or as a couple. Den Dulk (2001) provided a typology of family-friendly arrangements or organizational work–home policies, distinguishing between flexible work arrangements, leave arrangements, childcare arrangements, and supportive arrangements. Employers often expect that by offering family-friendly arrangements they have an edge in winning the war for talent (Barnett and Hall, 2001), and that they will be perceived in a positive light by important stakeholders (customers as well as future employees) (Casper and Harris, 2007). Relevant organizational outcomes of the presence and utilization of family-friendly arrangements are retention, representation of women at different hierarchical levels, and organizational performance (Kelly et al., 2008). These organizational indicators of careers are affected by the implementation of family-friendly policies and arrangements, which, in turn, are informed by normative beliefs about career and care of employers and supervisors. Allowing unconventional careers and customization may not automatically generate the intended beneficial effects on attrition rates, when underlying notions of a career system tied to a breadwinner model are not challenged (Van Kleef, 2014).

At the *individual* layer of the integrative framework (see Figure 9.1), we focus on the career consequences of the utilization of family-friendly arrangements by parents or others who provide informal care to dependents as our main concern. Gender roles and internalized normative beliefs about care responsibilities may affect the gendered use that care providers make of these arrangements, and many fear negative career consequences and flexibility stigma (Kossek et al., 2010; Leslie et al., 2012; Lyness and Judiesch, 2008; Williams et al., 2013). In particular the behaviour of the direct supervisor, team members and certain aspects of the organizational culture (Thompson et al., 1999) may actively encourage or discourage a gendered utilization of a specific arrangement. This behaviour may also pressure employees to be continuously available via email or phone, which may play a crucial role in supporting and/or hindering employees to combine career and care (see also Frye and Breaugh, 2004; Major et al., 2007; Pederson et al., 2010). Where breadwinner norms or one-and-a-half-income-models are dominant, mothers may feel a strong need to 'choose' to (partly) opt out of a career during the child-bearing and rearing years (Den Dulk, 2005; Orloff, 2006), which may be enabled by their organizations' work–family culture. That very same work–family culture may cause those who work part-time to be perceived as less ambitious which, in the long run, is likely to negatively affect their career advancement (Benschop et al., 2013; Peters et al., 2010). When supervisors make personal life, rather than productivity, attributions for employees' use of flexible arrangements, it is likely to result in career penalties rather than premiums (Leslie et al., 2012).

Hence, both the individual decision regarding whether or not to utilize family-friendly arrangements as well as the consequences of that decision are likely to be influenced by gendered beliefs about ideal workers and ideal parents. These consequences may be ironic or mixed, and depend on the context. As an illustration, mothers are rewarded for trying to adhere to both the ideal mother and the ideal worker norm, whereas fathers who openly combine work and care are penalized (Vinkenburg et al., 2012). Individual career consequences of the (non-)utilization of family-friendly arrangements typically include objective indicators of career success (for example, salary growth and career advancement; see Briscoe and Kellogg, 2011); and subjective indicators of career success (for example, career satisfaction and turnover intentions; see Eby et al., 2005). However, more distal consequences such as the wellbeing of children and other dependents as well as life and marital satisfaction could be included in a long-term perspective on combining career and care. Negative outcomes of combining career and care over time may reinforce traditional (and gendered) notions of the ideal parent and the ideal worker, whereas positive outcomes may challenge and, ultimately, change such beliefs. Of course, not all behaviours will lead to similar outcomes for everyone, which makes it important to consider individual and organizational moderators and mediators of the interplay between beliefs, behaviours and outcomes at the work–family interface.

POLICIES ON PART-TIME WORK AND FLEXIBLE WORKING: THE NETHERLANDS AS A CRITICAL CASE STUDY

In this section, we focus on policies on and utilization of flexible work arrangements in the Netherlands, with part-time work being the most frequently offered arrangement (Plantenga and Remery, 2005). Other common flexible work arrangements are flexible hours (often labelled flextime or flexitime), compressed workweeks (for example, 4 × 9 hours), job sharing, and telecommuting or teleworking (Den Dulk, 2001; Peters, 2011; Plantenga and Remery, 2005).

Part-time Work

Almost ten years ago, Mainiero and Sullivan (2005) mentioned flexibility as a means for organizations to find and retain talented employees.

> By creating more acceptable nontraditional career paths within the firm; by broadening compensation policies to encompass alternative forms of work; by abolishing obsolete norms such as face time, long hours, or travel as a surrogate measure for commitment and promotability; by rewarding managers who provide support to the development of women; and by creating cultures that truly support work/life balance, corporations will have an easier time recruiting, retaining, and shaping talent (Mainiero and Sullivan, 2005: 120).

One of the possible initiatives that Mainiero and Sullivan (2005: 120) suggested was: 'reducing the length of the paid workweek and [. . .] creating quality part-time jobs, with prorated benefits and pension plans.' Mainiero and Sullivan (2005: 120) mentioned the Netherlands as one of the prime examples of those few countries that 'have initiated policies that provide considerable support for working parents.' Indeed, the Netherlands has often been heralded for successfully creating flexible working arrangements that allow employees, particularly parents and others with care responsibilities, to integrate work and personal lives (Plantenga, 1997; Visser, 2002). Repeatedly, the *New York Times* (2010; 2013) has featured the Netherlands when reporting on employees' pleas for more flexibility. However, the career consequences of flexibility in general and part-time work in particular are not always positive. Let us, therefore, focus on flexible work arrangements in the Netherlands, viewed as a critical case study, in which women are known as 'part-time queens of the world' and attention for flexibility is rising (Peters, 2011).

Currently, more than 60.7 per cent of Dutch women work part-time and male part-time work is 18 per cent. The Netherlands has the highest rates of female and male part-time work throughout the OECD countries (OECD, 2012). Far-reaching legislation, for example, the 'Equal Treatment in Working Hours Act', the 'Equal Treatment of Temporary and Permanent Employees Act', and the 'Adjustment of Working Hours Act' (Peters, 2011: 2), also guarantees employees the right to adjust their working hours. The latter Act, introduced in 2000, gives all employees the legal right to adjust their current working hours, either reducing or extending these. As a rule, employers in large and medium-sized enterprises must grant the requested adjustment, unless this can be shown to seriously affect their business interests. Furthermore, a 16-week period of pregnancy and maternity leave is compulsory by law (with wages fully guaranteed), and parental leave is regulated. Clearly, data on labour force participation of women show that smaller part-time jobs allow work and care to be combined, reducing work–life conflict (Peters et al., 2009), which translates into relatively high female labour force participation in the Netherlands (Eurostat, 2015). In an analysis of policies affecting female labour force participation in OECD countries, Jaumotte (2003b) showed that besides other predictors, the share of part-time work in female employment boosts female participation, especially in the Netherlands.

However, as Orloff (2006) argued, one of the downsides of the Dutch model of supporting women's employment through stimulating work–home policies is that it implicitly reproduces maternalism, resulting in sex segregation on the labour market, both by level and by functional area. The so-called 'one-and-a-half income model' in Dutch society persists (Merens and Ross, 2011), at the expense of women's representation in decision-making bodies and higher management. In comparison to the USA, where 43 per cent of all managers, senior officials and legislators are women, in the Netherlands this figure is 27 per cent (Hausmann et al., 2012). Fuchshuber et al. (2004), comparing welfare regimes based on an analysis of ILO and OECD data, showed that among other factors, nations' number of full-time working women has a positive effect on the share of women in managerial positions. Again, the Netherlands stands out. However, over the past decade, besides the category of part-time workers working no more than three days per week, the Netherlands has witnessed the emergence of a 'new' labour-market category of part-time workers working four days per week. In contrast, this new part-time category is no longer exclusively female and may face less severe career consequences, depending on the economic situation. However, part-time work that is less than three days per week is still exclusively associated with women who are care providers, and continues to suffer from negative labour-market connotations (Mescher, 2011), and especially from stereotypical perceptions of reduced or non-existent career ambition (Benschop et al., 2013; Peters et al., 2010).

In the current situation, however, promoting part-time work through policies is a double-edged sword in terms of sustainable careers. On the one hand, it may boost female labour participation by allowing women to combine work and care, but on the other hand the career advancement of women is hindered. In contrast, in the USA, with a lack of social provisions concerning caretaking, but with 'flourishing equal opportunity feminism and their legal and regulatory victories' (Orloff, 2006: 251), women's employment has expanded and sex segregation on the labour market is much smaller.

As a direct consequence of the dominant and normative one-and-a-half-income-model, most Dutch women depend on the income of a partner apart from their own earnings. This is troublesome as currently 37 per cent of marriages in the Netherlands dissolve (Statistics Netherlands, 2014) and women, particularly single mothers, have a higher risk of poverty than men (Poverty Index, 2012). Equally important, Dutch men do not share care responsibilities with their spouses to the extent that some of them may want to. The 'Dutch Labour Force Survey' repeatedly reports that fathers would prefer to work four days a week and share care responsibilities with their partner. Yet in fact fathers with a partner work the most hours, and mothers work the least hours of all (Cloïn and Bierings, 2012). Vinkenburg et al. (2012) showed how normative beliefs about parenting dictate that we continue to applaud mothers – and punish fathers – who equally share career and care responsibilities with their partner by both working reduced hours. These ironic effects, reproducing a one-and-a-half-income-model in favour of an equal-sharing model, can only be resolved if the underlying beliefs are challenged.

Alternative Flexible Work Arrangements

It is because part-time work is so normalized that, up until now, there have been few initiatives in Dutch society aimed at tackling any obstacles to women working more hours and, hence, to stimulate men and women to take up an equal share of work and care. In order to change this situation and enable both women and men to have access to sustainable work and care careers, in 2011 the Dutch Social and Economic Council (SER, 2011) advocated a new 'time-spatial' organization of work and services (for example, schools, child care, council offices, libraries, hospitals, family doctors, dentists and pharmacies). This would allow both men and women to combine paid and private activities on a daily basis and over the life course (Peters, 2011; Van Engen et al., 2009).

In view of this, Dutch policy makers have increasingly pushed flexibility and customization of work arrangements as alternatives for part-time work (Peters, 2011). Flexible work has been called a recipe for career success of ambitious parents (Dikkers et al., 2010). In particular, flexible work arrangements that promote time-spatial flexibility, such as teleworking and New Ways of Working have attracted a lot of attention in the Dutch debate over the last decade. Telework allows employees to perform tasks away from the primary or central work location, for example at home, for part of their work schedule, often using electronic media to interact with others inside and outside the organization (Gajendran and Harrison, 2007). New Ways of Working (NWW) refers to a new job design and has gained particular momentum since the introduction of the concept in 2005 by Microsoft's CEO Bill Gates (Gates, 2005; Peters, 2011; Peters et al., 2014). The idea of NWW is giving employees – within certain limits – room and freedom to decide how, where, when, with what and with whom they work (Bijl, 2009: 27). In the research by Peters et al. (2014), NWW refers to a set of HRM practices reflecting the NWW conditions (that is, employee empowerment, teleworking, and creating trust relationships). In fact, remote working (from home) and the intensified use of IT to collaborate with colleagues associated with NWW may further stimulate the blurring of boundaries, allowing employees to potentially work '24/7' outside of centralized workplaces.

In 2008, the Ministry of Social Affairs and Employment set up a temporary 'Taskforce Part-Time Plus' (2010) aimed to stimulate flexibility and customization rather than part-time work to encourage women (particularly those holding part-time jobs of less than 24 hours per week) to extend their working hours. Women will consider increasing their contractual hours only when their employer offers them flexible working conditions, and even then, only by working two to four more hours per week (Keuzenkamp et al., 2009). An initiative of the Ministry of Education, Culture and Science, called 'Customized Working', therefore, is aiming to stimulate employers to both adopt and foster a culture supporting flexible working and a healthy work–life balance as an integral part of organizational objectives (cf. Peters, 2011). The focus is on all aspects of working life (flexible working, health, informal care, personal development, culture, leave intentions, and so on). The initiative uses self-assessment gauges that indicate whether companies are ahead in this regard based on their HR-practices and work–life culture. Employers judged positively are awarded the quality mark of 'The Modern Employer' and are given 1 to 5 stars, depending on their scores, with 1 being supportive, and 5 being very supportive. The award is assumed to be an important incentive for organizations to address human resource development and gender equality issues in general. Moreover, it is believed that it offers other employers examples of good practice and stimulates or supports employers to include flexible working (currently promoted under the heading of New Forms of Working) (Peters, 2011).

Despite the intentions of the policy initiatives in the Dutch context to stimulate women's labour participation and work–life balance, however, it should be realized that promoting flexibility is not always driven by issues such as gender equality or to facilitate the combination of career and care. Although employers widely acknowledge the gains that telework might have for combining career and care, the prime driver for teleworking appears to be enhanced productivity (Peters and Batenburg, 2014). In fact, due to the empowerment of workers to take responsibility for the outcomes of their work, flexible work environments are often very demanding (Peters et al., 2009; Van Echtelt et al., 2009) and may rather lead to overtime, work–home conflict, unpredictable working hours, permanent accessibility, time competition, job insecurity, or health issues. In view of women's traditional care roles, women (and men) might not feel comfortable in such environments and may even leave the organization (see also Van Echtelt et al., 2009).

Because of deeply rooted norms of ideal workers and ideal care providers, matching 'choices' and career patterns of men and women, policy initiatives such as 'Customized Working' and other forms of customization should particularly monitor any potential gendered (side) effects of flexible working, should stimulate organizations to take gender issues into account and to improve their policies and practices accordingly. Stimulating gender equality and new norms on combining career and care to foster more sustainability for all, regardless of sex, is of utmost importance. This holds especially true in the increasingly flexible and ever-demanding 24/7 work contexts, where the sky has become the limit and work intensification and permanent accessibility is key, due to the loss of traditional checks and balances, such as opening hours and weekends off.

Although flexibility and customization might have the potential to foster sustainability in the combination of career and care for men and women alike, it also demands serious attention from policy makers at all levels (government, social partners, employers, employees, other parties), as it opens up the possibility of rather reproducing traditional gender patterns at the cost of gender equality, even leading to more work–family conflict and threats to sustainability.

LEVERS FOR CHANGE: BENDING NORMATIVE BELIEFS AND PROMOTING TRUE FLEXIBILITY

In previous sections, building on our integrative framework, we exposed normative beliefs concerning the ideal worker and the ideal parent or care provider that affect 'choices' combining career and care, and looked at societal, organizational and individual outcomes. It is important to realize that such normative beliefs are not set in stone across time and place, but are contextual and subject to change (Lück, 2006; Sjöberg, 2004; Crompton and Lyonette, 2006). Bending normative beliefs while being sensitive to the local context is a way forward in promoting sustainable careers. Here we distinguish three different ways in which society, organizations and individuals can contribute to bending norms affecting the work–family interface in a more sustainable direction: by focusing on trailblazers, by talking differently and openly negotiating norms, and by promoting true flexibility.

First, we need to focus our attention on trailblazers: the small but growing numbers of men and women in most industrialized nations that more or less equally share career and care responsibilities and thus defy traditional notions of breadwinners and caretakers. For the diffusion of innovation, putting the beneficial consequences of this constellation for careers, couples and children of such early adopters in the spotlight is a simple 'trick' that marketing communication specialists and organizational change agents have long discovered (Rogers, 1962; Zimmerman, 2004). Such 'learning by seeing' inspirational role models have the added benefit of reflecting on otherwise implicit norms, and making room for alternative 'choices'. Future research on trailblazers, instead of the majority of the population, is important, but perhaps portraying and profiling such trailblazers in the media is much more instrumental in bending norms.

Second, we need to realize that language is a crucial tool for promoting new norms. Rather than reproducing and normalizing traditional norms, particularly in the popular media, we invite journalists to ask questions about combining career and care to men and women politicians, CEOs, athletes and actors. The 'drench' effect of a positive role model who demonstrates this new behaviour can be a source of inspiration for those who write and produce television series and movies (Reep and Dambrot, 1989). In addition, openly negotiating norms by talking differently and more equally to colleagues, family members, friends and neighbours about men and women who care and work is something we all can do (Herschberg et al., 2014).

Third, we argue that organizational practices and policies can be improved to promote true flexibility, reflecting an individual adult worker model rather than gender-specialized arrangements (Daly, 2011), by acknowledging the realities of all employees with care responsibilities, and by not penalizing customization or 'unconventional' career and care choices. For example, by compensating for 'time to care' in performance evaluation and output assessment, employers can sustain performance, bend normative beliefs, and change organizational cultures into one where employees openly dare to care (Herschberg et al., 2014).

IN CONCLUSION

This chapter started from a conceptual integrative framework on sustainability in combining career and care. To facilitate long-term solutions to all who are faced with the challenge of combining work and care responsibilities, and in this sense promote sustainability, we argue that it is of vital importance to expose, challenge and renegotiate underlying normative beliefs, both in future research and in practice. Such normative beliefs pertain not only to gender roles, but also to the notions of ideal workers, permanent accessibility, visibility and presenteeism. Understanding the importance of reframing and bending norms and beliefs requires continued attention to language, images, assumptions and conventions that reproduce and normalize the way we tend to manage the work–family interface. However, promoting true flexibility, openly negotiating norms, and showcasing trailblazers in studies, corporate communication and the media generates insight into alternative choices and win–win solutions for various stakeholders. This asks for double-loop learning, recalibrating the standard, moving beyond fixing, and creating truly inclusive cultures for all who work and care.

ACKNOWLEDGEMENTS

This *Handbook* chapter is an adaptation and integration of earlier work published as: Van Engen, M.L., C.J. Vinkenburg and J.S.E. Dikkers (2012), 'Sustainability in combining career and care: challenging normative beliefs about parenting', *Journal of Social Issues*, **68** (4), 645–64; Dikkers, J.S.E., M.L. Van Engen and C.J. Vinkenburg (2010), 'Flexible work: ambitious parents' recipe for career success in the Netherlands', *Career Development International*, **15** (6), 562–82; and Peters, P. (2011), 'Flexible working time arrangements: exchange of good practice', Discussion Paper, the Netherlands, available at: http://ec.europa.eu/justice/gender-equality/tools/good-practices/index_en.htm.

REFERENCES

Acker, J. (1990), 'Hierarchies, jobs, bodies: a theory of gendered organizations', *Gender and Society*, **4** (2), 139–58.

Ajzen, I. (1985), 'From intentions to actions: a theory of planned behavior', in J. Kuhl and J. Beckmann (eds), *Action Control: From Cognition to Behavior*, Heidelberg: Springer, pp. 11–39.

Barnett, R.C. and D.T. Hall (2001), 'How to use reduced hours to win the war for talent', *Organizational Dynamics*, **29** (3), 192–210.

Bassin, D., M. Honey and M.M. Kaplan (1994), *Representations of Motherhood*, New Haven, CT: Yale University Press.

Benschop, Y., M. Van den Brink, H. Doorewaard and J. Leenders (2013), 'Discourses of ambition, gender and part-time work', *Human Relations*, **66** (5), 699–723.

Bijl, D. (2009), 'Aan de slag met het nieuwe werken', available at http://www.aandeslagmethnw.nl/Libraries/Boek_concepten/Aan_de_slag_met_Het_Nieuwe_Werken_pdf.sflb.ashx [in Dutch].

Bongaarts, J. (1998), 'Demographic consequences of declining fertility', *Science*, **282** (5388), 419–20.

Brescoll, V.L. and E.L. Uhlmann (2005), 'Attitudes toward traditional and non-traditional parents', *Psychology of Women Quarterly*, **29** (4), 436–45.

Briscoe, F. and K.C. Kellogg (2011), 'The initial assignment effect: local employer practices and positive career outcomes for work–family program users', *American Sociological Review*, **76** (2), 291–319.

Casper, W.J. and C.M. Harris (2007), 'Work–life benefits and organizational attachment: Self-interest utility and signaling theory models', *Journal of Vocational Behavior*, **72** (1), 95–109.

Christensen, K., G. Doblhammer, R. Rau and J.W. Vaupel (2009), 'Ageing populations: The challenges ahead', *The Lancet*, **374** (9696), 1196–208.

Cloïn, M. and H. Bierings (2012), 'De combinatie van betaalde arbeid en zorgtaken', in A.Merens, M. Hartgers and M. Van den Brakel (eds), *Emancipatiemonitor 2012*, The Hague: Sociaal en Cultureel Planbureau and Centraal Bureau voor de Statistiek.

Crompton, R. and C. Lyonette (2006), 'Work–life "balance" in Europe', *Acta Sociologica*, **49** (4), 379–93.

Crosby, F.J., J.C. Williams and M. Biernat (2004), 'The maternal wall', *Journal of Social Issues*, **60** (4), 675–82.

Cuddy, A.J.C., S.T. Fiske and P. Glick (2004), 'When professionals become mothers, warmth doesn't cut the ice', *Journal of Social Issues*, **60**, 701–18.

Daly, M. (2011), 'What adult worker model? A critical look at recent social policy reform in Europe from a gender and family perspective', *Social Politics: International Studies in Gender, State and Society*, **18** (1), 1–23.

Den Dulk, L. (2001), *Work–Family Arrangements in Organizations. A Cross-National Study in the Netherlands,*

Italy, the United Kingdom and Sweden, PhD thesis, University of Amsterdam, Amsterdam: Rozenburg Publishers.

Den Dulk, L. (2005), 'Workplace work–family arrangements: a study and explanatory framework of differences between organizational provisions in different welfare states', in S.A.Y. Poelmans (ed.), *Work and Family: An International Research Perspective*, Mahwah, NJ: Lawrence Erlbaum, pp. 211–38.

Dikkers, J.S.E., M.L. Van Engen and C.J. Vinkenburg (2010), 'Flexible work: ambitious parents' recipe for career success in the Netherlands', *Career Development International*, **15** (6), 562–82.

Eagly, A.H. and S.J. Karau (2002), 'Role congruity theory of prejudice toward female leaders', *Psychological Review*, **109**, 573–98.

Eby, L.T., W.J. Casper, A. Lockwood, C. Bordeaux and A. Brinley (2005), 'Work and family research in IO/OB: Content analysis and review of the literature (1980–2002)', *Journal of Vocational Behavior*, **66** (1), 124–97.

Ehnert, I. (2009), *Sustainable Human Resource Management: A Conceptual and Exploratory Analysis from a Paradox Perspective*, Berlin-Heidelberg: Physica-Verlag HD.

Ellingsæter, A.L. (2009), 'Leave policy in the Nordic welfare states: a "recipe" for high employment/high fertility?', *Community, Work and Family*, **12** (1), 1–19.

Eurostat (2015), 'Employment rates', available at http://appsso.eurostat.ec.europa.eu.

Feldman, D.C. (1984), 'The development and enforcement of group norms', *Academy of Management Review*, **9** (1), 47–53.

Frye, N.K. and J.A. Breaugh (2004), 'Family-friendly policies, supervisor support, work–family conflict, family–work conflict, and satisfaction: A test of a conceptual model', *Journal of Business and Psychology*, **19** (2), 197–220.

Fuchshuber, E., L. Den Dulk and A. Van Doorne-Huiskes (2004), 'Explanations for differences in women's representation in managerial positions across countries: The impact of welfare states', paper presented at EIASM workshop on female managers, entrepreneurs and the social capital of the firm, Brussels.

Fuegen, K., M. Biernat, E. Haines and K. Deaux (2004), 'Mothers and fathers in the workplace: How gender and parental status influence judgments of job-related competence', *Journal of Social Issues*, **60** (4), 737–54.

Gajendran, R.S. and D.A. Harrison (2007), 'The good, the bad, and the unknown about telecommuting: Meta-analysis of psychological mediators and individual consequences', *Journal of Applied Psychology*, **92** (6), 1524–41.

Gates, W. (2005), 'The new world of work', available at http://www.microsoft.com/mscorp/execmail/2005/05-19newworldofwork.mspx. (accessed 3 April 2011).

Greenberger, E., W.A. Goldberg, T.J. Crawford and J. Granger (1988), 'Beliefs about the consequences of maternal employment for women', *Psychology of Women Quarterly*, **12**, 35–59.

Gregory, A. and S. Milner (2009), 'Editorial: Work–life balance: A matter of choice?', *Gender, Work and Organization*, **16** (1), 1–13.

Hausmann, R., L.D. Tyson and S. Zahidi (2012), The Global Gender Gap Report, World Economic Forum, available at http://www3.weforum.org/docs/WEF_GenderGap_Report_2012.pdf.

Heilman, M.E. and T.G. Okimoto (2008), 'Motherhood: A potential source of bias in employment decisions', *Journal of Applied Psychology*, **93** (1), 189–98.

Herschberg, C., C.J. Vinkenburg, I.L. Bleijenbergh and M.L. Van Engen (2014), 'Dare to care: Negotiating organizational norms on combining career and care in an engineering faculty', in D. Bilimoria and L. Lord (eds), *Women in STEM Careers: International Perspectives on Increasing Workforce Participation, Advancement and Leadership*, Cheltenham, UK and Northampton, MA, USA: Edward Elgar.

Jaumotte, F. (2003a), 'Female labour force participation: Past trends and main determinants in OECD countries', Organisation for Economic Co-operation and Development (OECD) Economics Department Working Papers No. 376.

Jaumotte, F. (2003b), 'Labour force participation of women: Empirical evidence on the role of policy and other determinants in OECD countries', *OECD Economic Studies*, **37** (2), 51–108.

Kelliher, C. and J. Richardson (2012), *New Ways of Organizing Work, Developments, Perspectives and Experiences*, New York: Routledge.

Kelly, E.L., E. Kossek, L.B. Hammer, M. Durham, J. Bray, K. Chermack, L.A. Murphy and D. Kaskubar (2008), 'Getting there from here: Research on the effects of work–family initiatives on work–family conflict and business outcomes', *The Academy of Management Annals*, **2** (1), 305–49.

Keuzenkamp, S., C. Hillebrink, W. Portegijs and B. Pouwels (2009), *Deeltijd (g)een Probleem: Mogelijkheden om de Arbeidsduur van Vrouwen met een Kleine Deeltijdbaan te Vergroten*, The Hague: SCP.

King, E.B. (2008), 'The effect of bias on the advancement of working mothers: Disentangling legitimate concerns from inaccurate stereotypes as predictors of advancement in academe', *Human Relations*, **61** (12), 1677–711.

Kossek, E.E. and L. Van Dyne (2008), 'Face-time matters: A cross level model of how work–life flexibility influences work performance of individuals and groups', in K. Korabik, D.S. Lero and D.L. Whitehead

(eds), *Handbook of Work–Family Integration: Research, Theory, and Best Practices*, San Diego, CA: Elsevier, pp. 305–30.
Kossek, E.E., S. Lewis and L.B. Hammer (2010), 'Work–life initiatives and organizational change: Overcoming mixed messages to move from the margin to the mainstream', *Human Relations*, **63** (1), 3–19.
Leslie, L.M., C.F. Manchester, T.Y. Park and S.A. Mehng (2012), 'Flexible work practices: A source of career premiums or penalties?', *Academy of Management Journal*, **55** (6), 1407–28.
Lewis, J. (2001), 'The decline of the male breadwinner model: Implications for work and care', *Social Politics: International Studies in Gender, State and Society*, **8** (2), 152–69.
Lewis, J., T. Knijn, C. Martin and I. Ostner (2008), 'Patterns of development in work/family reconciliation policies for parents in France, Germany, the Netherlands, and the UK in the 2000s', *Social Politics: International Studies in Gender, State and Society*, **15** (3), 261–86.
Lück, D. (2006), 'The impact of gender role attitudes on women's life courses', in Hans-Peter Blossfeld and Heather Hofmeister (eds), *Globalization, Uncertainty and Women's Careers: An International Comparison*, Cheltenham, UK and Northampton, MA, USA: Edward Elgar.
Lyness, K.S. and M.K. Judiesch (2008), 'Can a manager have a life and career? International and multisource perspectives on work–life balance and career advancement potential', *Journal of Applied Psychology*, **93** (4), 789–805.
Mainiero, L.A. and S.E. Sullivan (2005), 'Kaleidoscope careers: An alternative explanation for the "opt-out" revolution', *Academy of Management Executive*, **19** (1), 106–23.
Major, D.B., T.D. Fletcher, D.D. Davis and L.M. Germano (2007), 'The influence of work–family culture and workplace relations on work interference with family: A multilevel model', *Journal of Organizational Behavior*, **29** (7), 881–97.
Marks, G. and D.M. Houston (2002), 'Attitudes towards work and motherhood held by working and non-working mothers', *Work, Employment & Society*, **16** (3), 523–36.
McKenzie-Mohr, D. and S. Oskamp (1995), 'Psychology and sustainability: An introduction', *Journal of Social Issues*, **51** (4), 1–14.
Merens, J.G.F. and J.A. Ross (2011), *Emancipatiemonitor 2010*, Sociaal en Cultureel Planbureau.
Mescher, S. (2011), 'Ambiguities in work–life balance support', PhD thesis, Radboud University, Nijmegen.
New York Times (2010), 'Working (part-time) in the 21st century', available at: http://www.nytimes.com/2010/12/30/world/europe/30iht-dutch30.html.
New York Times (2013), 'Sunday dialogue: flexible work hours', available at: http://www.nytimes.com/2013/01/20/opinion/sunday/sunday-dialogue-flexible-work-hours.html.
OECD (2006), *Live Longer, Work Longer*, Paris: OECD Publishing.
OECD (2011), *Doing Better for Families*, Paris: OECD Publishing.
OECD (2012), 'Incidence of FTPT employment', available at: http://stats.oecd.org/Index.aspx?DatasetCode=FTPTC_I.
Orloff, A.S. (2006), 'From maternalism to "employment for all": State policies to promote women's employment across the affluent democracies', in J.D. Levy (ed.), *The State after Statism: New State Activities in the Age of Liberalization*, Cambridge, MA: Harvard University Press, pp. 230–368.
Oskamp, S. (2000), 'Psychology of promoting environmentalism: Psychological contributions to achieving an ecologically sustainable future for humanity', *Journal of Social Issues*, **56** (3), 373–90.
Özbilgin, M.F., T.A. Beauregard, A. Tatli and M.P. Bell (2011), 'Work–life, diversity and intersectionality: A critical review and research agenda', *International Journal of Management Reviews*, **13**, 177–98.
Pederson, D.E., K.L. Minnotte and S.E. Mannon (2010), 'Getting by with a little help from workplace friends: Workplace culture, social support and family cohesion', *Marriage and Family Review*, **46** (6–7), 400–419.
Peters, P. (2011), 'Flexible working time arrangements: Exchange of good practice', Discussion Paper, the Netherlands, available at http://ec.europa.eu/justice/gender-equality/tools/good-practices/index_en.htm.
Peters, P. and R. Batenburg (2014, forthcoming), 'Telework adoption and formalization in organizations from a knowledge transfer perspective', *International Journal of Work Innovation* (www.inderscience.com/ijwi).
Peters, P., I. Bleijenbergh and E. Oldenkamp (2009), 'Cultural sources of variance in telework adoption in two subsidiaries of an ICT-multinational', *International Journal of Employment Studies*, **17** (2), 66–101.
Peters, P., L. Den Dulk and T. Van der Lippe (2009), 'The effects of time-spatial flexibility and new working conditions on employees' work–life balance: The Dutch case', Special issue edited by J. Haar, *Community, Work and Family*, **12** (3), 279–98.
Peters, P., I. Bleijenbergh, B. Pas and I. Gremmen (2010), 'De deeltijdval: Beeldvorming over ambitie en deeltijdwerk bij Nederlandse vrouwen en hun leidinggevenden. Themanummer Betaald Werk', *Tijdschrift voor Genderstudies*, **13** (4), 21–32.
Peters, P., E. Poutsma, B.I.J.M. Van der Heijden, A.B. Bakker and T. De Bruijn (2014), 'Enjoying new ways to work: An HRM-process approach to study flow', *Human Resource Management*, **53** (2), 271–90.
Plantenga, J. (1997), 'Part-time work in the Netherlands: facts, figures and policies', in M. Klein (ed.),

Part-time Work in Europe: Gender, Jobs and Opportunities, Frankfurt/Main and New York: Campus Verlag, pp. 151–67.

Plantenga, J. and C. Remery (2005), 'Reconciliation of work and private life: A comparative review of thirty European countries', EGGSIE report for the European Commission, available at http://www.mbs.ac.uk/research/europeanemployment/projects/gendersocial/publications.aspx (accessed 27 September 2007).

Poverty Index (2012), 'Armoedesignalement 2012' ['Poverty index 2012'], The Hague: Sociaal en Cultureel Planbureau and Centraal Bureau voor de Statistiek, available at: http://www.cbs.nl/NR/rdonlyres/21B02627-A155-4E33-A660-C12FBA856211/0/2012armoedesignalement.pdf.

Ray, R., J.C. Gornick and J. Schmitt (2010), 'Who cares? Assessing generosity and gender equality in parental leave policy designs in 21 countries', *Journal of European Social Policy*, **20** (3), 196–216.

Reep, D.C. and F.H. Dambrot (1989), 'Effects of frequent television viewing on stereotypes: "Drip, drip" or "drench"?', *Journalism and Mass Communication Quarterly*, **66** (3), 542–56.

Rogers, E.M. (1962), *Diffusion of Innovations*, New York: The Free Press.

SER (2009), *Een Kwestie van Gezond Verstand: Breed Preventiebeleid binnen Arbeidsorganisaties*, The Hague: Sociaal Economische Raad.

SER (2011), *Tijden van de Samenleving: Slimmer Organiseren van Tijd en Plaats van Arbeid en Dienstverlening*, The Hague: Sociaal Economische Raad.

Sjöberg, O. (2004), 'The role of family policy institutions in explaining gender-role attitudes: A comparative multilevel analysis of thirteen industrialized countries', *Journal of European Social Policy*, **14** (2), 107–23.

Statistics Netherlands (2014), 'Huwelijksontbindingen', available at: http://statline.cbs.nl/StatWeb/publication/?VW=T&DM=SLNL&PA=37425ned&D1=3-9&D2=(l-11)-l&HD=100526-0713&STB=G1,T.

Stephens, N.M. and C.S. Levine (2011), 'Opting out or denying discrimination? How the framework of free choice in American society influences perceptions of gender inequality', *Psychological Science*, **22** (10), 1231–6.

Taskforce Part-Time Plus (2010), 'De discussie voorbij. Eindrapport Taskforce DeeltijdPlus', The Hague: Ministerie van Sociale Zaken en Werkgelegenheid.

Thompson, C.A., L.L. Beauvais and K.S. Lyness (1999), 'When work–family benefits are not enough: The influence of work–family culture on benefit utilization, organizational attachment, and work–family conflict', *Journal of Vocational Behavior*, **54**, 392–415.

Van Echtelt, P., A. Glebbeek, S. Lewis and S. Lindenberg (2009), 'Post-Fordist work: A man's world?: Gender and working overtime in the Netherlands', *Gender and Society*, **23**, 188–214.

Van Engen, M.L., C.J. Vinkenburg and J.S.E. Dikkers (2012), 'Sustainability in combining career and care: Challenging normative beliefs about parenting', *Journal of Social Issues*, **68** (4), 645–64.

Van Engen, M.L., J.S.E. Dikkers, C.J. Vinkenburg and E. de Rooy (2009), 'Carrièresucces van vaders en moeders: De rol van moederschapsideologie, werk-thuis-cultuur en werk-thuis-arrangementen', *Gedrag en Organisatie*, **22** (2), 146–71.

Van Kleef, Marco C. (2014), 'Customizing careers: De impact van een loopbaan op maat', PhD thesis, VU University Amsterdam.

Van Marrewijk, M. and M. Werre (2003), 'Multiple levels of corporate sustainability', *Journal of Business Ethics*, **44** (2), 107–19.

Vinkenburg, C.J., M.L. Van Engen, J. Coffeng and J.S.E. Dikkers (2012), 'Bias in employment decisions about mothers and fathers: The (dis)advantages of sharing care responsibilities', *Journal of Social Issues*, **68**, 725–41.

Visser, J. (2002), 'The first part-time economy in the world: A model to be followed?', *Journal of European Social Policy*, **12** (1), 23–42.

Williams, J.C., M. Blair-Loy and J.L. Berdahl (2013), 'Cultural schemas, social class, and the flexibility stigma', *Journal of Social Issues*, **69**, 209–34.

Zimmerman, J. (2004), 'Leading organizational change is like climbing a mountain', *The Educational Forum*, **68** (3), 234–42.

10 Sustainable labour participation and sustainable careers

Judith H. Semeijn, Karen Van Dam, Tinka Van Vuuren and Beatrice I.J.M. Van der Heijden

INTRODUCTION

Over the past decades, the context of work has changed dramatically; global developments and some severe crises (Gratton, 2011) in combination with demographic changes (Eurostat, 2013) and changing work relations (see, for example, Katz et al., 2004) have forced and inspired us to think about more sustainable solutions and goals for work. Moreover, these changes have led towards an increasing scholarly interest in concepts and perspectives in which sustainability is a key issue. For example, governmental institutions have integrated sustainability in their policies, such as those promoted by the European Commission (EC, 2013). Similarly, scholars and practitioners in the field of management and organization have contributed to the increasing attention in both research and practice by attaching major significance to concepts such as Corporate Social Responsibility (CSR) (Lindgreen and Swaen, 2010) and sustainable Human Resource Management (HRM) (see, for example, Ehnert and Wes, 2012). CSR refers to a process of continuous improvement in which companies voluntarily and systematically integrate economic (profit), environmental (planet) and social considerations (people) into their overall business operations (Brundtland Commission, 1987). In line with these considerations, the sustainable labour participation of individual workers is currently a major topic of concern (for example, De Lange et al., forthcoming).

The primary objective of this chapter is to provide more insight into the concept of sustainable labour participation and to explore important factors at the micro and meso level that might stimulate or impede individuals' and organizations' efforts to bring sustainable labour participation within reach. By providing a conceptual framework for (micro-level) sustainable labour participation, accompanied by an overview of important antecedents (at the micro and meso level), this chapter aims to contribute to theory development in the scholarly field of sustainable careers. Moreover, this chapter has practical relevance. For many organizations, it is still difficult to obtain a more sustainable perspective, that is, a perspective that is explicitly including the longer-term interests for not only the organization itself (profit), but also for employees (people) and diverse stakeholders (planet) as well (for the three P's, see Fisk, 2010). The insights from this chapter may therefore also contribute to a better understanding of what employers and employees can do to realize more sustainable organizational practices.

Specifically, in this chapter, we will first explore the concept of sustainable labour participation by further elaborating on its three components: employability, vitality and work ability. Next, an overview of antecedents of sustainable labour participation at different levels will be given: individual characteristics, task and socio-environmental characteristics, and organizational characteristics. After this overview, conclusions will be drawn on the available knowledge, and consequences for sustainable careers are considered. Finally, avenues for further research will be explored, and more practical implications for organizations will be discussed.

SUSTAINABLE LABOUR PARTICIPATION: CONCEPTUALIZATION AND OPERATIONALIZATION

In the literature, several conceptualizations of sustainable labour participation have been proposed. Van der Klink et al. (2010) noted that the concept of sustainable labour participation refers to a continuous availability of achievable possibilities and conditions to (continuously) function in current and future work, while keeping healthy and fit. Van Vuuren (2011; 2012) defined sustainable labour participation as the extent to which people are able and willing to conduct their current and future work. In scholarly literature, three specific aspects have been distinguished that are considered to reflect employees' sustainable labour participation, referring to workers' employability, vitality, and work ability (De Lange and Van der Heijden, 2013; Van Vuuren, 2011; 2012). In this chapter, we will adhere to this distinction, which is further sustained by the Dutch Social and Economic Council (SER) (2009), reflecting its relevance for policies aimed at sustainable labour participation and for organizational practice.

Sustainable labour participation can be considered a multi-disciplinary conceptual framework that includes employees, their work, employers, HRM, and broader stakeholders (see also Van der Klink et al., 2011). This concept can be viewed from various angles that are related to, or include, different levels of analysis, that is the macro (political, economic and societal), meso (organizational or firm-related), and micro (individual) levels (De Lange and Van der Heijden, 2013). In this chapter, we will focus on the concept of sustainable labour participation as defined at the individual level, in terms of workers' sustainable employability, vitality and work ability. Although this focus refers to a micro-level perspective, we will take both micro and meso-level factors into account (the individual and his/her direct organizational work environment) that might affect these individual (micro) level outcomes. More specifically, we intend to discuss factors that are in the sphere of influence of employees and employers; therefore, macro-level factors will not be included in the context of this chapter.

Employability, the first aspect of sustainable labour participation, refers to individuals' ability to adequately fulfil work in their current and future jobs (Van der Heijden, 2011; Van Vuuren, 2011). As such, employability is considered to be important for dealing with job insecurity (see, for example, De Cuyper et al., 2009). In research, different approaches to employability can be found (Berntson et al., 2006). The competence-based approach views employability in terms of different competencies, skills and other attributes that are necessary for employees to sustain their labour participation (Van der Heijde and Van der Heijden, 2006). For instance, Fugate et al. (2004) argued that employability encompasses four aspects: career identity, personal adaptability, and social and human capital. Similarly, Van der Heijde and Van der Heijden (2006) developed a five-dimensional conceptualization of employability: occupational expertise, anticipation and optimization, personal flexibility, corporate sense, and balance. These authors added that, in the case of a lack of employment or fear of losing one's job, employability includes the ability to *create* work through the optimal use of available competencies. In general, the competence-based approach to employability stresses the importance of continuous learning and expertise development for two reasons: first, as a necessity to meet the changing needs of organizations, and, secondly, to realize personal aspirations and potential in work (De Vos et al., 2011; Van der Heijde and Van der Heijden, 2006).

Another approach to employability focuses on workers' opportunities to move into and within, or across, the labour market (McQuaid and Linsday, 2005). In this case, employability is viewed in terms of either subjective perceptions or objective indicators of employees' opportunities in the labour market (for example, Berntson et al., 2006; De Cuyper et al., 2011). Rothwell and Arnold (2007), for instance, defined perceived employability as the individual's beliefs about how easy it is to find new employment. As De Cuyper et al. (2011) have noted, this conceptualization of employability parallels previous theoretical and empirical developments concerning perceived ease of movement (March and Simon, 1958), and perceived job alternatives (Griffeth and Hom, 1988). In addition to subjective perceptions of labour market opportunities, researchers have looked at more objective indicators of workers' employability, that is, in terms of *actual obtained* work or jobs (Forrier and Sels, 2003). In this case, the number of career steps or realized mobility have been used as indicators of workers' employability.

Vitality, the second aspect of sustainable labour participation, refers to being able to work in an energetic, resilient, tireless, fit and persistent manner (Bakker et al., 2008). In previous literature, vitality has often been described and studied as an element of work engagement, next to absorption and dedication (Schaufeli and Bakker, 2007). According to Van Vuuren (2011), vitality is a combination of being energetic and motivated. In general, vitality is considered to indicate employees' intrinsic motivation for their work (Bakker et al., 2008). Earlier, Ryan and Frederick (1997) referred to the conceptual relationship between vitality and organismic wellness, including both psychological well-being and physical health. Vitality implies a certain amount of self-reinforcement; vital people tend to engage in activities that enhance their feelings of aliveness and being active (Kark and Carmeli, 2009; Ryan and Bernstein, 2004).

Work ability, the third aspect of sustainable labour participation, refers to the physical, psychological and sociological ability of people to work (Ilmarinen et al., 2005). It closely aligns with the notion and meaning of health, as put forward by the World Health Organization: 'Health is a state of complete physical, mental and social well-being and not merely the absence of disease or infirmity' (WHO, 1948). Since the bases for work ability are health and functional capacity, work ability has also been defined as 'the degree to which an employee, given his health, physically and mentally is able to meet the demands of the work' (Van den Berg, 2010, p. 135). Otherwise stated, work ability is built on the balance between a person's resources and work demands (Ilmarinen, 2005). Whereas employability can be mostly associated with competence, and vitality with energy and motivation, work ability puts the largest focus on health and functional capacity.

Now that we have differentiated between the main aspects of the concept of sustainable labour participation and their common operationalizations, the next section will elaborate on important antecedents of sustainable labour participation.

ANTECEDENTS OF EMPLOYEES' SUSTAINABLE LABOUR PARTICIPATION

In order to enhance sustainable labour participation, it is important to better understand the factors that contribute to workers' employability, vitality and work ability. In the literature, possible antecedents of these three aspects of sustainable labour participation have been studied at several levels, relating to characteristics of the individual, his or her task and social work environment, the organization, and society as a whole. The next sections will provide an overview of some important antecedents at the micro and meso level that may facilitate or hinder employees' sustainable labour participation. In this sense, these antecedents can be interpreted as job resources versus job demands, as put forward by the *Job Demands-Resources (JD-R) Model*, developed in the field of occupational health (Demerouti et al., 2001; Bakker and Demerouti, 2007). This model is often used to distinguish strain factors (that is, job demands) and motivational factors (that is, job resources) in employees' work situation. Some antecedents actually originate from the literature on this model, while other factors originate from different theoretical notions. The antecedents are: age, health, personal resources, task characteristics, social-environmental characteristics, and finally, culture and HR practices in organizations.

Individual Characteristics

Age

Related to an ageing workforce, researchers have set out to investigate age-related changes in older employees. Although ageing is often associated with general decline, previous empirical findings have indicated that this assumption is too simple and therefore misleading (Kanfer and Ackerman, 2004). On the one hand, reviews outline that there is little evidence that performance and motivation decrease with employees' age (Kanfer et al., 2013). On the other hand, it is well-established that there is a gradual decline in cognitive abilities, starting in the early twenties, and continuing over the lifespan, which especially affects the intellectual abilities associated with working memory, attention, and the processing of novel information (Salthouse, 2011). One explanation for why this decline in so-called fluid intelligence does not impair performance points to an increase in accumulated experiential knowledge (or crystallized intelligence) (Ackerman, 1996; Cattell, 1963). This combination of declined fluid intelligence and increased crystallized intelligence also explains why older employees can experience more difficulty when learning completely new material compared to learning materials that match their previous knowledge (Warr, 2001). Other explanations hold that employees rarely need to perform at their cognitive maximum, that cognition is not the only determinant of performance, and that employees make age-related accommodations in their work situation (Salthouse, 2011). Still, as cognitive capacities decline with age, the cognitive costs of performing at the same level will increase (Kanfer and Ackerman, 2004). Consequently, long working hours will exhaust older workers more in comparison with younger workers, while older workers might also have a greater need for recovery (Kiss, De Meester, and Braeckman, 2008). Given these differences between older workers and their younger counterparts, it is possible that age-related changes can endanger employees' sustainable labour participation, in all three aspects (employability, vitality and work ability). Yet, as Warr (2001) notes, the variability between older workers is large (see also Chapter 20 in this volume). Therefore, it is difficult to draw any valid inference about a specific employee's cognitive functioning based on age alone.

Health

Van den Berg (2010) showed that good health is an important antecedent for sustainable labour participation, especially related to work ability (see also Chapter 17 in this volume). Health may affect restrictions regarding work ability, depending on the requirements of the work at hand and the specific capabilities of the individual worker. In a large-scale study among construction and other workers, Burdorf and Elders (2007) found that diseases and health conditions, from all types of antecedents, had the largest impact on employees' work ability. In a systematic review by Van den Berg et al. (2009), lack of physical activity, poor musculoskeletal capacity and obesity appeared to be individual health factors that were associated with poor work ability, as defined by the Work Ability Index (WAI) (Ilmarinen, 2005). Besides obesity, other chronic diseases, such as diabetes, lung diseases, some forms of cancer and heart disease, might also affect the working population. These factors are more prevalent among older workers, and are responsible for over half the deaths in the world (Suhrcke et al., 2006). As regards employability and vitality, health effects are significant as well, since health problems can negatively affect workers' employability (for example, Hamilton et al., 1997) and undermine their vitality (Ryan and Frederick, 1997; Schaufeli and Bakker, 2007; 2010).

Personal resources

Evidence indicates that employees' personal resources are important antecedents of sustainable labour participation. Personal resources are positive state-like human strengths that function as a means of dealing with the world (Hobfoll, 2002). Research has generally shown that personal resources are important for handling change, uncertainties and work stress (Luthans et al., 2007; Van Dam, 2013). Different personal resources have been investigated, including the four resources that are known as 'psychological capital' (PsyCap) (Luthans et al., 2007): hope, resilience, optimism and self-efficacy. Hope refers to a positive motivational state that is based on a sense of successful agency (goal-directed energy) and pathways to meet goals (Snyder et al., 1991). Resilience is generally defined as the capacity to bounce back from adversity, conflict and failure or even positive events (Luthans et al., 2007). Optimism refers to a positive outcome outlook in which positive events are attributed to personal, permanent and pervasive causes and negative events to external, temporary and situation-specific causes. Self-efficacy, finally, concerns the extent to which people believe they can perform the behaviour required in any given situation to obtain certain goals (Bandura, 2001). Research using these PsyCap resources, either as separate predictors or as a combined predictor, indicates that they indeed affect indicators of employability, vitality and work ability (Avey et al., 2009), and therefore appear to be important precursors of sustainable labour participation (see Avey et al., 2011).

Task Characteristics

In the past decades, characteristics of the task environment have received extensive research attention. Over time, a substantial number of theoretical approaches have been developed (see, for instance, Kompier, 2003), each emphasizing the importance of task characteristics and job design for employee well-being, motivation and performance, and thus for sustainable labour participation. Developed in the 1970s and focusing on job (re)design, the *job characteristics model* (Hackman and Oldham, 1976; Oldham and Hackman, 2010) sets out to explain how job enrichment can have beneficial outcomes for employees and organizations, such as reduced sickness absence and turnover. More recently, the JD-R model (Demerouti et al., 2001; Bakker and Demerouti, 2007) is often used. This model is an elaboration of Karasek's (1979) *Job Demand-Control (JD-C) Model*, which focuses on the impact of job demands and job control on employee health and learning. In this section, aiming to facilitate sustainable labour participation, the concept of enriched jobs will be discussed, building upon the JD-R and JD-C models.

Job demands

Job tasks usually entail demanding characteristics that require sustained physical and psychological effort and skills, and therefore can have a negative impact on employee health (Bakker and Demerouti, 2007). Demanding characteristics have been studied for decades; the concept of job demands attracted a lot of research attention upon Karasek's (1979) introduction of the JD-C model. This model predicts that employees' health is especially at risk in high strain jobs, that is, when job demands are high and job control (or autonomy) is low. Subsequent research has supported the importance of job demands, showing that high levels of, for instance, workload, time pressure, and emotionally demanding work situations, are associated with negative health outcomes, and even relate to burnout (Bakker and Demerouti, 2007). Negative effects can be expected when meeting those demands requires too much physical and psychological effort, and overcharges the employees' capacities in such a way that their goals and health are at stake. At the same time, the JD-C model predicts that job demands can enhance learning – and thus employability – in the case of active jobs, that is, when both job demands and job control are high. This effect, however, is seldom found. In fact, Taris et al. observed that job demands actually decreased learning, and that learning was highest in jobs with low demands and high control (Taris et al., 2003). Thus, it appears that a situation of excessive job demands can negatively affect sustainable labour participation, because it increases the risk that employees will leave the work process owing to physical and/or psychological health complaints, while limiting workers' employability through reduced learning.

Job resources

Job resources are defined as those aspects of the job that are functional in achieving work goals, reducing job demands and the associated physiological and psychological costs, and stimulating personal growth and development (Bakker and Demerouti, 2007; Schaufeli and Taris, 2013). Examples of job resources are autonomy (or job control), feedback, rewards, job security, and development opportunities. In 1976, Hackman and Oldham referred to so-called 'job enrichments' indicating several of these job resources (for example, autonomy, feedback). Because job resources are instrumental for performance and foster employee development, they are expected to instigate a motivational process that results in high work engagement (including vitality), involvement and performance. Subsequent research of the JD-R model has indeed shown that job resources can have positive effects, including high levels of vitality, and can counteract the negative effects of job demands (Bakker et al., 2003). Additionally, research of the JD-C model has found that job resources (for example, job control) enhance employee health and learning (Taris et al., 2003). In sum, we can conclude that job resources contribute to workers' employability, motivation and health. Hence, they appear to be important conditions for sustainable labour participation.

Social-environmental Characteristics

The social environment is a crucial aspect of employees' work situation that can affect their sustainable labour participation. Extensive empirical evidence shows that interaction with and support from others, such as clients, colleagues and the supervisor, can be a source of both joy and strain, and can stimulate and hinder employees' employability, vitality and work ability.

Social support

Social support comprises a concept that emphasizes the importance of other people for employees' functioning. Social support can be provided in different ways (House, 1981): through instrumental support (doing something for the employee), emotional support (giving care and sympathy), informational support (giving relevant information), and appraisal support (feedback focused on enhancing the employee's self-esteem). Social support enables employees to better cope with difficult work situations, because they feel valued and they are part of a network of communication and mutual obligations as a result of the support (House, 1981). As such, social support has been included as a job resource in a number of stress models. Research indicates that support from near colleagues and one's direct supervisor impact employees' levels of well-being and vitality, either directly or indirectly, by buffering the effects of work demands (Demerouti et al., 2001). Besides affecting employees' health and vitality, social support at work can impact employability, the other aspect of sustainable labour participation. For instance, both colleague and supervisor support have been related to employees' participation in learning activities and training transfer (for example, Chiaburu et al., 2010), and as such contribute to enhanced employability. Moreover, social support at work can influence employees' retirement decision-making; in a study by Van Dam et al. (2009) it was found that employees who perceived positive support from their social work environment were more likely to postpone their (early) retirement.

Leadership

Leadership refers to an important factor that can affect many aspects of employees' work situation. For instance, leaders can decide about the work schedule, how much autonomy employees will have, whether employees receive promotion or engage in learning opportunities, and whether they are treated fairly and with respect. Quality of leadership therefore appears crucial for employees' sustainable labour participation through enhancing employee career development, employability and health (Van der Heijden et al., 2009). For example, Van der Heijden et al. (2009) found that leadership quality was negatively related to nurses' intention to leave the profession. Additionally, the exchange relationship between a supervisor and an individual employee (LMX relationship) matters. LMX has been associated with important outcomes such as performance, job satisfaction, career progress, retention and openness to change (Gerstner and Day, 1997). Research evidence indicates that a high-quality LMX relationship is associated with higher levels of learning, motivation and health (for example, Bezuijen et al., 2010; Gerstner and Day, 1997). Therefore, leadership in general, and LMX specifically, appears to be an important predictor of employees' sustainable labour participation.

Interactions with clients

Besides interactions with colleagues and supervisors, many jobs entail interactions with clients, such as customers, patients and students. Client interactions usually require that employees are polite, sympathetic, and that they express organizationally desired (positive) emotions and suppress undesirable (negative) emotions. This so-called emotional labour (or emotion work) has received increased research attention in the past decade (for example, Grandey, 2000). Although emotional labour is functional in enhancing the client–employee relationship, research indicates that it can be dysfunctional for employees' well-being, and can lead to emotional exhaustion and lowered job satisfaction (for example, Brotheridge, 2006). Ybema and Van Dam (2014) found that the requirement to suppress negative emotions and express positive emotions was related to indicators of health (emotional exhaustion) and motivation (engagement). Although, to the best of our knowledge, the relationship with employability has not been studied up to now, research evidence does indicate that interactions with clients can have consequences for workers' sustainable labour participation. In particular, when these interactions cause negative emotions that need to be suppressed, employees' health and motivation are endangered.

Organizational Characteristics

Next to the importance of factors at the individual and task and social-environmental level, factors at the organizational level have been recognized for their impact on the sustainable labour participation of workers as well. In this section, we will focus upon two organizational antecedents, namely, organizational culture and Human Resource practices.

Organizational culture

Schein (2004, p. 17) described organizational culture as: 'A pattern of shared basic assumptions that the group learned as it solved its problems that has worked well enough to be considered valid and is passed on to new members as the correct way to perceive, think, and feel in relation to those problems.' Ilmarinen et al. (2005) recognized the importance of organizational culture and stated that the interaction between values and attitudes of employees with the perceived organizational characteristics influences their work ability. More specifically, a stronger organizational learning culture has a positive impact on motivation (job satisfaction) of workers as well as their employability (motivation to transfer learning and lower turnover intention) (Egan et al., 2004). Hence, we could expect that all three aspects of sustainable labour participation will be affected by organizational culture or climate (see also Van Vuuren, 2011). In this respect, a phenomenon in relation to organizational culture that is called age-related stereotyping is worth mentioning here.

Age-related stereotyping refers to schema or cognitive categories that people use to evaluate others based on their age (Ng and Feldman, 2012). Stereotypes can be negative and positive, but in many organizations a negative image of older workers is present (Finkelstein et al., 2013). In spite of the fact that most stereotypes about older workers are not accurate (Ng and Feldman, 2012), they lead to an age-discriminatory climate with unfair and often unwise workplace decisions in the context of hiring, performance reviews and career and training opportunities (Finkelstein et al., 2013).

Human Resource practices

To date, literature on HRM and Human Resource practices (HR practices) does not systematically study its impact on sustainable labour participation of workers. So far, ample research supports the view that HRM influences performance of workers and organizations (see, for example, Guest and Conway, 2011; Huselid, 1995). This outcome is also confirmed in reviews and meta-analytic approaches (for example, Boselie et al., 2005). Recently, studies have also gained insights into the relation between HR practices and outcomes in terms of well-being of personnel. In this respect, Kroon et al. (2009) showed that High Performance Work System (HPWS) HR practices can enhance burnout symptoms by means of an intensification of job demands. Conversely, Bal et al. (2013) have shown that developmental HRM can generically enhance employees' engagement at work. So far, only a few studies have explicitly dealt with the relationship between (perceived) HR practices and sustainable outcomes in terms of employability, vitality and work ability.

For example, in the study by Dorenbosch (2009), some HPWS HR practices appeared to have a positive impact on employee vitality. In particular, flexible internal personnel solutions, training and development, and horizontal and vertical mobility activities appeared beneficial. Kooij (2010) focused on the importance of HR bundles for motivating older workers to continue to work, and found that HR bundles aimed at learning and development of employees are especially profitable for workers' motivation, regardless of their age (Kooij, 2010). A study among employees of Dutch primary schools confirmed the importance of learning and development in relation to their employability, vitality and work ability, and this was especially true for older workers (Van Vuuren et al., 2011). From this previous empirical work, it appeared that older workers in particular maintained their employability and work ability when they had more interest in, and more opportunities for life-long learning.

Sustainable labour participation and sustainable careers require a thorough concern of HRM, especially when it comes to longer-term outcomes. Analogous to the sustainable use of nature and energy, nowadays employers need to manage their human resources in such a way that they have a long shelf life. However, in reality, organizations appear to pay less attention to the sustainability of their workforce than to environmental or societal interests (see, for example, Pfeffer, 2010). One might think that organizations that claim to conduct their everyday work practice according to CSR principles would pay attention to this. In practice, this is not the case, at least not yet (Ehnert and Wes, 2012; Pfeffer, 2010). To explicitly integrate sustainability of the workforce in everyday practice, social responsibility and CSR need to be included as well (Müller-Camen et al., 2010).

CONCLUSION AND IMPLICATIONS FOR SUSTAINABLE CAREERS

Theoretical Implications

From the overview of aspects (or ingredients) and antecedents related to sustainable labour participation, several conclusions can be drawn. In the first place, a large range of antecedents can be distinguished, at different levels of influence, for employee outcomes, which vary from personal resources and skills to task characteristics and social and organizational factors. In this respect, the overview presented in this chapter reflects a significant, but by no means comprehensive selection. Second, antecedents often appear to be interrelated, or show conceptual overlap with outcomes, such as, for example, health and work ability (see, for example, Van den Berg, 2010). Conceptual overlap is also present to a certain extent between the aspects of sustainable labour participation themselves (employability, vitality and work ability). For example, vitality appears to be also included in the work ability concept (see also Brouwer et al., 2012). Conceptual clarity is an important concern in further research (see also Ryan and Frederick, 1997; Van der Klink et al., 2011). Future studies on sustainable labour participation therefore need to be clear and concise on the perspective they take. The same accounts for their conceptual and analytical focus. Next to this, an integral approach, in both research and practice, is advocated that incorporates curative, preventive, as well as amplition-related measures taken by HRM representatives (see also Van Vuuren, 2011; 2012). Unlike curative interventions (aimed at lower scoring employees) and preventive measures (aimed at risk groups), amplition is aimed at all employees, regardless of age. This latter type of intervention is intended to strengthen the employability, vitality and work ability of all workers (see also Ouweneel et al., 2009). Previous research has indicated that so-called *vitalizing* HR activities, such as training possibilities, internal and external mobility, and coaching and feedback of the supervisor (Feldman and Ng, 2007) can stimulate sustainable labour participation, which is needed for sustainable careers. Vitalizing HR activities are thus focused on 'amplition', meaning, after the Latin word '*amplio*', to enlarge, increase or magnify. Interventions focused on amplition aim to enhance positive work-related well-being.

The JD-R model (Demerouti et al., 2001) offers a fruitful, although a rather broad starting-point for a further investigation of the impact of possible antecedents and their effects upon important sustainable labour participation outcomes. In particular the impact of specific HR (bundles of) practices on sustainable labour participation and careers needs to be further explored, as only very limited findings for this type of organizational antecedents are available.

Next to clear conceptual choices and more insight into the impact of HR practices, there is a third research avenue that will be explicitly helpful; relevant factors for sustainable labour participation need to be studied in terms of their (interrelated) working mechanisms, especially over time. Up till now, the interrelatedness of antecedents of sustainable labour participation has only rarely been addressed. Furthermore, the different types of antecedents and outcomes ought to be further investigated using a multi-level perspective, focusing upon interactions and possible counterintuitive effects, such as the example that HR can enhance burnout symptoms (Kroon et al., 2009). Further research can elaborate on testing different perspectives and thereby contribute to insights into different routes for the working mechanisms of sustainable labour participation.

As sustainable careers reflect the longer-term outcomes of sustainable labour participation of individuals, longitudinal designs will be a necessary ingredient for future research. However, in-depth analyses into what types of concepts and developments should be, perhaps additionally, taken into account along this road of scholarly work, also seem necessary. In this respect, future studies can profit from different lines of research into sustainable careers as well. It is important to integrate both previous and new insights to capture the characteristics and dynamics of the multi-dimensional phenomena of sustainable labour participation and careers. In this way, their developmental nature can be addressed. Specifically, future research into sustainable labour participation should also incorporate more systematic knowledge from different HRM and careers subfields, such as HR development, labour market studies, employment relations, occupational health and safety (see also Ehnert, 2009). Also, more research into the impact of contextual factors, such as cultural value orientation or institutional influences, is needed using cross-country approaches. Cultural and institutional contexts differ widely across the globe, and it is assumed that a better understanding of these differences will increase the possibilities of coming up with tailor-made practices (Ehnert, 2009).

Practical Implications

From a more practical point of view, some conclusions can be drawn as well. So far, the literature in the field has shown that there are many individual antecedents for sustainable outcomes. It is therefore worth the effort to consciously foster and nurture people's psychological resources in order to optimize human functioning, both at work and in private life (Muster and Schrader, 2011). It is often argued, but also assumed, that individuals should take their own responsibility for these resources as well, and to invest in further development in the context of their careers (see, for example, Clarke and Patrickson, 2008). However, it is clear that employers and organizations should take responsibility as well, not only in the light of optimizing task characteristics, but also in terms of social support and specific Human Resource activities. When organizations set their agendas for a more sustainable future for people at work, they will have to consider what actions need to be taken. Although these conclusions are preliminary based on the overview above, the following recommendations seem beneficial.

Organizations may have to re-focus on interventions, from cure and prevention to amplifying positive effects of work. These may be aimed at performance, but should also be aimed at employability, vitality (engagement), work ability and other indicators of well-being at work. In addition, organizations should include all workers for interventions, and be alert to the presence and consequences of (age-) stereotyping. And finally, interventions can be useful at all levels of influence at work; the job, team and organizational level.

All in all, we look forward to putting the available knowledge to use for further research as well as practice, to gain insights in what consequences can be expected for sustainable careers in the longer run. As has become clear, many factors are '*at work*'.

REFERENCES

Ackerman, P. (1996), 'A theory of adult intellectual development: Process, personality, interests, and knowledge', *Intelligence*, **22** (2), 227–57.
Avey, J.B., F. Luthans and S.M. Jensen (2009), 'Psychological capital: A positive resource for combating employee stress and turnover', *Human Resource Management*, **48**, 677–93.
Avey, J.B., R.J. Reichard, F. Luthans and K.H. Mhatre (2011), 'Meta-analysis of the impact of positive psychological capital on employees' attitudes, behaviors, and performance', *Human Resource Development Quarterly*, **22**, 127–52.
Bakker, A.B. and E. Demerouti (2007), 'The job demands-resources model: State of the art', *Journal of Managerial Psychology*, **22**, 309–28.
Bakker, A.B., W.B. Schaufeli, M.P. Leiter and T.W. Taris (2008), 'Work engagement: An emerging concept in occupational health psychology', *Work & Stress*, **22**, 187–200.
Bakker, A.B., E. Demerouti, T. Taris, W.B. Schaufeli and P. Schreurs, (2003), 'A multi-group analysis of the Job Demands-Resources model in four home care organizations', *International Journal of Stress Management*, **10**, 16–38.
Bal, M., D. Kooij and S. de Jong (2013), 'How do developmental and accommodative HRM enhance employee engagement and commitment? The role of psychological contract and SOC strategies', *Journal of Management Studies*, **50** (4), 545–72.
Bandura, A. (2001), 'Social cognitive theory: An agentic perspective', *Annual Review of Psychology*, **52**, 1–26.
Berntson, E., M. Sverke and S. Marklund (2006), 'Predicting perceived employability: Human capital or labour market opportunities?', *Economic and Industrial Democracy*, **27**, 223–44.
Bezuijen, X., K. Van Dam, P.T. Van den Berg and H. Thierry (2010), 'How leaders stimulate employee learning: A leader–member exchange approach', *Journal of Occupational and Organizational Psychology*, **83**, 673–93.
Boselie, J.P., G. Dietz and C. Boon (2005), 'Commonalities and contradictions in research on human resource management and performance', *Human Resource Management*, **15** (3), 67–94.
Brotheridge, C.M. (2006), 'A review of emotional labor and its nomological network: Practical and research implications', *Ergonomia IJE&HF*, **28**, 295–309.
Brouwer, S., A. de Lange, S. Van der Mei, M. Wessels, W. Koolhaas, U. Bültmann, B. Van der Heijden and J. Van der Klink (2012), 'Duurzame inzetbaarheid van de oudere werknemer: stand van zaken. Overzicht van determinanten, interventies en meetinstrumenten vanuit verschillende perspectieven' ['Sustainable labour participation of the older worker: state of the art. Overview of determinants, interventions and measures from different perspectives'], Financed by Stichting Instituut Gak. Universitair Medisch Centrum Groningen/Radboud Universiteit, Nijmegen.
Brundtland Commission (1987), *Report of the World Commission on Environment and Development: Our Common Future*, Annexe to document A/42/427 – Development and International Co-operation: Environment, United Nations.
Burdorf, A. and L. Elders (2007), 'Het instrument Werkvermogen wetenschappelijk bekeken' ['The instrument work ability from a scientific perspective'], in D. Molenaar (ed.), *Werkvermogen. Verantwoord Werken aan Duurzame Inzetbaarheid* [*Responsibly Working Towards Sustainable Labour Participation*], Enschede: PreventNed.
Cattell, R.B. (1963), 'Theory of fluid and crystallized intelligence: A critical experiment', *Journal of Educational Psychology*, **54**, 1–22.
Chiaburu, D., K. Van Dam and H.M. Hutchins (2010), 'Social support in the workplace and training effectiveness: A longitudinal analysis', *International Journal of Selection and Assessment*, **18**, 187–200.
Clarke, M. and M. Patrickson (2008), 'The new covenant of employability', *Employee Relations*, **30** (2), 121–41.
De Cuyper, N., G. Notelaers and H. de Witte (2009), 'Job security and employability in fixed-term contractors, agency workers, and permanent workers: Associations with job satisfaction and affective organizational commitment', *Journal of Occupational Health Psychology*, **14** (2), 193–205.
De Cuyper, N., S. Mauno, U. Kinnunen and A. Mäkikangas (2011), 'The role of job resources in the relation

between perceived employability and turnover intention: A prospective two-sample study', *Journal of Vocational Behavior*, **78**, 253–63.

De Lange, A. and B.I.J.M. Van der Heijden (eds) (2013), *Een Leven Lang Inzetbaar? Duurzame Inzetbaarheid op het Werk: Interventies, Best Practices en Integrale Benaderingen* [*Lifelong Employability? Sustainable Employability at Work: Interventions, Best Practices and Comprehensive Approaches*], Vakmedianet, Alphen aan den Rijn, the Netherlands.

De Lange, A.H., D.T.A.M. Kooij and B.I.J.M. Van der Heijden (2015), 'Human Resource Management and sustainability across the lifespan: An integral perspective', in L. Finkelstein, D. Truxillo, F. Fraccaroli and R. Kanfer (eds), *Facing the Challenges of a Multi-Age Workforce: A Use-Inspired Approach*, SIOP Society for Industrial and Organizational Psychology, New York: Routledge, pp. 50–79.

De Vos, A., S. Hauw and B.I.J.M. Van der Heijden (2011), 'Competency development and career success: The mediating role of employability', *Journal of Vocational Behavior*, **79**, 438–47.

Demerouti, E., A.B. Bakker, F. Nachreiner and W.B. Schaufeli (2001), 'The job demands-resources model of burnout', *Journal of Applied Psychology*, **86**, 499–512.

Dorenbosch, L. (2009), 'Management by vitality. Examining the 'active' well-being and performance outcomes of high performance work practices at the work unit level', PhD thesis, Tilburg University, Tilburg, the Netherlands.

Egan, T.M., B. Yang and K.R. Barlett (2004), 'The effects of organizational learning culture and job satisfaction on motivation to transfer learning and turnover intention', *Human Resource Development Quarterly*, **15** (3), 297–301.

Ehnert, I. (2009), *Sustainable Human Resource Management: A Conceptual and Exploratory Analysis from a Paradox Perspective*, Berlin, Heidelberg: Physica-Verlag.

Ehnert, I. and H. Wes (2012), 'Recent developments and future prospects on sustainable Human Resource Management: Introduction to the special issue', *Management Revue*, **23** (3), 221–38.

European Commission (2013), *A Decent Life for All: Ending Poverty and Giving the World a Sustainable Future*, COM.92 final, Brussels.

Eurostat (2013), *Smarter, Greener, More Inclusive? Indicators to Support the Europe 2020 Strategy*, Eurostat statistical books, Luxembourg: Publications Office of the European Union.

Feldman, D.C. and T.W.H. Ng (2007), 'Careers: mobility, embeddedness, and success', *Journal of Management*, **33** (3), 350–77.

Finkelstein, L.M., K.M. Ryan and E.B. King (2013), 'What do the young (old) people think of me? Content and accuracy of age-based meta-stereotypes', *European Journal of Work and Organizational Psychology*, **22**, 633–57.

Fisk, P. (2010), *People, Planet, and Profit: How to Embrace Sustainability for Innovation and Business Growth*, London: Kogan Page.

Forrier, A. and L. Sels (2003), 'The concept employability: A complex mosaic', *International Journal of Human Resources Development and Management*, **3** (2), 102–23.

Fugate, M., A.J. Kinicki and B.E. Ashforth (2004), 'Employability: A psycho-social construct, its dimensions, and applications', *Journal of Vocational Behavior*, **65**, 14–38.

Gerstner, C.R. and D.V. Day (1997), 'Meta-analytic review of leader–member exchange theory: Correlates and construct issues', *Journal of Applied Psychology*, **82**, 827–44.

Grandey, A.A. (2000), 'Emotion regulation in the workplace: A new way to conceptualize emotional labor', *Journal of Occupational Health Psychology*, **5**, 50–110.

Gratton, L. (2011), 'Workplace 2025: What will it look like?', *Organizational Dynamics*, **40**, 246–54.

Griffeth, R.W. and P.W. Hom (1988), 'A comparison of different conceptualizations of perceived alternatives in turnover research', *Journal of Organizational Behavior*, **9**, 103–11.

Guest, D. and N. Conway (2011), 'The impact of HR practices, HR effectiveness, and a "strong HR system" on organizational outcomes: A stakeholder perspective', *The International Journal of Human Resource Management*, **22** (8), 1686–702.

Hackman, J.R. and G.R. Oldham (1976), 'Motivation through the design of work: Test of a theory', *Organization Behavior and Human Performance*, **16**, 250–79.

Hamilton, V.H., P. Merrigan and E. Dufresne (1997), 'Down and out: Estimating the relationship between mental health and unemployment', *Health Economics*, **6** (4), 397–406.

Hobfoll, S.E. (2002), 'Social and psychological resources and adaptation', *Review of General Psychology*, **6**, 307–32.

House, J.S. (1981), *Work Stress and Social Support*, Reading, MA: Addison-Wesley.

Huselid, M.A. (1995), 'The impact of human resource management practices on turnover, productivity, and corporate financial performance', *Academy of Management Journal*, **38** (3), 635–72.

Ilmarinen, J. (2005), *Towards a Longer Worklife*, Helsinki: FIOH Bookstore.

Ilmarinen, J., T.K. Tuomi and J. Seitsamo (2005), 'New dimensions of work ability', *International Congress Series 1280*, 3–7.

Kanfer, R. and P.L. Ackerman (2004), 'Aging, adult development, and work motivation', *Academy of Management Review*, **29**, 440–58.

Kanfer, R., M.E. Beier and P.L. Ackerman (2013), 'Goals and motivation related to work in later adulthood: An organizing framework', *European Journal of Work and Organizational Psychology*, **22**, 253–64.

Karasek, R.A. (1979), 'Job demand, job decision latitude, and mental strain: Implications for job redesign', *Administrative Science Quarterly*, **24**, 285–308.

Kark, R. and A. Carmeli (2009), 'Alive and creating: The mediating role of vitality and aliveness in the relationship between psychological safety and creative work involvement', *Journal of Organizational Behavior*, **30** (6), 785–804.

Katz, H., W. Lee and J. Lee (eds) (2004), *The New Structure of Labor Relations: Tripartism and Decentralization*, New York: ILR Press, Cornell University Press.

Kiss, P., M. de Meester and L. Braeckman (2008), 'Differences between younger and older workers in the need for recovery after work', *International Archive of Occupational and Environmental Health*, **81**, 311–20.

Kompier, M. (2003), 'Job design and well-being', in M.J. Schabracq, J.A.M. Winnubst and C.L. Coopere (eds), *The Handbook of Work and Health Psychology*, Chichester: Wiley, pp. 429–54.

Kooij, D. (2010), 'Motivating older workers. A lifespan perspective on the role of perceived HR practices', PhD thesis, Vrije Universiteit Amsterdam.

Kroon, B., K. Van der Voorde and M. Van Veldhoven (2009), 'Cross-level effects of high-performance work practices on burnout: Two counteracting mediating mechanisms compared', *Personnel Review*, **38** (5), 509–25.

Lindgreen, A. and V. Swaen (2010), 'Corporate social responsibility (editorial)', *International Journal of Management Reviews*, **12** (1), 1–7.

Luthans, F., B.J. Avolio, J.B. Avey and S.M. Norman (2007), 'Positive psychological capital: Measurement and relationship with performance and satisfaction', *Personnel Psychology*, **60**, 541–72.

March, J.G. and H.A. Simon (1958), *Organizations*, New York: Wiley.

McQuaid, R. and M. Lindsay (2005), 'The concept of employability', *Urban Studies*, **42** (2), 197–219.

Müller-Camen, M., S. Parsa and I. Roper (2010). 'The sustainable business and human resource practices: What is the link?', paper presented at the BAM HRM Conference, London, 22 April.

Muster, V. and U. Schrader (2011), 'Green work–life balance: A new perspective for green HRM', *Zeitschrift für Personalforschung*, **25** (2), 140–56.

Ng, T.W.H. and D.C. Feldman (2012), 'Evaluating six common stereotypes about older workers with meta-analytical data', *Personnel Psychology*, **65**, 821–58.

Oldham, G.R. and J.R. Hackman (2010), 'Not what it was but what it will be: The future of job design research', *Journal of Organizational Behavior*, **31**, 463–79.

Ouweneel, E., W. Schaufeli and P. LeBlanc (2009), 'Van preventie naar amplitie: Interventies voor optimaal functioneren' ['From prevention to amplition: Interventions for optimal functioning'], *Gedrag & Organisatie*, **22** (2), 118–35.

Pfeffer, J. (2010), 'Building sustainable organizations: The human factor', *Academy of Management Perspectives*, **24** (1), 34–45.

Rothwell, A. and J. Arnold (2007), 'Self-perceived employability: Development and validation of a scale', *Personnel Review*, **36**, 23–41.

Ryan, R.M. and J.H. Bernstein (2004), 'Vitality', in C. Peterson and M.E.P. Seligman (eds), *Character Strengths and Virtues: A Handbook and Classification*, New York: Oxford University Press, pp. 273–90.

Ryan, R.M. and C. Frederick (1997), 'On energy, personality and health: Subjective vitality as a dynamic reflection of well-being', *Journal of Personality*, **65** (3), 529–65.

Salthouse, T. (2011), 'Consequences of age-related cognitive declines', *Annual Review of Psychology*, **63**, 201–26.

Schaufeli, W.B. and A.B. Bakker (2007), 'Burnout en bevlogenheid' ['Burnout and work engagement'], in W.B. Schaufeli and A.B. Bakker (eds), *De Psychologie van Arbeid en Gezondheid* [*The Psychology of Work and Health*], Houten, the Netherlands: Bohn Stafleu van Loghum, pp. 341–58.

Schaufeli, W.B. and A.B. Bakker (2010), 'Defining and measuring work engagement: Bringing clarity to the concept', in A.B. Bakker and M.P. Leiter (eds), *Work Engagement: A Handbook of Essential Theory and Research*, New York: Psychology Press, pp. 10–24.

Schaufeli, W. and T. Taris (2013), 'Het job demands-resources model: Overzicht en kritische beschouwing' ['The job demands-resources model: Review and critical considerations'], *Gedrag & Organisatie*, **26**, 182–204.

Schein, E.H. (2004), *Organizational Culture and Leadership*, San Francisco: Jossey-Bass.

Snyder, C.R., L. Irving and J. Anderson (1991), 'Hope and health: Measuring the will and ways', in C.R. Snyder and D.R. Forsyth (eds), *Handbook of Social and Clinical Psychology*, Elmsford: Pergamon, pp. 285–305.

Social and Economic Council (SER) (2009), *Een Kwestie van Gezond Verstand. Breed Preventiebeleid binnen Arbeidsorganisaties* [*A Matter of Common Sense. Broad Policies for Prevention in Labour Organizations*], The Hague: Sociaal Economische Raad.

Suhrcke, M., R.A. Nugent, D. Stuckler and L. Rocco (2006), *Chronic Disease: An Economic Perspective*, London: Oxford Health Alliance.
Taris, T.W., M.A.J. Kompier, A.H. de Lange, W.B. Schaufeli and P.J.G. Schreurs (2003), 'Learning new behaviour patterns: A longitudinal test of Karasek's active learning hypothesis among Dutch teachers', *Work & Stress*, **17**, 1–20.
Van Dam, K. (2013), 'Employee adaptability to change at work: A multidimensional, resource-based framework', in S. Oreg, A. Michel and R.T. By (eds), *The Psychology of Organizational Change: Viewing Change from the Employee's Perspective*, Cambridge: Cambridge University Press, pp. 123–42.
Van Dam, K., J. Van der Vorst and B.I.J.M. Van der Heijden (2009), 'Employees' intentions to retire early: A case of planned behavior and anticipated work conditions', *Journal of Career Development*, **35** (3), 265–89.
Van den Berg, T. (2010), 'The role of work ability and health on sustaining employability', PhD thesis, Erasmus University Rotterdam, the Netherlands.
Van den Berg, T.I.J., L.A.M. Elders, B.C.H. de Zwart and A. Burdorf (2009), 'The effects of work-related and individual factors on the Work Ability Index: A systematic review', *Occupational Environmental Medicine*, **6**, 211–20.
Van der Heijde, C. and B. Van der Heijden (2006), 'A competence-based and multidimensional operationalization and measurement of employability', *Human Resource Management*, **45**, 449–76.
Van der Heijden, B.I.J.M. (2011), 'Als het getij verloopt, verzet men de bakens', Inaugural lecture about lifelong employability management, 18 March, Radboud University, Nijmegen, the Netherlands.
Van der Heijden, B.I.J.M., K. Van Dam and H. Hasselhorn (2009), 'Social work environment and work–home interference and their impact upon nurses' intention to leave the profession', *Career Development International*, **14**, 616–35.
Van der Klink, J., A. Burdorf, W. Schaufeli, G. Van der Wilt, F. Zijlstra, S. Brouwer and U. Bultmann (2010), 'Duurzaam inzetbaar: Werk als waarde' ['Sustainable labour participation: work as value'], Research report commissioned by ZonMW, the Netherlands.
Van der Klink, J., U. Bültmann, S. Brouwer, A. Burdorf, W. Schaufeli, F. Zijlstra and G. Van der Wilt (2011), 'Duurzame inzetbaarheid bij oudere werknemers, werk als waarde' ['Sustainable labour participation for older people, work as value'], *Gedrag & Organisatie*, **24**, 341–55.
Van Vuuren, T. (2011), 'Je hoeft niet ziek te zijn om beter te worden!' ['You don't have to be ill to get better!'], Inaugural address, Open Universiteit Heerlen, the Netherlands.
Van Vuuren, T. (2012), 'Vitaliteitsmanagement: je hoeft niet ziek te zijn om beter te worden! Vergroot de duurzame inzetbaarheid van werknemers door hun vitaliteit, werkvermogen en employability te versterken' ['Vitality management: you don't have to be ill to get better! Enlarge the sustainable labour participation of workers by strengthening their vitality, work ability and employability'], *Gedrag & Organisatie*, **25** (4), 400–418.
Van Vuuren, T., M. Caniëls and J.H. Semeijn (2011), 'Een leven lang leren en duurzame inzetbaarheid' ['Life long learning and sustainable labour participation'], *Gedrag & Organisatie*, **24** (4), 356–73.
Warr, P.B. (2001), 'Age and work behaviour: Physical attributes, cognitive abilities, knowledge, personality traits and motives', *International Review of Industrial and Organizational Psychology*, **16**, 1–36.
World Health Organization (1948), 'Preamble to the Constitution of the World Health Organization, entered into force on 7 April 1948, Official Records of the World Health Organization, no. 2, p. 100', adopted by the International Health Conference, New York, 19–22 June, 1946.
Ybema, J.F. and K. Van Dam (2014), 'The importance of negative and positive emotional display rules for emotional exhaustion and work engagement: A multi-group comparison', *Journal of Positive Psychology*, **9** (4), 366–76.

11 Perceived employability in times of job insecurity: a theoretical perspective

Nele De Cuyper, Anja Van den Broeck and Hans De Witte

INTRODUCTION

Job insecurity and employability seem to be naturally related in the current Flexicurity discourse (Green, 2011). Flexicurity combines labour market flexibility and employment security. Labour market flexibility also implies flexible contractual arrangements and work organizations, which leads to insecurity among an increasing contingent of the workforce (Reisel and Probst, 2010; Sverke et al., 2010). Employability is advocated as the new way to secure one's labour market position (DiRenzo and Greenhaus, 2011).

Surprisingly, the discussion on the relationship between job insecurity and employability has remained fairly speculative (De Cuyper et al., 2008). This prompts the question whether the idea of an insecure but highly employable workforce is realistic or, more generally, how job insecurity and employability are related. We address this question from the perspective of employee perceptions: felt job insecurity, perceived employability and their interrelationship. The reason is that perceptions drive employees' attitudes and behaviours (Lazarus and Folkman, 1984) and thus they are critical for sustainable career development and the success of labour market policies, including measures aimed at installing Flexicurity (Chung and Van Oorschot, 2011).

The existing studies to date see perceived employability as a potential buffer against the negative effects associated with felt job insecurity, which has been established in recent studies (Berntson et al., 2010; Green, 2011; Kalyal et al., 2010; Kang et al., 2012; Kirves et al., 2011; Silla et al., 2009; Sora et al., 2010). While these studies have brought felt job insecurity and perceived employability to the fore, they remain silent about their possible interrelationship. A detailed inspection of the relationship between felt job insecurity and perceived employability should account for the nature of the relationship (negative or positive) and issues related to causality (from felt job insecurity to perceived employability, from perceived employability to felt job insecurity or reciprocal causation).

In response, our aim is to provide a theoretical discourse on the relationship between felt job insecurity and perceived employability that may serve future studies. We discuss each of six possible relationships (Table 11.1). A particular strength is that we introduce mediators derived from theories from different fields. The evidence to date is limited and mainly cross-sectional and hence it may not convincingly point to one of the six possibilities as 'the winner'. To fuel future research, we conclude with potential routes for integration. We set out with an outline on similarities and differences in the definitions of felt job insecurity and perceived employability.

Table 11.1 Relationship between felt job insecurity and perceived employability

	The relationship is . . .	
Causality is . . .	negative	positive
from felt job insecurity ➔ perceived employability	Route 1 Self Determination Theory	Route 4 Hindrance vs. Challenge
from perceived employability ➔ felt job insecurity	Route 2 Human Capital Theory	Route 5 Social Comparison
reciprocal	Route 3 Appraisal Theory	Route 6 Social Exchange

DEFINITION: SIMILARITIES AND DIFFERENCES

There has been some debate about potential overlap in the definitions of felt job insecurity and perceived employability. This overlap is sometimes seen as substantial, even to the extent that some authors have lumped the concepts together in the notion of 'subjective employment insecurity': the employees' perceptions about the risk of losing their job in the near future and being unable to find another position with relative ease (Chung and Van Oorschot, 2011; Green, 2011). We take a different stance and see the concepts as clearly distinct. Felt job insecurity is defined as the employee's perception and/or concern about potential involuntary job loss (Vander Elst et al., 2014). Perceived employability refers to the individual's perception about alternative job opportunities that are readily available (Vanhercke et al., 2014). These definitions are similar in some respects but different in others.

A first similarity is that felt job insecurity and perceived employability are both based upon individual sense-making and thus inherently subjective. The implication of subjectivity is that individuals may perceive the same objective situation differently (De Witte, 1999; Sverke et al., 2002): a particular situation is filtered and coloured by the individual.

A second similarity is a focus upon the future: felt job insecurity concerns the possibility of future job loss (De Witte, 1999; Sverke et al., 2002), and perceived employability possible job transitions in the future (Vanhercke et al., 2014). The reference to the future in most definitions is fairly general, but a focus upon the near future is made explicit in most instruments on felt job insecurity and is implied in many instruments on perceived employability. For example, Vander Elst et al. (2014) validated the Job Insecurity Scale with items such as 'Chances are, I will *soon* lose my job' and 'I think I might lose my job *in the near future*'. Similarly, Hellgren and Sverke (2003) use items such as 'I feel uneasy losing my job *in the near future*' and 'There is a risk that I would have to leave my job *in the year to come*'. Perceived employability measures generally highlight how easy it is to make transitions, for example 'I could easily switch to another employer, if I wanted to' (De Cuyper et al., 2008) or 'How easy would it be for you to acquire new and comparable employment?' (Berntson, 2008). This reference to ease of transitions can be interpreted as meaning transitions in the near future that require little effort in terms of job search.

The definitions are also similar in the sense that they take a specific perspective in ongoing debates. Our definition of felt job insecurity highlights concerns about potential loss of the job as opposed to other definitions that include potential loss of important job features (Greenhalgh and Rosenblatt, 1984; Hellgren et al., 1999). This difference is referred to as 'quantitative' versus 'qualitative' job insecurity, respectively. The debate now concerns the relative impact of quantitative versus qualitative felt job insecurity (De Witte et al., 2010). Along similar lines, our definition of perceived employability concerns perceived alternative job opportunities. This highlights a quantitative approach: it refers to all possible job opportunities (De Cuyper and De Witte, 2011) or more conservatively to job opportunities that are equal to the present job (Berntson, 2008). Though less well established in the literature, De Cuyper and De Witte (2011) introduced qualitative perceived employability, namely job opportunities that are in some way better than the present job. The distinction between quantitative and qualitative perceived employability was demonstrated empirically and in relation to both antecedents and consequences in the studies by De Cuyper and De Witte (2011) and Van den Broeck et al. (2013). In line with the definitions presented earlier, our focus is upon quantitative felt job insecurity and quantitative perceived employability: these have been used most often in existing studies.

There are also differences. First, felt job insecurity concerns the future of the present job, and perceived employability concerns potential other jobs (Wittekind et al., 2010). This emphasis has a number of implications. To start with, felt job insecurity relates to the present job and thus also the present organization. Perceived employability relates to other jobs in the internal labour market (that is, with the present organization) or in the external labour market (that is, with other organizations or from a position as (unemployed) job seeker). This relates to the distinction between perceived internal and external employability (Rothwell and Arnold, 2007). The critical difference is that internal perceived employability concerns transfer of skills across jobs but within organizational boundaries and external perceived employability across organizational boundaries (De Cuyper et al., 2012) or across positions (for example, from unemployment/student to employment). Most studies have concerned perceived external employability, as this is perhaps most relevant in today's volatile labour market and in the context of increasing feelings of job insecurity. Therefore, the focus is also upon perceived external employability in our discourse.

Second, and on a related note, felt job insecurity is conditional upon having a job: thus, felt job insecurity is studied among the employed. Perceived employability is not conditional upon having a job, but instead is relevant for different groups on the labour market and throughout an individual's career (Vanhercke et al., 2014). Perceived employability has been studied among (graduate) students mainly as a means to facilitate labour market entry (Rothwell et al., 2009), the employed as a means to secure employment (Rothwell and Arnold, 2007) and the unemployed as a means of transitioning to employment (McArdle et al., 2007).

Third, felt job insecurity is generally portrayed as a demand, and perceived employability as a personal resource (De Cuyper et al., 2009). Felt job insecurity concerns involuntary loss that is beyond the individual's control, and that is likely to induce strain (De Witte, 1999). Evidence for this perspective is plentiful: job insecurity has been associated with poorer health and well-being, undesirable attitudes and reduced effort at work (for meta-analyses, see Cheng and Chan, 2008; Sverke et al., 2002). In contrast, perceived employability concerns choice between different potential alternatives that are within the individual's reach and that leads to gain (Chen and Lim, 2012; De Cuyper et al., 2012). The idea of perceived employability as a personal resource is based on the argument that perceived employability is similar to some resources, self-efficacy in particular (Berntson et al., 2008). Another argument is that perceived employability forms the output of other resources (Forrier et al., 2009), among them employability dispositions (Fugate et al., 2004) and competences (Van der Heijde and Van der Heijden, 2006).

In conclusion, felt job insecurity and perceived employability are related in the sense that they both focus upon individuals' perceptions and on the (near) future. They are different in two important ways. First, felt job insecurity concerns the present job in the current organization, while perceived employability may concern any possible job transition. Second, felt job insecurity is conceived as a demand with associated losses, and perceived employability as a personal resource with possible gains.

THE RELATIONSHIP BETWEEN FELT JOB INSECURITY AND PERCEIVED EMPLOYABILITY

Most studies to date hint at a negative relationship between felt job insecurity and perceived employability. The strength of the relationship varies from weak (Berntson et al., 2010: $r = -.22$; De Cuyper et al., 2008: $r = -.14$; Peiró et al., 2012: $r = -.17$) to moderate (Kang et al., 2012: $r = -.37$; Kirves et al., 2011: $r = -.29$; Sora et al., 2010: $r = -.28$). The negative relationship between felt job insecurity and perceived employability is corroborated in the study by Mäkikangas et al. (2013), who used a person-centred approach to investigate individual development of perceived employability over time, so-called 'trajectories'. High felt job insecurity characterized those trajectories that signalled weaker employability profiles, namely workers who perceived their employability as continuously low or decreasing over time. In contrast, low felt job insecurity was characteristic for trajectories in which perceived employability was continuously high or increasing over time.

Though a negative relationship is plausible, we believe some caution is warranted. First, most studies are cross-sectional and hence causality is an issue of concern. One exception is the study by De Cuyper et al. (2012): they established a negative relationship from perceived employability at Time 1 to felt job insecurity at Time 2 ($\gamma = -.08$) but also a negative relationship from felt job insecurity at Time 1 to perceived employability at Time 2 ($\gamma = -.05$). This highlights the possibility of reciprocal causation. Second, roughly half of the studies did not establish a negative relationship, without yet accounting for a possible publication bias: instead, the relationship in some studies was not significant (Kalyal et al., 2010; Kirves et al., 2011; Sora et al., 2010) and in other studies positive (Griffeth et al., 2005; Silla et al., 2009). Third, the evidence to date is largely atheoretical. In response, we discuss the relationship between felt job insecurity and perceived employability accounting for potential negative and positive relationships and causality along the six alternatives in Table 11.1. Our focus is upon theoretical development: to that aim, we selected a set of theories with demonstrated impact in the field and which hint at mediators to explain the relationship.

Route 1: Felt job insecurity negatively affects perceived employability through need satisfaction.

Reactions to felt job insecurity are likely to hamper an active attitude and the investments needed to feed employability. This can be understood with reference to Self-Determination Theory (Deci and Ryan, 2000) as applied in the realm of job insecurity research by Vander Elst et al. (2012). Self-Determination Theory advances basic psychological need satisfaction as the core motivational force for individuals to become active agents at work. Vander Elst et al. (2012) argued and demonstrated that felt job insecurity leads to the frustration of these basic psychological needs, while perceived employability is conditional upon need satisfaction.

First, felt job insecurity frustrates the three innate needs that are advanced in Self Determination Theory, namely, the need for autonomy, belongingness and competence. Felt job insecurity frustrates the need for autonomy: felt job insecurity is by definition involuntary, whereas the need for autonomy concerns the inherent desire for volition and authorship over one's decisions and acts (Deci and Ryan, 2000). Furthermore, felt job insecurity frustrates the need for belongingness: it induces a negative atmosphere at work with gossip, rumour, conflicts and competition among colleagues (Bordia et al., 2006; De Cuyper et al., 2009). In contrast, the need for belongingness is defined as the inherent need to feel connected to others in a positive fashion (Baumeister and Leary, 1995). Finally, job insecurity frustrates the need for competence. Job insecure workers do not know what to expect from the future, dismissal or not, and hence they find it difficult to select the most appropriate response vis-à-vis job insecurity (Dekker and Schaufeli, 1995; De Witte, 1999). In contrast, outcome expectancy and self-efficacy are critical facets of the need for competence (Deci and Ryan, 2000).

Second, frustration of the basic psychological needs reduces perceived employability or, otherwise, basic psychological needs satisfaction is critical to promote perceived employability. The degree to which an individual is experiencing needs satisfaction is predictive for optimal functioning and psychological flourishing (Van den Broeck et al., 2010), much in line with the growth perspective that is perhaps most characteristic for Self-Determination Theory. There is convincing evidence that psychological need satisfaction leads to employability-enhancing outcomes, most notably school engagement and achievement (Filak and Sheldon, 2008; Jang et al., 2012), (willingness for) learning and training participation (Park et al., 2012) and proactivity (Parker et al., 2010). Thus, need satisfaction may promote perceived employability and need frustration may reduce perceived employability.

In all, this suggests that felt job insecurity frustrates the basic psychological needs, which then negatively affects perceived employability: felt job insecurity → reduced basic psychological need satisfaction → reduced perceived employability.

Route 2: Perceived employability negatively affects felt job insecurity through human capital investments.

A leading idea in the realm of employability research is that employability empowers the individual in matters of career development (Pruijt and Dérogée, 2010) and in general (De Cuyper et al., 2009). The implication is that perceived employability may lead to reduced feelings of job insecurity. This can be understood theoretically using insights from Human Capital Theory (Becker, 1993; see, for example, De Cuyper et al., 2008; De Cuyper et al., 2012).

A central tenet in Human Capital Theory is that investments are made in view of potential revenues. Employable workers have made considerable investments, for example, in terms of acquiring and accumulating human and/or social capital (Wittekind et al., 2010). They may then seek revenues for these investments. These revenues can take the form of financial but also non-financial incentives (Brown et al., 2003; Worth, 2002). The result is that employable workers may pursue jobs with, for example, high earnings or considerable job security (Gracia et al., 2011; Peiró et al., 2012). Job security has particular resonance today: workers are committed to the ideal of long-term employment as a return on earlier investments in human capital (Worth, 2002). Employable workers are likely to establish such revenues too: employers seek to attract and retain workers with strong profiles, like highly employable workers who are also wanted by competitors. Employers may try to bind these workers to the organization by offering them high quality jobs and inducements, job security, for example. In this respect, previous studies have shown that this could be an effective strategy (De Cuyper et al., 2011).

In conclusion, perceived employability may negatively affect felt job insecurity: employable workers have made investments in their human and social capital which then may help them to acquire more security, so that perceived employability ➔ human capital investments ➔ reduced job insecurity.

Route 3: Negative reciprocal causation between felt job insecurity and perceived employability through perceived control.

A plausible assumption is that the negative path goes in two ways, from felt job insecurity to perceived employability and vice versa, much in line with assumptions made in Appraisal Theory (Lazarus and Folkman, 1984) as applied in the context of felt job insecurity by Vander Elst (2013).

Appraisal theory is built on the assumption that individuals first appraise a given situation or experience as either irrelevant, benign-positive or stressful, and they continue with appraisals about the resources available to control the situation. Felt job insecurity is likely to be seen as stressful as it implies a threat. Job insecure workers may furthermore feel that available resources are insufficient: felt job insecurity implies uncertainty about the future and is often the result of external factors, so that workers find it difficult to control the situation or to select the most appropriate response for effective problem-solving (De Witte, 1999). The result is that workers are likely to engage in emotion-focused coping that forestalls employability-development in two ways. Job insecure workers may withdraw from the organization (Berntson et al., 2010) or from the job (Peiró et al., 2012) so as to psychologically increase the distance between themselves and the stressor. Withdrawal often implies passivity (De Witte, 1999), while perceived employability is built on proactive attitudes (Wittekind et al., 2010). Second, job insecure workers may show strong negative emotions (for example, anger, fear; Kiefer, 2005) to express discontentment. These emotions consume energy that is needed for employability-development. Earlier studies have shown a negative relationship between felt job insecurity and aspects that are critical inputs to perceived employability, for example, career planning (Klehe et al., 2011) and commitment to change (Kalyal et al., 2010). In all, the argument is that felt job insecurity reduces perceptions of being in control while control is a critical input to perceived employability (DiRenzo and Greenhaus, 2011): felt job insecurity ➔ reduced control ➔ reduced perceived employability.

Conversely, workers are likely to appraise employability as benign-positive, and employable workers are equipped with many resources, control in particular. Control is mostly seen as inherent to the general notion of employability (Fugate et al., 2004) and likewise applies to the more specific notion of perceived employability (De Cuyper et al., 2008). For example, DiRenzo and Greenhaus (2011, p. 571) defined employability as 'the capacity to *control* one's employment options through the creation, identification and realization of career opportunities'. Such feelings of control promote effective coping, both emotion-wise and problem-wise (Chen and Lim, 2012). Emotion-focused coping means that workers are able to alleviate immediate or emotional distress. Perceived employability implies a sense of choice between different alternatives and thus less dependence on the current job (Sora et al., 2010). The result is that highly employable workers are less concerned about potential job loss or they may find job loss less threatening (Fugate et al., 2004), which then may reduce feelings of job insecurity (De Cuyper et al., 2008). Problem-focused coping means that highly employable workers are able to eliminate the source of distress: here felt job insecurity. Highly employable workers may feel that other employment is within reach and thus they may adopt strategies that are targeted at pursuing alternative employment, job search, for example. This then may lead to a transition towards a more secure job. Chen and Lim (2012) established among a sample of job seekers that perceived employability induces both emotion-focused and problem-focused coping, and that these strategies, particularly when used in tandem, are successful. The bottom line seems to be that perceived employability provides opportunities for control that then reduce (through emotion- and problem-focused coping) feelings of job insecurity: perceived employability ➔ perceived control ➔ reduced felt job insecurity.

In terms of reciprocity, felt job insecurity may negatively affect perceived employability through reduced control and associated downsides, such as ineffective emotional-focused coping, withdrawal and strong negative emotions. Lower levels of perceived employability, in turn, may add to the perception of powerlessness, which may then feed feelings of insecurity. Or conversely, perceived employability may prompt feelings of being in control. This leads to effective emotion-focused and problem-focused coping that may prevent workers from feeling insecure. Workers may feel they have the necessary resources to control their present job situation, which then may spill over to feelings of control over their career, that is, perceived employability. This suggests that job insecurity ➔ reduced control ➔ reduced perceived employability, or that perceived employability ➔ increased control ➔ reduced felt job insecurity.

Route 4: Felt job insecurity positively affects perceived employability through job search.

The idea that felt job insecurity leads to increased employability is provocative among the dominant group of mostly occupational health scholars, but not among career scholars: career scholars see perceived employability as the alternative for job security and implicitly assume that felt job insecurity may lead workers to invest in employability or to engage in job search. This can be understood as follows.

Job insecurity is traditionally seen as a demand that depletes energy (De Witte, 1999). Some authors go one step further, and argue that job insecurity, though always energy-consuming and hence demanding, may sometimes be appraised as challenging (DiRenzo and Greenhaus, 2011; Staufenbiel and König, 2010; Stynen et al., 2014). They draw on the earlier distinction between demands as hindrances versus challenges advanced by Cavanaugh et al. (2000). Hindrances are demands that are seen as threatening and that result in distress. Challenges are demands that are stimulating and motivating. When felt job insecurity is appraised as challenging, employees may overcome felt job insecurity by engaging in job search. Job search provides the workers with opportunities to gauge their employability (DiRenzo and Greenhaus, 2011). A similar argument has been made in the realm of unemployment research (for example, Klehe et al., 2011): redundancy related positively to career adaptability. In all, this suggests that felt job insecurity may increase perceived employability through job search: felt job insecurity ➔ job search ➔ perceived employability.

Route 5: Perceived employability positively affects felt job insecurity through social comparison.

While the other scenarios have at least some theoretical and empirical background, the idea that perceived employability may induce feelings of job insecurity is novel, but nevertheless plausible based on social comparison mechanisms. Employable workers are generally well informed about the labour market. The result is that they may readily and fairly accurately compare their present situation with jobs elsewhere: indeed, social comparison is a strong urge among most people (Festinger, 1954). This comparison may in some cases lead to a negative evaluation of the present job; for example, when workers see that competitors are doing better financially, attract more personnel or offer more inducements, also in terms of security of employment. This may lead to doubts about their present organization and job, hence insecurity. The conclusion is that perceived employability ➔ negative social comparison ➔ increasing feelings of job insecurity.

Route 6: Positive reciprocal causation between felt job insecurity and perceived employability through withdrawal.

Felt job insecurity and perceived employability may reinforce each other through mechanisms of social exchange, as applied by De Cuyper and De Witte (2006) in the context of felt job insecurity.

The argument raised by De Cuyper and De Witte (2006) is that felt job insecurity breaches the relational psychological contract employees hold with their employer; indeed, most employment relationships today and particularly in Europe are based on permanent employment contracts with the expectation of long-term employment. As a result, insecure workers may withdraw from their part of the deal: they may reduce their loyalty to the present employer. Instead, they may be driven by self-interest and become oriented towards the external labour market. Such an orientation is a critical condition for perceived employability. This aligns with our earlier argument on the relationship between felt job insecurity and perceived employability through job search cognitions and behaviours. It also ties in with the reasoning from Kang et al. (2012): felt job insecurity may induce a sense of self-interest in an attempt to avoid the associated downsides and an opportunity to establish career breakthroughs. This suggests that felt job insecurity ➔ withdrawal ➔ increased perceived employability.

Perceived employability, in turn, may further strengthen this self-interested orientation (De Cuyper et al., 2009). This is particularly likely in today's changing career environment and volatile labour market. New career models, for example, the boundaryless and the protean career (DeFillippi and Arthur, 1996; Hall, 2004), are built around employability and emphasize the role of the individual in setting and then pursuing specific career goals in their own best interest. Volatile labour markets encourage quick transitions and quick wins: workers may readily compare their situation with what they would have elsewhere. When perceived employability induces such self-interest, this is likely to undermine the traditional employee–employer relationship based on job security on the part of the employer in exchange for strong commitment on the part of the employee: when highly employable workers decide to pursue their own interest, the employer may no longer feel obligated to provide job security, which ultimately may leave the workers insecure about their jobs. Furthermore, self-interest may reduce collective actions and social protection; for example, in the form of union participation, which has traditionally been a way to secure jobs (Sverke and Hellgren, 2002). In all, perceived employability ➔ withdrawal ➔ increased job insecurity.

TOWARDS INTEGRATION

The empirical evidence to date seems to suggest that a negative relationship between felt job insecurity and perceived employability is most plausible, but also signals two unresolved issues. First, we arrived at the conclusion that also other than negative relationships between felt job insecurity and perceived employability have been observed. This highlights the need to account for more complex relationships based on multiple mediators. Second, an obvious question is how to reconcile the positive and negative paths. We believe the answer lies in an account of potential moderators. In the following, we address the aspect of multiple mediators and moderators.

Multiple Mediators

A potential and legitimate criticism of our earlier theoretical discourse is that we discussed the mechanisms underlying the six possible relationships between felt job insecurity and perceived employability as if they existed in isolation. In reality, complex models involving multiple mediators are more plausible. In response, we advance a model with multiple mediators according to Figure 11.1 and our earlier theoretical considerations.

The upper part of Figure 11.1 concerns the negative relationship between felt job insecurity and perceived employability. Felt job insecurity may negatively affect perceived employability (Route 1) through need frustration, in line with insights from Self-Determination Theory: felt job insecurity frustrates the basic psychological needs

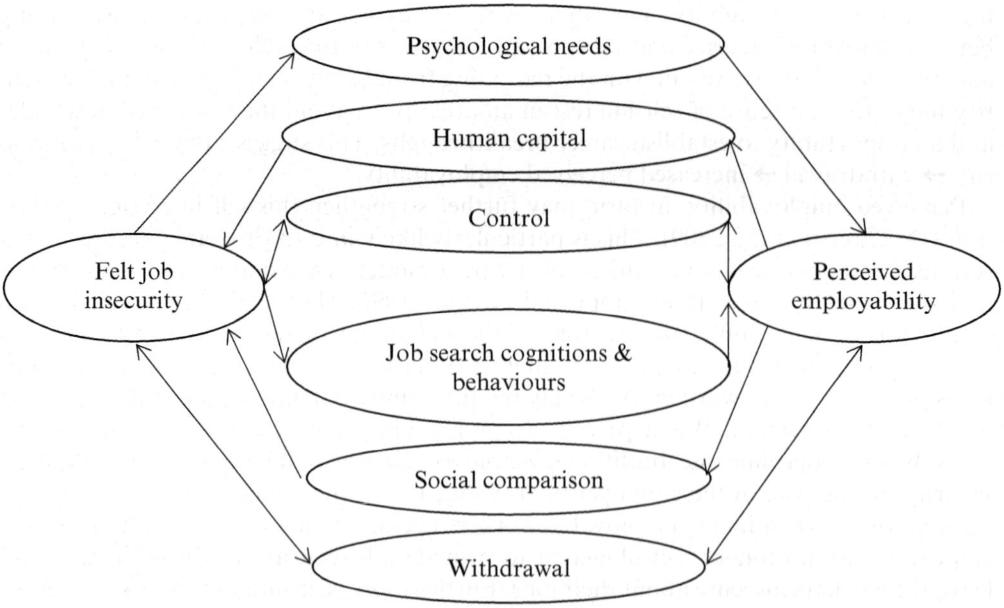

Figure 11.1 Multiple mediators

which then forestall all employability-development. Conversely, perceived employability may reduce feelings of job insecurity (Route 2) through returns on human capital investments: highly employable workers seek and get a return for their highly valued profile in the form of job security much in line with insights from Human Capital Theory. Appraisal Theory suggests reciprocal causation through perceived control (Route 3). Felt job insecurity is a stressor that is difficult to control and that may prompt ineffective emotional coping that forestalls all employability-development. Lower levels of perceived employability may contribute to feelings of uncontrollability, and hence to felt job insecurity. Conversely, high perceived employability provides the workers with a sense of control which may prevent feelings of job insecurity. Relative security may strengthen the individual's perception that she/he has an impact on the environment which then fosters perceived employability.

The lower part in Figure 11.1 displays the positive relationship between felt job insecurity and perceived employability. Felt job insecurity may positively affect perceived employability (Route 4): felt job insecurity may prompt job search cognitions and behaviour, which then feed perceived employability. This can be understood in terms of the idea of felt job insecurity as a challenge: felt job insecurity appraised as a challenge activates workers, for example, in the form of job search. In contrast, perceived employability may positively affect felt job insecurity when employable workers compare their present situation negatively to situations elsewhere (Route 5). Finally, felt job insecurity and perceived employability may mutually reinforce each other (Route 6) through mechanisms of social exchange: workers may see job insecurity as a breach of their psychological contract with the employer, and they may withdraw from their part of the deal by reducing loyalty and instead invest in becoming employable. The employer may see such investments as a signal that employees are planning to leave, and may refrain from further investments in the form of job security.

Possible Moderators

The idea that the paths between felt job insecurity and perceived employability can be both negative and positive may appear counterintuitive and conflicting. We believe that the negative and positive paths can be reconciled by accounting for possible moderators: the nature of the relationship may depend upon personal factors and upon structural factors related to the organization, the sector, the labour market and the general economy (De Cuyper et al., 2012). The underlying idea is that the negative paths might be more likely in situations that are based upon the traditional career model of job security provided by the employer, and the positive paths in situations that ease transition in line with newer and more flexible career models.

An example from the category of personal factors is age: younger workers may see job insecurity as part of the career phase of exploration they are in: upon felt job insecurity, they may engage in job search to increase the number of job opportunities and thus their perceptions of employability. In contrast, job insecurity might be particularly problematic among older workers (Stynen et al., 2014): older workers may feel powerlessness when they experience job insecurity and this may lead to lower perceived employability.

An example from the category of structural factors concerns differences in mobility rates between organizations and sectors. A plausible assumption in this respect is that the relationship between felt job insecurity and perceived employability is negative in most organizations and sectors but positive in organizations and sectors that promote quick transitions, such as organizations that promote quick exit along the in-and-out or up-or-out idea or in the information technology sector. Similarly, labour markets differ in the extent to which they promote active policies (Chung and Van Oorschot, 2011): active labour market policies may ease job search and thus promote employability upon feeling insecurity. Finally, the general economic condition may affect the relationship between felt job insecurity and perceived employability (Berntson et al., 2006): insecure workers may perceive themselves to be relatively employable when the economy is flourishing and many transitions are possible, while they may be fairly pessimistic about alternative labour market opportunities in times of recession.

CONCLUSION

We aimed at a thorough discussion on the nature and causality of the relationship between felt job insecurity and perceived employability, which led to an integrative model as depicted in Figure 11.1 and incorporating the idea of moderators. We see contributions at different levels. Theoretically, we have shown that the relationship between felt job insecurity and perceived employability is complex, and that different theoretical perspectives and an account of personal and structural factors are needed to understand this complexity. Methodologically, our discussion highlights the need for more longitudinal studies in order to establish causality. Practically, our discussion highlights that the idea of Flexicurity, namely a job insecure but highly employable workforce, and the idea of sustainable career development in times of insecurity are plausible. However, other routes are equally plausible. For example, high levels of felt job insecurity may lead to a reduced sense of employability that may hinder further career development. Furthermore, one should be aware of potential unintended side-effects: perceived employability may lead to a sense of self-interest that may change or even undermine the employee–employer relationship.

We also integrated some novel aspects into the discussion within this scholarly field. First, what is unique in the field of felt job insecurity and perceived employability research is that we combine theories from different fields: motivational psychology, social psychology, economy and career research. Second, we highlighted the importance of structural next to personal factors. Many studies provided a contextual background to understand study results. However, few studies have incorporated structural factors in their design, while this could be critical in understanding the relationship between felt job insecurity and perceived employability. Third, we call for more longitudinal studies that combine the idea of reciprocal causation along with multiple mediators. We believe and hope that these aspects may inspire future research.

REFERENCES

Baumeister, R. and M. Leary (1995), 'The need to belong: Desire for interpersonal attachments as a fundamental human motivation', *Psychological Bulletin*, **117**, 497–529.

Becker, Gary S. (1993), *Human Capital: A Theoretical and Empirical Analysis with Special Reference to Education*, Chicago, IL: National Bureau of Economic Research, The University of Chicago Press.

Berntson, E. (2008), 'Employability perceptions: Nature, determinants, and implications for health and well-being', doctoral thesis, Stockholm University, Sweden, available at http://www.diva-portal.org/smash/get/diva2:198489/FULLTEXT01.pdf.

Berntson, E., K. Näswall and M. Sverke (2008), 'Investigating the relationship between employability and self-efficacy: A cross-lagged analysis', *European Journal of Work and Organizational Psychology*, **17**, 413–25.

Berntson, E., K. Näswall and M. Sverke (2010), 'The moderating role of employability in the association between job insecurity and exit, voice, loyalty and neglect', *Economic and Industrial Democracy*, **3**, 1–16.

Berntson, E., M. Sverke and S. Marklund (2006), 'Predicting perceived employability: Human capital or labour market opportunities?', *Economic and Industrial Democracy*, **27**, 223–44.

Bordia, P., E. Jones, C. Gallois, V. Callan and N. DiFonzo (2006), 'Management are aliens! Rumors and stress during organizational change', *Group & Organization Management*, **31**, 601–21.

Brown, P., A. Hesketh and S. Williams (2003), 'Employability in a knowledge-driven economy', *Journal of Education and Work*, **16**, 107–26.

Cavanaugh, M.A., W.R. Boswell, M.V. Roehling and J.W. Boudreau (2000), 'An empirical examination of self-reported work stress among US managers', *Journal of Applied Psychology*, **85**, 65–74.

Chen, D.J.Q. and V.K.G. Lim (2012), 'Strength in adversity: The influence of psychological capital on job search', *Journal of Organizational Behavior*, **33**, 811–39.

Cheng, G.H.L. and D.K.S. Chan (2008), 'Who suffers more from job insecurity? A meta-analytic review', *Applied Psychology: An International Review*, **57**, 272–303.

Chung, H. and W. Van Oorschot (2011), 'Institutions versus market forces: Explaining the employment insecurity of European individuals during (the beginning of) the financial crisis', *Journal of European Social Policy*, **21**, 287–301.

Deci, E.L. and R.M. Ryan (2000), 'The "what" and "why" of goal pursuits: Human needs and the self-determination of behavior', *Psychological Inquiry*, **11**, 227–68.

De Cuyper, N. and H. De Witte (2006), 'The impact of job insecurity and contract type on attitudes, well-being and behavioural reports', *Journal of Occupational and Organizational Psychology*, **79**, 395–409.

De Cuyper, N. and H. De Witte (2011), 'The management paradox: Employability and organizational commitment and performance', *Personnel Review*, **40**, 152–72.

De Cuyper, N., E. Baillien and H. De Witte (2009), 'Job insecurity, perceived employability, and targets' and perpetrators' experiences of workplace bullying', *Work & Stress*, **23**, 206–24.

De Cuyper, N., S. Mauno, U. Kinnunen and A. Mäkikangas (2011), 'The role of job resources in the relation between perceived employability and turnover intention: A prospective two-sample study', *Journal of Vocational Behavior*, **78**, 253–63.

De Cuyper, N., C. Bernhard-Oettel, E. Berntson, H. De Witte and B. Alarco (2008), 'Employability and employees' well-being: Mediation by job insecurity', *Applied Psychology: An International Review*, **57**, 488–509.

De Cuyper, N., A. Mäkikangas, U. Kinnunen, S. Mauno and H. De Witte (2012), 'Cross-lagged associations between perceived employability, job insecurity and exhaustion: Testing gain and loss spirals according to the COR theory', *Journal of Organizational Behavior*, **33**, 770–88.

DeFillippi, Robert J. and Michael B. Arthur (1996), 'Boundaryless contexts and careers: A competency-based perspective', in Michael B. Arthur and Denise M. Rousseau (eds), *The Boundaryless Career: A New Employment Principle for a New Organizational Era*, New York: Oxford University Press, pp. 116–31.

Dekker, S.W.A. and W.B. Schaufeli (1995), 'The effects of job insecurity on psychological health and withdrawal: A longitudinal study', *Australian Psychologist*, **30**, 57–63.

De Witte, H. (1999), 'Job insecurity and psychological well-being: Review of the literature and exploration of some unresolved issues', *European Journal of Work and Organizational Psychology*, **8**, 155–77.

De Witte, H., N. De Cuyper, Y. Handaja, M. Sverke, K. Näswall and J. Hellgren (2010), 'Associations between qualitative and quantitative job insecurity and well-being: A test in Belgian banks', *International Studies of Management & Organization*, Special issue on job insecurity, **40**, 40–57.

DiRenzo, M.S. and J.H. Greenhaus (2011), 'Job search and voluntary turnover in a boundaryless world: A control theory perspective', *Academy of Management Review*, **36**, 567–89.

Festinger, L. (1954), 'A theory of social comparison processes', *Human Relations*, **7**, 117–42.

Filak, V. and K.M. Sheldon (2008), 'Teacher support, student motivation, student need satisfaction, and college teacher course evaluation: Testing a sequential path model', *Educational Psychology*, **28**, 711–24.

Forrier, A., L. Sels and D. Stynen (2009), 'Career mobility at the intersection between agent and structure: A conceptual model', *Journal of Occupational of Organizational Psychology*, **82**, 739–59.

Fugate, M., A.J. Kinicki and B.E. Ashforth (2004), 'Employability: A psychosocial construct, its dimensions, and applications', *Journal of Vocational Behavior*, **65**, 14–38.

Gracia, F.J., J. Ramos, J.M. Peiró, A. Caballer and B. Sora (2011), 'Job attitudes, behaviours and well-being among different types of temporary workers in Europe and Israel', *International Labour Review*, **150**, 235–54.

Green, F. (2011), 'Unpacking the misery multiplier: How employability modifies the impacts of unemployment and job insecurity on life satisfaction and mental health', *Journal of Health Economics*, **30**, 265–76.

Greenhalgh, L. and Z. Rosenblatt (1984), 'Job insecurity: Toward conceptual clarity', *Academy of Management Review*, **9**, 438–48.

Griffeth, R.W., R.P. Steel, D.G. Allen and N. Bryan (2005), 'The development of a multidimensional measure of job market cognitions: The Employment Opportunity Index (EOI)', *Journal of Applied Psychology*, **90**, 335–49.

Hall, D.T. (2004), 'The protean career: A quarter-century journey', *Journal of Vocational Behaviour*, **65**, 1–13.

Hellgren, J. and M. Sverke (2003), 'Does job insecurity lead to impaired well-being or vice versa? Estimation of cross-lagged effects using latent variable modelling', *Journal of Organizational Behavior*, **24**, 215–36.

Hellgren, J., M. Sverke and K. Isaksson (1999), 'A two-dimensional approach to job insecurity: Consequences for employee attitudes and well-being', *European Journal of Work and Organizational Psychology*, **8**, 179–95.

Jang, H., E.J. Kim and J. Reeve (2012), 'Longitudinal test of Self-Determination Theory's motivation mediation model in a naturally occurring classroom context', *Journal of Educational Psychology*, **104**, 1175–88.

Kalyal, H.J., E. Berntson, S. Baraldi, K. Näswall and M. Sverke (2010), 'The moderating role of employability on the relationship between job insecurity and commitment to change', *Economic and Industrial Democracy*, **3**, 327–44.

Kang, D., J. Gold and D. Kim (2012), 'Responses to job insecurity: The impact of discretionary extra-role and impression management behaviors and the moderating role of employability', *Career Development International*, **17**, 314–32.

Kiefer, T. (2005), 'Feeling bad: Antecedents and consequences of negative emotions in ongoing change', *Journal of Organizational Behavior*, **26**, 875–97.

Kirves, K., N. De Cuyper, U. Kinnunen and J. Nätti (2011), 'Perceived job insecurity and perceived employability in relation to temporary and permanent workers' psychological symptoms: A two samples study', *International Archives of Occupational and Environmental Health*, **84**, 899–909.

Klehe, U., J. Zikic, A.E.M. Van Vianen and I.E. De Pater (2011), 'Career adaptability, turnover, and loyalty during organizational downsizing', *Journal of Vocational Behavior*, **79**, 217–29.

Lazarus, Richard S. and Suzan Folkman (1984), *Stress Appraisal and Coping*, New York: Springer.

Mäkikangas, A., N. De Cuyper, S. Mauno and U. Kinnunen (2013), 'A longitudinal person-centred view on perceived employability: The role of job insecurity', *European Journal of Work and Organizational Psychology*, **22**, 490–503.

McArdle, S., L. Waters, J.P. Briscoe and D.T. Hall (2007), 'Employability during unemployment: Adaptability, career identity and human and social capital', *Journal of Vocational Behavior*, **71**, 247–64.
Park, S., S.D. Holloway, A. Arendtsz, J. Bemechat and J. Li (2012), 'What makes students engaged in learning? A time-used study of within- and between-individual predictors of emotional engagement in low-performing high schools', *Journal of Youth and Adolescence*, **41**, 390–401.
Parker, S.K., U.K. Bindl and K. Strauss (2010), 'Making things happen: A model of proactive motivation', *Journal of Management*, **36**, 827–56.
Peiró, J.M., B. Sora and A. Caballer (2012), 'Job insecurity in the younger Spanish workforce: Causes and consequences', *Journal of Vocational Behavior*, **80**, 444–53.
Pruijt, H. and P. Dérogée (2010), 'Employability and job security, friends or foes? The paradoxical reception of employacurity in the Netherlands', *Socio-Economic Review*, **8**, 437–60.
Reisel, W.D. and T.M. Probst (2010), 'Twenty-five years of studies of job insecurity', *International Studies of Management and Organization*, **40**, 3–5.
Rothwell, A. and J. Arnold (2007), 'Self-perceived employability: Development and validation of a scale', *Personnel Review*, **36**, 23–41.
Rothwell, A., S. Jewell and M. Hardie (2009), 'Self-perceived employability: Investigating the responses of post-graduate students', *Journal of Vocational Behavior*, **75**, 152–61.
Silla, I., N. De Cuyper, F.J. Gracia, J.M. Peiró and H. De Witte (2009), 'Job insecurity and well-being: Moderation by employability', *Journal of Happiness Studies*, **10**, 739–51.
Sora, B., A. Caballer and J.M. Peiró (2010), 'The consequences of job insecurity for employees: The moderator role of job dependence', *International Labour Review*, **149**, 59–72.
Staufenbiel, T. and C.J. König (2010), 'A model for the effects of job insecurity on performance, turnover intention, and absenteeism', *Journal of Occupational and Organizational Psychology*, **17**, 101–17.
Stynen, D., A. Forrier, L. Sels and H. De Witte (2014), 'The relationship between qualitative job insecurity and OCB: Differences across age groups', *Economic and Industrial Democracy*, published online 2 December 2013, doi: 10.1177/0143831X13510326.
Sverke, M. and J. Hellgren (2002), 'The nature of job insecurity: Understanding employment uncertainty on the brink of a new millennium', *Applied Psychology: An International Review*, **51**, 23–42.
Sverke, M., J. Hellgren and K. Näswall (2002), 'No security: A meta-analysis and review of job insecurity and its consequences', *Journal of Occupational Health Psychology*, **7**, 242–64.
Sverke, M., H. De Witte, K. Näswall and J. Hellgren (2010), 'European perspectives on job insecurity: Editorial introduction', *Economic and Industrial Democracy*, **31**, 175–8.
Van den Broeck, A., M. Vansteenkiste, H. De Witte, B. Soenens and W. Lens (2010), 'Capturing autonomy, competence and relatedness at work: Construction and initial validation of the Work-Related Basic Need Satisfaction Scale', *Journal of Occupational and Organizational Psychology*, **83**, 981–1002.
Van den Broeck, A., N. De Cuyper, E. Baillien, E. Van Belle, D. Vanhercke and H. De Witte (2013), 'Perceptions of organization's value support and perceived employability: Insights from Self-Determination Theory', *International Journal of Human Resource Management*, published online 5 December 2013, doi:10.1080/09585192.2013.860385.
Vander Elst, T. (2013), 'Towards an explanation of the job insecurity–outcome relationship: The role of perceived control', doctoral thesis, KU Leuven, Belgium.
Vander Elst, T., H. De Witte and N. De Cuyper (2014), 'The Job Insecurity Scale: A psychometric evaluation across five European countries', *European Journal of Work and Organizational Psychology*, **23**, 364–80.
Vander Elst, T., A. Van den Broeck, H. De Witte and N. De Cuyper (2012), 'Explaining the relationship between job insecurity and work-related well-being by psychological need frustration', *Work & Stress*, **26**, 256–71.
Van der Heijde, C.M. and B.I.J.M. Van der Heijden (2006), 'A competence-based and multidimensional operationalization and measurement of employability', *Human Resource Management*, **45**, 449–76.
Vanhercke, D., N. De Cuyper, E. Peeters and H. De Witte (2014), 'Perceived employability: A conceptual review', *Personnel Review*, **43**, 592–605.
Wittekind, A., S. Raeder and G. Grote (2010), 'A longitudinal study of determinants of perceived employability', *Journal of Organizational Behavior*, **31**, 566–86.
Worth, S. (2002), 'Education and employability: School leavers' attitudes to the prospect of non-standard work', *Journal of Education and Work*, **15**, 163–79.

12 Psychological mobility during unemployment: an outplacement study

Marijke Verbruggen, Nicky Dries, Anke Milissen and Sarah Vansteenkiste

The global economic crisis, along with the enduring trend of decreasing loyalty between employers and employees, has increased the occurrence and prevalence of bouts of unemployment throughout people's careers (Eby et al., 2003; Rousseau, 1997; Van Hoye and Lootens, 2013). Labor market researchers believe that psychological mobility – the extent to which people are *prepared* to and even *prefer* to explore a variety of career options and to cross different career boundaries (Forret et al., 2010; Sullivan and Arthur, 2006) – may help people to better navigate (recurrent) transitions from unemployment back into work (Koen et al., 2010; Van den Broeck et al., 2010).

People who are psychologically mobile are said to assess periods of unemployment more positively – for instance, as opportunities to make a positive change rather than as negative events interrupting their pathway to success (Forret et al., 2010). More specifically, psychological mobility is believed to positively affect people's self-perceived employability (Sullivan and Arthur, 2006) and their likelihood of reemployment (Vansteenkiste et al., 2013).

Yet little is known about the actual value of psychological mobility for unemployed job seekers. Only a few studies have examined the impact of psychological mobility to date (for example, Verbruggen, 2012). In addition, all but one of these studies have used samples of employed people, linking psychological mobility to outcomes such as career satisfaction and organizational commitment (Vansteenkiste et al., 2013). The one study that examined the impact of psychological mobility among unemployed job seekers (Vansteenkiste et al., 2013) focused on the impact of people's *preparedness* to explore a variety of career options. It was found that psychologically mobile individuals searched for jobs more intensely. They did not receive more job offers as a result of this, however.

In this empirical study, we want to extend our understanding of the impact of psychological mobility among unemployed job seekers by focusing on another aspect of psychological mobility – people's *preference* for making job transitions (Verbruggen, 2012) – and examining its impact on perceived employability. Although both preparedness to be mobile and preference for mobility are facets of psychological mobility, we believe that the latter may have stronger positive effects than the former because preferences are more intrinsic than preparedness, which is more situation-driven (Verbruggen, 2012).

In addition, if psychological mobility – in the sense of preference to be mobile – is indeed a valuable attitude for unemployed individuals, it is also important to understand which factors contribute to having or developing this attitude. Individuals who face an objectively similar career transition, such as the transition into unemployment, often demonstrate varying degrees of psychological mobility (Sullivan and Arthur, 2006). In this chapter, we will therefore examine a host of possible antecedents to psychological mobility, grouped together under the construct label of 'career competences' (Sullivan and Arthur, 2006). Shedding light on the specific career competences that encourage psychological mobility may help career counselors and employment officers to develop interventions aimed at enhancing psychological mobility among job seekers.

The present chapter makes three distinct contributions. First, we extend the understanding of psychological mobility by examining both its antecedents (that is, career competences) and outcomes (that is, perceived employability). Second, while most studies on psychological mobility have used samples of employees (Vansteenkiste et al., 2013), we focus on unemployed job seekers, in so doing shedding light on the potential value of psychological mobility for this particularly precarious group in the labor market. Third, as perceived employability can be seen as an indicator of career success for unemployed job seekers (Mäkikangasa et al., 2013) and therefore as an indicator of sustainable careers, we not only answer to the call for more integration between career success research and research on 'non-traditional' career attitudes (Arthur et al., 2005), but also shed light on the value of psychological mobility for the sustainability of a career.

PSYCHOLOGICAL MOBILITY

The concept of psychological mobility originates from the literature on the boundaryless career. Rather than representing any single form of career, the boundaryless career encompasses 'a range of possible forms that defy traditional employment assumptions' (Arthur and Rousseau, 1996, p.6). Although the original conceptualization of the boundaryless career by Arthur and Rousseau encompassed both physical and psychological boundary crossing, over time, research on the boundaryless career has come to focus mostly on the topic of changing employers (Sullivan and Baruch, 2009). In an effort to encourage researchers to acknowledge the broader meaning of the boundaryless career construct, Sullivan and Arthur introduced the psychological mobility construct in 2006, urging researchers to focus not only on the physical dimension of career mobility, but also on its psychological dimension.

Psychological mobility refers to people's *attitudes towards* physically crossing career boundaries (Lazarova and Taylor, 2009). Just as there are different types of physical mobility depending on the type of boundary that is crossed – organizational, occupational, geographic – variations in psychological mobility are conceivable, depending on the kind of transition the attitude relates to (Lazarova and Taylor, 2009; Forret et al., 2010). It makes sense that people would feel significantly different about becoming unemployed than they would about, for instance, changing organizations or functional domains.

Empirical research on the boundaryless career has largely ignored psychological mobility (Lazarova and Taylor, 2009; Sullivan and Baruch, 2009). This is in part due to the fact that psychological mobility is a hard construct to grasp (Rodrigues and Guest, 2010). Across different publications, psychological mobility has been defined as a preference to cross boundaries (Lazarova and Taylor, 2009; Marler et al., 2003), as perceived capability to move (Arthur et al., 2005; Sullivan and Arthur, 2006), as readiness to move (Vansteenkiste et al., 2013) and as the way people interpret a particular career move (Forret et al., 2010). Moreover, until recently, no measures of the construct could be found in the literature (Rodrigues and Guest, 2010; Sullivan and Baruch, 2009). To this end, Briscoe et al. (2006) developed and validated two scales measuring distinct aspects of psychological mobility: 'boundaryless mindset' and 'organizational mobility preference'.

Boundaryless mindset refers to people's preference towards initiating and pursuing work-related relationships across departmental and organizational boundaries. A person with this attitude is enthusiastic about creating and sustaining active relationships beyond departments and organizations. *Organizational mobility preference* refers to a person's inclination towards physically crossing organizational boundaries. Someone with high ratings on this attitude prefers a career that plays out across several employers (Briscoe et al., 2006). Both aspects of psychological mobility thus assess people's preference to cross specific career boundaries – the construct of interest in our study.

Boundaryless Mindset and Organizational Mobility Preference

Research on boundaryless mindset and organizational mobility preference, so far, has found that employees with a boundaryless mindset are more engaged in continuous job search behavior (Briscoe et al., 2012) and, on average, obtain a higher salary and more promotions (Verbruggen, 2012). Employees with high organizational mobility preference have been found to show less organizational commitment (Briscoe and Finkelstein, 2009; Çakmak-Otluoğlu, 2012) and to feel less easily satisfied with their job and career in general (Enache et al., 2011; Verbruggen, 2012).

Much less is known about the consequences of these types of psychological mobility among *unemployed* job seekers. As unemployed job seekers by definition are going through an important career transition, adopting a more positive stance towards crossing boundaries may be particularly valuable for this group (Forret et al., 2010). Being psychologically mobile might help them to maintain confidence in their ability to find a new job (Sullivan and Arthur, 2006) and to persevere in exploring different job opportunities (Briscoe et al., 2012) – all of which might enhance their likelihood of reemployment. As we discussed earlier, we consider career competences as an important antecedent to psychological mobility and perceived employability as an important outcome.

In what follows, we develop our hypotheses on the role of career competences – in particular, 'knowing why', 'knowing how' and 'knowing whom' competences (DeFillippi and Arthur, 1994) – in enhancing boundaryless mindset and organizational mobility preference and on the impact of these two aspects of psychological mobility on perceived employability (see Figure 12.1).

CAREER COMPETENCES AS ANTECEDENTS OF PSYCHOLOGICAL MOBILITY

In defining the possible antecedents of psychological mobility, we follow the typology of career competences developed by DeFillippi and Arthur (1994). They identified three broad types of career competences: knowing why, knowing how and knowing whom.

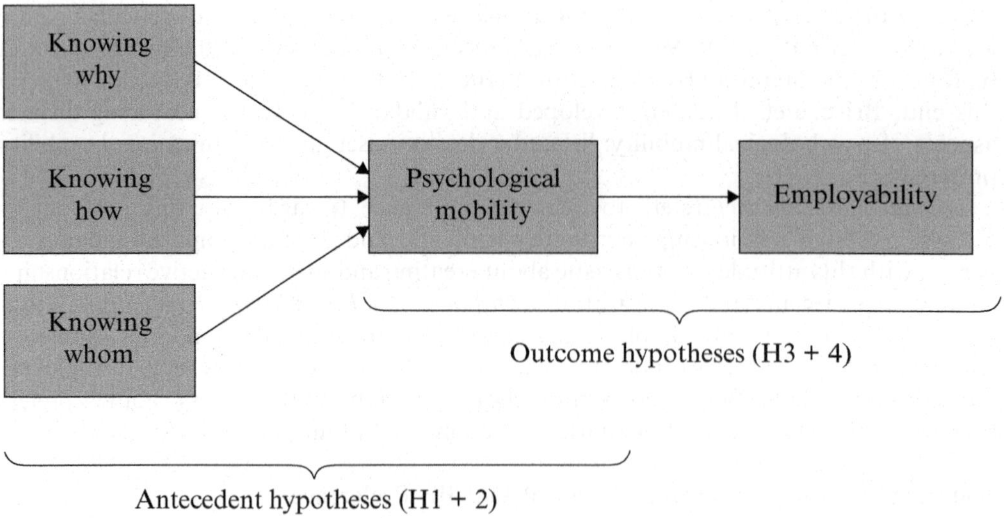

Figure 12.1 Research model

Knowing why competences give people direction when navigating their career (Sullivan and Arthur, 2006) and include people's self-awareness, opportunity awareness and ability to adapt to changing work situations (Arthur et al., 1999). Knowing how competences refer to people's job- and career-related knowledge and skills which are transferable across organizational boundaries (Eby et al., 2003). Knowing whom competencies concern people's professional and amicable relationships that provide information, visibility and access to new career opportunities (Sullivan and Arthur, 2006).

Sullivan and Arthur (2006) identified career competences as important antecedents of psychological mobility. We therefore expect knowing why, knowing how and knowing whom competences to be positively related to boundaryless mindset and organizational mobility preference. First, we expect a positive impact of knowing why. When people are more aware of their strengths and what they want in their career, they may have a stronger motivation to initiate relationships with people across functional domains and organizations, which may result in a stronger boundaryless mindset. In addition, a higher degree of self-awareness and of proactivity may make people more positive towards crossing organizational boundaries, since this could often help to realize their goals. So, knowing why may also be positively related to organizational mobility preference.

Second, we expect a positive impact of knowing how. People with more job-related skills and expertise may feel stronger in the labor market (Eby et al., 2003) and are often more open towards developing their competences even further (Storen, 2013). This may make them more positive towards initiating relationships across the functional and organizational domain ('boundaryless mindset') and towards actually crossing organizational boundaries ('organizational mobility preference'), as these could be viewed as new learning opportunities.

Finally, we also expect knowing whom competences to be positively related to the two psychological mobility indicators. Indeed, people who have a large network and who have experience with using their contacts may be better able to appreciate the value of initiating new relationships ('boundaryless mindset') and are likely to feel more comfortable with and take a more positive stance towards crossing organizational boundaries ('organizational mobility preference'). For these reasons, we expect knowing why, how and whom career competences to be positively related to boundaryless mindset and organizational mobility preference.

Hypothesis 1: Knowing why, how and whom competences are positively related to boundaryless mindset.

Hypothesis 2: Knowing why, how and whom competences are positively related to organizational mobility preference.

PERCEIVED EMPLOYABILITY AS AN OUTCOME OF PSYCHOLOGICAL MOBILITY

Perceived employability refers to individuals' perceptions of their likelihood of obtaining and retaining a job (for example, De Cuyper et al., 2008) and is assumed to be beneficial for individuals, especially in a context of unemployment. As individuals are likely to act upon their perceptions, perceived employability is believed to be conditional for people's effort to search for a new job, which may in turn affect their reemployment likelihood. Perceived employability may also be related to future career success, particularly in times when job vacancies are scarce (Arnold and Cohen, 2008; Mäkikangas et al., 2013) and has been shown to positively affect individuals' well-being (Berntson and Marklund, 2007; De Cuyper et al., 2008). Therefore, we believe perceived employability to be an important and highly relevant outcome for unemployed job seekers.

In line with Sullivan and Arthur (2006), we expect psychological mobility – and more specifically boundaryless mindset and organizational mobility preference – to be positively related to perceived employability. Since individuals with a boundaryless mindset prefer to build relationships across departments and organizations, they may be inclined to explore employment opportunities in many different organizations. Similarly, since people with a high mobility preference prefer their time with any employer to be limited, they may be inclined to explore and invest in their external career opportunities. This is likely to positively affect their expectations of their own employability. In addition, both types of psychological mobility indicate that people hold a positive view towards crossing boundaries (Briscoe et al., 2006). Having this type of mindset has been shown to positively affect unemployed job seekers' perceived employability and to motivate them to keep seeking reemployment despite setbacks (Chen and Lim, 2012). We therefore expect a positive association between boundaryless mindset and organizational mobility preference on perceived employability.

Hypothesis 3: Boundaryless mindset is positively related to perceived employability.

Hypothesis 4: Organizational mobility preference is positively related to perceived employability.

MEDIATING ROLE OF PSYCHOLOGICAL MOBILITY

Since we expect career competences to be positively related to boundaryless mindset and organizational mobility preference and the latter two, in turn, to be positively related to perceived employability, we assume the two psychological mobility indicators to mediate the relationship between career competences and perceived employability. Earlier research (Eby et al., 2003) has indeed found an impact of career competences on perceived employability.

Hypothesis 5: Boundaryless mindset and organizational mobility preference mediate the relationship between career competences and perceived employability.

METHOD

Procedure

Data were collected using a sample of Belgian unemployed job seekers who were participating in outplacement counseling at the time of data collection. We collaborated with a large outplacement firm located in Brussels, the capital of Belgium, which offers both individual and collective outplacement counseling. The outplacement firm provides counseling to job seekers who have been unemployed for a maximum of two years, specifically.

Clients of the outplacement firm were contacted by email to complete our questionnaire. We also provided hard copies of the questionnaire which were distributed at the outplacement office for clients who preferred to answer on paper. Of the 1079 unemployed job seekers invited, 466 (43 percent) filled in the questionnaire. After deleting records with missing values, we retained a final sample of 306 individuals.

About 57 percent of respondents were male and 43 percent were female. The average age of the respondents was 50 (SD = 6.05). Most respondents (63 percent) either held a bachelor's or master's degree. The respondents had been unemployed for on average five months (SD = 4.39) and they had been following the outplacement counseling for an average of four months (SD = 3.98).

Measures

Career competences

Knowing why was assessed with two indicators which have also been used as knowing why indicators in earlier studies (for example, Eby et al., 2003; Verbruggen and Sels, 2008), that is, proactive personality and self-awareness. Proactive personality was measured with the scale of Seibert et al. (1999). Respondents had to evaluate ten items on a seven-point Likert scale (1: Does not apply to me at all; 7: Fully applies to me). Example items were: 'I am constantly on the lookout for new ways to improve my life' and 'I excel at identifying opportunities'. The scale was found to be highly reliable (Cronbach's alpha = .92). Self-awareness was measured using two items from Day and Allen (2004), which respondents had to evaluate on a seven-point Likert scale (1: Does not apply to me at all; 7: Fully applies to me). A sample item is: 'I know my strengths'. Cronbach's alpha was .76.

Knowing how was measured with a five-item scale developed by Eby et al. (2003), which assesses people's career- and job-related skills. The scale includes items like: 'I possess a varied set of job-related skills' and 'I look for opportunities for training and development'. Respondents had to assess the items on a seven-point Likert scale (1: Does not apply to me at all; 7: Fully applies to me). We found the scale to be highly reliable (Cronbach's alpha = .89).

To measure *knowing whom*, we used the networking scale by Eby et al. (2003). This scale comprises four items (for example, 'I networked regularly with people from outside the organization where I was employed'), which respondents had to assess on a seven-point Likert scale (1: Does not apply to me at all; 7: Fully applies to me). The scale turned out to have a good internal consistency (Cronbach's alpha = .85).

Psychological mobility

We measured boundaryless mindset and organizational mobility preference using the scales of Briscoe, Hall and Demuth (2006). The items were slightly adapted to the situation of unemployed job seekers. The boundaryless mindset scale consists of eight items which respondents had to rate on a seven-point Likert scale (1: Totally disagree; 7: Totally agree). Sample items were: 'When I work for an organization, I like to accept tasks that require me to work beyond my own department' and 'When I work for an organization, I enjoy working with people outside of the organization'. After excluding two items due to cross-loadings (i.e. 'When I work for an organization, I look for job assignments which allow me to learn new things' and 'I am energized in new experiences and situations'), we found the scale to be highly reliable (Cronbach's alpha = .91). The mobility preference scale consists of five items measuring the strength of interest in having multiple (as opposed to a single) employers. Respondents had to rate the items on the same seven-point Likert scale. Example items included: 'I like the predictability that comes with working continuously for the same organization (Reverse Coded)' and 'I prefer to stay in a company I am familiar with rather than look for employment elsewhere (Reverse Coded)'. The scale had good internal consistency (Cronbach's alpha = .84).

Perceived employability

Perceived employability was measured with the reemployment efficacy scale of Wanberg et al. (2010). This scale aims to capture unemployed individuals' beliefs about their possibilities of getting new employment (Wanberg et al., 2010) and is therefore a good measure of self-perceived employability for the specific group of unemployed job seekers (cf. Berntson, 2008). The scale consists of four items (for example, I can find a job when I look for one) which respondents had to rate on a five-point Likert scale (1: no confidence at all; 5: fully confident). Reliability analysis revealed a Cronbach's alpha of .89.

Control variables

We controlled for gender (1: female, 0: male), age, the extent to which the dismissal was expected (1: not at all; 4: very much), unemployment duration and the duration of the outplacement counseling.

RESULTS

We first tested the measurement model comprising the four career competences, the two psychological mobility indicators and perceived employability. Estimation of this measurement model with seven latent factors yielded an acceptable fit (RMSEA=.06; SRMR=.06; CFI=.90 and NNFI=.90). All observed variables had significant loadings on their corresponding latent factor (.47 to .92; $p < .001$). Table 12.1 shows that this seven-factor model had a better fit to the data than models with fewer factors. In addition, given the poor fit of the single-factor model (see Table 12.1), common method bias is unlikely to be a serious concern for this study (Podsakoff et al., 2003).

Table 12.2 presents the descriptive statistics and correlations. We see that our respondents scored relatively high on knowing why and knowing how competences, but only moderately on knowing whom competences. In addition, they perceived themselves as having a boundaryless mindset, although their preference to switch organizations appeared to be rather moderate. They were on average relatively confident in their ability to find a new job.

To test our hypotheses, we conducted hierarchical regression analyses. First, we performed hierarchical regression analyses to examine the impact of the knowing why, how and whom competences on the two indicators of psychological mobility (see Table 12.3). Boundaryless mindset turned out to be significantly related to one of the two knowing why indicators – that is, proactive personality ($\beta = .18$; $p < .05$) – as well as to the

Table 12.1 Fit indices of different measurement models

	X^2(df)	P(X^2)	SRMR	RMSEA	CFI	NNFI
1-factor model	4035(664)	<.0001	.113	.129	.54	.51
2-factor model[1]	3381(661)	<.0001	.115	.116	.63	.61
3-factor model[2]	2749(657)	<.0001	.096	.102	.72	.70
4-factor model[3]	2212(652)	<.0001	.082	.089	.78	.77
5-factor model[4]	2567(646)	<.0001	.097	.099	.74	.71
6-factor model A[5]	1920(639)	<.0001	.076	.081	.83	.81
6-factor model B[6]	1493(639)	<.0001	.059	.066	.88	.87
7-factor model[7]	1376(631)	<.0001	.056	.062	.90	.89

Notes:

1. The 2-factor model contains 1 factor for the career competences and 1 factor for the 2 psychological mobility variables and perceived employability.
2. The 3-factor model contains 1 factor for the career competences, 1 for the 2 psychological mobility variables and 1 factor for perceived employability.
3. The 4-factor model contains 1 factor for the career competences, 1 factor for boundaryless mindset, 1 factor for organizational mobility preference and 1 factor for perceived employability.
4. The 5-factor model contains 4 factors for the 4 career competences and 1 factor for the 2 psychological mobility variables and perceived employability.
5. The 6-factor model A contains 4 factors for the 4 career competences and 1 factor for the 2 psychological mobility variables and 1 factor for perceived employability.
6. The 6-factor model B contains 1 factor for the knowing why competences, 1 factor for career insight, 1 factor for networking, 1 factor for boundaryless mindset, 1 factor for organizational mobility preference and 1 factor for perceived employability.
7. The 7-factor model contains 1 factor for the 4 career competences, 1 factor for boundaryless mindset, 1 factor for organizational mobility preference and 1 factor for perceived employability.

Table 12.2 Descriptives of and correlations among key variables

	M	SD	1	2	3	4	5	6
1. Knowing why 1: Proactive personality	5.1	1.0	–					
2. Knowing why 2: Self-awareness	5.7	1.0	.48**	–				
3. Knowing how	5.1	1.2	.67**	.52**	–			
4. Knowing whom	4.2	1.5	.39**	.23**	.39**	–		
5. Boundaryless mindset	4.8	1.4	.49**	.29**	.58**	.48**	–	
6. Organizational mobility preference	4.3	1.6	.19**	.07	.23**	.28**	.33**	–
7. Perceived employability	3.6	1.0	.37**	.29**	.48**	.37**	.33**	.26**

Note: ** $p < .01$; * $p < .05$.

Table 12.3 Hierarchical regression analyses with psychological mobility as the dependent variable

	Boundaryless mindset		Organizational mobility preference	
Female	−.33*	−.07	.12	.33(*)
Age	−.02	.00	−.03(*)	−.02
Expectedness of dismissal	.11	.06	−.30**	−.32**
Unemployment duration	−.01	−.01	.04	.05(*)
Duration counseling	−.00	−.00	−.03	−.04
Knowing why				
• Proactive personality		.18*		−.02
• Self-awareness		−.05		−.15
Knowing how		.46**		.33**
Knowing whom		.25**		.24**
R^2	2%	42%**	5%**	16%**
Change in R^2		40%**		11%**

Note: ** $p < .01$; * $p < .05$; (*) $p < .10$.

knowing how ($\beta = .46$; $p < .01$) and knowing whom variables ($\beta = .25$; $p < .01$). We found no significant relationship with the second knowing why indicator, self-awareness. Organizational mobility preference, on the other hand, was only significantly related to knowing how ($\beta = .33$; $p < .01$) and knowing whom ($\beta = .24$; $p < .01$), not to the knowing why indicators. We can therefore only partially accept Hypotheses 1 and 2.

Second, we examined the impact of the two psychological mobility indicators on perceived employability. As can be seen in Table 12.4, both boundaryless mindset ($\beta = .18$; $p < .01$) and organizational mobility preference ($\beta = .10$; $p < .01$) were found to be positively related to perceived employability. Our findings thus provide support for Hypotheses 1 and 2.

Finally, we tested whether psychological mobility mediated the relationship between career competences and perceived employability. Since we had already performed the

Table 12.4 Hierarchical regression analyses with perceived employability as the dependent variable

	Perceived employability	
Female	−.02	.03
Age	−.03**	−.03**
Expectedness of dismissal	.05	.06
Unemployment duration	−.03(*)	−.03*
Duration counseling	−.02	−.03
Boundaryless mindset		.18**
Organizational mobility preference		.10**
R^2	10%**	22%**
Change in R^2		12%**

Note: ** $p < .01$; * $p < .05$; (*) $p < .10$.

first necessary step to test mediation – that is, testing the impact of career competences on psychological mobility (Baron and Kenny, 1986) – what remained to be done was to test the two remaining steps: (1) examining the impact of career competences on perceived employability in a regression without the psychological mobility indicators; and (2) examining the impact of career competences and psychological mobility together. The results of these analyses are found in Table 12.5.

The mediation analyses revealed a significant impact of knowing how ($\beta = .29$; $p < .01$) and knowing whom ($\beta = .12$; $p < .01$) on perceived employability when the psychological mobility indicators were not included in the analysis. Neither of the two knowing why indicators were found to have an impact. Table 12.5 further shows that the impact of knowing how ($\beta = .28$; $p < .01$) and knowing whom ($\beta = .11$; $p < .01$) is slightly reduced when the psychological mobility indicators are included in the regressions, which suggests a partial mediation by psychological mobility. This is supported by the results of the Sobel tests ($p_{\text{knowing how}} = .071$; $p_{\text{knowing whom}} = .051$), although the mediation effects were only slightly significant. As can be seen in the right-hand column of Table 12.5, the mediation is fully accounted for by organizational mobility preference ($\beta = .07$; $p < .05$), not by boundaryless mindset. We thus found only partial support for Hypothesis 5. The fact that we found no impact of boundaryless mindset when the career competences were entered into the regression further suggests that the impact we found initially (see Table 12.3) is likely to be spurious and accounted for by the career competences knowing how and knowing whom, rather than by boundaryless mindset itself.

DISCUSSION

In this study, we examined a specific set of antecedents (career competences) and outcomes (perceived employability) of two aspects of psychological mobility (boundaryless mindset and organizational mobility preference) among unemployed job seekers participating in outplacement counseling. The overall aim of the study was to improve

Table 12.5 Additional analyses to test the mediating role of psychological mobility

	Perceived employability		
Female	−.02	.11	.09
Age	−.03**	−.02**	−.02**
Expectedness of dismissal	.05	.02	.05
Unemployment duration	−.03(*)	−.02	−.02
Duration counseling	−.02	−.03*	−.03(*)
Knowing why			
• Proactive personality		.04	.05
• Self-awareness		.02	.03
Knowing how		.29**	.28**
Knowing whom		.12**	.11**
Boundaryless mindset			−.26
Organizational mobility preference			.07*
R^2	10%**	34%**	36%**
Change in R^2		25%**	1%(*)

Note: ** $p < .01$; * $p < .05$; (*) $p < .10$.

understanding of psychological mobility with the population of unemployed jobseekers, specifically.

We first of all examined the impact of career competences on psychological mobility. We found the expected impact of knowing how and knowing whom on boundaryless mindset and organizational mobility preference. The knowing why 'proactive personality' indicator was found to affect boundaryless mindset, but not organizational mobility preference. No impact was found of the second knowing why indicator, 'self-awareness'.

In addition, we found indications that, as expected, psychological mobility was positively related to perceived employability. Our supplementary analyses, however, showed that for boundaryless mindset, this relationship was likely to be spurious. More specifically, the fact that the impact of boundaryless mindset disappeared once career competences were included in the analysis indicates that the impact we found initially is likely to be accounted for by career competences, rather than by people's preference for initiating relationships across functional and organizational boundaries as such. It is likely that people believe that their competences are more visible than their mindset to future employers and therefore base their expectations of their own employability more on their competences than on their general attitude towards mobility. For organizational mobility preference, we still found an impact after including career competences in the analysis although this impact, as well, was found to be much lower than in the regression where career competences were not included. As individuals with a high organizational mobility preference prefer to switch employers regularly, they are likely to view unemployment, to a lesser extent, as a distinctly negative experience, which may translate into a more optimistic assessment of reemployment odds (Forret et al., 2010).

Implications

Our findings indicate that, when developing hypotheses about the antecedents and outcomes of psychological mobility, researchers should take into account that results can be expected to differ based on the population upon which psychological mobility studies are conducted. For instance, our findings indicate that in our (very specific) sample of unemployed job seekers going through outplacement counseling, psychological mobility is only to a certain extent related to self-perceived employability. Furthermore, boundaryless mindset appeared to have little impact at all, which is an unexpected result when we compare our findings to those of earlier studies done in working populations (Briscoe et al., 2012; Verbruggen, 2012). In fact, studies on psychological mobility using employed samples tend to find that having a boundaryless mindset has more positive outcomes than reporting high organizational mobility preference, especially for career success-related outcomes such as job level, promotion speed and wage (Briscoe et al., 2012; Verbruggen, 2012). We have found opposite results for our unemployed sample, however, which implies that the relationship between psychological mobility and career outcomes may be markedly different for different groups in the labor market. As we discussed earlier in this chapter, although psychological mobility is in fact a topic of specific interest to researchers looking at unemployment and reemployment, the question remains as to whether the theory on psychological mobility at present is capable of explaining its effects in employed and unemployed populations alike. Previously, Vansteenkiste et al. (2013) and Forret et al. (2010) have done some work in the way of developing psychological mobility measures specifically for the unemployed, but further research is necessary to test these measures and to assess the validity of choosing one measure over another depending on the population under study. In addition, it is important to acknowledge that our population was not only unemployed but also in the specific situation of being enrolled in outplacement counseling, which is only the case for around 15 000 people in Belgium (Federgon, 2012).

Our finding regarding the lack of a relationship between self-awareness and psychological mobility is particularly remarkable since self-awareness is generally considered to be an important career competence (DeFillippi and Arthur, 1994; Hall, 1996), as it provides direction when people are faced with less-than-straightforward career transitions (Bright and Pryor, 2005). Better self-awareness provides a clearer self-concept and the clearer the self-concept, the easier it should be to filter and process information in a consistent way (Cabral and Salomone, 1990). In turbulent times, when people are confronted with an 'overkill' of information, self-awareness would appear to be an essential competency in terms of decision making and coping. It is therefore remarkable that we did not find a relationship between self-awareness and people's attitude towards change and turbulence. The lack of a relationship with self-awareness might be explained by the specific forms of psychological mobility we focused on in this study: people's preference for mobility. Perhaps self-awareness relates first and foremost to people's *readiness* to be mobile, or to their *capability* to handle changes rather than to their mobility *preferences*. Further research into the role of self-awareness in how psychological mobility shapes sustainable careers seems warranted. A good starting point may be the work of McArdle et al. (2007), in which a clear distinction is made between career adaptability (that is, the willingness and ability to change behaviors, feelings and thoughts in response to environmental demands) and career identity (that is, the way individuals define themselves in the career context, which acts as a 'cognitive compass' used to navigate career opportunities).

Limitations and Directions for Further Research

Our study was obviously not without limitations. First, our findings are based on self-report data and therefore run the risk of common-method variance. To validate our findings, future research might consider including more objective (non-self-reported) measures. Secondly, because we used cross-sectional data, we need to proceed with caution in making causal attributions. It is possible, for instance, that being more psychologically mobile is related to a higher motivation for ongoing career competence development and improvement, because the person wants to keep his or her options open and not become too narrowly skilled for one specific occupation or organizational context. Third, it is important to recognize the specificity of our sample. Although we explicitly set out to examine the potential effects of psychological mobility for unemployed job seekers, not all job seekers participate in outplacement counseling. It is highly likely that this type of setting creates both increased self-awareness and increased social and practical support in finding a new job. Therefore, our findings cannot be generalized to the broader population of the unemployed.

As for further research, it appears that first and foremost there is a need for further work to dig deeper into what the most adequate operationalization of psychological mobility is, or should be: is it a readiness, a capability, a preference, all of the above, or none of these? And to what extent, and how, do results differ when we use different measures of psychological mobility? Second, future studies could look at outcome variables beyond self-perceived employability. Variables such as time to reemployment, job quality and skill utilization in the first job, or sequence of jobs, after a period of unemployment appear of particular interest. Third, future research might examine whether the three career competences, knowing why, knowing how, or knowing whom, are to be seen as complementary or supplementary resources to individuals. Can people compensate for a lack of specific knowledge and skills (knowing how) by having an exceptionally large, tight, or loyal network (knowing whom), for instance? Finally, as careers are by definition longitudinal, it seems of particular interest to examine the value of psychological mobility over extended periods of time.

REFERENCES

Arnold, J. and L. Cohen (2008), 'The psychology of careers in industrial and organizational settings: A critical but appreciative analysis', in G.P. Hodgkinson and J.K. Ford (eds), *International Review of Industrial and Organizational Psychology*, New York: Wiley, pp. 1–44.

Arthur, M. and D. Rousseau (1996), *The Boundaryless Career: A New Employment Principle for a New Organizational Era*, New York: Oxford University Press.

Arthur, M., K. Inkson and J. Pringle (1999), *The New Careers: Individual Action and Economic Change*, London: Sage.

Arthur, M., S. Khapova and C. Wilderom (2005), 'Career success in a boundaryless career world', *Journal of Organizational Behavior*, 26, 177–202.

Baron, R.M. and D.A. Kenny (1986), 'The moderator–mediator variable distinction in social psychological

research: Conceptual, strategic and statistical considerations', *Journal of Personality and Social Psychology*, 51, 1173–82.
Berntson, E. (2008), *Employability Perceptions*, Stockholm: Department of Psychology, Stockholm University.
Berntson, E. and S. Marklund (2007), 'The relationship between perceived employability and subsequent health', *Work and Stress*, 21, 279–92.
Bright, J. and R. Pryor (2005), 'The chaos theory of careers: A user's guide', *Career Development Quarterly*, 53, 291–305.
Briscoe, J. and L. Finkelstein (2009), 'The "new career" and organizational commitment: Do boundaryless and protean attitudes make a difference?', *Career Development International*, 14, 242–60.
Briscoe, J., D.T. Hall and R. DeMuth (2006), 'Protean and boundaryless careers: An empirical exploration', *Journal of Vocational Behavior*, 69, 30–47.
Briscoe, J., S. Henagan, J. Burton and W. Murphy (2012), 'Coping with an insecure employment environment: The differing roles of protean and boundaryless career orientations', *Journal of Vocational Behavior*, 80, 308–16.
Cabral, A. and P. Salomone (1990), 'Chance and careers: Normative versus contextual development', *The Career Development Quarterly*, 39, 5–17.
Çakmak-Otluoğlu, K. (2012), 'Protean and boundaryless career attitudes and organizational commitment: The effects of perceived supervisor support', *Journal of Vocational Behavior*, 80, 638–46.
Chen, D. and V. Lim (2012), 'Strength in adversity: The influence of psychological capital on job search', *Journal of Organizational Behavior*, 33, 811–39.
Day, R. and T.D. Allen (2004), 'The relationship between career motivation and self-efficacy with protégé career success', *Journal of Vocational Behavior*, 64, 72–91.
De Cuyper, N., C. Bernhard-Oettel, E. Berntson, H. De Witte and B. Alarco (2008), 'Employability and employees' well-being: Mediation by job insecurity', *Applied Psychology: An International Review*, 57, 488–509.
DeFillippi, R.J. and M. Arthur (1994), 'The boundaryless career: A competency-based perspective', *Journal of Organizational Behavior*, 15, 307–24.
Eby, L., M. Butts and A. Lockwood (2003), 'Predictors of success in the era of the boundaryless career', *Journal of Organizational Behavior*, 24, 689–708.
Enache, M., J. Sallan, P. Simo and V. Fernandez (2011), 'Career attitudes and subjective career success: Tackling gender differences', *Gender in Management: An International Journal*, 26, 234–50.
Federgon (2012), 'Federgon Annual Report 2012', available at: http://www.federgon-annualreport.be/nl/economisch-rapport?t=outplacement.
Forret, M., S. Sullivan and L. Mainiero (2010), 'Gender role differences in reactions to unemployment: Exploring psychological mobility and boundaryless careers', *Journal of Organizational Behavior*, 31, 647–66.
Hall, D. (1996), 'Protean careers of the 21st century', *Academy of Management Executive*, 10, 8–16.
Koen, J., U.C. Klehe, A. Van Vianen, J. Zikic and A. Nauta (2010), 'Job-search strategies and reemployment quality: The impact of career adaptability', *Journal of Vocational Behavior*, 77, 126–39.
Lazarova, M. and S. Taylor (2009), 'Boundaryless careers, social capital and knowledge management: Implications for organizational performance', *Journal of Organizational Behavior*, 30, 119–39.
Mäkikangas, A., N. De Cuyper, S. Mauno and U. Kinnunen (2013), 'A longitudinal person-centred view on perceived employability: The role of job insecurity', *European Journal of Work and Organizational Psychology*, 22 (4), 490–503.
Marler, J., M. Barringer and G. Milkovich (2003), 'Boundaryless and traditional contingent employees: Worlds apart', *Journal of Organizational Behavior*, 23, 425–53.
McArdle, S., L. Waters, J.P. Briscoe and D.T. Hall (2007), 'Employability during unemployment: Adaptability, career identity and human and social capital', *Journal of Vocational Behavior*, 71 (2), 247–64.
Podsakoff, P.M., S.B. MacKenzie, J.Y. Lee and N.P. Podsakoff (2003), 'Common method biases in behavioral research: A critical review of the literature and recommended remedies', *Journal of Applied Psychology*, 88 (5), 879–903.
Rodrigues, R. and D. Guest (2010), 'Have careers become boundaryless?', *Human Relations*, 63, 1157–75.
Rousseau, D. (1997), 'Organizational behavior in the new organizational era', *Annual Review of Psychology*, 48, 515–46.
Seibert, S.E., J.M. Crant and M.L. Kraimer (1999), 'Proactive personality and career success', *Journal of Applied Psychology*, 84, 416–27.
Storen, L. (2013), 'Who attends work-related training five years after graduation? A comparison across European countries', *International Journal of Lifelong Education*, 32, 165–89.
Sullivan, S. and M. Arthur (2006), 'The evolution of the boundaryless career concept: Examining physical and psychological mobility', *Journal of Vocational Behavior*, 69, 19–29.
Sullivan, S. and Y. Baruch (2009), 'Advances in career theory and research: A critical review and agenda for future explorations', *Journal of Management*, 35, 1542–71.

Van den Broeck, A., M. Vansteenkiste, W. Lens and H. De Witte (2010), 'Unemployed individuals' work values and job flexibility: An explanation from expectancy-value theory and self-determination theory', *Applied Psychology: An International Review*, 59, 296–317.
Van Hoye, G. and H. Lootens (2013), 'Coping with unemployment: Personality, role demands and time structure', *Journal of Vocational Behavior*, 82, 85–95.
Vansteenkiste, S., M. Verbruggen and L. Sels (2013), 'Being unemployed in the boundaryless career era: Does psychological mobility pay off?', *Journal of Vocational Behavior*, 82, 135–43.
Verbruggen, M. (2012), 'Psychological mobility and career success in the "New" career climate', *Journal of Vocational Behavior*, 81, 289–97.
Verbruggen, M. and L. Sels (2008), 'Can career self-directedness be improved through counseling?', *Journal of Vocational Behavior*, 73, 318–27.
Wanberg, C.R., J. Zhu and E.A.J. Van Hooft (2010), 'The job search grind: Perceived progress, self-reactions and self-regulation of search effort', *Academy of Management Journal*, 53, 788–807.

13 The role of employee adaptability, goal striving and proactivity for sustainable careers

Karen Van Dam, Tanja Bipp and Joris Van Ruysseveldt

INTRODUCTION

Today's organizations are characterized by dynamic and uncertain environments that require organizations to be increasingly adaptive and innovative (Van Dam, 2013). Globalization, rapid technological changes, and economic crises are some of the factors forcing organizations to engage in continuous change. As a consequence, the labor market has changed substantially, emphasizing flexible contracts, employee development, and proactive career management (Berntson et al., 2006). The time when employees would enter an organization and remain with this organization seems over (Klehe et al., 2011). Instead of the traditional career that was largely managed by the organization, employees are nowadays engaging in self-managed careers that comprise of frequent changes in tasks, jobs, work roles and work environments (Hall, 2002; Sullivan and Baruch, 2009).

This dynamic and constantly changing world has important implications for workers' sustainable careers. Sustainability implies that employees (and organizations) should act in such a way that workers' resources are retained for the future (Docherty et al., 2009). Given that change has become an ever-present feature of organizational life, the question arises as to how employees should respond to this dynamic work environment and changed career perspectives in order to secure a sustainable career. In this chapter, we argue that a satisfying and sustainable career requires employees to engage in adaptive and self-regulated (that is, goal-directed, proactive) behavior (see also Savickas, 1997; Savickas and Porfeli, 2012; Wanberg and Kammeyer-Mueller, 2008). Accordingly, the goal of the present chapter is to explore the role of three personal aspects that appear crucial for sustainable careers: workers' adaptability, goal striving and proactivity. In line with the positive psychology framework that focuses on conditions and processes contributing to optimal functioning (Seligman and Csikszentmihalyi, 2000), we emphasize the positive side of dynamic work contexts. As such, we aim to contribute to the insights of employees' sustainable careers by discussing some important self-regulatory behaviors and conditions underlying employees' adaptation to dynamic work contexts.

The chapter first focuses on adaptation in general and employee adaptation in particular. Both concepts refer to self-regulatory processes and emphasize the importance of goal-directed and proactive behavior. Therefore, in the following sections, we will explore and discuss research on goal-directed striving and proactive behavior. Throughout the chapter, we will show how adaptability, goal striving and proactivity relate to workers' sustainable careers.

INDIVIDUAL ADAPTATION AT WORK

Nowadays, most organizations operate in dynamic, competitive and/or uncertain environments and therefore need to be flexible and adaptive in order to survive. As a consequence, today's employees are facing dynamic work contexts that are defined by continuous change and uncertainty. These dynamics have also changed the nature of careers, which have become increasingly discontinuous and boundaryless, with career paths less prescribed (Strauss et al., 2012). In order to sustain their career, employees need to become (pro)active career-managers who define their own career goals, maintain their employability and engage in career transitions (Fugate et al., 2004). Together, these developments imply new requirements regarding employees' ability to adapt effectively to new or uncertain work situations. But what does effective adaptation imply?

Effective Adaptation

The concept of adaptation has been extensively addressed in evolutionary biology, where it relates to the evolutionary process whereby a population becomes better suited to its habitat. Adaptation is supposed to help organisms adjust to a changing and/or demanding environment, and as such contribute to the survival of the species (King et al., 2006). In the work context, 'survival' might not be an adequate outcome indicator for effective adaptation; very few people would consider working for an organization whose workers 'manage to survive'. Still, the emphasis on survival stresses the importance of a long-term perspective when looking at adjustment processes. A response can only be considered adaptive when it is successful in the long run. For example, conforming oneself to a new bossy supervisor or an aversive work environment might only work in the beginning but is likely to undermine employee motivation and health when it is continued for a longer period. This long-term perspective highlights that adaptation is different from conforming and accommodating, concepts that emphasize employees' efforts to align themselves with the environment (Savickas, 1997). Whereas adaptation is associated with positive outcomes, efforts to conform and accommodate might result in negative outcomes. As Block and Kremen (1996, p. 350) noted, a person who has conformed to the environment might not be a happy person, but just a person 'who has settled for less'.

Central to the concept of adaptation is the fit between the individual and the environment. Research on Person–Environment (P–E) fit suggests that discrepancies between aspects of the individual and the environment can have severe, negative consequences, while individuals fare better when personal and environmental aspects are well-matched (for example, Deci and Ryan, 2000; Kristof-Brown et al., 2005). Perceptions of discrepancies between the person and the work environment are expected to trigger adaptive responses that can involve both the person and the environment (Ployhart and Bliese, 2006; Van Dam, 2013). That is, employees can try to improve P–E fit by changing some personal aspects, work environmental aspects, or both. It should be noted that misfit can develop in different ways; besides changes in the work environment, employees can change as well (Griffin and Hesketh, 2003; Nicholson, 1984). Employees might experience evolving developmental needs and career aspirations while working in their job or going through different life stages. Consequently, they might feel a need to address and/or develop different aspects and competencies, prepare themselves for future career roles, or search for a new career opportunity.

Effective adaptation in the long run is considered to enhance employee health, motivation, human capital and career opportunities (Kristof-Brown et al., 2005; Van Dam, 2013). Therefore, instead of focusing on 'survival', we could very well use these aspects of sustainable employability (or sustainable labor participation, see also Chapter 10 in this volume) as indicators of effective adaptation. Employees who deal effectively with changing work situations or evolving personal needs will stay healthy, motivated and competent during their careers, and accordingly will be able to remain in the work force until – and even beyond – the official retirement year. In other words, effective adaptation can be considered a crucial condition for employees' sustainable careers.

Approaches to Adaptation

Although the importance of adaptation for individual and organizational outcomes has been emphasized in both the academic and popular press (Griffin and Hesketh, 2003; Ployhart and Bliese, 2006). Besides this apparent agreement, many different definitions and labels have been used when referring to adaptation. Still, a number of general approaches can be distinguished. Evolutionary biologists, for example, distinguish between adaptation as (1) the process of adjustment; (2) the state of being adapted; and (3) an underlying ability that enhances the probability that the organism will survive and reproduce (Orr, 2005). In the same vein, organizational and career researchers have studied employee adaptation using behavioral approaches on the one hand, and individual differences approaches on the other hand (Van Dam, 2013).

Within the behavioral approach of employee adaptation, researchers have generally focused on what employees do when work tasks and/or the work context change, or when a P–E misfit occurs. Experimental studies have investigated, for instance, how employees perform when some features of the task are altered, and whether knowledge and skills transfer to new work tasks (for example, LePine et al., 2000). Similarly, field studies have examined how workers adjust to new work roles and work processes (for example, Griffin et al., 2010; Niessen et al., 2010; Wanberg and Kammeyer-Mueller, 2008). Some studies have tried to establish which behaviors are needed in specific adaptive situations. Within the US Army, for example, a taxonomy of adaptive behaviors has been developed that is used to select and develop Army recruits (Pulakos et al., 2006). It should be noted that other research fields have similarly focused on employees' responses to changing, stressful or uncertain work situations, yet without directly referring to the concept of adaptation. Workplace learning, employability development, coping with stress, career self-management, job search and new entrants' socialization tactics are all examples of behaviors involved in employees' efforts to adapt to new or changing work situations (Ployhart and Bliese, 2006; Van Dam, 2013).

Within the individual differences approach to employee adaptation, the focus has been on employee adaptability as an underlying adaptive potential (for example, Griffin and Hesketh, 2003; Ployhart and Bliese 2006; Van Dam, 2013). Adaptability has been conceptualized in several different ways, relating to adaptability in general (Fugate et al., 2004; Ployhart and Bliese, 2006; Van Dam, 2013), and to more specific forms of adaptability, such as task adaptiveness (Griffin et al., 2007), leader adaptability

(Mueller-Hanson et al., 2005), and career adaptability (Savickas, 1997; Savickas and Porfeli, 2012). Whereas some definitions emphasize employees' willingness to change aspects of themselves (for example, Fugate et al., 2004), other definitions include the possibility to change the person as well as the environment (Ployhart and Bliese, 2006; Van Dam, 2013). This position holds that whereas individuals can modify their behavior and competencies to fit the environment, the environment is also malleable and subject to change (Ashford and Taylor, 1990; Nicholson, 1984).

Adaptation and Sustainable Careers

Most approaches to adaptability emphasize the importance of self-regulation for employees' sustainable careers. Self-regulation is considered a critical competency that underlies the mindful, intentional and thoughtful behaviors of individuals. Generally, self-regulation refers to proactive, goal-directed behavior, that is behavior that is personally initiated and aimed at accomplishing a valued, long-term goal. Especially in dynamic work environments where career paths are created by employees individually, employees have to be proactive, engage in career planning by setting career goals and formulating strategies to achieve these goals (Seibert et al., 2001). At the same time, they need to invest in continuous development of skills and core competencies, and engage in consultation with senior colleagues regarding career opportunities and personal development (King, 2004). In short, employees should engage in self-regulated, proactive career management instead of being passive, reactive respondents to career opportunities and environmental developments (Parker et al., 2010). The next two sections will further explore the importance of employees' goal striving and proactivity for enhancing sustainable careers.

GOAL STRIVING AND SUSTAINABLE CAREERS

Goal striving can be considered an important self-regulatory behavior contributing to the sustainability of careers. Effective goal striving has been found to strengthen workers' motivation, performance, career advancement and career satisfaction (for example, Locke and Latham, 1990; 2013). Goals have been an important topic of empirical research since Locke (1968) proposed that individuals' intention to work towards a goal is a major source of work motivation. The goals employees are trying to obtain at work are crucial for energizing, directing and guiding behavior in achievement situations (DeShon and Gillespie, 2005; Locke and Latham, 1990). In the past, a plethora of studies has delineated how goals affect motivation and behavior, and which conditions are important for such effects.

Also with regard to careers, goals have received considerable attention, for example, with regard to career stage transitions, career decision making and career success (for example, Abele and Spurk, 2009; Dik et al., 2008; Wanberg and Kammeyer-Mueller, 2008). Because today's careers are characterized by lifelong learning and dealing with change, conceptualizations of career development and career adaptability refer to the central role of self-regulatory strategies that facilitate the achievement of one's career goals (for example, Savickas, 1997). Several authors have stressed the role of goal setting and goal striving as core competencies with regard to (modern) careers (for example, Kuijpers et al., 2006).

Goal Setting

An important impetus to goal research was the introduction of goal setting theory by Locke and Latham (1990; 2013). The main proposition of this theory holds that goals that are specific (that is, expressed in terms of a clearly defined performance level) and challenging (that is, difficult but not impossible to achieve) will lead to higher motivation and performance in comparison to do-your-best goals, easy goals, or an absence of goals. Numerous studies have supported the premises of goal-setting theory, showing that goals direct attention to goal-relevant activities, increase effort and persistence while working towards goal attainment, and prompt the development and use of effective task strategies in order to reach these goals (Kanfer, 2005; Locke and Latham, 2013). Moreover, goal-setting theory has led to various successful interventions in the workplace.

Goal setting plays a crucial role in career decision-making and career enhancement. Because goals are supportive in directing and maintaining behavior on tasks that provide only distant awards, they can support these complex career processes requiring workers to delay immediate gratification, and to plan, prioritize and act over time (Dik et al., 2008). Several studies have reported support for the application of goal-setting theory to career success. Mento et al. (1992), for example, found in a sample of graduate business students that high goals (in terms of grade goals in their study program) were associated with anticipated future benefits in life, such as higher starting salary after graduation or later career success. In a longitudinal study (Howard, 2013), managers' goals (in terms of highest management level to be attained) were strongly and positively related to the actual advancement these managers had made and the salary level they had reached some years later.

Although these studies provide support for a positive effect of high goals with regard to career outcomes, they have emphasized only one type of goal. That is, mainly goals with regard to achievement, prestige or power (that is, performance goals) have been found to positively relate to objective career success. This raises the question whether these goals will contribute to subjective career success as well. Abele and Spurk (2009) found positive effects of such personal occupational goals, from the time of graduation, on salary and status of employees three years later. However, they also noticed that persons pursuing such goals were less satisfied with their careers later in their lives. Although this could indicate that a high aspiration level might lead to lower levels of subjective career success in the long run (because high career goals might not be met), this result also points towards the relevance of what kind of goals a person pursues in his or her career. Therefore, it is important to consider the content of the goals that are being set and pursued as well.

Goal Orientation

Goal content has been extensively addressed in research on goal orientation (for example, DeShon and Gillespie, 2005; Payne et al., 2007). Goal orientation refers to individuals' goal preferences in achievement situations (for example, Elliot and Dweck, 1988). Originating in the educational psychology literature, goal orientation was rapidly embraced by organizational researchers, who established an important role of goal orientation for work outcomes (for example, Payne et al., 2007). A distinction has been made between performance goals, which focus on proving oneself through high performance, and learning goals, which focus on self-development and mastering new tasks (Elliot and Dweck, 1988). Whereas goal orientation was initially considered an individual difference variable, it soon became apparent that the sources for goal striving can also reside in the work context (for example, DeShon and Gillespie, 2005). Work contexts can hold specific goal orientations that emphasize the achievement of particular goals, and contain pressures and cues regarding the adoption of these goals (Van Dam, 2015). For example, when companies apply an up-or-out career system, they emphasize the importance of performance and excellence, which in turn might stimulate employees to hold a performance goal orientation. Conversely, companies that aim to become a learning organization will emphasize learning and experimentation, and thus will stimulate employees to develop a learning goal orientation.

Research generally indicates that learning goals are beneficial for employees' sustainable careers. Employees with a learning goal orientation report a higher motivation to participate in development activities or training, and prefer work situations that challenge them or enhance their personal development (for example, Payne et al., 2007). Furthermore, employees holding learning goals engage more in goal setting, effort and planning (VandeWalle et al., 1999), and are more willing to seek feedback (VandeWalle, 2001), a self-regulatory strategy suggested to be essential for career adaptability (Callister et al., 1999).

Especially for careers in changing environments that require employees to rapidly adapt their skills and knowledge, and for careers that are non-routine and emphasize the relevance of long-term outcomes in terms of development, the pursuit of learning goals should provide an advantage. By now, several studies support the relevance of learning goals for subjective (for example, career satisfaction, Godshalk and Sosik, 2003) and objective career success (for example, promotion, Lin and Chang, 2005). Furthermore, learning goals are associated with central aspects of career adaptability. For example, Creed et al. (2009) demonstrated that employees' learning goal orientation was associated with lower levels of career concerns via higher levels of career and self-exploration, career decision-making, and career planning to reach these goals. The adoption of learning goals therefore seems essential for employees' sustainable careers in today's changing labor market.

Goal Striving

As the previous sections suggest, goal striving is an essential self-regulatory behavior for enhancing sustainable careers. Goal-striving behaviors, such as monitoring one's progress towards career goals and, if necessary, the adjustment of behavior to facilitate goal attainment, have shown positive associations with career orientations that reflect today's continuing changes in the workplace (Creed et al., 2011). Furthermore, research findings indicate that people profit from goal striving in transition periods, like from school to work (Dietrich et al., 2013), or reemployment after job loss (Wanberg, 2012).

In order to understand how these positive effects come about, we will take a closer look at the process of goal striving.

According to Gollwitzer's (1990) Rubicon model of action phases, once a goal is chosen, a phase of planning starts in which plans are being made and strategies developed defining how the goal can be accomplished. With regard to careers, Savickas (1997) has emphasized the role of career planning as an adaptive strategy. In their meta-analysis, Ng et al. (2005) found a positive effect of making personal career plans on salary and career satisfaction, both indicators of career success. It therefore seems essential that workers not only formulate career goals, but that they also develop effective strategies or plans for obtaining these goals. Career planning has shown to be beneficial for employees in general and in transition periods more specifically. For instance, several studies indicate the importance of using effective job-search strategies in times of unemployment (for example, Wanberg, 2012; Wanberg and Kammeyer-Mueller, 2008).

The next phase of the Rubicon model of action phases relates to goal pursuit. When an opportunity to pursue a chosen career goal opens up, the individual starts acting towards goal attainment and has to deal with implementation problems, such as distractions or conflicts between competing goals (Gollwitzer, 1990). In the phase of goal pursuit, attention has to be paid to processes that support goal commitment and goal implementation (Oettingen et al., 2013). Goal commitment, that is, one's attachment to a goal, has been shown to support the effect of high, difficult goals on behavioral outcomes (Locke and Latham, 1990; 2013). Goal commitment will be higher if the goal is considered attractive, and when the individual expects that the specific goal is attainable (Klein et al., 1999). Moreover, employees' self-efficacy, or their confidence to successfully accomplish career goals, has been outlined as an important resource for effective career adaptation (Ashford and Taylor, 1990; Savickas, 1997; Van Dam, 2013); several researchers emphasize that employees need to develop broad self-efficacy beliefs in order to deal with unpredictable adjustments in their career (Parker, 1998; Van Vianen et al., 2009).

Moreover, the explication of implementation intentions appears an effective self-regulatory strategy in this phase of the action process. Implementation intentions link specific situational features to certain goal-directed behaviors, as they specify what to do when a specific situation arises. Forming such intentions helps to ensure goal attainment as they support the goal-striving process in terms of 'getting started, staying on track, avoiding resource depletion, and disengaging from futile goal intentions' (Oettingen et al., 2013, p. 532). Especially in times of changes or transition, forming such intentions might help to implement career goals by anticipating obstacles and continuing to work on a goal even when confronted with setbacks. For instance, Koen et al. (2012) reported positive long-term effects on career adaptability of training that focused on the transition period from university to work, and included modules on implementation planning.

Whereas setting and planning career goals are considered important self-regulatory behaviors in career self-management, the ability to *adapt one's goals* forms a similar central component in terms of career adaptability. The development and adaptation of career goals should be seen as a dynamic process that takes, for example, personal interests and values or situational opportunities and limitations into account. Especially when goals appear unattainable, goal adjustment is considered adaptive, because it may help to release personal resources that were tightened up with the unrealistic goal, prevent the helplessness associated with an unattainable goal, and provide purpose through developing new goals and challenges (Creed and Hood, 2014). Research provides clear evidence of the positive outcomes of career goal adjustment. For instance, Hirschi and Vondracek (2009) showed in a longitudinal study that students focused on fewer goals over time and adapted their career goals according to environmental factors. Research on career transition periods indicates that adjustment of work-related goals might lead to higher rates of goal attainment and goal progress (Dietrich et al., 2013). Moreover, Creed and Hood (2014) found that disengagement from an unattainable career goal was associated with lower distress.

Together, theoretical and empirical evidence indicates that the pursuit of challenging but attainable goals, goals that focus on learning, and goal adjustment through time, are key competencies for adaptation and sustainable careers. This evidence also highlights the importance of employee proactivity for sustainable careers, which will be elaborated in the next section.

PROACTIVITY AND SUSTAINABLE CAREERS

The concept of proactivity is central to career research (for example, Seibert et al., 1999; Parker and Collins, 2010) and has shown to be a strong predictor of career success (for example, Seibert et al., 2001). It was introduced to organizational research by Bateman and Crant (1993) who defined proactive personality as 'the relative stable tendency to effect environmental change' (p. 103). Proactive individuals seek to initiate change in their environment while being relatively unconstrained by situational forces, whereas passive individuals react to, conform to, or are shaped by their environment (Bateman and Crant, 1993; Parker et al., 2010). More recently, the focus has shifted from proactive personality to proactive behavior, which refers to self-initiated, anticipatory action that aims to change and improve the situation or oneself (Parker et al., 2006). This behavior has also been addressed as personal initiative (Frese et al., 2007; Tornau and Frese, 2013).

As Grant and Ashford (2008) have noted, any behavior can be carried out proactively (or reactively). Hence, also 'bad' behaviors such as aggression and violence (Griffin and Lopez, 2005), and counterproductive behaviors, such as lateness and absence from work, could be conducted proactively. However, the literature on proactivity is predominantly focused on 'good' behaviors such as individual innovation (Scott and Bruce, 1994), taking charge (Morrison and Phelps, 1999), career initiative (Seibert et al., 2001), voice (Van Dyne and LePine, 1998), and problem prevention (Frese and Fay, 2001). These behaviors are considered to be 'good' because their intended target of impact is positive; proactive behavior is, for instance, aimed at an improvement in work conditions, job performance or career success.

Two characteristics are thought to distinguish proactive behavior from more general motivated behavior, and from more reactive, passive behavior (Grant and Ashford, 2008). The first characteristic is acting in advance; proactive behavior encompasses a domain of behavior in which individuals are agentic and anticipatory in their actions. The second characteristic is intended impact: employees behave with the explicit intent to have a discernible effect on the self and/or the environment. Since proactivity is not limited to a unique set of actions (for example, career initiative) but can be applied to any set of actions, it should be considered foremost as a process in which individuals anticipate, plan and subsequently strive for intended impact on the self and/or the environment (Grant and Ashford, 2008). From this perspective, the attention shifts from specific behavior, such as innovation, to 'the sequence of interrelated acts and phases' (Grant and Ashford, 2008, p. 9). Similar to the Rubicon model of action phases (Gollwitzer, 1990), Grant and Ashford (2008) distinguish several phases in proactive behavior: (1) anticipation, that is, thinking ahead to anticipate future outcomes or goals through envisioning; (2) planning, that is, developing plans for action to implement ideas; and (3) proactive goal striving, that is, enacting and reflecting in order to obtain self-set goals (see also Parker et al., 2010). Obviously, these phases of proactivity apply to career behavior as they imply reflecting on one's current and future career, considering future career goals, developing plans to reach those goals, and taking action directed to realize the envisioned future career path.

Different Proactive Behaviors

Over time, a large number of different proactive behaviors have been studied, reflecting the importance of proactivity for today's workplace. In an effort to clarify the similarities and differences among these behaviors, Parker and Collins (2010) distinguished three types of proactive behaviors that differ in the intended target of impact. The first type refers to proactive work behavior, and encompasses behaviors targeted at taking control of and bringing about change within the internal organizational environment. Examples of these behaviors are taking charge (Morrison and Phelps, 1999), and problem prevention (Frese and Fay, 2001). The second type relates to proactive strategic behavior, which is targeted at changing the organization's strategy and its fit with the external environment. Example behaviors are strategic scanning, issue selling and entrepreneurial behavior (Becherer and Maurer, 1999; Morrison and Phelps, 1999). Finally, the third type of proactive behavior refers to P–E fit behavior, which covers all actions targeted anticipatively at changing the individual's fit with the organizational environment. Example behaviors are job change negotiation and career initiative (Nicholson, 1984; Seibert et al., 2001).

As noted previously, P–E fit is indicative of successful adaptation and, therefore, this last type of proactive behavior, P–E fit behavior, is of utmost importance for employees' sustainable careers. Several career theories emphasize the relevance of the fit between the individual and the work environment. Holland (1997), for instance, argued that people choose vocations that match their personality. Employees can engage in a range of proactive behaviors in order to increase P–E fit. These behaviors can be targeted at both the individual and the environment (Nicholson, 1984). For instance, employees can seek developmental feedback, participate in learning activities, or apply socialization tactics with the objective of better fitting their present or future work environment (for example, Seibert et al., 1999). Additionally, employees can try to change their work environment through job crafting, job change negotiations and career initiatives (for example, Nicholson, 1984). Research suggests that people with a stronger proactive personality are more likely to show these proactive P–E fit behaviors (for example, Chiaburu et al., 2006; Parker and Collins, 2010). Consequently, proactivity has been shown to relate strongly to perceived person–job fit (Erdogan and Bauer, 2005).

Proactivity: Antecedents and Consequences

Research has identified a number of antecedents that influence general as well as more specific proactive behaviors (see Fuller and Marler, 2009; Thomas et al., 2012; Tornau and Frese, 2013). These antecedents relate to individual differences in personality, such as openness, conscientiousness, extraversion, learning goal orientation, role breadth self-efficacy, responsibility for change, and proactive personality, as well as differences in job experience, education and domain-relevant knowledge. Additionally, several contextual variables have been found to affect proactive behavior, including both general (for example, leadership, interpersonal climate and social processes) and more specific (for example, autonomy, ambiguity, job enrichment and job stressors) aspects of the work environment (Erdogan and Bauer, 2005; Parker et al., 2010). In their proactivity dynamics framework, Grant and Ashford (2008) have specified how individual and situational characteristics might interact to stimulate employees' proactive behavior. For example, whereas proactive behavior generally is more likely to happen in situations of ambiguity and uncertainty, they argue that especially employees who are more open to experiences will engage in proactive behavior in these situations. This would imply that proactivity is a matter of both the person and the work environment. A similar argument could be made concerning sustainable careers.

In turn, proactivity has been found to contribute to a number of beneficial outcomes with regard to work behavior and careers. Erdogan and Bauer (2005) argued that proactive individuals will be more satisfied with their jobs because they remove obstacles that can prevent job satisfaction. Additionally, proactivity has been found to predict job performance, organizational commitment, tolerance for stress in demanding jobs, leadership effectiveness, entrepreneurship, innovation, and learning and development activity (for example, Bateman and Crant, 1993; Major et al., 2006; Parker and Sprigg, 1999; Tornau and Frese, 2013).

Besides these positive organizational outcomes, proactivity (both proactive personality and behavior) is important for career outcomes. As Seibert et al. (2001, p. 847) noted, proactive employees are more likely to 'select, create, and influence work situations that increase the likelihood of career success'. Ng et al. (2005) found proactivity to be positively associated with objective (salaries and promotions) and even more strongly related to subjective (career satisfaction) career success. With regard to sustainable careers, Seibert et al. (2001) showed that proactive personality enhanced career progression (salary increase and number of promotions in a two-year period of time) and career satisfaction, and also found evidence for the mechanisms (in terms of proactive behaviors) underpinning this relationship. They noticed that proactive workers were more actively engaged in innovation, political knowledge and career initiative; in turn, these proactive behaviors all had a positive effect on objective and subjective career success. Parker and Collins (2010) found career initiative, as a type of proactive P–E fit behavior, to be significantly predicted by consideration of future consequences. Individuals who attributed a greater value to future benefits compared to immediate results engaged more frequently in career initiative actions, such as career planning, skill development and consultation with senior co-workers. Finally, proactivity is a central concept in dispositional employability (Fugate and Kinicki, 2008), which refers to effective adaptation at work and dealing with organizational changes. Furthermore, a recent study (Öncel, 2014) supports the finding that proactive personality is strongly and positively related to curiosity, one of the dimensions of career adaptability.

Proactivity and Sustainable Careers: Some Considerations

Whereas empirical evidence has convincingly shown that proactivity can contribute to career success, some findings indicate the importance of specific conditions that should be considered. Most researchers implicitly assume that proactive behavior is individually rewarding. Although there might be temporary setbacks and failures, proactivity will pay off in the long run, for example, in terms of higher salaries and promotions (Seibert et al., 2001), or more generally in terms of a desirable future (Parker et al., 2010). This might not always be the case, however (Bolino et al., 2010). As Grant and Ashford (2008) have argued, the potential image costs of proactive behavior might be considerable if employees fail, underperform or make errors. Accordingly, employees might avoid proactive behavior in order to protect their image (Grant and Ashford, 2008). This would especially be the case under conditions of low accountability, where employees do not need to explain their behavior and motives. Moreover, Seibert et al. (2001) found a negative impact of voice, which refers to proactive behavior that constructively challenges the status quo with the intent of improving the situation rather than merely criticizing (Van Dyne and LePine, 1998). The results of their longitudinal study showed that voice negatively affected objective career success (salary growth and number of promotions in a two-year period of time). They reasoned that people who use voice without offering innovative solutions to the problems they have identified 'may experience negative repercussions in terms of career success' (Seibert et al., 2001, p. 866). Hence, voice may upset rather than improve personal relations at work. Furthermore, proactive behavior may result in resource depletion and therefore threaten employee health (Bolino et al., 2010), and as such undermine employees' sustainable careers. And what will happen with employees' proactivity when they realize that their valued career path will not materialize, and how will this impact their well-being and career aspirations (Strauss et al., 2012)? As Strauss et al. (2012) note, future research on proactivity should deal with potential negative effects on employee motivation, health and career behavior.

CONCLUSION

In this chapter, we have focused on the role of employee adaptation, goal striving and proactivity for sustainable careers. Because change is inherent in both the environment and the person, employees need to continuously engage in adaptive, goal-striving and proactive behaviors in order to obtain effective adaptation and secure their career's sustainability. At this point, we would like to note that career sustainability requires adaptive behavior that is balanced; it should be aimed at establishing or restoring the balance between the goals, interests, values and expectations of the organization *and* those of the employee. Balanced adaptive behavior is effective if the organizational and personal goals are strived for at the same time, or – at least – the pursuit of personal goals, interests and values is not frustrated or hampered by the realization of organizational goals, and vice versa. Both the individual employee and the organization should strive to attain this balance (for example, by stimulating adaptive resources and effective self-regulatory behaviors), since it is a prerequisite for effective adaptation and sustainable careers.

REFERENCES

Abele, A.E. and D. Spurk (2009), 'The longitudinal impact of self-efficacy and career goals on objective and subjective career success', *Journal of Vocational Behavior*, **74**, 53–62.

Ashford, S.J. and M.S. Taylor (1990), 'Adaptation to work transitions: An integrative approach', in G.R. Ferris and K.M. Rowland (eds), *Research in Personnel and Human Resources Management* (Vol. 8), Greenwich, CT: JAI Press, pp. 1–39.

Bateman, T. and J. Crant (1993), 'The proactive component of organizational-behavior: A measure and correlates', *Journal of Organizational Behavior*, **14**, 103–18.

Becherer, R. and J. Maurer (1999), 'The proactive personality disposition and entrepreneurial behavior among small company presidents', *Journal of Small Business Management*, **38**, 28–36.

Berntson, E., M. Sverke and S. Marklund (2006), 'Predicting perceived employability: Human capital or labour market opportunities?', *Economic and Industrial Democracy*, **27**, 223–44.

Block, J. and A.M. Kremen (1996), 'IQ and ego-resiliency: Conceptual and empirical connections and separateness', *Journal of Personality and Social Psychology*, **70**, 349–61.

Bolino, M., S. Valcea and J. Harvey (2010), 'Employee, manage thyself: The potentially negative implications of expecting employees to behave proactively', *Journal of Occupational and Organizational Psychology*, **83**, 325–45.

Callister, R.R., M.W. Kramer and D.B. Turban (1999), 'Feedback seeking following career transitions', *Academy of Management Journal*, **42**, 429–38.

Chiaburu, D., V.L. Baker and A.H. Pitariu (2006), 'Beyond being proactive: What (else) matters for career self-management behaviors?', *Career Development International*, **11**, 619–32.

Creed, P.A. and M. Hood (2014), 'Disengaging from unattainable career goals and reengaging in more achievable ones', *Journal of Career Development*, **41**, 24–42.

Creed, P.A., T. Fallon and M. Hood (2009), 'The relationship between career adaptability, person and situation variables, and career concerns in young adults', *Journal of Vocational Behavior*, **74**, 219–29.

Creed, P.A., J. Macpherson and M. Hood (2011), 'Predictors of "new economy" career orientation in an Australian sample of late adolescents', *Journal of Career Development*, **38**, 369–89.

Deci, E.L. and R.M. Ryan (2000), 'The "what" and "why" of goal pursuits: Human needs and the self-determination of behavior', *Psychological Inquiry*, **11**, 227–68.

DeShon, R.P. and J.Z. Gillespie (2005), 'A motivated action theory account of goal orientation', *Journal of Applied Psychology*, **90**, 1096–127.

Dietrich, J., M. Jokisaari and J.E. Nurmi (2013), 'Work-related goal appraisals and stress during the transition from education to work', *Journal of Vocational Behavior*, **80**, 82–92.

Dik, B.J., A.M. Sargent and M.F. Steger (2008), 'Career development strivings: Assessing goals and motivation in career decision-making and planning', *Journal of Career Development*, **35**, 23–41.

Docherty, P., M. Kira and A.B. Shani (2009), 'What the world needs now is sustainable work systems', in P. Docherty, M. Kira and A.B. Shani (eds), *Creating Sustainable Work Systems: Developing Social Sustainability*, London: Routledge, pp. 1–21.

Elliot, A.J. and C.S. Dweck (1988), 'Goals: An approach to motivation and achievement', *Journal of Personality and Social Psychology*, **54**, 5–12.

Erdogan, B. and T. Bauer (2005), 'Enhancing career benefits of employee proactive personality: The role of fit with jobs and organizations', *Personnel Psychology*, **58**, 859–91.

Frese, M. and D. Fay (2001), 'Personal initiative (PI): An active performance concept for work in the 21st Century', in B.M. Staw and R.M. Sutton (eds), *Research in Organizational Behavior* (Vol. 23), Amsterdam: Elsevier Science, pp. 133–87.

Frese, M., H. Garst and D. Fay (2007), 'Making things happen: Reciprocal relationships between work characteristics and personal initiative (PI) in a four-wave longitudinal structural equation model', *Journal of Applied Psychology*, **92**, 1084–102.

Fugate, M. and A.J. Kinicki (2008), 'A dispositional approach to employability: Development of a measure and test of implications for employee reactions to organizational change', *Journal of Occupational and Organizational Psychology*, **81**, 503–27.

Fugate, M., A.J. Kinicki and B.E. Ashforth (2004), 'Employability: A psycho-social construct, its dimensions, and applications', *Journal of Vocational Behavior*, **65**, 14–38.
Fuller, J.B. and L.E. Marler (2009), 'Change driven by nature: A meta-analytic review of the proactive personality literature', *Journal of Vocational Behavior*, **75**, 329–45.
Godshalk, V.M. and J.J. Sosik (2003), 'Aiming for career success: The role of learning goal orientation in mentoring relationships', *Journal of Vocational Behavior*, **63**, 417–37.
Gollwitzer, P.M. (1990), 'Action phases and mind-sets', in E.T. Higgins and R.M. Sorrentino (eds), *The Handbook of Motivation and Cognition* (Vol. 2), New York: Guilford Press, pp. 53–92.
Grant, A.M. and S.J. Ashford (2008), 'The dynamics of proactivity at work', *Research in Organizational Behavior*, **28**, 3–34.
Griffin, B. and B. Hesketh (2003), 'Adaptable behaviours for successful work and career adjustment', *Australian Journal of Psychology*, **55**, 65–73.
Griffin, M.A. and Y. Lopez (2005), '"Bad behavior" in organizations: A review and typology for future research', *Journal of Management*, **31**, 988–1005.
Griffin, M.A., A. Neal and S.K. Parker (2007), 'A new model of work role performance: Positive behavior in uncertain and interdependent contexts', *Academy of Management Journal*, **50**, 215–24.
Griffin, M.A., S.K. Parker and C.M. Mason (2010), 'Leader vision and the development of adaptive and proactive performance: A longitudinal study', *Journal of Applied Psychology*, **95**, 174–82.
Hall, D.T. (2002), *Careers In and Out of Organizations*, Thousand Oaks, CA: Sage.
Hirschi, A. and F.W. Vondracek (2009), 'Adapation of career goals in early adolescence to self and opportunities', *Journal of Vocational Behavior*, **75**, 120–28.
Holland, J.L. (1997), *Making Vocational Choices: A Theory of Vocational Personalities and Work Environment*, 3rd edn, Odessa, FL: Psychological Assessment Resources Inc.
Howard, A. (2013), 'The predictive validity of conscious and subconscious motives on career advacement', in E.A. Locke and G.P. Latham (eds), *New Developments in Goal Setting and Task Performance*, New York: Routledge, pp. 246–61.
Kanfer, R. (2005), 'Self-regulation research in work and I/O psychology', *Applied Psychology: An International Review*, **54**, 186–91.
King, R.C., W.D. Stansfield and P. Mulligan (2006), *A Dictionary of Genetics*, 7th edn, Oxford: Oxford University Press.
King, Z. (2004), 'Career self-management: Its nature, causes and consequences', *Journal of Vocational Behavior*, **65**, 112–33.
Klehe, U.C., J. Zikic, A.E.M. Van Vianen and I.E. De Pater (2011), 'Career adaptability, turnover and loyalty during organizational downsizing', *Journal of Vocational Behavior*, **79**, 217–29.
Klein, H.J., M.J. Wesson, J.R. Hollenbeck and B.J. Alge (1999), 'Goal commitment and the goal-setting process: Conceptual clarification and empirical synthesis', *Journal of Applied Psychology*, **84**, 885–96.
Koen, J., U.C. Klehe and A.E.M. Van Vianen (2012), 'Training career adaptability to facilitate a successful school-to-work transition', *Journal of Vocational Behavior*, **81**, 395–408.
Kristof-Brown, A.L., R.D. Zimmerman and E.C. Johnson (2005), 'Consequences of individuals' fit at work: A meta-analysis of person–job, person–organization, person–group, and person–supervisor fit', *Personnel Psychology*, **58**, 281–342.
Kuijpers, M.A.C.T., B. Schyns and J. Scheerens (2006), 'Career competencies for career success', *Career Development Quarterly*, **55**, 168–78.
LePine, J.A., J.A. Colquitt and A. Erez (2000), 'Adaptability to changing task contexts: Effects of general cognitive ability, conscientiousness, and openness to experience', *Personnel Psychology*, **53**, 563–93.
Lin, S.C. and J.N. Chang (2005), 'Goal orientation and organizational commitment as explanatory factors of employees' mobility', *Personnel Review*, **34**, 331–53.
Locke, E.A. (1968), 'Motivation through conscious goal setting', *Applied & Preventive Psychology*, **5**, 117–24.
Locke, E.A. and G.P. Latham (1990), *A Theory of Goal Setting and Task Performance*, Englewood Cliffs, NJ: Prentice Hall.
Locke, E.A. and G.P. Latham (2013), 'Goal settting theory. The current state', in E.A. Locke and G.P. Latham (eds), *New Developments in Goal Setting and Task Performance*, New York: Routledge, pp. 623–30.
Major, D., J. Turner and T. Fletcher (2006), 'Linking proactive personality and the big five to motivation to learn and development activity', *Journal of Applied Psychology*, **91**, 927–35.
Mento, A.J., E.A. Locke and H.J. Klein (1992), 'Relationship of goal level to valence and instrumentality', *Journal of Applied Psychology*, **77**, 395–405.
Morrison, E.W. and C.C. Phelps (1999), 'Taking charge at work: Extrarole efforts to initiate workplace change', *Academy of Management Journal*, **42**, 403–19.
Mueller-Hanson, R.A., S.S. White, D.W. Dorsey and E.D. Pulakos (2005), *Training Adaptable Leaders: Lessons from Research and Practice*, Alexandria, VA: US Army Research Institute, Report No. 1844.

Ng, T.W.H., L.T. Eby, K.L. Sorensen and D.C. Feldman (2005), 'Predictors of objective and subjective carreer success: A meta-analysis', *Personnel Psychology*, **58**, 367–408.
Nicholson, N. (1984), 'A theory of work role transitions', *Administrative Science Quarterly,* **29**, 172–91.
Niessen, C., C. Binnewies and J. Rank (2010), 'Disengagement in work role transitions', *Journal of Occupational and Organizational Psychology*, **83**, 695–715.
Öncel, L. (2014), 'Career adapt-abilities scale: Convergent validity of subscale scores', *Journal of Vocational Behavior*, **85**, 13–17.
Oettingen, G., M. Wittchen and P.M. Gollwitzer (2013), 'Regulating goal pursuit through mental contrasting with implementation intentions', in E.A. Locke and G.P. Latham (eds), *New Developments in Goal Setting and Task Performance*, New York: Routledge, pp. 523–48.
Orr, H. (2005), 'The genetic theory of adaptation: A brief history', *National Review of Genetics*, **6**, 119–27.
Parker, S. (1998), 'Role breadth self-efficacy: Relationships with work-enrichment and other organizational practices', *Journal of Applied Psychology*, **83**, 835–52.
Parker, S. and C. Collins (2010), 'Taking stock: Integrating and differentiating multiple forms of proactive behavior', *Journal of Management*, **36**, 633–62.
Parker, S. and C. Sprigg (1999), 'Minimizing strain and maximizing learning: The role of job demands, job control, and proactive personality', *Journal of Applied Psychology*, **84**, 925–39.
Parker, S., U. Bindl and K. Strauss (2010), 'Making things happen: A model of proactive motivation', *Journal of Management*, **36**, 827–56.
Parker, S., H. Williams and N. Turner (2006), 'Modeling the antecedents of proactive behavior at work', *Journal of Applied Psychology*, **91**, 636–52.
Payne, S.C., S.S. Youngcourt and J.M. Beaubien (2007), 'A meta-analytic examination of the goal orientation nomological net', *Journal of Applied Psychology*, **92**, 128–50.
Ployhart, R.E. and P.D. Bliese (2006), 'Individual Adaptability (I-Adapt) theory: Conceptualizing the antecedents, consequences, and measurements of individual differences in adaptability', *Advances in Human Performance and Cognitive Engineering Research*, **6**, 3–39.
Pulakos, E.D., D.W. Dorsey and S.S. White (2006), 'Adaptability in the workplace: Selecting an adaptive workforce', *Advances in Human Performance and Cognitive Engineering Research*, **6**, 41–71.
Savickas, M. (1997), 'Career adaptability: An integrative construct for life-span, life-space theory', *Career Development Quarterly*, **45**, 247–59.
Savickas, M.L. and E.J. Porfeli (2012), 'Career Adapt-Abilities Scale: Construction, reliability, and measurement equivalence across 13 countries', *Journal of Vocational Behavior*, **80**, 661–73.
Scott, S. and R. Bruce (1994), 'Determinants of innovative behavior: A path model of individual innovation in the workplace', *Academy of Management Journal*, **37**, 580–607.
Seibert, S., J. Crant and M. Kraimer (1999), 'Proactive personality and career success', *Journal of Applied Psychology*, **84**, 416–27.
Seibert, S., M. Kraimer and J. Crant (2001), 'What do proactive people do? A longitudinal model linking proactive personality and career success', *Personnel Psychology*, **54**, 845–74.
Seligman, M.E.P. and M. Csikszentmihalyi (2000), 'Positive psychology: An introduction', *American Psychologist*, **55**, 5–14.
Strauss, K., M. Griffin and S.K. Parker (2012), 'Future work selves: How salient hoped-for identities motivate proactive career behaviors', *Journal of Applied Psychology*, **97**, 580–98.
Sullivan, S.E. and B. Baruch (2009), 'Advances in career theory and research: A critical review and agenda for future exploration', *Journal of Management*, **35**, 1542–71.
Thomas, J.P., D.S. Whitman and C. Viswesvaran (2012), 'Employee proactivity in organizations: A comparative meta-analysis of emergent proactive constructs', *Journal of Occupational and Organizational Psychology*, **83**, 275–300.
Tornau, K. and M. Frese (2013), 'Construct clean-up in proactivity research: A meta-analysis on the nomological net of work-related proactivity concepts and their incremental validities', *Applied Psychology, An International Review*, **62**, 44–96.
Van Dam, K. (2013), 'Employee adaptability to change at work: A multidimensional, resource-based framework', in S. Oreg, A. Michel and R.T. By (eds), *The Psychology of Organizational Change: Viewing Change from the Employee's Perspective*, Cambridge: Cambridge University Press, pp. 123–42.
Van Dam, K. (2015), 'Workplace goal orientation: Development of a measure', *European Journal of Psychological Assessment*, **31**, 62–8.
Van Dyne, L. and J.A. LePine (1998), 'Helping and voice extra-role behaviors: Evidence of construct and predictive validity', *Academy of Management Journal*, **41**, 108–19.
Van Vianen, A.E.M., I.E. De Pater and P.T.Y. Preenen (2009), 'Adaptable careers: Maximizing less and exploring more', *Career Development Quarterly*, **57**, 304–9.
VandeWalle, D. (2001), 'Why wanting to look successful doesn't always lead to success', *Organizational Dynamics*, **30**, 162–71.

VandeWalle, D., S.B. Brown, W.L. Cron and J.W. Slocum (1999), 'The influence of goal orientation and self-regulation tactics on sales performance: A longitudinal field test', *Journal of Applied Psychology*, **84**, 249–59.
Wanberg, C. (2012), 'The individual experience of unemployment', *Annual Review of Psychology*, **63**, 369–96.
Wanberg, C. and J. Kammeyer-Mueller (2008), 'A self-regulatory perspective on navigating career transitions', in R. Kanfer, G. Chen and R.D. Prichard (eds), *Work Motivation: Past, Present, and Future*, New York: Routledge, pp. 433–69.

14 Career control

David E. Guest and Ricardo Rodrigues

INTRODUCTION

The concept of control is central to much research in organizational behaviour. For example, it is embedded in theories about motivation, job design and coping with stress at work. It is also implicit in the study of careers. Debates about the shift from the old to the new career (Arthur et al., 1999) and the growth of protean careers (Hall, 2004) are predicated on the assumption that control over careers and career decisions has shifted from organizations to individuals. A parallel assumption is that individuals' ability to control their careers will have a positive impact on their ability to have sustainable careers and on positive career-related outcomes.

Despite the rhetoric of the new career, there is good evidence that organizations remain eager to control the careers of the 'A Players' (Michaels et al., 2001) they wish to attract and retain. There is also evidence that those entering graduate programmes in organizations expect some degree of career control by the organization (Sturges et al., 2002).

These contrasting perspectives raise the question of who is in control of careers and career management. While the literature on careers occasionally refers to career control, the concept is rarely explicitly considered within career theory or in the wider careers literature (for an exception see DiRenzo and Greenhaus, 2011). We believe this omission is a mistake and that an analysis of careers utilizing control theories can provide valuable insights. The aim of this chapter is therefore to explore the concept of career control and to examine its implications for contemporary careers, career sustainability and career outcomes. This will be achieved in three ways. The first is a review of some relevant literature on the concept of control, highlighting different but potentially relevant perspectives. The second is the development of an analytic framework designed to place career control in its wider career context and demonstrate its value in the study of careers. The third is to present the findings of a study examining the role of perceptions of career control for outcomes including career satisfaction, job satisfaction and life satisfaction.

THE CONCEPT OF CONTROL

Control, when applied to behaviour at work, has been approached from a variety of perspectives. Here we will outline four major perspectives which have implications for career theory and research. They are cybernetic models, industrial relations perspectives, individual control and individual differences.

Cybernetic Models

A well-established approach to control in organizations adopts a cybernetic feedback model typically described as a systems perspective. The core argument is that systems, including human systems, have self-regulating tendencies and through perceptual and behavioural processes seek to exercise control to ensure either a sense of homeostasis or to achieve a specified goal (for a review see Carver and Scheier, 1982). Any disturbance to an existing or planned path creates a search for information and feedback which in turn can lead to a modification of behaviour to ensure a return to a more comfortable state. Control systems that fit broadly within the cybernetic model are commonly found in a range of standard management processes such as accounting and engineering. Exercising appropriate control is a central management activity and there is an extensive body of literature on processes managers use to ensure that they control work systems and processes (see, for example, Giglioni and Bedeian, 1974).

Barney (1991) argued that a top priority is to control and effectively manage the key resources that provide the basis for competitive advantage and, as he has subsequently argued (Barney and Wright, 1998), human resources have the greatest potential to provide distinctive competitive advantage. As a result, organizations will be eager to ensure effective management of their human resources and this will include seeking control through effective talent management of the careers of key employees. This leads to the proposition that organizations will seek to control the careers of valued employees.

From an individual perspective, DiRenzo and Greenhaus (2011) adopt a control theory approach, based on a cybernetic model, to theorize about job mobility in a boundaryless world. They suggest that the opportunity to exert individual control is enhanced through possession of 'movement capital' reflected in levels of education, training and relevant experience. This, in turn, enhances employability, which they define as 'the capacity to control one's employment options through the creation, identification, and realization of career opportunities' (p. 571). This leads to the counter proposition that many individuals will seek to control their own careers.

Industrial Relations and the Frontier of Control

Industrial relations is centrally concerned with institutions that address the management of relations between employers and employees with respect to control of workplace activities and the distribution of surplus value (Clegg, 1979). Organizations typically seek to exert control over the provision of goods and services including the cost of this provision. This usually extends to control over staff and staff costs, including wages. However, organizations rely on staff to produce the goods and services and therefore have to manage with their consent. From a pluralist perspective, there are likely to be differences of interest concerning the allocation and utilization of resources, and part of the role of industrial relations systems is to manage these competing interests. Within this context, there may be conflicts around issues where control is contested. The concept of the 'frontier of control' (Goodrich, 1920), refers to areas of contention in the workplace where employers and workers battle to exert control.

Within an industrial relations framework, the frontier of control is a moving boundary between areas of management and worker control. Ramsay (1977) argued that there are 'cycles of control' in industrial relations, as power shifts from one side to the other. Marchington et al. (1993) prefer the metaphor of 'waves of control', reflecting the ebb and flow of relations. The concept of a frontier of control implies a zero sum game but an alternative perspective suggests this need not be the case. Tannenbaum (1968), for example, demonstrated that organizations with participative systems that included an element of joint decision-making had a higher overall perceived level of control, as reported by managers and workers, than organizations with unilateral management decision-making.

The relevance of this for careers is that there may be competition between the organization and the individual concerning control of personal careers. Employers engaging in the 'war for talent' may seek to control the careers of those they regard as most talented. These highly marketable individuals may wish to control their own career paths. This raises questions about who controls careers, whether there can be fundamental differences of interest in this respect and the relative emphasis given to organizational and self-management of careers. The work of Tannenbaum and others suggests that joint management of careers may lead to mutual gains. However, the broad proposition to emerge from an industrial relations perspective on control is that there will often be competing interests between the organization and the individual with respect to the control of careers.

Personal Control

An extensive body of research within psychology, increasingly applied to organizational behaviour, emphasizes the importance of personal control. A comprehensive model of personal control has been presented by Greenberger and Strasser (1986). They defined personal control as 'a psychological construct reflecting an individual's beliefs, at a given point in time, in his or her ability to effect a change, in a desired direction, on the environment' (p. 165). They emphasized that this is a cognitive construct and that it can change over time. Ganster and Fusilier (1989) highlighted the importance of distinguishing, where possible, between perceived control and actual or objective control. The psychological construct of cognitive control therefore differs from managerial concepts of control that reside in organizational systems and can be viewed as more objective and relatively stable over time.

A second central component of personal control theory is a belief that the exercise of personal control is desired by individuals and beneficial for their well-being. White (1959), among others, has argued that humans have an instinctive need to master and control their environment. Deci (1975) located personal control at the centre of his theory of intrinsic motivation. In the extension of this approach, self-determination theory (Gagne and Deci, 2005) highlights the importance of three core components of competence, relatedness and autonomy, with autonomy implying a significant degree of personal control. Control is also central to the expectancy theory of motivation (Vroom, 1964). Bazerman (1982) distinguished between control over activities and control over outcomes where outcome control reflects a link between performance and rewards. Therefore, those eager to advance their career may be able to control the activities necessary to gain an interview for a new job but they may not be able to control factors influencing the outcome, including, for example, the quality of competing applicants.

Much research has been devoted to the questions of what happens when control is reduced or when individuals fail to achieve the desired outcome. Brehm (1966) has argued that a threat to control results in a process of reactance, reflected in extra effort to regain control. Therefore, in the short term at least, there may be heightened motivation. However, if the renewed efforts end in failure, then a further stage of learned helplessness may ensue (Seligman, 1975). This is viewed as a learning process, reflecting a perception that there is no further point in exerting effort. As a result, the individual gives up any attempt to gain control. Relating this to careers, we can imagine young unemployed workers who seek to control their prospects by applying for endless jobs but who never even gain an interview. After a while, they come to believe that the effort of completing applications is a waste of time and they stop applying for work.

Theories of control have been extensively utilized in the study of stress at work. There are two main elements to this. First, the central argument in the influential job demands–resources model (Karasek, 1979) is that high demand and low control is a recipe for stress. Work should therefore be organized to ensure that employees have sufficient control to be able to manage demand. Secondly, the way people cope with stressful events reveals variations in the extent and type of control that people exert. Responses can range from exercising control by taking direct action to address the source of stress through to use of palliatives or simply passive acceptance. Direct action is the most likely to be associated with better outcomes including reductions in stress levels and improved well-being (Dewe et al., 2010). In the context of careers, and stress caused by, for example, frustration at lack of career development and progress, direct action might entail engaging in career self-management rather than waiting for the organization to decide on the next career step. Alternatively, it is possible that people seek to change their career preferences so as to regain control over their career.

In their model of personal control, Greenberger and Strasser (1986) recognized the need to take account of organizational factors and individual differences. They propose that the desire to exert control will depend on the salience of the issue and argue that there will be a potentially important distinction between desired and actual perceived levels of control. Implicit in this model is an assumption that some event or information triggers a desire to assess and then potentially assert personal control. In the context of careers, a graduate might feel that she is making satisfactory career progress until a reunion of fellow students makes it apparent that she is falling behind in the 'career tournament' (Rosenbaum, 1979), triggering a desire to exercise control and ensure career progress. The broad proposition to emerge from this analysis is that many individuals desire career control, and that where personal control over careers is threatened, individuals will take steps to assert personal control.

Individual Differences and Personality

Models of personal control acknowledge a role for individual differences in both the extent to which individuals desire control and in beliefs that they are able to exert control. There are also likely to be differences in the tendency to be proactive and seek control. For example, there is a well-established stream of research on locus of control (Rotter, 1966; Lefcourt, 1976) that draws an initial distinction between beliefs about internal or external locus of control. The simple prediction, well-supported by a large body of research (Spector, 1982), is that those with an internal locus of control are more likely to seek to exert control than those with an external locus of control. These differences are judged to be a function of social learning and to be a relatively stable feature of personality.

One of the factors that might influence exertion of control is the attribution for outcomes. Attribution theory (Kelley and Michela, 1980) proposes that individuals have a need to explain events that affect them and typically cite a limited number of broad factors influencing outcomes, some of which are controllable and others not. Internal attributions include ability and effort, and whereas the former is relatively stable, the latter is not. External attributions typically allude to the nature of the task or to factors associated with luck. The former is stable while the latter is highly unstable. Control, including control over careers, is more likely to be exerted by those who believe they have ability but need to combine it with more effort.

A further individual factor concerns proactivity (Parker et al., 2010). Proactive behaviour goes beyond the conventional boundaries of a role by using initiative; in other words, by exercising control. The key antecedents of the propensity to engage in proactive behaviour are a proactive personality, jobs designed to permit autonomy and initiative, and organizational support (Parker et al., 2010). Job crafting (Wrzesniewski and Dutton, 2001) is one example of proactive behaviour. By implication, some people will be more proactive in seeking to manage their careers and therefore will be more likely to take the initiative in finding a mentor or obtaining developmental assignments. Furthermore, not everyone will feel equally comfortable managing their own careers, leaving a role for management control. This analysis of individual differences leads to the proposition that there will be individual differences in the extent to which individuals seek to control their careers.

In this section, we have briefly reviewed four bodies of literature on control that lie outside career theory. They have highlighted the rationale for organizational control of careers, for the role of personal control and of individual differences in control and the potential for conflict between organizational and individual interests in career management. We have provided some preliminary illustrations of how the varying perspectives on control might be relevant to careers. Ganster and Fusilier (1989) have provided a comprehensive overview of the literature on control in organizations. They highlight relevant research relating to participation at work, to job design and autonomy, to machine pacing and decision latitude, and to stress. What is notable in this and in almost all the research on the role of personal control at work is that the focus is on the nature of the work. Only DiRenzo and Greenhaus (2011) come close to career issues with their focus on control over job mobility. One consequence is that control with respect to careers has been largely neglected. Yet, as noted at the outset, control is central to, but often only implicit in, many aspects of the career discourse. Given this neglect, we therefore utilize the four perspectives outlined above to develop an analytic framework that places career control more centrally in the study of careers.

TOWARDS A MODEL OF CAREER CONTROL

In this section, we outline a model of career control that builds on the four perspectives on control outlined above. It reflects the propositions that most individuals seek some control over their careers and their employment more generally and that organizations seek to manage the employment relationship (Shore et al., 2012) including careers, particularly the careers of those identified as key employees. However, it is essential to recognize that a wider range of external factors can influence and, to varying degrees, exercise control over careers, career opportunities and career-related decisions. Finally, the model builds on the proposition that at the intersection between the individual desire for control and the external influences on control there is what we term the career control frontier.

The full model is illustrated in Figure 14.1. We start by considering external controls and influences.

External Influences on Career Control

Mayrhofer et al. (2007) have presented a framework for analysing the context that shapes careers. They identify three main classes of context. The first they term the context of work, which includes external labour markets, new ways of working and organizing and social relationships. The second they term context of origin, which includes class and social origin, educational socialization and individual work history. Thirdly, they identify the context of society and culture, in which they include the influence of gender, ethnicity, demography and community. This classification provides a useful starting-point for the analysis of external influences that help to determine career control. While certain external influences may be pervasive throughout the career, including the structure of opportunity determined by class and education, other influences become more or less salient at different career stages. Here we identify some of the key stages at which different types of external control may exert a controlling influence over careers. Specifically, adopting a career stages approach, we identify family and social influences prior to entering employment; organizational influences once in employment; family commitments in mid-career; and specific legislative issues in the closing stages of a career. We also consider wider macro-contextual influences.

The parental/childhood context

Research on career preferences and orientations to work reveals that prior to entering employment, the family, social and educational context can help to shape career orientations and choices (Rodrigues et al., 2013). Families can exert control by supporting or disapproving of potential career choices and by providing funding for education. They can serve as career models, for example, in a family firm or in a profession. Research has revealed, for example, that parents in ethnic minority families can put considerable pressure on female children, in particular, to pursue a 'respectable' career, which in practice usually means a recognized profession (Phillips and Imhoff, 1997). Prior to entering employment, some people, uncertain about their career ambitions, may be happy to accept strong external control over preliminary career-related decisions. Others will have a clearer idea about their career aspirations and will exert control to achieve their aims.

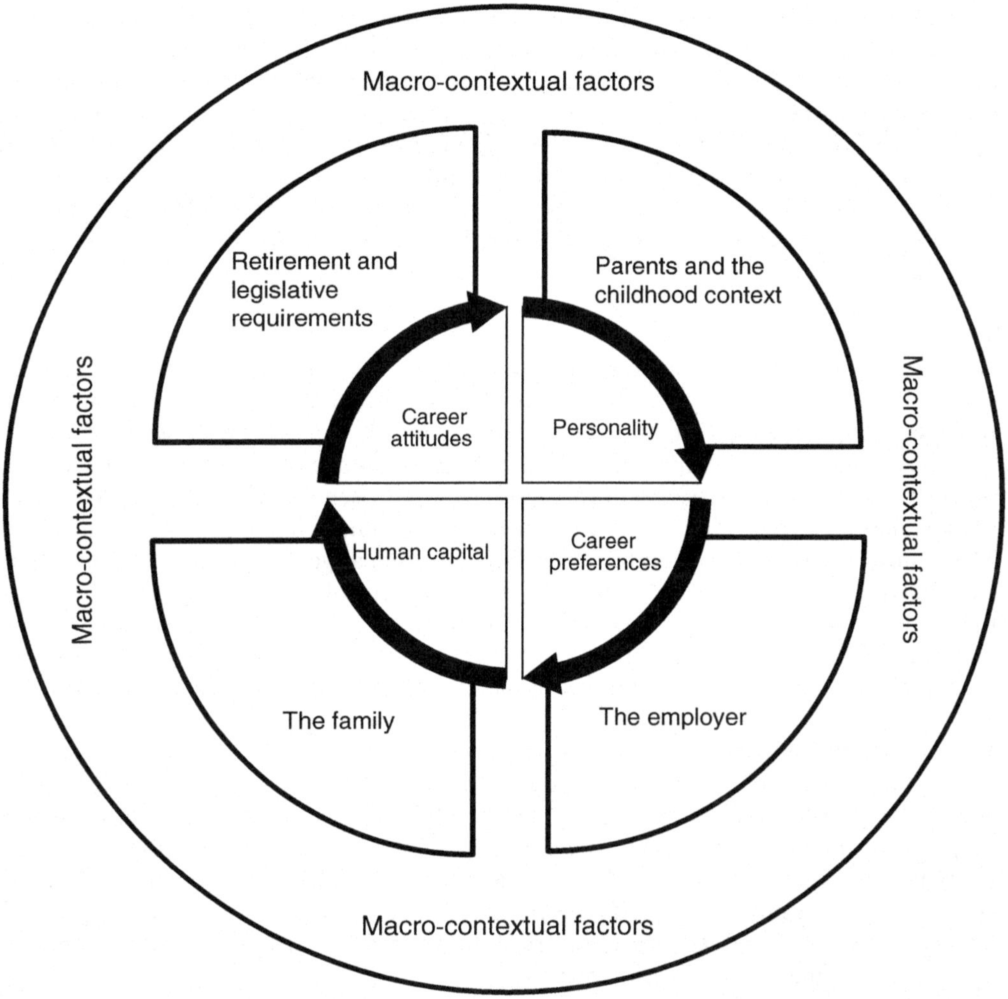

Figure 14.1 A model of career control

The employer

Employers will generally have a range of policies and practices to manage the employment relationship, including the opportunities for career progress within an organization. These can include the determination of internal labour markets, the development of the graduate intake and succession planning. This control is designed to ensure that organizations are able to attract, develop, utilize and retain suitable talent at all levels in the hierarchy. How far organizations actively seek to control careers will vary depending on how highly employees are valued. Advocates of talent management (Michaels et al., 2001) and of a strategic approach to the management of human resources (see, for example, Lepak and Snell, 1999) recommend a selective approach. What this can mean in practice is a heavy investment in the management and control of the careers of those who are identified as strategic human resources by virtue of their value and scarcity, while other employees may have their careers controlled by imposing limits on their opportunities for development and advancement within the organization. The challenge for employers is to align these control processes with what may be a desire for career self-management (King, 2004). Indeed, employers may actively encourage career self-management, both to limit their own responsibilities to those employees they do not view as justifying investment and in the recognition that the most able employees will seek a degree of control over their own careers irrespective of what the organization may seek to do.

The family

At a certain point in many careers, the family becomes an influence on career priorities and decisions. The family can exercise control by 'demanding' more time diverting attention from career activities, creating pressure on work–life balance (Kossek and Lautsch, 2012). The challenge of managing work–life balance can be more acute for women, particularly around the time of child-bearing, since it has been shown that time away from work can affect career progress of both men and women (Schneer and Reitman, 1997). The family can also exercise control over decisions such as geographical mobility, due to embeddedness in a particular location, especially when children are at a critical stage in their education (Feldman and Ng, 2007). Finally, the growth of dual-career families can affect career decisions of one or both partners (Moen and Yu, 2000), further illustrating how family membership can compete for and exert control over career decisions.

Retirement and legislative requirements

The ending of a career may be something that individuals can do little to control. Many countries have fixed retirement ages against which individuals and companies have little scope to act. There are exceptions, including the USA and more recently the UK, where many people, either through desire to continue to do work they enjoy or through financial necessity, continue to work beyond the traditional retirement age, suggesting that in countries where a retirement age is enforced, individuals experience a significant loss of control at this final stage of their careers.

Macro-contextual factors

The role of legislation highlights the influence and control over careers exercised by external factors that individuals and organizations can do little to affect. These factors can also be highly unpredictable. At the organizational level, there are risks of major changes in markets, takeovers, changes in governments and a range of other factors that can affect specific organizations. Once seemingly secure career prospects can disappear overnight. Government legislation and policy guidelines can also affect career prospects. For the individual, constraining factors can include the availability and ease of access to education and training opportunities. For example, restricted access to a particular educational programme can force individuals to consider alternative opportunities, leading to long-term career regret. Forrier et al. (2009) identified a number of structural factors that can constrain career mobility. These include levels of demand and the match between supply and demand for jobs, labour market segmentation, labour costs, values and norms and institutional incentives and barriers.

Observers such as Cappelli (1999) have argued that the levels of turbulence in the economic and organizational environment mean that we now live in a boundaryless and inherently insecure world in which organizations have lost control over their ability to manage their own destiny and that of their employees. Cappelli argues that this is a secular trend and that one thing that is predictable is that careers will be played out in an increasingly unpredictable context. The key implication of this, so he argues, is that individuals must take control of their own careers and, in particular, ensure their employability.

Internal Personal Factors Influencing Career Control

We locate personal control at the centre of our model. There is likely to be variation in both the motivation to exert control and the ability to do so effectively, influenced partly by characteristics of the individual and partly by the range of external factors already outlined.

Forrier et al. (2009) have emphasized the important role of self-determination theory for understanding career mobility. They note a continuum from external regulation to self-regulation. Cultural and other factors may result in an internalized acceptance of external regulation and this will affect careers as much as other issues. Examples might include acceptance of a certain view about what is a suitable role for women with children and views among certain ethnic groups about what constitute suitable careers. However, based on a sizeable body of evidence, they argue that there are demonstrated benefits for individuals of exercising personal career choices.

The first set of personal factors likely to affect the desire for control over careers are features of individual personality. As already noted, those with a high internal locus of control and a proactive personality are more likely to want to control their careers. Research by Seibert et al. (2001) found a positive relationship between a proactive personality and behaviour associated with the promotion of their career. However, in a review of the relationship between various facets of personality and career success, Judge and Kammeyer-Mueller (2007) urged caution in emphasizing the significance of specific personality factors since they are usually explored in isolation rather than in the context of other dimensions of personality. This is not to deny the importance of a proactive personality and proactive behaviour, but it is a call for more research that takes account of a fuller range of personality variables.

A range of relevant attitudes and preferences are likely to affect individual efforts to control careers. The interest in personal agency with respect to careers allied to a belief that values have changed as we move from the era of baby boomers through Generation X to Millennials has resulted in an argument that there has been a growth in a protean career orientation and a boundaryless career mindset. The protean orientation has been defined by Hall (2004: p.4) as a belief that 'the person, not the organization, is in charge, the core values are freedom and growth, and the main success criteria are subjective (psychological success) versus objective success (position, salary).' The boundaryless career mindset involves navigating 'the changing work landscape by enacting a career characterized by different levels of physical and psychological movement' (Sullivan and Arthur, 2006: p.9). Both emphasize an independence from the constraints and controls imposed by specific organizations and a desire to move beyond organizational controls through the exercise of career self-management (King, 2004).

A further individual factor that will have an influence on the ability to control career decisions is the possession of relevant human capital. Those with what have been described as scarce, valuable and hard to imitate or replace qualities will have a wider range of career opportunities and therefore potentially greater control over career choices. This is increasingly seen as critical for effective human resource management (Carmeli and Schaubroeck, 2005) and, as DiRenzo and Greenhaus (2011) highlight, movement capital.

The focus on personality and individual differences implies that there will be considerable variation in the extent to which individuals seek to exert control over their careers. The more proactive and those with a strong protean mindset may typically wish to retain full control. Others may be more content to take control only when confronted with important decisions while still others may be largely passive, allowing external controls to dominate. However, reactance theory (Brehm, 1966) proposes that for many people, when control over important outcomes is threatened, they will seek to reassert control. We can predict that this is likely to be the case when the career is threatened and it is on such occasions that conflicts over control can arise.

In summary, therefore, there will be differences in the general desire to exert career control, due to differences in personality, attitudes and career preferences, different circumstances in which individuals will seek to exert control and, based partly on human capital, differences in the likely success of efforts to exert control.

The Boundaries of Career Control

At the boundary between external and internal individual influences on careers lies the career control frontier. This frontier will be flexible and will move between predominantly individual or external influences at different points in a career. The frontier will also vary according to external circumstances such as the state of relevant labour markets and according to individual differences in motivation and ability to control careers. For example, in considering a choice of career, some individuals from quite an early age seem to have a 'calling' (Berg et al., 2010) and are clear about the sort of career they wish to pursue. Others drift into a career, perhaps because they performed strongly in certain subjects at school, and this led to a progression into a degree subject or a certain kind of apprenticeship which channelled the potential career choices.

The frontier of career control between the individual and organization can become a contentious issue. Organizations may encourage the rhetoric of career self-management while remaining eager to control the careers of high-potential employees (King, 2004). There is a widely disseminated view that the 1950s to the 1970s was the era of the organizational career control, with sophisticated career planning and career management systems, and an underlying assumption of organizational stability and continuity. Thereafter, external factors such as increasing global competition, oil crises and market changes meant that organizations began to lose control over their own destiny and over their ability to manage the careers of their staff (Cappelli, 1999). Given the growing unpredictability of organizational careers, Hall (2004) proclaimed the emergence of the protean career and a shift in control of careers from the organization to individuals. However, the extent to which 'new' careers and their associated mindset now dominate is unclear (Pringle and Mallon, 2003) and there is evidence that the kind of behaviour typically associated with organizational boundarylessness, namely more frequent voluntary moves across organizational boundaries, had not occurred, at least up to the time of the 2008 recession, in most advanced industrial countries (Rodrigues and Guest, 2010).

There are certain points in life where individuals may seek to exert more control over their careers in the face of organizational opposition. An early example can occur soon after initial organizational entry. Graduates who believe that the promises made to them when they joined an organization have not been kept may opt to leave their employer in search of alternative opportunities (Sturges et al., 2000). Poorly qualified entrants to the labour market may be uncertain about the kind of work to which they are best suited and therefore use their early years to move from job to job until they find the kind of work that fits their interests and aspirations. Of course the feasibility of initiating movement depends to an important extent on the state of the labour market, so that exerting career control in this way is not without its risks.

The boundaries of career control can become even more complex when family demands increase and work–life balance becomes a priority. There may be conflict, both between the individual and their organization, between the individual and their family and in addition an element of internal conflict as attempts are made to reconcile competing demands on time and attention. There has been extensive research highlighting the conflicts that can occur in dual-career families when the organization of one partner plans a move which conflicts with the career plans of the other partner (Greenman, 2011).

In many cases, it may be unclear who is controlling careers and career decisions. This may not be an issue most of the time and only becomes salient when provoked by an external event such as a company takeover, a threat of redundancies or being overlooked for promotion. At this point, reactance may occur and the scope for exerting control comes to the fore. At the same time, we must acknowledge that many people do not think about their career as a planned process or as something over which they might want to have control. They are, in effect, disengaged from the career process. Furthermore, there is likely to be an important distinction between who or what actually controls career decisions and individual perceptions of control. The research on control and autonomy highlights the benefits of the perception of control for individual well-being in most circumstances (Karasek, 1979). We would hypothesize that a perception of career control is likely to be associated with greater satisfaction with the career and with associated outcomes. However, this has rarely been tested. Therefore, in the final part of this chapter, we present a study that explores this assumption.

A TEST OF THE ASSOCIATION BETWEEN CAREER CONTROL AND CAREER OUTCOMES

There has been almost no prior research exploring the relationship between career control and career-related outcomes. In other research, an association has been found between perceptions of autonomy and control and a range of positive outcomes. For

Table 14.1 Sample demographics

	Gender		Age			Ethnicity		Marital Status		Dependent Children	
	Men	Women	25–30	40–45	55–60	White	Non-White	Married	Single	Yes	No
No.	435	990	563	451	311	827	598	1007	375	559	820
%	30.5	69.5	42.4	34	23.5	58	42	73.7	27.3	40.5	59.5

example, a study by Greenberger et al. (1989) found an association between perceptions of control over work and both job satisfaction and supervisor ratings of performance.

There are no established measures of career control. We adapted two items from a scale developed by Millar and Shevlin (2007) designed to measure career locus of control among schoolchildren and deductively developed an additional two items to form a preliminary measure of career control. After pilot testing and amendment, the items demonstrated good internal consistency (Cronbach's alpha = .72) (The four items were: 'I have always been in control of the direction of my career'; 'My career is the result of my own actions, choices and decisions'; 'I have deliberately developed certain skills and abilities in order to get where I wanted'; 'I deliberately seek to control and manage my own career'.)

This measure was applied as part of a study of UK pharmacists' careers (see Rodrigues et al., 2013). Questionnaires were sent to 3942 members of the Royal Pharmaceutical Society of Great Britain, a professional body to which all practising pharmacists must belong. A total of 1425 completed questionnaires were returned. Details of all background information can be found in Table 14.1.

Responses to all relevant items were provided on a five-point scale ranging from: 'strongly agree' (5) to 'strongly disagree' (1). The average score on the measure of career control was 3.86 (SD = 0.65), suggesting relatively high levels of perceived control, as might be expected with a professional group. Data were collected on three relevant dependent variables using established measures. These were job satisfaction (Kim et al., 1996), career satisfaction (Greenhaus et al., 1990) and life satisfaction (Diener et al., 1985). The mean scores were, respectively, 3.91 (SD = 0.81), 3.94 (SD = 0.85) and 3.38 (SD = 0.90). Life satisfaction falls well below levels of career and job satisfaction. Inspection of the correlations in Table 14.2 suggests that life satisfaction is significantly lower among those who are single, those from ethnic minorities and those working long hours.

The antecedents of career control were examined by regressing career control on a wide range of background variables. The results, shown in Table 14.3, reveal that those with a higher income and those working in the community sector rather than the hospital sector report higher levels of career control. No biographical factors had any significant influence on perceptions of career control, and background factors appear to explain only 5 per cent of the variance.

Further analysis explored the role of career control in explaining the three relevant outcomes. This was achieved using a step-wise regression with the personal characteristics entered in a first step (Model 1) followed in a second step by work-related

Table 14.2 Means, standard deviations and correlations between study variables

	Mean	SD	Age	Gender	Ethnic group	Marital status	Dep. children	Income	Empl. tenure	Occup. tenure	Sector (1= hosp.)	Sector (1= other)	Hours	Contract (1= temp.)	Contract (1= Part-time)	Job sat.	Life sat.	Career sat.
Age	40.04	12.05																
Gender (0 = women)	.32	.46	.02															
Ethnic group (0 = white)	.37	.48	−.07**	.02														
Marital status (0= single)	.73	.44	.25**	.01	−.06*													
Dependent children (0 = no.)	.41	.49	.22**	.01	.10**	.36**												
Income	3.35	1.53	.08**	.33**	.05	−.02	−.01											
Employer tenure in years	7.93	8.56	.60**	.07**	−.02	.15**	.16**	.13**										
Occupational tenure in years	17	12.42	.96**	.00	−.13**	.24**	.20**	.09**	.61**									
Sector (1= hospital)	.23	.42	−.15**	−.13**	−.11**	−.03	−.10**	−.09**	−.04	−.13**								
Sector (1= other)	.20	.39	.11**	−.08**	−.06*	.06*	.08**	.02	−.08**	.14**	−.27**							
Hours of work	35.06	11.48	−.24**	.34**	.06*	−.17**	−.20**	.51**	−.10**	−.26**	−.02	−.06*						
Contract (1= temporary)	.23	.41	.08**	.07**	.12**	−.00	−.00	−.22**	.03	.07*	−.19**	−.08**	−.21**					
Contract (1= part-time)	.31	.46	.34**	−.21**	−.02	.20**	.30**	−.45**	.17**	.34**	−.07*	.06*	−.77**	.20**				
Job satisfaction	3.91	.81	.10**	−.08**	−.04	.06*	.05*	.09**	.07**	.10**	.07**	.09**	−.05	−.14**	.00			
Life satisfaction	3.38	.90	.01	−.09**	−.10**	.17**	.04	−.00	.03	.03	.02	.03	−.15**	−.04	.07*	.49**		
Career satisfaction	3.94	.85	.01	−.03	−.09**	.02	−.05	.17**	.07**	.01	.06*	.08**	.04	−.14**	−.05	.55**	.45**	
Career control	3.86	.65	−.03	.08**	.06*	−.00	−.03	.19**	.01	−.05	−.10**	.04	.12**	−.02	−.08**	.27**	.24**	.42**

Notes: * $p < 0.05$; ** $p < 0.01$; *** $p < 0.001$.

Table 14.3 Hierarchical regression of demographic and employment experience variables on career control

Independent Variables	Career Control
	β
Age	−.06
Gender (0 = women)	−.01
Ethnic group (0 = white)	.01
Marital status (0 = single)	.03
Dependent children (0 = no.)	−.05
Income	.16***
Employer tenure	.02
Occup. tenure	−.05
Sector (1= hospital)	−.10**
Sector (1= other)	.04
Hours of work	−.00
Contract (1= temporary)	−.01
Contract (1= part-time)	.00
Total R^2	.05***

Notes: * $p < 0.05$; ** $p < 0.01$; *** $p < 0.001$.

background factors (Model 2) and finally in the third step by career control (Model 3). The results are presented in Table 14.4.

The results for job satisfaction, based on Model 3, reveal that women, those working in hospitals and those with permanent employment contracts report significantly higher job satisfaction. However, much the most important influence is perceived career control. This is reflected in the change in R^2 which rises from .04 between Models 1 and 2 to .08 between Models 2 and 3. Taken together, the biographical, work-related and career control variables explain 15 per cent of the variance in job satisfaction.

Career satisfaction is significantly higher among women, those with a higher income, those working in hospitals rather than in community pharmacy and those with permanent rather than temporary jobs. There is also evidence of a significant association between longer tenure and career satisfaction and between belonging to a black and minority ethnic group and lower career satisfaction. Once again, perceptions of career control are much the most important influence on career satisfaction, explaining 18 per cent of the variance where the three sets of factors combined explain 25 per cent of the variance in career satisfaction.

The third outcome variable is life satisfaction. Biographical factors are relatively more important in this case. Life satisfaction is significantly higher among those who are married and have a higher income but lower among men and those belonging to a black or minority ethnic group. Life satisfaction is also lower among those with longer working hours. Finally, life satisfaction is higher among those reporting higher levels of career control.

In summary, these results support the hypothesis that those reporting higher levels of

Table 14.4 Hierarchical regression of career control on career, job and life satisfaction controlling for demographic and employment experience variables

Independent Variables	Job Satisfaction			Career Satisfaction			Life Satisfaction		
	β			β			β		
	Model 1	Model 2	Model 3	Model 1	Model 2	Model 3	Model 1	Model 2	Model 3
Age	.10**	.21	.20	.00	.07	.09	−.04	−.22	−.20
Gender (0 = women)	−.10***	−.11**	−.10**	−.06	−.08*	−.07**	−.10**	−.08**	−.08**
Ethnic group (0 = white)	−.04	−.02	−.02	−.08**	−.06*	−.06*	−.09**	−.08**	−.08**
Marital status (0 = single)	−.00	−.00	−.01	.01	.01	.00	.17***	.16***	.15***
Dependent children (0 = no.)	.00	−.00	.01	−.06	−.07*	−.05	−.00	−.02	−.00
Income		.12**	.06		.21***	.14***		.13**	.08*
Employer tenure		.04	.03		.08*	.07*		.04	.03
Occupational tenure		−.15	−.10		−.14	−.12		.10	.12
Sector (1= Hospital)		.09**	.12***		.08*	.12***		.00	.03
Sector (1= Other)		.07*	.06		.07*	.05		−.03	−.05
Working hours		−.03	−.01		−.07	−.07		−.18**	−.17**
Contract (0 = Permanent)		−.09**	−.09**		−.08**	−.08**		−.02	−.01
Contract (0 = Full-time)		.00	.01		.00	−.00		−.01	−.01
Career control			.30***			.43***			.27***
ΔR^2	.03***	.04***	.08***	.01**	.06***	.18***	.05***	.02**	.07***
Total R^2		.15			.25			.14	

Notes: * $p < 0.05$; ** $p < 0.01$; *** $p < 0.001$.

perceived control will report more positive outcomes. In this case, we examined three outcomes: job satisfaction, career satisfaction and life satisfaction. Career control was the strongest explanatory variable and the association with life satisfaction suggests some spillover into life outside work.

CONCLUSIONS

In this chapter we have argued that an analysis of careers based on the concept of career control can provide new insights for career theory. Drawing on the utilization of the control concept in management, employment relations and organizational psychology, we have presented a model designed to highlight the dynamics of career control and how these dynamics, including potential conflicts at the frontier between individual and external control, might play out. We have also described a range of internal and external factors that can influence control over career outcomes.

More generally, what this analysis highlights is the importance of an inter-disciplinary approach to the study of careers, with a predominantly psychological perspective on internal aspects of control and a predominantly socio-economic perspective on external influences on control. The interplay and sometimes the conflict between individual agency and structural context are central to any analysis of career control (see also Forrier et al., 2009). However, the analysis confirms that a simple dichotomy between agency and structure is not appropriate for the analysis of the range of dynamic and often subjectively perceived aspects of careers. A control framework helps to highlight features of this dynamism and complexity and also the challenges of ensuring sustainable careers in the face of a range of individual and contextual factors affecting careers.

What we have offered is a preliminary model and analysis designed to draw attention to the potential importance and value of the career control concept in helping to understand the nature of the so-called 'new' career world. We have also outlined an initial test of the influence of career control. Despite the potential shortcomings of the research design, including common-method variance and the adoption of a novel measure, the findings appear to confirm that perceptions of career control are significantly associated with job, career and life satisfaction. Given the importance of these outcomes for general well-being, we believe the concept of career control merits further development and research.

REFERENCES

Arthur, M., K. Inkson and J. Pringle (1999), *The New Careers: Individual Action and Economic Change*, Thousand Oaks, CA: Sage.

Barney, J. (1991), 'Firm resources and sustained competitive advantage', *Journal of Management*, **17**, 99–120.

Barney, J. and P. Wright (1998), 'On becoming a strategic partner: The role of human resources in gaining competitive advantage', *Human Resource Management*, **37**, 31–46.

Bazerman, M. (1982), 'Impact of personal control on performance: Is added control always beneficial?', *Journal of Applied Psychology*, **67**, 472–9.

Berg, J., A. Grant and V. Johnson (2010), 'When callings are calling: Crafting work and leisure in pursuit of unanswered occupational callings', *Organization Science*, **21**, 973–94.

Brehm, J. (1966), *A Theory of Psychological Reactance*, New York: Academic Press.

Cappelli, P. (1999), 'Career jobs are dead', *California Management Review*, **42**, 146–67.

Carmeli, A. and J. Schaubroeck (2005), 'How leveraging human resource capital with its competitive distinctiveness enhances the performance of commercial and public organizations', *Human Resource Management*, **44**, 391–412.

Carver, C. and M. Scheier (1982), 'Control theory: A useful conceptual framework for personality-social, clinical and health psychology', *Psychological Bulletin*, **92**, 111–35.

Clegg, H. (1979), *The Changing System of Industrial Relations in Great Britain*, Oxford: Blackwell.

Deci, E. (1975), *Intrinsic Motivation*, New York: Plenum Press.

Dewe, P., M. O'Driscoll and C. Cooper (2010), *Coping with Work Stress: A Review and Critique*, Chichester: Wiley.

DiRenzo, M. and J. Greenhaus (2011), 'Job search and voluntary turnover in a boundaryless world: A control theory perspective', *Academy of Management Review*, **36**, 567–89.

Diener, E., R. Emmons, R. Larsen and S. Griffin (1985), 'The satisfaction with life scale', *Journal of Personality Assessment*, **49**, 71–5.

Feldman, D. and T. Ng (2007), 'Careers: Mobility, embeddedness, and success', *Journal of Management*, **33**, 350–77.

Forrier, A., L. Sels and D. Stynen (2009), 'Career mobility at the intersection between agent and structure: A conceptual model', *Journal of Occupational and Organizational Psychology*, **82**, 739–60.

Gagne, M. and E. Deci (2005), 'Self-determination theory and work motivation', *Journal of Organizational Behavior*, **26**, 331–62.

Ganster, D. and M. Fusilier (1989), 'Control in the workplace', in C. Cooper and I. Robertson (eds), *International Review of Industrial and Organizational Psychology, 1989*, Chichester: Wiley.

Giglioni, G. and A. Bedeian (1974), 'A conspectus of management control theory: 1900–1972', *Academy of Management Journal*, **17**, 292–305.
Goodrich, C. (1920), *The Frontiers of Control: A Study of British Workshop Relations*, London: Bell.
Greenberger, D. and S. Strasser (1986), 'Development and application of a model of personal control in organizations', *Academy of Management Review*, **11**, 164–77.
Greenberger, D., S. Strasser, L. Cummings and R. Dunham (1989), 'The impact of personal control on performance and satisfaction', *Organizational Behavior and Human Decision Processes*, **43**, 29–51.
Greenhaus, J., S. Parasuraman and W. Wormley (1990), 'Effects of race on organizational experiences, job performance evaluations, and career outcomes', *Academy of Management Journal*, **33**, 64–86.
Greenman, E. (2011), 'Asian American–White differences in the effect of motherhood on career outcomes', *Work and Occupations*, **38**, 37–67.
Hall, D. (2004), 'The protean career: A quarter century journey', *Journal of Vocational Behavior*, **65**, 1–13.
Judge, T. and J. Kammeyer-Mueller (2007), 'Personality and career success', in H. Gunz and M. Peiperl (eds), *Handbook of Career Studies*, Thousand Oaks, CA: Sage, pp. 59–78.
Karasek, R. (1979), 'Job demands, job decision latitude, and mental strain: Implications for job design', *Administrative Science Quarterly*, **24**, 285–306.
Kelley, H. and J. Michela (1980), 'Attribution theory and research', *Annual Review of Psychology*, **31**, 457–501.
Kim, S., J. Price, C. Mueller and T. Watson (1996), 'The determinants of career intent among physicians at a US Air Force hospital', *Human Relations*, **49**, 947–76.
King, Z. (2004), 'Career self-management: Its nature, causes and consequences', *Journal of Vocational Behavior*, **65**, 112–33.
Kossek, E. and B. Lautsch (2012), 'Work–family boundary management styles in organizations: A cross-level model', *Organizational Psychology Review*, **2**, 152–71.
Lefcourt, H. (1976), *Locus of Control*, Hillsdale, NJ: Lawrence Erlbaum.
Lepak, D. and S. Snell (1999), 'The human resource architecture: Towards a theory of human capital allocation and development', *Academy of Management Review*, **24**, 31–48.
Marchington, M., A. Wilkinson, P. Ackers and J. Goodman (1993), 'The influence of managerial relations on waves of employee involvement', *British Journal of Industrial Relations*, **31**, 553–76.
Mayrhofer, W., M. Meyer and J. Steyrer (2007), 'Contextual issues in the study of careers', in H. Gunz and M. Peiperl (eds), *Handbook of Career Studies*, Thousand Oaks, CA: Sage, pp. 215–40.
Michaels, E., H. Handfield-Jones and B. Axelrod (2001), *The War for Talent*, Boston, MA: Harvard Business Review Press.
Millar, R. and M. Shevlin (2007), 'The development and factor structure of a career locus of control scale for use with school pupils', *Journal of Career Development*, **33**, 224–49.
Moen, P. and Y. Yu (2000), 'Effective work/life strategies: Working couples, work conditions, gender, and life quality', *Social Problems*, **47**, 291–326.
Parker, S., U. Bindl and K. Strauss (2010), 'Making things happen: A model of proactive behaviour', *Journal of Management*, **36**, 827–56.
Phillips, S. and A. Imhoff (1997), 'Women and career development: A decade of research', *Annual Review of Psychology*, **48**, 31–59.
Pringle, J. and M. Mallon (2003), 'Challenges for the boundaryless career odyssey', *The International Journal of Human Resource Management*, **14**, 839–53.
Ramsay, H. (1977), 'Cycles of control: Worker participation in sociological and historical perspective', *Sociology*, **11**, 481–506.
Rodrigues, R. and D. Guest (2010), 'Have careers become boundaryless?', *Human Relations*, **63**, 1157–75.
Rodrigues, R., D. Guest and A. Budjanovcanin (2013), 'From anchors to orientations: Towards a new theory of career preferences', *Journal of Vocational Behavior*, **82**, 142–52.
Rosenbaum, J. (1979), 'Tournament mobility: Career patterns in a corporation', *Administrative Science Quarterly*, **24**, 220–41.
Rotter, J. (1966), 'Generalized expectancies for internal and external control of reinforcement', *Psychological Monographs*, **80** (whole of No. 609).
Schneer, J. and F. Reitman (1997), 'The interrupted managerial career path: A longitudinal study of MBAs', *Journal of Vocational Behavior*, **51**, 411–34.
Seibert, S., M. Kraimer and J. Crant (2001), 'What do proactive people do? A longitudinal model linking proactive personality and career success', *Personnel Psychology*, **54**, 845–74.
Seibert, S., M. Kraimer and R. Liden (2001), 'A social capital theory of career success', *Academy of Management Journal*, **44**, 219–37.
Seligman, M. (1975), *Helplessness: On Depression, Development and Death*, San Francisco, CA: W.H. Freeman.
Shore, L., J. Coyle-Shapiro and L. Tetrick (eds) (2012), *The Employee–Organization Relationship*, London: Routledge.

Spector, P. (1982), 'Behavior in organizations as a function of employees' locus of control', *Psychological Bulletin*, **91**, 482–97.
Sturges, J., D. Guest and K. MacKenzie Davey (2000), 'Who's in charge? Graduates' attitudes to and experiences of career management and their relationship with organizational commitment', *European Journal of Work and Organizational Psychology*, **9**, 351–70.
Sturges, J., D. Guest, N. Conway and K. MacKenzie Davey (2002), 'A longitudinal study of the relationship between career management and organizational commitment among graduates in their first ten years of work', *Journal of Organizational Behavior*, **23**, 731–48.
Sullivan, S. and M. Arthur (2006), 'The evolution of the boundaryless career concept: Examining physical and psychological mobility', *Journal of Vocational Behavior*, **69**, 19–29.
Tannenbaum, A. (1968), *Control in Organizations*, New York: McGraw-Hill.
Vroom, V. (1964), *Work and Motivation*, New York: Wiley.
White, R. (1959), 'Motivation reconsidered: The concept of competence', *Psychological Review*, **66**, 297–333.
Wrzesniewski, A. and J. Dutton (2001), 'Crafting a job: Revisioning employees as active crafters of their work', *Academy of Management Review*, **26**, 179–201.

15 Building a sustainable career: the role of work–home balance in career decision making

Sara De Hauw and Jeffrey H. Greenhaus

As discussed throughout this book, the current career landscape has changed dramatically during the past 25 years (Arthur et al., 1989). This change has been the complex result of a number of emerging economic, organizational and societal trends (Greenhaus and Kossek, 2014).

First, driven by globalization and technological advancements, the current economic environment has been transformed into a rapidly changing and highly uncertain, global playing field in which organizations aim to adhere to the ever-increasing and continuously shifting market demands, while trying to outdo competitors from all over the world. To do so, organizations have undergone substantial changes, becoming more lean and flexible, enabling them to respond more quickly and efficiently to changing market demands (De Vos et al., 2011; Greenhaus et al., 2008). They have flattened their structures, limiting the possibility for upward promotions (Arthur and Rousseau, 1996), and have engaged in more short-term transactional contracts, which provide more mobility and flexibility, but also more uncertainty (Forrier and Sels, 2003; Rousseau, 1995). To survive in this world of uncertainty in which promises of lifetime employment and upward career paths have diminished, employees need to take charge and create their own successful career path based on what they value and aspire to (Hall, 2002). In order to do so, employees need to make sure that they remain attractive for their current and future employers by continuously developing their competencies, and as such remain employable (De Vos et al., 2011; Fugate et al., 2004).

Second, we also note a number of societal changes that have shaped contemporary careers. One of the most prominent changes has been the entrance of women in the workforce (Marks, 2006). Since the 1960s, women have started to work outside the home, leading today to nearly 50 per cent of managers and professionals being female (Lee et al., 2011). This evolution has significantly changed the outlook of the modern family, replacing the traditional male-breadwinner/female-homemaker roles with dual-career families and single-parent families in which both men and women are simultaneously confronted with work and domestic responsibilities (Marks, 2006; Moen and Sweet, 2004). As a result, work and home domains are no longer seen as separate entities, but as entangled strands that continuously influence each other (Greenhaus and Powell, 2012; Lee et al., 2011). However, career researchers have only recently recognized the influence of the personal and family life on careers (for example, customized careers; Valcour et al., 2007), and have begun to look at careers within the constraints and opportunities of the broader life context (Greenhaus and Kossek, 2014). Next to the rise of women, we also observe a rise of older workers in the workforce (Johnston, 1991). Thanks to improvements in hygiene and medical care, we have been able to prolong our lives. As a consequence, many employees prolong their careers to contribute to the household income, experience satisfaction derived from work, or secure their pension when retiring (Cappelli and Novelli, 2010). The question remains, however, how we can lengthen our careers, making sure that we have the energy, drive and competence to keep working effectively, while simultaneously building a satisfactory home life.

All in all, economic, organizational and societal trends emphasize the need for employees to take charge and build a sustainable career.

DEFINING A SUSTAINABLE CAREER

In this chapter, we define a sustainable career as a career in which employees remain healthy, productive, happy and employable throughout its course and that fits into their broader life context.

This definition is based upon the work of Greenhaus and Kossek (2014), who stated that a sustainable career is successfully integrated into a satisfying personal and family life, and provides employees a sense of security and well-being. A sense of security is obtained through employees' efforts to remain employable (Forrier and Sels, 2003), developing the necessary expertise to secure their job and financial income, as well as the necessary flexibility to change their career paths to suit the labour market's and their own needs (Fugate et al., 2004; Van der Heijde and Van der Heijden, 2006). The sense of well-being, on the other hand, is obtained by preserving and enhancing employees' physical and mental health by, for example, regularly creating opportunities for rejuvenation (Newman, 2011) and making sure that their job and career fit with the core values in their life (Greenhaus and Kossek, 2014).

Moreover, creating a sustainable career also benefits organizations by assuring high levels of productivity through a continual high performance of their employees. As noted by Van der Heijde and Van der Heijden (2006), employees remain employable by enhancing their expertise and flexibility. To do so, employees develop their competencies, and make sure that they stay up-to-date. This heightened level of relevant competencies boosts employees' performance (Van der Heijde and Van der Heijden, 2006), and as such, increases organizations' productivity. In addition, a recent meta-analysis by Lyubomirsky et al. (2005) debunks the myth that good performance leads to happiness, but shows that the reverse is true in that happiness leads to good performance. Being healthy and happy is thus an important prerequisite for employees' long-term performance, as it gives them the necessary energy and drive to work effectively throughout the course of their career.

BUILDING A SUSTAINABLE CAREER VIA CAREER DECISION MAKING

Building a sustainable career that is characterized by employability, physical health and mental well-being is today primarily the responsibility of the employee (Arthur and Rousseau, 1996; Hall, 2002). It is the employee who steers his/her career in the preferred direction and who needs to make sure that it stays aligned with the demands from the labour market and his/her own physical and psychological needs. As both labour market demands and individual needs continuously change (Greenhaus et al., 2008; Sullivan and Mainiero, 2007), employees need to periodically adjust their current work experiences to keep their career on track. As such, building a sustainable career requires employees to make a series of decisions about their current work role, such as accepting or quitting a job, starting to work part-time, becoming self-employed, or staying put. These decisions have been defined by Greenhaus and Powell (2012) as 'a choice between alternative courses of action when the decision maker has sufficient control over the situation to have a choice' (p. 247).

To build a sustainable career through a series of career decisions, employees thus need multiple alternatives from which to choose. In prior decades (for example, the 1950s), careers were rather straightforward and consisted of a full-time, continuous involvement in the workforce (generally by men), in which a steady advancement via upward moves was presumed (Valcour et al., 2007). These traditional careers often took place within the context of a single employer and a single profession, and were orchestrated almost entirely by the employer (Arthur and Rousseau, 1996; Valcour et al., 2007). Employees hence had few alternatives, and thus few career decisions to make. Nowadays, however, employees are stimulated to move across professions, organizations and national borders (Ng et al., 2007), and to look beyond the limited upward possibilities and take initiative to pursue their personal values and goals when mapping out their careers (Hall, 2002). These contemporary trends have created a plethora of different career paths for employees to follow (Greenhaus and Kossek, 2014; Valcour et al., 2007) and, hence, a wide variety of possible career decisions for them to make.

A Taxonomy of Contemporary Career Decisions

To understand the diverse set of career decisions employees can engage in, we created a non-exhaustive taxonomy. Following the literature on job crafting (Wrzesniewski and Dutton, 2001) and Idiosyncratic deals or I-deals (Rosen et al., 2013), we distinguish two ways in which employees can alter their current work experiences (next to the decision of staying put), being: (1) a change in work content; and (2) a change in work arrangements.

First, a change in work content represents a change in what employees do in their work, such as the type and number of tasks or the level of responsibility. Creating an overall categorization of job mobility, Ng et al. (2007) recognized that in addition to the presence or absence of inter-organizational mobility, there are two dimensions on which work content can change, namely status and function. *Status* refers to the level of responsibility at work, which can increase (for example, upward move), decrease (for example, downward move) or stay the same (for example, lateral move). *Function*, on the other hand, refers to the type of tasks that need to be fulfilled, which can remain rather similar (for example, upward move from junior manager to middle manager) or change drastically (for example, lateral move from sales representative to HR officer). In sum, changes in work content are described through their change in responsibility level (for example, increase or decrease responsibility) and their change in tasks (for example, similar or different tasks).

Second, a change in work arrangements describes a change in how employees perform their work, such as the number of working hours, the type of employment contracts, and the location of work. In their customized careers concept, Valcour et al. (2007)

distinguished three dimensions on which work arrangements can differ from traditional arrangements, being time, continuity and employment relation. *Time* refers to the number of hours employees work. Traditionally, employees worked during standard full-time work schedules, but recently deviations from these schedules have been observed (for example, job sharing, part-time work). These deviations indicate that employees today can alter their working hours, and hence choose to either decrease or increase their current hours. *Continuity*, on the other hand, refers to when work experiences are scheduled into the broader life cycle. Whereas in former times, employees worked on a continuous basis from their twenties (after education) until their sixties (before retirement), employees' careers are today characterized by interruptions and discontinuities in the work experience, such as temporary career breaks to take care of the children or to travel around the world. The *employment relation* refers to the type of contract under which employees perform their work. Traditionally, employees worked under permanent contracts negotiated with a single organization. Nowadays, however, employees can work under a variety of employment contracts, which can differ based on the duration (for example, temporary contracts) and the strength of the dependence relation (for example, independent employment). In addition to time, continuity and employment relation (Valcour et al., 2007), previous research also pointed out that current work experiences differ from traditional arrangements in terms of *location* and *personalization* of work. As noted by Shaffer et al. (2012), contemporary work environments are largely characterized by globalization, leading to a proliferation of multinationals, expatriate experiences and international careers. This trend created, in contrast to former times, both the opportunity and the demand for employees to engage in global work experiences by, for example, taking on short-term international assignments or working as a (permanent) expatriate. Furthermore, the rise of technological innovations and so-called New Ways of Working also created a trend towards an increased personalization in terms of, for example, the time and location of work. As a result, contrary to former times, employees today can (partially) shape their own work conditions by taking up flex-arrangements, such as flex-time or telework (Peters et al., 2009). In sum, changes in work arrangements are described through changes in time (for example, decrease or increase working hours), changes in continuity (for example, interrupt work experiences), changes in employment relations (for example, engage in more independent employment), changes in location (for example, engage in global work experiences), and changes in the personalization of work (for example, take up flex-arrangements).

How Do Contemporary Career Decisions Influence the Sustainability of Careers?

The career decisions described above are assumed to influence the sustainability of careers by impacting employees' health and/or employability.

A first set of career decisions, being the decisions to increase responsibility, to change tasks, to engage in global work experiences, to engage in independent employment and to increase working hours, are primarily assumed to enhance employability by increasing job resources. More specifically, a decision to *increase responsibility* (for example, making an upward move) challenges employees to take on a broader set of different tasks, in which a higher performance level is expected. Likewise, a decision to *change tasks* (for example, making a lateral move to a new function) requires employees to deal with new, though not necessarily higher-level, tasks. But also engaging in *global work experiences* and engaging in *independent employment* confronts employees with new and challenging situations (Hundley, 2001; Shaffer et al., 2012). As such, these four career decisions offer employees ample opportunities to further develop their competencies. As noted by Bakker et al., (2011), opportunities for competency development are an important job resource, which can help employees broaden their expertise and stimulate their flexibility, and thus enhance their employability (De Vos et al., 2011; Van der Heijde and Van der Heijden, 2006). In addition, *increasing working hours* expands the personal resources, such as time, attention and intellectual capital, that employees can devote to work, allowing them to learn more from the job and to more easily achieve their work goals (Ten Brummelhuis and Bakker, 2012). Consequently, the decision to increase working hours can also contribute to employees' perceived employability.

A second set of career decisions, being the decisions to lower responsibility, to reduce working hours, to interrupt work experiences and to take up flex-arrangements, are, on the other hand, primarily assumed to stimulate physical and mental health by reducing job demands. More specifically, by *lowering responsibility*, employees scale down their cognitive involvement in the work domain, limiting the demands for intellectual capital and continuous attention. *Reducing working hours*, on the other hand, allows employees to scale back their physical presence at work, and as such limit the time demands that their work puts on them. By *interrupting work experiences*, employees can terminate both by fully withdrawing from the workforce for a certain period of time. These three career decisions thus enable employees to directly reduce their job demands. As an excess of these demands has been noted in previous research to cause exhaustion as well as strain (Bakker and Demerouti, 2007), reducing job demands is an important way to protect and boost physical and mental health. Besides these direct approaches, employees can also choose to reduce their job demands by using available job resources as a buffer (Bakker and Demerouti, 2007). By *taking up flex-arrangements* (for example, flex-time or telework), employees gain autonomy (Gajendran and Harrison, 2007) and can hence choose how they deal with their job demands. As a result, they perceive their job demands as less hindering, and hence as causing less exhaustion and strain (Podsakoff et al., 2007). As such, taking up flex-arrangements also contributes to employees' physical and mental health.

Next to these positive effects on employability and/or health, we recognize that career decisions might also have less desirable effects, which can threaten the sustainability of careers. Increasing responsibility, changing tasks, engaging in global experiences, engaging in independent employment or increasing working hours do not only create opportunities for growth, but also the demand to develop more expertise and to be highly involved at work. Consequently, these career decisions not only increase job resources, but also job demands (for example, Prottas and Thompson, 2006), which might make employees more vulnerable to exhaustion and stress (Bakker and Demerouti, 2007), and therefore could hamper their physical and mental health. Lowering responsibility, reducing working hours, interrupting work experiences or taking up flex-arrangements, on the other hand, decrease job demands, which not only limits the experience of stress and exhaustion, but also the opportunities to learn from work experiences and to keep up-to-date with new developments, as such enabling employees to stay employable. Moreover, career decisions, such as taking a career break or using flex-arrangements, can have detrimental effects on future career advancement (Judiesch and Lyness, 1999; Valcour and Ladge, 2008). As a result, decisions to lower responsibility, reduce working hours, interrupt work experiences or take up flex-arrangements can hamper employability.

Career decisions can thus both facilitate and hinder the creation of sustainable careers, depending on whether the positive or negative effects prevail. According to behavioural decision making theory (March, 1994), employees make a certain career decision assuming that the positive outcomes will outweigh negative side-effects. As such, career decisions are assumed to facilitate a sustainable career. However, as stated by Poelmans (2005), decisions are not always fully rational and are bounded by imperfect information and an impossibility to know in advance all alternatives, required inputs and associated rewards and costs. Decision making is hence imperfect, and as a result, employees might overestimate a decision's positive outcomes and/or underestimate its negative side-effects. When this occurs, career decisions can hinder a sustainable career.

DRIVERS OF CAREER DECISIONS

Although employees' career decisions can play an essential role in facilitating (or hindering) the sustainability of their careers, it is unclear how employees make these career decisions. For example, how do employees choose between a variety of career paths and decide to move upwards or downwards, to work full-time or part-time, to become self-employed, or take up an international assignment?

Previous research uncovered a complex set of work-related (for example, salary), home-related (for example, partner's work) and personal (for example, health) factors that influence career decisions. The majority of studies thereby focused on work-related factors, such as pay (Griffeth et al., 2000), job satisfaction (Ostroff and Clark, 2001) or work stressors (Podsakoff et al., 2007). Though these studies provide interesting insights into how current work experiences influence career decisions, they largely neglect the influence that employees' home and personal lives have on their career (Greenhaus and Powell, 2012). As new trends at work (for example, 24/7 economy) and home (for example, dual-career couples) increasingly blur the boundaries between both domains (Marks, 2006; Wharton, 2006), it becomes more prevalent that work influences home decisions (for example, when to start a family) and that home influences work decisions (for example, accepting or declining a promotion) (Greenhaus and Kossek, 2014). As a result, an increasing number of studies started to investigate the impact of home life on work decisions (Lyness and Judiesch, 2008; Powell and Greenhaus, 2010; Van Vianen and Fischer, 2002) and this area of research may grow further in light of the Family-Relatedness of Work Decisions framework (Greenhaus and Powell, 2012). This growing interest for the influence of home life on work decisions embodies a positive evolution in career decision making that is vital to building a sustainable career (Greenhaus and Kossek, 2014). By considering home and personal lives in career decision making, employees can help to assure that their careers fit into their broader life context and keep them happy (for example, by securing marital satisfaction) and healthy (for example, by keeping the total sum of work and home demands manageable). As such, employees experience the necessary energy and drive to keep working effectively and efficiently, and hence build a sustainable career based on long-term employability and well-being.

Values Play a Key Role in Career Decision Making

Research and theory have thus shown that an extensive set of work-related, home-related and personal factors influence career decisions. To better understand how these factors, such as salary or the birth of a child, influence career decision making, we need to take a look at employees' core values (Sullivan and Mainiero, 2007). According to behavioural decision making theory (March, 1994), employees make a choice between alternative (career) actions by evaluating them on a set of different criteria. These criteria are not equally important to all employees, but get different weights based on the employees' values (Poelmans, 2005). As such, employees' values determine the importance of factors, such as partners' work, in making a career decision. Therefore, employees' values lie at the heart of career decisions (Judge and Bretz, 1992; Sullivan and Mainiero, 2007). A model of career values that takes both work and the broader life domain into account is the Kaleidoscope career model.

The Kaleidoscope career model discerns three values that drive career decisions by acting as a signpost guiding people throughout their career (Sullivan and Mainiero, 2007). These values are authenticity, balance and challenge. *Authenticity* refers to the need to be genuine and true to oneself, while *balance* refers to the need to be successful and satisfied in multiple life roles, and *challenge* describes the need to learn, grow and find stimulating work. All three values are simultaneously active over the course of an employee's career, but one type of value takes priority, expressing the largest influence over career decisions. Which value this is shifts over time, depending on what is happening in an employee's life at that given moment (Sullivan and Mainiero, 2007).

In this chapter, we focus on balance as a driver of career decisions, as work–home balance has been recognized by several contemporary career theories as a key motivator of career transitions (Hall, 2002; Valcour et al., 2007), and is an important prerequisite for building a sustainable career. To build a sustainable career in which employability, energy and drive remain high, employees need to build a career that fits into a satisfying personal and family life (Greenhaus and Kossek, 2014), and as such brings balance between work and home.

WORK–HOME BALANCE AS A DRIVER OF CAREER DECISIONS

To understand how work–home balance drives career decisions, we first need to have a comprehensive insight into what work–home balance means. Despite its popularity and frequent usage, the meaning of work–home balance still remains ambiguous today (Greenhaus and Allen, 2011). This is partially due to both popular and academic writings, which often assume that the meaning of work–home balance is self-evident, and therefore neglect to properly define it (Valcour, 2007). Only recently, a handful of definitions have been proposed (for example, Greenhaus and Allen, 2011; Grzywacz and Carlson, 2007), mostly originating from different theories or frameworks. Though these different perspectives are all valuable in their own right, we follow a subjective, individual-based approach and define work–home balance as 'individuals' overall evaluative judgement of how successful they are in and how satisfied they are with their multiple roles at work and home'.

This definition is based on three recurring elements that are observed in (almost) all balance definitions, being: (1) an overall appraisal; (2) a cognitive component; and (3) an affective component. First, in contrast to work–home conflict and enrichment describing events in which experiences in one role (for example, having to work overtime) directly affect experiences in the other role (for example, not being able to put your children to bed), work–home balance describes a global evaluation that examines multiple work and home roles simultaneously (Grzywacz and Carlson, 2007). This global evaluation is assumed to influence career decisions, as these decisions are not taken lightly based on a single event, but are often thoroughly reflected upon based on more holistic evaluations.

Holistic evaluations of work–home balance thereby tap into two dimensions: cognitive and affective. The cognitive dimension describes the degree to which employees believe they are successful in their work and home roles. Following Baltes and Carstensen (1996), we define success as goal attainment. More specifically, we focus on attaining personal goals rather than other-defined goals. This is in line with the protean view on career decisions as being primarily driven by personal values, instead of corporate or societal standards (Hall, 2002). Hence, the cognitive dimension describes the degree to which employees believe their achievement in their roles meet the personal goals they have set for these roles. The affective dimension, on the other hand, describes employees' feelings about their multiple work and home roles, and hence refers to how satisfied employees are with their roles. Though inconsistencies might exist between the cognitive and affective component, most often a strong positive relation can be observed in which both dimensions strengthen each other (Huskinson and Haddock, 2006; Van den Berg et al., 2006). As such, we assume that employees experience high work–home balance when they are able to reach the goals they have set for themselves in their work and home roles and when they are satisfied with their roles, while they experience low work–home balance when they are unable to reach their goals and when they are dissatisfied with their roles at work and home.

How Does Experiencing Low Work–Home Balance Drive Career Decisions?

According to frustration theory (Maier, 1949), the experience of unrealized goals and dissatisfaction induces frustration, a state of discomfort. In response to this state of discomfort, employees may retaliate by engaging in negative behaviours, such as workplace deviance (Lawrence and Robinson, 2007), but they might also engage in more positive change-oriented behaviours in an effort to move away from frustration (Young, 2009). As such, employees experiencing low work–home balance are assumed to engage more in career changes or career decisions that are specifically aimed at releasing frustration. Depending on the source of frustration, different types of career decisions are made.

First, frustration can originate from *unrealized goals and dissatisfaction at home*. According to the work–home resources model (Ten Brummelhuis and Bakker, 2012), these unsatisfactory home outcomes can be (partially) explained by job demands, defined as all aspects at work that require excessive physical and mental input or energy (Bakker and Demerouti, 2007). By putting excessive claims on, for example, employees' time and attention, employees have only a limited amount of these resources they can spend at home, hindering them from accomplishing their home goals (Ten Brummelhuis and Bakker, 2012) and causing strain and frustration (Bakker and Demerouti, 2007). According to the recent job crafting literature, one way in which employees can deal with this situation is by trying to reduce excessive claims or job demands (Demerouti, 2014; Tims et al., 2012).

Reducing job demands is an important job crafting strategy that employees use in an effort to reduce hindrances (which cause frustration), by, for example, lowering time demands, workload and other demanding aspects of work (Demerouti, 2014; Petrou et al., 2012; Tims et al., 2012). A career decision aimed at specifically reducing cognitive demands (such as attention) without reducing physical presence at work requires solely a change in work content. More specifically, a decision to lower responsibility aims to free up mental energy by confronting employees with work that limits the need for them to take accountability and that is less challenging and intellectually demanding. Next to that, a career decision aimed at specifically reducing physical or time demands at work requires a change in the physical environment of work, or hence the work arrangements. More specifically, by reducing working hours, employees reduce the time they devote to work, freeing up more time to spend in other life domains. As such, employees can take on the often-heard frustration of having insufficient time to do it all, without however fully taking away the interesting challenges and intellectual stimulation that work can bring. Finally, by deciding to interrupt work experiences, employees aim to take both a physical and mental break from work. As such, they can free up both their time and attention to be fully committed to the other life domains.

In addition to these direct approaches, employees can also indirectly reduce their job demands by using available job resources as a buffer. As mentioned by Bakker and Demerouti (2007), job resources reflect all aspects at work that help employees achieve their work goals, reduce their job demands and/or stimulate their personal growth and development. Job resources can thus be used for three distinct but important goals, one of which is the reduction of job demands. Though several types of job resources can be discerned (for example, participation in decision making, opportunities for development, leader–member exchange), we focus on only one of these job resources, which is known to reduce job demands, namely autonomy (Bakker and Demerouti, 2007). Two career decisions aimed at increasing autonomy are the decisions to take up flex-arrangements and to engage in independent employment. By taking up flex-arrangements, such as flex-time or telework, and by engaging in independent employment, employees gain autonomy over when, where and how they work, and can thus choose how they deal with their job demands. By organizing their job demands to also fit their needs at home, employees perceive these demands as less hindering, and hence experience less frustration due to these demands.

Second, frustration can also originate from *unrealized goals and dissatisfaction at work*. To release this frustration, employees can increase their job resources (Demerouti, 2014; Tims et al., 2012), which are described above as all aspects at work that help employees to achieve their work goals (Bakker and Demerouti, 2007). As such, increasing job resources is an important strategy for employees to reduce frustration caused by unrealized work goals. A career decision directly aimed at enhancing job resources is the decision to increase working hours. By increasing working hours, employees can devote more time and possibly other resources (for example, attention or intellectual capital) to the work domain, enabling them to more easily achieve their work goals (Ten Brummelhuis and Bakker, 2012).

In addition to this rather quantitative approach driving up the time, attention and resources spent at work, employees can also take a more qualitative approach and get closer to their work goals by finding a job that better fits with their work values. Two career decisions can help employees to increase this fit, being the decision to change tasks and the decision to engage in independent employment. First, by changing tasks, employees engage in a new set of roles and expectations, which might align better with who they are (referring to their self-image) and who they want to be (referring to their values). Consequently, by changing tasks, employees can create a better person–job fit (Edwards and Rothbard, 1999), enabling them to more easily achieve their work goals. Second, by engaging in independent employment, employees gain autonomy, which not only gives them control over their work arrangements (for example, when and where they work), but also over their work content. Therefore, by becoming independent, employees have the power to adjust their work to better fit their values and self-image, and hence create a better person–job fit (Edwards and Rothbard, 1999) to facilitate their achievement of work goals.

In sum, we assume that employees with a low work–home balance experience a sense of frustration and discomfort, and, as a result, engage more in career changes or career decisions aimed at releasing frustration. These career decisions can be aimed at releasing frustration caused by unrealized goals and dissatisfaction at home, via a reduction of job demands that are currently hindering home outcomes. Career decisions that are reducing job demands are decisions to lower responsibility (limiting cognitive demands at work), to reduce working hours (limiting time demands at work), to interrupt work experiences (limiting time and cognitive demands at work), to take up flex-arrangements (buffering work demands via autonomy), and to engage in independent employment (buffering work demands via autonomy). In addition, career decisions can also be aimed at releasing frustration caused by unrealized goals and dissatisfaction at work, via an enhancement of job resources that are known to stimulate the achievement of work goals. Career decisions enhancing such job resources are decisions to increase working hours (enhancing the amount of resources), to change tasks (enhancing person–job fit) and to engage in independent employment (enhancing person–job fit).

How Does Experiencing High Work–Home Balance Drive Career Decisions?

Employees experiencing high work–home balance, on the other hand, do not feel frustrated or uncomfortable. Rather, they feel pleased as they are able to reach their goals and are satisfied with their roles, both at work and home (Maier, 1949; Pinder, 1998). For them, the need to achieve a balance between work and home has been fulfilled (at least for the time being), leaving them in a satisfactory situation (Pinder, 1998). In contrast to frustrating situations, this satisfactory situation does not urge employees to change, or hence to take (sometimes drastic) career decisions aimed at breaking away from frustrating circumstances (Young, 2009). On the contrary, a favourable situation puts employees in a state of comfort and satisfaction that people aim to prolong. However, experiencing comfort and satisfaction does not mean that no career changes will take place. It only means that career changes or decisions will not be stimulated by an urge to release frustration, but will instead be characterized by a desire for a steady career development (Young, 2009). As mentioned by Lee et al. (2011), employees can (partially) control and shape their careers via two dynamics: individual actions and gradual development. Individual actions, displayed as responses or choices, are described as reactions to certain circumstances, like, for instance, hindering situations. Internal gradual development, on the other hand, has a more proactive and lower pace characteristic and involves, for example, more carefully rolled out plans for reaching long-term career goals (Lee et al., 2011). Gradual career development is thus triggered by a need to further develop and keep your competencies up-to-date to work towards the attainment of long-term goals. One way to do this is by increasing job resources (Demerouti, 2014; Tims et al., 2012).

As mentioned by Bakker and Demerouti (2007), increasing job resources helps employees not only to achieve their work goals or reduce their job demands, but also to stimulate their personal growth and development, which is essential in creating a steady career development. Four career decisions are assumed to stimulate growth and career progression by creating opportunities for competency development. First, the decision to increase responsibility challenges employees to bring their performance to a new level and to execute new tasks, creating ample opportunities for employees to further develop their competencies. Second, by changing tasks, employees perform new but not necessarily more difficult tasks, and as a result develop new competencies needed to perform these tasks. Hence, a change of tasks also generates opportunities for competency development. Third, engaging in global work experiences broadens employees' horizons by confronting them with new work and life situations. Though global work experiences do not necessarily involve new tasks or higher competency levels, they do create the opportunity and necessity for employees to develop global competencies (for example, intercultural understanding), which are seen as increasingly important in the business world (Shaffer et al., 2012). Finally, engaging in independent employment loosens the ties between employee and organization, and, as such, makes employees increasingly responsible for securing a continuous stream of work and assignments. To do this, employees need to remain attractive in the labour market by keeping their competencies up-to-date and by showing to be flexible in terms of both work arrangements and work content (Valcour et al., 2007). This presses employees to seek out the ample opportunities for competency development that exist in the work space and take on challenging assignments to differentiate themselves from their competitors.

In sum, we assume that employees with a high work–home balance experience a certain level of comfort and satisfaction, and, as a result, are more inclined to engage in career decisions aimed at a gradual career development. This gradual career development is triggered by an increment of job resources known to stimulate personal growth and development. Career decisions that increase such job resources are decisions to increase responsibility (creating opportunities to develop a higher level of competencies), to change tasks (creating opportunities to develop new competencies), to engage in global work experiences (creating opportunities to develop global competencies), and to engage in independent employment (creating opportunities to constantly develop relevant competencies).

CONCLUSION

Nowadays, both the career literature (Harrington and Hall, 2007) and the work–home literature (Dorio et al., 2008) increasingly recognize the importance of work–home balance in shaping employees' careers. Unfortunately, despite that, surprisingly little is known about how this process unfolds. In this chapter, we have built a model that can shed some light on the process by explaining how work–home balance stimulates employees to make certain career decisions that might facilitate or hinder them in creating a sustainable career. The model is summarized in Figure 15.1.

In short, the model shows that when employees experience low work–home balance, they feel frustrated, and, as a result, engage more in career decisions aimed at releasing frustration via a reduction of job demands or an enhancement of job resources. When employees experience high work–home balance, on the other hand, they feel satisfied, and, as a result, engage more in career decisions aimed at stimulating growth via an enhancement of job resources. An enhancement of job resources is primarily aimed at boosting employability by helping employees further develop their competencies, and thus broaden their expertise and flexible deployment, while a reduction of job demands is primarily aimed at enhancing health as an excess of these demands has been shown to cause exhaustion and strain.

The model furthers our current knowledge on the links between work–home balance and careers. To date, previous research on career decisions mainly consisted of fragmented studies, indicating whether or not a relationship exists between work–home balance and a single decision, such as becoming self-employed (Mallon and Cohen, 2001). These fragmented studies created a scattered insight dispersed over multiple disciplines, and provided limited insight into why the effect exists and why different effects can be found for different career decisions. The model in this chapter overcomes these limitations by providing a more comprehensive and theory-driven understanding of how work–home balance influences career decisions. However, the question remains whether this theoretical model accurately describes real-life situations. To address this question, we encourage future research to subject the theoretical model to a profound and wide-ranging empirical investigation.

Furthermore, though we emphasize the active role that employees play in mapping out their careers via the various decisions they make, we also recognize that there are boundaries to their decision latitude, and that a number of personal and contextual factors can influence the extent to which work–home balance impacts career decisions (Lee et al., 2011). For example, based on the theory of planned behaviour (Ajzen, 1991) and the Family-Relatedness of Work Decisions theory (Greenhaus and Powell, 2012), we assume that perceived behavioural control and perceived organizational support might moderate relations between work–home balance and career decisions. Future research is needed to explore these and other moderating influences.

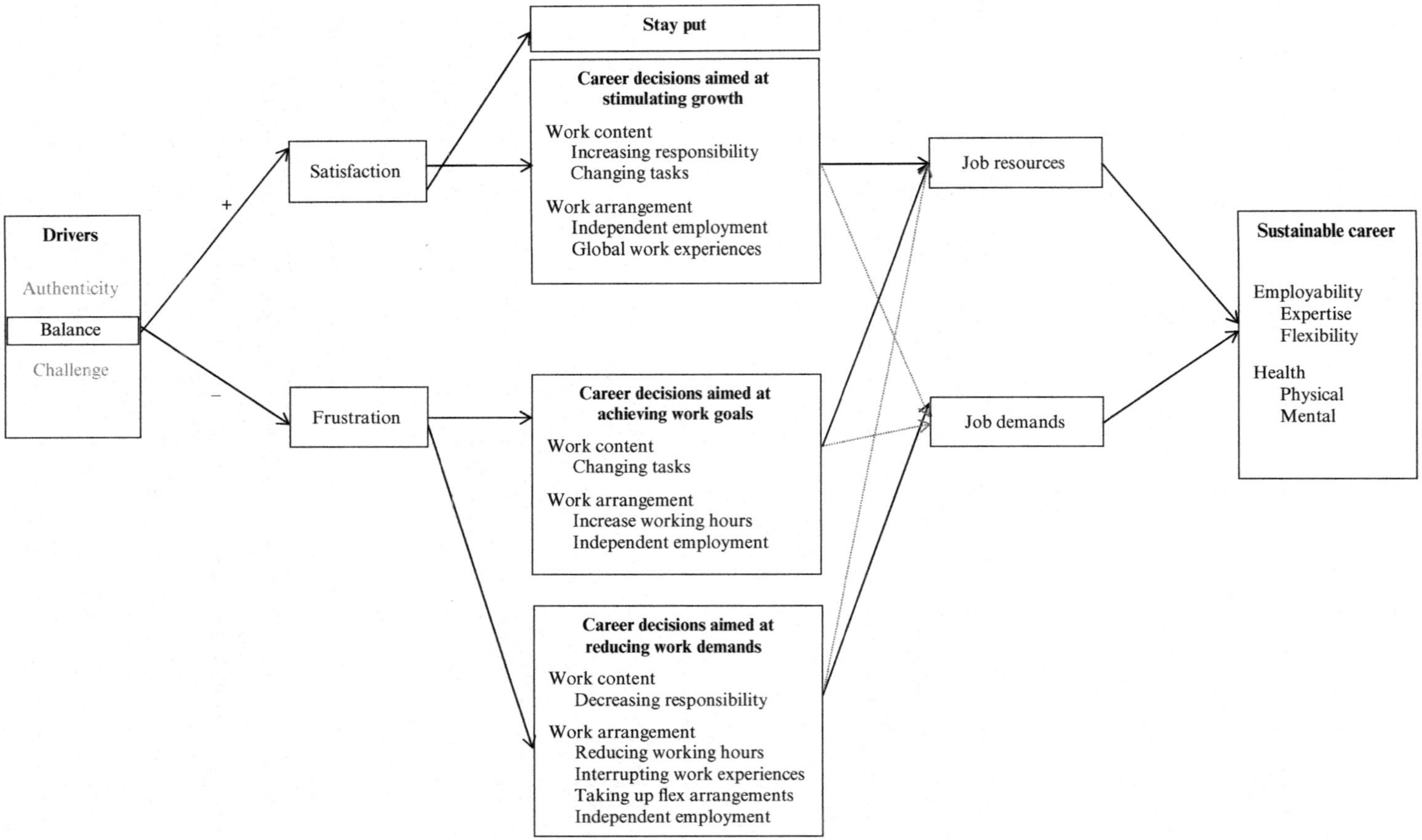

Figure 15.1 *Conceptual model explaining the role of work–home balance in career decisions and the creation of sustainable careers*

REFERENCES

Ajzen, I. (1991), 'The theory of planned behavior', *Organizational Behavior and Human Decision Processes*, **50**, 179–211.

Arthur, M.B. and D.M. Rousseau (eds) (1996), *The Boundaryless Career*, New York: Oxford University Press.

Arthur, M.B., D.T. Hall and B.S. Lawrence (eds) (1989), *Handbook of Career Theory*, New York: Cambridge University Press.

Bakker, A.B. and E. Demerouti (2007), 'The job demands-resources model: State of the art', *Journal of Managerial Psychology*, **22**(3), 309–28.

Bakker, A.B., L.L. Ten Brummelhuis, J.T. Prins and B.I.J.M. Van der Heijden (2011), 'Applying the job demands-resources model to the work–home interface: A study among medical residents and their partners', *Journal of Vocational Behavior*, **79**(1), 170–80.

Baltes, M.M. and L.L. Carstensen (1996), 'The process of successful ageing', *Ageing and Society*, **16**, 397–422.

Cappelli, P. and B. Novelli (eds) (2010), *Managing the Older Worker: How to Prepare for the New Organizational Order*, Boston, MA: Harvard Business Press.

De Vos, A., S. De Hauw and B.I.J.M. Van der Heijden (2011), 'Competency development and career success: The mediating role of employability', *Journal of Vocational Behavior*, **79**(2), 438–47.

Demerouti, E. (2014), 'Individual strategies to prevent burnout', in M.P. Leiter, A.B. Bakker and C. Maslach (eds), *Burnout at Work: A Psychological Perspective*, Hove: Psychology Press, pp. 32–55.

Dorio, J.M., R.H. Bryant and T.D. Allen (2008), 'Work-related outcomes of the work–family interface: Why organizations should care', in K. Korabik, D.S. Lero and D.L. Whitehead (eds), *Handbook of Work–Family Integration: Research, Theory and Best Practices*, London: Elsevier Publishing, pp. 157–76.

Edwards, J.R. and N.P. Rothbard (1999), 'Work and family stress and well-being: An examination of person–environment fit in the work and family domains', *Organizational Behavior and Human Decision Processes*, **77**(2), 85–129.

Forrier, A. and L. Sels (2003), 'The concept of employability: A complex mosaic', *International Journal of Human Resources Development and Management*, **3**(2), 102–24.

Fugate, M., A.J. Kinicki and B.E. Ashforth (2004), 'Employability: A psycho-social construct, its dimensions, and applications', *Journal of Vocational Behavior*, **65**(1), 14–38.

Gajendran, R.S. and D.A. Harrison (2007), 'The good, the bad, and the unknown about telecommuting: Meta-analysis of psychological mediators and individual consequences', *Journal of Applied Psychology*, **92**(6), 1524–41.

Greenhaus, J.H. and T.D. Allen (2011), 'Work–family balance: A review and extension of the literature', in J.C. Quick and L.E. Tetrick (eds), *Handbook of Occupational Health Psychology*, Washington, DC: American Psychological Association, pp. 165–83.

Greenhaus, J.H. and E.E. Kossek (2014), 'The contemporary career: A work–home perspective', *Annual Review of Organizational Psychology and Organizational Behavior*, **1**(1).

Greenhaus, J.H. and G.N. Powell (2012), 'The family-relatedness of work decisions: A framework and agenda for theory and research', *Journal of Vocational Behavior*, **80**, 246–55.

Greenhaus, J.H., G.A. Callanan and M. DiRenzo (2008), 'A boundaryless perspective on careers', in J. Barling and C. Cooper (eds), *Handbook of Organizational Behavior*, Thousand Oaks, CA: Sage Publications, pp. 277–99.

Griffeth, R.W., P.W. Hom and S. Gaertner (2000), 'A meta-analysis of antecedents and correlates of employee turnover: Update, moderator tests, and research implications for the next millennium', *Journal of Management*, **26**(3), 463–88.

Grzywacz, J.G. and D.S. Carlson (2007), 'Conceptualizing work–family balance: Implications for practice and research', *Advances in Developing Human Resources*, **9**(4), 455–71.

Hall, D.T. (ed.) (2002), *Careers In and Out of Organizations*, Thousand Oaks, CA: Sage Publications.

Harrington, B. and D.T. Hall (eds) (2007), *Career Management and Work–Life Integration: Using Self-Assessment to Navigate Contemporary Careers*, Thousand Oaks, CA: Sage Publications.

Hundley, G. (2001), 'Why and when are the self-employed more satisfied with their work?', *Industrial Relations: A Journal of Economy and Society*, **40**(2), 293–316.

Huskinson, T.L.H. and G. Haddock (2006), 'Individual differences in attitude structure and the accessibility of the affective and cognitive components of attitude', *Social Cognition*, **24**(4), 453–68.

Johnston, W.B. (1991), 'Global workforce 2000: The new world labor market', *Harvard Business Review*, **69**(2), 115–27.

Judge, T.A. and R.D. Bretz (1992), 'Effects of work values on job choice decisions', *Journal of Applied Psychology*, **77**(3), 261.

Judiesch, M.K. and K.S. Lyness (1999), 'Left behind? The impact of leaves of absence on managers' career success', *Academy of Management Journal*, **42**, 641–51.

Lawrence, T.B. and S.L. Robinson (2007), 'Ain't misbehavin: Workplace deviance as organizational resistance', *Journal of Management*, **33**(3), 378–94.
Lee, M.D., E.E. Kossek, D.T. Hall and J. Litrico (2011), 'Entangled strands: A process perspective on the evolution of careers in the context of personal, family, work, and community life', *Human Relations*, **64**(12), 1531–53.
Lyness, K.S. and M.K. Judiesch (2008), 'Can a manager have a life and a career? International and multisource perspectives on work–life balance and career advancement potential', *Journal of Applied Psychology*, **93**(4), 789–805.
Lyubomirsky, S., L. King and E. Diener (2005), 'The benefits of frequent positive affect: Does happiness lead to success?', *Psychological Bulletin*, **131**(6), 803.
Maier, N.R.F. (ed.) (1949), *Frustration: The Study of Behavior without a Goal*, New York: McGraw-Hill Book Company.
Mallon, M. and L. Cohen (2001), 'Time for a change? Women's accounts of the move from organizational careers to self-employment', *British Journal of Management*, **12**(3), 217–30.
March, J.G. (ed.) (1994), *Primer on Decision Making: How Decisions Happen*, New York: The Free Press.
Marks, S.R. (2006), 'Understanding diversity of families in the 21st century and its impact on the work–family area of study', in M. Pitt-Catsouphes, E.E. Kossek and S. Sweet (eds), *The Work and Family Handbook: Multi-Disciplinary Perspectives and Approaches*, Mahwah, NJ: Erlbaum Associates, pp. 41–65.
Moen, P. and S. Sweet (2004), 'From "work–family" to "flexible careers". A life course reframing', *Community, Work & Family*, **7**(2), 209–26.
Newman, K.L. (2011), 'Sustainable careers: Lifecycle engagement in work', *Organizational Dynamics*, **40**(2), 136–43.
Ng, T.W., K.L. Sorensen, L.T. Eby and D.C. Feldman (2007), 'Determinants of job mobility: A theoretical integration and extension', *Journal of Occupational and Organizational Psychology*, **80**(3), 363–86.
Ostroff, C. and M.A. Clark (2001), 'Maintaining an internal market: Antecedents of willingness to change jobs', *Journal of Vocational Behavior*, **59**(3), 425–53.
Peters, P., L. Den Dulk and T. Van der Lippe (2009), 'The effects of time–spatial flexibility and new working conditions on employees' work–life balance: The Dutch case', *Community, Work & Family*, **12**(3), 279–97.
Petrou, P., E. Demerouti, M.C. Peeters, W.B. Schaufeli and J. Hetland (2012), 'Crafting a job on a daily basis: Contextual correlates and the link to work engagement', *Journal of Organizational Behavior*, **33**(8), 1120–41.
Pinder, C.C. (ed.) (1998), *Work Motivation in Organizational Behavior*, Upper Saddle River, NJ: Prentice Hall Publishing.
Podsakoff, N.P., J.A. LePine and M.A. LePine (2007), 'Differential challenge stressor-hindrance stressor relationships with job attitudes, turnover intentions, turnover, and withdrawal behavior: A meta-analysis', *Journal of Applied Psychology*, **92**(2), 438–54.
Poelmans, S.A.Y. (2005), 'The decision process theory of work and family', in E.E. Kossek and S.J. Lambert (eds), *Work and Life Integration: Organizational, Cultural, and Individual Perspectives*, Mahwah, NJ: Erlbaum Associates, pp. 263–86.
Powell, G.N. and J.H. Greenhaus (2010), 'Sex, gender and decisions at the family-to-work interface', *Journal of Management*, **36**(4), 1011–39.
Prottas, D.J. and C.A. Thompson (2006), 'Stress, satisfaction, and the work–family interface: A comparison of self-employed business owners, independents, and organizational employees', *Journal of Occupational Health Psychology*, **11**(4), 366–78.
Rosen, C.C., D.J. Slater and R.E. Johnson (2013), 'Let's make a deal: development and validation of the ex post I-deals scale', *Journal of Management*, **39**(3), 709–42.
Rousseau, D. (ed.) (1995), *Psychological Contracts in Organizations: Understanding Written and Unwritten Agreements*, Thousand Oaks, CA: Sage Publications.
Shaffer, M.A., M.L. Kraimer, Y.-P. Chen and M.C. Bolino (2012), 'Choices, challenges, and career consequences of global work experiences: a review and future agenda', *Journal of Management*, **38**(4), 1282–327.
Sullivan, S.E. and L.A. Mainiero (2007), 'Kaleidoscope careers: Benchmarking ideas for fostering family-friendly workplaces', *Organizational Dynamics*, **36**(1), 45–62.
Ten Brummelhuis, L.L. and A.B. Bakker (2012), 'A resource perspective on the work–home interface: The work–home resources model', *American Psychologist*, **67**(7), 545–56.
Tims, M., A.B. Bakker and D. Derks (2012), 'Development and validation of the job crafting scale', *Journal of Vocational Behavior*, **80**(1), 173–86.
Valcour, M. (2007), 'Work-based resources as moderators of the relationship between work hours and satisfaction with work–family balance', *Journal of Applied Psychology*, **92**, 1512–23.
Valcour, M. and J.J. Ladge (2008), 'Family and career path characteristics as predictors of women's objective and subjective career success: Integrating traditional and protean career explanations', *Journal of Vocational Behavior*, **73**, 300–309.

Valcour, M., L. Bailyn and M.A. Quijada (2007), 'Customized careers', in H.P. Gunz and M. Peiperl (eds), *Handbook of Career Studies*, London: Blackwell Publishing, pp. 188–210.
Van den Berg, H., A.S.R. Manstead, J. Van der Pligt and D.H.J. Wigboldus (2006), 'The impact of affective and cognitive focus on attitude formation', *Journal of Experimental Social Psychology*, **42**, 373–9.
Van der Heijde, C.M. and B.I.J.M. Van der Heijden (2006), 'A competence-based and multidimensional operationalization and measurement of employability', *Human Resource Management*, **45**(3), 449–76.
Van Vianen, A.E.M. and A.H. Fischer (2002), 'Illuminating the glass ceiling: The role of organizational culture preferences', *Journal of Occupational and Organizational Psychology*, **75**, 315–37.
Wharton, A.S. (2006), 'Understanding diversity of work in the 21st century and its impact on the work–family area of study', in M. Pitt-Catsouphes, E.E. Kossek and S. Sweet (eds), *The Work and Family Handbook: Multi-Disciplinary Perspectives and Approaches*, Mahwah, NJ: Erlbaum Asociates, pp. 17–39.
Wrzesniewski, A. and J.E. Dutton (2001), 'Crafting a job: Revisioning employees as active crafters of their work', *Academy of Management Review*, **26**(2), 179–201.
Young, A.M. (2009), 'Frustration-instigated career decisions: A theoretical exploration of the role of frustration in career decisions', *Human Resource Development Review*, **8**(3), 281–99.

16 Work–family interface in atypical working arrangements

Saija Mauno, Ulla Kinnunen, Johanna Rantanen and Anne Mäkikangas

INTRODUCTION

Work–family interface has received considerable research attention in recent decades. For example, it has convincingly been shown that the successful integration of work and family roles relates to many positive career- and health-related outcomes, such as job satisfaction and psychological health (for reviews, see Amstad et al., 2011; McNall et al. 2010; Shockley and Singla, 2011). However, less interest has been shown in work–family interface in the context of atypical working arrangements. Investigation of work–family interface in these more challenging types of working arrangements is nevertheless of crucial importance, as, in part due to globalization, they appear to be on the increase. The so-called 24/7 society imposes extra demands on workers, in the form, for example, of lengthening the average working day or reducing recovery time. In addition, workers are expected to show higher flexibility, in turn, implying more flexible job contracts and irregular working hours. These changes are very likely to pose challenges to sustainable, life-long careers via their effects on work–family interface since work and family constitute two main life domains for most adults.

In this chapter, we focus on two forms of atypical working arrangements. First, we look at *non-standard working hours*, which refer to working outside of the traditional 8 to 5 working day (including shift work). The overall negative health effects of non-standard working hours are well-documented (Costa, 1996; Knutsson, 2003; Merkus et al., 2012). Therefore, non-standard working hours can be expected to be relevant also from the perspective of work–family interface. Second, we introduce findings on *temporary work* and its associations with work–family interface. Generally speaking, temporary work refers to dependent employment of limited duration (for example, fixed-term contract, agency work, on-call work). Despite its increasing prevalence in the labor market, temporary work has received little attention in contemporary work–family research.

The main goal of this chapter is to review previous studies in which atypical work has been examined either in the form of non-standard working hours or temporary work. We start by defining the key concepts with which work–family interface has been examined and operationalized in this research domain. Next, we briefly argue the case for relating non-standard working hours and temporary work to experiences of work–family interface, that is, we introduce the theoretical underpinnings behind the empirical findings. We then review some of the main findings on the effects of non-standard working hours and temporary work on work–family interface. Finally, we suggest an integrative model for future research and present some of the implications of the findings for policy makers and organizations.

Defining Work-to-family Conflict and Spillover as Experiences of Work–Family Interface

Work–family interface, describing the interaction between work and family roles, can be positive or negative and may occur in two directions, from work to family and from family to work (Frone, 2003). In this chapter, we concentrate mostly on negative work–family interface. This is because, thus far, experiences of positive work–family interface, such as work–family enrichment and facilitation, have been a rather neglected topic of research in this domain. However, it is very likely that atypical working arrangements would bear costs for positive work–family interface as it describes how quality of work (family) affects positively the quality of family (work) life via different processes (Greenhaus and Powell, 2006). These processes have many forms (affective, developmental, skills) that are likely to be permeable to atypical working arrangements.

In addition, although work–family interface is typically bi-directional, our main focus here is the work-to-family direction. This is because non-standard working hours and temporary work are located in the work domain, and hence should be most strongly reflected in the work-to-family direction. Moreover, empirical studies in this field have typically investigated work–family interface in the work-to-family direction. Negative interface between work and family is captured by such terms as *work-to-family conflict* and *negative spillover from work to family*, which are also used in this chapter. However, their overall definitions, which we introduce below, take into account bi-directionality.

Overall, the most often applied definition of work–family conflict is that proposed by Greenhaus and Beutell (1985), who state that work–family conflict is 'a form of inter-role conflict in which the role pressures from the work and family domains are mutually incompatible in some respect. That is, participation in the work (family) role is made more difficult by virtue of participation in the family (work) role' (p. 77). This definition is typically operationalized using items in which an employee reports the extent to which this cause–effect relation applies to his/her situation, that is, how often/much work demands hinder his/her participation in the family domain (for example, 'When I get home from work I am often too frazzled to participate in family activities/responsibilities', Carlson et al., 2000). Therefore, the term 'work-to-family conflict' as used here refers to a subjective cause–effect evaluation made by an individual that his/her work exerts a negative effect on his/her family/private life.

The term 'negative work–family spillover' refers to negative carry-over effects from one life domain to another that generate similarity between different life domains, such as between work and family (Edwards and Rothbard, 2000; Lambert, 1990). According to Edwards and Rothbard (2000), a positive relationship between a work-related construct (for example, supervisor-subordinate conflict) and a distinct but related construct in the family domain (for example, marital disagreement) must exist before spillover can be said to occur. For example, if a worker has had an exhausting day at work, he/she is likely to come home in a bad mood. This bad mood may then result in tense interaction and a poor family climate. Thus, the worker's work-related distress is positively linked to his/her family distress.

More specifically, Lambert (1990) distinguished between direct and indirect spillover. In her model, direct spillover is expected to occur when the objective conditions of one life domain, such as an irregular work schedule, directly affect outcomes in another life domain, for example, difficulties in arranging childcare. Indirect spillover, in turn, occurs when an individual's subjective reactions (for example, frustration) to objective conditions (for example, an irregular work schedule) mediate the effect of these conditions on the outcomes (for example, discord with family members). Thus, in negative spillover, negative experiences are carried over by an individual from work to family without any cause–effect evaluation, as in the case of work–family conflict. Therefore, the term 'work-to-family negative spillover' refers here to work-related objective conditions and experiences, moods, skills, behaviors that transfer, either directly or indirectly, via subjective experiences from work to the family, producing negative outcomes in the latter. However, it should be noted that negative work-to-family spillover and conflict are occasionally used as synonyms.

In sum, both *work-to-family conflict* and negative *work-to-family spillover* describe the situations in which work can have detrimental effects on family or private life. The difference between these terms is that the former emphasizes the negative experience of incompatibility and conflict between the work and family roles, and is self-evaluated. The latter term focuses on negative carry-over effects and processes from work to family that emerge as significant correlative relationships between work-related and family-related constructs. In earlier spillover studies, the family-related constructs that have most typically served as outcomes include marital satisfaction/adjustment, parental satisfaction/adjustment, and children's behavioral, emotional or cognitive symptoms (as effects of parents' work on their children). These family outcomes have also been studied in atypical work research.

Why May Non-standard Hours and Temporary Work Affect Employees' Work–Family Interface?

Non-standard working hours and temporary work may affect work–family interface because they are likely to present an employee and his/her family with extra challenges, as they may make more demands on the employee and yield fewer compensatory resources. A situation of high demands and low resources are key determinants of negative experiences of work–family interface such as work–family conflict (Byron, 2005; Frone, 2003; Michel et al., 2011). Among all employees, high workload is the most typical work-related demand, whereas lack of support and control at work or low flexibility are the most typical resource deficits that affect negatively employees' work–family interface, particularly in the work-to-family direction. More specifically, among those employees who work non-standard hours, it is reasonable to assume that non-standard working hours allow less time for family- and home-related activities, complicate the organizing of one's family life or other close relationships, allowing less support, and also mean less control or flexibility over one's work and family time (La Valle et al., 2002; Presser, 2003). All this may then directly increase employees' work–family conflict or spillover negatively to employees' family life, for instance, via work-related fatigue or depression.

Another atypical working arrangement focused on here is temporary work. Generally, temporary workers are conceived as periphery workers in organizations, and according to the core-periphery hypothesis (Atkinson, 1985; Kallenberg, 2009) do not have the same resources or benefits as their permanently employed colleagues, who typically belong to the core staff, and hence are also the beneficiaries of high investment, resources and other benefits bestowed by their employer. Moreover, temporary workers may also accept more tasks or extra work if they believe that this is one route to securing more permanent employment in their organization. These factors, which often characterize temporary work, may well have negative impacts on temporary workers' work–family interface in terms of higher work–family conflict or negative spillover effects from work to family.

To conclude, both non-standard working hours and temporary working arrangements often bring with them fewer resources and also sometimes more demands, which factors can be assumed to have a negative influence on work–family interface among these employee groups. This line of argumentation is also supported by empirical findings. It is these that we turn to next.

NON-STANDARD WORKING HOURS AND WORK–FAMILY INTERFACE: EMPIRICAL FINDINGS

We conducted a search for empirical studies on non-standard working hours and their family-related outcomes from the Web of Science and PSYCinfo databases. We utilized several keywords and their relevant combinations in the search: non-standard hours/schedule, shift work, irregular hours/schedule, (to describe forms of non-standard working hours), and work–family/work–non-work conflict/interference/balance, spill-over, family, marital, parental, children (to describe work–family interface). It should be noted that our review is not systematic but qualitative, and that it focuses on quantitative studies published in English. Thus, our aim is to present some of the most interesting findings of the research to date. Specifically, we seek to offer a content-rich picture on various family-related outcomes, rather than restricting our focus to a specific set of outcomes. It should also be noted that, in this chapter, the concept of non-standard working hours covers a range of atypical schedule arrangements, mainly evening and weekend work, night shifts and variable shifts, to capture working hours outside of the hours worked during the traditional 8 to 5 working day. Next, we will present the findings of empirical studies on the effects of non-standard hours on work–family conflict and marital relationship. After that, we will introduce studies on their effects on children. Some moderator effects (for example, gender, age, parenting status) will also be reported.

Effects on Work–Family Conflict and Marital Relationship

The effects of non-standard working hours on family life began to attract the attention of work–family interface scholars in the 1980s. A pioneer study conducted by Staines and Pleck (1984) indicated that working non-standard hours or shifts (weekends or variable days) was related not only to less time spent in family roles (child care, housework) but also to higher perceived work-to-family conflict. However, the effects of non-standard hours were not totally negative; the study also revealed that working a non-day shift did not have negative effects on family adjustment, which was described via an index comprising marital satisfaction, marital happiness and family satisfaction. However, a few years later, White and Keith (1990) found that shift work, and night shifts in particular, was related to lower marital quality and an increased likelihood to divorce.

Later, Davis et al. (2008) showed that working nights was related to greater marital instability and higher levels of work-to-family and family-to-work (one's family life is perceived to interfere with one's working life) conflict. However, working weekends, without night shifts, was not related to any negative family outcomes. Employees' age and parenting status moderated the associations: night shift was more detrimental for marital instability among the younger respondents and among fathers with small children than in older respondents and fathers with older children. Some moderator effects were also detected for work–family conflict: a combination of night shift and small children in men predicted higher family-to-work conflict. Thus, this study suggests that working night shifts might have more adverse family outcomes in men, particularly fathers. Interestingly, in order to compare daily experiences, this same study also included a separate diary study. The diary study revealed that those who worked on weekends reported more daily work stressors, such as being late, being understaffed, or making mistakes at work, than weekday workers. However, no differences were found between weekend and weekday workers in spouse- or home-related stressors.

Overall, the results indicate that night shifts in particular impose the greatest costs on families. These results also support Presser's (2003) often-cited findings that, among both sexes, a night shift plus rotating shift, in particular, was associated with poorer family outcomes in terms of marital instability (for similar findings, see Dunifon et al., 2013; Han and Miller, 2009; Han et al., 2010).

In the late 2000s, Barnett et al. (2008) published a study on working couples where the wife worked either day shifts or evening shifts. Specifically, they compared experiences of work–family conflict and marital role quality in couples according to the spouses' working hours. Barnett and Gareis (2007) had found earlier, based on the same data, that for the (amount of) mother–child interaction it did not matter whether the mother worked evening or day shifts. In this later study, Barnett and her co-researchers focused on the differences between day and evening shift workers at the couple level and found that the wife's evening shift was related to her own, elevated, work–family conflict, but not to her husband's work–family conflict. In addition, the wife's evening shift was not associated with her own marital role quality or her husband's marital role quality. These results indicate that no crossover occurred between spouses. In sum, the study highlights that the family-related outcomes of working an evening shift can be relatively limited and that these effects are not easily transmitted between spouses, at least not from wife to husband. Unfortunately, possible family-related effects of the husband's work schedule were not examined in this study, but other studies have indicated that some of these effects may be gender-specific.

Craig and Powell (2011) recently conducted a study in which they examined the gender-specific effects of non-standard working hours. They showed that both mothers and fathers who worked non-standard hours also tended to spend more time on paid work and less time on housework and childcare than those who worked standard (day) hours. In their study, spouses' working schedules had more effect on mothers' than fathers' family time (see also Joshi and Bogen, 2007): when fathers worked non-standard hours, mothers did more housework and childcare, whereas if mothers worked non-standard hours, fathers' input at home did not increase. These findings suggest that non-standard working hours may intensify the traditional pattern of gendered division of housework in families. On the other hand, Haines et al. (2008) reported earlier that non-standard hours (including various types of shifts) were related to increased work-to-family conflict in men and women alike, which, in turn, were related to elevated depression, again to a similar extent among both sexes. Thus, the findings on gender differences are not consistent and may depend on various contextual factors (for example, country, type of organization and work measures).

The debate on the harmful effects of the 24/7 economy (Presser, 2003) has also raised the question whether long (non-standard) shifts, in particular, have negative family-related consequences. A few empirical studies have focused on this topical issue. Loudoun (2008) found no difference in work–family conflict in comparing workers who worked either an 8- or 12-hour shift. Similarly, Estryn-Behar and Van der Heijden (2012) found no empirical evidence of an extended shift (12 hours) increasing work–family conflict in a large sample of European nurses. A more important factor in their study was individual employee control over the shifts worked. Thus, based on this study, flexibility in an employee's schedule seems to be a crucial determinant of the impact of shift work.

Morningness–eveningness, that is, a tendency to be a morning or evening type of person, can be another important factor affecting how an employee copes with different shifts or irregular schedules. Willis et al. (2008) investigated how the morningness–eveningness typology related to irregular working hours and their outcomes. They found that evening types (a personal tendency to function best/be most alert in the afternoons and evenings) reported more work–family conflict than morning types (a personal tendency to function best/be most alert in the mornings). Altogether, there seem to be many potential moderators or confounding factors, such as schedule control, personal chronobiological/circadian tendencies, and family situation, which ultimately determine the effects of non-standard working hours on employees and their families (see also Dunifon et al., 2013; Merkus et al. 2012).

Effects on Children's Mood, Behavior and Performance

Some studies on family-related outcomes of non-standard working hours have focused on their influences on employees' children. Altogether, these studies have found both positive and negative results, thus providing an inconclusive overall picture. On the positive side, it has been indicated that parents who work non-standard hours spend more time with their children (Han et al., 2010). This finding was recently verified by Täht and Mills (2012), who showed that parents with non-standard work schedules spent more time in joint activities with their children. In addition, in families with non-standard schedules, fathers participated more often in child care, implying better gender equality at home. Wood and Repetti (2004) had established even earlier that, in families where mothers worked non-standard schedules, fathers were more involved with their children's care. However, we should remember that other studies, such as Craig and Powell's (2011) study discussed above, suggested the possibility of an association between non-standard hours and more traditional gender roles at home. It has occasionally also been proposed that families may use non-standard schedules to avoid institutionalized child care and to ensure that one parent is always available at home (LaValle et al., 2002; Täht and Mills, 2012). Thus, non-standard hours might constitute a coping strategy that families apply in balancing work and family life and in seeking to optimize their family situation.

On the other hand, negative effects on children have also been reported. Typically, non-standard hours or irregular schedules have been considered 'unhealthy' and 'unsociable' parental working arrangements. This refers to the argument that non-standard working hours are very likely to be associated with parental health problems, such as depression, anxiety and strain (Härmä, 2006), resulting, in turn, in poor parenting behavior, for instance, in the form of lower or less qualified parent–child interaction (Dunifon et al., 2013; Han et al., 2010; Hsueh and Yoshikawa, 2007). This can have negative implications, which are transmitted within families, causing behavioral and socio-emotional problems in children as negative endpoints of this chain. A relatively large number of studies support this argumentation. For example, Joshi and Bogen (2007) found that children whose parents worked non-standard hours experienced more social and emotional difficulties than children whose parents worked standard hours. Moreover, they also observed that these negative effects were mediated through parental depression, higher parenting stress, and poorer parenting behavior. However, this was not confirmed by Dunifon et al. (2005): the children of shift-working mothers did not exhibit concurrent behavioral problems.

Nevertheless, the most recent evidence suggests that night shift(s), in particular, would have the most effects on children in shift-working families. Both Han et al. (2010) and Dunifon et al. (2013) showed that, if a parent (mother) worked nights, her child(ren) showed more risk behaviors (for example, aggression) and negative mood (see also Han and Miller, 2009). Furthermore, some studies have found evidence that parents' non-standard working hours may also be related to their children's poorer cognitive performance at school (see Han, 2005; Hsueh and Yoshikawa, 2007). However, it should be pointed out that according to some scholars, there is no really strong evidence of a direct association between parents' non-standard working hours and children's lower level of well-being or cognitive performance (Dunifon et al., 2005; 2013; Han et al., 2010). There are numerous personal and contextual 'third factors', such as schedule preferences, schedules, adjustment, chronobiological tendency, and access to family care arrangements that may determine the circumstances in which non-standard hours are most likely to have a negative effect on employees' family life or their children.

Summary: The Effects of Non-standard Working Hours on Family-related Outcomes

In conclusion, strong empirical evidence has not been found in support of the argument that non-standard working hours inevitably have negative family-related outcomes, such as work–family conflict, marital instability or children's socio-emotional or cognitive problems. Similarly, empirical evidence on the effects of non-standard working hours on other health-related outcomes is not wholly negative; for instance, working on a night shift did not relate to increased sickness absence in a recent review (Merkus et al., 2012). Altogether, the results on family-related outcomes are rather conflicting, while longitudinal evidence is scarce.

Interestingly, in some situations, working non-standard hours may even have positive outcomes for families; for example, they may allow more interaction between parent and child, at least in families with school-aged children. In the future, more attention should be paid to the accumulation of risks that might co-occur with non-standard working hours, such as economic hardship, other atypical working arrangements, or maladaptive coping skills, and hence exacerbate the negative effects on the family of non-standard working hours. It should also be noted that regulations and laws on working hours vary considerably across countries and welfare regimes. Clearly, workers and their families are more at risk in countries where formal legislation on working hours is less strict or is even totally lacking. It has been stated that low-income families in low-income societies might be the families most at risk if parent(s) work non-standard hours (Dunifon et al., 2013).

TEMPORARY WORK AND WORK–FAMILY INTERFACE: EMPIRICAL FINDINGS

We also conducted our search for empirical studies on family-related outcomes of temporary work via the Web of Science and PSYCinfo databases. Again, we used several keywords and their relevant combinations: temporary work/employment, atypical work, contingent work, non-standard work, precarious work (to describe temporary work), and work–family/work–non-work conflict/interference/balance, spillover, family, marital, parental, children (to describe work–family interface). However, we found only two published studies in which temporary employment was examined in relation to experiences of work–family interface (for example, work–family conflict, spillover effects). Therefore, we also present the findings of two studies recently conducted by our research group. It should be noted that the studies introduced below concern all kinds of temporary working arrangements without differentiating between them, as none of the earlier studies on work–family interface have distinguished or compared the various forms of temporary employment.

Thus far, only three empirical published studies have examined whether and, if so, how temporary work relates to experiences of work–family interface. The study by Scherer (2009), conducted in 16 EU countries, indicated that temporary employees reported higher work–family conflict, more disagreement with their marital partner, and less frequent intentions to have children in the future than permanent employees. Thus, in this study, temporary employment was associated with poorer family-related outcomes. In line with Scherer's last finding, Artazcoz et al. (2005) had earlier shown that partnered (fixed-term) temporary workers in Spain were less likely to have children than partnered permanent workers; unfortunately, however, their study did not cover perceived work–family conflict or spillover effects on family life.

Some additional research evidence has been obtained in Finland, where temporary work is relatively common (15–20 percent), especially in the public sector. Heponiemi et al. (2010) examined temporarily and permanently working Finnish nurses, but did not find any significant relationship between temporary contracts and work–family conflict. Similarly, another very recent Finnish study, which also sampled nurses (Mauno and Ruokolainen, 2015), found that temporarily and permanently employed nurses did not differ in their level of work-to-family or family-to-work conflict. Although the groups did not differ in the prevalence of work–family conflict(s), the study indicated that temporarily employed nurses who reported high work-to-family conflict benefited most from high emotional support from co-workers: these temporary nurses showed a higher energy level (vigor) at home and at work than either the temporary or permanent nurses with low support in this high stress situation. Thus, the study proposes that certain resources at work, such as co-worker support, are important, particularly for temporary workers, if an employee encounters challenges in balancing the work and family roles. The buffering effects of work-related resources, in the presence of stress, may thus vary according to contract type.

Very preliminary evidence on longitudinal effects has also been reported from Finland. Namely, in a recent two-year follow-up study with three measurement points (Mauno et al., 2015), which focused on Finnish university employees, temporary employees reported higher work-to-family conflict, although only in the first wave of the study, compared to permanent employees. However, whereas permanent employees perceived an increase in work-to-family conflict over time, this was not the case for temporary employees. One potential explanation for this finding is the higher workload borne by permanent employees (Mauno et al., 2012), which is one of the best predictors of work-to-family conflict (see Byron, 2005; Michel et al., 2011). Specifically, in the university context, permanent employees may have more longer-lasting assignments (for example, student supervision), along with more administrative work, because these are not duties that can readily be assigned to temporary workers, implying a higher workload – and thus higher work-to-family conflict in the long-term – among permanent workers.

Notably, this Finnish longitudinal study also included a measure of positive work–family interface, that is, work-to-family enrichment, which describes the extent to which the quality of one's work positively affects the quality of one's family life (Greenhaus and Powell, 2006). A comparison between permanent and temporary workers found that the temporary workers, at each measurement point, reported lower work-to-family enrichment; thus they experienced a positive effect of their work on their family life more seldom than their permanent colleagues. Moreover, Mauno and her co-researchers (2015) also found that a high level of work-to-family enrichment was more beneficial for temporary than for permanent workers across time: when reporting high work-to-family enrichment, temporary employees experienced lowered job exhaustion one and two years later, whereas permanent employees did not benefit from high enrichment over time. In this study, the respondents were either permanently or temporarily employed throughout the follow-up period, two years or even more, and thus the findings highlight the effects of longer-term temporary (vs. permanent) employment.

Summary: The Effects of Temporary Work on Family-related Outcomes

It seems that researchers have only recently started to pay attention to whether and, if so, how temporary work arrangements are associated with family-related outcomes, and only a few empirical studies have explored this issue. In addition, the findings to date are rather inconclusive, with only some evidence for the detrimental effects of temporary work on the experiences of work–family interface (work–family conflict, enrichment). Thus, not all studies have shown that temporary employment has negative implications for an employee's family life. This is well in line with what we know about other psychosocial consequences of temporary working arrangements: contrary to general expectations, some studies have found no negative effects of temporary work on health, well-being or motivation (for reviews, see De Cuyper et al., 2008; Virtanen et al., 2005).

As was found in the case of non-standard working hours, several confounding factors are likely to complicate the picture regarding the family-related outcomes of temporary work. For example, contract preferences, length and type of temporary employment, and other contextual factors both at the macro- (labor laws, organizational policies, cultural context and so on) and micro-level (age, socio-economic status, family situation, coping skills and strategies and so on) may operate as confounding factors. However, these factors have rarely been studied as moderators in research on the effects of temporary employment on family outcomes, and never in studies where the focus has been on the consequences of temporary work for work–family conflict or for work–family spillover effects.

Consequently, future studies in this field should pay more attention to potential moderators/confounding factors which may reveal what type(s) of temporary work are related to adverse family-related outcomes, and under what circumstances. Moreover, as the core-periphery hypothesis (Atkinson, 1985; Kallenberg, 2009) suggests, temporary employment brings with it lower work-related resources, and sometimes also higher work demands, and therefore future studies should examine these factors as mediators between temporary work and family-related outcomes. Finally, the scope of family outcomes should become much broader, so as to cover, for instance, experiences of marital role quality, parenting quality or stress, as well as family members' reports (for example, spouses' or children's experiences) of life with temporarily employed individuals. These types of family outcomes have already been studied in connection with non-standard working hours but not in relation to temporary work.

DISCUSSION

An Integrative Model for Future Research

This review has shown that two relatively common forms of atypical working arrangements, that is, non-standard working hours and temporary employment, may in some, but not all, occasions be associated with negative family-related outcomes, such as an employee's higher risk for work–family conflict, poorer marital and parental role quality or dissatisfaction, and children's lowered well-being and cognitive performance. However, most of this evidence comes from cross-sectional studies, and therefore we cannot draw firm conclusions on causality or speak about 'real impacts', but only 'tendencies'. This also implies that the so-called 'healthy worker effect' cannot be ruled out, and thus it remains plausible that an employee ends up with poorer working conditions, for example, in temporary work, because (s)he is not healthy or competent enough to cope with the contemporary demands of the labor market, which seem to be constantly on the increase. We need more longitudinal (with full-panel design) studies with different time lags to be better able to reveal the causal associations, signifying a need for an improvement in the overall research designs used in this field. Furthermore, shorter follow-ups, for example, diary studies, would better reveal how the negative effects of atypical work accumulate within work periods and spill over to the family domain. Diary studies would be suited to examining family-related outcomes of non-standard working hours, which typically vary more daily or weekly than temporary employment.

Researchers and policy makers, but also ethically responsible employers (who truly care about their employees' well-being), should be able to screen out so-called 'risk

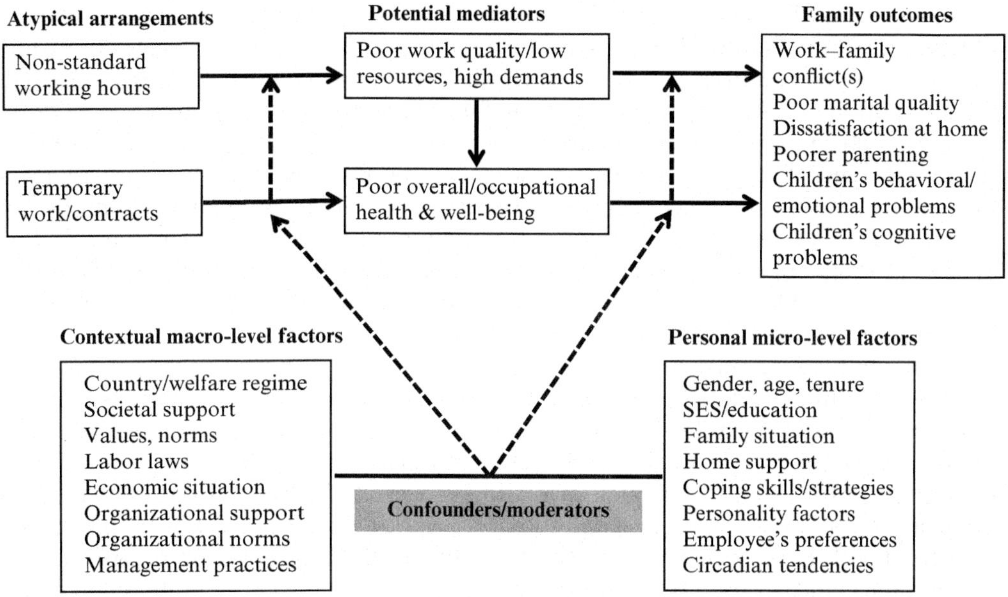

Figure 16.1 Factors affecting the relationship between atypical working arrangements and family-related outcomes

employees', that is, those who have higher risks for negative family-related consequences when working non-standard hours or on temporary contracts. These elevated risks may relate to various micro- and macro-level risk factors, which we have summarized in Figure 16.1 as 'confounders/moderators'. *Demographic risk factors* include, at least, higher age, lower job tenure, lower socioeconomic status/education, as well as a more demanding family situation (for example, more children, single parenting, or economic hardship). Certain *individual differences and life circumstances*, which may also be more psychosocial in nature, may also add to the risk for negative family-related outcomes in atypical work: lack of emotional or instrumental support at home, inadequate coping strategies or skills, certain personality factors (for example, high neuroticism, poor self-efficacy) and biological or even genetic/circadian tendencies (for example, morningness/eveningness types) are examples of personal-related psychosocial risk factors that may strengthen the negative family-domain effects of non-standard hours and temporary work. For example, a recent systematic review showed that young age, low morningness, high flexibility in circadian rhythm, and high extroversion and high internal locus of control as personality factors, related to better shift work adjustment and tolerance (Saksvik et al., 2011). Such individual differences have not yet been systematically reviewed in research on the effects of temporary work.

Moreover, in our model (Figure 16.1), certain macro-level factors may also increase the risk for an association between negative family-related outcomes and non-standard hours and temporary work. First, an *overall broader context*, covering country/welfare regime, support, policies and laws at the societal level, and the overall economic situation, may reveal particular risk factors. For example, in the Nordic countries, various laws and standards regulate scheduling and rest periods in shift works, and also the use of temporary labor, which may have positive implications for an employee's family life. In less developed countries and regimes, legislation may be lacking or poorly enforced, thereby putting atypical workers and their families at risk. Second, an *organizational context* in which atypical work occurs in everyday life may increase risks for negative family outcomes if support in balancing work and family is lacking or if the organization's norms, values or management practices are not family-friendly, that is, they do not allow employees to take their family needs into account at work. Clearly, these factors are risks for all employees alike, but might be greater for those working non-standard hours and/or on temporary contracts, as these employee groups may have less flexibility, choice, decision-making latitude and, overall, less 'voice' at work.

Furthermore, our model in Figure 16.1 suggests that non-standard hours or temporary work do not directly relate to negative family-related outcomes but that this association is *mediated* by poorer psychosocial working conditions (lower resources/higher demands or both) as well as poorer occupational health and well-being, such as job dissatisfaction or burnout. Moreover, two related mediating processes are likely: first, non-standard hours and temporary work are related to poorer working conditions, which, in turn, are connected with lower well-being in the work domain (for example, job dissatisfaction, job burnout), and, second, this occupational ill-being is reflected in family-related well-being in the form of work–family conflict and the other types of negative work-to-family spillover effects discussed in this chapter. A core argument in the work–family interface spillover theory (Edwards and Rothbard, 2000; Lambert, 1990) is that similar types of feelings and experiences, such as dissatisfaction at work, are very likely to be transmitted to other domains, such as dissatisfaction at home. These kinds of mediating processes merit more attention in research on the effects on the family of atypical work.

Finally, we encourage researchers in this field to test this model empirically and to explore other currently hidden psychosocial risk or resource factors that were not included in our model so as to gain a more comprehensive picture of the effects of non-standard hours and temporary work on the family domain. This is best approached via long-term longitudinal studies or short-term diary studies, as noted above. We also have to take into account that an individual employee may also face more than one form of atypical working arrangement: for instance, (s)he does shift work but has also a temporary contract. In such 'double-risk' situations, not only researchers but also employers should be better aware of the risks associated with accumulative atypical working arrangements. If atypical work arrangements continue to increase, as we might reasonably predict, their combined forms also become more prevalent.

Implications

We propose that, first of all, legislation/labor laws have to accord similar rights and benefits to employees with atypical working arrangements, and that employers should act accordingly by providing equal treatment for their 'typical' and 'atypical' workers. Services for working families, for example, day care, after-school care, home aid, should also be equally available for all workers, including those working non-standard hours or on temporary contracts. For instance, in the Nordic countries, which we know best, many public work–family policies are widely available for uptake by all workers.

However, globalization and the 24/7 economy pose new, also unpredictable, challenges, not only for employees themselves but also for those who are organizing services for working families.

It is reasonable to argue that good societal and legislative measures will eventually decrease the risks for negative family-related consequences that might otherwise accompany non-standard working hours or temporary work. Such sociopolitical measures will also set the agenda for employers, who will have to act accordingly. Compliant employers could then offer a combination of formal (for example, allowing more flexible hours) and informal (for example, providing emotional support for their employees) family-friendly arrangements (discussed briefly in relation to Figure 16.1). They should also be aware that such family-friendly arrangements may be even more important for those of their employees working non-standard hours or on temporary contracts.

Finally, it is important to highlight that measures described above should also consider a career-span perspective. If non-standard working hours or temporary employment is an employee's own choice or acceptable at certain career stages, these working arrangements may not be optimal at later stages. For instance, younger parents, who have small children, may want to work irregular hours in order to care for their children at home (when one parent works, another can be at home). Thus, this arrangement works as an adaptive coping strategy in this life situation. However, the same arrangement may not work so well for older working parents, who may have adjustment problems to variable hours and changeable work sites or assignments (in temporary work) due to their greater age and different life stage. For them, normal working hours or working in (more) permanent jobs would be better alternatives. Thus, different life and career stages need different kinds of 'family-friendly' policies, which should also be considered in organizational and societal interventions. This would also be the best avenue for sustainable working careers, in which an employee's broader life context and varying needs for work–family balance are considered by taking into account different life stages.

REFERENCES

Amstad, Fabienne, L.L. Meier, J. Elfering and N.K. Semmer (2011), 'A meta-analysis of work–family conflict and various outcomes with a special emphasis on cross-domain versus matching-domain relations', *Journal of Occupational Health Psychology*, **16** (2), 151–69.

Artazcoz, Lucia, J. Benach, C. Borrell and I. Cortes (2005), 'Social inequalities in the impact of flexible employment on different domains of psychosocial health', *Journal of Epidemiology and Community Health*, **59** (9), 761–7.

Atkinson, John (1985), *Flexibility, Uncertainty, and Manpower Management*, Brighton: Institute for Employment Studies.

Barnett, Rosalind and Karen Gareis (2007), 'Shift work, parenting behaviors, and children's socioemotional well-being: A within-family study', *Journal of Family Issues*, **28** (6), 727–48.

Barnett, Rosalind, K.L. Gareis and R.T. Brennan (2008), 'Wives' shift work schedules and husbands' and wives' well-being in dual-earner couples with children: A within-couple analysis', *Journal of Family Issues*, **29** (3), 396–421.

Byron, Kristin (2005), 'A meta-analytic review of work–family conflict and its antecedents', *Journal of Vocational Behavior*, **67** (2), 169–98.

Carlson, Dawn, K.M. Kacmar and L.J. Williams (2000), 'Construction and initial validation of a multidimensional measure of work–family conflict', *Journal of Vocational Behavior*, **56** (2), 249–76.

Costa, Giovanni (1996), 'The impact of shift work and night work on health', *Applied Ergonomics*, **27** (1), 9–16.

Craig, Lyn and Abigail Powell (2011), 'Non-standard work schedules, work–family balance and the gendered division of childcare', *Work, Employment, & Society*, **25** (2), 274–91.
Davis, Kelly, B.D. Goodman, A.E. Pirretti and D.M. Almeida (2008), 'Non-standard work schedules, perceived family well-being, and daily stressors', *Journal of Marriage and the Family*, **70** (4), 991–1003.
De Cuyper, Nele, J. de Jong, H. De Witte, K. Isaksson, T. Rigotti and R. Schalk (2008), 'Literature review of theory and research on the psychological impact of temporary employment: Towards a conceptual model', *International Journal of Management Reviews*, **10** (1), 25–51.
Dunifon, Rachel, A. Kalil and A. Bajracharya (2005), 'Maternal working conditions and child well-being in welfare-leaving families', *Developmental Psychology*, **41** (6), 851–9.
Dunifon, Rachel, A. Kalil, D.A. Crosby and J. Houston Su (2013), 'Mothers' night work and children's behavior problems', *Developmental Psychology*, **49** (10) 1874–85.
Edwards, Jeffrey and Nancy Rothbard (2000), 'Mechanisms linking work and family: Clarifying the relationships between work and family constructs', *Academy of Management Review*, **25** (1), 178–99.
Estryn-Behar, Madeleine and Beatrice Van der Heijden (2012), 'Effects of extended work shifts on employee fatigue, health, satisfaction, work/family balance, and patient safety', *Work – A Journal of Prevention Assessment & Rehabilitation*, **41** (1), 4283–90.
Frone, Michael (2003), *Work–family balance*, in James Quick and Louis Tetrick (eds), *Handbook of Occupational Health Psychology* (pp. 143–62). Washington, DC: American Psychological Association.
Greenhaus, Jeffrey and Nicholas Beutell (1985), 'Sources of conflict between work and family roles', *Academy of Management Review*, **10** (1), 76–88.
Greenhaus, Jeffrey and Gary Powell (2006), 'When work and family are allies: A theory of work–family enrichment', *Academy of Management Review*, **31** (1), 72–92.
Haines, Victor, A. Marchand, V. Rousseau and A. Demers (2008), 'The mediating role of work-to-family conflict in the relationship between shiftwork and depression', *Work and Stress*, **22** (4), 341–56.
Han, Wen-Jui (2005), 'Maternal nonstandard work schedules and child cognitive outcomes', *Child Development*, **76** (1), 137–54.
Han, Wen-Jui and Daniel Miller (2009), 'Parental work schedules and adolescent depression', *Health Sociology Review*, **18** (1), 36–49.
Han, Wen-Jui, D.P. Miller and J. Waldfogel (2010), 'Parental work schedules and adolescent risky behaviors', *Developmental Psychology*, **46** (5), 1245–67.
Härmä, Mikko (2006), 'Workhours in relation to work stress, recovery and health', *Scandinavian Journal of Work, Environment, and Health*, **32** (6), 502–14.
Heponiemi, Tarja, A. Kouvonen, T. Sinervo and M. Elovainio (2010), 'Do psychosocial factors moderate the association of fixed-term employment with work interference with family and sleeping problems in registered nurses?', *International Journal of Nursing Studies*, **47** (9), 1096–104.
Hsueh, JoAnn and Hirokazu Yoshikawa (2007), 'Working nonstandard schedules and variable shifts in low-income families: Associations with parental psychological well-being, family functioning and child well-being', *Developmental Psychology*, **43** (3), 620–32.
Joshi, Pamela and Karen Bogen (2007), 'Nonstandard schedules and young children's behavioral outcomes among working low-income families', *Journal of Marriage and the Family*, **69** (1), 139–56.
Kallenberg, Arne (2009), 'Precarious work, insecure workers, employment relations in transition', *American Sociological Review*, **74** (1), 1–22.
Knutsson, Anders (2003), 'Health disorders of shift workers', *Occupational Medicine*, **53** (2), 103–8.
Lambert, Susan (1990), 'Processes linking work and family: A critical review and research agenda', *Human Relations*, **43** (3), 239–57.
La Valle, Ivana, Sue Arthur, Christine Millward, James Scott and Marion Clayden (2002), *Happy Families? Atypical Work and its Influence on Family Life*, Bristol: Policy Press.
Loudoun, Rebecca (2007), 'Balancing shiftwork and life outside work: Do 12-h-shifts make a difference?', *Applied Ergonomics*, **39** (5), 572–9.
Mauno, Saija and Mervi Ruokolainen (2015), 'Does organizational work–family support benefit temporary and permanent employees alike in a work–family conflict situation? Evidence from Finnish Nurses', *Journal of Family Issues* (in press).
Mauno, Saija, N. De Cuyper, U. Kinnunen and H. De Witte (2012), 'Work characteristics in long-term temporary workers and temporary-to-permanent workers: A prospective study among Finnish health care personnel', *Economic and Industrial Democracy*, **33** (3), 357–77.
Mauno, Saija, N. De Cuyper, U. Kinnunen, J. Rantanen, M. Ruokolainen and A. Mäkikangas (2015), 'The prospective effects of work–family conflict and enrichment on job exhaustion and turnover intentions: Comparing long-term temporary vs. permanent workers across three waves', *Work & Stress*, **29** (1), 75–94.
McNall, Laurel, J.M. Nicklin and A.L. Masuda (2010), 'Meta-analytic review of the consequences associated with work–family enrichment', *Journal of Business & Psychology*, **25** (3), 381–96.
Merkus, Suzanne, A. Van Drongelen, K.A. Holte, M. Labriola, T. Lund, W. Van Mechelen and

A.J. Van der Beek (2012), 'The association between shift work and sick leave: a systematic review', *Occupational and Environmental Medicine*, **69** (10), 701–12.
Michel, Jesse, L. Kotrba, J. Mitchelson, M. Clark and B. Baltes (2011), 'Antecedents of work–family conflict: A meta-analytic review', *Journal of Organizational Behavior*, **32** (5), 689–725.
Presser, Harriet (2003), *Working in a 24/7 Economy*, New York: Russell Sage.
Saksvik, Ingvild B., B. Bjorvatn, H. Hetland, G.M. Sandal and S. Pallesen (2011), 'Individual differences in tolerance to shift work – A systematic review', *Sleep Medicine Reviews*, **15** (4), 221–35.
Scherer, Stefani (2009), 'The social consequences of insecure jobs', *Social Indicator Research*, **93** (3), 527–47.
Shockley, Kristen and Neha Singla (2011), 'Reconsidering work–family interactions and satisfaction: A meta-analysis', *Journal of Management*, **37** (3), 861–86.
Staines, Graham and Joseph Pleck (1984), 'Nonstandard work schedules and family life', *Journal of Applied Psychology*, **69** (3), 515–23.
Täht, Karin and Melinda Mills (2012), 'Nonstandard work schedules, couple desynchronization, and parent–child interaction: A mixed-method analysis', *Journal of Family Issues*, **33** (8), 1054–87.
Virtanen, Marianna, M. Kivimäki, M. Joensuu, P. Virtanen, M. Elovainio and J. Vahtera (2005), 'Temporary employment and health: A review', *International Journal of Epidemiology*, **34** (3), 610–22.
White, Lynn and Bruce Keith (1990), 'The effects of shift work on the quality and stability of marital relations', *Journal of Marriage and the Family*, **52** (2), 453–62.
Willis, Thomas, D.B. O'Connor and L. Smith (2008), 'Investigating effort–reward imbalance and work–family conflict in relation to morningness–eveningness and shift work', *Work & Stress*, **22** (2), 125–37.
Wood, Jeffrey and Rena Repetti (2004), 'What gets dad involved? A longitudinal study of change in parental child caregiving involvement', *Journal of Family Psychology*, **18** (1), 237–49.

17 Sustainable work ability and cognitive functioning through lifestyle improvement

Teun Aalbers and Annet H. De Lange

INTRODUCTION

In the previous chapters, important insights have been offered concerning the theme of sustainable careers. This chapter aims to describe the role of (online) lifestyle interventions in facilitating sustainable work ability, especially in terms of cognitive functioning. We will start with discussing the concept of sustainable work ability, subsequently we address the relationship between healthy lifestyle behavior and cognitive functioning and we will conclude this chapter with the role that lifestyle behavior interventions can have in improving the lifestyle and work ability of aging workers and their contribution to more sustainable careers.

SUSTAINABLE WORK ABILITY AND COGNITIVE FUNCTIONING

Work ability expresses the extent to which a worker is capable of working in the present and in the near future, taking his or her own physical and cognitive resources, as well as the requested level of work demands, into account (Ilmarinen, 2001; Ilmarinen and Tuomi, 1992). In line with the work ability theory and elaborating on the notion of P–E fit (Edwards et al., 2006), De Lange et al. (2015) assume that work ability of workers will become sustainable if their (future) physical and cognitive capacity as well as personal needs and interests are congruent with aspects and (future) requirements of their current (and future) work environment. More specifically, in line with their view, we argue that sustainability at work involves parallel accomplishment of three different objectives, namely: (a) the maintenance of workers' cognitive as well as physical working capacity within their current or future organization; (b) the improvement of the working environment to create work settings that are conducive to health, development, motivation and internal or external mobility of workers; and (c) the development of work organizations and working cultures (that is, management systems and personnel policy) in a direction which supports positive development of worker health and capacities, mobility and safety at work, and in doing so promoting a sound social climate that positively influences organizational performance (De Lange et al., 2015).

As a result, we may argue that sustainable work ability is determined by retaining an optimal capacity in terms of physical, cognitive and social skills to work across time (Ilmarinen and Rantanen, 1999). For example, recent statistics reveal that the absolute number of people suffering from neurocognitive diseases such as dementia is rapidly growing on a global scale. Approximately 5–7 percent of the world's population over

60 years of age has a form of dementia. This adds up to a staggering 35.6 million people in 2010 and is estimated to grow to 115.4 million in 2050 (Prince et al., 2013). In this chapter we will focus on the maintenance of cognitive functioning of workers to perform well at work (Gajewski et al., 2010).

Cognitive control concerns the internal representation, maintenance and updating of context information in the service of exerting control over thoughts and behavior (Diestel and Schmidt, 2011). The prefrontal cortex, the brain area that is responsible for functions such as planning, working memory, spatial ability, abstract thinking, and assessing risks is fully developed around the 20th to 25th birthday. These functions, also called executive functions, are very important in cognitively processing complex environmental cues and information in the work environment. Unfortunately the 'last in, first out'-principle applies to these executive functions. This means that they take the longest to reach full maturity and they decline first when cognitive decline sets in.

As workers age, they face a risk of declining physical and cognitive capacity (Dittmann-Kohli and Van der Heijden, 1996; De Frias and Schaie, 2001; Kanfer and Ackerman, 2004). For example, aging workers reveal, in comparison to younger workers, a weakening of precision and speed perception as well as a slower cognitive processing of sensory input and memory systems (Ilmarinen, 2001; Rizzuto et al., 2012). British research shows that the deterioration of our cognitive functioning can already be measured at the age of 40 (Singh-Manoux et al., 2012). So from this age onwards, there is reason to believe that there is work to be done to prevent fast or further decline.

Prevention through Improving Lifestyle Behavior

In determining the sustainable nature of cognitive functioning of older workers, earlier research has pointed to the pivotal role or preventive function of individual differences in lifestyle characteristics, for example, nutritional habits and exercise (Maertens et al., 2012). There is also a growing body of research that shows inter-individual diversity in cognitive functioning at older ages (Maertens et al., 2012; Staff et al., 2004). In this chapter, we therefore want to provide a more fine-graded overview of the possible effects of healthy lifestyle behaviors in relation to cognitive functioning by providing a brief overview of relevant figures and norms as well as results of earlier research on lifestyle behavior change programs.

Lifestyle Behavior and Cognitive Functioning

Since work ability relies on good cognitive functioning at work, it becomes important to maintain a high level of cognitive functioning up until an advanced age. The section 'Health behavior change theory' presents an overview of important and well-researched health behavior theories that can form the basis of lifestyle programs to facilitate cognitive aging at work. For six major lifestyle areas there is increasing evidence of a positive effect on the way the brain ages. In the following paragraphs, a brief outline of the current state of the scientific literature on these different lifestyle areas will be given. This is just a sample of the literature and certainly not intended to be a comprehensive systematic review of all the available literature.

Exercise

Exercise or physical activity not only leads to improved cardiovascular function, but is also related to a reduced loss of brain tissue due to aging (Miller et al., 2012). The damage to our aging brain is largely caused by an accumulation of oxidative stress. The amount of oxidative stress that is found in our brain is reduced by physical activity. Additionally, exercise also stimulates the production of neurotrophins. Neurotrophins are responsible for the maintenance of the plastic properties of the brain. Because of this, the brain maintains its plasticity and is able to adapt to the environment up to an old age, learning new things, and recovering from damage caused by aging (Radak et al., 2010). This reduced amount of oxidative stress and increased amount of neurotrophins lead to a better functioning of the memory and a reduced risk of developing mild cognitive impairment (Erickson et al., 2011; Geda et al., 2010).

Nutrition

In the field of healthy nutrition, scientists are currently focusing their research on the promising Mediterranean diet and caloric restriction. A Mediterranean diet consists of a lot of unsaturated fats such as olive oil, vegetables, fruits, nuts and seeds, and fish (Box 17.1). Separate nutrients are often studied extensively, such as folic acid and various vitamins. Unfortunately, these nutrients were found to have little positive effect on brain aging when singled out. However, the Mediterranean diet as a package seems to have more potential. In any case, the Mediterranean diet leads to a reduction in a number of risk factors for cardiovascular disease, vascular dementia and cardiovascular seizures (Barnes, 2011). For this reason alone, it is a positive investment which reduces the risk of non-age-related cognitive decline. The principle behind caloric restriction, or simply put, to eat less, is that this will lead to a reduced production of harmful substances such

BOX 17.1 THE MEDITERRANEAN DIET

In many countries around the Mediterranean sea, a number of health problems such as heart disease and obesity are significantly less prevalent. Researchers suspect that the diet of these populations has a preventive effect. This diet is significantly different from that of northern European countries. However, the researchers say that it is not only the diet that differs. The rest of the southern European lifestyle could play a role too. The Mediterranean diet basically consists of:

- Using fruits and vegetables as the basis for every meal.
- Eating fish or poultry at least twice a week.
- Eating red meat only a few times a month.
- Using herbs and spices instead of salt to season your food.
- Using olive oil instead of butter or margarine.
- Eating lots of nuts, seeds and whole grains.
- Moderate alcohol consumption (and when drinking, preferably drinking red wine).
- Taking sufficient exercise.
- Enjoying your food, taking your time, and having your meals with friends or family.

as insulin (Witte et al., 2009). In their study Witte et al. (2009) found that participants in the caloric restriction condition scored as much as 20 percent higher on a verbal memory task than control subjects.

Smoking

In addition to exercise and diet, smoking cessation is one of the most studied behaviors. Only recently have researchers also started to research whether or not smoking cessation has a positive effect on brain aging. The probability of getting dementia of the Alzheimer's type increases as a person has a longer history of smoking behavior (Tyas et al., 2003), and depending on the amount of cigarettes a person smokes, the risk of various forms of dementia increases by 1.59 up to 2.72 times (Anstey et al., 2007; Peters et al., 2008; Rusanen et al., 2011). In addition to an increased risk of getting dementia, smokers generally have a lower level of cognitive functioning to begin with and they experience faster decline as they age (Nooyens et al., 2008).

Alcohol

Alcohol consumption is a tricky area in comparison with the behaviors discussed above. The healthy recommendation when it comes to alcohol consumption is not black and white. Moderate alcohol consumption may very well have positive effects, but too much alcohol is very harmful to the brain. Cross-sectional studies show that moderate alcohol consumption (up to three units a day) has beneficial effects on episodic memory, executive functioning and processing speed of the brain (Anstey et al., 2009; Luchsinger et al., 2004; Ngandu et al., 2007; Ruitenberg et al., 2002). However, these results should be interpreted with care. There are no systematic or controlled-trial intervention studies available that examine the influence of alcohol consumption on cognitive functioning at work, but earlier research has shown that alcohol consumption higher than three units per day is very harmful to the brain and can cause Korsakoff's syndrome (Letenneur, 2004). In addition, it is not clear whether the positive cognitive effects are the direct result of the alcohol consumption itself. It may also be that people who have a lifestyle that includes moderate alcohol consumption also know how to moderate themselves in other lifestyle areas, making them better cognitive agers.

Sleep

The amount of sleep a person gets affects many aspects of daily life. In general a person knows how much sleep he or she needs to function properly during the day, but for adults the National Institutes of Health recommend between 7 and 8 hours of sleep for adults and the elderly. When we get too little sleep, our attention is lacking and we are less alert (Chee and Chuah, 2008), making us more liable to make work-related errors or to experience injuries at work (Uehli et al., 2014). In addition, all of our memory functions benefit from a good night's sleep (Walker and Stickgold, 2006). In this respect not only the quantity of sleep, but also the quality of the sleep is important.

Stress

Sleep and stress have a lot of common ground (Åkerstedt et al., 2012; De Lange et al., 2009; Petersen et al., 2012). An increase in psychosocial stress is increasingly associated with absence from work. Too much stress can even lead to burnout or depression, which have a negative effect on the cognitive functioning of people. Amongst others, attention, concentration, flexibility and memory deteriorate with higher amounts of perceived stress (Jonsdottir et al., 2013; Wolf, 2009). Epidemiological research shows a connection between the tendency to experience stress and the risk of mild cognitive impairment and Alzheimer's disease (Wilson et al., 2003; Wilson et al., 2006; Wilson et al., 2007). Also, the speed at which older people experience cognitive decline is correlated with the tendency to experience stress (Wilson et al., 2006).

Taken together, the major lifestyle decisions people make throughout their lives can have a severe impact on their brain integrity. For employers, it becomes increasingly evident that investing time and money in promoting healthy lifestyles in the active workforce can gain important physical and mental health benefits and provides a better basis for a lifelong career. Researchers and HR departments alike have been in search of effective lifestyle intervention programs. Before we discuss these intervention programs we will take a look at the theories that underlie behavior change into healthy lifestyle behavior.

HEALTH BEHAVIOR CHANGE THEORY

For developers, it is important to maximize the odds of developing effective intervention programs. In order to do so, they can use health behavior change theories. In this section, we elaborate on several relevant theories on human health behavior change. For the most part, human behavior is habitual. Changing these habits usually is a laborious affair. Anybody will recognize this from his or her own life experience. Altering routine behavior that has been taken for granted for years or even decades can prove to be extremely difficult. It makes little difference whether this concerns working out to stay in shape or eating healthy foods. Any change is difficult. And changing behavior is just the first step. Maintaining newly learned behavior is at least equally challenging. Breaking down old habits and building new ones requires a lot of patience, flexibility, endurance and mental toughness from the person undergoing the changes.

An intervention, be it online or offline, has to focus on facilitating this process of change. Creating circumstances that are stable, clear and simple enables the participant to adopt healthy behavior as smoothly as possible. The ultimate responsibility of the change will always lie with the individual, but a program can significantly ease the process of breaking down old and building new habits. By developing an intervention guided by relevant and established health behavior change theory, program developers can increase the odds of their program being successful. Next, summaries of some of the best known and most used health behavior change theories are presented.

The Transtheoretical Model (TTM)

The Transtheoretical Model by Prochaska and Velicer (1997), also known as the 'Stages of Change Model', is defined by five different stages in the behavior change process.

- The *precontemplation phase* in which a person is not planning on changing any behavior or may not yet be aware of the risky behavior.
- The *contemplation phase* in which a person becomes aware of his behavior and starts thinking about the possibility of change.
- The *preparation phase* in which a person starts making concrete plans for their behavior change and is planning on initiating this change within the next 30 days.
- The *action phase* in which the actual change has been initiated within the last six months.
- The *maintenance phase* in which a person attempts to internalize the newly learned behavior that has been initiated at least six months ago.

Progression through these five stages is not necessarily linear and is accomplished by using ten processes of change. For a more detailed description of these processes of change we refer to Prochaska and Velicer (1997). Whether or not the change in behavior occurs is a simple weighing of pros and cons concerning current and future behavior (the decision scale). The amount of self-efficacy is of great importance to this decisional scale (Bandura, 1991). Self-efficacy is a measure of confidence in one's ability to deal with difficult life situations especially during times of (behavior) change. Therefore, it also is a direct predictor of success.

The TTM, amongst others, has been used as a theoretical background for programs to quit smoking (Prochaska and Velicer, 1997), exercise programs (Hutchison et al., 2009) and stress management (Prochaska et al., 2008), and alters its approach towards a participant as they progress through the different stages of change.

The Health Belief Model (HBM)

The central belief in the Health Belief Model of Rosenstock et al. (1988) is that one's decision to behave in a healthy manner is heavily influenced by the perceived threat of disease, and the perceived benefits of behavior change to one's health. People are more likely to adapt their behavior when:

- they consider themselves to be at risk;
- they feel that this risk may possibly have a severe negative health impact;
- they judge that their possible actions significantly reduce the risk on negative health outcomes;
- the pros and cons of healthy behavior outweigh the pros and cons of the current unhealthy behavior.

The lack of a self-efficacy measure is generally considered to be a weakness of the HBM. The HBM has so far been used for, amongst others, the development of screening programs for cancer (Champion and Skinner, 2008), unsafe sexual behavior (Champion and Skinner, 2008), and the development of health dietary plans (Abood et al., 2003).

The Social Cognitive Theory

According to the Social Cognitive Theory (SCT) by Bandura (1991), human behavior is mostly explained by the expectations somebody has about certain behavior. Different expectations play a role in this decision:

- expectations about the consequences that the new behavior will exert on the social and physical surroundings of the person;
- expectations about what the consequences are of one's personal actions;
- the amount of self-efficacy: does a person think he is capable of successfully making a behavioral change?

In addition to helping people to (re-)learn their own behavior, the SCT also takes role models into account. This means that significant others can give the right example for others to copy. The SCT is used in developing programs for chronic diseases (Bandura, 1998), cardiovascular disease (Bandura, 1998), and exercise in the workplace (Hallam and Petosa, 2004).

The Theory of Planned Behavior

The Theory of Planned Behavior of Fishbein and Ajzen (2010) states that to predict behavior you have to ask if people plan to exhibit that behavior. This is called the behavioral intention. A person forms the behavioral intention on the basis of:

- their attitude towards the new behavior;
- the subjective norms that a person has about the desired behavior (smoking, for example, is socially accepted in some social environments, but may also be socially unacceptable behavior in another social environment);
- the fact that they are or are not in possession of the required set of skills to exhibit the new behavior.

In addition to the behavioral intention, the way a participant assesses whether he or she has the necessary preconditions to realize the behavioral change is important, as is the consideration of whether they believe they are able to overcome the barriers that are predicted to be on the road towards a healthier life. The TPB is used to develop smoking cessation programs, to encourage exercise regimes, self-checks, stop alcohol abuse, and encourage healthy eating (Armitage and Conner, 2001).

The aforementioned theories share certain (core) ideas, and none of them is without its critics. Some of them lack essential thought processes and others prove to be hard to refute. They will therefore remain aids in the development of new programs, not natural laws.

LIFESTYLE INTERVENTIONS

Now that we are familiar with the major health behavior change theories we will use this section to take a look at global norms on healthy behavior and we will examine the percentage of people that does not meet these norms. We start this section with some important statistics on exercising, diet, smoking, alcohol consumption, sleep, and stress of older employees. We then explore offline and online interventions for healthy living in the workplace.

Health Norms

A healthy lifestyle can improve health and longevity (Rimm and Stampfer, 2004). Table 17.1 gives an overview of the most important lifestyle factors for cognitive functioning, relevant health norms, and the extent to which populations currently comply with these norms. It shows that there is much to be gained when it comes to healthy living.

Offline Lifestyle Interventions in the Workplace

Table 17.1 clearly states the ongoing need for a societal effort to strive towards a healthier workforce. Research on lifestyle and health promotion shows that there are four different types of interventions: (1) programs aimed to cure diseases (curative); (2) programs aimed at prevention (primary prevention); (3) programs for people with an increased risk of health problems, detecting them or encouraging them to visit screenings (secondary prevention); and (4) programs that try to guide people with a diagnosis to cope with the disease or condition as best as possible (tertiary prevention). Most of the existing programs are aimed at promoting enough exercise, a healthy diet, smoking cessation, regulating alcohol consumption and coping with chronic diseases (such as diabetes). Encouraging healthy behavior can be done from home or at the workplace. This section will focus on encouraging healthy behavior in the workplace. Table 17.2 gives an overview of successful intervention components in offline behavioral studies in the workplace. The programs often cover both preventive and curative strategies. Furthermore, the most frequently used methods for behavior change are goal setting and self-monitoring, which also have been proven to be most effective (Aalbers et al., 2011). In the following section we look at the way the components from Table 17.2 are processed using eHealth programs.

Online Lifestyle Interventions in the Workplace

When programs are digitized they become eHealth interventions. In this section we will discuss eHealth interventions that are aimed at promoting healthy lifestyle factors in the workplace.

Exercise and nutrition

Table 17.2 shows that intervention studies promoting nutrition and exercise show improvements in percentage of body fat, endurance, amount of exercise, waist

Table 17.1 Health markers on key lifestyle domains

Lifestyle domain	Health norm	Current situation
Weight	BMI of 20–25[1]	Globally approximately 1.4 billion people are overweight; another 500 million people are obese[1]
Physical activity	150 minutes of moderate-intensity aerobic physical activity per week OR 75 minutes of vigorous-intensity physical activity per week[2]	>52% of Americans don't meet the guidelines for physical activity[3]
Nutrition	– no more than 2500 daily kcal for men – no more than 2000 daily kcal for women – two pieces of fruit per day – two servings of vegetables per day – two servings of fish per week – daily breakfast[4]	– Only 24% of US adults report eating 5 or more daily servings of fruit and vegetables – Globally approximately 1.4 billion people are overweight; another 500 million people are obese[1]
Smoking	No smoking	– 21.6% of US adult males smoke – 16.5% of US adult females smoke[5]
Alcohol	– For men no more than two standard servings of alcohol per day; – For women no more than one standard serving of alcohol per day; – Preferably no alcohol is drunk on at least two days a week to avoid alcohol dependency[4]	Worldwide approximately 2.5 million alcohol-attributed deaths occur on an annual basis Approximately 11.5% of drinkers have heavy episodic drinking behaviors People over 15 years of age average 6.13 liters of pure alcohol per year[6]
Sleep	For 65% of all adults 7–8 hours of sleep per night is sufficient to function properly[7]	33% of the population present at least one symptom given by the DSM-IV definition of insomnia[8]
Stress	For example: working at too high speed[9]	22% of the European Union workforce reports stress-related health problems[10]

Notes:

1. WHO, Fact Sheet No. 311 (2013).
2. WHO, Global recommendations on physical activity for health (2010).
3. Allen and Morey (2010).
4. US Dietary Guidelines (US Department of Agriculture and US Department of Health and Human Services, 2010).
5. Center for Disease Control, Fact Sheet Adult Cigarette Smoking in the US: Current Estimate 2011.
6. WHO, Global status report on alcohol and health (2011).
7. Banks and Dinges (2007).
8. Ohayon (2002).
9. Eurofound (2012), Sustainable work and the ageing workforce.
10. European Agency for Safety and Health at Work.

Table 17.2 Short overview of offline studies on intervention programs aimed at health behavior change in the workplace

Lifestyle area	Study and population	Outcomes and study period	Intervention design: preventive/ curative complex/ simple[1]	Active components
Exercise and nutrition	Descriptive review health promotion in the workplace (Goetzel and Ozminkowski, 2008)	Tailored interventions are more effective than creating awareness and general information dissemination	Preventive and curative, complex and simple	– Tailored interventions that use goal setting, reflection and monitoring, and motivational interviewing
	Review on 47 mostly randomized controlled studies on weight loss programs in the workplace for employees aged 18 and over (Anderson et al., 2009)	Weight loss- and exercise programs at work achieve an average loss of 0.5 BMI points or 1.3 kg after 6–12 months.	Preventive, complex and simple	– Use of a complex program is more effective than simple programs. – Structured, professionally led programs are more effective than self-help programs. – Adding behavioral counseling adds value to generic information dissemination.
	12-week exercise program in the workplace for 1442 employees from large Construction company (Dishman et al., 2009)	An increase in moderate and intense physical activity of 60% when comparing experimental and control groups	Preventive, complex	– Personally relevant goal setting – Generate broad support within higher management.
	Review on 27 intervention programs using pedometers in different populations (Tudor-Locke and Lutes, 2009)	Pedometers are effective in increasing physical activity.	Preventive and curative, complex and simple	– Goal setting – Self-monitoring in combination with feedback on behavior. – Pedometers

Table 17.2 (continued)

Lifestyle area	Study and population	Outcomes and study period	Intervention design: preventive/ curative complex/ simple[1]	Active components
	Randomized intervention study at the workplace with 98 overweight women (Christensen et al., 2011)	Weight loss of 3.6 kg after 12 months	Curative, complex	– Individual dietary plan – Strength exercises – Cognitive behavioral training
Smoking	Review study on 26 studies with employees in different age groups (Fichtenberg and Glanz, 2002)	The effect of a smoke-free workplace on percentage successful quit attempts (+ 3.8%) and number of cigarettes smoked (−3.1 cigarettes per day per smoker). Combined effect: a reduction of 29% in cigarette consumption	Preventive, complex and simple	– Smoke-free workplace
	Cohort study amongst 6179 Finnish employees with an average age of 44 years (Kouvonen et al., 2012)	Moderate and heavy smokers find it easier to quit smoking when employer offers pharmaceutical treatment and financial compensation	Preventive	– Financial compensation – Pharmacological treatment (with the exception of nicotine replacement therapy)
	Intervention study amongst 109 male Korean employees with an average age of 35 years (Hwang et al., 2012)	Smoking cessation program was successful in 53.2% of participants after 3 months	Preventive, simple	– Education – Free fitness when quit attempt was maintained over time as an incentive
	Intervention study with 185 participants (Koffman, Lee, Hopp, and Emont, 1998)	Smoking cessation program was successful in 41% of participants after 6 months	Preventive, complex	– Self-help course – Phone counseling – Financial compensation – Team competition

Table 17.2 (continued)

Lifestyle area	Study and population	Outcomes and study period	Intervention design: preventive/ curative complex/ simple[1]	Active components
	Review on 51 intervention studies with employees, aged 18 or older (Cahill and Lancaster, 2014)	Offering smoking cessation programs doubles the amount of quitters. However, the net result remains small because the number of participants at the workplace is relatively low	Preventive, complex and simple	– Personal coaching – Group coaching – Pharmacological treatment
Alcohol	Intervention study in 990 employees of a large transport firm (Hermansson et al., 2010)	Screening on alcohol use is enough to reduce alcohol consumption by about 50%	Preventive, simple	– Screening on alcohol consumption
	Descriptive review of different intervention types against alcohol abuse (Ames and Bennett, 2011)	Prevention of alcohol abuse at the workplace	Preventive, simple and complex	– Stress management – Individual counseling – Social support at workplace – Team building – Attitude change towards alcohol consumption during working hours

Note: 1. See Box 17.2.

circumference, blood pressure, body composition, and risk of several chronic diseases such as Type 2 diabetes mellitus and cardiovascular disease (Verweij et al., 2010). In addition, results from more recent research seem to indicate that participants in health promotion programs generally perceive less stress from work and take fewer leaves of absence (Conn et al., 2009; Freak-Poli et al., 2011).

Just like the offline studies, online studies focus on nutrition and exercise programs as well. The generally more successful intervention components are also identifiable on the Internet. These include setting achievable personal goals, disseminating information about behavior, identifying risk situations, triggers for behavior, and the monitoring of behavior (Aalbers et al., 2011; Cook et al., 2007). Personal counseling is used less

BOX 17.2 COMPLEX VERSUS SIMPLE INTERVENTIONS

The design of an intervention may vary. For example, complex and simple interventions can be distinguished. A simple intervention consists of only a single component (such as setting goals or providing a peer support forum) that focuses on a single behavior or condition. A complex intervention consists of more than one active ingredient, and can potentially target multiple behaviors and disorders (Craig et al., 2008; Perera et al., 2007).

A complicating factor in the use of complex interventions is the analysis of the results. Pinpointing the active ingredient during evaluation is often difficult. In the studies listed in Table 17.2 this was often the case. Isolating effective components and building programs consisting solely of active entities is an ongoing challenge. There are a number of theoretical frameworks developed to aid in development, implementation and evaluation of complex interventions (for example, the MRC Framework (www.mrc.ac.uk), Craig et al., 2008; Lehto and Oinas-Kukkonen, 2011) A review of Aalbers et al. (2011) showed that, with lifestyle interventions via the Internet, in an age group above 50 years, relatively complex interventions are more likely to succeed.

frequently online than face-to-face counseling, but it may be replaced to some extent (for example, by video contact or email counseling).

Smoking

Smoking cessation programs in the workplace can have a significant impact on the number of successful quitting attempts (see Table 17.2; Cahill and Lancaster, 2014). Encouraging smoking cessation not only brings health benefits to the person that quits, the company also reaps organizational benefits from successful quit attempts. For example, it increases productivity and reduces absenteeism (Halpern et al., 2001).

However, cessation programs on the Internet have not yet led to a uniform set of principles that are most effective. A plausible explanation for this is the difficulty for researchers to maintain high adherence rates among their study populations (Hutton et al., 2011), and the complexity of evaluating complex interventions (see Box 17.2). Differences in successful smoking cessation in programs using websites with multiple components versus programs using personal counseling seem minimal. However, websites with multiple components seem to be more effective than not providing treatment. Offering personal information does seem to lead to a higher number of successful quit attempts (Hutton et al., 2011). The percentage of expected quitters is between 21 and 30 percent when an information brochure, a cigarette counter, an online diary (supplemented by email), a social forum, and cognitive behavioral therapy (eight sessions) on mood management are combined (Leykin et al., 2012).

Alcohol

Health programs in the workplace that focus on alcohol can effectively control the amount of alcohol consumed (see Table 17.2). Alcohol interventions should especially address the social component that is associated with alcohol consumption. It is also important to continually address the association with relaxation and de-stressing. Often employees go for drinks after hours, which is a perfect opportunity to talk about something other than work. This is, however, behavior that would not occur if the individuals were unemployed (Ames and Bennett, 2011).

BOX 17.3 GENERIC VERSUS TAILORING AND FOLLOW-UP PERIODS

In addition to simple and complex interventions, we can distinguish between interventions that use generic information or that adapt their information to the needs and circumstances of the particular participant (tailoring). Although it has not yet been shown that tailored interventions are effective, it appears that the more personalized message conveyed to the participant results in a more extensive adoption of the program (Aalbers et al., 2011). So with an equally effective program this does increase the ultimate effect on public health.

Many of the studies discussed above make use of a limited intervention period. However, sustaining a healthy working population does not stop at positively changing behavior alone. After behavior change comes behavior maintenance. A temporary change in behavior is difficult, but actually developing new habits appears to be at least as difficult (Ory et al., 2010). Sustaining health behavior change appears to be based on a principle other than the initial change of behavior (Rothman, 2000). Only measuring the change of behavior thus seems inadequate for being able to determine a program's long-term effects.

Effective Internet-mediated programs are based on the assessment of personal risk (Doumas and Hannah, 2008). Assessing personal risk may require tailoring instead of a program with generic information (see Box 17.3). With the addition of a 15-minute motivational interviewing session, an extra positive impact can be made. A website aimed at preventing the use of drinking as a method of stress management proved successful by offering a stress and mood course (Billings et al., 2008). This website made use of videos and narration and let the participants go through the program at their own pace. Unlike the trend in smoking (where many studies try to reach full smoking cessation), a study which was aimed at drinking less also was effective (Hester et al., 2009). This website increased motivation and confidence and made use of goal setting, self-monitoring, and assistance in developing alternative behaviors and identifiable triggers for drinking.

Sleep and stress

No sleep interventions in the workplace have been conducted and only the first study protocol has surfaced in the scientific literature (Thiart et al., 2013). The number of online stress reduction programs is, quite surprisingly, limited as well. The Internet has been used to estimate occupational stress (Muhonen and Torkelson, 2008), and study protocols are available too (Heber et al., 2013). But study results are scarce. Cook et al. (2007) found that both the control group (using print materials) and the experimental group (using the online intervention) had slightly reduced stress levels. There was no difference in stress reduction rate between the control and intervention group.

CONCLUSION

We have seen that a healthy life style has definite benefits to both physical and cognitive well-being later in life, which increases the chances of having a long and healthy career. As of yet, no sure shot interventions have been developed that are scalable and cost-effective. However, it has become evident that behavior change can be accomplished at the workplace for various target populations and various target behaviors, resulting in a more sustainable workforce. The lack of an overarching success story emphasizes the need for program developers to not only focus on program content per se but to keep taking program context into account. Which contextual or individual factors determine the successful adherence to and outcomes of life style programs and subsequently positively impact cognitive functioning and work ability at work? The commitment of the company, HR department and line manager and the unique context in which the program is implemented will always be part of its effectiveness. Be it offline or online, prevention through healthy life style behavior programs has important social, organizational and societal outcomes and should be on the agenda of every organization to ensure sustainability at work and prolonged healthy careers, but also to prevent cognitive decline later in life.

REFERENCES

Aalbers, T., M.A.E. Baars and M.O.R. Olde Rikkert (2011), 'Characteristics of effective Internet-mediated interventions to change lifestyle in people aged 50 and older: A systematic review', *Ageing Research Reviews*, **10**, 487–97.

Abood, D.A., D.R. Black and D. Feral (2003), 'Nutrition education worksite intervention for university staff: Application of the Health Belief Model', *Journal of Nutrition Education and Behavior*, **35**(5), 260–67.

Åkerstedt, T., N. Orsini, H. Petersen, J. Axelsson, M. Lekander and G. Kecklund (2012), 'Predicting sleep quality from six weeks and prior sleep – A study of day-to-day covariation across six weeks', *Sleep Medicine*, **13**(6), 674–9.

Allen, Kelli and Miriam C. Morey (2010), 'Physical activity and adherence', in H. Bosworth (ed.), *Improving Patient Treatment Adherence*, New York: Springer Science, pp. 9–38.

Ames, G.M. and J.B. Bennett (2011), 'Prevention interventions of alcohol problems in the workplace: a review and guiding framework', *Alcohol Research & Health*, **34**(2), 175–87.

Anderson, L.M., T.A. Quinn, K. Glanz, G. Ramirez, L.C. Kahwati, D.B. Johnson and D.L. Katz (2009), 'The effectiveness of worksite nutrition and physical activity interventions for controlling employee overweight and obesity', *American Journal of Preventive Medicine*, **37**(4), 340–57.

Anstey, K.J., H.A. Mack and N. Cherbuin (2009), 'Alcohol consumption as a risk factor for dementia and cognitive decline: Meta-analysis of prospective studies', *American Journal of Geriatric Psychiatry*, **17**(7), 542–55.

Anstey, K.J., C. Von Sanden, A. Salim and R. O'Kearney (2007), 'Smoking as a risk factor for dementia and cognitive decline: A meta-analysis of prospective studies', *American Journal of Epidemiology*, **166**(4), 367–78.

Armitage, C.J. and M. Conner (2001), 'Efficacy of the Theory of Planned Behavior: A meta-analytic review', *The British Psychological Society*, **40**, 471–99.

Bandura, A. (1991), 'Social Cognitive Theory of Self-Regulation', *Organizational Behavior and Human Decision Processes*, **50**, 248–87.

Bandura, A. (1998), 'Health promotion from the perspective of social cognitive theory', *Psychology and Health*, **13**(4), 623–49.

Banks, S. and D.F. Dinges (2007), 'Behavioral and physiological consequences of sleep restriction', *Journal of Clinical Sleep Medicine*, **3**(5), 519–28.

Barnes, D.E. (2011), 'The Mediterranean diet: Good for the heart = good for the brain', *Annals of Neurology*, **69**(2), 226–8.

Billings, D.W., R.F. Cook, A. Hendrickson and D.C. Dove (2008), 'A web-based approach to managing stress and mood disorders in the workforce', *Journal of Occupational and Environmental Medicine*, **50**(8), 960–68.

Cahill, K. and T. Lancaster (2014), 'Workplace interventions for smoking cessation', *The Cochrane Library*, **2**, 1–126.

Champion, Victoria, L. and Celette S. Skinner (2008), 'The health belief model', in K. Glanz, B.K. Rimer and K. Viswanath (eds), *Health Behavior and Health Education: Theory, Research, and Practice*, San Francisco: Jossey-Bass, pp. 45–66.

Chee, M.W.L. and L.Y.M. Chuah (2008), 'Functional neuroimaging insights into how sleep and sleep deprivation affect memory and cognition', *Current Opinion in Neurology*, **21**, 417–23.

Christensen, J.R., A. Faber, D. Ekner, K. Overgaard, A. Holterman and K. Sogaard (2011), 'Diet, physical exercise and cognitive behavioral training as a combined workplace based intervention to reduce body weight and increase physical capacity in health care workers, a randomized controlled trial', *BMC Public Health*, **11**, 671–82.

Conn, V.S., A.R. Hafdahl, P.S. Cooper, L.M. Brown and S.L. Lusk (2009), 'Meta-analysis of workplace physical activity interventions', *American Journal of Preventive Medicine*, **37**(4), 330–39.

Cook, R.F., D.W. Billings, R.K. Hersch, A.S. Back and A. Hendrickson (2007), 'A field test of a web-based workplace health promotion program to improve dietary practices, reduce stress, and increase physical activity: Randomized controlled trial', *Journal of Medical Internet Research*, **9**(2), e17.

Craig, P., P. Dieppe, S. Macintyre, S. Mitchie, I. Nazareth and M. Petticrew (2008), 'Developing and evaluating complex interventions: The new Medical Research Council guidance', *The British Medical Journal*, **337**, 979–83.

De Frias, C.M. and K.W. Schaie (2001), 'Perceived work environment and cognitive style', *Experimental Aging Research*, **27**(1), 67–81.

De Lange, A.H., T.A.M. Kooij and B.I.J.M. Van der Heijden (2015), 'Human resource management and sustainability at work across the lifespan: An integrative perspective', in L. Finkelstein, D. Truxillo, F. Fraccaroli and R. Kanfer (eds), *Facing the Challenges of a Multi-Age Workforce. A Use-Inspired Approach*, SIOP Organizational Frontiers Series, London: Routledge pp. 50–79.

De Lange, A.H., M.A.J. Kompier, T.W. Taris, S. Geurts, D. Beckers, I. Houtman and P. Bongers (2009), 'A hard day's night. A longitudinal study on the relationships among job demands and job control, sleep quality and fatigue', *Journal of Sleep Research*, **18**, 374–83.

Diestel, S. and K.H. Schmidt (2011), 'The moderating role of cognitive control deficits in the link from emotional dissonance to burnout symptoms and absenteeism', *Journal of Occupational Health Psychology*, **16**(3), 313–30.

Dishman, R.K., D.M. DeJoy, M.G. Wilson and R.J. Vandenberg (2009), 'Move to Improve, a randomized workplace trial to increase physical activity', *American Journal of Preventive Medicine*, **36**(2), 133–41.

Dittmann-Kohli, F. and B.I.J.M. Van der Heijden (1996), 'Performance capacity of elderly workers: Internal and external influencing factors', *Zeitschrift Für Gerontologie Und Geriatrie: Organ Der Deutschen Gesellschaft Für Gerontologie Und Geriatrie*, **29**(5), 323–7.

Doumas, D.M. and E. Hannah (2008), 'Preventing high-risk drinking in youth in the workplace: A web-based normative feedback program', *Journal of Substance Abuse Treatment*, **34**(3), 263–71.

Edwards, J.R., D.M. Cable, I.O. Williamson, L.S. Lambert and A.J. Shipp (2006), 'The phenomenology of fit: Linking the person and environment to the subjective experience of person–environment fit', *Journal of Applied Psychology*, **91**, 802–27.

Erickson, K.I., M.W. Voss, R.S. Prakash, C. Basak, A. Szabo, L. Chaddock and F. Kramer (2011), 'Exercise training increases size of hippocampus and improves memory', *Proceedings of the National Academy of Sciences*, 1–6.

Eurofound (2012), 'Sustainable work and the ageing workforce', Luxembourg: Publications Office of the European Union.

Fichtenberg, C.M. and S.A. Glantz (2002), 'Effect of smoke-free workplaces on smoking behavior: Systematic review', *British Medical Journal*, **325**(27), 188–95.

Fishbein, Martin and Icek Ajzen (2010), *Predicting and Changing Behavior: The Reasoned Action Approach*, New York: Psychology Press.

Freak-Poli, R., R. Wolfe, K. Backholer, M. de Courten and A. Peeters (2011), 'Impact of a pedometer-based workplace health program on cardiovascular and diabetes risk profile', *Preventive Medicine*, **53**, 162–71.

Gajewski, P.D., N. Wild-Wall, S.A. Schapkin, U. Erdmann, G. Freude and M. Falkenstein (2010), 'Effects of aging and job demands on cognitive flexibility assessed by task switching', *Biological Psychology*, **85**(2), 187–99.

Geda, Y.E., R.O. Roberts, D.S. Knopman, T.J. Christianson, V.S. Pankratz, R.J. Ivnik and W.A. Rocca (2010), 'Physical exercise, aging, and mild cognitive impairment', *Archives of Neurology*, **67**(1), 80–86.

Goetzel, R.Z. and R.J. Ozminkowski (2008), 'The health and cost benefits of work site health-promotion programs', *Annual Reviews of Public Health*, **29**, 303–23.

Hallam, J.S. and R. Petosa (2004), 'The long-term impact of a four-session work-site intervention on selected social cognitive theory variables linked to adult exercise adherence', *Health Education & Behavior*, **31**(1), 88–100.

Halpern, M.T., R. Shikiar, A.M. Rentz and Z.M. Khan (2001), 'Impact of smoking status on workplace absenteeism and productivity', *Tobacco Control*, **10**, 233–8.

Heber, E., D.D. Ebert, D. Lehr, S. Nobis, M. Berking and H. Riper (2013), 'Efficacy and cost-effectiveness of a web-based and mobile stress-management intervention for employees: Design of a randomized trial', *BMC Public Health*, **13**, 655.

Hermansson, U., A. Helander, L. Brandt, A. Huss and S. Ronnberg (2010), 'Screening and brief intervention for risky alcohol consumption in the workplace: Results of a 1-year randomized controlled study', *Alcohol & Alcoholism*, **45**(3), 252–7.

Hester, R.K., H.D. Delaney, W. Campbell and N. Handmaker (2009), 'A web application for moderation training: Initial results of a randomized clinical trial', *Journal of Substance Abuse Treatment*, **37**(3), 266–76.

Hutchison, A.J., J.D. Breckon and L.H. Johnston (2009), 'Physical activity behavior change interventions based on the transtheoretical model: A systematic review', *Health Education & Behavior*, **36**(5), 829–45.

Hutton, H.E., L.M. Wilson, B.J. Apelberg, E.A. Tang, O. Odelola, E.B. Bass and G. Chander (2011), 'A systematic review of randomized controlled trials: Web-based interventions for smoking cessation among adolescents, college students, and adults', *Nicotine & Tobacco Research*, **13**(4), 227–38.

Hwang, G.S., H.S. Jung, Y. Yi, C. Yoon and J.W. Choi (2012), 'Smoking cessation intervention using stepwise exercise incentives for male workers in the workplace', *Asia-Pacific Journal of Public Health*, **24**(1), 82–90.

Ilmarinen, J.E. (2001), 'Aging workers', *Occupational and Environmental Medicine*, **58**(8), 546.

Ilmarinen, J.E. and K. Tuomi (1992), 'Work ability of aging workers', *Scandinavian Journal of Work, Environment & Health*, **18**, 8–10.

Ilmarinen, J.E. and J. Rantanen (1999), 'Promotion of work ability during ageing', *American Journal of Industrial Medicine*, **36**(1), 21–3.

Jonsdottir, I.H., A. Nordlund, S. Ellbin, T. Ljung, K. Glise, P. Währborg and A. Wallin (2013), 'Cognitive impairment in patients with stress-related exhaustion', *Stress*, **16**(2), 181–90.

Kanfer, R. and P.L. Ackerman (2004), 'Aging, adult development and work motivation', *Academy of Management Review*, **29**, 440–58.

Koffman, D.M., J.W. Lee, J.W. Hopp and S.L. Emont (1998), 'The impact of including incentives and competition in a workplace smoking cessation program on quit rates', *American Journal of Health Promotion*, **13**(2), 105–11.

Kouvonen, A., M. Kivimäki, T. Oksanen, J. Pentti, T. Heponiemi, A. Väänänen and J. Vahtera (2012), 'Implementation of workplace-based smoking cessation support activities and smoking cessation among employees: The Finnish public sector study', *Research and Practice*, 102(7), e56.

Lehto, T. and H. Oinas-Kukkonen (2011), 'Persuasive features in web-based alcohol and smoking interventions: A systematic review of the literature', *Journal of Medical Internet Research*, **13**(3), e46.

Letenneur, L. (2004), 'Risk of dementia and alcohol and wine consumption: A review of recent results', *Biological Research*, **37**, 189–93.

Leykin, Y., A. Aguilera, L.D. Torres, E.J. Pérez-Stable and R.F. Muñoz (2012), 'Interpreting the outcomes of automated Internet-based randomized trials: Example of an international smoking cessation study', *Journal of Medical Internet Research*, **14**(1), e5.

Luchsinger, J.A., M.X. Tang, M. Siddigui, S. Shes and R. Mayeux (2004), 'Alcohol intake and risk of dementia', *Journal of the American Geriatric Society*, **52**, 540–46.

Maertens, Julie, A., Stefanie E. Putter, Peter Y. Chen, Manfred Diehl and Emily Huang (2012), 'Physical capabilities and occupational health of older workers', in J.W. Hedge and W.C. Borman (eds), *The Oxford Handbook of Work and Aging*, New York: Oxford University Press, pp. 215–35.

Miller, D.I., V. Taler, P.S. Davidson and C. Messier (2012), 'Measuring the impact of exercise on cognitive aging: Methodological issues', *Neurobiology of Aging*, **33**(3), 622.e29–622.e43.

Muhonen, T. and E. Torkelson (2008), 'Collective and individualistic coping with stress at work', *Psychological Reports*, **102**(2), 450–58.

Ngandu, T., E.L. Helkala, H. Soininen, B. Winblad, J. Tuomilehto, A. Nissinen and M. Kivipelto (2007), 'Alcohol drinking and cognitive functions: Findings from the cardiovascular risk factors aging and dementia (CAIDE) study', *Dementia and Geriatric Cognitive Disorders*, **23**, 140–49.

Nooyens, A.C., B.M. Van Gelder and W.M. Verschuren (2008), 'Smoking and cognitive decline among middle-aged men and women: The Doetinchem cohort study', *American Journal of Public Health*, **98**(12), 2244–50.

Ohayon, M.M. (2002), 'Epidemiology of insomnia: What we know and what we still need to learn', *Sleep Medicine Reviews*, **6**(2), 97–111.

Ory, M.G., M. Lee Smith, N. Mier and M.M. Wernicke (2010), 'The science of sustaining health behavior change: The health maintenance consortium', *American Journal of Health Behavior*, **34**(6), 647–59.

Perera, R., C. Heneghan and P. Yudkin (2007), 'A graphical method for depicting randomised trials of complex interventions', *British Medical Journal*, **334**(7585), 127–9.

Peters, R., R. Poulter, J. Warner, N. Beckett, L. Burch and C. Bulpitt (2008), 'Smoking, dementia and cognitive decline in the elderly, a systematic review', *BMC Geriatrics*, **8**(36).

Petersen, H., G. Kecklund, P. D'Onofrio, J. Nilsson and T. Akerstedt (2012), 'Stress vulnerability and the effects of moderate daily stress on sleep polysomnography and subjective sleepiness', *Journal of Sleep Research*, **22**(1), 50–57.

Prince, M., R. Bryce, E. Albanese, A. Wimo, W. Ribeiro and C.P. Ferri (2013), 'The global prevalence of dementia: A systematic review and meta-analysis', *Alzheimer's & Dementia*, **9**(1), 63–75.
Prochaska, J.O. and W.F. Velicer (1997), 'The transtheoretical model of health behavior change', *American Journal of Health Promotion*, **12**(1), 38–48.
Prochaska, J.O., S. Butterworth, C.A. Redding, V. Burden, N. Perrin, M. Leo, M. Flaherty-Robb and J.M. Prochaska (2008), 'Initial efficacy of MI, TTM tailoring and HRI's with multiple behaviours for employee health promotion', *Preventive Medicine*, **46**(3), 226–31.
Radak, Z., N. Hart, L. Sarga, E. Koltai, M. Atalay, H. Ohno and I. Boldogh (2010), 'Exercise plays a preventive role against Alzheimer's Disease', *Journal of Alzheimer's Disease*, **20**, 777–83.
Rimm, E.B. and M.J. Stampfer (2004), 'Diet, lifestyle, and longevity – The next steps?', *Journal of the American Medical Association*, **292**(12), 1490–92.
Rizzuto, Tracey, E., Katie E. Cherry and Jared A. LeDoux (2012), 'The aging process and cognitive capabilities', in J.W. Hedge and W.C. Borman (eds), *The Oxford Handbook of Work and Aging*, New York: Oxford University Press, pp. 236–56.
Rosenstock, I.M., V.J. Strecher and M.H. Becker (1988), 'Social learning theory and the health belief model', *Health Education Quarterly*, **15**(2), 175–83.
Rothman, A.J. (2000), 'Toward a theory-base analysis of behavioral maintenance', *Health Psychology*, **19**(1), 64–9.
Ruitenberg, A., J.C. Van Swieten, J.C.M. Witteman, K.M. Mehta, C.M Van Duijn, A. Hofman and M.M.B. Breteler (2002), 'Alcohol consumption and risk of dementia', *The Lancet*, **359**, 281–6.
Rusanen, M., M. Kivipelto, C.P. Quesenberry, J. Zhou and R.A. Whitmer (2011), 'Heavy smoking in midlife and long-term risk of Alzheimer Disease and vascular dementia', *Archives of Internal Medicine*, **171**(4), 333–9.
Singh-Manoux, A., M. Kivimaki, M.M. Glymour, A. Elbaz, C. Berr, K.P. Ebmeier and A. Dugravot (2012), 'Timing of onset of cognitive decline: Results from Whitehall II prospective cohort study', *British Medical Journal*, **344**(7622).
Staff, R.T., A.D. Murray, I.J. Deary and L.J. Whalley (2004), 'What provides cerebral reserve?', *Brain*, **127**, 1191–9.
Thiart, H., D. Lehr, D.D. Ebert, B. Sieland, M. Berking and H. Riper (2013), 'Log in and breathe out: Efficacy and cost-effectiveness of an online sleep training for teachers affected by work-related strain – study protocol for a randomized controlled trial', *Trials*, **14**(169).
Tudor-Locke, C. and L. Lutes (2009), 'Why do pedometers work?: A reflection upon the factors related to successfully increasing physical activity', *Sports Medicine*, **39**(12), 981–93.
Tyas, S.L., L.R. White, H. Petrovich, G. Webster Ross, D.J. Foley, H.K. Heimovitz and L.J. Launer (2003), 'Mid-life smoking and late-life dementia: The Honolulu–Asia aging study', *Neurobiology of Aging*, **24**, 589–96.
Uehli, K., A.J. Mehta, D. Miedinger, K. Hug, C. Schindler, E. Holsboer-Trachsler, J.D. Leuppi and N. Kunzli (2014), 'Sleep problems and work injuries: A systematic review and meta-analysis', *Sleep Medicine Reviews*, **18**(1), 61–73.
US Department of Agriculture and US Department of Health and Human Services (2010), 'Dietary guidelines for Americans', 7th edn, Washington, DC: US Government Printing Office.
Verweij, L., A. Weel, C. Hulshof, K. Proper and W. Van Mechelen (2010), 'Richtlijn in ontwikkeling: Balans in beweging en voeding op de werkplek', *TBV*, **18**(3), 110–13.
Walker, M.P. and R. Stickgold (2006), 'Sleep, memory, and plasticity', *Annual Reviews in Psychology*, **57**, 139–66.
Wilson, R.S., S.E. Arnold, J.A. Schneider, J.F. Kelly, Y. Tang and D.A. Bennett (2006), 'Chronic psychological distress and risk of Alzheimer's disease in old age', *Neuroepidemiology*, **27**, 143–53.
Wilson, R.S., D.A. Evans, J.L. Bienias, C.F. Mendes de Leon, J.A. Schneider and D.A. Bennett (2003), 'Proneness to psychological distress is associated with risk of Alzheimer's disease', *Neurology*, **61**, 1479–85.
Wilson, R.S., J.A. Schneider, P.A. Boyle, S.E. Arnold, Y.A. Tang and D.A. Bennett (2007), 'Chronic distress and incidence of mild cognitive impairment', *Neurology*, **68**, 2085–92.
Witte, A.V., M. Fobker, R. Gellner, S. Knecht and A. Flöel (2009), 'Caloric restriction improves memory in elderly humans', *Proceedings of the National Academy of Sciences*, 106(4), 1255–60.
Wolf, O.T. (2009), 'Stress and memory in humans: Twelve years of progress?', *Brain Research*, **1293**, 142–54.

18 Older workers and sustainable late careers: job characteristic effects

Sara Zaniboni, Franco Fraccaroli and Donald M. Truxillo

INTRODUCTION

Aging is a complex multidimensional process (for example, Shultz and Adams, 2007) that includes the interplay of contextual and individual dynamics. It is influenced by chronological age, historical events, expectations derived from roles played, and by generational membership (for example, Hedge and Borman, 2012). In a historical moment in which societies need a higher participation rate of older workers in the job market, we still face difficult social issues around aging, largely rooted in prejudices and stereotypes (WHO, 2002). Indeed, it is common to associate the adult life cycle and especially older age with progressive psychophysical decline, illness and dependency. The urgent need for research and interventions to sustain active and healthy careers for older workers has already been underlined (for example, Wang et al., 2013).

This chapter will make a contribution in this direction. We will describe the socio-demographic changes that drive a need for higher and more flexible participation of older workers in the job market, and a redefinition of the career path during the lifespan. Theories related to the careers of older workers will be considered, followed by an examination of different factors that can play an important role in late career paths. In particular, we will focus on job characteristics and related organizational interventions that can reinforce the creation of more sustainable careers for the older workforce, enhancing the opportunities for keeping older workers satisfied, healthy and productive at work. Future research suggestions will also be addressed.

AGE AND CAREERS, AN UPSET BALANCE: A SOCIO-DEMOGRAPHIC FRAME

The relationship between age and work has been rendered increasingly complex by the great demographic upheavals characterizing the first decades of the twenty-first century. The baby-boomer generation (born between 1945 and 1964) is approaching retirement age, swelling the ranks of pensioners and the costs of pensions systems with its demographic surge. The improvement in life expectancy, the slowing of aging processes, and the improving of health conditions among the elderly, particularly in economically developed countries, also play an important role in modifying the traditional balance between age and work (Vaupel, 2010; Wheaton and Crimmins, 2013).

The effects of this demographic transition are summarized by data from Eurostat, the statistical office of the European Commission, using the projected old age dependency ratio evolution from 1960 to 2060 in Europe. First, the total population in the

European Union (27 countries) will become older, with an average age increasing from 40.4 years in 2008 to 47.9 years in 2060. Second, the portion of people aged 65 years or over is projected to become 30.0 percent of the entire population in 2060 (151.5 million units), from 17.1 percent in 2008. Third, the age dependency ratio is expected to increase to 53 percent in 2060 from 25.9 percent in 2010. That means that while today in the EU there are four working people for every retired person, in 50 years this ratio will be two working persons for one retired. Similar estimates are made for Japan, whereas the demographic impact in the USA seems less pronounced (from about 19.5 'older dependent' in 100 'workers' in 2010, to 36.8 percent in 2060). These projections, if confirmed, clearly indicate that a new quantitative equilibrium is expected between working and retired people, and between people at the beginning of their career and people in the late career.

Also noteworthy are the marked imbalances which persist at the international level in the labor market participation of people aged between 55 and 64 (the age at which people can obtain voluntary early retirement under certain conditions). A single figure is indicative: in Southern European countries (for example, Italy, Spain, France) the proportion of active 55–64-year-olds is equal to around 40 percent of the total; in Central and North European countries (for example, Germany, UK, Sweden) and in the USA and Japan it is over 60 percent. Such imbalances in activity levels, probably due to contextual and cultural factors, have important repercussions for the competitiveness of country systems and social security budgets. Moreover, these imbalances strongly interact with the aging process in the working population previously described. Countries with a higher old age dependency ratio and with a lower level of activity at the age of 55–64 will be exposed to greater risk of financial unsustainability in the pension and welfare systems. These imbalances are then often corrected through policies that force people to work longer, postpone retirement, and lengthen their work career.

The increase in life expectancy (which today in Europe and USA is 20 and 17 years at age 65, respectively, for women and men) and an overall improvement in health also make work possible at an advanced age, and a growing proportion of people continue to work even after reaching pensionable age. In Europe, a survey conducted by Eurofound (2012) shows that among retired people aged 65–69, 10.5 percent were still working in 2011 (it was 8.8 percent in 2005). At the age of 70–74, the number of people still working after retirement was 5.2 percent in 2011 (and 4.3 percent in 2005). A growing participation in the labor market is foreseen for the US older workforce, where from 2006 to 2016, the number of people at work after retirement is expected to increase by 84 percent (US Bureau of Labor Statistics). Working after retirement seems to be more characteristic of the North American labor market, and less frequently seen in other areas such as Europe; for instance, Beck (2013) reports that the number of workers above retirement age doubled in 2011 in the UK, but this is mostly due to people that remain in their employment rather than returning to employment after retirement.

Disengagement from work and from the primary career in later years is becoming more gradual, with different assignments (temporary, part-time, occasional, irregular). This 'buffer' between full-time primary employment and full retirement makes it possible to think about a 'job career' after retirement (Arnold, 1997; Wang et al., 2013). Different forms of gradual retirement (phased or partial retirement, re-entry) are now developing, giving older workers many opportunities to continue their career after retirement age.

The most studied option is 'bridge employment' (Alcover et al., forthcoming), which refers to jobs that follow the principal career and precede complete job withdrawal.

In fact, these trends are also evident in the current economic recession. As Beck (2013) points out, the current recession is the first one in which the position of older workers is more protected than in past recessions. Although they have suffered redundancies and a loss of quality in their employment, they have not been targeted disproportionally relative to other age groups. Particularly in the UK, new forms of flexibility in working hours and new adjustments in work tasks have been important alternatives to redundancies among older workers. But the effect of the financial crisis is evident for the 55–65 and 65+ age groups in the USA, considering that the unemployment rates for these groups are the highest since data were first recorded in 1948.

The continued changes in workforce demographics and health improvement are also expected to lead to significant changes in the relationship between age, work and career. As Vaupel (2010) pointed out:

> If progress in reducing mortality continues at the same pace as it has over the past two centuries, which is a matter of debate, then in countries with high life expectancies most children born since the year 2000 will celebrate their 100th birthday – in the twenty-second century. Longer lifespans will alter the way individuals want to allocate time during their lives and will require radical revision of employment, retirement, health, education and other policies' (Vaupel, 2010, p. 536).

People living in healthy conditions for 80 or 90 years, as is expected in the future, could lead to an actual re-definition of working life-seasons and career steps extending and blending education, work, parenting and leisure across more years of life.

All these data and forecasts illustrate that the 'traditional' career path, related to chronological age (until 15–20 years, education; from 20 to 55 years, career development; from 55 to 65 career decline and exit) is a less useful way to describe people's work experiences, particularly for the final part of the career. New research and new theories are needed. On an international level there is a call for supportive interventions and policies in favor of creating sustainable careers for older workers. By sustainable careers we mean a career path that fits with the needs and aspirations of the person, together with the opportunities and constraints of organizations and societies. In particular, regarding older workers, this could mean staying longer in the labor market and staying satisfied, engaged, productive and healthy. In order to design and implement efficient and effective interventions to support sustainable careers for older workers, it is necessary to gain a better knowledge of specific processes and aspects that characterize older workers' careers.

This chapter will present career theories relevant to late careers of older workers, focusing on how these theories may help clarify the issues related to late careers. We will then discuss factors that affect the careers of older workers, with particular attention to job design and job characteristics, integrating both lifespan development theories and the existing empirical research. Based on this discussion, we will then describe possible organizational policies and interventions that may support or impede sustainable careers for older workers.

CAREER THEORIES AND LATE CAREER ISSUES

In dynamic theories of career and career development, a strong link is usually made between chronological age and career. One of the most widely used models, the life span approach to career development (Super, 1957), frames the careers of people as falling into life stages typical in the life course: *growth*, when children and pre-adolescents gain a first representation of the world of work; *career exploration*, during adolescence with first choices and exploration during first jobs; *career establishment*, in the middle of work life when workers try to establish a fit between job and personal characteristics; *career maintenance*, during the late career stage, when people try to preserve the position and to balance career experiences with other life domains; and finally, *career decline* at the pre-retirement and retirement age with the transition to full retirement. Super himself in his life-span life space model (1980) was more attentive to examining the short cycle of careers inside the large-stage model. Similarly, Schein (1978) developed a typology of career stages related to age that defines the movement of individuals from outside to the inner core of an organization.

Beginning with Arthur et al. (1989), a deep theoretical rework of the career concept has been developed to better understand the dynamics of career in a changing labor market and in emerging organizational models.

Some theorists advocated for a 'new science' in the career field which would consider as core concepts the non-linearity, interdependence and emergence of the dynamic of careers in the current labor market and in work organizations (Lichtenstein and Mendenhall, 2002).

Non-linearity refers to non-stable and non-fixed times between actions and their outcomes. Non-linearity explains why the quantity of efforts, engagement and actions don't generate the same results in terms of career outcomes at all times and for all people. For instance, at the beginning of a career, the relationship between learning processes and performance is not the same as in the middle phase. Later, after one has reached a certain level of competence and visibility, professional reputation will cause performance and career outcomes to have increased effects (Hall, 1996).

Interdependence refers to the mutual causality between elements, with cause and effect appearing simultaneously. In career studies, interdependence could be assessed when people reconstruct their career after downsizing: the use of old and the construction of new competences happen in interaction with new organizational demands.

Emergence refers to how new unexpected properties emerge to shape the dynamic system. For instance, high work engagement and a deep learning could lead to a boundaryless, autonomous career. The career emerges over time from these work attitudes and behaviors as a result of the dynamic interaction between the person and the organizational contexts (Lichtenstein and Mendenhall, 2002).

The recent changes in the economic and cultural context of careers (Arnold, 1997; Khapova et al., 2009; Wang et al., 2013) show that the linear and interconnected link between age, life stage, organizational position and career can no longer describe the complexity and the multi-dimensionality of the dynamics of careers throughout the lifespan (Arthur and Rousseau, 1996; Hall, 2004). Careers unfold, not necessarily in a cumulative way, along a sequence of experiences in relationship with a large variety of contexts and as a result of individual networks. Moreover, if the life events that characterize the life course today are even more unpredictable and uncertain, then the causal link between age and career is even less strong. In other words, when considering the last 20 years, chronological age and career stages for many individuals no longer correspond.

Following this perspective, the metaphor of 'spiral careers' seems appropriate: people enter new career contexts many times during their lives; they explore new organizational settings and accumulate knowledge to master their job. Today, it is increasingly common for people to move to other jobs and/or organizations to improve their professional opportunities. They then restart the cycle, but from a new starting-point (Hall, 1996): the past choices and the previous experiences have an impact on the future paths, and people can use past knowledge and evaluate established networks for developing future work experiences. A more recent metaphor of 'entangled strands' (Lee et al., 2011) accurately describes the idea of non-linearity and interdependence of careers. A person builds their career in an overall life context following different 'strands' (work, family, community, personal interests) during the entire life. The career trajectories are the results of key dynamic elements that are catalysts for changes and choices.

This theoretical development of careers notion grew up in a dynamic context characterized by high levels of growth, speedy development of new industries (the knowledge-intensive economy), and was particularly relevant to professional careers in the computer science industry (Arthur and Rousseau, 1996). Today, the same principles could be applied to characteristics of the current labor market: high levels of unemployment; downsizing; layoffs; job uncertainty; and frequent career transitions. At the same time, these principles could be used to understand the dynamics of careers for older workers and transition to retirement (Wang et al., 2013). As the authors point out, in analyzing the mid- and late-career of people, 'no one traditional mid and late career worker framework exists. Instead, consistent with the lifespan perspective on careers, there are many pathways to a successful career and many of those are forged based on the unique approaches taken by the individual as they progressed through their respective careers' (p. 4). And 'later career workers have increased freedom of choice and also have the resources to make personal choices and search for self-fulfillment' (p. 7).

The model of the protean career could be applied to the final stage of careers and to the study of the progressive transition to retirement. Kim and Hall (2013) show that the late career and working after retirement could be seen as a career stage where individuals have a variety of options. This particular stage is intense in terms of 'career mini-cycles' of exploration, trial, establishing and mastery. A person in their late career or after retirement may start new experiences, explore new job opportunities, and develop new competences and skills. Moreover, following Kim and Hall (2013), the degree of protean career orientation could be higher in this stage, as in the beginning phase of the career. Older workers have a high degree of self-awareness, they can select the skills to improve and the networks to develop more appropriately, they are better able to optimize their learning experiences, and to compensate for weaknesses and emphasize strengths (see the discussion of the Selective Optimization with Compensation Theory (SOC; Baltes and Baltes, 1990) in the next section).

To understand the dynamics of the late career (working during the last stage of the career; working longer after retirement age; restarting or continuing to work after retirement), it is important to consider a wide set of factors as possible attractors for people to continue their job or develop their career. Usually these factors are organized into three categories: individual-level factors, job-level factors, and organizational-level factors (Wang et al., 2013). This categorization, even if simplistic and incomplete, is useful for understanding different influences (subjective and contextual) that characterize the career experience of people. Among these factors, some are specifically salient for studying the late career.

The individual level includes motivational structures and their change with age; experiences and expertise; individual differences in aging; and the uniqueness of life span circumstances. At this level, Social Cognitive Career Theory (SCCT; Lent et al., 1994) has been applied by Wöhrmann et al. (2013) to post-retirement career planning. The theory considers two cognitive mechanisms especially relevant for career development and career planning processes: self-efficacy and outcome expectations. Using a multilevel approach, the authors examined the effects of outcome expectations regarding post-retirement employment as well as two characteristics of work design (physical demands and social support at work) on post-retirement work planning. Outcome expectations are considered as the expected benefit people would receive from engagement and are predictors of intentions and behavior. Wöhrmann et al. (2013) found that people with higher outcome expectations and stronger intentions to continue work are more likely to engage in planning a job career after retirement. These results support the application of SCCT in early career, late career, and after retirement. Moreover, the two work design characteristics, physical demands and social support, mediated the relationship between outcome expectations and intention to continue a career after retirement.

At the job level, the types of jobs done in the past (complexity; physical, mental and social demands; job design) and the number and variety of past jobs could be considered as possible attractors for continuing the career. While studying post-retirement work in Australia, Griffin and Hesketh (2008) showed the importance of people's evaluation of their previous employment in predicting post-retirement work activities. Using image theory, the authors considered the *trajectory image*, which is the preferred course of action or future outcomes that people think is appropriate and want to achieve. This trajectory image is built on the self-image of people (beliefs, values, attitudes) and consists of the anticipated future state of people and on the image of plans and behaviors that are needed to achieve this state. In this particular study, trajectory image included engagement in post-retirement work. The intention to engage in post-retirement work was dependent on people's evaluation of their pre-retirement work.

Applying the conservation of resources theory (Hobfoll, 1989) to post-retirement career choices, Armstrong-Stassen et al. (2012) proposed that retirement-related resource losses (financial loss; role loss) and organization-related resource gains (gain in life satisfaction) would be positive predictors of interest in returning to the previous organization after retirement. The loss factors could facilitate restarting a career; the gain factors could inhibit the interest in a new restart.

At the organizational level, factors such as perceived organizational support, the degree of organizational commitment, and the human resource management system (particularly in reference to older workers) are the main predictive elements in explaining late career choices of people (Wang et al., 2013).

At this level, many studies have started to show the importance of managing the late career as a key to integrating older workers, to maintain them in the organization in a productive and satisfactory way, and to promote the continuation of careers after retirement. A recent contribution is the research of Böhm et al. (forthcoming) on age diversity climate. The authors hypothesized that age-inclusive human resource management practices (for example, equal training opportunities; equal opportunities for promotion) could affect organizational age diversity climate (shared perceptions of a non-discriminatory treatment of employees by age), the collective perceptions of social exchange inside the organization, and turnover intentions.

Taken together, these studies show how different factors could intervene in the dynamics of late career and transition to retirement. In the following section we devote particular attention to job characteristics as a possible factor that could influence the career choice and the psychosocial experience of people during their late career.

FACTORS THAT AFFECT THE CAREER OF OLDER WORKERS: JOB CHARACTERISTICS

Many career studies have dealt with the identification of factors that provide meaning and purpose in a person's work (Hall, 2002). These factors can contribute to objective and subjective career success. Studies of objective career success are frequently focused on outcomes that can be seen and evaluated objectively by others, for example, occupational status (for example, Ganzeboom and Treiman, 1996; Ng and Feldman, 2010) or pay (for example, Ng and Feldman, 2010; O'Reilly and Chatman, 1994). Research on subjective career success is focused on outcomes related to the individual's perception of the extent to which a person can achieve personal goals (Hall, 2002), for example, career and job satisfaction (for example, Judge and Hurst, 2008) or career and job attachment (for example, Adams and Beehr, 1998). Moreover, other outcomes may be relevant to late career workers as well, for example, physical and psychological well-being and career-related decisions (for example, career change, retirement, bridge employment).

There are different factors that can enhance older workers' employability, reinforcing the creation of more sustainable careers for the older workforce. By employability we refer to 'the continuous fulfilling, acquiring, or creating of work through the optimal use of competences' (Van Der Heijde and Van Der Heijden, 2006, p. 453). These factors can help or impede in keeping older workers satisfied, healthy and productive at work. Job characteristics may be an important factor that influence the late career (Wang et al., 2013). For example, job demands and work stress are important factors for career change and retirement decisions (for example, Wang et al., 2008). On the other hand, workers tend to retire later if the organization focuses on creating an opportunity for growth and development in the job (for example, Zaniboni et al., 2010) and the supervisors consider older workers' capacity when assigning tasks (for example, Zappalà et al., 2008).

Job characteristics are related to a wide range of important individual, group and organizational outcomes (Morgeson and Campion, 2003; Morgeson and Humphrey, 2006), and can affect important career processes (Hall and Las Heras, 2010). In a conceptual paper, Hall and Las Heras (2010) integrated the research on job design and career, showing the connections between them. The authors suggested that people make career decisions based on the characteristics that they expect their jobs to have. Therefore, people at different stages in their careers make decisions by prioritizing certain job characteristics over others so that those job characteristics will help them pursue subjective career success (Hall and Las Heras, 2010).

Lifespan aging theories, such as Socioemotional Selectivity Theory (SST; Carstensen, 1991) and SOC (Baltes and Baltes, 1990), support what Hall and Las Heras (2010) suggested. SOC posits that people use three strategies to adapt effectively to the aging process. *Selection* refers to selecting specific goals that match the person's resources and that are demanded to pursue the selected outcomes. *Optimization* refers to allocating time, effort and resources to achieve desired results. *Compensation* refers to coping with losses to maintain positive functioning, such as using different methods to get the same results. Older workers can use these strategies to enhance their employability: they select job aspects that give them the opportunity to use their accumulated experience, allowing them to optimize their efforts to achieve the desired results, and compensating for any decline through their experience. SST suggests that people become progressively more selective during the aging process, perceiving their time as limited, prioritizing present-oriented goals to pursue emotionally and socially-gratifying experiences. Therefore, older workers will be interested in different job characteristics compared to their younger counterparts. Older workers should benefit from a job that gives them the opportunity to maximize socially gratifying working experiences.

The understanding of job characteristics that benefit older workers has received relatively little scrutiny, and has only just begun to be raised as a research question (Truxillo et al., 2012a; Truxillo et al., 2012b; Zaniboni et al., 2013; Zaniboni et al., forthcoming). Truxillo et al. (Truxillo et al., 2012a; Truxillo et al., 2012b) used lifespan aging theories (Baltes and Baltes, 1990; Carstensen, 1991) to suggest that different job characteristics should have different outcomes in terms of well-being, performance, satisfaction and engagement for older and younger workers. Using the work design model of Morgeson and Humphrey (2006), the authors discuss how specific task characteristics (that is, the range and the nature of tasks associated with a specific job), knowledge characteristics (that is, knowledge, skills, and abilities required of workers as a function of their jobs), and social characteristics (that is, social and relational aspects related to work), interact with age, affecting such work outcomes as satisfaction, engagement and performance. Of the 21 characteristics described by Morgeson and Humphrey (2006), the authors suggest that 10 can be beneficial for older workers.

Specifically, among the task characteristics, they suggested that *autonomy* (the extent to which a job allows freedom and discretion to schedule work, make decisions, and choose the methods to perform tasks) and *task significance* (the degree to which one's job influences the lives and work of others) will lead to more positive working outcomes for older workers. Older workers may prefer to work autonomously given their work experience and crystallized intelligence; work autonomy allows them to craft their jobs and to choose roles to fit their strengths. Regarding task significance, keeping in mind the generativity motives that begin to develop in late-career, older workers may prefer to be more focused on meaning in their job rather than gaining job skills (Kanfer and Ackerman, 2004).

Regarding the knowledge characteristics, Truxillo (2012b) considered *job complexity* (the extent to which job tasks are complex and challenging to perform), *information processing* (the degree to which a job requires processing data and information), *problem solving* (the extent to which a job requires innovative ideas or solutions), *skill variety* (the extent to which a job requires an individual to use a variety of different skills), and *specialization* (the extent to which a job involves performing specialized tasks and requires in-depth knowledge and skills). The authors suggested that if *job complexity*, *information processing* and *problem solving* require fluid intellectual abilities which may decline later in life this will result in more negative working outcomes for older workers such as decreased satisfaction, engagement and performance. However, when older workers are able to successfully apply their accumulated knowledge and skill or SOC strategies, complex jobs can lead to positive work outcomes (see, for example, Zacher and Frese, 2009; 2011; Zacher et al., 2010). For the same reason, older workers benefit more from *skill variety* compared to their younger colleagues because it allows them to use their accumulated skills (Zaniboni et al., 2013). Moreover, older workers may prefer the *specialization* characteristic since it can allow them to focus on a single specialty in which they have gained deep expertise.

Among the social and relational characteristics examined by Morgeson and Humphrey (2006), *social support* – particularly giving support – (that is, the extent to which a job provides opportunities for advice and assistance from and given to others), and *interdependence* – both initiated and received (that is, which reflects how connected one's job is to others' jobs) should lead to more positive outcomes for older workers. Giving social support could potentially lead to emotional and social gratifying experiences, as suggested by SST, and may be more beneficial for older workers because they are more motivated by present-oriented goals. For a similar reason, interdependence should be more attractive to older workers since it makes the job more relational, fulfilling the desire to be emotionally and socially integrated with other people.

Considering the aging of the workforce, it seems particularly important that jobs are designed to fit preferences and needs of older workers. Therefore, providing a job with characteristics in which people can meet their own personal goals is useful to create conditions in which people successfully master their career (Hall and Las Heras, 2010).

ORGANIZATIONAL POLICIES AND INTERVENTIONS THAT MAY SUPPORT OR IMPEDE A SUSTAINABLE CAREER FOR OLDER WORKERS

In the previous section, we described how job characteristics and age may interact to affect worker outcomes, as well as some empirical support for this model. Unfortunately, there is a dearth of research that examines actual interventions to support workers in middle and late careers. In fact, although there has been much talk about 'active aging' (promoting activity and participation among older people) particularly in Europe, there has been little work on specific interventions that can be used by employers (Walker and Maltby, 2012). Nevertheless, research on job characteristics can provide significant guidance as to what types of interventions may support workers in mid and late careers. Furthermore, the rich theoretical basis for this work – in the areas of both job design and careers – provides a strong basis for intervention research. This provides a significant advantage to scholars.

First, research on job characteristics suggests that there are age-related differences with respect to the desire for task variety and skill variety (Zaniboni et al., 2013; Zaniboni et al., forthcoming), which are based in models of age-related job design (Truxillo et al., 2012b) and theories of lifespan development (Baltes and Baltes, 1990; Carstensen et al., 1999). Specifically, older workers may have better attitudinal and well-being outcomes when provided with greater skill variety, and younger workers may do best where their jobs provide greater task variety. This is because older workers will value the opportunity to apply accumulated knowledge and skills, while younger workers will value the opportunity to gain skills by performing a variety of tasks. Moreover, research has shown that job characteristics such as skill variety can lead to successful aging outcomes like generativity and sense of control (Sanders and McCready, 2010). This suggests that organizations, managers and supervisors should actively address the differing needs of older and younger workers with regard to the job duties and responsibilities. Moreover, capitalizing on older workers' accumulated skills might be enacted through a number of workplace interventions, such as mentoring programs that help younger workers, thus providing older workers with a chance to use their rich skills and abilities, at the same time preserving institutional knowledge and memory (for example, Wang et al., 2013).

Relatedly, younger workers seem to have stronger learning goals than their older counterparts (Hertel et al., 2013). This makes sense, as early career is a time for accumulating needed skills and abilities. In contrast, mid- and late-career workers may feel that they have accumulated most of the knowledge, skills and abilities that they need to perform their jobs (Truxillo et al., 2012b). However, given the changing nature of work in the twenty-first century, workers in later career stages do need to continue to learn to keep up with changes. Therefore, while supervisors and managers should recognize these differences between older and younger workers in their desire to learn, they also need to support late-career workers in gaining necessary skills to adapt to workplace changes. They should also allow older workers additional time needed to acquire new skills.

Some empirical findings point out the potential importance of job design to keep workers employed longer prior to retirement. For instance, Robroek et al., (2013) found that lack of control can lead to increased probability of retirement. Nevertheless, a dose of realism is in order when weighing the relative value of organizational interventions that encourage workers to work longer, as contextual issues may outweigh what can be done by organizations. For instance, Engelhardt (2012), in a study of retirement patterns across European countries, found that pension issues outweigh financial incentives in predicting retirement. In other words, interventions should take into account employees' non-work contexts such as family and the cultural and country context (Ilmarinen, 2012).

Hertel et al. (2013) present a number of recommendations for practice based on their findings from a series of empirical studies. These include providing greater autonomy for older workers, as older workers appear to value autonomy more than their younger counterparts and may be more effective at using autonomy for dealing with work stressors. These scholars also illustrate the importance of addressing the different motivational needs of older and younger workers. Importantly, they recommend that organizations carefully monitor the needs of older (late career) workers through surveys and performance ratings. In other words, organizations should 'keep an eye' on the evolving needs of workers throughout the development of their careers. This is consistent with recommendations to assess employees' current work ability (for example, Ilmarinen, 2012) to determine how workers are doing and finding ways that management can address these issues through redesign of the job (Wang et al., 2013). Finally, Hertel et al. (2013) suggest that workplace flexibility be provided to assure that non-work needs are addressed across the career.

One important issue to keep in mind when considering interventions to address career-stage issues is that although there may be differences between early- and late-career workers in terms of skills, abilities and motivation, there is still significant variability among employees within career groups. For this reason, managers and supervisors should provide careful attention to the needs of individual workers. Second, although we advocate for age-sensitive interventions, we caution against separate interventions and privileges for workers in different career stages, for reasons of legality and fairness.

Finally, we cannot leave the issue of career-focused interventions without emphasizing the need not only for intervention research but also for greater understanding of the process involved in specific interventions, that is, understanding how interventions work (for example, Nielsen et al., 2010). Moreover, it is important to acknowledge the contextual issues that can enhance or inhibit the effectiveness of workplace interventions, such as employee and manager support and organizational resources (Egan et al., 2009). We call for a deeper understanding of processes in intervention research in general, as well as for interventions focused on career stage. Thankfully, such understanding should be bolstered by the theoretically rich literature on career stages and age-related needs at work.

FUTURE RESEARCH NEEDS

As suggested by Hall and Las Heras (2010), in addition to examining the effects of job characteristics on satisfaction, motivation and performance, it is important to study the effects of job characteristics on longer-term career variables such as career orientation, career intentions, and subjective success *over time*. This time dimension in studying the effect of job characteristics on careers is critical. Indeed, the effect on certain career outcomes can be expected only under conditions of long-term exposure to jobs with specific characteristics (Hall and Las Heras, 2010). Moreover, longitudinal studies are needed for a deeper understanding of how age and job characteristics interact, examining how a person's preferred job characteristics change over time (Truxillo et al., 2012b).

Future research may also take into consideration the interaction of job characteristics and job crafting on late career outcomes. Job crafting has been defined as self-initiated change that employees make with the aim of fitting their jobs with their preferences and goals (Tims et al., 2012; Wrzesniewski and Dutton, 2001). For example, certain job characteristics such as autonomy give workers more opportunity to craft their job, and this can affect career decisions such as retirement. Moreover, job characteristic preferences can change with age, and job crafting can help a successful adjustment to the workplace, affecting longer-term career outcomes. Job crafting may allow workers to change the characteristics of their jobs, as they perceive misfit with their age needs. Similarly, SOC (Baltes and Baltes, 1990) suggests adaptive strategies that people can use to fit their current resources to demands throughout the aging process.

Work–life issues can be particularly important for workers in middle and late careers.

Work–life balance may have different meanings and facets for people at different ages; however, there is a paucity of research examining these issues. Work–life factors such as family, roles played outside work, friends and leisure activities are considered important elements in affecting career decisions of older workers such as retirement (Wang et al., 2013). For example, Zaniboni et al. (2010) found that the anticipation of lost social integration upon retirement (that is, a general fear of losing work relationships and being lonely after retirement) was positively related to the intention to take part-time retirement and job mobility. Research is needed on job characteristics that take career experiences into account along with work–life issues. Various aspects of work, such as flexible work schedules, job control, autonomy and social support, can help to craft the required balance between professional and personal life, considering the age of the worker. Jobs might be redesigned to enable older workers to choose a working pattern that suits their aspirations and life needs.

CONCLUSION

Recent demographic changes are heavily influencing workforce composition, forcing developed countries to deal with the sustainability of retirement systems. Reduced birth rates, the economic crisis, and the increased life expectancy are challenging older people to be more flexible in terms of postponing their retirement. Moreover, career paths have changed dramatically over recent decades, and individuals have to take responsibility for the nature and course of their careers. Late-career workers need to take charge of their own career paths: on the one hand, they need to define success for themselves, while on the other they need to have many more career-related options provided by the environment/employers.

There are numerous processes which can lead individuals to efficient and satisfying adjustment to life-long, aging-related changes. There are different factors which can promote or discourage successful aging at work, thus affecting positively or negatively middle- and late-career workers. However, there is little empirical and theoretical work on the career issues faced by workers in their late career stages and the factors that affect late career outcomes and success. With the aging of the workforce, we need a deeper understanding of the aspects that affect older worker careers. In this chapter, we illustrate the role that job characteristics can play in middle- and late-career workers, and the importance of empirical research in this field. Age-diverse job design interventions can become an important approach for creating more sustainable late careers.

REFERENCES

Adams, G.A. and Beehr, T.A. (1998). Turnover and retirement: A comparison of their similarities and differences. *Personnel Psychology*, 51, 643–65.

Alcover, C.M., Topa, G., Perry, E., Fraccaroli, F. and Depolo, M. (forthcoming). *Bridge Employment: A Research Handbook*. London: Routledge.

Armstrong-Stassen, M., Schlosser, F. and Zinni, D. (2012). Seeking resources: Predicting retirees' return to their workplace. *Journal of Managerial Psychology*, 27, 615–35.

Arnold, J. (1997). *Managing Careers into the 21st Century*. London: Paul Chapman Publishing.
Arthur, M.B. and Rousseau, D.M. (1996). *The Boundaryless Career. A New Employment Principle for a New Organizational Era*. New York: Oxford University Press.
Arthur, M.B., Hall, D.T. and Lawrence, B.S. (1989). *Handbook of Career Theory*. Cambridge: Cambridge University Press.
Baltes, P.B. and Baltes, M.M. (1990). Psychological perspectives on successful aging: The model of selective optimization with compensation. In P.B. Baltes and M.M. Baltes (eds), *Successful Aging: Perspectives from the Behavioral Sciences* (pp. 1–34). New York: Cambridge University Press.
Beck, V. (2013). Employers' use of older workers in the recession. *Employee Relations*, 35, 257–71.
Böhm, S.A., Kunze, F. and Bruch, H. (forthcoming). Spotlight on age-diversity climate: The impact of age-inclusive HR practices on firm-level outcomes. *Personnel Psychology*.
Carstensen, L.L. (1991). Selectivity theory: Social activity in life-span context. In K.W. Schaie (ed.), *Annual Review of Gerontology and Geriatrics* (Vol. 11, pp. 195–217). New York: Springer.
Carstensen, L.L., Isaacowitz, D.M. and Charles, S.T. (1999). Taking time seriously: A theory of socioemotional selectivity. *American Psychologist*, 54, 165–81.
Egan, M., Bambra, C., Petticrew, M. and Whitehead, M. (2009). Reviewing evidence on complex social interventions: Appraising implementation in systematic reviews of the health effects of organisational-level workplace interventions. *Journal of Epidemiology and Community Health*, 63, 4–11.
Engelhardt, H. (2012). Late careers in Europe: Effects of individual and institutional factors. *European Sociological Review*, 28, 550–63.
Eurofound (2012). *Income from Work after Retirement in the EU*. Luxembourg: Publications Office of the European Union.
Ganzeboom, H.B.G. and Treiman, D.J. (1996). Internationally comparable measures of occupational status for the 1988 International Standard Classification of Occupations. *Social Science Research*, 25, 201–39.
Griffin, B. and Hesketh, B. (2008). Post-retirement work: The individual determinants of paid and volunteer work. *Journal of Occupational and Organizational Psychology*, 81, 101–21.
Hall, D.T. (1996). Protean careers of the 21st century. *The Academy of Management Executive*, 10, 8–16.
Hall, D.T. (2002). *Careers In and Out of Organizations*. Thousand Oaks, CA: Sage.
Hall, D.T. (2004). The protean career: A quarter-century journey. *Journal of Vocational Behavior*, 65, 1–13.
Hall, D.T. and Las Heras, M. (2010). Reintegrating job design and career theory: Creating not just good jobs but smart jobs. *Journal of Organizational Behavior*, 31, 448–62.
Hedge, J.W. and Borman, W.C. (2012). *The Oxford Handbook of Work and Aging*. New York: Oxford University Press.
Hertel, G., Thielgen, M., Rauschenbach, C., Grube, A., Stamov-Roßnagel, C. and Krumm, C. (2013). Age differences in motivation and stress at work. In C. Schlick, E. Frieling and J. Wegge (eds), *Age-Differentiated Work Systems* (pp. 119–47). Berlin: Springer.
Hobfoll, S.E. (1989). Conservation of resources: A new attempt at conceptualizing stress. *American Psychologist*, 44, 513–24.
Ilmarinen, J. (2012). Promoting active ageing in the workplace. European Agency for Safety and Health at Work. Available at: http://www.ipbscordoba.es/uploads/Documentos/promoting-active-ageing-in-the-workplace.pdf.
Judge, T.A. and Hurst, C. (2008). How the rich (and happy) get richer (and happier): Relationship of core self-evaluations to trajectories in attaining work success. *Journal of Applied Psychology*, 93, 849–63.
Kanfer, R. and Ackerman, P.L. (2004). Aging, adult development, and work motivation. *Academy of Management Review*, 29, 440–58.
Khapova, S.N., Vinkenburg, C.J. and Arnold, J. (2009). Careers research in Europe: Identity and contribution. *Journal of Occupational and Organizational Psychology*, 82, 709–19.
Kim, N. and Hall, D.T. (2013). Protean career model and retirement. In M. Wang (ed.), *The Oxford Handbook of Retirement* (pp. 102–16). New York: Oxford University Press.
Lee, M.D., Kossek, E.E., Hall, D.T. and Litrico, J.-B. (2011). Entangled strands: A process perspective on the evolution of careers in the context of personal, family, work, and community life. *Human Relations*, 64, 1531–53.
Lent, R.W., Brown, S.D. and Hackett, G. (1994). Toward a unifying social cognitive theory of career and academic interest, choice, and performance. *Journal of Vocational Behavior*, 45, 79–122.
Lichtenstein, B.M.B. and Mendenhall, M. (2002). Non-linearity and response-ability: Emergent order in 21st century careers. *Human Relations*, 55, 5–32.
Morgeson, F.P. and Campion, M.A. (2003). Work design. In W.C. Borman, D.R. Ilgen and R.J. Klimoski (eds), *Handbook of Psychology: Industrial and Organizational Psychology* (Vol. 12, pp. 423–52). Hoboken, NJ: John Wiley & Sons.
Morgeson, F.P. and Humphrey, S.E. (2006). The Work Design Questionnaire (WDQ): Developing and

validating a comprehensive measure for assessing job design and the nature of work. *Journal of Applied Psychology*, 91, 1321–39.
Ng, T.W.H. and Feldman, D.C. (2010). Human capital and objective indicators of career success: The mediating effects of cognitive ability and conscientiousness. *Journal of Occupational and Organizational Psychology*, 83, 207–35.
Nielsen, K., Taris, T.W. and Cox, T. (2010). The future of organizational interventions: Addressing the challenges of today's organizations. *Work & Stress*, 24, 219–33.
O'Reilly, C. and Chatman, J.A. (1994). Working smarter and harder: A longitudinal study of managerial success. *Administrative Science Quarterly*, 39, 603–27.
Robroek, S.J.W., Schuring, M., Croezen, S., Stattin, M. and Burdorf, A. (2013). Poor health, unhealthy behaviors, and unfavorable work characteristics influence pathways of exit from paid employment among older workers in Europe: A four year follow-up study. *Scandinavian Journal of Work, Environment, and Health*, 39, 125–33.
Sanders, M.J. and McCready, J.W. (2010). Does work contribute to successful aging outcomes in older workers? *The International Journal of Aging and Human Development*, 71, 209–29.
Schein, E.H. (1978). *Career Dynamics: Matching Individual and Organizational Needs*. Reading, MA: Addison-Wesley.
Shultz, K.S. and Adams, G.A. (2007). *Aging and Work in the 21st Century*. Mahwah, NJ: Lawrence Erlbaum Associates Publishers.
Super, D.E. (1957). *The Psychology of Careers*. New York: Harper & Row.
Super, D.E. (1980). A life-span, life-space approach to career development. *Journal of Vocational Behavior*, 16, 282–98.
Tims, M., Bakker, A.B. and Derks, D. (2012). Development and validation of the job crafting scale. *Journal of Vocational Behavior*, 80, 173–86.
Truxillo, D.M., Cadiz, D.A. and Rineer, J.R. (2012a). Designing jobs for an aging workforce: An opportunity for occupational health. In J. Houdmont, S. Leka and R.R. Sinclair (eds), *Contemporary Occupational Health Psychology: Global Perspectives on Research and Practice, Volume 2* (pp. 109–25). Oxford: Oxford University Press.
Truxillo, D.M., Cadiz, D.M., Rineer, J.R., Zaniboni, S. and Fraccaroli, F. (2012b). A lifespan perspective on job design: Fitting the worker to the job to promote job satisfaction, engagement, and performance. *Organizational Psychology Review*, 2, 340–60.
Van Der Heijde, C.M. and Van Der Heijden, B.I.J.M. (2006). A competence-based and multidimensional operationalization and measurement of employability. *Human Resource Management*, 45, 449–76.
Vaupel, J.W. (2010). Biodemography of human ageing. *Nature*, 464, 536–42.
Walker, A. and Maltby, T. (2012). Active ageing: A strategic policy solution to demographic ageing in the European Union. *International Journal of Social Welfare*, 21, 117–30.
Wang, M., Olson, D.A. and Schultz, K.S. (2013). *Mid and Late Career Issues: An Integrative Perspective*. New York: Routledge Academic Press.
Wang, M., Zhan, Y., Liu, S. and Shultz, K.S. (2008). Antecedents of bridge employment: A longitudinal investigation. *Journal of Applied Psychology*, 93, 818–30.
Wheaton, F. and Crimmins, E.M. (2013). The demography of aging and retirement. In M. Wang (ed.), *The Oxford Handbook of Retirement* (pp. 22–41). New York: Oxford University Press.
WHO (2002). *Active Ageing. A Policy Framework*. Geneva: World Health Organization.
Wöhrmann, A.M., Deller, J. and Wang, M. (2013). Outcome expectations and work design characteristics in post-retirement work planning. *Journal of Vocational Behavior*, 83, 219–28.
Wrzesniewski, A. and Dutton, J.E. (2001). Crafting a job: Revisioning employees as active crafters of their work. *Academy of Management Review*, 26, 179–201.
Zacher, H. and Frese, M. (2009). Remaining time and opportunities at work: Relationships between age, work characteristics, and occupational future time perspective. *Psychology and Aging*, 24, 487–93.
Zacher, H. and Frese, M. (2011). Maintaining a focus on opportunities at work: The interplay between age, job complexity, and the use of selection, optimization, and compensation strategies. *Journal of Organizational Behavior*, 32, 291–318.
Zacher, H., Heusner, S., Schmitz, M., Zwierzanska, M.M. and Frese, M. (2010). Focus on opportunities as a mediator of the relationships between age, job complexity, and work performance. *Journal of Vocational Behavior*, 76, 374–86.
Zaniboni, S., Sarchielli, G. and Fraccaroli, F. (2010). How are psychosocial factors related to retirement intentions? *International Journal of Manpower*, 31, 271–85.
Zaniboni, S., Truxillo, D.M. and Fraccaroli, F. (2013). Differential effects of task variety and skill variety on burnout and turnover intentions for older and younger workers. *European Journal of Work and Organizational Psychology*, 22, 306–17.

Zaniboni, S., Truxillo, D.M., Fraccaroli, F., McCune, E. and Bertolino, M. (forthcoming). Who benefits from more tasks? Older versus younger workers. *Journal of Managerial Psychology*.
Zappalà, S., Depolo, M., Fraccaroli, F., Guglielmi, D. and Sarchielli, G. (2008). Postponing job retirement? Psychosocial influences on the preference for early or late retirement. *The Career Development International*, 13, 150–67.

19 Sustainability in the second half of the career

René Schalk, Marloes L. Van Engen and Dorien Kooij

Because of demographic workforce changes, the relative number of employees in the second half of their career (that is, from mid-career to retirement) will grow substantially in the near future. Therefore, sustainability or maintaining health, performance, motivation and well-being (Van Engen et al., 2012) in the second career half is an important topic for employees and for employers as well. In this chapter, we present an overview of issues associated with sustainability in the second career half for women and men. We provide suggestions for how to improve sustainability in the second career half for employees, employers and governments.

Most industrialized nations face a substantial aging of the working population. In 2013, 38 percent of the population in the European Union were 50 and older (Eurostat, 2014). It is estimated that this percentage will increase considerably in the future. Many older people (in the second half of their career) are employed, and the employment rate in this group has steadily increased over time. In the EU, 50 percent of people in the 55 to 59 age group were employed in 2000. This percentage increased to 61 percent in 2010. The same trend is observed among people aged 60 to 64 years: 23 percent were employed in 2000, and 31 percent in 2010. It is interesting to note that the growth in the labor market participation of people aged 50 and older is higher for women (Otten et al., 2010). Due to changing demographics, it is less acceptable that older workers leave the workforce at their own discretion before the official retirement age. Workers are confronted with a rising retirement age, and organizations feel a stronger need to hold on to their older workers.

In recent years, a growing number of studies have examined the effects of the aging of the workforce on health, performance, motivation and well-being, as well as the role of stereotyping of older workers in this respect (see for an overview Schalk et al., 2010; Kanfer and Ackerman, 2004; Posthuma and Campion, 2009). In the next section, we provide a concise overview of the changes that play a role in the second half of the career. After that we focus on gender differences. Since workers in the second career half also experience changes in the way they perceive themselves and in the way they are perceived, we discuss how stereotypes and meta-perceptions of older workers in general, and older working women in particular, affect experiences at work. We then address the person–organization interaction. We will describe typical career patterns, and the role of both older workers themselves and organizations in dealing with issues in the second career half. Finally, in our concluding section, we discuss possible ways to improve sustainability in the second career half.

HEALTH, PERFORMANCE, MOTIVATION AND WELL-BEING IN THE SECOND HALF OF THE CAREER

The link between age and health has been studied in many ways. Since it is impossible to give a short, comprehensive review of studies, we discuss some exemplary issues here. Health refers to the physical state as well as to mental and cognitive abilities. Physical work capacity (Ilmarinen, 2006) and information processing (Salthouse, 1996; Verhaegen and Salthouse, 1997) decrease with age. The general trend is more health problems with age. However, it is less important to assess *whether* there are changes than to identify *how* these changes have effects on performance.

The relationship between age and performance is complex. Performance is an umbrella construct covering many different forms (Sonnentag and Frese, 2002). A considerable body of literature is available on the relation between age and individual performance. Schalk et al. (2010) noted that reviews of psychological studies on the relationship between overall job performance and age found mixed or contradictory results. On the one hand, this is due to the fact that individual differences become larger in the second career half. On the other hand, this is due to the fact that age-related changes can be negative and positive at the same time. Whereas physical work capacity (Ilmarinen, 2006) as well as information processing decrease with age, work experience, wisdom and more complex mental capacities improve with age. Work experience plays a large role in compensating for diminishing capacities (Ilmarinen, 2006; Spirduso, 1995). In line with this reasoning, Ng and Feldman (2008) found that task performance is unrelated to age, but that citizenship performance increased and counterproductive performance decreased with age.

Salthouse (2012) discusses the consequences of age-related differences in cognitive abilities. He states that although many cognitive abilities are found to be associated with work performance in laboratory studies, field studies seldom find lower levels of real-world performance at work among older workers. This means that although abilities declined with age, this did not impact job performance. Although employees in the second career half are more likely to experience health problems, it is important to put this into perspective. Differences are not large, and the potential negative impact of health differences on work performance is in most cases compensated by other factors (Salthouse, 2012).

With respect to well-being, several meta-analytic overviews of the literature have been published on the relationship between age and work-related attitudes, encompassing hundreds of articles (for example, Ng and Feldman, 2010). These articles concluded that age had a significant, however not strong, relationship with work-related attitudes. The size of the relationships depended on the specific attitude that is concerned. Job involvement and organizational commitment generally increased with age, although the effect was small (Ng and Feldman, 2010). Regarding the less studied concepts of reliability, loyalty and proactivity, a positive effect of age was found (Bertolino et al., 2011; Ng and Feldman, 2010; 2013; Posthuma and Campion, 2009; Thomas et al., 2010).

With respect to work motivation, it was found that this changes over time (Barnes-Farrell and Matthews, 2007; De Lange et al., 2010; Finegold et al., 2002; Smola and Sutton, 2002; Kanfer and Ackerman, 2004). Workers in the second half of their career are likely to have different work-related goals and motives than workers in the first half of their career. These changes result from changes in age-related factors, such as physical and cognitive abilities, perceptions of time, and career stage. As proposed by lifespan theories, such as the Selection Optimization and Compensation (SOC) model (Baltes and Baltes, 1990) and Socioemotional Selectivity Theory (SST; Carstensen, 1995), life goals change as people age. Because older people have to deal with losses in physical abilities and shorter perceptions of time, for example, their goal focus will shift away from growth and knowledge acquisition towards maintenance, regulation of losses, and more affective goals, such as generativity and social embeddedness.

These shifting goals have important implications for work motives. Kooij et al. (2011) conducted a meta-analysis of 86 studies and found that work-related growth and extrinsic motives decreased and that intrinsic motives increased with age (see also Ng and Feldman, 2010). More specifically, they found that motives related to development, advancement, working with people, getting recognition and compensation decreased, and that motives related to accomplishment, use of skills, autonomy, helping people or contributing to society, and job security increased with age.

Further, since lifespan theories propose that age-related changes, in physical abilities, for example, explain why work-related motives change with age, Kooij et al. (2013) examined the mediating role of self-perceived health and future time perspective in the relationship of age with security, esteem, generativity and growth work motives. In line with lifespan theories, they demonstrated in two Dutch samples that the relationships of age with work-related growth, esteem and security motivations were mediated by an open-ended future time perspective and a good subjective general health. The association between age and generativity motivations was not mediated by a limited future time perspective.

GENDER AND THE SECOND CAREER HALF

Although in general men and women experience similar changes in performance, health, motivation and well-being, women face additional challenges. First, women go through the menopause in the second half of their career, which affects their health (Goldman, 2010). Second, women in present-day society might face additional demands because of care responsibilities for children and the elderly, which might lead to work–family conflict (Riley and Bowen, 2005). In addition, there are differences in how motivation changes with age between men and women (Kooij et al., 2013).

Although the working life of both women and men in the second half of their career is affected by hormonal changes, this is particularly the case for women going through the menopause transition. The menopause starts between the ages of 48 and 58 (Goldman, 2010), and can have a length of more than ten years (Dennerstein, 1996). Hot flushes, tiredness, mood swings, aches and pains, night sweats that lead to insomnia, urinary frequency, menstrual irregularities, irregular heartbeats, headaches, depression and anxiety, lack of energy, difficulties in concentrating, and dizzy spells are frequently reported as being part of the menopause (Goldman, 2010; Matthews and Bromberger, 2005; Soares and Taylor, 2007; Utian et al., 2002).

These complaints influence the well-being of women in the workplace and therefore the retention and performance of women in this life phase. Several studies confirmed that women who experience hot flushes on a regular basis have a lower general well-being and lower quality of life (Kronenberg, 1994; Oldenhave et al., 1993; Utian et al., 2002). Hot flushes can cause physical discomfort, disturbed sleep, fatigue, irritability and depression (Kronenberg, 1994; Oldenhave et al., 1993). Sleep problems, or difficulties with falling asleep can result in daytime sleepiness, cognitive difficulties, poor job performance, higher risk of depression, and a low overall quality of life (Kronenberg, 1994; Matthews and Bromberger, 2005). It is highly likely that these complaints affect the working life of women undergoing the menopause, yet research on how the menopause affects women at work is still scarce. In a pilot project collecting data among 428 working women in the Netherlands of 40 years and older (see Van Engen et al., 2011), Van Ginneken (2011) found that women who reported more menopausal complaints also had a higher need for recovery from work, which in turn affected their occupational well-being. Of the several menopausal complaints that were measured (depression, sleeping, vasomotor and somatic complaints) it was menopausal depression that was the strongest predictor of decreased occupational well-being. This pilot study found that menopausal complaints were predictive for burnout (Peeters, 2011; Smeur, 2011) and decreased engagement (Strijbosch, 2011). Smeur (2011) reported that social support of colleagues and the supervisor buffered the relationship between menopausal complaints and burnout. Other studies too found that demands and resources at work affected the influence of menopause at work. In a study among Egyptian teaching staff (Hammam et al., 2012) it was found that a poor working environment functions as a source of work stress, and this was aggravated by menopausal complaints. Further, in a large-scale study in the UK among 896 working women aged 45–55 in white collar jobs in 10 organizations, Griffiths et al. (2013) found that women going through the menopausal transition indicated that their work performance had been negatively affected as a result of concentration and memory loss, tiredness, feeling depressed and lowered confidence. This study also revealed that the majority of women did not disclose menopause-related health problems to their line managers, and that organizational-level support was absent.

Another gender-related issue is work–family conflict. Work–family conflict is often associated with gender and younger age. Work conflict research has been mainly focused on the problems that young parents experience when they combine work and family roles. Because of demographic developments, and the higher life expectancies of elderly people, however, employees in the second half of the career are more often confronted with having to take care of family responsibilities. They not only have to support and care for their own children, but more often they also have to fulfill obligations in the care for their elderly relatives. Therefore, they are increasingly confronted with being in a 'sandwich' position (Riley and Bowen, 2005), which is likely to lead to work–family conflicts.

Recently, Huffman et al. (2013) published a study on two substantial samples (more than 6000 employees in total), in which they examined the occurrence of work–family conflicts at different ages. The results 'supported a curvilinear relationship, with youngest and oldest workers having the fewest conflicting demands between work and home' (Huffman et al., 2013, p. 761). In the 65–70 age group, work–family conflict was lowest, whereas it was highest among workers in age category 45–55 years. This study did not report on gender differences, however. Although women take the larger share of care responsibilities, both for children and in the care for the elderly, meta-analyses found that in samples with more men the instance of work–family conflict was higher (Michel et al., 2011). This finding is perhaps counterintuitive considering women's larger share in care responsibilities but may be explained by the fact that men usually work in less family-friendly sectors compared to women. Also, the type of work–family conflict matters. In a meta-analysis by Byron (2005), it was found that men had slightly more work-to-family conflict, whereas women had slightly more family-to-work conflict, although the differences between men and women were small.

Regarding motivation, in their study on the relationships of age with work-related growth, esteem and security motivations Kooij et al. (2013) found interesting gender differences. One of their samples consisted mainly of women workers (89 percent). The results for this sample differed from the other sample in which gender was evenly distributed (that is, 52 percent female workers). More specifically, among the health care workers who were mostly women, age was not related to health, and health was not related to growth motives. One reason for this, as mentioned by Kooij et al. (2013), is that health care workers have more psychologically and physically demanding jobs. Therefore, biological constraints might be due to job position and not age, and health care workers experiencing a deterioration in their subjective health try to advance to higher and physically less demanding job positions, which might offset the tendency to reduce resource allocation towards growth motivations. Another reason, however, might be that female workers have already learned to deal with losses (for example, in time and energy), because they have the largest share in care responsibilities, and hence they can deal with losses, in subjective health, for example, without reducing their resource allocation towards growth motives. Baltes and Heydens-Gahir (2003) found, in their predominantly female sample, that use of SOC strategies results in lower job and family stressors and subsequently lower work–family and family–work conflict. Thus, selecting fewer goals, modeling successful others, or using external aids help in dealing with work–family conflict. Since these strategies are also used to age successfully (Abraham and Hansson, 1995), women workers might age more successfully at work and have enough resources to allocate also to growth. Moreover, Young et al. (2007) found that engaging in SOC strategies was particularly helpful for workers in the most demanding situations, such as workers in their mid-life and workers having younger children working at home.

THE INFLUENCE OF STEREOTYPES

With respect to stereotypes about older working men and women, as early as 1952 Tuckman and Lorge reported that:

> It is claimed that older workers are slow, increase production costs, have a higher accident rate, are a poor investment, resent younger supervisors, resist new procedures and work methods, have a higher rate of absenteeism, are hard to get along with, etc. There is very little evidence to justify these complaints (p. 149).

Stereotypes for older workers seem to be long-lasting. More recently, Posthuma and Campion (2009) stated that there are six main categories of older worker stereotypes, which are: low performing; resistant to change; less able to learn; close to retirement and thus not worth the investment; more costly; and more dependent. All these stereotypes are related to lower competence.

Stereotypes of social groups can lead to two kinds of discrimination at work, namely description-based bias and prescription-based bias. Description-based bias refers to discrimination of stereotyped groups in, for instance, hiring, selection and promotion decisions. Decision-makers base their judgments on stereotypes and not individuating information (for instance, by overlooking older workers for IT jobs from the stereotypical view that older workers do not keep up with IT developments). Prescription-based bias refers to rejection of individuals of stereotyped groups when members of these individuals do not adhere to stereotypical expectations, for instance, when women behave in a firm and assertive manner (Heilman, 2012). These description- and prescription-based biases might lead to self-categorization and thus to negative effects. The more workers over 45+ self-categorized as 'older workers', the more they were willing to retire early and tended to disengage themselves from the work domain (Desmette and Gaillard, 2008).

Older working women are not only confronted with stereotypes of older workers, but also with stereotypes about women that do not fit with ideas of the ideal worker. The stereotype of women is that of being warm and caring, but incompetent. The stereotype of men is competent, but not warm (Fiske et al., 2002). Gender stereotypes give rise to biased judgments and decisions that impede women's advancement in the workplace (Heilman, 2012). Rudman and Phelan (2008) concluded in an overview that gender stereotypes led to workplace discrimination in many respects, such as hiring and selection decisions, negotiation outcomes, compensation and benefits and first and foremost career progression. Agars (2004) argued that there is a cumulative effect of stereotypes that hamper women's progress. Although a small bias in, for instance, hiring decisions for a job may not seem consequential, a number of such tiny biases in multiple decisions of hiring and promotion over the course of a life add up and have substantial consequences, not only in personnel decisions, but also in allocating resources and rewards that play a role in career progression.

Stereotypes thus hamper career progression, yet, interestingly, research suggested that these stereotypes are far from accurate. Roth et al. (2012), in a meta-analysis of gender differences in job performance, noted that in contrast to the stereotypical view, women generally performed slightly better than men. However, although job performance ratings favored women, ratings of promotion potential were higher for males. With respect to stereotypes for older workers, Ng and Feldman (2012) found that the only negative stereotype for older workers for which some support was found was a lower willingness to engage in training and development.

In summary, societal expectations about the typical characteristics of older people, women and men, influence how people see themselves, what they expect of others and how people evaluate others. Together, these processes hamper the development of individuals and organizations alike. Thus, organizations are wise to make policies, practices and particularly the organizational culture sensitive to bias stemming from stereotypes.

CAREER PATTERNS AND THE ROLE OF ORGANIZATIONS AND OLDER WORKERS

From an organizational perspective, employees are dynamic resources. Employees enter and leave the organization. During the time they are employed with an organization, employees can switch jobs, tasks, workplace, and/or working times. These shifts may be associated with climbing up the career ladder (promotion), making lateral moves on the same level, or with a demotion (lower-level job). From an employee perspective, a career is a sequence of work-related periods with upward or downward moves, as well as lateral changes (Arnold, 2001). A traditional career refers to long-term employment in one firm (Eby et al., 2003). This type of career can display many forms: upward, at the same level, or downward. With respect to the second half of the career, stagnation (plateauing), and demotion occur more often compared to earlier career phases.

Note that the traditional career is only one of many career forms. In a panel study on German data spanning 20 years, Biemann et al. (2012) applied optimal matching analysis to discover typical career patterns. Their data showed seven career patterns which were labeled: stable (traditional) career; full-time self-employed career; a full-time employment career with more cross-organizational mobility; a career marked by a switch from full-time to part-time work; a career composed of some periods of self-employment; a career largely composed of part-time employment; and a fragmented career. Biemann et al. (2012) noted that there was a shift away from traditional career trajectories, interestingly, especially for women.

The diversity in career patterns is probably associated with shifts in priorities among employees in the second half of the career. Levinson et al. (1978) and Levinson (1986) provided a typology of stages in male adult development which illustrate typical changes that occur in the second half of the career. Levinson conceived of the adult life course as a sequence of structure-building periods and structure-changing periods (or transitions). After each structure-building period, there is a period of transition to a next structure-building period. Much of the structure of the previous phase is then abolished. The person's views of self and the world are reexamined, and choices are made, creating a new life structure. The phases discerned by Levinson and relevant for the second half of the career are: (a) Mid-life transition 40–45; (b) Entry structure for middle adulthood 45–50; (c) Age 50 transition 50–55; (d) Culminating life structure for middle adulthood 55–60; (e) Late adult transition 60–65.

Similarly (see also Ornstein et al., 1989), Super (1957) proposed that employees pass through three stages with different goals in their career before they start detaching from work. In the late 'maintenance stage', employees have a great concern for peer and professional relationships (for example, helping others and mentoring) and involvement in organization decision-making. Employees in this stage will seek greater opportunities for involvement, more meaningful assignments, and more interesting jobs. Freese and Schalk (1995) indeed found that employees in the second half of the career attached a different value to having a career and to the sacrifices they had to make to reach their goals in their social lives. Work pleasure, self-actualization, social recognition, and being able to use creative sources seemed to be more important for employees in later career stages.

Women appear to have a different career of development as well as different correlates of development (Gallos, 1989). The central issues for women with respect to growth and career are that they are based on interdependence and relationships. According to Bardwick (1980), at age 40–50, the mid-life transition and middle adulthood, women feel more secure and settled in their relationship and are moving toward more autonomy. This is in line with the Kaleidoscope Model (Mainiero and Sullivan, 2005), which suggests that authenticity, balance and challenge predominate at different points in the lifespan for women. According to Sullivan and Mainiero (2008), in the late career the desire for authenticity plays a key role among women. Challenge was found to be still of interest, but women created their own challenges and their own terms.

Men become more sensitive to interpersonal relationships and to their internal psychological needs (comparable to authenticity) as career and task demands diminish. Both genders move toward a greater balance of autonomy and interdependence (Sekaran and Hall, 1989).

Organizations play an important role in shaping the careers of their workers, for example, by offering HR practices such as internal promotion and training. However, motives and abilities change with age and over people's career (Kooij et al., 2008; Kooij et al., 2011). In addition, universal or mainstream HR practices are particularly aimed at employees in the first career half, and might therefore not be suitable for workers in the second half of their career (for example, Armstrong-Stassen and Schlosser, 2011; Bal et al., 2013). Kooij and Boon (2013) found indeed that high performance HR practices particularly led to person–organization fit among employees in their mid-career stage. Similarly, Conway (2004) found that different HR practices were related to organization commitment in different career stages. Fair rewards, opportunities for involvement and training aimed at increasing employability were associated with organizational commitment in late career, but not in early (except opportunities for involvement) and mid-career.

Kooij et al. (2010) also found that the association between HR practices and work-related attitudes changed with age. They distinguished two types of HR practices, that is, development HR practices (HR practices related to advancement, growth and accomplishment that help individual workers to achieve higher levels of functioning, such as promotion) and maintenance HR practices (HR practices related to protection, safety and responsibility that help individual workers to maintain their current levels of functioning in the face of new challenges, such as flexible work schedules). They found that development HR practices were less strongly, and that maintenance HR practices were more strongly, related to affective commitment in old age. Armstrong-Stassen and Ursel (2009), on the other hand, found that development HR practices tailored to the needs of older workers did have a positive influence on their motivation to continue working, via perceived organizational support. Kooij et al. (2014) argued and found with a mixed methods study that HR practices for older workers could be categorized in four HR bundles, based on the four goals of successful lifespan development as described by SOC theory (Baltes et al., 1999): (1) development HR practices, such as promotion, help individual workers to reach higher levels of functioning; (2) maintenance HR practices, such as flexible work schedules, help individual workers to maintain their current levels of functioning in the face of new challenges; (3) utilization HR practices, such as participation in decision-making, help individual workers to recover to previous levels of functioning after a loss; and (4) accommodative HR practices, such as additional leave, help individual workers to function adequately at lower levels when maintenance or recovery is no longer possible.

In line with lifespan and career theories, earlier research found that development HR practices (for example, promotion) were less important and that maintenance (for example, flexible work schedules) and utilization (for example, opportunities for involvement) were more important for older worker commitment (Conway, 2004; Kooij et al., 2010). In addition, Kooij (2010) demonstrated that the association between accommodative HR practices and affective commitment strengthened with age among male workers but not among female workers. Hence, it seems that female workers in the second career half do not need accommodative HR practices. This finding again suggests that female workers are better capable of dealing with losses in resources that are part of the aging process, and are thus more likely to age successfully at work.

In addition to managing and motivating employees in their second career half, organizations can use HR practices to stimulate an active role for employees in the pursuit of their own career. One way through which employees can influence their career pattern is by being ready to change. A performance aspect that is of increasing importance in the context of the ever-changing world of work and organizations is the way workers can deal flexibly with change (Sonnentag and Frese, 2002). This also relates to the employability of the worker (Van Dam, 2004; Van der Heijde and Van der Heijden, 2006). With aging, the opportunities for development offered by organizations diminish (Birdi et al., 1997). In addition, older workers' preparedness to develop might be lower than in younger employees (Warr and Fay, 2001). These situational and personal factors result in less flexibility and employability among older workers (Maurer et al., 2003; Van Dam, 2004). At the same time, flexibility and employability are more important for employees in their second career half, because of experience concentration and career plateauing (for example, Thijssen et al., 2013). Therefore, organizations should aim at increasing this readiness for change among their employees.

Career patterns can also be influenced by job crafting. Job crafting is a specific form of proactive work behavior defined as the self-initiated changes individuals make in the task or relational boundaries of their work aimed at improving person–job fit (Tims et al., 2012; Wrzesniewski and Dutton, 2001). Wrzesniewski and Dutton (2001) proposed three forms of job crafting: altering the view of the job; altering the type or number of tasks; and altering the number or nature of interactions with others. Task boundaries are changed when employees alter the type, number, content or scope of tasks that they carry out, relational boundaries are changed when employees alter the range, nature, or number of their interactions at work (for example, talking more with colleagues who are helpful and inspiring), and cognitive boundaries are adapted when employees alter their views on work. For example, employees can view work as a set of discrete tasks or as a whole piece. Recent studies have further specified these forms of job crafting (for example, Tims et al., 2012) and proposed that job crafting entails increasing one's job resources and challenging job demands, and decreasing one's hindering job demands when necessary or desirable.

Although research on job crafting is in its infancy, studies indicated that job crafting was positively associated with work engagement and job performance at the individual level (Petrou et al., 2012; Tims et al., 2012; 2013) and at the team level (Leana et al., 2009; Tims et al., 2013). In addition, job crafting was positively associated with employability

(Tims et al., 2012). Workers who craft their job were better able to continuously fulfill, acquire or create work, that is, to stay employable (Van der Heijde and Van der Heijden, 2006). Older workers can thus influence their career by, for example, adding tasks they find enjoyable, expanding their job to include additional responsibilities or by establishing more frequent or closer ties with members of certain occupational groups. These self-initiated changes of the job are likely to influence the career patterns of the job crafter.

Organizations could stimulate workers in the second half of their career to take initiative, for example, through implementing High Involvement Management (HIM). HIM refers to HRM that encourages greater proactivity, flexibility and collaboration among workers (Wood et al., 2012). HIM thus includes practices such as extensive training, teamwork, decentralized decision making, information sharing, flexible job descriptions, career development, participation in decision-making, feedback, and job rotation (Vandenberg et al., 1999; Wood et al., 2012). Earlier studies indeed demonstrated that these types of HR practices resulted in psychological empowerment (for example, self-efficacy and self-determination; Messersmith et al., 2011), which in turn could lead to proactive behaviors at work, such as job crafting.

HOW TO PROMOTE SUSTAINABILITY IN THE SECOND HALF OF THE CAREER?

How organizations and governments can improve the sustainability of workers in the second half of their career remains an important issue that needs attention. Interventions that only address current needs may not be aimed at prevention and overlook long-term consequences. From a sustainability perspective, interventions need to address present needs without compromising the ability to meet future needs (McKenzie-More and Oskamp, 1995; Oskamp, 2000). In the context of organizations, this implies that individuals, employers and the government have to take the future performance, health, motivation and well-being of workers into account (Van Engen et al., 2012).

In this section, we develop an agenda for individuals, organizations and governments to work towards sustainable careers. Change towards more sustainability can be envisioned in different life domains: work, health, the interface of work and life, and the community. This is summarized in Figure 19.1.

The Work Domain

The work domain is most closely associated with sustainability in the second half of the career, since the quality of work and the fit between work and individual capabilities are major drivers for sustainability. For individual employees, it is important to try to maintain a good fit between their work and their capabilities. Since motives of employees shift over time, keeping a good fit requires changes in tasks. With respect to job design and mobility of employees, employees themselves can, for example, craft their job to increase its fit with personal interests and capabilities.

Most crucial in this domain is the role of the organization, in other words, the way 'sustainable HR' is implemented. As for other employees, for employees who are in the second half of their career it is important that they are confronted with fair employment

Domains	Levers for Change: Individuals/families	Levers for Change: Organization/Network/HR	Levers for Change: Society/Government
Work	Job content, job crafting Development and learning Career	Job design, training and development Mobility and employability	Facilitating lifelong learning Retirement schemes
Health	Healthy lifestyle Awareness of body	Health promotion (food, fitness, health checks, shift work regulations, ...)	Food, leisure, infrastructure, ...
Work–life	Taking care (children, elderly, dependents) Making a career Taking leisure	⇔ Work–home arrangements Work–home culture Employee time off	⇔ Work time policies Care facilities Leisure facilities (sports and culture)
Community	Being part of a meaningful social network Alignment of values Refraining from stereotyping self and others	Coordination and cooperation mechanisms Corporate social responsibility, ethics, i-deals Fair employment practices Valuing differences Climate for inclusion	Social capital Networking guilds Care-giving guilds Equal treatment legislation Access to fair employment practices Inclusive society

Figure 19.1 *Levers for change towards more sustainability in the second half of the career*

practices, that they feel that differences are valued instead of stereotyped in the company, and that there is a 'climate of inclusion' (Nishii, 2012). In addition, HR practices could take the different motives and different career perspectives of men and women into account. In short, HR practices play an important role in sustainability because, on the one hand, they have a signaling role (Sonnenberg, 2006) that the company is behaving in an ethical way and that the practices are fair, and, on the other hand, they provide opportunities for alignment with personal needs (for example, I-deals; see Rousseau, 2005) and values.

On the societal level, the government can enable sustainability in the career by providing regulations that stimulate companies and employees to behave in ways that promote sustainability, for example, by facilitating the use of training and development programs, as well as regulations that set the boundary conditions for what is acceptable regarding, for example, the quality of work.

Health

Regarding the health domain, employee health is influenced by individual lifestyle and behavior. A healthy lifestyle leads to physical fitness and lower chances of obesity and diseases that can be the outcome of, for example, excessive smoking and drinking.

In HR practices of modern organizations, more attention could be devoted to promoting healthy employee behavior at work and at home. Freese et al. (2013) interviewed HR managers of companies that were listed as best employers in the Netherlands and concluded that promoting employee health was listed often as a much-needed innovative HR practice by these HR managers (Freese et al. 2012; Freese et al. 2013). With respect to specific health problems in the second half of the career, such as the menopause, Griffiths et al. (2013) suggest that there are four ways in which organizational-level support can be provided. That is by creating a greater awareness among managers about the menopause as a possible occupational health issue, by giving access to information and sources of support at work, by implementing flexible working hours, and by regulating workplace temperature and ventilation. The last two practices would fit in the category of practices that are aimed at ensuring or improving health and safety at work. Time and shift schedules as well as HR practices that are aimed at preventing accidents and health hazards are important in this respect.

Societal factors and government regulations play a very important role in this domain. The importance that is attached to facilities for sports as well as the attention paid to food quality, physical fitness, and health and safety at work are important drivers for organizations and individuals to promote and maintain a healthy life style.

Work–Life Domain

In the work–life domain, it is important for individual employees and their families to be able to maintain a balance between work life and private life, and to prevent work–life conflict. Balance in this domain refers to having opportunities both for development at work as well as for leisure and family obligations. Currently, in many countries governments are cutting budgets for care for children as well as care for elderly people. This implies that more employees will have to deal with the question of how to care for their children, parents or other dependents when they are in need of care that is not provided by the government.

The work–life issue is increasingly becoming an important point to consider for organizations. The work–home arrangements companies offer are a potential source of competitive advantage that they can use when they are trying to acquire scarce (human) resources. Organizations should realize that the war for talent does not only apply to younger employees who are at the start of their career. The war for talent will increasingly be fought for by more experienced employees with specialized knowledge who are in the second half of their career. To attract and retain both groups of talent, work–life practices of companies should try to foster a culture that promotes a balance between home and work through policies such as taking time off, including time off for longer periods to provide care for dependents (children, parents), or time off for a sabbatical or unpaid leave period.

As in the work and health domain, the role of government is to provide the opportunities for work–life balance and to implement regulations that set the boundaries or create solutions. Taking care of facilities for sports, culture, child care and elderly care is an important challenge for the government. Regulations for work time policies have to make sure that employees get the opportunity to negotiate appropriate work times with their employers.

Community Domain

The community domain is often neglected as an important determinant of sustainability. Whereas work, health and work–life are often mentioned as factors that exert an important influence on sustainability, the community level seems to be mostly overlooked. In our view, the community level is essential for ensuring sustainability in the second half of the career. The social community network can support sustainability in a broader way than the individual experiences of body, work and family do. Being part of a meaningful social network, being respected and not stereotyped, and experiencing a fit of values are all very important.

Organizations can not only influence the sustainability of their human capital, they also need to take their social capital into account and make sure that their organizational social capital is sustainable. With respect to employees in the second half of their career, it can be said that often these employees are the carriers of the core organizational values and often possess valuable organization-specific specialized knowledge. Through cooperation and coordination mechanisms organizations can create opportunities for exchange, and by doing so increase social capital and knowledge exchange in the company, but also decrease stereotypical ideas.

On the societal level, values are the basics for formal legislation (for example, equal treatment legislation, provision of employee benefits). In addition, the culturally driven opinions and customs that determine the degree of inclusiveness in society, as well as provisions for networking and connecting, are associated with social capital.

CONCLUSION

Sustainability of the second half of the career is of increasing importance because of the aging workforce. This chapter has highlighted specific issues that are prominent in the second career half, such as the differences in motives, career perspectives, the role of stereotypes, and health issues, especially for women. Maintaining a good fit between work and the changing needs of the employee requires an active role on the part of the employee, as well as the availability of HR practices that facilitate this and provide opportunities for differentiation in career wishes and gender-specific preferences, and that counteract the stereotypical but incorrect view that older workers are less productive.

Future research is needed on which policies and practices indeed foster sustainability. Which practices create a climate of inclusion so that the organizational culture is sensitive to bias from stereotypes? Which practices have an impact on career patterns by facilitating the active role of the employee? Moreover, regarding the age–performance relationship, more research is needed on the interplay between positive and negative changes and how compensating mechanisms work.

REFERENCES

Abraham, J.D. and Hansson, R.O. (1995). Successful aging at work: An applied study of selection, optimization, and compensation through impression management. *Journal of Gerontology*, 50, 94–103.

Agars, M.D. (2004). Reconsidering the impact of gender stereotypes on the advancement of women in organizations. *Psychology of Women Quarterly*, 28, 103–11.

Armstrong-Stassen, M. and Ursel, N.D. (2009). Perceived organizational support, career satisfaction, and the retention of older workers. *Journal of Occupational and Organizational Psychology*, 82, 201–20.

Armstrong-Stassen, M. and Schlosser, F. (2011). Perceived organizational membership and the retention of older workers. *Journal of Organizational Behavior*, 32, 319–44.

Arnold, J. (2001). Careers and career management. In: Anderson, N., Sinangil, H.K. and Viswesvaran, C. (eds). *Handbook of Industrial, Work & Organizational Psychology*. Vol. 2 (pp. 115–32). London: Sage.

Bal, P.M., Kooij, D.T.A.M. and De Jong, S.B. (2013). How do developmental and accommodative HRM enhance employee engagement and commitment? The role of psychological contract and SOC-strategies. *Journal of Management Studies*, 50, 545–72.

Baltes, B.B. and Heydens-Gahir, H.H. (2003). Reduction of work–family conflict through the use of selection, optimization, and compensation behaviors. *Journal of Applied Psychology*, 88, 1005–18.

Baltes, P.B. and Baltes, M.M. (1990). Psychological perspectives on successful aging: The model of selective optimization with compensation. In: Baltes, P.B. and Baltes, M.M. (eds). *Successful Aging: Perspectives from the Behavioral Sciences* (pp. 1–34). New York: Cambridge University Press.

Baltes, P.B., Staudinger, U.M. and Lindenberger, U. (1999). Lifespan psychology: Theory and application to intellectual functioning. *Annual Review of Psychology*, 50, 471–507.

Bardwick, J. (1980). The seasons of a woman's life. In: McGuigan, D.G. (ed.). *Women's Lives: New Theory, Research and Policy* (pp. 35–55). Ann Arbor, MI: University of Michigan, Center for Continuing Education of Women.

Barnes-Farrell, J. and Matthews, R. (2007). Age and work attitudes. In: Shultz, K. and Adams, G. (eds). *Aging and Work in the 21st Century* (pp. 139–62). Mahwah, NJ: Lawrence Erlbaum Associates.

Bertolino, M., Truxillo, D.M. and Fraccaroli, F. (2011). Age as moderator of the relationship of proactive personality with training motivation, perceived development from training, and training behavioral intentions. *Journal of Organizational Behavior*, 32, 248–63.

Biemann, T., Zacher, H. and Feldman, D.C. (2012). Career patterns: A twenty-year panel study. *Journal of Vocational Behavior*, 81, 159–70.

Birdi, K., Allan, C. and Warr, P. (1997). Correlates and perceived outcomes of four types of employee development activity. *Journal of Applied Psychology*, 82, 845–57.

Byron, K. (2005). A meta-analytic review of work–family conflict and its antecedents. *Journal of Vocational Behavior*, 67, 169–98.

Carstensen, L.L. (1995). Evidence for a life span theory of socioemotional selectivity. *Current Directions in Psychological Science*, 4, 151–6.

Conway, E. (2004). Relating career stage to attitudes towards HR practices and commitment: Evidence of interaction effects?. *European Journal of Work and Organizational Psychology*, 13, 417– 46.

De Lange, A.H., Van Yperen, N.W., Van der Heijden, B.I.J.M. and Bal, P.M. (2010). Dominant achievement goals of older workers and their relations with motivation-related outcomes. *Journal of Vocational Behavior*, 77, 118–25.

Dennerstein, L. (1996). Well-being, symptoms and the menopausal transition. *Journal of the Climacteric & Postmenopause*, 23 (2), 145–56.

Desmette, D. and Gaillard, M. (2008). When a 'worker' becomes an 'older worker': The effects of age-related social identity on attitudes towards retirement and work. *Career Development International*, 13, 168–85.

Eby, L.T., Butts, M. and Lockwood, E. (2003). Predictors of success in the era of the boundaryless career. *Journal of Organizational Behavior*, 24, 689–708.

Eurostat (2014). Population on 1 January by five years age groups and sex [demo_pjangroup]. Accessed 27 March 2014 at http://epp.eurostat.ec.europa.eu/portal/page/portal/statistics/search_database.

Finegold, D., Mohrman, S. and Spreitzer, G.M. (2002). Age effects on the predictors of technical workers' commitment and willingness to turnover. *Journal of Organizational Behavior*, 23, 655–74.

Fiske, S.T., Cuddy, A.J.C., Glick, P. and Xu, J. (2002). A model of (often mixed) stereotype content: Competence and warmth respectively follow from perceived status and competition. *Journal of Personality and Social Psychology*, 82, 878–902.

Freese, C. and Schalk, R. (1995). Het psychologisch contract en leeftijdsbewust personeelsmanagement. In: Schalk, R. (ed.). *Oudere werknemers in een veranderende wereld*. (pp. 207–23). Utrecht: Lemma.

Freese, C., Paauwe, J. and Schalk, R. (2012). Perceptie van werkgevers en werknemers over de ideale arbeidsrelatie. *Economisch Statistische Berichten*, 97(4647S), 50–55.

Freese, C., Schalk, R. and Paauwe, J. (2013). Flexicurity in organisaties: Innovatieve HR-activiteiten. *Tijdschrift voor HRM*, 4, 53–68.

Gallos, J.V. (1989). Exploring women's development: Implications for career theory, practice, and research. In: Arthur, M.B., Hall, D.T. and Lawrence, B.S. (eds). *Handbook of Career Theory* (pp. 110–32). Cambridge: Cambridge University Press.

Goldman, N. (2010). Managing the menopause in the workplace environment. *Occupational Health*, 62, 13.

Griffiths, A., MacLennan, S.J. and Hassard, J. (2013). Menopause and work: An electronic survey of employees' attitudes in the UK. *Maturitas*, 76, 155–9.

Hammam, R.A., Abbas, R.A. and Hunter, M.S. (2012). Menopause and work: The experience of middle-aged female teaching staff in an Egyptian governmental faculty of medicine. *Maturitas*, 71, 294–300.

Heilman, M.E. (2012). Gender stereotypes and workplace bias. *Research in Organizational Behavior*, 32, 113–35.

Huffman, A., Culbertson, S.S., Henning, J.B. and Goh, A. (2013). Work–family conflict across the lifespan. *Journal of Managerial Psychology*, 28, 761–80.

Ilmarinen, J.E. (2006). Aging workers. *Occupational and Environmental Medicine*, 58, 546–52.

Kanfer, R. and Ackerman, P.L. (2004). Aging, adult development, and work motivation. *Academy of Management Review*, 29, 440–58.

Kooij, D.T.A.M. and Boon, C.T. (2013). HR practices, Person–organization fit, and turnover intentions: The moderating role of career stage. Paper presented at the Academy of Management meeting, Orlando, USA

Kooij, D., De Lange, A., Jansen, P. and Dikkers, J. (2008). Older workers' motivation to continue to work: Five meanings of age. A conceptual review. *Journal of Managerial Psychology*, 23, 364–94.

Kooij, D.T.A.M., De Lange, A.H., Jansen, P.G.W. and Dikkers, J.S.E. (2013). Beyond chronological age. Examining perceived time and subjective health as age-related mediators in relation to occupational well-being. *Work & Stress*, 27, 88–105.

Kooij, D.T.A.M., Jansen, P.G.W., Dikkers, J.S.E. and De Lange, A.H. (2010). The influence of age on the associations between HR practices and both affective commitment and job satisfaction: A meta-analysis. *Journal of Organizational Behavior*, 31, 1111–36.

Kooij, D.T.A.M., Jansen, P.G.W., Dikkers, J.S.E. and De Lange, A.H. (2014). Managing aging workers: A mixed methods study on bundles of HR practices for aging workers. *International Journal of Human Resource Management*, 25, 2192–212.

Kooij, D.T.A.M., De Lange, A.H., Jansen, P.G.W., Kanfer, R. and Dikkers, J.S.E. (2011). Age and work-related motives: Results of a meta-analysis. *Journal of Organizational Behavior*, 32, 197–225.

Kronenberg, F. (1994). Hot flashes: Phenomenology, quality of life, and search for treatment options. *Experimental Gerontology*, 29, 319–36.

Leana, C., Appelbaum, E. and Shevchuk, I. (2009). Work process and quality of care in early childhood education: The role of job crafting. *Academy of Management Journal*, 52, 1169–92.

Levinson, D.J. (1986). A conception of adult development. *American Psychologist*, 41, 3–13.

Levinson, D.J., Darrow, C.N., Klein, E.B., Levinson, M.H. and McKee, B. (1978). *The Seasons of a Man's Life*. New York: Knopf.

Mainiero, L.A. and Sullivan, S.E. (2005). Kaleidoscope careers: An alternate explanation for the 'opt-out' revolution. *Academy of Management Executive*, 19, 106–23.

Matthews, K.A. and Bromberger, J.T. (2005). Does the menopausal transition affect health-related quality of life? *The American Journal of Medicine*, 118 (12B), 25S–36S.

Maurer, T.J., Weiss, E.M. and Barbeitte, F.G. (2003). A model of involvement in work-related learning and development activity: The effects of individual, situational, motivational, and age variables. *Journal of Applied Psychology*, 88, 707–24.

McKenzie-Mohr, D. and Oskamp, S. (1995). Psychology and sustainability: An introduction. *Journal of Social Issues*, 51, 1–14.

Messersmith, J.G., Patel, P.C. and Lepak, D.P. (2011). Unlocking the black box: Exploring the link between High-Performance Work Systems and performance. *Journal of Applied Psychology*, 96, 1105–18.

Michel, J.S., Kotrba, L.M., Mitchelson, J.K., Clark, M.A. and Baltes, B.B. (2011). Antecedents of work–family conflict: A meta-analytic review. *Journal of Organizational Behavior*, 32, 689–725.

Ng, T.W.H. and Feldman, D.C. (2008). The relationship of age to ten dimensions of job performance. *Journal of Applied Psychology*, 93, 392–423.

Ng, T.W.H. and Feldman, D.C. (2010). The relationships of age with job attitudes: A meta-analysis. *Personnel Psychology*, 63, 677–718.

Ng, T.W.H. and Feldman, D.C. (2012). Evaluating six common stereotypes about older workers with meta-analytical data. *Personnel Psychology*, 65, 821–58.

Ng, T.W.H. and Feldman, D.C. (2013). A meta-analysis of the relationships of age and tenure with innovation-related behaviour. *Journal of Occupational and Organizational Psychology*, 86, 585–616.

Nishii, L.H. (2012). The benefits of climate for inclusion for gender diverse groups. *Academy of Management Journal*, 56, 1754–74.
Oldenhave, A., Jaszmann, J.B., Haspels, A.A. and Everaerd, W.T. (1993). Impact of climacteric on well-being. *American Journal of Obstetrics and Gynecology*, 168, 772–80.
Ornstein, S., Cron, W.L. and Slocum, J.W. (1989). Life stage versus career stage: A comparative test of the theories of Levinson and Super. *Journal of Organizational Behavior*, 10, 117–33.
Oskamp, S. (2000). A sustainable future for humanity? How can psychology help? *American Psychologist*, 55, 496–508.
Otten, F., Arts, K., Siermann, C. and Ybema, J.F. (2010). Vijftigplussers op de arbeidsmarkt. [Workers of 50 years and above]. Available at Centraal Bureau voor de Statistiek website: http://www.cbs.nl/NR/rdonlyres/06B75497-072B-41E2-AD9D-6E723A91FBD/0/2010k2v4p31art.pdf.
Peeters, J. (2011). Consequences of the menopause in older working women: The relationship between job demands and burnout. Master's thesis, Tilburg University.
Petrou, P., Demerouti, E., Peeters, M.C.W., Schaufeli, W.B. and Hetland, J. (2012). Crafting a job on a daily basis: Contextual correlates and the link to work engagement. *Journal of Organizational Behavior*, 33, 1120–41.
Posthuma, R.A. and Campion, M.A. (2009). Age stereotypes in the workplace: Common stereotypes, moderators, and future research directions. *Journal of Management*, 35, 158–88.
Riley, L.D. and Bowen, C. (2005). The sandwich generation: Challenges and coping strategies of multigenerational families. *The Family Journal*, 13, 52–8.
Roth, P.L., Purvis, K.L. and Bobko, A. (2012). A meta-analysis of gender group differences for measures of job performance in field studies. *Journal of Management*, 38, 719–39.
Rousseau, D.M. (2005). *I-deals: Idiosyncratic Deals Employees Bargain for Themselves*. Armonk, NY: M.E. Sharp.
Rudman, L. and Phelan, J.E. (2008). Backlash effects for disconfirming gender stereotypes in organizations. In: Brief, A.P. and Straw, M. (eds). *Research in Organizational Behavior*, Vol. 4 (pp. 61–79). New York: Elsevier.
Salthouse, T.A. (1996). The processing-speed theory of adult age differences in cognition. *Psychological Review*, 103, 403–28.
Salthouse, T. (2012). Consequences of age-related cognitive declines. *Annual Review of Psychology*, 63, 201–26.
Schalk, R. et al. (2010). Moving European research on work and ageing forward: Overview and agenda. *European Journal of Work and Organizational Psychology*, 19, 76–101.
Sekaran, U. and Hall, D.T. (1989). Asynchronism in dual-career and family linkage. In: Arthur, M.B., Hall, D.T. and Lawrence, B.S. (eds). *Handbook of Career Theory* (pp. 159–80). Cambridge: Cambridge University Press.
Smeur, E. (2011). The effect of menopausal complaints on burnout: Social support and menopausal taboo. Master's thesis, Tilburg: Tilburg University.
Smola, K.W. and Sutton, C.D. (2002). Generational differences: Revisiting generational work values for the new millennium. *Journal of Organizational Behavior*, 23, 363–82.
Soares, C.N. and Taylor, V. (2007). Effects and management of the menopausal transition in women with depression and bipolar disorder. *Journal of Clinical Psychiatry*, 68, 16–21.
Sonnenberg, M. (2006). *The Signaling Effect of HRM on Psychological Contracts of Employees*. Rotterdam: ERIM.
Sonnentag, S. and Frese, M. (2002). Performance concepts and performance theory. In: Sonnentag, S. (ed.). *Psychological Management of Individual Performance* (pp. 3–26). Chichester, UK: Wiley.
Spirduso, W.W. (1995). Job performance of the older worker. In: Spirduso, W.W. (ed.). *Physical Dimensions of Aging* (pp. 367–87). Champaign, IL: Human Kinetics.
Strijbosch, A. (2011). The influence of menopausal complaints on employee well-being and the moderating effect of HR practices. Master's thesis, Tilburg: Tilburg University.
Sullivan, S.E. and Mainiero, L.A. (2008). Using the Kaleidoscope career model to understand the changing patterns of women's careers. *Advances in Human Resources*, 10, 32–49.
Super, D.E. (1957). *The Psychology of Careers: An Introduction to Vocational Development*, New York: Harper & Rowe.
Thijssen, J., Knies, E. and Leisink, P. (2013), Aging as a career challenge. In: Chalofsky, N., Rocco, T. and Morris, L. (eds). *The Handbook of HRD: Theory and Application*, San Francisco, CA: Jossey-Bass.
Thomas, J.P., Whitman, D.S. and Viswesvaran, C. (2010). Employee proactivity in organizations: A comparative meta-analysis of emergent proactive constructs. *Journal of Occupational and Organizational Psychology*, 83, 275–300.
Tims, M., Bakker, A.B. and Derks, D. (2012). Development and validity of the job crafting scale. *Journal of Vocational Behavior*, 80, 173–86.

Tims, M., Bakker, A.B., Derks, D. and Van Rhenen, W. (2013). Job crafting at the team and individual level: Implications for work engagement and job performance. *Group and Organization Management*, 38, 427–54.
Tuckman, J. and Lorge, I. (1952). Attitudes toward older workers. *Journal of Applied Psychology*, 36, 149–53.
Utian, W.H., Janata, J.W., Kingsberg, S.A., Schluchter, M. and Hamilton, J.C. (2002). The Utian Quality of Life (UQOL) Scale: Development and validation of an instrument to quantify quality of life through and beyond menopause. Menopause: *The Journal of The North American Menopause Society*, 9, 402–10.
Van Dam, K. (2004). Antecedents and consequences of employability orientation. *European Journal of Work and Organizational Psychology*, 13, 29–51.
Vandenberg, R.J., Richardson, H.A. and Eastman, L.J. (1999). The impact of high involvement work processes on organizational effectiveness. *Group and Organization Management*, 24, 300–339.
Van der Heijde, C.M. and Van der Heijden, B.I.J.M. (2006). A competence-based and multidimensional operationalization and measurement of employability. *Human Resource Management*, 45, 449–76.
Van Engen, M.L., Pantlin, S. and Schalk, M.J.D. (2011). Pilot study to menopausal symptoms, complaints and work related antecedents and outcomes. Tilburg University.
Van Engen, M.L., Vinkenburg, C.J. and Dikkers, J.D. (2012). Sustainability in combining career and care: Challenging normative beliefs about parenting. *Journal of Social Issues*, 68, 645–64.
Van Ginneken, L. (2011). Menopausal women and their occupational well-being: The role of menopausal complaints, need for recovery and internal recovery opportunities. Master's thesis, Tilburg: Tilburg University.
Verhaegen, P. and Salthouse, T.A. (1997). Meta-analyses of age-cognition relations in adulthood: Estimates of linear and non-linear age effects and structural models. *Psychological Bulletin*, 122, 231–49.
Warr, P. and Fay, D. (2001). Age and personal initiative at work. *European Journal of Work and Organizational Psychology*, 10, 343–53.
Wood, S., Van Veldhoven, M., Croon, M. and De Menezes, L.M. (2012). Enriched job design, high involvement management and organizational performance: The mediating roles of job satisfaction and well-being. *Human Relations*, 65, 419–46.
Wrzesniewski, A. and Dutton, J.E. (2001). Crafting a job: Revisioning employees as active crafters of their work. *Academy of Management Review*, 26, 179–201.
Young, L.M., Baltes, B.B. and Pratt, A.K. (2007). Using selection, optimization, and compensation to reduce job/family stressors: Effective when it matters. *Journal of Business and Psychology*, 21, 511–39.

20 Sustainable careers: enabling older workers to continue working through individualized work arrangements

P. Matthijs Bal

INTRODUCTION

Sustainability of contemporary careers over the life course implies a different perspective on how employees currently develop their careers. While sustainability can be defined as a long-term oriented approach of designing policies and practices regarding careers, it is inherent that governments, organizations and employees rethink the dominant approach towards the establishment and development of contemporary careers. There are two trends that have caused the need for a different approach: the aging of the workforce and increased life expectancy of people nowadays.

The rapid aging of the workforce throughout the Western world and parts of Asia, including Japan and China, poses many challenges for contemporary organizations (European Commission, 2010; Wang and Shultz, 2010). The baby boom generation, consisting of workers born between 1945 and 1965, constitutes a large part of the current workforce. Due to decreased fertility rates, there are fewer younger workers entering the labor market, as a consequence of which the percentage of older workers is rapidly increasing (Truxillo and Fraccaroli, 2013). Moreover, life expectancies are increasing, which causes current retirement ages to become outdated when it comes to the affordability of pensions.

When people retire at the age of 65, they may live for another 25–30 years, which not only means that society has to pay for 25 years of pension, but this also leads to an increasing older generation who is not active on the labor market and, hence, do not actively contribute to society any more if they do not engage in volunteer work (see Chapter 6 in this volume). Hence, because people tend to live longer, governments are increasing the retirement age, through which careers are automatically extended; a person who graduates at 25 can nowadays expect to work for 45 to 50 years. These extended periods that people have to work demands a different approach towards the development of careers: the assumption that people can have a career within a single domain or occupation becomes rapidly obsolete. In contrast, there are few occupations that can be fulfilled for 45 to 50 years while maintaining high intrinsic motivation. Even though there may be people who in certain situations can work in a single occupation for the entire career without losing motivation in their work, this principle cannot be maintained as guiding career development paradigms for the future. Hence, a new paradigm is needed to facilitate and form contemporary careers that may last for these 50 years.

It is therefore advisable to distinguish two parts of the career: on the one hand, a person can work within an occupation or an organization and build a career within that occupation. In this sense, career refers to the development within an occupation, such as a PhD student who becomes assistant professor, associate and subsequently full professor. In this sense, career refers to the development of a person within an occupation. On the other hand, career refers to the total period a person spends from graduating from education until full retirement from the labor force. In this sense, career entails all the decisions a person makes during the working life, for instance, to choose a certain occupation, to go back to school and retrain, to engage in volunteer work or eldercare. While the former used to be equated to the latter, the extended period people now face as constituting their working lives implies that the former should be separated from the latter perspective, and that they should be regarded as two distinct features of contemporary careers.

Moreover, because working lives are extended, it is no longer possible to take a universalistic, generalized approach to careers (Purcell, 1999). In this chapter, I will therefore argue that one should take an individualized approach, because the older people become, the more heterogeneous the peer group becomes. Choices for career development increasingly differentiate when people become older and, hence, governments and organizations should take an individualized approach to ensure sustainable careers, especially when people become older. It is therefore also important that organizations adapt their policies and practices towards this increased need for individualization.

Organizations are increasingly aware that the employee population is changing, and that strategies to employ, motivate and retain workers have to be adapted. It is no longer sufficient for organizations to only focus on employing younger workers (for example, through designing traineeships for graduates), because there are fewer younger workers in the labor market, which is already particularly the case in certain sectors, such as health care (Polat et al., 2012). Hence, organizations will have to rely increasingly on older workers and try to retain them and motivate them to stay longer in the workforce. Similarly, governments across Europe are also focused on maintaining older workers in the labor market (European Commission, 2010).

Despite this heightened awareness of the need to retain older workers, there are only very few organizations who successfully achieve aims to retain older workers. However, it is important not only to keep them within the workforce, but also to ensure that older workers remain motivated, productive and healthy contributors to organizational performance (Wang and Shultz, 2010). Thus, employment becomes sustainable only when workers are able and willing to work for sustained periods of time, and do not drop out prematurely from the workforce. To do so, I argue that organizations should implement an individualized approach to treating workers (Bal et al., 2012). Due to the increased heterogeneity among older workers, implying that older workers have more heterogeneous needs in their work than younger workers, it is pivotal that older workers are treated as individuals rather than as a homogeneous group (Dannefer, 2003). Hence, individual arrangements targeting flexibility in the employment relationship will especially benefit older workers and keep them motivated in their work, productive, and healthy.

The current chapter will accordingly explore the opportunities and challenges of an individualized approach to treating older workers in organizations. I will first describe the theoretical basis for the increased individual heterogeneity among older people. Furthermore, I will discuss the rise of individualized arrangements in the employment relationship, after which I will go into the theoretical basis for individualized treatment of older workers in organizations. I will conclude the chapter by discussing how managers can negotiate and manage individualized agreements with (older) workers.

THE CONCEPT OF HETEROGENEITY IN CAREERS OF OLDER WORKERS

The majority of research that has focused on work motivation of older workers has largely ignored the notion of increased heterogeneity with age. Traditionally, research on aging at work has focused on age-related differences in various work attitudes and behaviors. For instance, the classic review of Rhodes (1983) investigated the relation between age and job attitudes and behavior, including satisfaction, commitment and performance. Moreover, more recent meta-analytic work has looked at similar relationships of age with various types of job performance (Ng and Feldman, 2008), work motives (Kooij et al., 2011), and turnover (Ng and Feldman, 2009). The basic assumption of most of these studies is that the aging process is associated with changes in the attitudes people hold regarding their jobs and their behavior at work. Similarly, recent research has increasingly focused on the moderating role of age (for example, Bal et al., 2008; Bal et al., 2013a; Zaniboni et al., 2013), assuming that older workers, in comparison with younger workers, respond differently to organizational treatment. For instance, Bal et al. (2008) found that younger workers in general tend to react more strongly to psychological contract breaches than older workers. All of these studies show that age may be directly related to work outcomes, but also indirectly, influencing the effects of job experiences (for example, contract breach and job demands) on work outcomes.

Hence, the foundation of this line of research is in *intergroup* differences; younger workers as a group differ in their attitudes, work behaviors and reactions to job experiences from older workers as a group of employees within the organization. However, previous research has traditionally shown mixed and inconsistent results regarding effects of age (Ng and Feldman, 2008; Rhodes, 1983), and usually (very) small effect sizes, which may be limited in relevance for theory and practice. One explanation of this lack of empirical relevance of age has been addressed by Kooij et al. (2008), who proposed that the aging process constitutes a combination of various age-related changes that people experience over time. Thus, age serves as an umbrella-variable in which various changes are captured that take place when people become older. For instance, while one 50-year-old employee may be very healthy and consequently motivated to work, another 50-year-old employee might be burnt out and not motivated to work. It is thus important to distinguish within groups of older workers. Consequently, in addition to a *between-groups* approach, looking at differences between younger and older workers, it is necessary to take a *within-group* approach, thus looking at differences within groups of employees in the same age range.

Therefore, I propose that future research should primarily focus on the heterogeneity within groups of workers of the same age (Bal et al., 2012; Nelson and Dannefer, 1992). Moreover, ample research has shown that heterogeneity increases with age, and that this process manifests itself in various domains (Light et al., 1996). To understand how older workers' motivation, productivity and health can be maintained at a greater age, it is crucial to understand the increased heterogeneity among older workers and, hence, the increased need to adopt an individualized approach to motivate older workers.

Nelson and Dannefer (1992) were among the first to point towards variability within age, and they found that increasing variability with age was present across physical, personality and cognitive domains. Follow-up research showed that even at the phenotypical level (thus the biochemical characteristics of a person), people have increased heterogeneity in genetic expression with age (Light et al., 1996; Somel et al., 2006). Moreover, even though it has been argued that personality develops primarily until young adulthood, research shows that personality changes across adulthood and that, with increasing age, personality differences within age groups increase as well (Caspi et al., 2005; Van Lieshout, 2000; 2006). Thus, people become more heterogeneous in personality when they become older, while younger people are more similar in terms of personality traits.

Furthermore, more recent research also showed that emotional experiences tend to become more complex and heterogeneous when people age; in an experimental study by Charles (2005), older people showed more complex emotions than younger people after viewing a film clip containing injustices (see also Kellough and Knight, 2012). Finally, reaction times, an important indicator of cognitive aging, also become more variable when people become older (Deary and Der, 2005). In sum, there is ample evidence to state that older people are more different from each other than younger people are different from other younger people.

There are a number of theoretical explanations for this increased heterogeneity. First, individuals select or are selected by specific environments which are similar to or suit their personality, through which their personality is reinforced over time. Hence, differences in personality among people tend to become greater over time (Light et al., 1996). Another explanation has been offered by sociologists, who have argued that social status characteristics, such as gender, social class and race, determine the social system in which an individual operates (Light et al., 1996). An individual is born within a social system, or a social environment, which predicts the extent to which personality is formed. Thus, the environment influences how personality is shaped over time, and the older people become, the more their personalities are further shaped by the characteristics of the social class they live in. Because classes differ among each other, such as socio-economic status, the influence of class on people's personalities will differ as well, giving rise to increasing differences over the life course.

A final explanation, as outlined shortly above, is genetic (Light et al., 1996; Somel et al., 2006). Genes not only influence how personality is shaped over the course of one's life (for example, a genetic disposition to be an introvert is amplified over the life course), but also how the environment shapes the personality of a child (for example, children with high intellectual skills are more likely to be raised by parents who are intellectual themselves). Thus, the expression of genotypes into behavior is strengthened such that differences in phenotypes will increase. Consequently, and in line with findings that phenotypes become more diverse over the life course (Somel et al., 2006), there is evidence for increased phenotypic variability among people over the life course.

Increased Heterogeneity in the Workplace

There is very little research available in career studies based on this notion of increased heterogeneity among older workers. The lifespan model of Kooij et al. (2008) includes age as a variable that captures various changes throughout life, and assumes that because people experience these changes in an idiosyncratic manner, the older people become, the more these underlying age-related changes will determine work motivation and not just chronological age. Kooij et al. (2008) did not explicitly assume that older workers are more heterogeneous, but only stated that individuals with the same chronological age may differ substantially in other operationalizations of age.

However, there is some evidence for the notion of increased heterogeneity among older workers. A study of Bal and Kooij (2011) showed that among younger workers, work centrality (that is, how central work is in the lives of people) was not a predictor of their psychological contract with their organization, while among older workers, the higher their work centrality, the more they were focused on a relational, long-term psychological contract with their organization. Their findings indicate that while younger workers were looking for relational contracts regardless of how central work was in their lives, for older workers the level of work centrality determined their relationship with and investment in the organization. This provides indirect evidence for the notion that among younger workers employment arrangements have a direct positive effect, while for older workers other aspects in life are important in ascertaining how they respond to employment arrangements. Furthermore, the study of Bal et al. (2012) explicitly integrated the heterogeneity perspective in their study on the effects of idiosyncratic deals (I-deals for short) on motivation to continue working. They found that I-deals indeed related to higher motivation to continue working after retirement, based on the idea that to be able to continue working, I-deals may help older workers to realize their needs.

In sum, although there is still a need for more research into greater heterogeneity among older workers, there is preliminary evidence that this perspective may contribute to a further understanding of the needs, attitudes and behaviors of older workers. In addition, organizations have already started implementing individualized career patterns and work arrangements for older workers (Benko and Weisberg, 2007; Pitt-Catsouphes and Matz-Costa, 2008). Based on the idea that older workers become more and more heterogeneous, it is no longer sufficient to assume that a single approach to maintaining older workers' motivation, health and productivity is enough.

However, although younger workers are more alike than older workers (Bal and Kooij, 2011), I observe that Human Resource Management (HRM) traditionally focuses more on the needs and wishes of younger workers than of older workers (Bal et al., 2013b). For instance, traineeships have traditionally been designed for younger workers. Therefore, there is no full integration of the knowledge about the heterogeneous aging process that has been generated in gerontology with the use of this knowledge in Organizational Behavior and HRM. I therefore propose that an individualized approach to older workers is necessary to be able to maintain older workers' motivation, productivity and health, while younger workers may still benefit from standardized work arrangements. Hence, individualized agreements about work arrangements, such as I-deals, are crucial for older workers. I-deals are defined as idiosyncratically negotiated agreements between an individual employee and the organization (Rousseau et al., 2006). In the next section, I will elaborate on the utility of I-deals in organizations as well as for older workers.

INDIVIDUALIZATION FOR OLDER WORKERS

The concept of individualization has gained increasing popularity in career research and in particular the notion on individually negotiated career trajectories (Benko and Weisberg, 2007; Rousseau, 2005). Individualization is a societal trend that more or less started in the late 1800s with the rise of psychology as a science of the individual human being and poetry aimed at the individual experience, as can be seen, for instance, in the work of Henry David Thoreau. In the early 2000s, career research, and HRM and OB research more generally, started to include a more individualized perspective on the employment relationship. Denise Rousseau, for instance, in her book on idiosyncratic deals (2005), focused specifically on how employees individually negotiate employment arrangements with their employers. The work of Wrzesniewski and Dutton (2001) on job crafting has been developed from the same principle of individualization: societies become more and more focused on the individual as center of the universe instead of the collective, and this is subsequently translated into how scientific research approaches careers. The career is a highly individualized experience, which differs for each human being. The disappearance of labor unions as a means to bring equality among workers has also made employees more dependent upon themselves.

Hence, individualization will increasingly become a paradox in career research. This paradox can be described as the need for people to be treated as an individual human being versus the lost protection of the group through an individualized approach (Bal, forthcoming; Rousseau, 2012). Individualization has led to a greater focus on the individual needs of employees in the workplace and, through individualized employment arrangements, employees are better able to align work demands with non-work demands (Baltes et al., 1999). Individualization may also allow employees to be treated with more respect for dignity of the employee. In this way individualization becomes the means to promote a more dignified treatment of employees in organizations, with respect for individual wishes, needs and capabilities of the employee.

However, at the same time individualization, and in particular in its dominant neoliberal form, has led to a greater focus on self-reliance, and thus people can no longer trust institutions to take care of their well-being. Governments using the neoliberal doctrine put a greater focus on privatization of social welfare as well as trust in the rule of the invisible hand of the market (Peck, Theodore and Brenner, 2009). People become responsible for their own welfare and well-being, and a lack of economic success (for example, unemployment) of an individual is increasingly attributed to the individual's own failure, ruling out the possibility of bad luck or simply the absence of capabilities to build a career. With governments and organizations retreating from the public sphere and labor unions rapidly becoming obsolete while representing only a specific group of older employees, people do not have a social safety net to protect them for the consequences of misfortunes in their lives.

Hence, individualization provides the more proactive people with the opportunity to negotiate favorable work arrangements but, at the same time, the less proactive people become subject to employer wishes and do not have the protection of any institutional body. The trend of individualization thus creates a dividing line between winners and losers in line with the principles of neoliberal capitalism, which still is the dominant economic–political ideology in Western countries (Peck et al., 2009). Hence, this division between the small group of winners (and primarily big companies) and the increasing group of losers who spend their lives in daily struggles to make enough money to live is increasing as a consequence of the combination between individualization and a dominant neoliberal ideology governing society.

A clear indication of this trend is the often found positive relation between quality of relation between employee and manager and I-deals: employees with better relationships get more I-deals (Rosen et al., 2013). Hence, individualized treatment becomes subject to corruption, cronyism and favoritism, and only those who are proactive get what they want, leaving the less proactive as victims of a self-reliant society. In sum, individualization constitutes a process that can both facilitate and hinder employment opportunities for older workers, because increased heterogeneity among older workers can be facilitated through an individualized approach to work, but at the same time can put them at a higher risk of becoming wholly self-reliant for their careers and employment. The question thus is how individual deals can be institutionalized or used by organizations, such that I-deals are implemented in a way that benefits all parties. To do so, I return to a more theoretical HRM perspective.

A HRM PERSPECTIVE ON INDIVIDUALIZATION

Delery and Doty (1996), in their paper on modes of theorizing in strategic HRM, explained that both a universalistic approach to HRM as well as a contingency approach to HRM may be necessary when designing human resource systems in organizations. A universalistic approach to HRM, which assumes that HR practices universally benefit employees, has become the primary mode of theorizing in HR research over time. For instance, a number of articles has focused on the main effects of 'high performance' HR practices on commitment and performance (Gardner et al., 2011; Kehoe and Wright, 2013). However, the contingency approach to HRM, which assumes that to be effective, HR practices have to be in line with other aspects of the organization, has received much less attention (Bal et al., 2013b; Boxall and Macky, 2009). This is strange because, with increasing diversity of workplaces, it seems imperative that organizations should take a diversified approach to motivate their workforce through HR practices. Especially with the increasing number of older workers in organizations, it is important that organizations are aware that the universalistic approach towards HRM is no longer sufficient, and should be replaced by a contingency approach (Bal et al., 2013b). This contingency approach dictates that organizations, when they design their strategic HR policies and practices, should take into account the diversity of the workforce and accordingly the diverse work-related needs of the workers in the organization (Delery and Doty, 1996).

With the increasing number of older workers in the workforce and, hence, the increasing heterogeneity in the needs and motivations of employees in organizations, organizations should therefore take a more individualized approach to motivating (older) workers. Some organizations have already started this, and inducements such as bonuses, training programs and individualized work schedules have been offered to employees, such that they remain with the company and increase their efforts to benefit the organization (Hornung et al., 2008).

These individualized arrangements, or I-deals, are not arrangements that are available to every employee, but they can be part of the contingent HR strategy of an organization that focuses on individualization of work arrangements for employees (Bal et al., 2012; Bal and Dorenbosch, 2015; Rousseau, 2005). According to Rousseau (2005), I-deals are heterogeneous among employees, such that employees may have negotiated different I-deals with the same employer. When an individual arrangement becomes available to every employee in the organization, the arrangement becomes an HR practice, and is no longer an I-deal (Rousseau, 2005). Hence, I-deals arise when employees negotiate work arrangements that deviate from organizational HR practices. I-deals should benefit both employee and employer; the employer may offer I-deals to attract or retain employees, and the employees' contract terms become more aligned towards personal preferences (Rousseau et al., 2009).

Finally, I-deals vary in scope, such that some employees might have negotiated a single specific agreement with the employer (for example, flexible working times to care for older parents), whereas other employees may have a completely individually negotiated set of employment arrangements. I-deals are not only idiosyncratic deals, but also *ideal* in the sense of benefiting both parties, since employees can fulfill their needs in their work while organizations benefit through greater employee motivation and retention of valuable employees (Rousseau, 2005).

I-deals can be negotiated before employment, such as during the recruitment process (*ex-ante* I-deals), but they can also be negotiated during employment (*ex-post* I-deals). *Ex-ante* I-deals will be primarily negotiated by (future) employees because of their valuable skills that the company wants to obtain, while *ex-post* I-deals will be negotiated when employees have skills that the company wants to retain, or as a way of rewarding loyal employees.

Research on I-deals has shown that, in general, employees tend to negotiate four different types of I-deals: task and work responsibilities; schedule flexibility; location flexibility; and financial incentives (Rosen et al., 2013). Task and work responsibilities I-deals refer to those arrangements employees negotiate concerning the tasks they conduct at work, as well as the responsibilities they have at work. Schedule flexibility concerns the working hours of the employee, and can be negotiated in relation to the number of hours worked during the week, or the time the employees will be at work. Location flexibility refers to the place where the work is conducted. For instance, employees can negotiate that they conduct part of their work from home or another location. Finally, financial I-deals concern the individual deals with respect to salary and received bonuses.

Theoretically, the effects of I-deals on employee outcomes have been explained using social exchange theory, and in particular the norm of reciprocity (Blau, 1964; Gouldner, 1960). According to social exchange theory, when an employee and an employer commit to each other in an exchange relationship, reciprocal obligations between the two parties drive behaviors of the two parties. I-deals serve as a basis for reciprocity between the employee and the organization, strengthening the employment relationship through the mutual obligations that have been agreed upon by the two parties. More specifically, the organization negotiates with the employee a certain arrangement and, in return, the employee becomes more committed, stays with the organization, and may perform at a higher level.

Moreover, the effects of I-deals can also be explained using work adjustment theory (Baltes et al., 1999), which postulates that through a customized set of work arrangements, employees achieve greater correspondence between work and private life, and hence avoid work–family conflict and retain a healthy work–life balance (Hornung et al., 2008). Because I-deals may create a fit between the needs and abilities of the employee and the demands of the job, employees are happier and better able to carry out their work. Previous research has indeed shown that employees who negotiate I-deals become more attached to the organization (Hornung et al., 2008), have a more favorable relationship with the organization (Rousseau et al., 2009) and contribute to a higher degree (Anand et al., 2010; Hornung et al., 2008). For instance, a study of Hornung et al. (2008) showed that flexibility I-deals reduced work–family conflict, while developmental I-deals enhanced commitment, performance expectations, and working overtime. Finally, recent research also showed that I-deals are important for the motivation to continue working beyond retirement (Bal et al., 2012). I-deals can thus enhance sustainable careers because, through individualization of work arrangements, people can be motivated both in the short term and in the long run.

Older Workers and I-deals

We propose that I-deals will be particularly important for older workers. Because younger workers are typically focused on building their career, they are likely to look for resources that enhance their wishes for career-building, such as high pay, fringe benefits including mobile phones and laptops, and developmental opportunities (Bal and Kooij, 2011). Extrinsic resources, such as salary and promotion, are indicators for younger workers that they are valued by their organization, while those resources become less important when people grow older (Kooij et al., 2011). Because older workers become more different from other older workers, their needs for the resources that they obtain from their organization also become more heterogeneous. Hence, the opportunity to negotiate I-deals with their organization will be more important for older workers than it is for younger workers.

Consequently, I-deals are the primary basis for designing strategic HR decisions among organizations that employ older workers. While there is very little direct evidence for the particular relevance of I-deals for older workers, there are a number of studies that do support this notion. In a study of Pitt-Catsouphes and Matz-Costa (2008) among almost 200000 employees in the US, it was found that the effect of flexibility on work engagement was stronger for older workers than for younger workers. In other words, they ascertained that flexibility in work schedules was more strongly related to higher work engagement among older workers, while younger workers did not profit that much from flexibility in their work schedules.

Another study of Bal et al. (2012) found that I-deals were related to motivation to continue working after retirement. It was expected that I-deals would create a stronger fit between the abilities of older workers and what they want from work, which consequently would enhance their motivation to continue working. The study indeed revealed that this was the case; among a sample of more than 1000 employees in a Dutch health care organization, I-deals related positively to motivation to continue working beyond retirement. Finally, in another study among almost 5000 Dutch organizations, Bal and Dorenbosch (2015) found that availability and use of I-deals were related to higher organizational performance as well as lower sickness absence and employee turnover. Moreover, it was found that in particular flexibility I-deals reduced sickness absence in organizations with many older workers. These studies show that the possibility of negotiating flexibility at work is important for older workers to be able to conduct their work. Moreover, I-deal negotiation can facilitate older workers in obtaining a more individualized relationship to their work; for instance, in prolonged careers lasting 50 years, people can negotiate career switches and job changes through I-deals. However, we also expect that these potential effects of I-deals for older workers are dependent upon a number of factors. More specifically, the extent to which I-deals will benefit older workers is likely to depend upon the type of I-deal negotiated, psychological characteristics of the older worker, and the context in which I-deals are negotiated. In the following section, I will elaborate on these issues.

The Role of Type of I-deals, and Psychological and Contextual Factors

Despite accumulating evidence that I-deals contribute to employee and organizational performance, and that I-deals may enhance commitment, motivation and retention, and reduce absence (Hornung et al., 2014), it is not self-evident that these effects of I-deals will always occur. Researchers normally do not find consistent effects of I-deals on work outcomes, as some I-deals may directly relate to outcomes, while others may only be related to outcomes under certain conditions (Hornung et al., 2008; Rousseau et al., 2009; Van der Meij and Bal, 2013). For instance, development I-deals may sometimes even have negative effects because development means investment in work, and hence less time for family and non-work concerns (Bal and Dorenbosch, 2015; Hornung et al., 2008). Moreover, researchers typically find few direct effects of financial I-deals on work outcomes (Rosen et al., 2013; Van der Meij and Bal, 2013). Thus, the question is also under which conditions types of I-deals are most beneficial for older workers. We argue that the strength of the effects of I-deals on work outcomes for older workers depends upon the type of I-deal, the team or department around the older worker, and the psychological processes underlying the utility of I-deals for older workers.

First, there is some recent evidence for different effects for younger and older workers of different types of I-deals on work outcomes. As argued earlier, younger workers have more similar needs in their work, such as salary, fringe benefits and career development (Bal and Kooij, 2011; Kooij et al., 2011). Hence, provision of I-deals is less important for them and, if younger workers are able to negotiate I-deals, they tend to value financial and developmental I-deals through which they contribute to and stay with the organization (Bal and Dorenbosch, 2015). However, due to the aging process, older workers experience gradual losses of physical abilities and gradually decreasing fluid intelligence, though progressing at different speeds (Baltes, 1997). Hence, and due to their more heterogeneous needs, older workers tend to value flexibility in their work more than younger workers. Subsequently, flexibility I-deals are more highly valued by older workers, because flexibility allows older workers to negotiate an individualized relation to work, and to obtain a better balance between what they find important in work and what they bring into their work, such as their abilities, experience and knowledge.

In line with this, Bal et al. (2012) found that flexibility I-deals were the strongest predictor of motivation to continue working after retirement, and hence can be regarded as the most important I-deal for older workers. However, research on I-deals has so far focused on a limited number of I-deal types (task and development, schedule flexibility, location flexibility, and financial I-deals; Rosen et al., 2013). Thus, it is important for further research that more specific deals are investigated that older workers tend to negotiate with their employer, such as reduced workload, in order to be able to conduct their work for a longer time.

Next to the I-deal type, it is also important to take into account the context in which I-deals are negotiated. For instance, there are three parties involved in negotiation of I-deals: the employee, the organization, and co-workers (Greenberg et al., 2004; Lai et al., 2009; Rousseau, 2005). This raises the issue of fairness: when an employee is able to negotiate an I-deal with the organization about, for instance, flexible working schedules, co-workers might react negatively when they perceive the I-deal as unfair. Therefore, co-workers' acceptance of I-deals is an important precondition for the successful implementation of I-deals in the workplace (Lai et al., 2009). When older workers are granted special arrangements because of their loyalty towards the organization, younger workers may see this as favoritism and may attribute this to undeserved entitlements of older workers that they cannot obtain themselves.

Based on this notion, Bal et al. (2012) indeed found that development I-deals only contributed to higher motivation to continue working beyond retirement when there was a supportive climate for older workers in the unit. When a climate was prevalent where older workers were encouraged to withdraw from their work roles when they were approaching their retirement, development I-deals were no longer predicting motivation to continue working. To be able to benefit from I-deals and transfer the benefit to the workplace, older workers need the support of their managers, co-workers, and to some extent, society. The study showed that when managers and co-workers were supportive of older workers developing themselves, development I-deals indeed related positively to continuing working (Bal et al., 2012).

Finally, it is not only the type of I-deal and the environment that predict the effectiveness of I-deal usage for older workers, but also, to a great extent, the psychological processes that take place within the older worker. As outlined above, people age differently, and the older people become, the more they differentiate in terms of their personalities, needs, attitudes and behaviors. Hence, 'the older worker' does not exist, and the way older workers perceive their work in their lives is important in ascertaining the investment of older workers in their work and organization. While some older workers mentally retire already long before they can retire and look forward to the date they can officially retire from work, others may be more successful in the strategies that they have employed to retain work motivation throughout the lifespan (Kooij et al., 2008).

The model of successful aging by Baltes (1997) indeed describes successful aging as being able to cope with age-related losses, such as declining physical capabilities and less fluid intelligence, by employing SOC strategies (Selection, Optimization and Compensation). SOC strategies include Selecting a narrower range of goals one will pursue at work, Optimizing the tasks one still carries out at work, while Compensation indicates employing alternative means when one is no longer able to conduct specific tasks to carry out the job (Bal et al., 2013b). Research has shown that when older workers use SOC strategies, they are more engaged, committed and show a higher focus on opportunities at work (Bal et al., 2013b; Zacher and Frese, 2011). Hence, the extent to which I-deals will be beneficial for older workers is also determined by the extent to which older workers engage in strategies that enable successful aging at work, such as SOC strategies. People who focus on SOC strategies as a way to cope with age-related losses will be particularly responsive to individualized agreements that help shape their job towards their capabilities and needs.

DISCUSSION

This chapter analyzed the need for I-deals for older workers. It set out to explain that the older people become, the more heterogeneous the peer group becomes, due to increased differences in personalities, needs and work-related attitudes and behaviors as people age. Hence, while a traditional approach to younger workers may be sufficient in organizations to attract and motivate these younger workers, for older workers this is no longer enough. Consequently, while younger workers may be motivated by economic rewards, developmental opportunities and possibilities to build their career (Bal and Kooij, 2011; Freund, 2006), older workers are motivated by different things at work, and become more differentiated.

Thus, an individualized approach to motivating older workers is crucial, and the use of I-deals in organizations may enable older workers to make individualized agreements with their organizations about how they will fill the time until their retirement. I-deals about accommodated work arrangements can be made, such as reduced work hours, lower job demands, and exemption from night shifts. Moreover, I-deals about job content can also be negotiated, such as I-deals on special projects, coaching roles and job shifts. So I-deals can be used to facilitate flexibility in how work is perceived, conducted and developed. Through these individualized agreements, older workers can maintain their health, work motivation and productivity (Bal and Dorenbosch, 2015; Kooij et al., 2008), and thus remain active until their (official) retirement age.

However, we also explained that the potential engaging effects of I-deals are also dependent upon the type of I-deal, the extent to which the environment around the older worker is supportive of the transfer of a negotiated I-deal to the workplace, and the psychological strategies that older workers follow to conquer age-related losses, such as selecting a narrower range of goals that older workers want to achieve in work (Zacher and Frese, 2011). Thus, I-deals do not operate within a social vacuum, but are influenced by many factors, including the direct environment (for example, co-workers), organizational structures (for example, size of the organization), and psychological factors of older workers themselves. Consequently, research on the benefits of I-deals for older workers should take a contextualized approach, in which the situation of the older worker within the team, organization and country should be taken into account.

Finally, as outlined above, individualization constitutes a paradoxical trend; on the one hand, it enables people to be treated individually, with the opportunity for the promotion of individual rights and dignity in the workplace, while at the same time, individualization endangers vulnerable employees because of the increasing need for self-reliance and the need for people to proactively shape their own careers. Thus, promotion of human dignity in the workplace may be hindered when a growing number of employees have marginalized jobs, because protection has disappeared in an individualized society. In all, I-deals can be an important strategy for workers to create sustainable employability, while at the same time it is essential to promote human dignity through individualization.

REFERENCES

Anand, S., P.R. Vidyarthi, R.C. Liden and D.M. Rousseau (2010), 'Good citizens in poor-quality relationships: idiosyncratic deals as a substitute for relationship quality', *Academy of Management Journal*, **53**, 970–88.

Bal, P.M. (forthcoming), 'Voorbij neoliberalisme in de arbeids- en organisatiepsychologie: menselijke waardigheid en organisatiedemocratie', manuscript under review.

Bal, P.M. and L. Dorenbosch (2015), 'Age-related differences in the relations between individualized HR practices and organizational performance: a large-scale employer survey', *Human Resource Management Journal*, **25**, 41–61.

Bal, P.M. and D. Kooij (2011), 'The relations between work centrality, psychological contracts, and job attitudes: the influence of age', *European Journal of Work and Organizational Psychology*, **20**, 497–523.

Bal, P.M., D.T.A.M. Kooij and S.B. De Jong (2013b), 'How do developmental and accommodative HRM enhance employee engagement and commitment? The role of psychological contract and SOC-strategies', *Journal of Management Studies*, **50**, 545–72.

Bal, P.M., S.B. De Jong, P.W.G. Jansen and A.B. Bakker (2012), 'Motivating employees to work beyond retirement: a multi-level study of the role of I-deals and unit climate', *Journal of Management Studies*, **49**, 306–31.

Bal, P.M., A.H. De Lange, P.G.W. Jansen and M.E. Van Der Velde (2008), 'Psychological contract breach and job attitudes: A meta-analysis of age as a moderator', *Journal of Vocational Behavior*, **72**, 143–58.

Bal, P.M., A.H. De Lange, H. Zacher and B.I.J.M. Van der Heijden (2013a), 'A lifespan perspective on psychological contracts and their relations with organizational commitment', *European Journal of Work and Organizational Psychology*, **22**, 279–92.

Baltes, P.B. (1997), 'On the incomplete architecture of human ontogeny. Selection optimization and compensation as foundation', *American Psychologist*, **52**, 366–80.

Baltes, B.B., T.E. Briggs, J.W. Huff, J.A. Wright and G.A. Neuman (1999), 'Flexible and compressed workweek schedules: a meta-analysis of their effects on work-related criteria', *Journal of Applied Psychology*, **84**, 496–513.

Benko, C. and A.A.C. Weisberg (2007), *Mass Career Customization: Aligning the Workplace with Today's Nontraditional Workforce*, Boston, MA: Harvard Business Press.

Blau, P.M. (1964), *Exchange and Power in Social Life*, New York: Wiley.

Boxall, P. and K. Macky (2009), 'Research and theory on high-performance work systems: progressing the high-involvement stream', *Human Resource Management Journal*, **19**, 3–23.

Caspi, A., B.W. Roberts and R.L. Shiner (2005), 'Personality development: Stability and change', *Annual Review of Psychology*, **56**, 453–84.

Charles, S.T. (2005), 'Viewing injustice: greater emotional heterogeneity with age', *Psychology and Aging*, **20**, 159–64.

Dannefer, D. (2003), 'Cumulative advantage/disadvantage and the life course: Cross-fertilizing age and social science theory', *The Journals of Gerontology Series B: Psychological Sciences and Social Sciences*, **58**, S327–S337.

Deary, I.J. and G. Der (2005), 'Reaction time, age, and cognitive ability: Longitudinal findings from age 16 to 63 years in representative population samples', *Aging, Neuropsychology, and Cognition*, **12**, 187–215.

Delery, J.E. and D.H. Doty (1996), 'Modes of theorizing in strategic human resource management: tests of universalistic contingency and configurational performance predictions', *Academy of Management Journal*, **39**, 802–35.

European Commission (2010), 'Green paper: Toward adequate, sustainable and safe European pension systems', Brussels: European Commission.

Freund, A.M. (2006), 'Age-differential motivational consequences of optimization versus compensation focus in younger and older adults', *Psychology and Aging*, **21**, 240–52.
Gardner, T.M., P.M. Wright and L.M. Moynihan (2011), 'The impact of motivation, empowerment, and skill-enhancing practices on aggregate voluntary turnover: the mediating effect of collective affective commitment', *Personnel Psychology*, **64**, 315–50.
Gouldner, A.W. (1960), 'The norm of reciprocity: A preliminary statement', *American Sociological Review*, **25**, 161–78.
Greenberg, J., M.E. Roberge, V.T. Ho and D.M. Rousseau (2004), 'Fairness in idiosyncratic work arrangements: Justice as an i-deal', *Research in Personnel and Human Resources Management*, **23**, 1–34.
Hornung, S., D.M. Rousseau and J. Glaser (2008), 'Creating flexible work arrangements through idiosyncratic deals', *Journal of Applied Psychology*, **93**, 655–64.
Hornung, S., D.M. Rousseau, M. Weigl, A. Muller and J. Glaser (2014), 'Redesigning work through idiosyncratic deals', *European Journal of Work and Organizational Psychology*, **23**, 608–26.
Kehoe, R.R. and P.M. Wright (2013), 'The impact of high performance HR practices on employees' attitudes and behaviors', *Journal of Management*, **39**, 366–91.
Kelley, H.H. and J.L. Michela (1980), 'Attribution theory and research', *Annual Review of Psychology*, **31**, 457–501.
Kellough, J.L. and B.G. Knight (2012), 'Positivity effects in older adults' perception of facial emotion: The role of future time perspective', *The Journals of Gerontology Series B: Psychological Sciences and Social Sciences*, **67**, 150–58.
Kooij, D., A. De Lange, P. Jansen and J. Dikkers (2008), 'Older workers' motivation to continue to work: five meanings of age', *Journal of Managerial Psychology*, **23**, 364–94.
Kooij, D., A.H. De Lange, P.G.W. Jansen, R. Kanfer and J. Dikkers (2011), 'Age and work-related motives: results of a meta-analysis', *Journal of Organizational Behavior*, **32**, 197–225.
Lai, L., D.M. Rousseau and K.T.T. Chang (2009), 'Idiosyncratic deals: coworkers as interested parties', *Journal of Applied Psychology*, **94**, 547–56.
Light, J.M., J.S. Grigsby and M.C. Bligh (1996), 'Aging and heterogeneity: Genetics, social structure, and personality', *The Gerontologist*, **36**, 165–73.
Nelson, E.A. and D. Dannefer (1992), 'Aged heterogeneity: Fact or fiction? The fate of diversity in gerontological research', *The Gerontologist*, **32**, 17–23.
Ng, T.W. and D.C. Feldman (2008), 'The relationship of age to ten dimensions of job performance', *Journal of Applied Psychology*, **93**, 392–423.
Ng, T.W. and D.C. Feldman (2009), 'Re-examining the relationship between age and voluntary turnover', *Journal of Vocational Behavior*, **74**, 283–94.
Peck, J., N. Theodore and N. Brenner (2009), 'Postneoliberalism and its malcontents', *Antipode*, **41**(s1), 94–116.
Pitt-Catsouphes, M. and C. Matz-Costa (2008), 'The multi-generational workforce: Workplace flexibility and engagement', *Community, Work and Family*, **11**, 215–29.
Polat, T., P.M. Bal and P.G.W. Jansen (2012), 'Hoe willen werknemers na hun pensioen blijven werken?', *Gedrag en Organisatie*, **25**, 66–86.
Purcell, J. (1999), 'Best practice and best fit: Chimera or cul-de- sac?', *Human Resource Management Journal*, **9**, 26–41.
Rhodes, S.R. (1983), 'Age-related differences in work attitudes and behavior: A review and conceptual analysis', *Psychological Bulletin*, **93**, 328–67.
Rosen, C.C., D.J. Slater, C.H. Chang and R.E. Johnson (2013), 'Let's make a deal: development and validation of the ex post I-deals scale', *Journal of Management*, **39**, 709–42.
Rousseau, D.M. (2005), *I-Deals: Idiosyncratic Deals Employees Bargain for Themselves*, New York: M.E. Sharpe.
Rousseau, D.M. (2012), 'Free will in social and psychological contracts', *Society and Business Review*, **7**, 8–13.
Rousseau, D.M., V.T. Ho and J. Greenberg (2006), 'I-deals: Idiosyncratic terms in employment relationships', *Academy of Management Review*, **31**, 977–94.
Rousseau, D.M., S. Hornung and T.G. Kim (2009), 'Idiosyncratic deals: testing propositions on timing, content, and the employment relationship', *Journal of Vocational Behavior*, **74**, 338–48.
Somel, M., P. Khaitovich, S. Bahn, S. Pääbo and M. Lachmann (2006), 'Gene expression becomes heterogeneous with age', *Current Biology*, **16**, R359–R360.
Truxillo, D.M. and F. Fraccaroli (2013), 'Research themes on age and work: Introduction to the Special Issue', *European Journal of Work and Organizational Psychology*, **22**, 249–52.
Van der Meij, K. and P.M. Bal (2013), 'De ideale "Idiosyncratic-deal"', *Gedrag en Organisatie*, **26**, 156–81.
Van Lieshout, C.F. (2000), 'Lifespan personality development: Self-organising goal-oriented agents and developmental outcome', *International Journal of Behavioral Development*, **24**, 276–88.

Van Lieshout, C.F.M. (2006), 'Lifespan development of personality and developmental outcome domains', *European Journal of Personality*, **20**, 515–24.
Wang, M. and K.S. Shultz (2010), 'Employee retirement: a review and recommendations for future investigation', *Journal of Management*, **36**, 172–206.
Wrzesniewski, A. and J.E. Dutton (2001), 'Crafting a job: Revisioning employees as active crafters of their work', *Academy of Management Review*, **26**, 179–201.
Zacher, H. and M. Frese (2011), 'Maintaining a focus on opportunities at work: The interplay between age, job complexity, and the use of selection, optimization, and compensation strategies', *Journal of Organizational Behavior*, **32**, 291–318.
Zaniboni, S., D.M. Truxillo and F. Fraccaroli (2013), 'Differential effects of task variety and skill variety on burnout and turnover intentions for older and younger workers', *European Journal of Work and Organizational Psychology*, **22**, 306–17.

21 Sustainable HRM for sustainable careers: introducing the 'Respect Openness Continuity (ROC)' model

Peggy De Prins, Ans De Vos, Lou Van Beirendonck and Jesse Segers

INTRODUCTION

In this chapter, the concept of sustainable careers is positioned within a broader framework of sustainable HRM. It broadens the scope from a single career-perspective to a more integrated HRM and Corporate Social Responsibility (CSR) perspective. The academic debate on sustainable HRM is relatively young but can count on an increasing interest (Clarke, 2013; Ehnert and Harry, 2012; Taylor et al., 2012). Following Ehnert and Harry (2012) and many others, we believe that sustainable HRM is a promising domain for HRM theory-building, research and practice, which also provides promising avenues to realize sustainable careers in organizations.

SUSTAINABLE HRM

Consistent with De Lange and Koppens (2007), we define sustainable HRM as a specific form of personnel management that is explicitly linked with the environment of the organization, which is focused on respect for the human workforce and in which the interests of the employer, the workers and societal interests are balanced with each other. Several definitions of sustainable HRM exist in the literature (Ehnert and Harry, 2012). The definition of De Lange and Koppens (2007) in which the triple P 'Planet, People and Profit' is 'translated' into 'Respect, Openness and Continuity' (ROC) offers a good starting-point in our opinion. In recent years, the triple P vocabulary has gained popularity in light of its practicality from the perspective of managers and scholars. Just as the triple P rhetoric has contributed to the mainstreaming of CSR, the ROC model has the potential to support the implementation and mainstreaming of sustainable HRM practices.

The Triple P Translated

According to De Lange and Koppens (2007), sustainable HRM differs from mainstream HRM because of the following characteristics:

1. a renewed focus on respect for the internal stakeholders in the organization, the employees (Respect);

2. environmental awareness and outside-in perspective on HRM (Openness);
3. a long-term approach, both with regard to economic and societal sustainability terms and also individual employability (Continuity).

Based on a critical review of three mainstream theoretical perspectives on strategic HRM, we discuss the building blocks of sustainable HRM in the sections that follow (see also Table 21.1). According to Paauwe (2012), the field of HRM, by nature, reflects developments in society and trends in the academic disciplines (psychology, strategic management and so on) that contribute to the field. During the 1990s, strategic HRM emphasized the following issues: (1) the link between HRM and financial performance; (2) the fit between HRM and strategy; and (3) HRM and sustainable competitive advantage (the resource-based view). The narrative style of many HRM articles focuses on 'strategy' and the 'search for strategic added value through people'. The HRM literature of that time was dominated by 'what employers want' (Boselie, 2010). In contrast to this unilateral strategic perspective, today's discussions concerning sustainable HRM are more balanced, recognizing the fact that 'what employers want' is not necessarily the same as 'what employees want' and 'what society/external stakeholders want'.

In this respect, the model responds to the plea by Janssens and Steyaert (2009) for R(econstructing)-reflexivity within the HRM field:

> R-reflexivity stands for reconstructing and reframing by bringing in issues of alternative paradigms, perspectives, and political values so that it illuminates what is left out and marginalized.

Table 21.1 The R(espect) O(penness) C(ontinuity) model of sustainable HRM: theoretical antecedents and overview of HRM practices

	People Respect	Planet Openness	Profit Continuity
Credo	'Searching for the human in HRM'	'HRM from the outside in'	'Long-term scope of HRM'
Theory			
Mainstream strategic HRM perspective revisited	Resourced-based view revisited	Strategic fit revisited	Long-term performance/long-term employment relationships revisited
Theoretical antecedents	Ethical and critical HRM theory	Institutional and stakeholder theory	
Practices			
Horizontal/thematic	Talent-Engagement-Empowerment- Health and Well-being-Employee Participation- . . .	Diversity-Ageing-Work–life Balance-Ecology-Stakeholders-Labor Market. . .	Employability-Careers-Succession-Learning organization-Workplace innovation-Workforce planning . . .
Vertical	Sustainable recruitment, selection, training, development, compensation, leadership, change, culture, . . .		

> It provides alternative descriptions, interpretations, vocabularies and voices that could be taken into account, aiming to open up new avenues, paths and lines of interpretations that produce 'better' research ethically, politically, empirically and theoretically (Janssens and Steyaert, 2009, p. 144).

For the R-reflexivity exercise within the mainstream strategic HRM field, we searched for innovative and critical streams of literature that provide a base for the principles of next-generation HRM and that correspond to the CSR tradition. In this search, we focused on aspects of stakeholders, institutional, ethical and critical theory.

In our inquiry for practical examples, many checklists, roadmaps and other instruments related to sustainable HRM appeared to be available (for example, the recent guidelines of the SHRM Foundation, 2012). Although the approach and tools described in these works are often not particularly new, framing them within the context of an integrated sustainability perspective is. For our examples in this chapter (for example, on sustainable people management, sustainable careers), we focus largely on horizontal HRM practices (that is, practices with a predominantly thematic approach). In vertical terms, classical HRM practices (for example, recruitment, selection, development, remuneration) could also be taken into account, given that they can also be reconsidered and re-oriented within a perspective of sustainability.

Before presenting the model in more detail, we address its primary underlying assumptions. These assumptions are related to the theoretical roots and foundations of the ROC model.

Revisionism Bis

The ROC model is based on the assumption that sustainable HRM forms the next, complementary stage in the tradition of HRM thinking (De Lange and Koppens, 2007; Ehnert, 2009). It reframes and revises the mainstream principles of strategic HRM, which were dominant in HRM thinking beginning in the 1980s. This kind of revision movement is not unique in the history of HRM. In the 1960s and 1970s, a revision approach emerged as well (Boselie, 2010). This approach criticized the highly 'rational' principles of Scientific Management, including the extreme division of labour, strong leadership and efficiency, as well as the far-reaching 'social' principles of the Human Relations Movement (with its strong focus on the social function of work, interactions between workers, personal attention to employees by supervisors, informal social systems and similar topics). Influenced by the changing climate of the 1960s, power and authority were no longer accepted as such. It was thought that employees would be able to work better if they had more independence, self-awareness and responsibility. Within the revisionist approach, the quality of working life, involvement and participation of employees became key issues.

The current shift towards sustainable HRM represents a second wave of revisionism. The assumption that a dominant perspective presently exists and that it should be identified is therefore important. The identification of a mainstream HRM perspective, along with its implicit assumptions, offers the possibility of more comprehensive critique and revision, both within and outside the perspective (Greenwood, 2012). Briefly stated, mainstream HRM assumes an objective, value-free reality. Humans are seen as objective, rational 'resources', whose beliefs and actions can and should be studied (and managed) with regard to how they should be directed in order to achieve organizational objectives (Greenwood, 2012). The unifying focus is a managerial orientation that prizes the functional and organizational benefits of HRM, particularly with regard to its potential contributions to strategy and organizational performance.

Mainstream HRM Revisited

Critical studies have extensively shown that HRM is impregnated by a unitarist approach in the management of the employment relationship (Janssens and Steyaert, 2009; Van Buren et al., 2011). The field of HRM apparently assumes that the well-being and organizational goals of employees can always be aligned, and that managers, employees and HRM professionals will all work together towards a common goal of efficiency and high performance levels. In a more pluralistic perspective, concepts are needed to account for the complexity of employment relationships, which are characterized by both shared and conflicting goals and interests. The primary assumption is that both parties to the employment relationship have divergent and sometimes conflicting interests, as well as common interests that provide the foundation for a voluntary (or largely voluntary) cooperative relationship.

A second assumption of mainstream HRM thinking concerns contingency and fit. According to Ehnert (2013) and Ehnert and Brandl (2013), the contingency view, with its focus on alignment and fit, is still the dominant logic in research on both organizations and HRM. Nevertheless, this view is being increasingly contested. The both/and approach or 'paradox lens' focuses on the idea of 'dynamic equilibrium' rather than on contingency (i.e. fit, alignment). Together with Ehnert (2013) and Ehnert and Brandl (2013), we criticize the excessively strong fit paradigm in HRM. We aim to contribute to the understanding of how HRM actors can address tensions proactively and positively, instead of being paralyzed by the fear of unfolding dynamics, instead of victimizing HRM managers or employees, and instead of ignoring or suppressing tensions. Sustainable HRM highlights the synthesis paradox (Clegg et al., 2002; Mariappanadar, 2013). In this both/and approach, organizations can use strategic HRM practices to maximize their profits in addition to reducing the harm of HRM practices on the stakeholders, given that these two polarities are not mutually exclusive but mutually reinforcing. In our further discussion of the ROC model, the synthesis approach will be illustrated.

THE ROC MODEL

The first building block of the ROC model stems from the ethical and critical tradition related to 'respect'. In addition to the ethical approach, CSR adds an outside-in perspective to sustainable HRM within the second building block 'openness'. The third building block, in its turn, is focused on continuity and adds a long-term scope on HRM. In the next paragraphs these three building blocks will be further developed.

First Building Block: Respect

With respect, we refer to the search for the 'Human' in HRM theory and practices. Respect calls for a smarter and more respectful attitude towards resources, and especially towards human resources. Given that 20 percent of European jobs are 'poor-quality jobs' with low levels of health and well-being (Eurofound, 2012), the Respect dimension should be a priority on the HRM agenda. The relationship between ethics and HRM has been the subject of considerable discussion in recent years as a response to what was previously dubbed an 'ethical turn' in HRM. The turning point was the subsequently well-established proposal that ethics should be considered central to the HRM function (Rhodes and Harvey, 2012). According to Guest and Woodrow (2012), HRM professionals should act as 'ethical stewards'. They might do this by aiming for a strong HRM system, forming alliances for the formulation and implementation of policy, seeking opportunities for promoting worker well-being and, more generally, seeking to make ethical choices whenever the opportunity arises (Guest and Woodrow, 2012). The latter is reflected in various contexts, including in the daily events within an organization, in conflicts between line managers and their subordinates and in situations in which a worker is transferred to another team.

Also the critical HRM literature contains many calls for bringing humanity back into HRM. According to Van Buren et al. (2011), the strategic business partnership role has made HRM more organization- than employee-focused, leading to a lack of concern for employee welfare and perspectives. In their book *Searching for the Human in Human Resource Management*, Bolton and Houlihan (2007) suggested that, even though people appear to be of central concern in HRM theory, HRM practice and the workplace experience, the rich, warm and unpredictable faces of humanity are all too clearly absent. By managing the employment relationship solely in economic terms, humanity is 'squeezed out' and the resource is therefore never seen in its full light. Scholars of CSR would refer to this as a tension between the logic of Profit and the logic of People. In the revision of the SHRM tradition, it implies the recognition and revaluation of the basic characteristics of the H(uman) within the resource-based view. As remarked by Lengnick-Hall et al. (2009): 'While SHRM research has drawn substantially from the resource-based view of the firm to emphasize the strategic and the resource factors in SHRM activities, at times it appears that the "human" element has been neglected' (Lengnick-Hall et al., 2009, p. 70).

Within the current more applied HRM/best practices debates, we recognize a similar search for a renewed attention to the human aspects of HRM. Van Beirendonck (2009) summarizes the evolution as follows (see Table 21.2): from competency management (organizational perspective, job fit), towards talent management (employee perspective, strengths) and sustainable management (perspective of both employee and organization, common terminology) (Van Beirendonck, 2009). Competency management proceeds from an organization's mission, vision and strategy, which are ultimately rendered as a profile of desired competencies, and which become the focal point for various HRM applications. Observed human behaviour is compared against the desired profile. The greatest opportunity for development is sought in the weakest competencies of people, and this demands considerable additional effort from them. One consequence of this conclusion is that many practitioners and scholars have sought refuge in an entirely

Table 21.2 A typology of competency, talent and sustainable people management approach

Competency approach	Talent approach	Sustainable approach
We start with the mission, vision and the 'desired' profile	We start with 'what is' in terms of strengths and talents	We start with what is and match it to profiles
Greater focus on the organizational perspective	Greater focus on the employee perspective	Combined perspectives of both employee and organization
Characteristics are competencies	Characteristics are 'talents'	Common terminology
Strengths, based on the competency profile	Strengths as characteristics that are conspicuously present/easily available	Observable characteristics that are useful
Focus on job fit, efficiency, ROI	Oriented towards 'utilizing', meaningfulness, development	Meaningful, partly based on objective observations
Gap analysis	Focus on strengths and 'making use of what is available'	Oriented towards using and fitting

Source: Van Beirendonck (2009).

different approach. This could explain the increasing popularity of talent management (Michaels et al., 2001), which proceeds from people's strengths. Talent management builds upon the strong aspects of an individual. Underlying interests and 'talents' are identified, with the goal of drawing relevant connections between these interests and competencies and the roles and/or positions in one or more organizational contexts. In a third, both/and, synthesis approach of sustainability, the challenge is to combine these different perspectives. This approach concerns dialogue, and is characterized by mutual respect and by the search for and discussion of possibilities and opportunities for both individual and organization. In this approach, the organization's mission is matched to the individual's passion.

Second Building Block: Openness

With openness, we refer to the connection of HRM with the external environment. First of all, it implies adding an outside-in perspective to HRM (Ulrich et al., 2012). Promoting an HRM with an outside-in character implies the adoption of a stakeholder perspective on HRM. Stakeholder theory represents a significant part of the debate in business ethics, and it shows many obvious connections to HRM (Greenwood and Freeman, 2011). The theory suggests that the organization's purpose, principles and relationship to society should be a shared process, in which employees are at the centre, in addition to social partners, customers and social movements (for example, the green movement). Along the same lines, it can be argued that every organization is like a mini-society, reflecting the same societal issues and trends. Dealing with diversity, work–life balance, ageing, scarcity, pollution and other issues should also be included on any HRM agenda.

Secondly, institutional theory can account for the societal embeddedness of HRM practices. Paauwe and Boselie (2003 and 2007) argue that, in addition to strategic (that is, vertical) fit and horizontal fit, organizational success through HRM depends upon environmental fit. They present a model of HRM based on the institutional mechanisms for organizational isomorphism developed by DiMaggio and Powell (1983). Three different types of institutional isomorphism can be distinguished: (1) coercive; (2) mimetic; and (3) normative. Coercive isomorphism results from formal and informal pressures on organizations exerted by other organizations upon which they are dependent and by cultural expectations in the societies in which they function. In HRM, coercive mechanisms include the influence of social partners (for example, trade unions and works councils), labour legislation and governments (Paauwe and Boselie, 2003). From a broader perspective, coercive isomorphism can also refer to a connection between the prevailing social norms and values and other processes (for example, the labour market participation of mothers, the elderly and immigrants). Mimetic isomorphism results from standard responses to uncertainty, leading to the imitation of structure, organizational design, or certain practices of similar organizations. Applied to HRM, mimetic mechanisms refer to imitations of the HRM strategies and practices of competitors due to uncertainty or a desire to follow trends in HRM (Paauwe and Boselie, 2003). Normative isomorphism is associated with professionalization. Formal education and professional networks lead to increasing homogeneity in the skills and knowledge of the entire workforce in a particular sector, which subsequently increases similarity between organizations.

The presence of these different isomorphic pressures on HRM, however, does not necessarily mean that organizations and their stakeholders see the institutional environment as restrictive. Organizations are able to create additional room by opting for specific HRM systems (Boon, 2008; Paauwe and Boselie, 2003). Institutional theorists have focused on structural conformity and isomorphism, while tending to overlook the role of active agency and resistance in organization–environment relationships. This active role of organizations has also been referred to as institutional entrepreneurship, which reintroduces agency, interests, power and stakeholders into the institutional analyses of organizations (Garud et al., 2007). For this reason, Lee (2011) calls for a theoretical framework that combines institutional and stakeholder theories in order to explain how firms choose their CSR and HRM strategies. According to Lee's argument, stakeholders play a critical role between institutional environments and organizations. On the one hand, stakeholders can amplify institutional pressure by directly channelling the message to the attention of organizational decision-makers. On the other hand, stakeholders can also smooth the institutional effect by acting as buffers between organizational and institutional pressure. A further assumption is that institutional forces and stakeholder influences are often issue-specific. For example, strong environmental norms or regulations do not necessarily entail equally pervasive norms on issues of employee diversity or human rights. Similarly, certain stakeholder groups with a strong interest in labour rights (for example, unions) may have no interest in other CSR-related issues (for example, pollution reduction). Organizational decision-makers should therefore identify and evaluate the strength of relevant institutional forces and stakeholder groups for each issue (Lee, 2011).

Third Building Block: Continuity

A third building block within the ROC model is the long-term perspective from the viewpoints of both the organizational relationship and the employee relationship. Companies strive to create conditions under which they can survive over a relatively long time, and HRM can contribute to this process. We begin this section with a discussion of the HRM and Performance debate. Second, we revisit the meaning of continuity within the employee relationship. We argue that, although 'careers for life' are a reality from a distant past, the organizational career is far from dead.

With the publications of Arthur (1994), Huselid (1995) and MacDuffie (1995), a decade of discussions on the added value of HRM started. Fifteen years and dozens of studies later, Boselie (2011) comes in his review article to a rather optimistic conclusion: there is growing evidence that HRM can lead to a better performance. Less optimistic is the author about the type of performance standards being used. The predominant theme is trying to understand how organizations manage their employees more effectively, so that productivity and profits are maximized. An important issue as such, yet rather one-sided since this approach ignores the importance of the employee perspective and the link with broader societal and institutional objectives. Within a more sustainable approach, research on three levels of performance is relevant: (1) the organization (for example, quality, efficiency, flexibility, innovation, profits); (2) society (for example, stakeholder satisfaction, employment growth, social inclusion); and (3) the individual (for example, work–life balance, engagement, employability). In a balanced approach, exclusively high scores on either financial, individual or social performance are considered as undesirable for the long-term survival of an organization. The latter approach combines the insights from an economic perspective with those from an institutional perspective in order to create a balanced and sustainable position for the organization (Paauwe et al., 2013). As such, sustainable HRM differs substantially from mainstream HRM.

The Continuity dimension can also be seen as an individual challenge within the employment relationship. The essence of the employment relationship is the supply of labour by the employee in return for a wage. The idea within exchange relationships is that these elements persist only as long as the exchange is in balance. Organizations can opt for HRM policies focused on mutual investments within a long-term perspective (Rousseau, 1995). Implications for the employer include investments in training or other forms of competence or career development initiatives. Implications for the employee include loyalty or the opportunity to develop skills that can be carried into the future (Tsui et al., 1997). In contrast, the exchanges in short-term labour relationships are limited to the provision of labour for a wage, without any guarantee of job security. The relational dimension is clearly missing in this context (Montes and Irving, 2008).

Within the literature on human capital (Lepak and Snell, 2002), these types of employment relationships are related to the strategic orientation and strategic importance of human capital. Current research shows that organizations whose workforces are characterized by low value and low uniqueness tend to be less concerned with the intra-organizational mobility of their employees and to offer fewer career management practices, while holding individual employees less accountable for managing their own careers (De Vos and Dries, 2013). Scholars have interpreted these findings as implying that such organizations tend to adopt a laissez-faire approach to career management, assigning organizational priority to neither career management nor continuity.

In contrast, this reality has been subjected to strong criticism within the literature on labour relations and stakeholder management. Questions concerning the treatment of low-wage, dependent workers are among the most central in ethical analyses of contemporary employment relationships (Van Buren and Greenwood, 2013). The ways in which organizations treat this group of stakeholders, who lack power and meaningful ways of changing the terms of exchange with their employers, should be a central focus of work in business ethics and stakeholder analysis. Given that stakeholders co-create value, one role of managers should be to create deals in which all of the firm's stakeholders – including low-wage workers – can ultimately win. Or as Hargreaves and Fink (2006) found: sustainable leadership is just. It does no harm to, and actively improves, the surrounding environment by finding ways to share knowledge and resources with other stakeholders.

SUSTAINABLE CAREER MANAGEMENT

Zooming in to the specific domain of sustainable career management forms a next step within our theoretical and conceptual reasoning on sustainable HRM. As career management is generally considered to be an important functional domain of HRM, consistent with the notion of sustainable HRM elaborated above, sustainable career management refers to all the processes and practices that manage the development of individuals along a path of experiences and jobs (Hall, 2002), with respect for employees, openness towards different stakeholders and in view of continuity. As mentioned in the introductory chapter of this Handbook, sustainability in careers does not equal lifetime employment in one single organization. If sustainability in careers also stems from inter-organizational mobility and employees taking charge of their own career development, what are the implications for sustainable career management? And how can we translate a sustainable career framework within the ROC model?

A career refers to the pattern of work-related experiences an individual encounters during his or her professional life (Greenhaus et al., 2010; Hall, 2002). It is a complex mosaic of objective situations and events, and subjective experiences. It is the individual who is considered as being the 'owner' of his or her career. At the same time, careers and the management of careers are highly relevant for organizations as for their continuity they depend – to a greater or lesser extent – on their human capital. Inversely, career management policies undertaken by organizations can have substantial implications for individuals. Differently stated, individuals' careers do not develop in a vacuum but are affected by the contexts in which they unfold; the organizational context as well as the broader labour market, but also the private context of individuals' personal lives. As described by Baruch in this Handbook (Chapter 24), careers can be conceived as 'eco-systems'. In this chapter, we will further elaborate on sustainable career management from an organizational perspective.

As outlined above, sustainable career management means more than designing an attractive career perspective for (core) employees. Underlying the notion of sustainable career management is the principle of balancing: a balance between organizational and individual needs; between support and active involvement of employees; between a tailor-made approach and inclusion of all employees; between the present and future. From this balancing perspective, six ingredients of sustainable career management can be discerned. In what follows, we will describe these six ingredients. Next, we will apply the ROC model to this framework of sustainable career management.

Ingredients of Sustainable Career Management

Focus on employability and work ability

Career management essentially comes down to a matching process of individual and organizational needs (Baruch, 2004). Sustainable career management addresses this matching process with a long-term view in mind by focusing on ways to ensure employability of employees in the short and the long run, with explicit attention also for their work ability and vitality, that is, the sustainable employment of employees. Sustainable employment is defined as employees having the opportunity to perform work while preserving their health and well-being during their working life, now and in the future (Van der Klink et al., 2011). The value aspect of work is emphasized: work must add value for the organization as well as for the employee in order to be sustainable. This implies that sustainable career management is more than matching current organizational needs with available competencies (De Vos and Dries, 2013). A focus on employability implies attention to the career potential of individuals, enabling their growth and facilitating their career security by investing in the development of competencies and talent (De Vos et al., 2011). By work ability, we mean focus on a sustainable work pressure in order to safeguard the physical, psychological and sociological ability of people to work (Ilmarinen et al., 2005). Careers imply a time frame and this is also connected to the idea of sustainable careers: no short-term view on overambitious challenges in a job today with the risk of burnout tomorrow, but focus on a workable career that will last even longer for the younger generations.

Anticipating for the future: a proactive approach

Career management that results in sustainable careers can only be effective when it operates proactively: looking forward to the future, thereby surpassing the so-called 'gravity law' and transcending the dominant tendency to selectively allocate our attention to what's needed here and now (De Vos, 2013). This tendency comprises reacting to problems stemming from the outflow of large groups of baby boomers, dealing with the sudden exit of a core employee or responding to the needs of specific target groups in order to ensure engagement and retention, which can take up a substantial part of the daily career management priorities (De Vos and Dries, 2013). However, the danger exists that the focus on these types of measures, which mainly aim to 'cure' a current situation, will undermine the focus on more anticipating and proactive measures. Proactivity implies, amongst other things, anticipating structural shortages on the labour market and changes in the business strategy or business environment and their implications for the need of human capital, changing expectations and attitudes of younger generations and so on. Sustainable career management means reconciling the dilemma between enacting a long-term vision and responding to the current situation by balancing these two different time frames.

Inclusive approach

From a strategic human capital approach, it seems to make sense that career management is focused on so-called 'critical talent' (Lepak and Snell, 2002). Sustainable career management, however, does not focus exclusively on those employee segments that are critical to the organization because of their shortages in critical skills, age-related concerns or other timely reasons. Sustainable career management entails policies directed to different target groups and avoids focused attention on only a limited percentage of the workforce, for whatever reason this might be. As a result of a too selective or exclusive focus on a limited part of the workforce, combined with a rather reactive approach, the gap between demand and supply on the internal labour market can become very wide.

Enabling a tailor-made and individualized approach

An inclusive approach does not mean uniformity or equality. Quite the opposite applies: career management that embraces all employees acknowledges at the same time that those employees are very diverse in their aspirations and talents. According to the life stage and the broader context of life, the needs of employees and their view on their career can vary (Mainiero and Sullivan, 2006). This calls for a dynamic perspective on careers, instead of a passive and inflexible system that aims to capture the dynamics of career expectations in one complex system. Rather, this dynamic perspective on careers implies an open view on careers and a culture that allows career development to be talked about in an open way also within the organizational context. This might, for instance, include facilitating I-deals or individualized agreements between individuals and their employers (Rousseau, 2005) and hence moving away from providing only standard career options that hold for all individuals. It means facilitating an 'n = 1 approach'. I-deals are voluntary, personalized agreements of a non-standard nature negotiated between individual employees and their employers regarding terms that benefit each party (Rousseau et al., 2006). These individual negotiated arrangements are becoming widespread in today's workplace as organizations and individuals experience a growing need for customization and individualization of various aspects of the employment relationship (Rousseau et al., 2006).

Active involvement of employees

Sustainable career management is not a 'taking care' policy but, on the contrary, acknowledges the employee in his or her role of 'career owner' (Hall, 2002; Greenhaus et al., 2010). In the end, it is the employee who is in the driving seat, not the organization. This means that facilitating self-awareness and self-directedness are intrinsic and inherent components of sustainable career management. Employees have to reflect themselves about their career needs, their competencies, their career identity. This requires a career management that acknowledges boundaryless careers – not limited to the boundaries of the organization – and that employees do not limit their reflections to these boundaries.

Career support

Career management that enables sustainable careers recognizes that self-awareness and self-directedness are meta-competencies that do not come as a given and that employees need to be supported in developing these career competencies. Sustainable career management hence involves supporting practices and processes, practices that develop employees' career competencies and that facilitate individuals in making their career choices, not making these choices on behalf of them.

Respect, Openness and Continuity as Building Blocks of Sustainable Career Management

In this section, we integrate the framework for sustainable career management with the broader ROC model for sustainable HRM. We discuss how respect, openness and continuity can be realized through sustainable career management practices. First, in the ROC model respect comes down to bringing the 'human' back to HRM and to balancing 'human' with 'resource'. This means recognizing the richness and complexity of the target focus, namely employees as human beings, and as a consequence the fact that this complexity cannot be brought down to economic indicators. Sustainable career management explicitly recognizes this complexity by embracing an inclusive approach, and facilitating the career development of all employees within the organization. It recognizes that all employees have careers, and that the long-term consequences of current job performance for outcomes like performance, retention, employability or engagement in the long run should not be overlooked. It departs from the principle of fairness, however, without evolving towards a uniform structure built on the premise of equality. Underscoring the individual nature of careers implies room for individualization by responding to individuals' career needs – or what Las Heras (2009) calls 'preferred success sets' – and by creating so-called 'smart jobs' (Hall and Las Heras, 2010) that stimulate not merely high performance but also learning, growth and employability. At the same time, however, this focus on the individual is balanced with organizational needs. By keeping track of organizational evolutions and evolutions in the broader socio-economic environment, organizational needs for competencies and implications for careers can be formulated and communicated towards employees, thereby contributing to a clear psychological contract (Sturges et al., 2005). Respect is also inherent in the dimension of active employee involvement, as this means that individuals get autonomy when it comes to their career development, and through career support systems that enhance the development of career competencies and that facilitate employees' career choices in line with their needs.

Openness brings the stakeholder perspective to HRM, it implies considering HRM from the 'outside in', recognizing the occurrence of societal issues and trends like diversity, the growing need for work–life balance and an ageing workforce, which require an organizational response. In other words, it recognizes the social embeddedness of the organization and considers relevant institutional forces and stakeholder groups. Applied to sustainable career management, this means that organizations anticipate, rather than merely react, to socio-economic trends, and formulate implications for the demand for and supply of human capital. This openness also implies consideration of the broader labour market and labour market regulations. It means tailoring to individuals' needs stemming from diverse factors such as gender differences, age-related needs, but also more deep-level differences such as career aspirations, personality and basic needs. In sustainable career management, the employee is recognized as being the central but not the only stakeholder. It balances individual ownership with organizational embeddedness, and a boundaryless view on careers incorporating support measures to facilitate career development. It also recognizes that careers contain many complex relationships both within the work context (for example, with supervisor, mentor, peers) and outside (for example, family, friends, community involvement) which together affect an individual's career choices at any given point in time. A tailored approach also means overcoming the tendency to develop one overarching career system that is applied to all employees.

Third, continuity encompasses a long-term perspective. For their continuity, organizations depend on their human capital, but depending on their strategic focus, their sector, and the wider labour market, this dependence on human capital might be more or less critical. In situations where dependence on human capital is critical, for instance, because competencies are difficult to find on the external labour market or because of their complexity of firm-specificity they require a long time before they are mastered, the need to ensure continuity through career management becomes a major concern (De Vos and Dries, 2013). Sustainable career management, however, encompasses more than a focus on retaining valuable human capital. It also implies a focus on employability and work ability as two critical factors enabling human capital to stay valuable not only today but also in the future. While employability is gaining increased attention in the career literature, work ability is often not considered from the viewpoint of career management (see also Chapter 10 in this Handbook). While a job reflects an employee's immediate work-related experiences, a career is the accumulation of these experiences over the entire working-life span (Hall and Las Heras, 2010). A job with high challenges, work pressure or stress today might hence have important consequences for an individual's work ability in the long run but is often not considered from that perspective. Sustainable career management balances a focus on today's needs with anticipation of future consequences by creating so-called 'smart jobs' which stimulate not merely performance but also learning, growth and employability (Hall and Las Heras, 2010). In doing so, it does not limit its attention to strategic workforce planning exercises for critical target groups, but complements this with a wider perspective on evolutions that can be expected amongst or will have impact on the total workforce both inside and outside the organization. In this regard, sustainable career management also has links with sustainable leadership. Sustainable leaders spread their leadership (that is, distributed leadership) and are heavily involved in making sure from day one that succession is ensured in the organization. They embrace and promote, however, cohesive diversity and avoid aligned standardization of policies, assessment, and staff development and training. Sustainable leaders foster and learn from diversity and try to create cohesion and networking among the different elements (Hargreaves and Fink, 2006). By doing so they contribute to continuity.

CONCLUSIONS

In this chapter, 'Respect', 'Openness' and 'Continuity' were introduced as the three building blocks of sustainable HRM. In the previous sections, we summarized theoretical and applied concepts and dynamics, and elaborated on their implications for sustainable careers. Although the attention for respect, openness and continuity is not new in itself, our contribution lies in the critical reflection upon and redirection of existing HRM practices, systems and themes towards the ROC model. As such, sustainable HRM should be seen as a complementary perspective. Its aim is not to substitute the strategic HRM perspective, but to offer a correction given the concretization of the latter from a unilateral business management point of view. It brings HRM into a next stage of maturity. For this, it uses inspiration derived from the CSR approach, ethical and critical HRM, and stakeholder and institutional theory. The ROC model aims to bridge theory and practice. It gives a framework and new vocabulary for classifying and (re)positioning both new initiatives and experiments as well as existing practices and traditions on the domain of sustainable HRM. Sustainable career management, as a specific domain of HRM, brings respect, openness and continuity into the management of employees' careers by balancing short-term and long-term needs, focusing on employability and work ability, following an inclusive approach, tailoring to individuals' needs and providing career support.

REFERENCES

Arthur, J.B. (1994), 'Effects of human resource systems on manufacturing performance and turnover', *Academy of Management Journal*, **37** (3), 670–87.

Baruch, Y. (2004), *Managing Careers. Theory and Practice*, Harlow, UK: Pearson.

Bolton, S. and Houlihan, M. (2007), *Searching for the Human in Human Resource Management*, London: Palgrave Macmillan.

Boon, C. (2008), 'HRM and fit: Survival of the fittest', Erasmus University Rotterdam, unpublished work.

Boselie, P. (2010), *Strategic Human Resource Management. A Balanced Approach*, London: McGraw-Hill.

Boselie, P. (2011), 'Human resource governance: Voorbij "Managerialism"', Utrecht University, unpublished work.

Clarke, M. (2013), 'Sustainable HRM: A new approach to people management', in M. Clarke (ed.), *Readings in HRM and Sustainability*, Prahran: Tilde University Press, pp. 1–6.

Clegg, R.S., Vieira Da Cunha, J. and Pina e Cunha, M. (2002), 'Management paradoxes: A relation view', *Human Relations*, **55** (5), 483–503.

De Lange, W. and Koppens, J. (2007), *De duurzame arbeidsorganisatie*, Amsterdam: WEKA uitgeverij.

De Vos, A. (2013), 'Over de (ir)rationaliteit van het loopbaanbeleid', *Gedrag en Organisatie*, **26** (4), 431–48.

De Vos, A. and Dries, N. (2013), 'Applying a talent management lens to career management: The role of human capital composition and continuity', *The International Journal of Human Resource Management*, **24** (9), 1816–31.

De Vos, A., De Hauw, S. and Van der Heijden, B.I.J.M. (2011), 'Competency development and career success: The mediating role of employability', *Journal of Vocational Behavior*, **79** (2), 438–47.

DiMaggio, P.J. and Powell, W. (1983), 'The iron cage revisited: Institutional isomorphism and collective rationality in organizational fields', *American Sociological Review*, **48** (2), 147–60.

Ehnert, I. (2009), *Sustainable Human Resource Management: A Conceptual and Explanatory Analysis from a Paradox Perspective. Contributions to Management Science*, Heidelberg: Springer-Verlag.

Ehnert, I. (2013), 'Paradox as a lens for theorizing sustainable HRM', in I. Ehnert, W. Harry and K.J. Zink (eds), *Sustainability and Human Resource Management. Developing Sustainable Business Organizations*, Heidelberg: Springer, pp. 247–72.

Ehnert, I. and Brandl, J. (2013), 'Towards a paradox perspective for HRM: Integrating research and moving ahead', unpublished paper presented at the 28th EIASM Workshop on Strategic HRM, 14–15 April, Copenhagen, Denmark.

Ehnert, I. and Harry, W. (2012), 'Recent developments and future prospects on sustainable human resource management: Introduction to the special issue', *Management Revue*, **23** (3), 221–38.

Eurofound (2012), 'Trends in job quality in Europe. A report on the fifth European Working Conditions', Luxembourg: Publications Office of the European Union.

Garud, R., Hardy, C. and Maguire, S. (2007), 'Institutional entrepreneurship as embedded agency', *Organization Studies*, **28** (7), 957–69.

Greenhaus, J.H., Callanan, G.A. and Godschalk, V.M. (2010), *Career Management*, 4th edn, Thousand Oaks, CA: Sage Publications.

Greenwood, M. (2012), 'Ethical analyses of HRM: A review and research agenda', *Journal of Business Ethics*, **111** (1), 109–19.

Greenwood, M. and Freeman, R.E. (2011), 'Ethics and HRM: The contribution of stakeholder theory', *Business and Professional Ethics Journal*, **30** (3–4), 269–92.

Guest, D.E. and Woodrow, C. (2012), 'Exploring the boundaries of Human Resource managers' responsibilities', *Journal of Business Ethics*, **111** (1), 109–19.
Hall, D.T. (2002), *Careers In and Out of Organizations*, Thousand Oaks, CA: Sage Publications.
Hall, D.T. and Las Heras, M. (2010), 'Reintegrating job design and career theory: Creating not just good jobs but smart jobs', *Journal of Organizational Behavior*, **31**, 448–62.
Hargreaves, A. and Fink, D. (2006), *Sustainable Leadership*, San Francisco, CA: Jossey-Bass.
Huselid, M.A. (1995), 'The impact of human resource management practices on turnover, productivity and corporate financial performance', *Academy of Management Journal*, **38** (3), 625–72.
Ilmarinen, J., Tuomi, T.K. and Seitsamo, J. (2005), 'New dimensions of work ability', *International Congress Series 1280*, 3–7.
Janssens, M. and Steyaert, C. (2009), 'HRM and performance: A plea for reflexivity in HRM studies', *Journal of Management Studies*, **46** (1), 143–55.
Las Heras, M. (2009), 'Psychological career success, preferred success set and its dynamism', Unpublished doctoral dissertation, Boston, MA: Boston University.
Lee, P.M.-D. (2011), 'Configuration of external influence: The combined effect of institutions and stakeholders and corporate social responsibility strategies', *Journal of Business Ethics*, **102**, 281–98.
Lengnick-Hall, M.L., Lengnick-Hall, C.A., Andrade, L. and Drake, B. (2009), 'Strategic human resource management: The evolution of the field', *Human Resource Management Review*, **19** (2), 64–85.
Lepak, D.P. and Snell, S.A. (2002), 'Examining the human resource architecture: The relationships among human capital, employment, and human resource configurations', *Journal of Management*, **28** (4), 517–43.
MacDuffie, J.P. (1995), 'Human resource bundles and manufacturing performance: Organizational logic and flexible production systems in the world auto industry', *Industrial and Labor Relations Review*, **48** (2), 197–221.
Mainiero, L.A. and Sullivan, S.E. (2006), *The Opt-Out Revolt. Why People are Leaving Companies to Create Kaleidoscope Careers*, Mountain View, CA: Davies-Black.
Mariappanadar, S. (2013), 'Stakeholder harm index: A method to capture the costs of harm of HRM practices on stakeholders', unpublished paper presented at the International Network of Business and Management Journals conference, Lisbon, Portugal, 17–19 June.
Michaels, E., Handfield-Jones, H. and Axelrod, B. (2001), *The War for Talent*, Boston, MA: Harvard Business School Press.
Montes, S.D. and Irving, P.G. (2008), 'Disentangling the effects of promised and delivered inducements: Relational and transactional contract elements and the mediating role of trust', *Journal of Applied Psychology*, **93** (6), 1367–81.
Paauwe, J. (2012), 'HRM als leer- en ontwikkelingstraject', *Tijdschrift voor HRM*, **15**, 11–12.
Paauwe, J. and Boselie, P. (2003), 'Challenging "strategic HRM" and the relevance of the institutional setting', *Human Resource Management Journal*, **13** (3), 56–70.
Paauwe, J. and Boselie, P. (2007), 'HRM and societal embeddedness', in P. Boxall, J. Purcell and P.M. Wright (eds), *The Oxford Handbook of Human Resource Management*, Oxford, UK: Oxford University Press, pp. 166–84.
Paauwe, J., Boon, C.T., Boselie, P. and den Hartog, D.N. (2013), 'Reconceptualizing fit in strategic human resource management: "Lost in translation"?', in J. Paauwe, D.E. Guest and P.M. Wright (eds), *HRM and Performance: Achievements and Challenges*, Chichester, UK: John Wiley and Sons, pp. 61–77.
Rhodes, C. and Harvey, G. (2012), 'Agonism and the Possibilities of Ethics for HRM', *Journal of Business Ethics*, **111** (1), 49–59.
Rousseau, D.M. (1995), *Psychological Contracts in Organizations: Understanding Written and Unwritten Agreements*, London: Sage Publications.
Rousseau, D.M. (2005), *I-Deals: Idiosyncratic Deals Employees Bargain for Themselves*, New York: M.E. Sharpe.
Rousseau, D.M., Ho, V.T. and Greenberg, J. (2006), I-deals: Idiosyncratic deals in employment relationships, *Academy of Management Review*, **31**, 977–94.
SHRM Foundation (2012), 'HRM's role in corporate social and environmental sustainability', available at www.shrm.org/about/foundation/products/documents/412%20csr%20report%20final%20for%20web.pdf, pp. 5–14.
Sturges, J., Conway, N., Guest, D. and Liefooghe, A. (2005), 'Managing the career deal: The psychological contract as a framework for understanding career management, organizational commitment and work behavior', *Journal of Organizational Behavior*, **26** (7), 821–38.
Taylor, S., Osland, J. and Egri, C. (2012), 'Guest editors' introduction: Introduction to HRM's role in sustainability: Systems, strategies, and practices', *Human Resource Management*, **51** (6), 789–98.
Tsui, A.S., Pearce, J.L., Porter, L.W. and Tripoli, A.M. (1997), 'Alternative approaches to the employee–organization relationship: Does investment in employees pay off?', *Academy of Management Journal*, **40** (5), 1089–121.

Ulrich, D., Younger, J., Brockbank, W. and Ulrich, M. (2012), *HR from the Outside In. Six Competences for the Future of Human Resources*, London: McGraw-Hill Education.
Van Beirendonck, L. (2009), 'Dieptezicht in competentie-management: Integratie van een modernistische en postmodernistische visie', PhD thesis, Tilburg: Tilburg University.
Van Buren, H.J. and Greenwood, M. (2013), 'Ethics and HRM education', *Journal of Academic Ethics*, **11** (1), 1–15.
Van Buren, H.J., Greenwood, M. and Sheehan, C. (2011), 'Strategic human resource management and the decline of employee focus', *Human Resource Management Review*, **21**, 209–19.
Van der Klink, J.J.L., Bültmann, U., Brouwer, S., Burdorf, A., Schaufeli, W.B., Zijlstra, F.R.H. and Van der Wilt, G.J. (2011), 'Duurzame inzetbaarheid bij oudere werknemers, werk als waarde', *Gedrag en Organisatie*, **24** (4), 342–56.

22 Studying retirement from a career perspective: are people who take charge of their career less inclined to retire?

An De Coen, Anneleen Forrier and Luc Sels

To deal with demographic changes in the labor market and an increasing life expectancy, it is important for older workers to extend their working lives (European Commission, 2012). In the past few decades, a significant amount of research has been conducted on factors impacting individuals' transition into retirement. Most of these studies looked at personal factors (for example, health or wealth), family factors (for example, spouse working status or care status), job and organizational factors (for example, job characteristics or age stereotypes at the workplace) and institutional factors (for example, early retirement schemes) influencing this transition (see, for instance, Feldman, 1994; Shultz et al., 1998; Wang and Schulz, 2010).

Surprisingly, few studies take a career perspective when studying the transition into retirement (De Vos and Segers, 2013; Topa et al., 2009). However, retirement is an important career transition (De Vos and Segers, 2013). Moreover, it is often argued that people with sustainable careers will postpone this career transition and remain longer in the labor market (Newman, 2011). Sustainable careers are flexible and adaptable, not only to employers' needs but also to individuals' needs (Newman, 2011). To build sustainable careers, people need the necessary career competencies to self-navigate their career (Eby et al., 2003). This enables them to pursue a satisfying career and to benefit from opportunities in the internal and external labor market (Eby et al., 2003). Both this career satisfaction (Hall and Mirvis, 1995) and employability (Armstrong-Stassen and Stassen, 2013; Gendron, 2011) are believed to extend people's working lives. Many active aging policies (OECD, 1998; Walker and Maltby, 2012) are based on these career-related assumptions. These policies aim to increase older workers' freedom to make personal choices and support their adaptability to deal with changing circumstances in the labor market in order to guarantee their employability (Moulaert and Biggs, 2013). Likewise, HR age policies supporting a developmental climate for older workers are based on the idea that this may enhance their competencies, increase their employability and consequently extend their working lives (Armstrong-Stassen and Schlosser, 2008; Bal et al., 2012; Leisink and Knies, 2011; Thijssen and Rocco, 2010).

Even though age policies are inspired by the idea that sustainable careers may extend individuals' working lives through their impact on career satisfaction and employability, empirical evidence remains scarce. Therefore, in this chapter we will investigate how career competencies influence the intention to retire through their impact on self-directedness, career satisfaction and employability. We thereby focus on two career competencies for which the current career literature has showed increasing attention (Hall, 1996; Hall and Chandler, 2005; Verbruggen and Sels, 2008). More specifically, Hall (1996; 2004) considered self-awareness and adaptability as career competencies that are crucial for self-directedness. While self-awareness facilitates self-evaluation, adaptability enables individuals to respond to changing demands from the environment and deal with new circumstances. We will examine how both career competencies, self-awareness and adaptability, impact self-directedness and how employability in the internal and external labor market as well as subjective career satisfaction mediate the relationship between self-directedness and the retirement intention of older workers.

Studying employee retirement from a career perspective, this study adds to the literature by testing the supposition that sustainable careers extend working lives (Newman, 2011). We test the assumption that older workers who are able to self-navigate their career will be less inclined to retire because they are more employable and more satisfied with their career. While these underlying ideas are widely accepted (Bal et al., 2012; Newman, 2011; Walker and Maltby, 2012), to the best of our knowledge there is little empirical research investigating this reasoning.

HYPOTHESES

Figure 22.1 depicts the research model. It shows how self-awareness and adaptability are hypothesized to relate to workers' retirement intention through diverse paths.

In this study, we consider retirement to be a career transition. The central idea behind the model is that older workers who are able to self-navigate their career will be less inclined to leave the labor market and retire (De Vos and Segers, 2013; Hall and Mirvis, 1995; Topa et al., 2009). Career self-directedness is a central dimension of a protean career orientation, and reflects a feeling of personal agency (Briscoe and Hall, 2006): individuals who are self-directed feel in charge of their own career and take an independent role in managing it (Briscoe et al., 2006). Self-awareness and adaptability are the two meta-competencies that equip people to obtain this protean career orientation of self-directedness (Hall, 2004). Since people with a self-directed career orientation are supposed to strive for psychological success in their career (Briscoe and Hall, 2006), we assume that older workers who are self-directed will be more satisfied with their career. This may decrease their intention to retire. Moreover, older workers with a self-directed

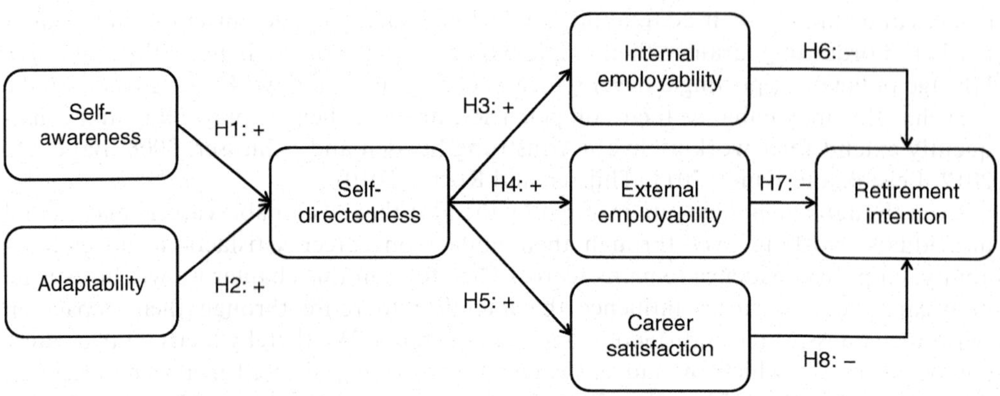

Figure 22.1 Research model

career orientation may be more able to safeguard their employability, both with their employer (internal employability) as in the external labor market (external employability), and this may also decrease their intention to retire. Below, we develop an argumentation for each hypothesis in the model.

Self-awareness and Adaptability Influence Self-directedness

Self-awareness relates to the knowing-why competencies of DeFillippi and Arthur (1994). It captures the extent to which people know their strengths, weaknesses, goals and values. Self-awareness offers individuals an 'internal career compass' that serves as a guide when making career decisions (Hall, 2002; McArdle et al., 2007). Adaptability is a key concept regarding career development. It reflects individuals' readiness to cope with predictable tasks related to aspects of work, but also with unpredictable work-related changes (Savickas, 1997). Adaptability comprises 'the willingness and ability to change behaviors, feelings and thoughts in response to environmental demands' (McArdle et al., 2007, p. 248). Adaptability serves as a self-correcting mechanism. Both self-awareness and adaptability may impact career self-directedness (Hall, 1996; 2004). Low levels of self-awareness may keep people from making their own career decisions due to a lack of direction and values to do so. Low levels of adaptability may prevent them from dealing with set-backs or changes they are confronted with. Empirical research from Verbruggen and Sels (2008) showed that self-awareness and adaptability relate positively to self-directedness in a relatively young sample. We assume this will also be the case for older workers. Older workers who are able to self-reflect and to change their behaviors, feelings and thoughts will feel more in charge of their own career compared to their peers who are lacking these career competencies (Hall and Mirvis, 1995).

Hypothesis 1: Self-awareness relates positively to self-directedness among older workers.

Hypothesis 2: Adaptability relates positively to self-directedness among older workers.

Self-directedness Relates to Perceived Employability

We assume that self-directedness may positively influence perceived employability. Perceived employability refers to individuals' perceived likelihood of retaining or obtaining a job, either with the current organization (that is, internal perceived employability) or with another employer (external perceived employability) (Berntson et al., 2006; De Cuyper et al., 2011; Forrier and Sels, 2003; Rothwell and Arnold, 2007; Silla et al., 2009). We focus on perceived employability for two reasons. First, we assume that individuals' perceptions of employability encompass their interpretation both of the labor market and of their own employability skills and attitudes. So perceived employability captures both contextual and individual factors of employability (Forrier et al., 2009). Second, actions of individuals are often more driven by their own perception of a situation than by the actual reality (De Witte and Näswall, 2003).

Individuals who feel in charge of their own career may be more concerned about identifying and creating career opportunities. Furthermore, they may be more likely to have realistic expectations and remain open to new career experiences. This may increase both their perceived internal and external employability (Kossek et al., 1998; Sturges et al., 2002; Zacher and Frese, 2011). Moreover, in the specific case of the late career, older workers who demonstrate a self-directed career attitude may counter employers' stereotypical belief of them being reluctant to change and focused on withdrawal or decline (Claes and Van Loo, 2011), and consequently strengthen their perceived employability. We therefore formulate the following hypotheses:

Hypothesis 3: Self-directedness relates positively to perceived internal employability among older workers.

Hypothesis 4: Self-directedness relates positively to perceived external employability among older workers.

Self-directedness Relates to Career Satisfaction

Hall (2002; 2004) stated that people take personal responsibility in managing their career to obtain psychological success. In this respect, self-directedness is theorized to relate positively to career satisfaction (Briscoe et al., 2006). Individuals who are self-directed in developing career paths are more likely to select those jobs enabling them to achieve personally meaningful career-related goals. This may promote career satisfaction since it is likely to enhance individuals' person-career fit, that is 'the extent to which an individual's career experiences are compatible with his or her values, interests and talents.' (Parasuraman et al., 2000, p. 70). Empirical studies (Colakoglu, 2011; De Vos and Soens, 2008; Verbruggen and Sels, 2008) supported the positive relationship between self-directedness and career satisfaction. Moreover, Hall and Mirvis (1995) assumed that self-directedness is the key for psychological success in the mid- and late career stage. They argued that older workers who are self-directed will be better able to navigate their career in the direction that satisfies them. Older workers who are not able to change and reflect on their career are more at risk of becoming dissatisfied. Therefore, we hypothesize that self-directedness contributes to career satisfaction.

Hypothesis 5: Self-directedness relates positively to career satisfaction among older workers.

Perceived Employability and Retirement Intention

Many strategies to retain older workers longer in the workforce are based on the idea that sustaining their employability is a way to extend working lives and delay retirement (Bal et al., 2012; Leisink and Knies, 2011; Thijssen and Rocco, 2010). The Conservation of Resources (COR) Theory (Hobfoll 1988; 1989) offers a framework to explain this relationship. In line with previous research, we consider perceived internal and external employability to be personal resources (for example De Cuyper et al., 2012). According to the COR Theory, people who have more personal resources have a stronger sense of control over their environment (Hobfoll et al., 2003). Following this line of reasoning, people with a higher perceived internal or external employability may still feel in control of their career (Wang et al., 2013) and may therefore be less inclined to end it. In contrast, the COR theory argues that people who lack personal resources or who are confronted with resource loss may shift their focus of attention (Hobfoll, 1989). They may focus on what they might gain instead of lose in a particular situation. In case of low perceived internal and external employability, older workers may shift their attention from their work and career to the alternative of retirement. An additional strategy to deal with a lack of resources is to reevaluate these resources (Hobfoll, 1989), so they may lower the value of work in their lives, which may increase their likelihood to retire. In a similar line, Brandstädter and Renner (1990) posited that individuals use accommodative coping processes like disengagement or reorientation when their appraisal of a situation is negative and they lack personal control for corrective action. In the case of low perceived employability, they may be more likely to disengage from work and intend to retire. We therefore hypothesize:

Hypothesis 6: Internal perceived employability relates to retirement intention in a negative way.

Hypothesis 7: External perceived employability relates to retirement intention in a negative way.

Career Satisfaction and Retirement Intention

The transition into retirement is often looked at as a form of turnover (Adams and Beehr, 1998). However, this transition into retirement is not just about quitting the organization or the current job but also about quitting one's career (Munderlein et al., 2013). According to the work role attachment theory, retirement involves detaching from all these work roles: job, organization and career (Adams et al., 2002). The more one is attached to a work role, the more one desires to remain in the work role. Leaving the work role may in that case more strongly imply the loss of self-identity. Following this line of reasoning, we assume that people who are more satisfied with their career will be more attached to their career and will therefore have a lower intention to retire. This is in line with empirical findings of Templer et al. (2010), who found that older workers with higher career satisfaction were more motivated to continue working The idea that career satisfaction may decrease the intention to leave one's career is also similar to the central idea in turnover literature that job satisfaction decreases one's intention to quit one's job (March and Simon, 1958).

Hypothesis 8: Career satisfaction relates to retirement intention in a negative way.

METHODS

Procedure and Sample

The data for this study originates from the survey 'Careers in Flanders' carried out by the Flemish Policy Research Centre Work and Social Economy (with Flanders being the

Table 22.1 Sample characteristics (n = 285)

Demographics		Percentage
Gender	Male	52.45
	Female	47.55
Age	50–54	53.71
	55–59	37.10
	60–64	9.19
Educational level	No high school degree	7.37
	High school degree	52.28
	Bachelor's or Master's degree	40.35
Functional level	Executive staff	50.53
	Clerical staff	16.49
	Professional staff	11.93
	Middle management	14.04
	Senior management	7.00

Dutch-speaking region of Belgium). The survey is based on two-stage stratified sampling to obtain a representative sample of the Flemish population. In a first step, 161 of the 308 Flemish municipalities were systematically selected; the possibility of being selected was proportional to the size of the municipality. In the second step, a random sample was selected that was stratified by age and gender. Hence, the sample is representative for the Flemish working population regarding workers' age, gender and geographical distribution. We conducted structured interviews with 1518 individuals about their labor market position and career attitudes. The majority of the respondents (1114 out of 1,18, that is, 73 percent) had a job at the time of the interview.

In Belgium, the legal retirement age is set at age 65. Furthermore, employee retirement is usually studied among individuals in late career, that is among workers aged 50 or older (see, for instance, Chan and Stevens, 1999; Claes and Van Loo, 2011; Herrbach et al., 2009). Therefore, this study uses the observations from the 285 employed respondents aged 50 to 64 years old with no missing values for the studied variables. Table 22.1 shows some sample characteristics.

Measures

Self-awareness

The six-item scale of Verbruggen and Sels (2008) was used to measure self-awareness (Cronbach's alpha = .85). Respondents had to indicate on a five-point Likert scale (1 = totally disagree; 5 = totally agree) to what extent they were aware of their strengths, weaknesses, values and motives. Items include: 'I know my strengths and weaknesses' and 'I am aware of what I value in my career and life'.

Adaptability

Five items (London, 1993) rated on a scale ranging from 1 (Low) to 5 (High) were used to measure adaptability (Cronbach's alpha = .75). The scale measures individuals' perceived ability and readiness to adapt to changing circumstances. Sample items are: 'To what extent are you able to adapt to changes in your career?' and 'To what extent do you welcome changes in your career?'.

Self-directedness

We used seven items from the scale developed by Briscoe et al. (2006) to measure self-directedness (Cronbach's alpha = .85). Respondents had to indicate on a five-point scale to what extent they agreed with each item. Sample items are: 'I am in charge of my own career' and 'Ultimately, I depend upon myself to move my career forward'.

Internal employability

Perceived employability in the internal labor market was measured by four items developed by De Cuyper and De Witte (2010). A sample item is: 'I am optimistic that I could find another job with this employer, if I looked for one'. The items were scored on a five-point Likert scale (1 = totally disagree; 5 = totally agree). The scale showed good internal consistency (Cronbach's alpha = .91).

External employability

Perceived employability in the external labor market was measured by four items developed by De Cuyper and De Witte (2010). A sample item is: 'I am optimistic that I could find another job elsewhere, if I looked for one'. The items were scored on a five-point Likert scale (1 = totally disagree; 5 = totally agree). The scale showed good internal consistency (Cronbach's alpha = .94).

Career satisfaction

Since Hofmans et al. (2008) found only one item of the Career Satisfaction Scale (Greenhaus et al., 1990) to have strong factorial invariance, that is 'I am satisfied with the success I have achieved in my career', we followed Heslin (2003) by measuring overall career success using a single item. Respondents were asked to answer the following question on a ten-point rating scale (1 = extremely unsatisfied; 10 = extremely satisfied): 'Everything considered, how successful do you consider your career to date?'.

Retirement intention

We developed four items for this study to assess workers' intention to leave the labor market: (1) 'If they propose that I leave the labor market tomorrow, I will seriously consider doing so'; (2) 'I would love to remain active in the labor market as long as possible' (reverse scored); (3) 'For a long time now, working is no longer my main concern'; and (4) 'If I were dismissed, I would immediately start searching for another job' (reverse scored). Respondents rated the items on a five-point Likert scale (1 = totally disagree; 5 = totally agree). The scale's reliability was acceptable (Cronbach's alpha = .61).

We performed confirmatory factor analysis on the 30 items comprising the six measures to verify whether the scales measured the distinct concepts. Consistent with previous research, we allowed for correlations between internal and external employability

(Rothwell and Arnold, 2007; Rothwell et al., 2008; Rothwell et al., 2009). The fit indices showed that the measurement model fits the data well ($\chi^2(400) = 709.66$ ($p < .001$); RMSEA = .051; SRMR= .097; CFI = .925). Because all items loaded significantly on their intended constructs ($p < .001$) and the sample was too small to test a model with latent factors, scale scores were calculated based on item averages.

Control variables

In the analysis, we controlled for gender, career length and functional level because of their known effects on workers' decision to stop working (Von Bonsdorff et al., 2010; Wang and Shultz, 2010). We chose to include career length rather than age as a control variable because it determines eligibility for early retirement in the Belgian labor market. The gender variable was dichotomous, with 0 = female and 1 = male. Career length was included as a continuous variable reflecting the number of years that have passed since starting in the first job after graduating. We distinguished five functional levels: senior management, middle management, professional staff (for example, experts, consultants), clerical staff and operational staff.

Analysis

The research model was tested using path analysis as it allows the hypothesized relationships to be estimated in a simultaneous way (Procedure CALIS in SAS Version 9). The analyses showed it fits the observed data well ($\chi^2(11) = 21.183$ ($p = .023$); RMSEA = .060; SRMR= .029; CFI =.966). Still, the fully mediated hypothesized model was compared with partially mediated models in order to assess whether direct paths from adaptability or self-awareness to retirement intention, career satisfaction, internal or external employability needed to be included. We furthermore verified whether self-directedness influenced retirement intention solely through its effect on career satisfaction, internal and external employability. Testing these alternatives, partially mediated models revealed that model fit significantly improved when including a direct relationship between adaptability and retirement intention ($\Delta\chi^2 = 8.583$; $\Delta DF = 1$). All other relationships turned out to be fully mediated, supporting the hypothesized model. After including this path, the revised model had an excellent fit to the data ($\chi^2(10) = 12.600$ ($p = .247$); RMSEA = .030; SRMR= .020; CFI =.992).

RESULTS

Table 22.2 presents the means, standard deviations and correlations between the studied variables. Figure 22.2 shows the significant standardized results of the path analysis for the revised model.

We found support for Hypotheses 1 and 2 as self-awareness ($\beta = .34$; p < .001) and adaptability ($\beta = .20$; $p < .001$) positively associate with self-directedness. Furthermore, in line with Hypothesis 4, self-directedness turned out to relate positively to external employability ($\beta = .21$; $p < .001$) and internal employability, yet the latter was only marginally significant ($\beta = .09$; $p < .10$; Hypothesis 3). Figure 22.2 further shows that self-directedness is positively associated with career satisfaction ($\beta = .34$; $p < .001$;

Table 22.2 Means, standard deviations and correlations (n = 285)

	M	SD	1	2	3	4	5	6	7
1. Retirement intention	2.72	.95	1						
2. Self-awareness	4.36	.48	−.09	1					
3. Adaptability	3.33	.76	−.24***	.17**	1				
4. Self-directedness	4.09	.60	−.15**	.38***	.24***	1			
5. Internal employability	2.31	1.15	−.10(*)	.09	.16**	.08	1		
6. External employability	2.71	1.24	−.19**	.10(*)	.11(*)	.24***	.21***	1	
7. Career satisfaction	7.58	1.82	−.16**	.18**	.18**	.34***	.10(*)	.07	1
8. Career length (in years)	35.22	5.14	.23***	.01	−.14*	.05	−.25***	−.14*	−.00

Note: (*) $p < 0.10$; * $p < 0.05$; ** $p < 0.01$; *** $p < 0.001$.

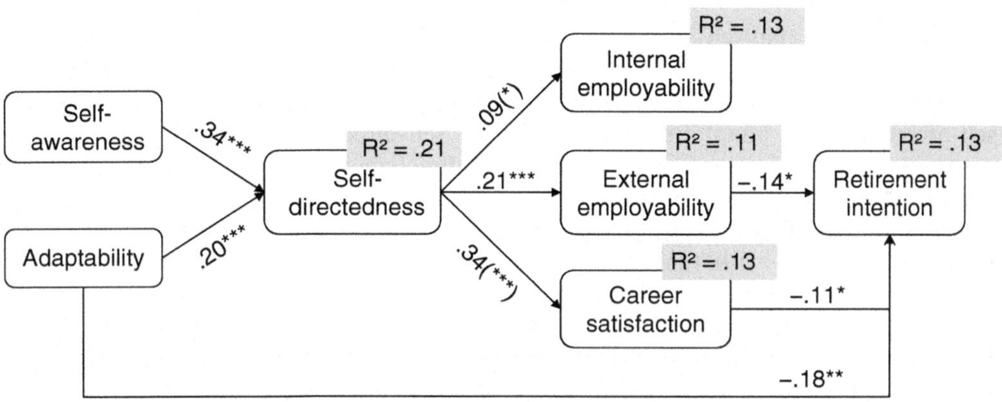

Note: (*) $p < .10$; *$p < .05$; ** $p < .01$; *** $p < .001$.

Figure 22.2 Results of the path analysis (standardized coefficients; n = 285)

Hypothesis 5). Providing support for Hypotheses 7 and 8, external employability (β = −.13; $p < .05$) and career satisfaction (β = −.13; $p < .05$) negatively relate to retirement intention. Contrary to what we expected, we found no relationship between internal employability and retirement intention (Hypothesis 6).

In addition to the assumed indirect relationship between adaptability and retirement intention, we also found a direct, negative relationship between adaptability and retirement intention (β = −.18; $p < .01$). As Table 22.3 shows, the indirect effects of self-awareness and adaptability on retirement intention are limited even though they are significant. However, since the relationship between adaptability and retirement intention appeared to be only partially mediated by employability and career satisfaction, adaptability has a considerable larger (total) effect on retirement intention than self-directedness.

Table 22.3 Indirect and total effects of self-awareness and adaptability

	Internal employability	External employability	Career satisfaction	Retirement intention
Self-awareness				
Indirect effect	.032	.073	.117	−.023
Total effect	.032	.073	.117	−.023
Adaptability				
Indirect effect	.018	.042	.066	−.013
Total effect	.018	.042	.066	−.195

DISCUSSION

Our results reveal that self-awareness and adaptability negatively relate to older workers' intention to retire via multiple paths. Consistent with the ideas of Hall (1996; 2004) and previous research (see, for example, Verbruggen and Sels, 2008), we find that both self-awareness and adaptability are drivers of self-directedness. Additionally, in line with our hypotheses, the results show that self-directedness is positively associated with individuals' perceived employability in the external labor market as it may enable them to create and identify career opportunities. As we expected, older workers' retirement intention decreases with their level of external employability. However, we find no similar path for internal employability. Our findings indicate that the positive relationship between self-directedness and internal employability is only marginally significant. Possibly, the relationship is weaker in the internal labor market since attitudes of supervisors or rigid career paths – rather than self-directedness – may determine the career opportunities individuals perceive within the organization. Moreover, self-directedness entails a feeling of independence from the current employer. Individuals who are self-directed may therefore be more focused on opportunities in the external labor market. Additionally, internal employability does not relate to workers' retirement intention. It is possible that, throughout their career, older workers ended up in a job that optimally matches their skills and knowledge. Hence, alternative jobs within the organization may not seem attractive or challenging enough to reduce their retirement intention. Consequently, among older workers, we find partial support for the idea behind active aging and development strategies. The basic principle that investing in older workers' employability will extend their working lives only holds for external employability. However, we have to put this somewhat in perspective. We only investigated employability to other jobs, and did not measure the extent to which individuals assessed their likelihood to remain employable within their current job. Future research may also want to focus on remaining employable within the current job.

Second, as we hypothesized, self-directedness relates positively to career satisfaction. This finding is consistent with career theory (Hall, 1996; 2004) and previous research (Colakoglu, 2011; De Vos et al., 2009; Verbruggen and Sels, 2008). Our results show a negative relationship between career satisfaction and retirement intention. While feeling satisfied at work may support older workers' self-concept and so motivate them to continue to work, feeling unsatisfied may push them into retirement (Kanfer and Ackerman, 2004).

Besides the indirect paths via external employability and career satisfaction, the results also show a direct, negative relationship between adaptability and retirement intention. Individuals with higher adaptability may perceive the changing working environment as challenging rather than threatening since they are willing and able to change their behavior, feelings and thoughts in response to environmental demands (Hall, 2002; McArdle et al., 2007). Higher adaptability may enable individuals to deal with factors that usually push older workers in retirement, like high job demands or deteriorating health. Therefore, being willing and able to cope with changes – be it personal or in the working environment – can reduce the perceived urge to retire.

Implications

From a practical perspective, our results underline the need to develop both self-awareness and adaptability when seeking to reduce older workers' retirement intention. In particular adaptability turns out to be a key competence in this respect. Adaptability is often at the center of the debate on late career issues. Older individuals are generally believed to be inflexible and unwilling or unable to deal with changes (Posthuma and Campion, 2009). Since self-awareness and, even more strongly, adaptability decrease the retirement intention, it is important to sustain these career competencies throughout the career. Diverse interventions may do so. Besides career counseling (Savickas et al., 2009; Verbruggen and Sels, 2008), training programs are put forward as effective interventions to increase self-awareness and adaptability (Clarke, 2008; Soresi et al., 2012). Furthermore, providing individuals with a variety of work experiences may increase their adaptability (Hall and Mirvis, 1995; Karaevli and Hall, 2006). Our results clearly show the need to invest in such interventions to promote older workers' adaptability. While workers may benefit from it by experiencing higher career satisfaction and employability, employers may gain an advantage from the lower intention to retire via career satisfaction and external employability.

This study also contributes to the literature in multiple ways. First, it contributes to the career literature since empirical research on career adaptability is scarce (Hartung, 2010) and self-directedness has hardly been linked to workers' retirement intention. Moreover, by studying retirement from a career perspective, we draw attention to antecedents that are rarely taken into account. Research aimed at identifying predictors of employee retirement tends to focus on negative factors pushing older workers into retirement or positive factors pulling them into retirement. In empirical studies, these factors are regularly related to workers' current situation rather than their entire career, for instance, by examining the impact of job satisfaction instead of career satisfaction. This study is a first step in filling this gap. It moreover responds to the call of Feldman and Beehr (2011) to examine how self-evaluations influence individuals' intention to retire rather than mainly focusing on factors like health and wealth. This study also contributes to research on aging by delivering empirical support for the basic reasoning behind active aging policies and a development strategy. Furthermore, it adds to the employability literature. While the distinction between internal and external employability is frequently discussed in the conceptual and theoretical literature (Hillage and Pollard, 1998; Sanders and De Grip, 2004; Van der Heijden, 2002), empirical studies hardly discern an internal and external dimension. Since external employability mediates the relationship between self-directedness and retirement intention while internal employability does not, our findings highlight the need to integrate the theoretical distinction into empirical studies on employability.

Limitations

Still, this study is not without shortcomings that future research may take into account. First, all data has been collected at one point in time. The cross-sectional nature of the data does not allow causal inferences to be made about the relationships in the research model. A longitudinal research design is needed to establish the causal nature of the relationships. Moreover, it can verify the stability of the studied variables over time and allows retirement to be studied as a process that occurs over time. Longitudinal data would also allow the evaluation of intervention strategies aimed at increasing individuals' employability or career satisfaction as our results show that these variables reduce workers' retirement intention. It would also provide valuable information on career trajectories and enable employee retirement to be studied as a career step.

Furthermore, the data was self-reported and collected from a single source. Consequently, common method bias may be an issue (Podsakoff et al., 2003; Spector 1994). However, in recent studies, several authors have noted that this methodological problem is less of a problem regarding self-report survey studies (for example, Lindell and Whitney, 2001; Spector, 2006). Furthermore, statistical observations argue against common method bias as an alternative explanation for our findings. First, the observed correlations are low to moderate since only 2 out of 28 correlations (7 percent) were higher than .30 (Spector, 2006). Second, we performed the 'Harman's single-factor test' (in Podsakoff et al., 2003), that is, we loaded all items into an exploratory factor analysis to see if a large factor accounted for the majority of the variance. Since multiple factors emerged, with the first factor only accounting for 20 percent of the variance, common method variance is unlikely to explain the findings of this study.

Moreover, the measurement of retirement intention was based on a self-developed scale with acceptable but moderate reliability (alpha = .61). A possible explanation for this reliability score of the scale could be that some items focused on the length of the career (for example, intention to leave the labor market), while others looked more at behavior (such as job search) or values (importance of work). Although all items loaded on one factor in the confirmatory factor analysis, future research might want to include other measures of retirement intention.

Finally, this study focused on workers' retirement intention instead of their actual retirement behavior. Yet in their review of the literature on employee retirement, Wang and Shultz (2010) point out that retirement intentions serve as one of the strongest predictors of actual retirement. Moreover, a focus on retirement intention provides organizations and governments with valuable information about older employees' retirement plans and on the factors that are related to these plans. Still, future research is needed to get more knowledge about workers' actual retirement age and to extend our research model with actual retirement behavior.

REFERENCES

Adams, G.A. and T.A. Beehr (1998), 'Turnover and retirement: a comparison of their similarities and differences', *Personnel Psychology*, **51**, 643–65.

Adams, G.A., J. Prescher, T.A. Beehr and L. Lepisto (2002), 'Applying work role attachment theory to retirement decision making', *International Journal of Aging and Human Development*, **54**, 125–37.

Armstrong-Stassen, M. and F. Schlosser (2008), 'Benefits of a supportive development climate for older workers', *Journal of Managerial Psychology*, **23** (4), 419–37.

Armstrong-Stassen, M. and K. Stassen (2013), 'Professional development, target-specific satisfaction, and old nurse retention', *Career Development International*, **18**, 673–93.

Bal, P.M., S.B. De Jong, P.G.W. Jansen and A.B. Bakker (2012), 'Motivating employees to work beyond retirement: A multi-level study of the role of I-deals and unit climate', *Journal of Management Studies*, **49**, 306–31.

Berntson, E., M. Sverke and S. Marklund (2006), 'Predicting perceived employability: Human capital or labour market opportunities?', *Economic and Industrial Democracy*, **27**, 223–44.

Brandstädter, J. and G. Renner (1990), 'Tenacious goal pursuit and flexible goal adjustment: Explication and age-related analysis of assimilative and accommodative strategies of coping', *Psychology and Aging*, **5** (1), 58–67.

Briscoe, J.P. and D.T. Hall (2006), 'The interplay of boundaryless and protean careers: Combinations and implications', *Journal of Vocational Behavior*, **69**, 4–18.

Briscoe, J.P., D.T. Hall and R.L. Frautschy DeMuth (2006), 'Protean and boundaryless careers: An empirical exploration', *Journal of Vocational Behavior*, **69**, 30–47.

Chan, S. and A.H. Stevens (1999), 'Employment and retirement following a late-career job loss', *The American Economic Review, Papers and Proceedings*, **89** (2), 211–16.

Claes, R. and K. Van Loo (2011), 'Relationships of proactive behaviour with job-related affective well-being and anticipated retirement age: An exploration among older employees in Belgium', *European Journal of Ageing*, **8**, 233–41.

Clarke, M. (2008), 'Understanding and managing employability in changing career contexts', *Journal of European Industrial Training*, **32** (4), 258–84.

Colakoglu, S.N. (2011), 'The impact of career boundarylessness on subjective career success: The role of career competencies, career autonomy and career insecurity', *Journal of Vocational Behavior*, **79**, 47–59.

De Cuyper, N. and H. De Witte (2010), 'Temporary employment and perceived employability: Mediation by impression management', *Journal of Career Development*, **37** (3), 635–52.

De Cuyper, N., S. Mauno, U. Kinnunen and A. Mäkikangas (2011), 'The role of job resources in the relation between perceived employability and turnover intention: A prospective two-sample study', *Journal of Vocational Behavior*, **78**, 253–63.

De Cuyper, N., S. Raeder, B. Van der Heijden and A. Wittekind (2012), 'The association between workers' employability and burnout in a reorganization context: Longitudinal evidence building upon the conservation of resources theory', *Journal of Occupational Health Psychology*, **17**, 162–74.

De Vos, A. and J. Segers (2013), 'Self-directed career attitude and retirement intentions', *Career Development International*, **18** (2), 155–72.

De Vos, A. and N. Soens (2008), 'Protean attitude and career success: The mediating role of self-management', *Journal of Vocational Behavior*, **73**, 449–56.

De Vos, A., K. Dewettinck and D. Buyens (2009), 'The professional career on the right track: A study on the interaction between career self-management and organizational career management in explaining employee outcomes', *European Journal of Work and Organizational Psychology*, **18** (1), 55–80.

De Witte, H. and K. Näswall (2003), '"Objective" vs. "subjective" job insecurity: Consequences of temporary work for job satisfaction and organizational commitment in four European countries', *Economic and Industrial Democracy*, **24**, 147–86.

DeFillippi, R. and M. Arthur (1994), 'The boundaryless career: A competency-based perspective', *Journal of Organizational Behavior*, **15** (5), 307–24.

Eby, L.T., M. Butts and A. Lockwood (2003), 'Predictors of success in the era of the boundaryless career', *Journal of Organizational Behavior*, **24**, 689–708.

European Commission (2012), 'The 2012 Ageing Report. Economic and budgetary projections for the 27 EU Member States', Brussels: European Union.

Feldman, D.C. (1994), 'The decision to retire early: A review and conceptualization', *The Academy of Management Review*, **19** (2), 285–311.

Feldman, D.C. and T.A. Beehr (2011), 'A three-phase model of retirement decision making', *American Psychologist*, **66**, 193–203.

Forrier, A. and L. Sels (2003), 'The concept employability: A complex mosaic', *International Journal of Human Resources Development and Management*, **3** (2), 102–214.
Forrier, A., L. Sels and D. Stynen (2009), 'Career mobility at the intersection between agent and structure: A conceptual model', *Journal of Occupational and Organizational Psychology*, **82**, 739–59.
Gendron, B. (2011), 'Older workers and active ageing in France: The changing early retirement and company approach', *The International Journal of Human Resource Management*, **22**, 1221–31.
Greenhaus, J.H., S. Parasuraman and W.M. Wormley (1990), 'Effects of race on organizational experiences, job performance evaluations and career outcomes', *Academy of Management Journal*, **33**, 64–86.
Hall, D.T. (1996), 'Protean careers in the 21st century', *Academy of Management Executive*, **10** (4), 8–16.
Hall, D.T. (2002), *Protean Careers In and Out of Organizations*, Thousand Oaks, CA: Sage.
Hall, D.T. (2004), 'The protean career: A quarter-century journey', *Journal of Vocational Behavior*, **65** (1), 1–13.
Hall, D.T. and D.E. Chandler (2005), 'Psychological success: When the career is a calling', *Journal of Organizational Behavior*, **26** (2), 155–76.
Hall, D.T. and P.H. Mirvis (1995), 'The new career contract: Developing the whole person at midlife and beyond', *Journal of Vocational Behavior*, **47**, 269–89.
Hartung, P.J. (2010), 'Practice and research in career counseling and development – 2009', *The Career Development Quarterly*, **59**, 98–142.
Herrbach, O., K. Mignonac, C. Vandenberghe and A. Negrini (2009), 'Perceived HRM practices, organizational commitment and voluntary early retirement among late career managers', *Human Resource Management*, **48** (6), 895–915.
Heslin, P.A. (2003), 'Self- and other-referent criteria of career success', *Journal of Career Assessment*, **11**, 262–86.
Hillage, J. and E. Pollard (1998), 'Employability: Developing a framework for policy analysis', Research Brief 85, London: DfEE.
Hobfoll, S.E. (1988), *The Ecology of Stress*, New York: Hemisphere Publishing Corporation.
Hobfoll, S.E. (1989), 'Conservation of resources. A new attempt at conceptualizing stress', *American Psychologist*, **44**, 513–24.
Hobfoll, S.E., R.J. Johnson, N. Ennis and A.P. Jackson (2003), 'Resource loss, resource gain and emotional outcomes among inner city women', *Journal of Personality and Social Psychology*, **84**, 632–43.
Hofmans, J., N. Dries and R. Pepermans (2008), 'The career satisfaction scale: Response bias among men and women', *Journal of Vocational Behavior*, **73**, 397–403.
Kanfer, R. and P.L. Ackerman (2004), 'Aging, adult development and work motivation', *The Academy of Management Review*, **29** (3), 440–58.
Karaevli, A. and D.T. Hall (2006), 'How career variety promotes the adaptability of managers: A theoretical model', *Journal of Vocational Behavior*, **69**, 359–73.
Kossek, E.E., K. Roberts, S. Fisher and B. Demarr (1998), 'Career self-management: A quasi-experimental assessment of the effects of a training intervention', *Personnel Psychology*, **51**, 935–62.
Leisink, P. and E. Knies (2011), 'Line managers' support for older workers', *The International Journal of Human Resource Management*, **22**, 1902–17.
Lindell, M.K. and D.J. Whitney (2001), 'Accounting for common method variance in cross-sectional research designs', *Journal of Applied Psychology*, **86**, 114–21.
London, M. (1993), 'Relationship between career motivation, empowerment and support for career development', *Journal of Occupational and Organizational Psychology*, **66**, 55–69.
March, J.G. and H.A. Simon (1958), *Organizations*, New York: Wiley.
McArdle, S., L. Waters, J.P. Briscoe and D.T. Hall (2007), 'Employability during unemployment: Adaptability, career identity and human and social capital', *Journal of Vocational Behavior*, **71**, 247–64.
Moulaert, T. and S. Biggs (2013), 'International and European policy on work and retirement: Reinventing critical perspectives on active ageing and mature subjectivity', *Human Relations*, **66** (1), 23–43.
Munderlein, M., J.F. Ybema and F. Koste (2013), 'Happily ever after? Explaining turnover and retirement intentions of older workers in the Netherlands', *Career Development International*, **18**, 548–68.
Newman, K.L. (2011), 'Sustainable careers: Lifecycle engagement in work', *Organizational Dynamics*, **40**, 136–43.
OECD (1998), *Maintaining Prosperity in an Ageing Society*, Paris: OECD.
Parasuraman, S., J.H. Greenhaus and F. Linnehan (2000), 'Time, person–career fit and the boundaryless career', in C.L. Cooper and D.M. Rousseau (eds), *Trends in Organizational Behavior*, vol. 7, Chichester: Wiley, pp. 63–78.
Podsakoff, P.M., S.B. MacKenzie, J.-Y. Lee and N.P. Podsakoff (2003), 'Common method biases in behavioral research: A critical review of the literature and recommended remedies', *Journal of Applied Psychology*, **88** (5), 879–903.

Posthuma, R.A. and M.A. Campion (2009), 'Age stereotypes in the workplace: Common stereotypes, moderators and future research directions?', *Journal of Management*, **35**, 158–88.
Rothwell, A. and J. Arnold (2007), 'Self-perceived employability: Development and validation of a scale', *Personnel Review*, **36** (1), 23–41.
Rothwell, A., I. Herbert and F. Rothwell (2008), 'Self-perceived employability: Construction and initial validation of a scale for university students', *Journal of Vocational Behavior*, **73**, 1–12.
Rothwell, A., S. Jewell and M. Hardie (2009), 'Self-perceived employability: Investigating the responses of post-graduate students', *Journal of Vocational Behavior*, **75** (2), 152–61.
Sanders, J. and A. de Grip (2004), 'Training, task flexibility and the employability of low-skilled workers', *International Journal of Manpower*, **25** (1), 73–89.
Savickas, M.L. (1997), 'Career adaptability: An integrative construct for life-span, life-space theory', *Career Development Quarterly*, **45**, 247–59.
Savickas, M.L., L. Nota, J. Rossier, J.P. Dauwalder, M.E. Duarte, J. Guichard, S. Soresi, R. Van Esbroeck and A.E.M. Van Vianen (2009), 'Life designing: A paradigm for career construction in the 21st century', *Journal of Vocational Behavior*, **75**, 239–50.
Shultz, K.S., K.R. Morton and J.R. Weckerle (1998), 'The influence of push and pull factors on voluntary and involuntary early retirees' retirement decision and adjustment', *Journal of Vocational Behavior*, **53** (1), 45–57.
Silla, I., N. De Cuyper, F.J. Gracia, J.M. Peiró and H. De Witte (2009), 'Job insecurity and well-being: Moderation by employability', *Journal of Happiness Studies*, **10** (6), 739–51.
Spector, P.E. (1994), 'Using self-report questionnaires in OB research: A comment on the use of a controversial method', *Journal of Organizational Behavior*, **15**, 385–92.
Spector, P.E. (2006), 'Method variance in organizational research: Truth or urban legend?', *Organizational Research Methods*, **9** (2), 221–32.
Soresi, S., L. Nota and L. Ferrari (2012), 'Career adapt-abilities scale – Italian form: Psychometric properties and relationships to breadth of interests, quality of life and perceived barriers', *Journal of Vocational Behavior*, **80**, 705–11.
Sturges, J., D. Guest, N. Conway and K. Mackenzie Davey (2002), 'A longitudinal study of the relationship between career management and organizational commitment among graduates in the first ten years at work', *Journal of Organizational Behavior*, **23** (6), 731–48.
Templer, A., M. Armstrong-Stassen and J. Cattaneo (2010), 'Antecedents of older workers' motives for continuing to work', *Career Development International*, **15** (5), 479–500.
Thijssen, J. and T. Rocco (2010), 'Development of older workers: Revisiting policies', in European Centre for the Development of Vocational Training (CEDEFOP), *Working and Ageing: Emerging Theories and Empirical Perspectives*, Luxembourg: Publications Office of the European Union, pp. 13–27.
Topa, G., J.A. Moriano, M. Depolo, C.-M. Alcover and J.F. Morales (2009), 'Antecedents and consequences of retirement planning and decision-making: A meta-analysis and model', *Journal of Vocational Behavior*, **75** (1), 38–55.
Van der Heijden, B.I.J.M. (2002), 'Individual career initiatives and their influence upon professional expertise development throughout the career', *International Journal of Training and Development*, **6**, 54–79.
Verbruggen, M. and L. Sels (2008), 'Can career self-directedness be improved through counseling?', *Journal of Vocational Behavior*, **73**, 318–27.
Von Bonsdorff, M., P. Huuhtanen, K. Tuomi and J. Seitsamo (2010), 'Predictors of employees' early retirement intentions: An 11-year longitudinal study', *Occupational Medicine*, **60**, 94–100.
Walker, A. and T. Maltby (2012), 'Active ageing: A strategic policy solution to demographic ageing in the European Union', *International Journal of Social Welfare*, **21**, S117–S130.
Wang, M. and K.S. Shultz (2010), 'Employee retirement: A review and recommendations for future investigation', *Journal of Management*, **36**, 172–206.
Wang, M., D.A. Olson and K. Shultz (2013), *Mid and Late Career Issues*, New York and London: Routledge.
Zacher, H. and M. Frese (2011), 'Maintaining a focus on opportunities at work: The interplay between age, job complexity and the use of selection, optimization and compensation strategies', *Journal of Organizational Behavior*, **32**, 291–318.

23 Managing the transition to retirement: from meaningful work to meaning in life at retirement

Ariane Froidevaux and Andreas Hirschi

INTRODUCTION

In the last decades, the vision of scholars on transition to retirement has shifted from a traditional withdrawal from work to pursuing multiple pathways and opportunities at a late career stage. Consequently, retirement issues need to be taken into account when considering career development and sustainable careers. Our aim in this chapter is to provide an understanding of retirement adjustment by specifically focusing on meaning in life for retirees and meaningful work for older workers who are close to retirement. To illustrate our point, we will present quotations from semi-structured interviews realized with French-speaking Swiss older workers, between 60 and 67 years old, who were going to retire within a few months. We approach transition to retirement from the standpoint of sustainable careers, thereby focusing on the elements of continuity and personal agency. In this regard, we describe ways to promote meaningful work for older workers and how to create a new meaning or to pursue a previous meaning as a retiree, from both individual and organizational standpoints.

CURRENT PERSPECTIVES ON AGING

Over the last few decades, scholars' understanding of aging has evolved. Whereas theories such as disengagement theory (Cummings and Henry, 1961) posited an inevitable process through which older persons would slowly disengage themselves from society and from many relationships, new gerontological perspectives propose a more positive view of aging. The deficit perspective is mainly rooted in the decline in physical abilities, which has been associated with a decline in cognitive and intellectual capabilities (Wechsler, 1944). However, scholars in several fields showed that this presupposition of general decline with age is far too simplistic. Research suggests that contrary to popular belief, the majority of older adults over 65 are both physically and psychologically healthy and are aging well (Williamson and Christie, 2009). Consequently, nowadays, aging is mostly understood as implying different patterns of development, such as loss (for example, fluid intellectual abilities), growth (for example, general knowledge), reorganization (for example, change of focus in time orientation), and exchange (for example, change in personality traits) (Kanfer and Ackerman, 2004).

This more nuanced view of aging also suggests that retirement should not just be viewed as a decline in activity generally and retreatment from work specifically. Rather, in this chapter, we suggest that the transition to retirement should be viewed as an active phase in the lifelong process of creating a sustainable career.

RETIREMENT CONCEPTUALIZED AS A PART OF SUSTAINABLE CAREERS

Newman (2011) proposed a conceptualization of sustainable careers as a lifecycle engagement in work. Her vision comprises that baby boomers, the current generation that is entering into retirement, 'present an opportunity to invent more sustainable, long term, fluid careers that engage people appropriately over the lifespan, well past the [official] retirement age' (p. 136). She further describes three characteristics that depict sustainable careers through the lifespan. First, the need for renewability that aims to support longer working lives and by doing so enhances work–life balance opportunities. In practice, this proposition could be translated into a sabbatical, in order to reinvigorate oneself, for instance by spending more time with one's family. Second, she describes the need for flexibility through continuous learning and increasing knowledge. To become more adaptable, one needs to build a protean career (Hall, 2004), which means a career driven by the individual's sources of satisfaction and values, rather than by those of the organization. Third, the need for the integration of different elements of the self-concept across life spheres is part of sustainable careers. Practically, it means that as people reach later career stages, they feel a greater need for integrity, congruence and meaning.

This conceptualization offers a general view of sustainable careers across the lifespan. In this chapter, we will focus on the specificity of the transition to the retirement stage – including the period before retirement, and the period thereafter when the new retirees' task is to find (new) meaning in their life. A first important element of sustainable careers is the idea of continuity throughout career episodes. This notion is in line with continuity theory (Atchley, 1999), which is one of the theories that explain the adjustment process needed after having retired. This theory posits that individuals generally tend to maintain consistency across their lifespan, despite the occurrence of disruptive events. Therefore, it predicts that only a severe amount of difficulties would cause an unpleasant quality of life and a more difficult adjustment in the transition to retirement. Continuity theory further suggests that retirees are likely to maintain their former lifestyle patterns and interpersonal relationships into their retirement (Wang and Shultz, 2010).

Flexibility skills based on continuous learning constitute a second important resource to foster a sustainable career, as we have presented above. Consequently, it can be assumed that it will be easier for retirees who have accumulated a great amount of knowledge to maintain their previous lifestyle. For instance, they might have more opportunities to continue working in the form of a part-time or on-demand job in their organization or professional field after retirement. As such, this greater flexibility increases personal agency, enabling these flexible retirees to shape their retirement according to their own preferences and be less constrained by environmental factors.

> I don't like talking about a new life because I think that it is still my life, with another direction. (Male, 70 years old)

> I see my life as being part of a unity [. . .] this is a growing process with a unity of life. (Female, 64 years old)

Another conceptualization of retirement in line with the sustainable career is to understand retirement not as the end of the career, but instead as a new, late career development stage. Here, retirement represents one of the different kinds of career episodes implied in sustainable careers. Specifically, this conceptualization recognizes the continued growth and renewal potentials of retired people and focuses on the numerous resources that retirees may still offer to the job market or work in volunteering (Wang and Shi, 2014).

> After a first year without any occupational life, I decided to divide my years in two: I hate winter, so from November to April I offer to work for replacements [for his employer before his official retirement] but part-time only. And from May to October I have six months completely free. (Male, 67 years old)

This kind of arrangement between complete retirement and complete working life has been called *bridge employment*, a type of employment which aims to facilitate the transition from full-time work to full retirement. Three kinds of bridge employment exist, namely working for the same organization as before official retirement, working in the same field but not the same organization, and working in a new career field. Numerous studies have investigated the different types and reasons for choosing bridge employment (for example, Müller et al., 2013). A specific kind of bridge employment was discussed by Freedman (2007), namely, the encore career, a purpose-driven career that makes a difference in the overall well-being of self and community. This idea of a career driven by personal values and goals is also consistent with the protean career model. Specifically, 'this conceptualization pays great attention to how retirees may align their career goals with their work and leisure activities in retirement life and emphasizes examining unique factors that are associated with retirees' career potential and career pursuit, which may inform retirees' workforce participation activities and patterns after they retire' (Wang, 2012, p. 573). Therefore, one can question the appropriateness of the term 'retirement', which literally means to retire from work, a withdrawal, and also implicitly implies to retire from either society, relationships, or both. Dennis and Fike (2012) described different attempts to find a new terminology. Propositions were made such as renewment, end-joy-ment, Gen R or Life 2.0, but thus far no consensus has been found to definitively replace the word 'retirement'.

THE IMPORTANCE OF MEANINGFUL WORK FOR OLDER WORKERS

After presenting conceptualizations of retirement that position retirement as a late career stage, we will now focus on how organizations and individuals can successfully foster meaning in work and life in their late career and during retirement. A focus on meaningful work is particularly pertinent because research has showed that performing meaningful work provides richer, more satisfying and more productive employment (Steger et al., 2013). Employees with meaningful work invest themselves in work more fully and benefit from greater job satisfaction, intrinsic motivation, and affective organizational commitment (Steger et al., 2013). Moreover, research suggests that for older workers and retirees conducting meaningful work and finding meaning in life are particularly important (Shacklock and Brunetto, 2011; Steger et al., 2009). In accordance with Rosso et al. (2010), we define meaningful work as work experienced as particularly significant and holding positive meaning for individuals.

Different models of how to conceptualize meaningful work have been suggested in the last decade. A three-dimension model proposed by Chalofsky (2003) consists of: (a) sense of self: bringing one's whole self to work, recognizing and developing one's potential, knowing one's purpose in life and how work fits into that purpose, and having a positive belief system about achieving one's purpose; (b) sense of work: the act of performing, learning, continuous growth, and autonomy; the opportunity to carry out one's purpose through work; and (c) sense of balance: the balance of work self and personal self, the balance of spiritual self and work self, and the balance of giving to oneself and giving to others.

A second model of meaningful work was proposed by Steger and Dik (2010), which posits meaningful work as being made of two dimensions: work comprehension and work purpose. The former involves people's ability to make sense of their self and work experiences, as well as their understanding of their fit with their organization, whereas the latter refers to people's identification with and intention to pursue personal and organizational goals. Rosso et al. (2010) introduced a model of meaningful work that specifically raises this issue of balance between self and others. Their two-dimensional model, placed in a continuum (self versus others and communion versus agency), suggests four major pathways to meaningful work: (1) Individuation (that is, meaningfulness of actions that distinguish the self as worthy); (2) contribution (that is, meaningfulness of actions perceived as done in service of the greater good); (3) self-connection (that is, meaningfulness of actions that make individuals feel closer to how they see themselves); and (4) unification (that is, meaningfulness of actions that make individuals feel in harmony with other beings).

Lastly, a recent model by Schnell et al. (2013) implies three levels in which meaning in work may occur. First, at a person-level self-efficacy is necessary to perceive one's acts as significant. Self-efficacy increases feelings of autonomy and mastery at work and therefore facilitates the perceived signification of one's work activities at an organizational and societal level, leading to a perception of one's actions as meaningful. Second, at a work-level task significance is supposed to be higher if the task is performed for a person other than oneself. Between the work and individual level lies the notion of work-role fit, implying a match between personal identities and work activities. Finally, at the organizational-level, socio-moral climate (that is, an open, appreciative and collaborative climate) and self-transcendent orientation (that is, a genuine organizational commitment to corporate values) are important to foster meaningful work.

We propose that these models may be summarized into three dimensions that constitute meaningful work (see Figure 23.1) by considering the three levels recommended by Chalofsky (2003): the sense of self, sense of work, and sense of balance. Steger and Dik's (2010) two-dimensional model of comprehension and purpose may also be translated into the sense of self, work and balance. In fact, they suggested that each of their two dimensions be distinguished into three sub-dimensions, concerning the level of self, work and the balance between these two levels. In a similar vein, the model by Schnell et al. (2013) also offers a three-level structure, referring to self, work and work-role, with the latter being closely related to sense of balance. By contrast, the model by Rosso et al. (2010) focuses only on the sense of balance through their distinction between the two dimensions of self versus other and communion versus agency.

Author	*Self level*	*Work level*	*Balance level*
Chalofsky (2003)	Self	Work	Balance between self and work
Steger and Dik (2010)	Comprehension (understanding self)	Comprehension (understanding organization)	Comprehension (understanding fit within organization)
	Purpose (personal purpose)	Purpose (organizational purpose)	Purpose (leadership)
Schnell et al. (2013)	Person (self-efficacy)	Work (task significance)	Work-role fit
		Organization (socio-moral climate, self-transcendence)	
Rosso et al. (2010)			Other <--> Self
			Communion <--> Agency

Figure 23.1 Comparison of the different existing models of meaningful work

Older Workers: How to Foster Meaningful Work?

We have seen different models of meaningful work and presented an integrative view by using the three levels introduced by Chalofsky (2003). We now turn to the question of how such models can be applied to the population of older workers. By doing so, it is also important to address the question of whether differences exist between meaningful work for older workers as compared to younger workers.

From a theoretical standpoint, few attempts exist to conciliate older workers and meaningful work. It seems helpful to look at the literature that has investigated *meaning of work* or *meaning of working* among older people. In contrast to *meaningful work*, meaning of work and working refers to the meaning attached to work per se, as an institution and life domain (Chalofsky, 2003) while it does not necessarily imply that the work performed itself is meaningful. A first international group of scholars was created in the 1980s to empirically study the *meaning of working* patterns also for older workers (MOWIRT, 1987). Specifically, they distinguished between the noun of work and the action of working. They defined meaning of working as 'the significance, beliefs, definitions and the value which individuals and groups attach to working as a major stream of human activity that occurs over much of their lives' (p. 13).

The respective scholars proposed the *heuristic meaning of working model*, which considers three conditional variables that give meaning to work: personal and family situation; present job and career history; and the macro-socioeconomic environment. These conditions then influence five central variables: centrality of working as a life role; societal norms about working; valued working outcomes; importance of work goals; and work-role identification. Together, these five dimensions are assumed to impact meaning of working patterns. Compared with the general models of meaningful work discussed above, most dimensions correspond to the self-level (that is, centrality of working, valued working outcomes, importance of work goals, and work-role identification), whereas only one is at a meso-level (that is, societal norms about working).

The heuristic meaning of working model would hence suggest that the self-level is particularly important for older workers. The group's empirical findings further reveal that other life domains have an important impact on the perception of meaning of working among older people, such as leisure, friends, family, community and spiritual development. This suggests that being able to conciliate work and other life domains is especially important for older workers, as we will discuss in more detail later.

More recently, a new model of the meaning of working for older workers (MOFOW) has been proposed by Baltes et al. (2012) with the aim to integrate different aging theories into a heuristic model. Mainly, they have described two components that determine meaning of working for older workers. First, rewards and expectations refer to how working may satisfy needs and wants at the extrinsic (working as a means to maintain standard of living and quality of life) and the intrinsic level (working as a means to achieve and maintain self-esteem). Research showed that the importance of extrinsic motivators for work generally tends to diminish with age while the importance of intrinsic motivators generally tends to increase (De Lange et al., 2010; Kooij et al., 2011).

The second component comprises identification with working, which is the global degree of importance of working compared to other life domains, at any time in the life course. Therefore, meaning of working depends on the subjective importance placed on extrinsic/intrinsic motivators and importance of work across time. According to Baltes et al. (2012), this importance may vary across the life course due to distal external influences (that is, macro-socioeconomic conditions) as well as proximal external influences, which can be organizational (for example, organizational culture) and individual (that is, age, education and training) ones.

Apart from addressing the issue of meaning of working, general theories of aging may also be used to specify significant sources of meaningful work for older workers. For instance, socio-emotional selectivity theory (Carstensen et al., 1999) predicts a growing importance for deep interpersonal relationships that support one's identity with age and would imply that older workers mostly derive meaning from significant relationships with co-workers. Because older workers are looking for deeper emotional interactions, working may represent an important source to satisfy this emotional need. This also would be an explanation of why more and more older workers decide to continue working after their official retirement age. Furthermore, as we have seen in the concept of encore careers, the aim to benefit the greater good in the second half of one's life, but especially during retirement, might mean that meaningful work for older workers could be derived not only from work itself but also from the significance of their work within society. From an empirical standpoint, research showed that older adults tend to have higher levels of identification with work, define working more positively, and place higher value on the outcomes of working as compared to younger employees (Baltes et al., 2012).

Meaningful work for older workers has also been linked with intentions to continue working past official retirement age (Shacklock and Brunetto, 2011). Rosso et al. (2010) pointed out the necessity to investigate the specificities of meaningful work for retirees working in bridge employment. Following this idea, Shacklock and Brunetto (2011) proposed that the subjective expectations about future working conditions after official retirement age are important in this regard (for example, attachment to work, working conditions). Moreover, personal attitudes have also been linked with meaningful work and the intention to continue working through bridge employment. Hall et al. (2013) suggested that a protean career orientation (a self-directed and values-driven approach to one's career) impacts workers' search for meaningful work. As employees with a high protean career orientation are more self-managed and tend to follow more their personal values, they are also hypothesized to be more likely to change jobs in order to attain meaningful work. This hypothesis would apply to every worker but might be especially important for older workers close to retirement.

In sum, theoretical and empirical research suggests that meaning of working for older workers might specifically depend on expectations and rewards of work (Baltes et al., 2012) and achieving valued working outcomes (MOWIRT, 1987). Specifically, as people age, the importance given to different types of rewards evolves from an importance given to extrinsic outcomes such as pay to a greater importance put on intrinsic rewards (De Lange et al., 2010). Socio-emotional selectivity theory (Carstensen et al., 1999) further suggests that older adults pay greater attention to the fulfillment of their emotional needs through work – that is, a need for deeper interpersonal relationships with co-workers. Moreover, the need for identification with working and work centrality as compared to other life domains is especially important for older workers for work to be meaningful (Baltes et al., 2012; MOWIRT, 1987). Finally, some authors have assumed an association between meaning of working and intentions to continue working after official retirement age (Shacklock and Brunetto, 2011), suggesting that meaning of working and its different sources (for example, importance of work-goals) would influence their subjective expectations about future working situations.

CONSTRUCTING MEANING IN LIFE AS A RETIREE

In this contribution so far, we have evoked different aspects of meaningful work for older workers. In a more general sense, meaningful work represents meaning for a specific life domain. Steger and Dik (2009) investigated the link between domain-specific meaning (that is, meaningful work) and meaning in life. Their results based upon studying a sample of students showed that individuals seeking global-level meaning in life showed greater well-being if they experienced work as meaningful (that is, as a calling). The specificity of the transition to retirement is that people lose their work-role as they are no longer workers. This has important implications in terms of meaning in life. Work as a source of meaning disappears, while meaning at a broader level (that is, meaning in life) is still possible to search for and/or to reach or maintain.

Before describing two important models of meaning in life, it is important to define this concept. According to Steger et al. (2009), the presence of meaning in life refers to 'the extent to which people comprehend, make sense of, or see significance in their lives, accompanied by the degree to which they perceive themselves to have a purpose, mission, or over-arching aim in life' (p. 43). This definition is quite close to the one used by Krause and Hayward (2014), which posits that meaning 'involves having a sense of purpose, order, and direction in life, as well as the belief that there is a reason for one's existence' (p. 7). Steger et al. (2009) proposed that the same two dimensions they suggested as comprising meaningful work also apply to overall meaning in life: purpose (highly motivating, long-term goals about which people are committed and highly passionate) and comprehension (the ability to find patterns, consistency and significance in the many events and experiences in their lives).

These two dimensions are also considered in the five factors model of meaning in life by Krause and Hayward (2014). The first factor is having values, which function as norms that describe behaviors and beliefs that are desirable. The second dimension is having a sense of purpose consisting of the affective evaluation following the successful implementation of behaviors which are consistent with one's values. The third factor comprises goals which give a line to follow along which people may invest their energy, efforts and ambitions. Fourth is being able to reconcile the past, derived from Erikson's (1959) identity theory. Fifth is the feeling that life makes sense; the ability to explain the events in one's life, as well as others' behaviors and one's own actions. In sum, the model of Steger et al. (2009) and Krause and Hayward (2014) are similar in that they both propose that meaning in life consists of (at least) two major dimensions: sense of purpose and comprehension. In addition, values, goals and reconciling with one's past are important to construct meaning in life.

Retirees: How to Foster Meaning in Life?

Based on this brief review of some principal models of meaning in life, we will now have a deeper look into the specificities of meaning in life for older adults who are either fully retired or have invested in bridge employment. We have seen that one dimension of meaning in life elaborated by Krause and Hayward (2014), being able to reconcile the past, is derived from Erikson's (1959) identity theory. This theory sheds light on the growing importance of meaning in life in late life stages. Erikson proposed eight developmental stages through the lifespan, each of them characterized by an identity crisis. The last developmental stage is characterized by the crisis of integrity versus despair. This stage necessitates a deep introspection, undertaken with the aim of accepting the kind of person one has become. In order to achieve integrity, older adults need to reconcile with the different parts of their life (for example, events, personal actions, and others' behavior). Consequently, a deep sense of meaning in life represents the successful resolution of this crisis (Krause, 2004). If not, the opposite result of this crisis would be despair, because one would evaluate one's life as lacking meaning (Baltes et al., 2012).

Another important theory for understanding meaning in life for older adults is socio-emotional selectivity theory (Carstensen et al., 1999). It considers that the time focus shifts to focusing on the 'time left' among older people. This places a growing importance on the most important, therefore meaningful, aspects of life. Nevertheless, it would be a misinterpretation to believe that older adults live more hedonistic lives compared to younger adults (Hershfield et al., 2013). By contrast, the emotional changes that occur with age – especially a decrease in negative affect – should lead older adults to 'a more eudemonic sense of meaningfulness and well-being in life' (Hershfield et al., 2013, p. 157).

> Of course there is the pleasure to do a lot of things. But, in itself, pleasure helps to find meaning but it doesn't completely give meaning to my life. (Female, 60 years old)

It is clear that the main difference concerning meaning in life for older versus younger adults is their position at the end versus the beginning of the life course. This different position has an impact on counterfactual reflection (Hershfield et al., 2013). Counterfactual reflection means thinking about what might have been if different events had happened in one's life as opposed to those that have actually happened. In other words, it conveys the idea of 'what if I had (not) done this or that?' or 'what would have been if this had (not) happened?' In their chapter, Hershfield et al. (2013) explain that counterfactual reflection plays a major role in the construction of personal meaning, giving a sense of who we are, reinforcing our deep values as well as our most valued relationships. Specifically, they propose two ways in which counterfactual thinking leads to meaning in life. First, it contributes to *connecting the dots* among life events. Second, it increases a sense of fate in one's life, because it leads to the idea that life took a path that was meant to be.

What is specific for older adults is that their longer life paths are likely to offer more instances of twists and turns, so counterfactual thinking may play a greater role for them regarding finding meaning in life as compared to younger adults. Moreover, as people age, they encounter numerous transitions, such as retirement, which imply a loss of something previously cherished (for example, work). This loss leads to a greater value placed on positive experiences, on the notion of enjoying life and the 'time left', and on paying less attention to potential regrets. In addition, research findings show that with age, specific events and details tend to vanish from memory, making individuals able to consider their life from a broader viewpoint (Hershfield et al., 2013).

Other studies have put a focus on this limited time perspective for older adults versus a future time perspective for younger adults. Hicks et al. (2012), for instance, asked their participants to mark an X on a lifeline that indicates where they think they currently are in their life course – in the beginning, middle or end. Their results show that for people who perceived themselves as having a limited amount of time left to live, positive affect was a stronger predictor of meaning in life. This is in line with socio-emotional selectivity theory (Carstensen et al., 1999) that posits that as people age, they place greater importance on positive emotions as an indicator of a meaningful life.

In addition, some studies have investigated changes of meaning in life across the lifespan. Krause and Hayward (2014) showed that not only does the way older adults tend to understand meaning in life remain relatively stable over time, but also that they are more likely to see meaning in life as a resource which helps them to cope with changes that arise as they age. Steger et al. (2009) differentiated between the search for and the presence of meaning. They discovered that presence of meaning in life was generally higher for older adults, while search for meaning in life was lower than for younger adults. These results suggest that meaning in life constitutes an important resource in later life stages, despite accumulation of interpersonal losses and declining physical capacity.

Fegg et al. (2007) also studied meaning in life differences across the lifespan in a German representative sample. Their results showed important differences in the content of what makes life meaningful across age groups. Across different ages, health, partnership and family were rated as the most important factors. However, compared with other age groups, for people aged between 60 and 69, health and altruism were found to be the most important dimensions, while for people aged 70 and above it was animals/nature and spirituality. Both generativity and spirituality have been linked with meaning in life (De St. Aubin, 2013; Steger et al., 2010), which is in line with the idea of a growing importance of meaning in life for older adults.

> I would like to do a long walk, a pilgrimage, to ask myself questions, find a new meaning [. . .] walking for one or two months would give meaning to my retirement. (Female, 60 years old)

Altruism may be linked with the idea of generativity, which is a stage occurring in midlife (Erikson, 1959), suggesting a developmental shift to other-orientedness with the aim of benefiting future mankind. The same idea lies behind Freedman's (2007) concept of encore career. Freedman proposed that a shift from freedom from work (before retirement) to freedom to work/engage in meaningful activities after retirement occurs among retirees.

> When I will be retired I think I could find meaning through helping others [. . .] It is great to be retired – also for other people, not only for oneself. (Male, 60 years old)

> I would like to reorient my working energy into an activity that would be both intellectually and socially stimulating, like being a volunteer who helps teenagers to do their homework. (Female, 62 years old)

Another specificity of retired adults is the important role played by leisure activities that partially replace the previous role of work before retirement. Liechty et al. (2012) offered the framework of innovation theory, suggesting that 'the adoption of new leisure activities in later life (leisure innovation) may facilitate healthy aging through personal growth, interest renewal, identity reconstruction and increased sense of meaning in life' (p. 389). Williamson and Christie (2009) have also pointed out the importance of daily activities or pastimes for older adults. They considered that aging well depends on the extent to which people are able to engage in personally meaningful activities, because it increases physical and psychological functioning of older adults. By contrast, they suggest that activity restriction, due to illness, for instance, constitutes a major factor for poorer mental health.

To summarize, theory suggests that meaning in life for retirees might specifically depend on their developmental stage at the end of the life course, which implies a specific search for integrity (Erikson, 1959), a greater need to reconcile with their past (Krause and Hayward, 2014), but also a greater use of counterfactual thinking with a shift from a focus on their life events in a detailed way to a focus on their life events in a broader scope (Hershfield et al., 2013). Furthermore, empirical research showed that older adults have higher scores on the presence of meaning in life and lower scores on the search for meaning in life, compared to younger adults (Steger et al., 2009), and that the elements that make their life meaningful are mostly health, nature, spirituality and altruism compared to their younger counterparts (Fegg et al., 2007). This last element can be linked with the concept of generativity (Erikson, 1959), that is, the desire to give to others, and that one's actions may benefit a larger community. This idea has also been developed by leisure innovation theorists (Liechty et al., 2012), who stress the importance of keeping meaningful activities (that is, leisure, volunteering, encore career or bridge employment) during one's retirement.

PRACTICAL IMPLICATIONS FOR CAREER COUNSELORS AND ORGANIZATIONS TO FACILITATE A MEANINGFUL TRANSITION TO RETIREMENT

In this last part of the chapter, we will describe practical ways in which both individuals and organizations may enhance meaningful work and meaning in life in the transition to retirement. We will organize our points along a timeline representing the transition to retirement (from being an older worker to being a retiree) and including individual (career counseling) and organizational (HR management) standpoints for each stage in this process.

First, during the first stage of transition, when people are still older workers approaching retirement, several interventions at the organizational level can be suggested. Cartwright and Holmes (2006) proposed that, especially for jobs that do not easily lead to a sense of benefiting the greater good, the organization could help their employees achieve a sense of meaning by actively supporting them to be involved in community work or donating a percentage of their profits to charity. Otherwise, organizations may also implement off-work periods for their employees in which they could engage in activities that would give them the opportunity to make a difference in the life of others as well as their own, for example, by working in a community project. Schnell et al. (2013) further insist on the importance for employees to know the short-, middle- and long-term consequences of their activities, and the ability to approach questions of responsibility, sustainability and global interconnectedness within the organization.

Another suggestion is that older workers clearly constitute a resource for their organization concerning training, supervision and mentoring of younger colleagues. These tasks allow older workers to stay fully engaged and may increase their perception of meaningful work, especially as this supervision includes generative motives and a closer emotional relationship with co-workers. Moreover, this strategy may be part of a global knowledge management in the firm, in order to keep specialized knowledge in the organization.

At the individual level, reflection about meaning in life and meaningful work can be enhanced and further developed through career counseling. This kind of counseling may help older workers to realize what their work goals and work values are and then to undertake actions so that work would be more aligned with their personal values. Career counseling may also help individuals to position themselves in an organization where their personal priorities fit their job tasks. This would increase intrinsic motivation, leading to greater meaningfulness at work (Rosso et al., 2010; Schnell et al., 2013). In addition, career counseling approaches that focus on identity construction through narrative techniques (Hartung, 2013) might be especially suitable. This type of career counseling aims at constructing a meaningful life story and then assisting clients in implementing and projecting their identity into their work.

During the second period of the transition, as people have just entered the retirement stage, an important human resource management practice to enable a meaningful transition is to facilitate work–life balance for older workers. Whereas work is a very important component for meaning in life, the gradual change between full employment to full retirement may begin with a slow decrease in workload. Employers should foster flexibility of employment for their older employees in order to help them follow personal interests and to find meaningful activities outside work that could continue after retirement. At the individual level, career counseling could support a reflection about work–life balance through specific exercises that enable older workers to determine their different life spheres and assess the relative importance of each of them compared to the others.

In the third phase, as the retirees get used to their new condition, career counseling approaches might also be useful to achieve meaning in life. Work values can be related to more general personal values that would direct older adults to life goals they would like to attain and describe what kind of life would be meaningful for them. Moreover, their reflection about work values may also help the retiree to define meaningful daily activities that are linked with their personal values and/or near to their previous work goals.

A final suggestion is to insist on the need for organizations to develop new HR management practices toward their retirees. Policies should be undertaken to give them the opportunity to continue working (bridge employment), either part time or full time for a specific period of time and projects. Apart from the clear benefit for the organization in terms of retaining knowledge and expertise, these policies may also be a way for retirees to get involved in meaningful activities and share their willingness regarding generativity.

CONCLUSION AND SUMMARY

We would like to summarize the main messages of this chapter. First, we have outlined global issues of aging and work. We have seen that age is no longer seen as a gradual and inevitable decline, but as consisting of different developmental patterns. Subsequently, we have discussed the transition to retirement from the standpoint of sustainable careers; specifically, its main dimensions of continuity and importance of personal agency (that is, retirement as a new career development stage and adjustment process). Next, we analyzed the literature on meaningful work and meaning in life and their different theoretical conceptualizations and empirical findings, distinguishing three levels that constitute meaningful work (that is, self, work, and balance between the former two) and five dimensions of meaning in life (that is, values, goals, purpose, reconciling with one's past, and making sense/comprehension). When applied to older workers and retirement issues, it appeared that both meaning in life and meaningful work are especially important for older adults, due to their developmental stage characterized by a growing importance of interpersonal motives and deep relationships, as well as a growing importance of meaning in life and a global aspiration for more eudemonic well-being. Finally, we distinguished different ways to foster meaning in life and meaningful work from the standpoint of individuals (that is, work and personal values, benefiting the greater good, narrative identity construction) and of organizations (that is, facilitating work–life balance, creating opportunities to benefit the greater good, knowledge transfer and mentoring within the organization) at different times in the transition process.

To conclude, our aim was to position the transition to retirement as a specific career stage within the larger notion of sustainable careers. We believe that focusing on meaningful work and meaning in life is of particular importance in this transition and that career counselors and organizations can help to make the transition to retirement a successful part of a sustainable career

REFERENCES

Atchley, R.C. (1999), 'Continuity theory, self, and social structure', in C.D. Ryff and V.W. Marshall (eds), *The Self and Society in Aging Processes*, Newbury Park, CA: Sage, pp. 145–58.

Baltes, B.B., C.W. Rudolph and A.C. Bal (2012), 'A review of aging theories and modern work perspectives', in J.W. Hedge and W.C. Borman (eds), *The Oxford Handbook of Work and Aging*, New York: Oxford University Press, pp. 117–36.

Carstensen, L.L., D.M. Isaacowitz and S.T. Charles (1999), 'Taking time seriously: A theory of socioemotional selectivity', *American Psychologist*, **54** (3), 165–81.

Cartwright, S. and N. Holmes (2006), 'The meaning of work: The challenge of regaining employee engagement and reducing cynicism', *Human Resource Management Review*, **16** (2), 199–208.

Chalofsky, N. (2003), 'An emerging construct for meaningful work', *Human Resource Development International*, **6** (1), 69–83.

Cummings, E. and W.E. Henry (1961), *Growing Old*, New York: Basic Books.

De Lange, A.H., N.W. Van Yperen, B.I. Van der Heijden, and P. Bal (2010), 'Dominant achievement goals of older workers and their relationship with motivation-related outcomes', *Journal of Vocational Behavior*, **77** (1), 118–25.

De St. Aubin, E. (2013), 'Generativity and the meaning of life', in J.A. Hicks and C. Routledge (eds), *The Experience of Meaning in Life: Classical Perspectives, Emerging Themes, and Controversies*, New York: Springer Science + Business Media, pp. 241–55.

Dennis, H. and K.T. Fike (2012), 'Retirement planning: New context, process, language, and players', in J.W. Hedge and W.C. Borman (eds), *The Oxford Handbook of Work and Aging*, New York: Oxford University Press, pp. 538–48.

Erikson, E.H. (1959), *Identity and the Life Cycle*, New York: International University Press.

Fegg, M.J., M. Kramer, C. Bausewein and G.D. Borasio (2007), 'Meaning in life in the Federal Republic of Germany: Results of a representative survey with the Schedule for Meaning in Life Evaluation (SMiLE)', *Health and Quality of Life Outcomes*, **5** (59), 133–41.

Freedman, M. (2007), *Encore: Finding Work that Matters in the Second Half of Life*, New York: Public Affairs.

Hall, D.T. (2004), 'The protean career: A quarter-century journey', *Journal of Vocational Behavior*, **65** (1), 1–13.

Hall, D.T., E. Feldman and N. Kim (2013), 'Meaningful work and the protean career', in B.J. Dik, Z.S. Byrne and M.F. Steger (eds), *Purpose and Meaning in the Workplace*, Washington, DC: American Psychological Association, pp. 57–78.

Hartung, P.J. (2013), 'Career as story: Making the narrative turn', in W.B. Walsh, M.L. Savickas and P.J. Hartung (eds), *Handbook of Vocational Psychology: Theory, Research, and Practice* (4th edn), New York: Routledge, pp. 33–52.

Hershfield, H.E., C.E. Brown and L.J. Kray (2013), 'Any second could be the second: How thinking about what might have been affects the emergence of meaning and commitment across the adult life span', in J.A. Hicks and C. Routledge (eds), *The Experience of Meaning in Life: Classical Perspectives, Emerging Themes, and Controversies*, New York: Springer Science + Business Media, pp. 151–62.

Hicks, J.A., J. Trent, W.E. Davis and L.A. King (2012), 'Positive affect, meaning in life, and future time perspective: An application of socioemotional selectivity theory', *Psychology and Aging*, **27** (1), 181–9.

Kanfer, R. and P.L. Ackerman (2004), 'Aging, adult development, and work motivation', *The Academy of Management Review*, **29** (3), 440–58.

Kooij, D.T., A.H. De Lange, P.G. Jansen, R. Kanfer and J.S. Dikkers (2011), 'Age and work-related motives: Results of a meta-analysis', *Journal of Organizational Behavior*, **32** (2), 197–225.

Krause, N. (2004), 'Stressors arising in highly valued roles, meaning in life, and the physical health status of older adults', *The Journals of Gerontology: Series B: Psychological Sciences and Social Sciences*, **59B** (5), S287–S291.

Krause, N. and R.D. Hayward (2014), 'Assessing stability and change in a second-order confirmatory factor model of meaning in life', *Journal of Happiness Studies*, **15**, 237–53.

Liechty, T., C. Yarnal and D. Kerstetter (2012), '"I want to do everything!": Leisure innovation among retirement-age women', *Leisure Studies*, **31** (4), 389–408.

MOWIRT (1987), *The Meaning of Working*, London: Academic Press.

Müller, A., A. De Lange, M. Weigl, C. Oxfart and B. Van der Heijden (2013), 'Compensating losses in bridge employment? Examining relations between compensation strategies, health problems, and intention to remain at work', *Journal of Vocational Behavior*, **83** (1), 68–77.

Newman, K.L. (2011), 'Sustainable careers: Lifecycle engagement in work', *Organizational Dynamics*, **40** (2), 136–43.

Rosso, B.D., K.H. Dekas and A. Wrzesniewski (2010), 'On the meaning of work: A theoretical integration and review', *Research in Organizational Behavior*, **30**, 91–127.

Schnell, T., T. Höge and E. Pollet (2013), 'Predicting meaning in work: Theory, data, implications', *The Journal of Positive Psychology*, **8** (6), 543–54.

Shacklock, K. and Y. Brunetto (2011), 'A model of older workers' intentions to continue working', *Personnel Review*, **40** (2), 252–74.

Steger, M.F. and B.J. Dik (2009), 'If one is looking for meaning in life, does it help to find meaning in work?', *Applied Psychology: Health and Well-Being*, **1** (3), 303–20.

Steger, M.F. and B.J. Dik (2010), 'Work as meaning: Individual and organizational benefits of engaging in meaningful work', in P. Linley, S. Harrington and N. Garcea (eds), *Oxford Handbook of Positive Psychology and Work*, New York: Oxford University Press, pp. 131–42.

Steger, M.F., S. Oishi and T.B. Kashdan (2009), 'Meaning in life across the life span: Levels and correlates of meaning in life from emerging adulthood to older adulthood', *The Journal of Positive Psychology*, **4** (1), 43–52.

Steger, M.F., H. Littman-Ovadia, M. Miller, L. Menger and S. Rothmann (2013), 'Engaging in work even when it is meaningless: Positive affective disposition and meaningful work interact in relation to work engagement', *Journal of Career Assessment*, **21** (2), 348–61.

Steger, M.F., N.K. Pickering, E. Adams, J. Burnett, J.Y. Shin, B.J. Dik and N. Stauner (2010), 'The quest for meaning: Religious affiliation differences in the correlates of religious quest and search for meaning in life', *Psychology of Religion and Spirituality*, **2** (4), 206–26.

Wang, M. (2012), 'Health and fiscal and psychological well-being in retirement', in J.W. Hedge and W.C. Borman (eds), *The Oxford Handbook of Work and Aging*, New York: Oxford University Press, pp. 570–84.

Wang, M. and J. Shi (2014), 'Psychological research on retirement', *Annual Review of Psychology*, **65**, 209–33.

Wang, M. and K.S. Shultz (2010), 'Employee retirement: A review and recommendations for future investigation', *Journal of Management*, **36** (1), 172–206.

Wechsler, D. (1944), *The Measurement of Adult Intelligence*, Baltimore, MD: Williams and Wilkins.

Williamson, G. and J. Christie (2009), 'Aging well in the 21st century: Challenges and opportunities', in F.G. Lopez and C.R. Snyder (eds), *Oxford Handbook of Positive Psychology*, New York: Oxford University Press, pp. 165–9.

24 Organizational and labor markets as career ecosystem

Yehuda Baruch

In this chapter, I present and discuss the phenomenon of careers and their management as part of a wide ecosystem which operates across internal and external labor markets. To fully understand labor markets, one has to understand the 'landscape' of careers and how it is changing, the career actors that take part in the play, and the dynamic nature of the system. The sustainability of careers relies not on their stability but on their ability to adjust, develop and fit into an ever-changing work environment. This applies both to individuals and to employers. Individuals need to take ownership of their career, and organizations should facilitate career systems to enable their employees to flourish where they can make the best contribution. In the past, people could rely on the traditional psychological contract of mutual commitment and job security, but this has changed (Rousseau, 1996; Herriot and Pemberton, 1995). The traditional commitment lost the basis for its existence and became transitional and conditional commitment (Baruch, 1998). Thus individuals understand that there is no career stability, and one cannot count on a false promise of future employment. For individuals, a sustainable career would mean, to start with, having high levels of employability and personal qualities such as career resilience (London, 1983) and proactivity (Seibert et al., 2001). Employability derives from the ability to acquire new jobs, and this necessitates constant learning and keeping up with new professional knowledge.

A career is typically referred to as 'an evolving sequence of a person's work experience over time' (Arthur et al., 1989, p. 8) or 'a process of development by [an] employee along a path of experience and roles in one or more organizations' (Baruch and Rosenstein, 1992, p. 478). A career system is the arena in which careers take place – the local, regional, sectorial, national and global labor markets.

Careers develop within labor markets in a way resembling an ecosystem (Baruch, 2013; Higgins, 2005). An ecosystem is 'a system that contains a large number of loosely coupled (interconnected) actors who depend on each other to ensure the overall effectiveness of the system' (Iansiti and Levien, 2004, p. 5). The career ecosystem operates in a constellation that is not merely economical but that is also part of a social political phenomenon in a global environment (Gunz et al., 2011). There is a significant 'flow of talent' across organizations, sectors and nations, all influenced constantly and simultaneously by various forces (in line with Lewin's field theory, 1951). Within an ecosystem, actors generate value through relationships, and within the career ecosystem, work and employment relationships define careers and their outcomes.

Compared with the past, career systems are more dynamic in many aspects. The system is influenced not just by the growing number of people in terms of global population, but also by other factors. Amongst the most prominent are the rapid changes and growth in professions (in particular IT and web-related), decline in others, changes in employment relationships (new psychological contracts), and shifting emphasis in sectors, such as the move of significant production capabilities from Western countries to the Far East (in particular to China – see Lemoine and Ünal-Kesenci, 2004, for example) or the move to automation (Rifkin, 1996). While having a fully boundaryless career system is probably a utopian idea, there is significant progress in the extent of boundary-crossing, boundary-blurring, and other forms of employment flexibility (Peiperl and Baruch, 1997). In many ways, the new system operates in a way that resembles natural ecosystems. Different career actors interact to reach an equilibrium of constant progress and development for individuals, organizations and nations.

Ecosystem mechanisms of adjustment, expansion and decline, and flow of talent, to name a few processes, are constantly evolving. The nature of contemporary careers offers more opportunities towards a 'boundaryless' career (Arthur and Rousseau, 1996), though in reality we are talking about more opportunities for boundary-crossing – a totally boundaryless career is not literally feasible (Inkson et al., 2012). Bearing in mind the relativity of the terminology, we use here the frequently applied term 'boundaryless career'. The boundaryless career can be depicted according to six possible, different meanings (Arthur and Rousseau, 1996):

1. careers that move across the boundaries of separate employers, sometimes within clusters or sectorial enclaves, like the stereotypical Silicon Valley career;
2. careers that draw validation – and marketability – from outside the present employer, like those of academics or craftsmen;
3. careers that are sustained by external networks or information like those of real-estate agents or sport agents;
4. careers that more generally break traditional organizational assumptions about hierarchy and career advancement;
5. careers that are typified or characterized by rejecting existing career opportunities for personal or family reasons; and
6. careers that are based on the interpretation of the career actor, who may perceive a boundaryless future regardless of structural constraints.

ORIGINS AND DEFINITIONS

An ecosystem is a scientific concept, originally developed within ecology studies (Golley, 1993). Within industrial and business settings, the ecosystem concept is concerned with systems and flow of people, knowledge and talent as fit for overall improvement and reaching socio- and economic balance. Applying an ecosystem perspective aims at understanding complex systems and how to manage the environment by understanding the function of ecological systems and predicting responsiveness to external interferences. Tansley (1935) introduced the concept of the ecosystem and defined it as a holistic and integrative ecological concept that combined living organisms and the physical environment into a system.

I define career ecosystems as a metaphorical use of the natural science ecosystem concept in the field of management and behavioral sciences, in which the organisms are replaced by human beings, and the physical environment is replaced by a complex system of labor markets – organizations, from small to large, from private to public, from national to global.

Amongst the characteristics of the labor markets as ecosystem are:

- a constant flow of human capital, prompted and influenced by push/pull factors;
- spiral learning processes, required for continuous adjustments and adaptation to new situations;
- ongoing change processes influencing the directions and magnitude of human capital flow;
- global labor markets, influenced by factors at many levels.

The main actors (and related domains) are:

- individuals (competence, needs, values and attitudes);
- organizations (nature of career system – traditional or dynamic, stage of globalization, sector and product type, knowledge management);
- nations/societies (culture, economy, legal, politics, social, technology).

Applying the ecosystem theory to career studies follows from what I consider a strong fit with the nature of careers – for individuals, organizations and the wider system. Career actors within each level are interrelated. They interact and mutually influence each other.

For individuals, a career is a salient life element, focusing on working life. About half of the average wake-up time of employees is dedicated to work or work-related activities. Work and professional status influence overall life status, self-perception and identification. Even when a person is unemployed, a career can be no less important, and can sometimes occupy that person's mind continuously (Chapter 12, this volume).

Yet, as work life and private life are interwoven, careers relate to most facets in the life of the individual actor. The career is planned and managed by different constituencies – first, the individual, but then the organization and the wider community – national, professional, and so on. At the basic level, careers are managed simultaneously by individuals and their employers, whereas the impact of the national system works via the education system, training mechanisms, legal constraints, and cultural attributes that shape the nature of what is considered a desirable, acceptable and fulfilling career.

Labor markets are the 'space' where human capital is bought and sold, as people enter, change or leave employment. In the past, they tended to be stable, closely controlled by organizations (Gutteridge et al., 1993), and typically with entry at the lower end of the organizational structure, upward progress until reaching a career plateau, and exit at retirement. In contrast, contemporary labor markets take place in increasingly dynamic (Hall, 2002) and global environments (Tams and Arthur, 2007). Entry and exit levels vary (Baruch, 2004a), and there are more career moves along individuals' life course (Cascio, 2000). Such career moves can involve a change of job, organization, occupation or sector of industry, as well as geographical mobility, be it local, national or global (Dickmann and Baruch, 2011).

THE CHANGING NATURE OF CAREER SYSTEMS AND EMERGING CAREER MODELS

It is claimed that career systems are 'boundaryless', though in practice, there is a continuum between two possible extremes: one is a very strict and rigid system (like the Catholic Church or army structure), stable and predictable, where careers remain within the boundaries of organizations, professions, and so on. The other one is a fluid system of employment with constant changes and moves, and where the lack of boundaries enables career shifts in various directions. Realizing that both extremes rarely exist in reality, Inkson et al. (2012) suggested the use of the more realistic and pragmatic term of 'boundary-crossing'.

Sullivan and Arthur (2006) posit the boundaryless careers alongside two dimensions: physical mobility and psychological mobility. Mobility and adjustments or adaptations are fundamental elements of ecosystems. Individuals change jobs, careers, country, profession, and above all, people can change their 'frame of mind'. Trust, loyalty and commitment can be established between individual people and between individuals and organizations. People and organizations can develop identities that will adjust to the changing work environment at the individual level (Ashforth and Mael, 1989) and the organizational level (He and Baruch, 2010). Organizations offer progress and development opportunities, working from different places (office, home, mobile work), and a revised psychological contract, which is more realistic and less committed (Rousseau, 1996). In layman's terms, the psychological contract is 'The unspoken promise, not present in the small print of the employment contract, of what an employer gives, and what employees give in return' (Baruch and Hind, 1999, p. 299). Such a contract is different from, though many times complementary to, the formal, legal employment contracts because of the differences in their context, 'audience', and in particular in their impact on human actions and organizational policies and practices (Kotter, 1973; Schein, 1980; Spindler, 1994). The new psychological contract adds dynamism to the overall labor market as it opens up more options for departure from organizations and a variety of career moves (Baruch, 2004a).

External factors, mostly economic, but also socio-cultural, shape and reshape the labor market system. Internal factors (for example, individual values and norms of conduct) and changes in organizations and nations add critical elements to these dynamics. One global reflection of this is the 'Brain Drain', defined as the occurrence of massive levels of outward migration of talented, educated and skilled individuals from one country to other countries. Under certain circumstances, brain drain can be transformed into 'brain circulation' (Saxenian, 2005). This is in line with the concept of the ecosystem when the actors change roles, where the playing field evolves, and when the rules of the game are rewritten (for example, the changes and breach of new psychological contracts). For a couple of decades, it appears that a new psychological contract has replaced the traditional one and, as presented in Table 24.1, this means a significant shift in the nature of careers, and manifests the way careers and their management have been transformed.

Table 24.1 Traditional vs. contemporary careers

Aspect	Traditional	Contemporary
Environment characteristic	Stability	Dynamism
Career choice being made	Once, at early career age	Series, at different career stages
Main responsibility for career planning and management lies with	Organization	Individual
Career horizon (workplace)	Within a single organization	Within and external to several organizations
Career horizon (time)	Long	Short
Psychological contract based on expectations of	Loyalty and commitment in return for job security	Empowerment and employability in return for freedom and flexibility
Progress criteria	Advance according to tenure	Advances according to competence and performance
Success means	Winning the tournament i.e. progress on the hierarchy ladder	Inner feeling of achievement
Training	Formal programs, generalist	On-the-job, company specific, sometimes ad hoc

Sources: Adapted from Baruch (2004b); Herriot and Pemberton (1995); Rousseau (1996).

Career Actors

A career actor is an entity that participates in the career system. It can be an individual, an organization, network, association, national or global body.

The career actors operate within internal and external labor markets – and influence each other. The primary actors are individuals, as the 'owners' of their own careers. Individuals look for career success, but the meaning of success is complex and multidimensional. It differs from person to person (Gunz and Heslin, 2005; Heslin, 2005) and within different career systems (Arthur et al., 2005). From this perspective, organizations can be taken as the internal labor market, whereas the wider environment is the external labor market. Labor markets become global, and there are growing options and opportunities for people to move across boundaries. Using a theater metaphor, one can recall Shakespeare (*As You Like It*, Act 2, Scene 7):

> All the world's a stage,
> And all the men and women merely players;
> . . .
> And one man in his time plays many parts . . .

In the theater business, the play progresses according to specific scripts written in advance, and the actors use a number of rehearsals to prepare for the 'live play'. In real business life, actors have to write their own scripts for their current role and anticipated future positions, and to manage transitions, which, using the theater metaphor, is more like improvisation. One cannot prepare for the future via rehearsals – the show goes on continuously. One can learn, though, from earlier experience; for example, when starting a second career, the experience in the first career is instrumental for success in the next career (Baruch and Quick, 2007).

Each career actor has a vested interest in their own career and in that of others: individuals are interested in their progress, in their work–life balance, in self-fulfilment, but also in the careers of others (for example, protégés). Organizations wish to gain the most from their talent, develop in new directions, get rid of dead wood, expand into new markets – as examples that manifest relevance of career systems to HRM outcomes, subsequently, to enhancing organizational effectiveness and performance. While individuals have careers, the career develops and evolves in various systems, most notably within organizations.

Career System

A career system is where interacting and interdependent actors form a complex integrated whole, including a set of 'components', relationships, and 'rules of the game'. Actors plan, act, and reflect upon their development and progress, and different actors are assigned with different roles.

Changes and developments occur for each actor – specifically and generally. For example, generally, at the individual level, there is more individualism – even in places in the Far East (and the 'single child' policy has made Chinese people more individualistic than ever; see Zhang and Shavitt, 2003). Specifically, each individual has his or her own view about the meaning of the career and what the career stands for (for example, what is 'progress', what is 'success'). At the organizational level, generally, organizational structures, hence, career systems, are characterized by perpetual changes (Baruch, 2004a). Specifically, organizations may grow fast, decline, merge or die (Sutton, 1987).

There is more to it than individual and organizational relationships only. Other actors in the wider systems are also significant stakeholders. Governments, unions, professional associations, legal systems and regulations, all play a part in shaping careers and career development within and outside organizations (Hall, 2002). The wider labor market and its globalization are part of an ecosystem (Baruch, 2013; Higgins, 2005). The large number of loosely coupled but interconnected actors depend on each other to ensure the overall effectiveness of the system, in line with the original view of Iansiti and Levien (2004).

Table 24.2 shows the actors, what they bring to the system, and what their actions are. There is significant dynamism and movement, different levels of organizational entry, globalization of 'flow of talent', more opportunities, either self-selected or imposed externally, of people opting for second careers (Baruch and Quick, 2007). People choose to move to a different location or country, either for a limited period or permanently (Carr et al., 2005; Mahroum, 2000). Many are sent to work abroad by their employers (Doherty and Dickmann, 2009); others are self-initiated expatriates (Bozionelos, 2009; Suutari and Brewster, 2000). More broadly, people are more open to change, or accept the necessity of change. This goes hand in hand with the individualization of societies, both in Western and Eastern societies.

Table 24.2 Actors, what they bring to the system and what they do

Individual	Organization	Society
What they bring to the system		
Needs, traits, values, attitudes, human capital	Organizational culture Organizational resources Organizational structure	Culture, values, education, legislation, professional associations
What they do		
Plan, learn, train, negotiate, network Perform Progress	Plan, support, inspire, monitor Train, negotiate	Educate, legislate, regulate, set norms

Career Actions: Individual, Institutional and National

The main actor is the individual. Increasingly, individuals take control of their own career, and plan and manage it according to their values and aspirations. Hall termed it a protean career (Hall, 1976), being a view or orientation that takes careers as driven by the values of career actors (that is, what individuals consider important and worthy) and directed through personal choice rather than by external agents (Hall, 1996; 2004; Hall and Moss, 1998). Individuals holding a protean career attitude will find the boundaryless career concept applicable and appealing (Baruch, 2014). A career can be considered protean according to the extent to which it is driven by values and the extent to which it is self-directed (Briscoe et al., 2006).

Apart from having a specific career orientation, traditional or protean, individuals acquire human capital, including social capital (Chapter 5, this volume). The 'knowing whom' is a critical part of gaining career capital (Arthur et al., 1995). Networking is a major element of 'knowing whom' and thus important for career progress and achievements. Mentoring is just one example of the well-proven contribution of networking (Baugh and Sullivan, 2005; Casciaro and Lobo, 2008; Higgins and Kram, 2001). Networking is a form of goal-directed behavior, both inside and outside of an organization, focused on meeting, cultivating and utilizing interpersonal relationships. It is concerned with individuals' attempts to develop and maintain relationships with those who may assist them in their work roles or in their career in general (Forret and Dougherty, 2004). Networking includes many types of behaviors that aim to develop informal interpersonal relationships with others, at a higher level, equal level or lower level within and outside the workplace. Networking typically involves the exchange of practical communication and power gains, but also of affective emotions (Michael and Yukl, 1993). Mentoring relationships are formed and developed for the mutual benefit of both sides in a similar way that relationships are developed in ecosystems (for example, symbiosis). The mentor–protégé relationship may transform into peer-mentoring, or end altogether. These relationships can evolve at different levels, and are not restricted to a single organization.

ORGANIZATIONAL PLANNING AND MANAGEMENT OF CAREERS

Human capital is a significant factor in firm resources (Becker, 1964) and performance (Combs et al., 2006; Huselid, 1995). The composition of human capital, be it specific versus generic, and its strategic value versus practical responsiveness, affects the way organizations design and implement their career management policies (De Vos and Dries, 2013). It also influences organizations' career management systems (Baruch, 1999; Baruch and Peiperl, 2000). While the career is the 'property' of individuals, for those employed by organizations, the planning and management of it is shared between both entities. Moreover, the process of negotiating careers is not bounded to a two-way contract (legal and psychological) between the employer and the employee: many other actors participate, directly and indirectly. A variety of organizations – employers, private and public bodies, associations, government, legal entities – all take part in this complex system that evolves continuously, like any other ecosystem. Furthermore, many careers are formed in the shape of self-employment or small business ownership, where the individual is the one negotiating with the self to form career direction and progress. The post-corporate career (Peiperl and Baruch, 1997) manifests what may be taken as a natural development to an ecosystem, when large organizations operate alongside a variety of other entities, many of them small organizations and personal enterprises (see Figure 24.1).

For example, education has a clear impact on an individual's aspirations and competence (Mayrhofer et al., 2005). The nature and quality of the national education system will influence competitiveness at the global level. Legislation may enable certain people to choose a certain profession or prevent them from doing so. For example, financial and banking regulations may be a critical factor in determining whether an entrepreneur can follow his or her dream.

NATIONAL LEVEL

The country in which careers take place is a significant actor in the ecosystem of careers. It has the major responsibility for economic progress and stability, for operating a legal system and its enforcement, for the educational system, and for human rights, as well as many other roles. National governance is responsible for and can influence norms of behavior, legal constraints (for example, the work permit system), and control over the economy, factors that relate to the career ecosystem. National culture sets norms, for example, social status ascribed to certain professions (Abbott, 1981). The status of engineers in Germany is considered to be very high, whereas in the US being a manager may be more prestigious. The government is also typically the largest employer in each country, and purely because of this scale of employing people, sets a clear benchmark for other industries. Within each country, there are factors such as employment vs. unemployment, education quality, physical infrastructure, national and personal security, and urbanization, which are determined and influenced by national characteristics and the governance in that country.

Different countries put different emphasis on industrial sectors, subject to the

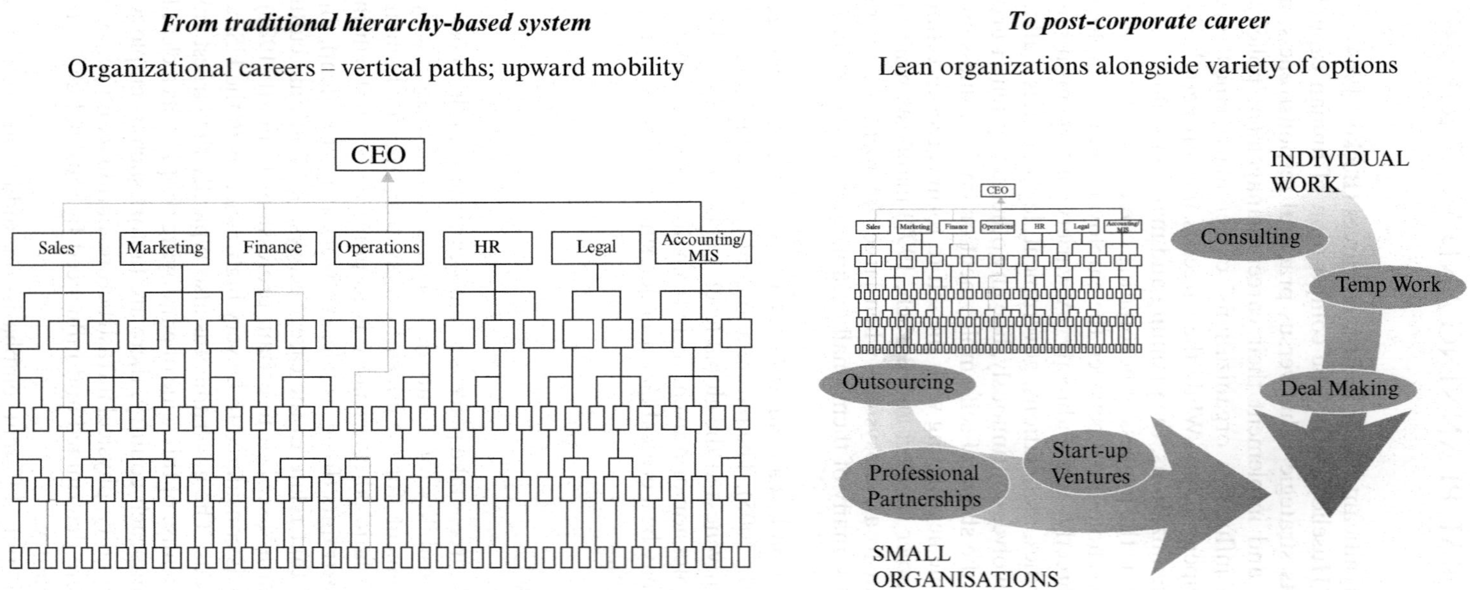

Figure 24.1 From traditional hierarchy-based system to post-corporate career

availability of natural and human resources. While Nigeria, Venezuela, Norway and Bahrain can base a significant share of their business market, hence their labor market, on the oil industry, countries like Bangladesh or the Philippines focus on textiles, where cheap labor is essential. In contrast, countries such as South Korea or Israel aim at the high-tech niche. This requires a differential education and infrastructure system (Rojewski, 2002).

INTEGRATIVE FRAMEWORK

All the parts of this system – individuals, organizations and societies – co-exist and interact with each other as an ecosystem that is balanced and functioning. The way the system controls itself and reaches equilibrium is not by sticking to a rigid status quo, but by aiming for stability in the shape of ever-evolving adjustments and adaptations, shaping and re-shaping relationships that are 'alive' and learning from constant interactions. The 'rules of the game' also change in line with the evolving needs of the different participants. The legal system forms the formal underpinning of those rules, but no less important are the culture and elements such as values and beliefs, which dictate norms of behavior. The dynamic nature and the responsiveness of its constituencies operate as a field force.

In the following section, I will use the push–pull model to manifest the dynamic and flexible nature of the career ecosystem. The idea of the push–pull model is based on Lewin's field theory (1951) and was widely applied to understand decision-making processes where different factors influence people's decisions.

REDUNDANCIES, RIGHT-SIZING, LEAN AND MEAN ORGANIZATIONS

Due to the highly competitive nature of the business environment, measures to keep costs under control have caused many organizations to try and do 'more with less'. Human costs make up a substantial part of the operating costs for organizations, and often comprise the main expense. The reduction of power of the unions and the relaxation of employment laws have made it easier for organizations to fire employees, even if their performance is not deteriorating. When some organizations use this practice, the herd phenomenon causes others to follow suit.

Top-down initiation occurs when executives cause their organization to fall into disarray by firing people en masse (Kets de Vries and Balazs, 1997), creating loss of knowledge and causing the 'survivor syndrome' for those remaining (Brockner et al., 1986). It can also lead to a cycle of reduction in the workforce, and when such cycles are consecutive, it can lead to 'organizational anorexia' (Bedeian and Armenakis, 1998). Yet, as unemployment rates remain quite steady, it means that most of these people find a different job or role to play in the economy (or retire); again, a clear manifestation of the ecosystem nature of processes (Cascio, 2000).

What is less obvious is that those leaving their employers, even if they were star performers, might not shine well in their new organizations. This was found in the knowledge industry, in particular within the financial sector (Groysberg, 2010; Groysberg et al., 2008). These studies found that people who flourished in a certain organization and believed they had unique and transferable competence found that in a different organization their human capital did not deliver the same results, probably due to the change in the environment, culture or luck.

In terms of psychological contracts, an environment of low job security and constant waves of redundancies requires employers to alter the psychological contract. Employers offer 'employability' (Fugate et al., 2004), 'empowerment' (Wilkinson, 1998), performance-related pay, and interesting roles. Furthermore, the employee is expected to be happy to have a job at all in times of turbulence.

Push–Pull Factors

First, at the organizational level people can be attracted to and can become alienated from their organization for many reasons. Remuneration can be one factor that attracts employees, but it is not the only factor. Type of job, (fit for personal interest, innovative culture), prospects of progress, fit with the organizational culture – all play a role in whether or not people are attracted to certain employers. Related to this, organizational reputation, in particular as 'investor in people' (with league tables for 'best place to work for') can operate as a pull factor, for example, by improving employability (Van der Heijden and De Lange, 2011). On the other hand, alienation can be a push factor (Chiaburu et al., 2013), causing people to leave or wish to leave, which ends in frustration if there is no viable way out. The ecosystem nature of the labor market enables new types of institutions to flourish. The temporary work niche of the workforce and employment, and the emergence of 'headhunter' firms are just two examples of the dynamic nature of a system where new needs and demands create and form new entities.

International Dynamics: Brain Drain Phenomenon

The business world is becoming global – and in terms of people's careers, people are becoming globally mobile. There is no single way to create a global career – Baruch et al. (2013a) listed a number of options that people utilize in becoming global. When people decide to move to another country, work-related issues form a significant factor in the decision-making process (though political and human rights issues may be the critical factors for some cases like asylum seekers). Work and career are taken into account by individuals and by organizations in mobility and relocation decisions (Baruch, 1995). This global push–pull model takes into account the economic, legal and cultural realms (see Figure 24.2). The set of motives (push or pull factors) are often multi-faceted – see, for example, Saxenian (2005) in her study about the connectivity and global mobility of scientists and entrepreneurs. Saxenian suggested that with the right attitude at the national level, brain drain can be transformed into 'brain circulation'. At the national level, governments aspiring to reach high-levels of sustained growth can compete in the global labor market to make gains in the process of 'brain circulation' (Baruch et al., 2007). A study of young graduates found that the talent flow can indeed be bi-directional (Carr et al., 2005).

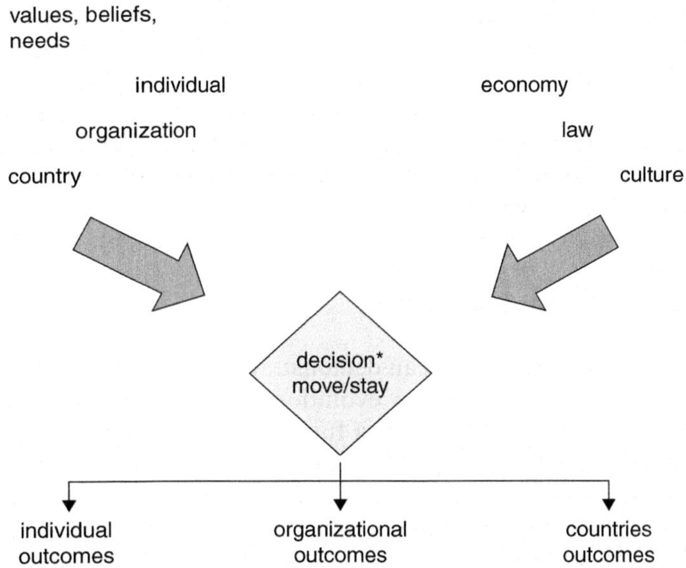

Note: * Can be taken in each level – usually the person.

Figure 24.2 The push–pull model for global career moves (Baruch, 1995)

At the individual level, globally oriented people often opt for a job and for maintaining a career in many regions. Organizations play a role in the process by assigning people to global assignments (expatriation) and bringing them back (repatriation). Nations can offer incentives to global migrants, like the case of the Arabian Gulf (Forstenlechner and Rutledge, 2011), creating the phenomenon of 'golden handcuffs' or 'golden cage' (Richardson and McKenna, 2002).

Gender and the Push–Pull Factors

From being a negligible section of the labor market, serving in low-prestige jobs, women have started to gain access to labor markets, and as years go by, have cracked, and later shattered the glass ceiling (Baruch, 2004b). Nevertheless, women tend to earn less and tend not to reach the higher echelons to the extent that men do. This is partially due to simple discrimination, but also due to self-restriction and self-perception (Hakim, 1996). A significant number of women take a career break to have children. Re-joining the 'rat-race' is challenging after being away for a few years. While taking a break for this purpose can be done by men too, it is usually not the case, for several reasons. Economically, if the female earns less, it makes less sense for the husband (or male partner) to take a career break (Baruch, 2004b, p. 256). For obvious reasons, the early days of parental leave in order to care for a child are typically taken by women and, with the return of the healthier option of breast feeding, the period of time that women take off increases, making it the preferred choice for families. This is a self-perpetuating system that reinforces gender gaps in employment and in promotion.

Many other factors exist; some push women out of the labor market whereas other factors pull them back, thereby reaching equilibrium. Compared with the past, more women are making it to the top or acquiring high earnings, but overall, there is strong gender bias in top positions, much of it due to societal values (Wigfield et al., 2002). Individual decision making on the part of women, for example, to enter the labor market, to re-enter employment after child bearing, or to pursue an executive career, depends on their values as well as on the view that society has on the role of females in modern society and many opt out (Mainiero and Sullivan, 2006).

Age Dynamism and the Push–Pull Factors

Another individual-level factor that can demonstrate how the ecosystem works in practice relates to individuals' age and how evolutions in the socio-economic environment have affected the meaning of a career as a function of age. In the industrial era, work started at the end of the education phase of the child – typically at the age of 14. Males would work and establish their career, often starting as an apprentice (industry) or post-boy (office), and progressing through the ranks. Females could start as secretaries, but were expected to stay at home once they got married. Work continued until the man retired at age 65, though age-related career decisions are subject to other factors, such as the intention to invest in career development (Simpson et al., 2002). Many, if not the majority, died before reaching the established age of 65. By the end of the twentieth century, a number of changes became apparent, emerging simultaneously at different levels of analysis. At the individual level, in developed societies, the majority of the younger generations follow formal education until the age of 18, and some 40 percent of them continue to university, entering working life at almost a decade later than earlier generations did. At the other end of the spectrum, due to continuous downsizing, many organizations 'release' employees to an early retirement. Coupled with increased longevity, the retirement phase of life is becoming significant in terms of duration. At a national level, such development means that the financial stability of pension funds will not be viable in the long term, and the future shape of the retirement age and retirement arrangements is facing changes – either evolving with a gradual increase of the retirement age, or taking the shape of abolition of retirement altogether (Baruch et al., 2013b).

Global Trends

The way wider labor markets operate as an ecosystem is reflected in global trends in business and industry, which are accompanied by employment trends (Baruch et al., 2013b). These include moving manufacturing to the Far East, mainly mainland China, establishing certain regions as leading in certain sectors (for example, Silicon Valley for high-tech), and emergence of new industries (such as green energy). These developments have strong implications for the type of employment and how employment in different professions and sectors is shifting under push and pull factors in a large ecosystem. Likewise, new professions are emerging – a clear example is the whole range of e-jobs such as 'web page designer', alongside the decline in other industries (such as travel agencies). A new set of training, qualifications, associations, and so on follows the introduction of each new profession. Economic considerations are determining the level of remuneration; social status is becoming associated with such jobs (Freidman, 2005).

DISCUSSION AND CONCLUSIONS

This chapter offers a view of career systems as ecosystems, where actors operate in internal and external labor markets, and constant flow of human capital characterizes the system. It highlights the micro- and macro-frames of reference for studying careers as ecosystems. In such a system, there is a constant development of human capital, dynamic talent flow at the individual level, and creation, re-shaping and dismantling of organizations, and national variations exist in the way labor markets operate. As time progresses, the whole system is becoming less local and more global (Dickmann and Baruch, 2011). Boundaries are becoming blurred, sometimes disappearing altogether, though the system is not becoming totally boundaryless (Inkson et al., 2012). A number of boundaries remain intact at all levels. Many individuals hold traditional career perceptions and, particularly for them, significant investment is required in order to make career moves, especially when a move involves a change of employer, profession or sector. Organizations are revising their structures, erasing complete layers of management, merging with other organizations, outsourcing activities, and becoming lean (and mean) in the process. Nations are more open for migration, but only within specific circumstances (such as within the EU). Reality does not match the rhetoric, as legal rules about immigration, and in particular the ability to acquire work permits, form a legal barrier for people who have the desire and ability to work in a different country.

Employment and labor markets are the landscape in which careers take place, and there are various 'rules of the game' for different segments of markets. The nature of career success is a critical aspect for the life of the individual actors, and forms a major factor in their performance in their employing organizations (or for their own enterprise, if self-employed). Contemporary career theories can be utilized to explicate the relevance and importance of considering labor markets as ecosystems for understanding and managing careers at the individual, organizational and national level. The lessons drawn here have been discussed and practical implications for people management have been presented. From the viewpoint of sustainable careers, the meaning of sustaining a career from an ecosystem perspective relies more on reaching equilibrium and being able to move and change as needed rather than to sticking to the idea of job stability, rigid structures and clear boundaries. Making career-related decisions is influenced by a number of factors at different levels, and the meaning of career stability is changing. In developed economies, individuals are interested in following their career calling, and use employability to replace job security as part of a constantly changing psychological contract (Fugate et al., 2004). New types of employment arrangements and flexibilities are emerging. The rules are changing continuously, for example, opening the labor market to minorities, reducing or eliminating the retirement age (Baruch et al., 2013b; Parry and Wilson, 2014). Coping with, adapting to, and initiating changes are critical factors, and career resilience is an asset for individuals' survival and sustainability. Organizations are learning to share the responsibility of career planning and management with their employees. Sustainable career systems are flexible systems that evolve continuously rather than staying stable and rigid.

REFERENCES

Abbott, A. (1981), 'Status and status strain in the professions', *American Journal of Sociology*, **86**, 819–35.

Arthur, M.B. and Rousseau, D.M. (1996), 'The boundaryless career as a new employment principle'. In M.G. Arthur and D.M. Rousseau (eds), *The Boundaryless Career*, New York: Oxford University Press, pp. 3–20.

Arthur, M.B., Claman, P.H. and DeFillippi, R.J. (1995), 'Intelligent enterprise, intelligent careers', *Academy of Management Executive*, **9** (4), 7–20.

Arthur, M.B., Hall, D.T. and Lawrence, B.S. (1989), 'Generating new directions in career theory: The case for a transdisciplinary approach'. In M.B. Arthur, D.T. Hall and B.S. Lawrence (eds), *Handbook of Career Theory*, Cambridge: Cambridge University Press, pp. 7–25.

Arthur, M.B., Khapova, S.N. and Wilderom, C.P.M. (2005), 'Career success in a boundaryless career world', *Journal of Organizational Behavior*, **26**, 177–202.

Ashforth, B.E. and Mael, F. (1989), 'Social identity theory and the organization', *Academy of Management Review*, **14**, 20–39.

Baruch, Y. (1995), 'Business globalization – the human resource management aspect', *Human Systems Management*, **14**, 313–26.

Baruch, Y. (1998), 'The rise and fall of organizational commitment', *Human System Management*, **17**, 135–43.

Baruch, Y. (1999), 'Integrated career systems for the 2000s', *International Journal of Manpower*, **20**, 432–57.

Baruch, Y. (2004a), 'Transforming careers – from linear to multidirectional career paths: Organizational and individual perspective', *Career Development International*, **9**, 58–73.

Baruch, Y. (2004b), *Managing Careers: Theory and Practice*, Harlow, UK: FT-Prentice Hall/Pearson.

Baruch, Y. (2013), 'Careers in academe: The academic labour market as an eco-system', *Career Development International*, **18**, 196–210.

Baruch, Y. (2014), 'The development and validation of a measure for protean career orientation', *The International Journal of Human Resource Management*, **25**, 2702–23.

Baruch, Y. and Hind, P. (1999), 'Perpetual motion in organizations: Effective management and the impact of the new psychological contracts on "Survivor Syndrome"', *European Journal of Work and Organizational Psychology*, **8**, 295–306.

Baruch, Y. and Peiperl, M.A. (2000), 'Career management practices: An empirical survey and theoretical implications', *Human Resource Management*, **39**, 347–66.

Baruch, Y. and Quick, J.C. (2007), 'Understanding second careers: Lessons from a study of US Navy admirals', *Human Resource Management*, **46**, 471–91.

Baruch, Y. and Rosenstein, E. (1992), 'Career planning and managing in high tech organizations', *International Journal of Human Resource Management*, **3**, 477–96.

Baruch, Y., Budhwar, P. and Khatri, N. (2007), 'Brain drain: Inclination to stay abroad after studies', *Journal of World Business*, **42**, 99–112.

Baruch, Y., Dickmann, M., Altman, Y. and Bournois, F. (2013a), 'Exploring international work: Types and dimensions of global careers', *International Journal of Human Resource Management*, **24**, 2369–93.

Baruch, Y., Sayce, S. and Gregoriou, A. (2013b), 'Abolition of the default retirement age', *Personnel Review*, **43**, 464–82.

Baugh, S.G. and Sullivan, S.E. (2005), 'Mentoring and career development', *Career Development International*, **10**, 425–8.

Becker, G.S. (1964), *Human Capital*, New York: National Bureau of Economic Research.

Bedeian, A.G. and Armenakis, A.A. (1998), 'The cesspool syndrome: How dreck floats to the top of declining organizations', *The Academy of Management Executive*, **12** (1), 58–67.

Bozionelos, N. (2009), 'Expatriation outside the boundaries of the multinational corporation: A study with expatriate nurses in Saudi Arabia', *Human Resource Management*, **48**, 111–34.

Briscoe, J.P., Hall, D.T. and Frautschy DeMuth, R.L. (2006), 'Protean and boundaryless careers: An empirical exploration', *Journal of Vocational Behavior*, **69**, 30–47.

Brockner, J., Greenberg, J., Brockner, A., Bortz, J., Davy, J. and Carter, C. (1986), 'Layoffs, equity theory, and work performance: Further evidence of the impact of survivor guilt', *Academy of Management Journal*, **29**, 373–84.

Carr, S.C., Inkson, K. and Thorn, K. (2005), 'From global careers to talent flow: Reinterpreting "brain drain"', *Journal of World Business*, **40**, 386–98.

Casciaro, T. and Lobo, M.S. (2008), 'When competence is irrelevant: The role of interpersonal affect in task-related ties', *Administrative Science Quarterly*, **53**, 655–84.
Cascio, W.F. (2000), 'New workplaces'. In Jean M. Kummerow (ed.), *New Directions in Career Planning and the Workplace* (2nd edn), Palo Alto, CA: Davies-Black Publishing.
Chiaburu, D.S., Diaz, I. and De Vos, A. (2013), 'Employee alienation: Relationships with careerism and career satisfaction', *Journal of Managerial Psychology*, **28**, 4–20.
Combs, J., Liu, Y., Hall, A. and Ketchen, D. (2006), 'How much do high-performance work practices matter? A meta-analysis of their effects on organizational performance', *Personnel Psychology*, **59**, 501–28.
De Vos, A. and Dries, N. (2013), 'Applying a talent management lens to career management: The role of human capital composition and continuity', *The International Journal of Human Resource Management*, **24**, 1816–31.
Dickmann, M. and Baruch, Y. (2011), *Global Careers*, New York: Routledge.
Doherty, N. and Dickmann, M. (2009), 'Exposing the symbolic capital of international assignments', *International Journal of Human Resource Management*, **20**, 301–20.
Forret, M.L. and Dougherty, T.W. (2004), 'Networking behaviors and career outcomes: Differences for men and women?', *Journal of Organizational Behavior*, **25**, 419–37.
Forstenlechner, I. and Rutledge, E.J. (2011), 'The GCC's demographic imbalance: Perceptions, realities and policy options', *Middle East Policy*, **18** (4), 25–43.
Freidman, T. (2005), *The World is Flat*, New York: Farrar, Straus and Giroux.
Fugate, M., Kinicki, A.J. and Ashforth, B.E. (2004), 'Employability: A psycho-social construct, its dimensions, and applications', *Journal of Vocational Behavior*, **65**, 14–38.
Golley, F.B. (1993), *A History of the Ecosystem Concept in Ecology: More than the Sum of the Parts*, New Haven, CT: Yale University Press.
Groysberg, B. (2010), *Chasing Stars: The Myth of Talent and the Portability of Performance*, Princeton, NJ: Princeton University Press.
Groysberg, B., Lee, L.-E. and Nanda, A. (2008), 'Can they take it with them? The portability of star knowledge workers' performance', *Management Science*, **54**, 1213–30.
Gunz, H.P. and Heslin, P.A. (2005), 'Reconceptualizing career success', *Journal of Vocational Behavior*, **26**, 105–11.
Gunz, H., Mayrhofer, W. and Tolbert, P. (2011), 'Careers as a social political phenomenon in the global economy', *Organization Studies*, **32**, 1613–20.
Gutteridge, T.G., Leibowitz, Z.B. and Shore, J.E. (1993), *Organizational Career Development*, San Francisco: Jossey-Bass.
Hakim, C. (1996), *Key Issues in Women's Work: Female Heterogeneity and the Polarisation of Women's Employment*, London: Athlone Press.
Hall, D.T. (1976), *Careers in Organizations*, Pacific Palisades, CA: Goodyear.
Hall, D.T. (1996), *The Career is Dead – Long Live the Career*, San Francisco: Jossey-Bass.
Hall, D.T. (2002), *Careers In and Out of the Organization*, Thousand Oaks, CA: Sage.
Hall, D.T. (2004), 'The protean career: A quarter-century journey', *Journal of Vocational Behavior*, **65**, 1–13.
Hall, D.T. and Moss, J.E. (1998), 'The new protean career contract: Helping organizations and employees adapt', *Organizational Dynamics*, **26** (3), 22–37.
He, H.-W. and Baruch, Y. (2010), 'Organizational identity narrative and legitimacy under major environmental changes: The case of UK building societies', *British Journal of Management*, **21**, 44–62.
Herriot, P. and Pemberton, C. (1995), *New Deals*, Chichester: John Wiley.
Heslin, P.A. (2005), 'Conceptualizing and evaluating career success', *Journal of Organizational Behavior*, **26**, 113–36.
Higgins, M. (2005), *Career Imprints. Creating Leaders Across an Industry*, San Francisco: Jossey-Bass.
Higgins, M.C. and Kram, K.E. (2001), 'Reconceptualizing mentoring at work: A developmental network perspective', *Academy of Management Review*, **26**, 264–88.
Huselid, M.A. (1995), 'The impact of human resource management practices on turnover, productivity, and corporate financial performance', *Academy of Management Journal*, **38**, 635–72.
Iansiti, M. and Levien, R. (2004), 'Strategy as ecology', *Harvard Business Review*, **82** (3), 68–81.
Inkson, K., Gunz, H., Ganesh, S. and Roper, J. (2012), 'Boundaryless careers: Bringing back boundaries', *Organization Studies*, **33**, 323–40.
Kets de Vries, M.F.R. and Balazs, K. (1997), 'The downsize of downsizing', *Human Relations*, **50**, 11–50.
Kotter, J. (1973), 'The psychological contract: Managing the joining-up process', *California Management Review*, **15** (3), 91–9.
Lemoine, F. and Ünal-Kesenci, D. (2004), 'Assembly trade and technology transfer: The case of China', *World Development*, **32**, 829–50.
Lewin, K. (1951), *Field Theory in Social Science*, New York: Harper & Row.
London, M. (1983), 'Toward a theory of career motivation', *Academy of Management Review*, **8**, 620–30.

Mahroum, S. (2000), 'Highly skilled globetrotters: Mapping the international migration of human capital', *R&D Management*, **30**, 23–31.
Mainiero, L.A. and Sullivan, S.E. (2006), *The Opt-Out Revolt: Why People are Leaving Companies to Create Kaleidoscope Careers*, Palo Alto, CA: Davis-Black.
Mayrhofer, W., Steyrer, J., Meyer, M., Strunk, G., Schiffinger, M. and Iellatchitch, A. (2005), 'Graduates' career aspirations and individual characteristics', *Human Resource Management Journal*, **15**, 38–56.
Michael, J. and Yukl, G. (1993), 'Managerial level and subunit function as determinants of networking behavior in organizations', *Group & Organization Management*, **18**, 328–51.
Parry, E. and Wilson, D.B. (2014), 'Career transitions at retirement age in the United Kingdom'. In C.-M. Alcover, G. Topa, E. Parry, F. Fraccaroli and M. Depolo (eds), *Bridge Employment: A Research Handbook*, Abingdon: Routledge, pp. 138–53.
Peiperl, M.A. and Baruch, Y. (1997), 'Back to square zero: The post-corporate career', *Organization Dynamics*, **25** (4), 7–22.
Richardson, J. and McKenna, S. (2002), 'Leaving and experiencing: Why academics expatriate and how they experience expatriation', *Career Development International*, **7**, 67–78.
Rifkin, J. (1996), *The End of Work*, Washington, DC: Social Planning Council of Winnipeg.
Rojewski, J.W. (2002), 'Preparing the workforce of tomorrow: A conceptual framework for career and technical education', *Journal of Vocational Education Research*, **27**, 7–35.
Rousseau, D.M. (1996), 'Changing the deal while keeping the people', *Academy of Management Executive*, **10** (1), 50–59.
Saxenian, A. (2005), 'From brain drain to brain circulation: Transnational communities and regional upgrading in India and China', *Studies in Comparative International Development*, **40** (2), 35–61.
Schein, E.H. (1980), *Organizational Psychology* (3rd edn), Englewood Cliffs, NJ: Prentice-Hall.
Seibert, S.E., Kraimer, M.L. and Crant, J.M. (2001), 'What do proactive people do? A longitudinal model linking proactive personality and career success', *Personnel Psychology*, **54**, 845–74.
Simpson, P.A., Greller, M.M. and Stroh, L.K. (2002), 'Variations in human capital investment activity by age', *Journal of Vocational Behavior*, **61**, 109–38.
Spindler, G.S. (1994), 'Psychological contracts in the workplace – a lawyer's view', *Human Resource Management*, **33**, 325–33.
Sullivan, S.E. and Arthur, M.B. (2006), 'The evolution of the boundaryless career concept: Examining physical and psychological mobility', *Journal of Vocational Behavior*, **69**, 19–29.
Sutton, R.I. (1987), 'The process of organizational death: Disbanding and reconnecting', *Administrative Science Quarterly*, **32**, 542–69.
Suutari, V. and Brewster, C. (2000), 'Making their own way: International experience through self-initiated foreign assignments', *Journal of World Business*, **35**, 417–36.
Tams, S. and Arthur, M.B. (2007), 'Studying careers across cultures: Distinguishing international, cross-cultural, and globalization perspectives', *Career Development International*, **12**, 86–98.
Tansley, A.G. (1935), 'The use and abuse of vegetational concepts and terms', *Ecology*, **16** (3), 284–307.
Van der Heijden, B.I.J.M. and De Lange, A.H. (2011), 'Employability across the life-span: Towards new pathways for age research'. In R. Ennals and R.H. Salomon (eds), *Older Workers in a Sustainable Society*, Frankfurt am Main: Peter Lang Verlag, pp. 19–31.
Wigfield, A., Battle, A., Keller, L.B. and Eccles, J.S. (2002), 'Sex differences in motivation, self-concept, career aspiration, and career choice: Implications for cognitive development'. In A. McGillicuddy-De Lisi and R. De Lisi (eds), *Biology, Society, and Behavior: The Development of Sex Differences in Cognition*, Westport, CT: Ablex Publishing, pp. 93–124.
Wilkinson, A. (1998), 'Empowerment: theory and practice', *Personnel Review*, **27**, 40–56.
Zhang, J. and Shavitt, S. (2003), 'Cultural values in advertisements to the Chinese X-Generation: Promoting modernity and individualism', *Journal of Advertising*, **32**, 23–33.

25 Career continuance and transfer of competencies after job transitions: insights from a Swedish study

Claudia Bernhard-Oettel and Katharina Näswall

Flexibility and adaptability have become important characteristics in organizations that have to keep pace with international competitors. Factors such as technology, costs and utilization of human resources are optimized in innumerable organizational changes, often crossing national boundaries. A well-known example is the outsourcing of service functions or the moving of entire production plants to countries with less expensive labor or resource costs. For employees, this considerably reduces the possibilities for building an entire career in one organization or occupation.Therefore, job changes, with or without periods of unemployment or re-training, are no longer exceptions but have become a new norm. Whilst a wealth of career literature has discussed the need for individual flexibility in order to secure employability and adaptability (Koen et al., 2012) and to handle boundaryless (Arthur, 2008) or protean careers (Hall and Moss, 1998), this chapter focuses on the related issues of job transitions and transfer of competencies following involuntary job loss.

Our point of departure is the assumption that any individual accumulates a wealth of competencies over the course of their career. These competencies result from formal training as well as daily experiences and learning on the job. Competency, that is, 'an individual's ability to act knowledgeably, effectively, deliberately, strategically, and reflectively in a situation' (Svensson et al., 2004, p. 480), also refers to a core facet of human capital (Becker, 1964). An individual's professional competencies are mainly inferred from his or her work experience (Huang et al., 2013), and reflect knowledge, skills, abilities and other characteristics, such as interests or years of experience (summarized as KSAO factors; see Peterson et al., 2001). The amount and characteristics of the accumulated competencies are important assets in building sustainable careers, which may entail a number of interruptions, changes, or re-orientations across different jobs and career paths. Experiences and competencies learned in earlier jobs are assumed to carry over – or transfer – to a new job to some extent. Such transfer of competencies may be valuable for both individuals and societies since the investment of time, money and energy in professional development is not wasted when competencies are re-used and further built upon. Transfer may even lead to innovations when competencies are carried across organizational or occupational boundaries (Inkson and Thorn, 2010). However, only a few career researchers have considered an individual's repository of knowledge in career transitions (cf. Arthur, 2008).

The career literature primarily focuses on how careers are planned, and assumes that job transitions are voluntary (Feldman and Ng, 2013), often building on the idea of the continuous career and implying that job changes are possible since an individual's competency profile is carried over to a new job and developed further. Studies considering the case of 'disrupted careers' are more often found in the unemployment literature, where competencies are taken into account as facets of human and social capital (for example, Wanberg et al., 2002), but without more closely studying overall career development and competency transfer mechanisms.

Given the different directions and limited overlap of previous research on careers, unemployment and knowledge transfer, many important questions related to transfer of competencies in the context of involuntary job transitions are left unanswered. In this chapter, we discuss some of these questions. A first central question concerns how individuals' competencies are transferable from one job context to another and how similar the contexts need to be for transfer to occur. First, we present a brief overview of essential findings from transfer studies in the field of education with respect to context similarity using the perspective of near–far transfer. We go into examples to discuss the implications of these findings for potential competency transfer in different types of job and career transitions. Second, we turn to the question of whether there are factors other than similarity which relate to competency transfer in job transitions. We discuss three important factors derived from the literature on training transfer: individuals' competency profiles; their willingness to transfer their competencies; and contextual factors in the new workplace that facilite or hinder possible job transitions and transfer of competencies. For each of these aspects, we provide empirical findings from data gathered as part of a larger research project studying job transitions among Swedish unemployed individuals receiving re-employment coaching after involuntary job loss. We conclude this chapter with a discussion of important findings and point out areas of future research to better understand competency transfer in work settings.

We believe that career sustainability is increased with a better understanding of the factors which may facilitate or hinder potential competency transfer. For example, job seekers, but also career coaches, employers and policy makers may benefit from being familiar with the framework of near and far transfer, and from understanding the role of job similarity or what competency transfer a certain job change would require.

TRANSFER OF COMPETENCIES

To transfer or to 'carry over' means to apply learning in similar and new situations and has mainly been studied in the educational field (Haskell, 2001). Much of the research on competency transfer *in the work context* has focused on how competencies gained in training transfer to the workplace (Grossman and Salas, 2011). In this chapter, we refer to the process of transfer of competencies, since we are interested in the nature of the mechanisms that enable existing competencies to be used in new situations. Another important distinction concerns the difference in researching transfer of competencies *between situations* or *between individuals*. Research on transfer *between individuals* taps into questions of knowledge sharing (Mura, 2013; Testa, 2013). In this chapter, however, we are concerned with transfer of competencies *between situations* (but within individuals), focusing on the investigation of how competencies acquired in one job can be used and built upon in the next. Such re-use of competencies may facilitate transitions and reduce needs for training in the new job.

A taxonomy of transfer can be framed in terms of content (what) and context (when and where) (Barnett and Ceci, 2002). This is similar to the general scheme presented by

Haskell (2001) that differentiates between what kind of knowledge is being transferred, and how the specific kind of transfer happens. In both frameworks there is an underlying gradient of generalizability from near to far transfer, which is based on similarity principles (Blume et al., 2010). Previous knowledge is transfered in a *near transfer* if it is applied to a similar, yet not exactly identical, context, for example a pre-school teacher who starts an after-school program for young children. *Far transfer* occurs when knowledge is used in contexts quite different from the original learning situation, for example a pre-school teacher who starts working as a project manager at a city council.

Though simple at first sight, the conceptualization of far and near transfer is rather complex. Barnett and Ceci (2002) argued that similarity builds upon dimensions such as the knowledge domain, or the modality that things are transfered to and from, and physical or temporal context. Accordingly, near transfer would be more likely to occur for a pre-school teacher who only switches to another pre-school, continues to teach children of the same age group and does so without a large time lag (for example, without a long period of unemployment). Transferable knowledge also interacts with context (Barnett and Ceci, 2002; Haskell, 2001). For example, knowing specific facts or an exact sequence of procedures may lead to successful near transfer, whereas for far transfer to occur, more abstract or general knowledge, concerning strategies, conditions or rules may be required. Consequently, whether an individual is capable of near or far transfer depends on the similarity of contexts, but also on the level of the individual's specific and generic skills and knowledge.

Before turning to a more detailed discussion of how these conceptual ideas about transfer can be used to understand career sustainability and job changes, we briefly discuss another important distinction between *lateral* and *vertical* transfer (Haskell, 2001). Lateral transfer more closely resembles a simple carry-over, meaning that previous learning is transferred to the same level of the hierarchy. A typical example could be working as a pre-school teacher in a private school before changing to a public school. Vertical transfer entails previous learning providing the basis for further learning at a higher level in the knowledge hierarchy, meaning that earlier skills and knowledge form a prerequisite to develop further knowledge, enhance skills or deepen understanding. An example of vertical transfer could be a pre-school teacher who aspires to become a team leader for other teachers at a school, which requires a good basic understanding of pre-school teachers' daily work, along with competencies related to leadership.

The brief review given above is by no means exhaustive. Rather, we have focused our review on essential concepts in transfer research and on clarifying the aspects that help in understanding how job and career transitions can be facilitated.

Types of Job Transitions

In the light of a lifelong or sustainable career, we suggest that the type of job transitions and the possibilities for (or requirements of) competency transfer are linked to different career trajectories. More specifically, changes may fall into one of the following four categories, differing in terms of job domain and level.

Transition to a very similar job

This job change is characterized by a horizontal move. The individual gets a new job at the same level in the hierarchy and there is neither a downgrading nor upgrading. Tasks and responsibilities are rather similar and the individual still works in the same job domain. Most of the competencies needed in the previous job can be used again, but since there are never two *identical* situations (Haskell, 2001), some learning needs to occur and new experiences are added to the competency profile. However, from the perspective of an individual's occupational trajectory, this type of job change between rather similar contexts can be described as career continuance that enriches and resembles a near transfer situation.

Transition to a job at a different level

This type of job change entails a change in the level of the job hierarchy. For example, individuals may make a vertical move to the next level in the organizational hierarchy as part of career development. The competencies acquired in the previous job are prerequisites for the new position but, also, other competencies are added to the employee's repertoire. Learning and adaptation of general and specific knowledge is needed and far rather than near transfer has to occur. Also, vertical transfer has to happen, usually in an upward direction, if the new job is higher in the hierarchy and requires more skills and competencies. There is also the possibility of downward mobility, where an individual moves downward on the career ladder, and takes on a job that requires less knowledge.

Transition to a different job domain

This transition resembles the first type of change described here: it is a horizontal move. However, in this case not only are organizational or job boundaries crossed, the job domain also changes, as the individual starts working in a new sector. Here, general processes or procedures allow far transfer, but specific knowledge about rules or regulations, for example, hygiene rules for food production or health-related issues in elder care need to be learned, limiting the possibilities of near transfer. In terms of career development, this sort of job change may be classified as a career re-direction.

Transition to a job that differs completely in level and job domain

This type of job transition is characterized by a career change, knowledge transfer is difficult and often only basic generic skills can be transferred. This type of job change often requires education and training as it crosses occupational boundaries (Feldman and Ng, 2007). A practical example which illustrates this type of unconventional change is the recent closure of the car manufacturer SAAB in Sweden, where a surprisingly large number of technical professionals have switched to work in the health care sector (Arbetet, 2013; Sveriges Radio, 2012). In these transitions, several boundaries were crossed – between a typically male to a typically female occupational domain, and between a processing and technical profession to a relational and caregiving occupation with other levels of seniority and hierarchies. Inevitably, this has implications for possible transfer of competencies and reflects transitions largely in line with the ideas of boundaryless career paths (Arthur, 2008).

WHAT IS REQUIRED TO TRANSFER COMPETENCIES?

In addition to the similarity of situations described above as a facilitating factor for transfer, are there other factors that are important? Following the seminal work of Baldwin and Ford (1988), distinguishing between the learner, the training and the work environment as important factors contributing to training transfer, several reviews and meta-analyses have provided overviews of the existing empirical evidence (for example, Blume et al., 2010; Burke and Hutchins, 2007; Grossman and Salas, 2011). From the perspective of job transitions and career sustainability, three major aspects should be highlighted, related to individuals' *competency profile*, their *willingness* to transfer these competencies, and the *possibilities* that the particular type of job transition and the new organization offer them for competency transfer. Below, we discuss each of these three aspects and illustrate what they may mean in the context of job and career transitions, with empirical findings from data gathered in interviews and online surveys.

Data collections were conducted between 2010 and 2013 in Sweden in a research project studying job tranisitions. Participants had received or were still receiving re-employment coaching after involuntary job loss. Most were trained in typically blue-collar or low-level white-collar professions, and only about one third had a university education. We collected data in four samples, consisting of individuals with a wide range of different working experiences and qualifications from different sectors, through purposefully approaching different outplacement agencies (who provided coaching during the job search) in different parts of Sweden (see Table 25.1 for a sample description). Participants in all four samples were invited to participate in the study (interview or online survey) via their outplacement agency during, or shortly after, their job transition.

The qualitative data was analyzed with thematic analysis combining bottom-up and top-down processes (Braun and Clarke, 2013) to explore how individuals going through job transitions experience and think about the content and processes in which they are able, want, and are given the opportunity to transfer their competencies from one job to another. Nvivo 10 was used to facilitate the analysis. The quantitative data (collected

Table 25.1 Sample description

Sample name	Data collection method	Time of data collection		Sample size N
		During transition	After transition	
Sample A	Open-ended, semi-structured interview	x		18
Sample B	Open-ended, semi-structured interview		x	11
Sample C	Online survey: open questions and scales; 8 subsequent weeks and one follow-up (1 year later)	x		33
Sample D	Online survey: open questions and scales		x	69

in the online survey) was analyzed (correlation, t-tests, means and standard deviations) using SPSS 20.

The results based on the data collected will be presented in conjunction with our discussion of previous research and theory. We do not aim to prove or disprove any of the previous research or theory, but to elucidate some important issues related to transfer of competencies in the context of job transitions.

Competency Profile: What Can be Transferred?

Concerning *competencies*, research has shown that individuals with higher cognitive abilities seem to be better at processing and retaining generalized and trained skills (Grossman and Salas, 2011), which is a prerequisite for being able to transfer them to a new setting. Also, training in general principles rather than specific skills (Blume et al., 2010), and training which provides possibilities for active learning (Burke and Hutchins, 2007), enhance transfer from the training context to the workplace. Furthermore, many studies have shown that individuals' self-efficacy is important; those who believe in their abilities to perform certain work tasks are more likely to make use of these competencies in other settings (Blume et al., 2010). Based on these findings, competency transfer to more dissimilar jobs should be facilitated if the type of knowledge is generic (concerning principles and rules) rather than specific.

To illustrate these ideas, we present some empirical results from the sample completing the online *survey after* a successful job transition (Sample D). After the transition about half of the sample worked in a new sector, while the other half found a job in the same sector as their previous job, and the differences between these groups in terms of the degree to which previous competencies could be applied and were useful in the new job are shown in Figure 25.1. It should be noted that the group changing sectors also reported that they changed occupations to a high degree.

All differences between these two groups were found to be significant using a t-test. A transition within the same job domain appears to allow for a higher degree of transfer of

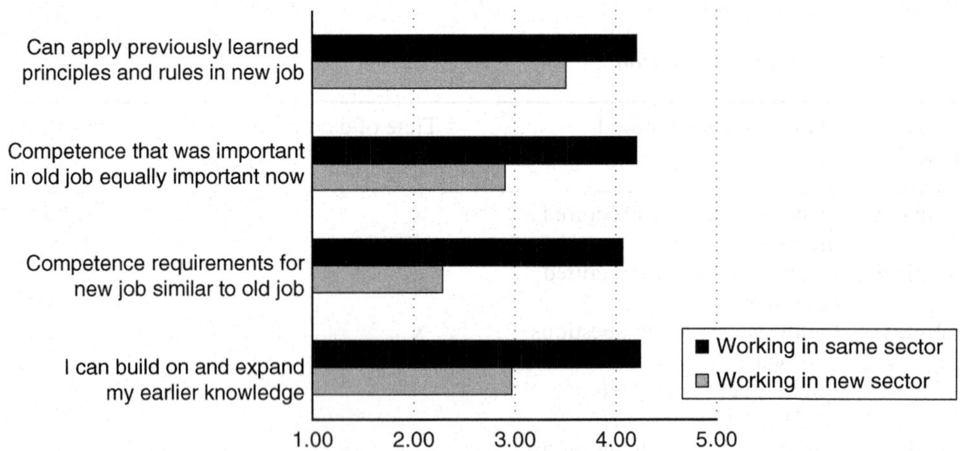

Figure 25.1 Competency transfer in relation to job transitions

existing competencies, and earlier competencies can be built on and expanded more than in a transition between different job domains. We also note that the group changing job domains reported that rules and principles were the easiest to transfer. Moving into a dissimilar job indeed appears to entail that only some of the previous competency profile can be expanded, and the type of competencies transferred seem to be generic, which is in accordance with far transfer (Barnett and Ceci, 2002). Also, transfer of competencies to a new job setting should be easier for knowledge and skills that have been used actively (and often) before the job transition and which the individual considers themselves to be good at. So what competencies do individuals consider transferable? Some preliminary answers to this question can be derived from the listed five most important competencies transferable to new jobs given by the sample of individuals responding to online *surveys during transitions* (Sample C). Thematic analysis of all answers to this open-ended question showed that respondents thought of their 'competency profile' in terms of four different aspects. Some answers reflected (1) *occupational knowledge and skills*, either in specific ways (for example, having a truck driver's license, speaking a specific language, understanding technical drawings) or at a more general level (for example, experience from working in different sectors, having technical knowledge, having analytic abilities). Furthermore, respondents listed (2) *social skills* (for example, being good at working in a team, being good listeners, being good at encouraging others); and (3) *attributes that described them as a person* (for example, being open, curious, positive) or (4) *in terms of their work ethic* (for example, being punctual, responsible).

These findings add to the discussion about far and near transfer in several ways. A very narrow view of one's own competencies may make it difficult to identify possibilities for job transitions into jobs that are dissimilar from the previous one. For example, thinking 'I am able to drive a truck' makes it easy to identify opportunities for near transfer, that is, to a new job as a truck driver. However, having a truck driver's license also means being knowledgeable about traffic rules, being capable of driving vehicles (for example, cars, smaller trucks), having knowledge about first aid or specific geographic areas. Broadening individuals' thoughts about their own competencies in these aspects may thus help them identify more opportunities for job transitions and transfer of their competencies. Generally, we thus expect that those who reflect upon more general abilities, such as 'analytical thinking' or social competencies, may identify a wider range of possible jobs to change to, which may even make it more likely for them to re-orient their career. A former data service technician who had become a bus driver after some months of training, and who was interviewed about the experiences of his job transition, provided an example of this when he highlighted that he could not transfer any specific knowledge from his former job other than skills used when giving service to customers with computer problems, which he now could make use of with his passengers (cf. Boklund and Eriksson, 2013).

A surprisingly large number of the respondents' comments in the online survey (Samples D and C) emphasized the A and O dimensions of the KSAO model (Peterson et al., 2001) in that many respondents identified general personal attributes and their ways of working as a transferable competency. These answers reflect a view of competencies that includes more than what is reflected in formal certificates or degrees, and such competencies can be aquired in other areas of life, not just working life. Furthermore, these competencies reflect general expectations that most employers have of their employees

(Guest et al., 2010). However, it is difficult to prove that one possesses these competencies, and being punctual, open, flexible, and willing to work hard may not differentiate one candidate from other applicants. Furthermore, jobs that only require such overall competencies may be just as hard to find as jobs that exactly match a very specific competency profile. This ties in with another important aspect required for transfer to occur and concerns willingness: individuals have different competency profiles, which they are willing to make use of to different degrees.

Willingness: What Do Individuals Want to Transfer?

Research on the transfer of training has suggested that successful transfer is contingent on individual *willingness*. Extant research has shown that training participants' motivation, voluntary participation in, and perceived utility of, the training in relation to their overall career orientation (Burke and Hutchins, 2007), as well as goal orientation and work involvement (Blume et al., 2010), play an important role for transfer of acquired competencies to occur. In other words, those who find the training useful for their work or overall career are more likely to transfer new competencies into their daily work. In the context of job and career transitions, this may mean that for competency transfer to occur between jobs, there needs to be an overlap between the competency profile that an individual has and the competency profile that this individual wants to utilize in the future. In our data from both interviews (Samples A and B) and surveys (Samples C and D), we found that individuals differed in their willingness to transfer competencies from previous jobs depending on whether the loss of job was truly involuntary, seen as an opportunity for change, or led to a career re-orientation during the job search process.

Cases of involuntary job change

Those who saw their earlier job as a step in their lifelong or sustainable career were still willing to transfer their competencies and looked for a similar job after dismissal to continue on the same career path. In such cases, being dismissed from an appreciated job often meant an abrupt end, and individuals often needed some time to let go (Blau, 2006). In the interview samples, being laid off was often described as a shock; even in cases when organizations had announced downsizing initiatives, few individuals believed this would affect them personally. During or after being laid off, many tried to get a similar job with their old employer, or would be willing to go back to this employer if there was a similar job available.

> Interviewer: 'If there was an opening, would you go back?'
> Respondent: 'Yeees [hesitatingly], I guess I would. . . yes, I would if, . . . I have no hard feelings or so. . . I would do this, for an acceptable salary, and so on. Sure.'

Continuing in a similar career path appears to be the preferred solution. This may be because making use of the accumulated competencies is seen as favorable for oneself, which is expressed in the following quote:

> 'Finally got a job in which I can not only use the experience I have accumulated during the last four years, but I also have higher job security and salary.'

Both quotes also suggest that competency transfer is an asset in the labor market; those who can transfer competencies from a previous job are, or expect to be, rewarded accordingly.

Data from all four samples furthermore show that job loss does not always mean an unwelcome job transition. As the following results of our material indicate, the boundaries between what is considered an involuntary versus voluntary job transition may be blurred (Feldman and Ng, 2013).

Cases of voluntary job change

In one of the organizations participating in the project, the lay-offs were announced along with an offer of 12 months' full salary and re-employment coaching to all those who quit voluntarily. We interviewed 11 individuals who had accepted this offer (Sample B), and a common denominator in their motives for voluntarily changing their jobs was that for a while they had felt that they wanted to change jobs, they wanted to develop their competencies and get new experiences, and, therefore, they saw this offer as a very safe opportunity to do so. Over the course of one year, one of the interviewees had started a business, but most crossed some organizational boundary, and even if they continued to work in similar jobs they had the opportunity to take on slightly different tasks in which they could make use of their earlier competencies, but also develop new ones. In terms of the individuals' career, most of these transitions can thus be described as continuing, leading to horizontal transfer.

Cases of re-orienting job change

Other participants in our project had been laid off (as opposed to voluntarily leaving their job), which may be classified as involuntary job loss. This, however, did not mean that all of them wanted to continue their career in a job similar to the one they had lost. The survey sample that had completed a transition included individuals who had accepted a job in a different sector, and they were asked for the reason for this change of sectors. A thematic analysis of their written answers showed that the reasons were either related to situational or individual factors (which we discuss below), or related to dissatisfaction with the previous job and career.

However, individuals may not be able to make job transitions entirely based on their competencies and willingness, because opportunities for competency transfer depend on available options that individuals have in the labor market.

Possibilities: What Job Transitions Make Transfer Possible?

The third important aspect for successful competency transfer relates to *possibilities* given to the individual to make use of their acquired skills in the new context. Also referred to as 'transfer climate' in the work environment, factors that facilitate training transfer are related to supervisor and peer support, as well as opportunities to apply learning and perform trained skills in daily work routines (Burke and Hutchins, 2007; Lancaster et al., 2013). Based on these findings, it may be suggested that the degree to which competencies can be transfered after a job transition not only relates to the individual's competency profile or the individual's willingness to transfer, but also to characteristics of the new work environment. For example, some individuals may be recruited to a new job because they have a specific competency that the organization needs. In such cases, the employing organization should be open to learn from the new employee and adopt new practices based on the competencies added by the employee, and the job changer may thus be given a great deal of opportunities to apply and re-use their competencies.

Another aspect of the transfer climate, supervisor and peer support for using competencies, may also play a role after a job change. If supervisors and colleagues are unaware of the newly recruited individual's competency profile, they are less likely to make use of it. A third aspect that restricts transfer is that to some extent, job tasks and responsibilities are organized differently in different organizations. This means that even if individuals make a job transition to a similar job, they may be restricted in their opportunities to make use of all their experiences and competencies or in their ability to make potential improvements in the new workplace, because what they are able to add is not part of their new job. In our study, there were several examples of this restriction provided in the interviews with those who had completed the job transitions and changed to dissimilar jobs. The job changers had competencies that they saw a need for in their new organization, for instance, because the IT system was suboptimal or the organization of work led to a lot of stress, but the job changers felt that they would have to work on improvements for free and in addition to their formal tasks, since there was no possibility of adding this type of work to their daily duties or to their job description.

Facilitators and Hindrances for Job-to-job Changes and Consecutive Transfer of Competencies

A discussion of an individual's opportunities to re-use competencies after a job transition does not, however, only include transfer climate in a certain job, but also what types of jobs an individual can get. By means of thematic analysis in the empirical material gathered after job transition (Samples B and D), we identified numerous references to factors that either facitilated or hindered optimal job transitions and consecutive competency transfer.

Hindrances could either be related to individual or situational constraints, facilitators were associated with possibilities for additional training and the support and information received through coaching. The themes are summarized in Table 25.2.

Individual constraints

Age was mentioned as a barrier hindering individuals from even being considered for suitable jobs. In some comments, those with ages as low as the early 50s experienced this as a hindrance to finding new employment, and our participants felt that it required a lot of effort to overcome this barrier, as illustrated in the following quote from an interview with a person aged 60:

> 'I have five years left until retirement and I am very proud of myself, that I could find a job on my own.'

Age discrimination has been identified as one aspect that may affect re-employment success negatively (Wanberg et al., 2002), and seems to be encountered by many older employees, despite research showing that most age-related stereotypes are wrong and

Table 25.2 Thematic analysis of diary material and online survey sample: open ended survey questions commenting on job search and job transitions

Category	Definition	Example citation
Hindrances		
1. Labor market related	Labor market does not offer jobs that fit either since timing or geographical area is problematic	'Right now, there are not many openings for my competencies'
2. Individual related	Individual's age, health, financial or family circumstances restrict job opportunities	'I am turning 59 next March, my chances to find a new job aren't that big'
Facilitators		
1. Coach contact network	Coach helps individual to get contacts for interesting job opportunities	'My coach had good contacts which has led to a job for me'
2. Coach knowledge of labor market and necessary job search skills	Coach can inform about job opportunities and help with practical job search behavior (writing a CV, interview training)	'I got help with my CV' 'They have knowledge about the labor market, and on what is required'
3. Courses to overcome competency gaps	Shorter course, education, certificates that enhance chances for individual to change to another job	'I had the chance to take a computer course'

that older persons generally make as good employees as younger persons (Ng and Feldman, 2012).

Another aspect that may be a barrier to finding a better job which allows the transfer of previous competencies relates to individual restrictions such as the need to find new employment, no matter in what type of job, that can accommodate the living circumstances of the candidate, as illustrated by the following quote:

> 'I knew that because of my family situation – I am single and have a kid – I needed to find a job close to my home, daytime and I was forced to take whatever I was offered at that moment.'

Other circumstances that were also mentioned as restricting the availability of a job were impaired health or financial problems. Under such circumstances, it was more likely that the individual accepted any job, which in turn may have led to career discontinuity and limited possibilities to transfer available competencies.

Situational constraints

External circumstances experienced as problematic were mainly related to fluctuating labor market demands (Wanberg et al., 2002). For example, several respondents emphasized that at that particular time of year, few, if any, jobs were available that suited their competencies. Others mentioned problems related to structural changes which resulted in limited job opportunities, particularly in the countryside as compared to urban areas. The *availability* of jobs that an individual is potentially suitable for is largely neglected in career research, which typically views individuals as free agents to initiate their own mobility and change jobs whenever they wish. Also, labor market constraints are less emphasized in career research, since the individuals under study can postpone their career moves should there be no job openings in positions they are interested in. However, the availability of jobs becomes a very salient factor for those who have lost their jobs and have low geographical mobility.

Facilitators

Facilitating factors appeared to relate first to possibilities to receive additional training, for example, to update computer skills or obtain additional driving licenses for machines (for example, lift truck). Opportunities for re-employment were enhanced for individuals who only needed shorter training to complement or update their competency profile. Secondly, since our empirical material was gathered among individuals who had received coaching, many of them emphasized the role of their coach. First of all, the coaches could, via the outplacement agency, provide training to improve job search skills. Second, coaches were helpful in identifying job opportunities that the individuals did not think of themselves. Third, coaches with networks and contacts utilized these in order to give job seekers previews of jobs in other organizations and/or sectors, for example, through study visits or short internships. Occasionally, this directly led to an employment offer. Naturally, changing to other sectors or occupational fields means that the individual's social capital, particularly in terms of networks containing valuable information and resources (Van Emmerik and Euwema, 2008), needs to be re-built. It is thus not surprising that the coaches and their contacts constitute a facilitating factor providing guidance and contact networks in the local labor market. Particularly for career re-orientation and far competency transfer, this seems to be a salient factor.

DISCUSSION

The study of job transitions from the perspective of competency transfer highlights the role of an individual's complete profile of competencies – the sum of all work-related knowledge and skills. In this chapter, we illustrated how an individual's competencies are useful for certain job transitions and discussed how they may be related to career sustainability. Applying the theory of competency transfer to a context of job transitions and individual careers adds new insights, but it also raises a number of questions relating both to theory as well as practice.

Competency Transfer and Career Sustainability

By introducing a more elaborate discussion which includes competency transfer, we emphasize an important aspect that much of the earlier literature on career and employment transitions often takes for granted, namely the ways in which individuals can make use of their human capital and how this may contribute to career sustainability.

First, the emphasis on the transferability of competencies raises the question of what competency is, how, where and when it is formed, and how aspects of the outdating of competencies (Wanberg et al., 2002) will be treated. Similar to conceptualizations of the competency construct used in the domain of work (cf. Svensson et al., 2004; Peterson et al., 2001), the examples given by our respondents regarding their transferable competencies illustrate that the understanding of competency is rather broad. Competency is expected to encompass specific knowledge, but also very general principles that facilitate the solving of a task, for example, by listening or being open-minded and motivated. While the possession of some of these competencies can be objectively indicated (for example, by certificates or degrees), others are harder to demonstrate to a potential employer. Also, whereas qualifications often stem from formal learning processes tied to work and education (Svensson et al., 2004), knowledge about the 'ways things are done' is often the result of informal learning, which can even take place outside of work, for example, in a role as a parent, a friend, or as a member of a sports team. Many of the answers given by the participants in our study reflected a holistic view about competencies from a lifelong perspective. This seems to contradict the commonly held view that competencies as human capital can become obsolete over time and reduce an individual's overall employability (Van Emmerik et al., 2012). Since competency transfer has not been studied much in job transitions, we believe that further research can fill important gaps. Here, the taxonomy of transfer (Barnett and Ceci, 2002) may be useful to understand which specific versus broad competencies may make near or far transfer possible, or which hinder transfer across jobs in the lifelong career perspective.

Second, while we referred to job transitions and subsequent competency transfer in the opening of this chapter, our findings illustrate more of an interactionistic pattern; even if the individual's competency profile may influence what job transitions are possible, the type of job transition dictates how former competencies can be re-used and developed.

Regarding possible job transitions, our empirical findings revealed that the transfer of competencies is not only dependent on competency profiles but also on willingness to transfer competencies and the possibilities given for transfer. Especially when job transitions are not purposefully initiated career moves but necessary due to job loss, we find that integrating research on training and knowledge transfer, careers and re-employment can provide useful information. In particular, literature on job loss and re-employment contributes with aspects of labor market structures and job availability to the career literature, which in turn adds aspects of volition and choice to re-employment studies. Adding a framework of transfer, that is, what competencies individuals actually are able, want and have opportunities to make use of, contributes to the understanding of re-employment and career development. For example, job transitions because of job loss, perhaps followed by some time in unemployment, have been studied in research on organizational change and unemployment (see, for example, Blau, 2006; Wanberg et al., 2002). Often, this research mainly concentrates on identifying factors that predict re-employment success (see Wanberg, 2012), and tends to portray individuals as having little, if any, choice. To illustrate this, the wheel of re-employment success (Wanberg et al., 2002) contains labor market needs, human and social capital, job search behaviors and individual constraints, but does not include individual interests and career goals. Thus, whereas the career literature perhaps paints an overly positive picture of individuals' possibilities and desire to create boundaryless careers (Verbruggen, 2012), re-employment research may need to consider individual willingness and career ideas to a greater extent. Based on the empirical data presented in this chapter, we argue that individuals' willingness to transfer competencies should be considered along with structural issues when studying re-employment and career development. While it is important for the unemployed to find a new job quickly to avoid increasing stigmatization and decreased well-being that follows from longer unemployment periods (Wanberg, 2012), creating institutional policies and economic pressure that force those who have lost their job to accept whatever job that comes their way may be rather short-sighted. Particularly if jobs neither fit a personal competency profile nor the individual's overall career aspirations, such choices seem rather unfavorable for individuals and society since they may create underemployment (for such findings and similar discussions, see Slocum Jr et al., 2000). Not having adequate opportunities for skill utilization and not being in a preferred job have earlier been found to be detrimental for employee attitudes, intrinsic motivation and health (Aronsson and Göransson, 1999; Lai, 2011). For future research, we therefore suggest that re-employment quality be discussed not only in terms of skill utilization and over- or under-qualification, but also in terms of how well a new job fits the overall career path and fulfills needs of competence as suggested in self-determination theory (Ryan and Deci, 2000). Of course, it may not be realistic for all career plans to continue since over the course of an occupational career individual circumstances as well as labor markets and competency requirements may change. Processes of adaptation are inevitably required, but these may be facilitated by considering an individual's overall career vision.

Practical Implications

This chapter has several practical implications. Obviously, re-employment and career coaching provide job seekers with information about the labor market and available jobs as well as local networks. By relying on experts in this area, job seekers are better prepared for the job search and better equipped to compete with others. Furthermore, re-employment coaches may benefit from knowing the principles of competency transfer to make a more fine-grained assessment of a particular case, and to suggest even more appropriate options for the job seeker. Re-employment coaches thus provide job seekers with a competitive edge, particularly in cases that require far transfer and transitions to different job domains.

Another practical implication of this chapter is that for some individuals, successful job transitions were made possible through shorter trainings (for example, getting a driver's license or learning specific computer skills). For the samples in our study, outplacement agencies often provided this type of competency development, and many respondents mentioned this as a factor facilitating transfer. Here the lessons for policy makers may be that even other groups of unemployed who have no access to outplacement coaching may need the same facilitators to become more employable. A further practical implication concerns organizational recruitment strategies and use of individual competency. First, during recruitment, applicants who do not fit a specific competency profile may be ignored despite some candidates being well-equipped for the job due to their generic knowledge and experiences. Hence, for organizations that find it difficult to fill vacancies, the framework of near and far, or even new and creative transfer (Haskell, 2001), may help in identifying job applicants with high potential even though their formal competency profiles do not fit at first glance. Second, after a new recruitment, organizations may not always have a good transfer climate to mobilize the newly employed person's full potential, although, in an era of more protean careers (Hall and Moss, 1998), many employees transition across organizational and occupational boundaries more often during their career and may thus have more competencies than are made use of by organizations.

Finally this chapter also adds to the overall discussion about career sustainability as it accentuates the question of what sustainability actually means. It may mean being able to pursue similar jobs and careers with high and near competency transfer. It may also mean being able to adapt and change by switching to more dissimilar jobs, leading to a broadening of competencies and increasingly far transfer. In a third scenario, sustainability may mean being able to continue working, even in most dissimilar jobs that allow for far transfer of rather general competencies only, but keeping the individual employed. The framework of competency transfer complements existing knowledge in both career and unemployment research, and suggests that sustainability can be found in each of the three scenarios. For some individuals, sustainability may be achieved because during their career they can accumulate and make use of and further develop their formal and informal competencies, thereby reaching mastery that makes them very sought-after in the labor market. Likewise, sustainability may be achieved when individuals can cross organizational boundaries or re-orientate their careers altogether, because remaining in jobs or career paths that are perceived as increasingly dissatisfying threatens long-term well-being. At worst, this could cause severe health problems, unemployment, or early retirement, and all of these are unsustainable career trajectories.

Limitations and Overall Conclusions

In all our samples, previous employers prompted individual job transitions through downsizing and lay-offs. However, these organizations also made re-employment coaching available, which is common practice in Swedish organizations. In some cases, organizations continued to pay salaries to their former employees for up to a year after job loss, and in most cases job coaching was provided for 6–12 months. Such a rather long time-span may have been favorable since it may take some time to get used to a new situation, assess competencies and reflect upon or adapt career ideas. These circumstances perhaps limit generalizability to other organizations and other countries.

Despite these limitations, our findings suggest that organizational needs for greater flexibility have important implications for individuals' (unplanned) job transitions and career paths. Our theoretical review and empirical findings call for a better integration of research on competency transfer in studies on successful job and career transitions. Increasing knowledge about the transferability of competencies will be useful for policy makers, employers, recruiters, coaches and job seekers themselves. It also provides one of the building blocks for sustainable career development.

ACKNOWLEDGEMENTS

This chapter was made possible by a grant from VINNOVA, Sweden. We would also like to thank Professor Gunnar Aronsson for inspiring and enabling our research on competency transfer and job transitions.

REFERENCES

Arbetet (2013), 'Männens väg in I omsorgen' ['Men's way into care professions'], available at: http://arbetet.se/2013/03/22/mannens-vag-in-i-omsorgen/.

Aronsson, G. and Göransson, S. (1999), 'Permanent employment but not in a preferred occupation: Psychological and medical aspects, research implications', *Journal of Organisational Health Psychology*, **4** (2), 152–63.

Arthur, M.B. (2008), 'Examining contemporary careers: A call for interdisciplinary inquiry', *Human Relations*, **61** (2), 163–8.

Baldwin, T.T. and Ford, J.K. (1988), 'Transfer of training: A review and directions for future research', *Personnel Psychology*, **41** (1), 63–106.

Barnett, S.M. and Ceci, S.J. (2002), 'When and where do we apply what we learn? A taxonomy for far transfer', *Psychological Bulletin*, **128** (4), 612–37.

Becker, G.S. (1964), *Human Capital: A Theoretical and Empirical Analysis, with Special Reference to Education*, Chicago: University of Chicago Press.

Blau, G.M. (2006), 'A process model for understanding victim responses to worksite/function closure', *Human Resource Management Review*, **16**, 12–28.

Blume, B.D., Ford, J.K., Baldwin, T.T. and Huang, J.L. (2010), 'Transfer of training: A meta-analytic review', *Journal of Management*, **36** (4), 1065–105.

Boklund, A. and Eriksson, A. (2013), 'Har du användning av dina erfarenheter? Kunskapsöverföring i arbet-

slivet' ['Can you make use of your experience? Competence transfer in working life'], Stockholm: Stockholm University, unpublished Bachelor's thesis.
Braun, V. and Clarke, V. (2013), *Successful Qualitative Research: A Practical Guide for Beginners*, London: Sage.
Burke, L.A. and Hutchins, H.M. (2007), 'Training transfer: An integrative literature review', *Human Resource Development Review*, **6** (3), 263–96.
Feldman, Daniel C. and Ng, T.W.H. (2007), 'Careers: Mobility, embeddedness, and success', *Journal of Management*, **33** (3), 350–77.
Feldman, D.C. and Ng, T.W.H. (2013), 'Theoretical approaches to the study of job transitions'. In *Handbook of Psychology, Vol. 12: Industrial and Organizational Psychology* (2nd edn), Hoboken, NJ: John Wiley & Sons, pp. 292–307.
Grossman, R. and Salas, E. (2011), 'The transfer of training: What really matters', *International Journal of Training & Development*, **15** (2), 103–20.
Guest, D., Isaksson, K. and De Witte, H. (2010), *Employment Contracts, Psychological Contracts, and Worker Well-being: An International Study*, Oxford: Oxford University Press.
Hall, D.T. and Moss, J.E. (1998), 'The new protean career contract: Helping organizations and employees adapt', *Organizational Dynamics*, **26** (3), 22–37.
Haskell, R.I. (2001), *The Transfer of Learning: Cognition, Instruction and Reasoning*, New York: Academic Press.
Huang, Y.-M., Chen, C.-C. and Lai, S.-Y. (2013), 'Test of a multidimensional model linking applicant work experience and recruiters' inferences about applicant competencies', *The International Journal of Human Resource Management*, **24** (19), 3613–29.
Inkson, K. and Thorn, K. (2010), 'Mobility and careers'. In S.C. Carr (ed.), *The Psychology of Global Mobility* (pp. 259–78). New York: Springer.
Koen, J., Klehe, U.-C. and Van Vianen, A.E.M. (2012), 'Training career adaptability to facilitate a successful school-to-work transition', *Journal of Vocational Behavior*, **81** (3), 395–408.
Lai, L. (2011), 'Employees' perceptions of the opportunities to utilize their competences: Exploring the role of perceived competence mobilization', *International Journal of Training & Development*, **15** (2), 140–57.
Lancaster, S., Milia, L. Di and Cameron, R. (2013), 'Supervisor behaviours that facilitate training transfer', *Journal of Workplace Learning*, **25** (1), 6–22.
Mura, M. (2013), 'Promoting professionals' innovative behaviour through knowledge sharing: The moderating role of social capital', *Journal of Knowledge Management*, **17** (4), 527–44.
Ng, T.W.H. and Feldman, D.C. (2012), 'Evaluating six common stereotypes about older workers with meta-analytical data', *Personnel Psychology*, **65** (4), 821–58.
Peterson, N., Mumford, M.D., Borman, W.C., Jeanneret, P.R., Fleishman, E.A. et al. (2001), 'Understanding work using the occupational information network (O*NET): Implications for practice and research', *Personnel Psychology*, **54**, 451–92.
Ryan, R.M. and Deci, E.L. (2000), 'Self-determination theory and the facilitation of intrinsic motivation, social development, and well-being', *The American Psychologist*, **55** (1), 68–78.
Slocum Jr, J.W., Feldman, D.C. and Leana, C.R. (2000), 'What ever happened to laid-off executives? A study of reemployment challenges after downsizing', *Organizational Dynamics*, **29** (1), 64–75.
Svensson, L., Ellström, P.-E. and Åberg, C. (2004), 'Integrating formal and informal learning at work', *Journal of Workplace Learning*, **16** (8), 479–91.
Sveriges Radio (2012), 'Saabare utbildas för EU-miljoner' ['Former SAAB employees: training funded with millions from EU'], available at: http://sverigesradio.se/sida/artikel.aspx?programid=125&artikel=5171439.
Testa, G. (2013), 'Knowledge transfer in vertical relationship: The case study of Val d'Agri oil district', *Journal of Knowledge Management*, **17** (4), 617–36.
Wanberg, C.R. (2012), 'The individual experience of unemployment', *Annual Review of Psychology*, **63**, 369–96.
Wanberg, C.R., Hough, L.M. and Song, Z. (2002), 'Predictive validity of a multidisciplinary model of reemployment success', *The Journal of Applied Psychology*, **87** (6), 1100–20.
Van Emmerik, I.J.H. and Euwema, M.C. (2008), 'The aftermath of organizational restructuring: Destruction of old and development of new social capital', *Journal of Managerial Psychology*, **23** (7), 833–49.
Van Emmerik, I.J.H., Schreurs, B., De Cuyper, N., Jawahar, I.M. and Peeters, M.C.W. (2012), 'The route to employability: Examining resources and the mediating role of motivation', *Career Development International*, **17** (2), 104–19.
Verbruggen, M. (2012), 'Psychological mobility and career success in the "New" career climate', *Journal of Vocational Behavior*, **81** (2), 289–97.

26 Career implications of job performance: persistence of OCB and CWB behaviors across domains

Thomas H. Stone and I.M. Jawahar

For two decades, researchers have recognized that work behavior extends beyond simply task performance (Campbell, 1990; Organ, 1988). More recently, some contend that employee job performance may be categorized into three broad classes of behavior: task performance; organizational citizenship (OCB); and counterproductive work behaviors (CWB) (Rotundo and Sackett, 2002; Sackett, 2002). That is, job performance is composed of prescribed role behaviors and both extra-role positive and negative work-related behaviors. OCB is employee behavior and activities that contribute 'to the maintenance and enhancement of the social and psychological context that supports task performance' (Organ, 1997, p. 91). Organ's (1997) conceptualization of OCB is very similar to Borman and Motowidlo's (1997) definition of contextual performance and therefore they may be considered nearly identical terms.

CWB or 'workplace deviance, on the other hand, consists of voluntary behavior of organizational members that violates significant organizational norms and, in so doing, threatens the well-being of the organization and/or its members' (Robinson and Bennett, 1995, p. 556). These behaviors include but are not limited to theft, excessive absence, production deviance, sabotage, interpersonal abuse and rule violations (Miles et al., 2002; Spector et al., 2006). Such misconduct violates organizational norms and jeopardizes the welfare of organizations and members (Gruys and Sackett, 2003; Robinson and Bennett, 1995).

Misconduct and pro-social behaviors can also be observed in academic settings. For instance, a substantial body of research has documented the severity and prevalence of academic misconduct (Christensen-Hughes and McCabe, 2006; Josephson Institute of Ethics, 2010; 2012; McCabe et al., 2012; Stone et al., 2010). We contend that reporting instances of cheating by other students helps maintain the integrity of the educational process (McCabe and Trevino, 1993) and is analogous to OCB in work organizations. Academic misconduct (for example, cheating), on the other hand, is similar to CWB as it is intentional behavior that violates university policies and undermines the educational process.

Some research suggests that those who cheat in school are also likely to engage in unethical work behaviors as well (for example, Ariely, 2012; McCabe et al., 1996; Nonis and Swift, 2001; Sims, 1993). Likewise, those who report cheating in school may be disposed to engage in citizenship behaviors, such as providing a 'voice' or showing individual initiative or persisting at work.

Behaviors learned while in school are likely to persist in the work environment, leading to important consequences for one's career. Engaging in OCB might well be one avenue for getting ahead in organizations. Getting ahead in organizations traditionally has been assessed in terms of how individuals 'track' through a series of jobs/positions in their careers over time, typically reflecting a vertical trajectory (for example, Ng et al., 2005). Thus, the promotions individuals receive serve as key indicators of such career success, and are valued by employees. Research on the consequences of promotion decisions (for example, Tzafrir and Hareli, 2008) indicates that individuals greatly value, and experience intense reactions to, promotion decisions that have implications for themselves as well as for organizations. On the other hand, engaging in CWB might well have negative consequences for one's health and well-being, job performance, and relations at work (Berry et al., 2007; Kisamore et al., forthcoming).

One of the best predictors of cheating and other unethical behaviors is past cheating (Whitley, 1998). There is evidence that cheating begins in high school, if not earlier (Josephson Institute, 2010; 2012); college cheating continues in graduate school (McCabe et al., 2006) and extends into the workplace (McCabe et al., 1996; Nonis and Swift, 2001; Sims, 1993).

The chapter is organized as follows. First, OCB and CWB research is reviewed, focusing on identifying antecedents common to both behaviors and unique to each. Second, we review academic integrity research that has focused on personality variables as antecedents of academic misconduct. Third, we integrate these streams of research, arguing that personality variables (adjustment, prudence and likeability) predict reporting cheating and cheating behavior in the academic world and desirable (OCB) and undesirable (CWB) behaviors in the work domain. Fourth, we show that behaviors learned in one domain (academic) spill over into another (work) domain. Fifth, a study conducted to investigate these predictions is described. Finally, we discuss implications of study results for theory and practice, and offer suggestions for future research.

OCB AND CWB RESEARCH

Personality as an Antecedent of OCB and CWB

Antecedents of OCB and CWB have been examined in studies examining both variables (Berry et al., 2007; Cohen-Charash and Spector, 2001; Colquitt et al., 2001; Dalal, 2005) and those examining either OCB (LePine et al., 2002; Meyer et al., 2002; Organ and Ryan, 1995; Riketta, 2002) or CWB separately (Barrick and Mount, 1991; Mount et al., 2006; Salgado, 2002). Dalal's (2005) meta-analysis found that conscientiousness has a similar magnitude of relationship to OCB ($\hat{\rho}$ = .34) as to CWB ($\hat{\rho}$ = −.36). His meta-analysis shows negative affectivity is much more strongly related to CWB, $\hat{\rho}$ = 0.41, than to OCB, $\hat{\rho}$ = − 0.10, but results for positive affectivity, though positive for OCB and negative for CWB were 'less clear' (Dalal, 2005, p. 1248).

Prior meta-analyses (Cohen-Charash and Spector, 2001; Colquitt et al., 2001; LePine et al., 2002; Meyer et al., 2002; Organ and Ryan, 1995; Riketta, 2002) of the dimensionality and antecedents of OCB found similar results to those of Dalal (2005). For instance, Organ and Ryan's (1995) analysis found the highest correlations were between conscientiousness and organizational compliance (***r*** = .30, corrected) and between conscientiousness and altruism (***r*** = .22, corrected). Borman et al. (2001) identified 20 studies conducted since Organ and Ryan's meta-analysis of the relationship between OCB and personality variables. Borman et al. (2001) found significant, uncorrected correlation coefficients between OCB and various personality constructs including other-oriented empathy (*r* = .28), conscientiousness (*r* = .24), helpfulness (*r* =. 22), positive affectivity (PA; *r* = .18), negative affectivity (NA; *r* = .14), and agreeableness (*r* = .13).

Major reviews (for example, Barrick and Mount, 1991; Berry et al., 2007; Cullen and Sackett, 2003; Ones et al., 1993; 2003; Salgado, 2002) of the association between personality and CWB conclude that of the Big Five personality constructs, conscientiousness, emotional stability and agreeableness best predict CWB. Salgado (2002) found conscientiousness (mean corrected correlation of −.26) was the best predictor of a composite measure of CWB that includes behaviors such as theft, rule violations, substance abuse, disciplinary problems, property damage and other irresponsible behaviors. Dalal's (2005) meta-analysis found conscientiousness had a mean corrected correlation of −. 38 although it was the only Big Five personality factor included. PA, however, had a mean corrected correlation of − .34 and NA .41 with CWB and, as mentioned above, Wilson and Gullone (1999) found the Positive and Negative Affect Scale (PANAS) significantly related to extroversion and emotional stability.

The Berry et al. (2007) meta-analysis found agreeableness more highly correlated with interpersonal deviance but not with organizational deviance in comparison with conscientiousness. Hogan and Hogan (1989) developed a Reliability scale from items of the Hogan Personality Inventory (HPI) predicting 'organizational delinquency' that included theft, substance abuse, insubordination and other behaviors associated with CWB. The HPI is based on the Five Factor model and the Reliability scale includes items from those identified as the best predictors of OCB: conscientiousness, emotional stability and agreeableness. Ones et al. (1993), in a study of integrity tests, found the average criterion-related validity between scores on the Hogan Reliability scale and CWB was .45. In summary, this stream of research has clearly established personality variables to be predictive of OCB and CWB.

ACADEMIC INTEGRITY AND MISCONDUCT

A significant body of research suggests that cheating, plagiarism and other forms of academic misconduct are prevalent in high schools (Josephson Institute of Ethics, 2010; 2012), in colleges and universities in the United States (for example, Davis et al., 1992), Canada (Christensen-Hughes and McCabe, 2006), Australia (Brimble and Stevenson-Clarke, 2005), England (Newstead et al., 1996) and many other countries (for example, Koljatic et al., 2003).

Although a voluminous body of research exists on academic integrity, relatively few studies of academic misconduct have relied on personality as an antecedent. In a number of studies, locus of control has been related to cheating behavior in academic settings (Houston, 1983; Karabenick and Srull, 1978; Forsyth et al., 1985). We are aware of only one study that relied on a measure of Big Five personality factors to predict academic misconduct. In a sample of 217 business students, Stone et al. (2008) reported correlations of −.21 between the HPI Reliability and intentions to cheat in college and .18 with likelihood of reporting cheating. The Reliability scale is a composite measure of items typically used to measure adjustment, prudence and likeability. Adjustment is similar to emotional stability, conscientiousness is highly correlated with prudence, and likeability is analogous to agreeableness from the Big Five Factor model of personality (Hogan and Hogan, 1989). Additionally, Stone et al. (2012) found that higher levels of two HPI subscales, moralistic and self-confidence, were associated with reporting cheating. This finding is consistent with high levels of self-confidence among whistle-blowers (Bjorkelo et al., 2010; LePine and Van Dyne, 2001).

SPILLOVER FROM SCHOOL TO WORK

As previously discussed, personality measures are consistently related to positive behaviors (reporting cheating at school, OCB at work) and to negative behaviors (cheating at school, CWB at work). In this section, we will integrate these disparate streams of research to build our rationale for using samples from one domain (school) to predict positive (OCB) and negative (CWB) behaviors in another domain (the workplace).

Personality, Academic Integrity, OCB and CWB

Personality is related to pro-social behaviors, such as reporting cheating by others and to academic misconduct, such as cheating and plagiarism (for example, Stone et al., 2008; Stone et al., 2012). Likewise, personality factors including conscientiousness (for example, Borman et al., 2001; Dalal, 2005) and agreeableness (for example, Berry et al., 2007) are related to OCB and to CWB.

Academic misconduct appears to be related to attitudes toward CWB. Indeed, some research suggests that people who cheat in school are more likely to engage in unethical behavior at work (McCabe et al., 1996; Nonis and Swift, 2001; Sims, 1993) later on. That is to say, cheating in school might well be a precursor to engaging in unethical behaviors at work, which has implications for one's career. For example, in early 2014, it was revealed that missile launch crews cheated on tests of their knowledge of launch procedures and some officers were complicit in the cheating (Burns, 2014). A relatively common form of cheating is exaggerations or false statements on résumés (Heneman et al., 2015). Such false claims can ruin dream job opportunities. For example, in 2001, George O'Leary resigned as US University of Notre Dame's head football coach within a week of his appointment when it was discovered that he had lied about his athletic and academic background (Fountain and Wong, 2001). Of course, cheating in college does not always block career success. For example, in 1951, future US senator Edward Kennedy was suspended from Harvard for having someone else take a Spanish test for him (Carmichael, 2012). We argue that such cheating is a relevant behavior sample that predicts illegal, unethical and counterproductive behavior at work.

Both theory and research suggest that academic misconduct is likely to be correlated with deviant work behavior (Gottfredson and Hirschi, 1990; Marcus and Schuler, 2004). Based upon their General Theory of Crime, Gottfredson and Hirschi (1990) argued that self-control, 'the tendency to avoid acts whose long-term costs exceed momentary advantages' (Hirschi and Gottfredson, 1994, p. 4), is the core explanation for crime.

Several studies (McCabe et al., 1996; Nonis and Swift, 2001; Sims, 1993) examined the relationship between academic misconduct and OCB and/or unethical behavior at work.

None of these studies, however, used established CWB measures and none examined personality as an antecedent of CWB or OCB. McCabe et al. (1996) found no difference in self-reported unethical work behaviors such as theft and lying between business graduates from schools with or without honor codes. Sims (1993) found, in a sample of 60 MBAs, a correlation of .48 between frequency ratings of cheating in school and work behaviors such as theft of materials and time and lying.

In a much larger sample of 1051 students, Nonis and Swift (2001) found a stronger correlation between frequency of cheating at school and at work for both undergraduate (r = .66) and graduate (r = .61) students. Work behaviors rated in Nonis and Swift's study were similar to those used in Sims (1993), with the addition of substance abuse and additional reasons for lying. The primary focus of both studies was not the relationship between academic misconduct and CWB, but rather agreement regarding perceptions of the severity of such behaviors. Therefore, this is the first study to address the relationship between academic misconduct and counterproductive work behavior using established measures of both cheating behavior and CWB.

As suggested earlier, employee performance can be viewed as including task performance, OCB and CWB (Rotundo and Sackett, 2002; Sackett, 2002; Viswesvaran and Ones, 2000). Therefore, it is appropriate to examine indicators of OCB and CWB in both the classroom and work contexts. We contend that just as misconduct in organizational settings violates organizational norms and jeopardizes the welfare of organizations and members (Gruys and Sackett, 2003; Robinson and Bennett, 1995), academic misconduct violates university policies and undermines the educational process and is, therefore, a form of counterproductive behavior. Similarly, we argue that reporting instances of cheating by other students helps maintain the integrity of the educational process (McCabe and Trevino, 1993). Thus, reporting cheating is an example of an OCB in an academic setting given that such behavior contributes 'to the maintenance and enhancement of the social and psychological context that supports task performance' (Organ, 1997, p.91). Indeed, we argue that students who would report cheating or plagiarism in school are more likely to demonstrate OCB at work and less likely to engage in CWB.

The present study extends previous OCB and CWB research in several ways. First, we examine the efficacy of three Big Five personality dimensions predicting OCB and CWB, academic cheating and report cheating. Second, the efficacy of cheating behavior and intent to report cheating in school to predict OCB and CWB is examined using structural equation modeling. The vast majority of OCB and CWB research (Berry et al., 2007; Dalal, 2005) has relied upon self, peer or supervisor responses to personality or perceptual measures. This study is the first to use a behavior sample (Campbell and Wernimont, 1968) as well as personality measures from one organizational setting, school, to predict OCB and CWB in a work setting.

We examined two structural equation models, a full and a partial mediation model. In the full mediation model, the three personality factors have paths to both cheating behavior and report cheating and each of these behaviors has direct paths to the three OCB and four CWB measures. If this model were to be accepted, it would suggest that samples of behavior in school mediate the effects of personality on OCB and CWB. In the partial mediation model, we also include direct paths from each of the personality measures to each of the OCB and CWB measures. If this model is a significantly better fit to the data, it would suggest personality variables account for variance in OCB and CWB not accounted for by cheating behaviors and report of cheating intentions.

METHOD

Sample and Procedure

Undergraduate business students (438) in seven marketing, management and economics classes at a large, mid-western public university in the US were recruited for participation in the current study. A total of 207 participants provided usable responses, yielding a response rate of 47 percent. Participants completed both the HPI and the integrity survey online outside of class. They were given a logon code and an individual password and assurance of confidentiality of their responses.

Approximately 21 percent of the participants were between the ages of 18 and 20, 43 percent between the ages of 21 and 23, and the rest were 24 or more years old. Forty-nine percent of the sample was male. Almost 75 percent of participants were full-time students. Of those reporting, 3.6 percent worked less than 10 hours per week, 30.2 percent worked between 11 and 20 hours per week, 28.8 percent worked between 21 and 30 hours per week, 18 percent worked between 31 and 40 hours per week and 19.4 percent reported working over 40 hours per week.

Measures

Hogan Personality Inventory (HPI)

The HPI is a measure of normal personality based on the socio-analytic theory of personality and was designed to parallel the Big Five personality factors (Hogan and Hogan, 1995). The HPI consists of seven personality scales: adjustment, ambition, likeability, school success, intellectance [*sic*], prudence and sociability. For the current study, the HPI was used to measure adjustment, prudence and likeability. The HPI manual lists the internal consistency reliability values for these three scales as .89, .78 and .71, respectively (Hogan and Hogan, 1995). Adjustment was highly correlated with the Big Five factor emotional stability (r = .70), prudence was correlated with conscientiousness (r = .36), and likeability was correlated with agreeableness (r = .56) (Hogan and Hogan, 1995).

Cheating behavior

Academic misconduct was measured using 10 items (a = .89) asking how often respondents engaged in behaviors such as cheating on a test themselves or helping others cheat, unauthorized collaboration on an assignment, plagiarism and others. Responses were made on a 5-point Likert type scale with response options ranging from ‘never’ to ‘many times’. Higher scores indicate greater levels of academic misconduct than lower scores. Items used to measure the constructs of cheating behaviors, report cheating, organizational citizenship behaviors and counterproductive work behaviors are reported in Column 1 of the Appendix.

Report cheating

The intent to report cheating was measured with four items (α = .85). Questions asked how likely respondents were to report cheating by others. Responses were made on a 5-point Likert type scale with response options ranging from 'very unlikely' to 'very likely'. Higher scores indicate a stronger intent to report academic misconduct by others.

Organizational citizenship behaviors

Moorman and Blakely's (1995) Organizational Citizenship Behavior Scale was used to measure citizenship behaviors. The three types of citizenship behaviors measured were interpersonal helping (α = .74), individual initiative (α = .82) and personal industry (α = .77). Responses were made on a 7-point Likert type scale with response options ranging from 'strongly disagree' to 'strongly agree'.

Counterproductive work behaviors

Counterproductive work behaviors were measured using items on the Counterproductive Work Behavior Checklist developed by Spector et al. (2006). On a 5-point scale, respondents indicated how often, ranging from 'never' to 'every day', that they engaged in various counterproductive behaviors. The four types of counterproductive behaviors measured were sabotage (α = .62), production deviance (α = .60), withdrawal (α = .70) and theft (α = .81).

RESULTS

Confirmatory Factor Analysis (CFA)

A CFA was conducted using LISREL 8.5 (Joreskog and Sorbom, 1993) and several models were compared. The hypothesized model in which items used to measure each of the nine constructs were specified to load on their respective constructs fit the data well (χ^2 (782, N = 207) = 1600.75, RMSEA = .071, RMSEA 90 percent confidence interval (.066, .076), CFI = .91, and SRMR = .08). In support of convergent validity, the paths from the latent constructs to individual indicators were all statistically significant ($p < .05$) and completely standardized factor loadings ranged in values from .31 to .96 (see Appendix). Results of chi-square tests and the non-overlapping confidence interval tests (Anderson and Gerbing, 1988) provided evidence of discriminant validity. Means, standard deviations, and correlations between study variables are reported in Table 26.1.

Structural Model

We tested two models, a full mediation model and a partial mediation model. In the full mediation structural model, we had paths from adjustment, prudence and likeability to cheating behavior and report cheating. These two variables, in turn, had direct paths to the citizenship behaviors of interpersonal helping, individual initiative and personal industry, and direct paths to the counterproductive behaviors of sabotage, production deviance, withdrawal and theft. The full mediation model provided an acceptable fit to the data (χ^2 (915, N = 207) = 1764.26, RMSEA = .067, RMSEA 90 percent

Table 26.1 Means, standard deviations and correlations between study variables

	M	SD	1	2	3	4	5	6	7	8	9	10	11	12
1. Adjustment	22.28	6.99	(.89[a])											
2. Prudence	17.86	4.04	.25**	(.78[a])										
3. Likeability	18.42	2.86	.47**	.17*	(.71[a])									
4. Report Cheating	2.30	0.91	.04	.08	.07	(.85)								
5. Cheating Behavior	1.75	0.67	−.19**	−.23**	−.01	−.27**	(.89)							
6. Interpersonal Helping	3.75	0.50	.21**	.09	.38**	−.06	−.09	(.74)						
7. Individual Initiative	3.75	0.58	.09	.03	.19**	.02	−.17*	.57**	(.82)					
8. Personal Industry	3.98	0.57	.06	.11	.03	−.09	−.14	.42**	.41**	(.77)				
9. Theft	1.12	0.25	−.16*	−.13	−.02	.10	.38**	−.09	−.03	−.10	(.81)			
10. Production Deviance	1.19	0.33	−.19**	−.13	.00	.04	.33**	−.10	−.06	−.09	.51**	(.60)		
11. Sabotage	1.17	0.31	−.20**	−.16*	−.01	.13	.32**	−.08	−.06	−.13	.69**	.55**	(.62)	
12. Withdrawal	1.53	0.51	−.14*	−.10	.04	.11	.28**	−.08	.02	−.18**	.47**	.46**	.42**	(.70)

Notes:
** $p < .01$, * $p < .05$; scale reliabilities are reported on the diagonal.
a. Scale reliabilities are based on those reported in the HPI manual (Hogan and Hogan, 1995, p. 17).

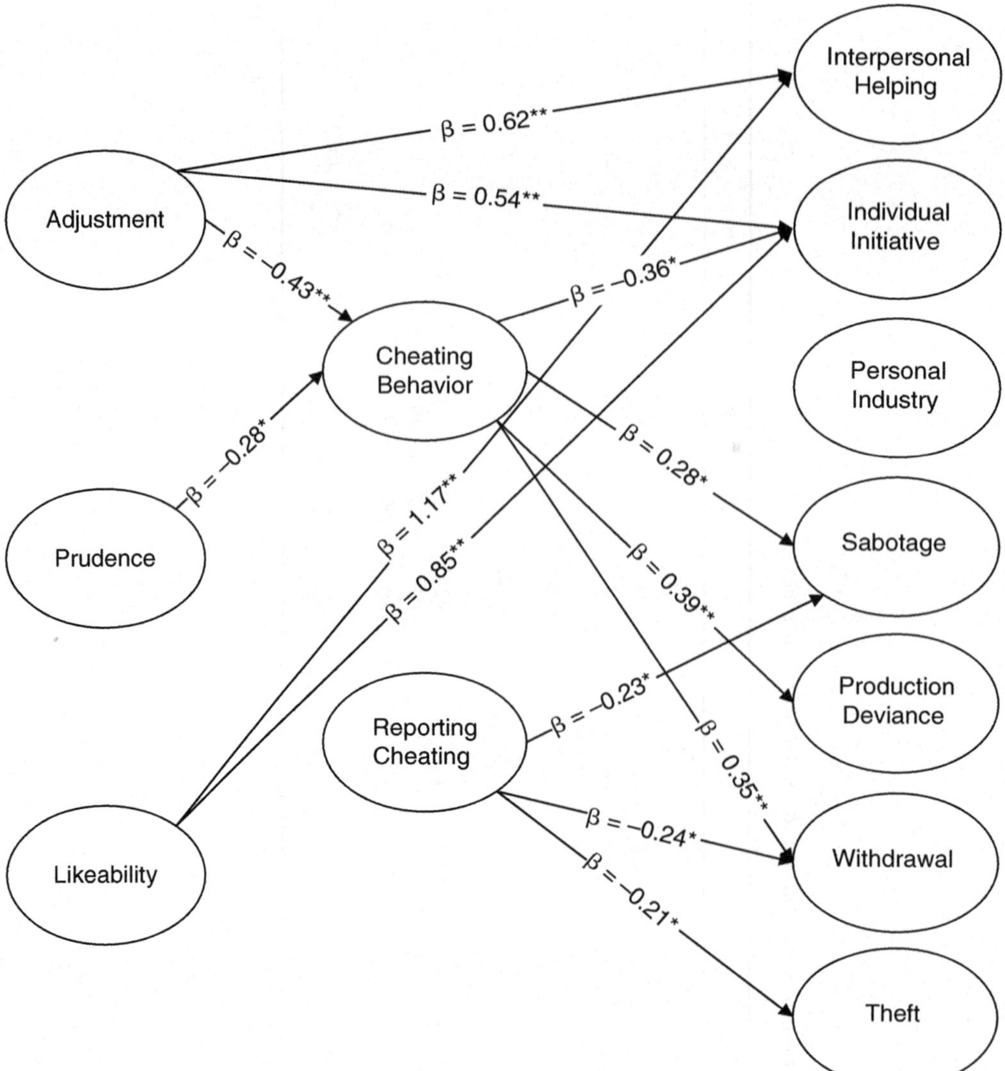

Notes: * $p < .05$, ** $p < .01$. Only significant relationships are reported. Completely standardized factor loadings of indicators on latent variables are reported in the Appendix and are not shown here.

Figure 26.1 Results of structural equation model – partial mediation model

confidence interval (.063, .072), CFI = .903, and SRMR = .084). A second, less restrictive model (see Figure 26.1) was tested that also included direct paths from adjustment, prudence and likeability to the three forms of citizenship behaviors and the four forms of counterproductive work behaviors. This partial mediation model also fit the data (χ^2 (8941, N = 207) = 1708.72, RMSEA = .067, RMSEA 90 percent confidence interval (.062, .071), CFI = .90, and SRMR = .08). The chi-square difference test was conducted between the full mediation and the partial mediation model. The obtained chi-square difference of 55.54 for 21 degrees of freedom was greater than the critical chi-square value of 32.67, indicating that the more restrictive full mediation model should be rejected and the partial mediation model retained.

In the partial mediation model, adjustment ($\beta = -.43, p < .01$) and prudence ($\beta = -.28, p < .05$) but not likeability ($\beta = .41$, ns) were related to cheating behavior and collectively explained 17 percent of the variance in cheating behavior at school. Adjustment ($\beta = .11$, ns), prudence ($\beta = -.08$, ns) and likeability ($\beta = -.17$, ns) were not significantly related to reporting cheating behaviors by others. Cheating in school was negatively related to citizenship behaviors of individual initiative ($\beta = -.36, p < .05$) but failed to reach statistical significance for interpersonal helping ($\beta = -.32$, ns) and personal industry ($\beta = -.14$, ns). Cheating in school was positively related to counterproductive work behaviors of sabotage ($\beta = .28, p < .05$), production deviance ($\beta = .39, p < .01$) and withdrawal ($\beta = .35, p < .01$) but not to theft ($\beta = .26$, ns). Reporting cheating by others at school was not significantly related to citizenship behaviors: interpersonal helping ($\beta = .25$, ns), individual initiative ($\beta = .13$, ns) and personal industry ($\beta = .15$, ns). It was negatively related to sabotage ($\beta = -.23, p < .05$), withdrawal ($\beta = -.24, p < .05$) and theft ($\beta = -.21, p < .05$) but not to production deviance ($\beta = -.17$, ns).

Of the three personality variables, only adjustment and likeability had direct effects. Adjustment was positively related to interpersonal helping ($\beta = .62, p < .01$) and to individual initiative ($\beta = .54, p < .01$). Likewise, likeability was also strongly related to interpersonal helping ($\beta = 1.17, p < .01$) and to individual initiative ($\beta = .85, p < .01$). Collectively, the entire partial mediation model explained 17 percent of the variance in cheating behavior in school, 61 percent of the variance in interpersonal helping, 31 percent in individual initiative, 6 percent in personal industry, 12 percent in sabotage, 23 percent in production deviance, 19 percent in withdrawal and 10 percent in theft. The inclusion of direct effects increased variance explained in interpersonal helping from 1 percent to 61 percent, in individual initiative from 2 percent to 31 percent, in personal industry from 5 percent to 6 percent, in sabotage 11 percent to 12 percent, in production deviance from 20 percent to 23 percent, in withdrawal from 18 percent to 19 percent, and variance explained in theft from 9 percent to 10 percent.

Results indicate that individuals with high scores on adjustment and prudence are less likely to cheat at school and the former are more likely to engage in interpersonal helping and show initiative at work. Individuals with high scores on likeability are more likely to help and show initiative at work. As expected, those who engage in cheating at school are more likely to engage in counterproductive work behaviors and less likely to engage in OCB. And, those who report cheating are less likely to engage in counterproductive work behaviors. These results indicate that habits persist from school to work.

DISCUSSION

Generally, results of the partial mediation model support the efficacy of behavioral samples of cheating behavior and report cheating as useful predictors of OCB and especially CWB behaviors. The lack of any significant direct effects for prudence to OCB is likely due to both the mediation by cheating behavior and the low overlap of OCB items with those of prudence. Specifically, the HPI prudence scale assesses adherence to conventional values, working hard, perfectionism, preference for predictability, avoidance of trouble and self-control (Hogan and Hogan, 1995). The items measuring OCB, listed in the Appendix, appear to tap into somewhat different behavioral domains. Therefore, these results suggest that samples of dysfunctional cheating behavior mediate the relationship between prudence and all four CWB components.

Comparison of increases in variance accounted for from the full to the partial mediation model offer insights into the efficacy of personality measures versus behavior samples. Consistent with the comparison of OCB and CWB above, the addition of direct paths for personality had a much larger effect for OCB than CWB. Specifically, interpersonal helping increased from 1 percent to 61 percent, individual initiative from 2 to 31 percent although personal industry changed little, from 5 to 6 percent. The betas and change in variance explained indicate that this result was due to adjustment and likeability, not prudence. For CWB, the results are quite different, with no significant direct effects from any personality variables to any CWB components.

In summary, both adjustment and prudence were negatively related to cheating behavior. Cheating behavior, in turn, was negatively related to individual initiative and positively to sabotage, production deviance and withdrawal. Also, report cheating was negatively related to sabotage, withdrawal and theft. Thus, cheating at school is related to cheating at work and report cheating is negatively related to cheating at work. Both adjustment and likeability are directly related to at least two dimensions of OCBs, interpersonal helping and individual initiative.

Those who report cheating at school may be disposed to engage in citizenship behaviors, such as providing a 'voice' or showing individual initiative or persisting at work. These behaviors, learned while at school, are likely to persist in the work environment, leading to important consequences for one's career. For instance, getting ahead in organizations traditionally has been assessed in terms of how individuals 'track' through a series of jobs/positions in their careers over time, typically reflecting a vertical trajectory (for example, Ng et al., 2005). Thus, the promotions that individuals receive serve as key indicators of such career success, and are valued by employees. Research on the consequences of promotion decisions (Tzafrir and Hareli, 2008) indicates that individuals greatly value, and experience intense reactions to, promotion decisions that have implications for themselves as well as for organizations.

Vertical mobility in organizations (that is, promotions) historically has been regarded as a key indicator of career success, and such promotion decisions typically are driven by supervisors' judgments of employee promotability. Results of one study by Jawahar and Ferris (2011) found that both task and contextual performance (OCB) explained unique variance in judgments of promotability. Thus, subordinates who exhibited higher levels of task performance and those demonstrating higher levels of contextual (OCB) performance were rewarded with higher ratings of promotability.

Limitations and Future Research

The generality of these findings is limited by several factors. First, although no strong causal attributions were made, the cross-sectional nature of the study renders causal attributions speculative. Second, the sample of primarily young, college students, many working less than full-time, may not represent the larger universe of older, non-college, full-time workers. Another potential limitation is that parts of the Moorman and Blakely (1995) OCB scale and the Spector et al. (2006) CWB measures were omitted. Ideally, future research would undertake a longitudinal examination of the relationship between Big Five personality factors, relevant behavior samples and work behaviors including task, OCB and CWB. A shortcoming of both this study and many other OCB and CWB studies is that actual job/task performance is not included. In the future, it is possible that measures of job performance, currently labeled task performance, will subsume some components of OCB and CWB.

Practical Implications

Clearly, one major implication of this study is that OCB and CWB research may benefit from examination of samples of OCB and CWB in non-work contexts. Indeed, the concept of 'past behavior as a valid predictor of future behavior' is well established in selection (Heneman et al., 2015). The methods of behavior description interviews (Janz et al., 1986), biographical inventory blanks (Shaffer et al., 1986) and reference checks (Gatewood et al., 2007) are all examples of samples of past behavior used to predict work behaviors.

Janz et al. (1986) state two principles relevant to behavior samples. First, the more recent past behavior is, the greater its predictive power, and second, the more longstanding a behavior, the greater its predictive power (Janz et al., 1986, p. 33). Although human resource practitioners and industrial psychologists have utilized behavior samples to predict work behaviors for decades, most OCB or CWB research has relied upon personality and perceptual ratings. Results of this study suggest that examination of samples of past behavior may contribute to future OCB and CWB research.

From a practical perspective, although research shows that cheating is common, both in the academic and business environments, some steps can reduce it. McCabe et al. (2012) noted that in the 20-plus years of their nationwide college integrity research, more students are indicating they have not engaged in cheating or plagiarism, but in open-ended comments they write justifications, such as the test was unfair, a personal emergency, or too much work. Because one of the best predictors of cheating is the perception that others cheat (Ariely, 2012; McCabe et al., 2012), a common justification is to 'level the playing field' (McCabe et al., 2012). The research of Ariely and his co-authors offers a number of suggestions to encourage honesty and reduce cheating. For example, providing moral reminders such as the 10 commandments in potential cheating situations and supervision. Additionally, consistent with McCabe's many studies, a culture of honesty could be created with pledges and signatures on honor codes. The importance of creating an ethical culture is highlighted by factors contributing to dishonesty such as seeing others benefit from cheating, a cheating tolerating culture, and conflicts of interest. Finally, one of Ariely's (2012) findings, that one immoral act leads to others, supports the importance of preventing cheating in school so it will not spill over to one's career.

Research Implications

Obviously, this study needs to be replicated with a sample of older working adults. We recommend a predictive design, such that measurement of cheating and report cheating behaviors precede measurement of OCB and CWB at work. Future OCB and CWB research may benefit from use of behavioral measures or objective indices of behavior such as school attendance, video rental records, driving records, and awards in sports and social groups. It might be worthwhile also to examine how the other two factors of the Big Five, namely, openness to experience and conscientiousness, relate to both positive and negative behaviors at school and at work to document the persistence of behaviors across domains.

REFERENCES

Anderson, J.C. and Gerbing, D.W. (1988), 'Structural equation modeling in practice: A review and recommended two-step approach', *Psychological Bulletin*, **103**, 411–23.

Ariely, D. (2012), *The Honest Truth about Dishonesty: How We Lie to Everyone – Especially Ourselves*, New York: Harper.

Barrick, M.R. and Mount, M.K. (1991), 'The "Big Five" personality dimensions and job performance: A meta-analysis', *Personnel Psychology*, **44**, 1–26.

Berry, C.M., Ones, D.S. and Sackett, P.R. (2007), 'Interpersonal deviance, organizational deviance, and their common correlates: A review and meta-analysis', *Journal of Applied Psychology*, **92**, 410–24.

Bjorkelo, B., Einarsen, S. and Matthíesen, S.B. (2010), 'Predicting proactive behaviour at work: Exploring the role of personality as an antecedent of whistle-blowing behaviour', *Journal of Occupational and Organizational Psychology*, **83**, 371–94.

Borman, W.C. and Motowidlo, S.J. (1997), 'Task performance and contextual performance: The meaning for personnel selection research', *Human Performance*, **10**, 99–109.

Borman, W.C., Penner, L.A., Allen, T.D. and Motowidlo, S.J. (2001), 'Personality predictors of citizenship performance', *International Journal of Selection and Assessment*, **9**, 52–69.

Brimble, M. and Stevenson-Clarke, P. (2005), 'Perceptions of the prevalence and seriousness of academic dishonesty in Australian universities', *Australian Educational Researcher*, **32**, 19–44.

Burns, R. (2014), 'Cooks saved nuke missile crews from failure. Associated Press', available at http://www.npr.org/templates/story/story.php?storyId=290068218 (accessed 14 March 2014).

Campbell, J.P. (1990), 'Modeling the performance prediction problem in industrial and organizational psychology'. In M.D. Dunnette and L.M. Hough (eds), *Handbook of Industrial and Organizational Psychology* (Vol. 1, pp. 687–732). Palo Alto, CA: Consulting Psychologists Press.

Campbell, J.P. and Wernimont, P.F. (1968), 'Signs, samples and criteria', *Journal of Applied Psychology*, **52**, 372–6.

Carmichael, M. (2012), 'Harvard accuses 125 students of cheating', available at http://www.boston.com/metrodesk/2012/08/30/harvard-investigates-students-for-cheating-final-exam/xA95LyxfyT2uKICbrNUjcO/story.html (accessed 6 January 2014).

Christensen-Hughes, J.M. and McCabe, D.L. (2006), 'Academic misconduct within higher education in Canada', *The Canadian Journal of Higher Education*, **36**, 1–21.

Cohen-Charash, Y. and Spector, P.E. (2001), 'The role of justice in organizations: A meta-analysis', *Organizational Behavior and Human Decision Processes*, **86**, 278–321.

Colquitt, J.A., Conlon, D.E., Wesson, M.J., Porter, C.O. and Ng, K.Y. (2001), 'Justice at the millennium: A meta-analytic review of 25 years of organizational justice research', *Journal of Applied Psychology*, **86**, 425–45.

Cullen, M.J. and Sackett, P.R. (2003), 'Personality and counterproductive workplace behavior'. In M. Barrick and A.M. Ryan (eds), *Personality and Work*, New York: Jossey-Bass-Pfeiffer.

Dalal, R.S. (2005), 'A meta-analysis of the relationship between organizational citizenship behavior and counterproductive work behavior', *Journal of Applied Psychology*, **90**, 1241–55.

Davis, S.F., Grover, C.A., Becker, A.H. and McGregor, L.N. (1992), 'Academic dishonesty: Prevalence, determinants, techniques, and punishments', *Teaching of Psychology*, **19**, 16–20.

Forsyth, D.R., Pope, W.R. and McMillan, J.H. (1985), 'Students' reactions after cheating: An attributional analysis', *Contemporary Educational Psychology*, **10**, 72–82.

Fountain, J.W. and Wong, E. (2001), 'Notre Dame coach resigns after 5 days and a few lies', *New York Times*, 15 December, accessed 5 February 2015 at: http://www.nytimes.com/2001/12/15/sports/notre-dame-coach-resigns-after-5-days-and-a-few-lies.html.

Gatewood, R.D., Field, H.S. and Barrick, M.R. (2007), *Human Resource Selection*, Dallas, TX: Southwestern.

Gottfredson, M.R. and Hirschi, T. (1990), *A General Theory of Crime*, Stanford, CA: Stanford University Press.

Gruys, M.L. and Sackett, P.R. (2003), 'The dimensionality of counterproductive work behavior', *International Journal of Selection and Assessment*, **11**, 30–42.

Heneman, H.G. III, Judge, T.A. and Kammeyer-Mueller, J.D. (2015), *Staffing Organizations* (8th edn), Irwin: McGraw Hill.

Hirschi, T. and Gottfredson, M.R. (1994), 'The generality of deviance'. In T. Hirschi and M.R. Gottfredson (eds), *The Generality of Deviance* (pp. 1–22). New Brunswick, NJ: Transaction Publishers.

Hogan, J. and Hogan, R. (1989), 'How to measure employee reliability', *Journal of Applied Psychology*, **74**, 273–9.

Hogan, R. and Hogan, J. (1995), *Hogan Personality Inventory Manual* (2nd edn). Tulsa, OK: Hogan Assessment Systems.

Houston, J.P. (1983), 'College classroom cheating, threat, sex, and prior performance', *College Student Journal*, **17**, 196–204.

Janz, T., Hellervik, L. and Gilmore, D.C. (1986), *Behavior Description Interviewing*, Boston, MA: Allyn Bacon.

Jawahar, I.M. and Ferris, G.R. (2011), 'A longitudinal investigation of task and contextual performance influences on promotability judgments', *Human Performance*, **24**, 1–20.

Joreskog, K.G. and Sorbom, D. (1993), *LISREL 8: Structural Equation Modeling with the SIMPLIS Command Language*, Hillsdale, NJ: Scientific Software International.

Josephson Institute of Ethics (2010), 'The ethics of American youth: 2010', available at http://charactercounts.org/programs/reportcard/2010/installment02_report-card_honesty-integrity.html (accessed 17 March 2012).

Josephson Institute of Ethics (2012), 'The ethics of American youth: 2012', available at http://charactercounts.org/programs/reportcard/2012/installment_report-card_honesty-integrity.html (accessed 5 January 2014).

Karabenick, S.A. and Srull, T.K. (1978), 'Effects of personality and situational variations in locus of control on cheating: Determinants of the congruence effect', *Journal of Personality*, **46**, 72–95.

Kisamore, J.L., Ligouri, E.W., Muldoon, J. and Jawahar, I.M. (forthcoming), 'Keeping the peace: An investigation of the interaction between personality, conflict and competence on organizational citizenship behaviors', *Career Development International*.

Koljatic, M., Silva, M. and Ardiles, J. (2003), 'Are student perceptions of parent acceptance of academic dishonesty associated with its occurrence?', *Psychological Reports*, **93**, 93–7.

LePine, J.A. and Van Dyne, L. (2001), 'Voice and cooperative behavior as contrasting forms of contextual performance: Evidence of differential relationships with Big Five personality characteristics and cognitive ability', *Journal of Applied Psychology*, **86** (2), 326–36.

LePine, J.A., Erez, A. and Johnson, D.E. (2002), 'The nature and dimensionality of organizational citizenship behavior: A critical review and meta-analysis', *Journal of Applied Psychology*, **87**, 52–65.

Marcus, B. and Schuler, H. (2004), 'Antecedents of counterproductive behavior at work: A general perspective', *Journal of Applied Psychology*, **89**, 647–60.

McCabe, D.L. and Trevino, L.K. (1993), 'Academic dishonesty: Honor codes and other contextual influences', *Journal of Higher Education*, **64**, 522–38.

McCabe, D.L., Butterfield, K.D. and Trevino, L.K. (2006), 'Academic dishonesty in graduate business programs: Prevalence, causes and proposed action', *Academy of Management Learning and Education*, **5**, 294–306.

McCabe, D.L., Butterfield, K.D. and Treviño, L.K. (2012), *Cheating in College: Why Students Do It and What Educators Can Do About It*, Baltimore, MD: Johns Hopkins Press.

McCabe, D.L., Trevino, L.K. and Butterfield, K.D. (1996), 'The influence of collegiate and corporate codes of conduct on ethics-related behavior in the workplace', *Business Ethics Quarterly*, **6**, 461–76.

Meyer, J.P., Stanley, D.J., Herscovitch, L. and Topolnytsky, L. (2002), 'Affective, continuance, and normative commitment to the organization: A meta-analysis of antecedents, correlates, and consequences', *Journal of Vocational Behavior*, **61**, 20–52.

Miles, D.E., Borman, W.E., Spector, P.E. and Fox, S. (2002), 'Building an integrative model of extra role work behaviors: A comparison of counterproductive work behavior with organizational citizenship behavior', *International Journal of Selection and Assessment*, **10**, 51–7.

Moorman, R.H. and Blakely, G.L. (1995), 'Individualism-collectivism as an individual difference predictor of organizational citizenship behavior', *Journal of Organizational Behavior*, **16**, 127–42.

Mount, M., Ilies, R. and Johnson, E. (2006), 'Relationship of personality traits and counterproductive work behaviors: The mediating effects of job satisfaction', *Personnel Psychology*, **59**, 591–622.
Newstead, S.E., Franklyn-Stokes, A. and Armstead, P. (1996), 'Individual differences in student cheating', *Journal of Educational Psychology*, **88**, 229–41.
Ng, T.W.H., Eby, L.T., Sorensen, K.L. and Feldman, D.C. (2005), 'Predictors of objective and subjective career success: A meta-analysis', *Personnel Psychology*, **58**, 367–408.
Nonis, S. and Swift, C.O. (2001), 'An examination of the relationship between academic dishonesty and workplace dishonesty: A multi-campus investigation', *Journal of Education for Business*, **77**, 69–77.
Ones, D.S., Viswesvaran, C. and Schmidt, F.L. (1993), 'Comprehensive meta-analysis of integrity test validities: Findings and implications for personnel selection and theories of job performance', *Journal of Applied Psychology*, **78**, 679–703.
Ones, D.S., Viswesvaran, C. and Schmidt, F.L. (2003), 'Personality and absenteeism: A meta-analysis of integrity tests', *European Journal of Personality*, **17**, S19–S38.
Organ, D.W. (1988), *Organizational Citizenship Behavior: The Good Soldier Syndrome*, Lexington, MA: Lexington Books.
Organ, D.W. (1997), 'Organizational citizenship behavior: It's construct clean-up time', *Human Performance*, **10**, 85–97.
Organ, D.W. and Ryan, K. (1995), 'A meta-analytic review of attitudinal and dispositional predictors of organizational citizenship behavior', *Personnel Psychology*, **48**, 775–802.
Riketta, M. (2002), 'Attitudinal organizational commitment and job performance: A meta-analysis', *Journal of Organizational Behavior*, **23**, 257–66.
Robinson, S.L. and Bennett, R.J. (1995), 'A typology of deviant workplace behaviors: A multidimensional scaling study', *Academy of Management Journal*, **38**, 555–72.
Rotundo, M. and Sackett, P.R. (2002), 'The relative importance of task, citizenship, and counterproductive performance to global ratings of job performance: A policy capturing approach', *Journal of Applied Psychology*, **87**, 66–80.
Sackett, P.R. (2002), 'The structure of counterproductive work behaviors: Dimensionality and relationships with facets of job performance', *International Journal of Selection and Assessment*, **10**, 5–11.
Salgado, J.F. (2002), 'The big five personality dimensions and counterproductive behaviors', *International Journal of Selection and Assessment*, **10**, 117–25.
Shaffer, G.S., Saunders, V. and Owens, W.A. (1986), 'Additional evidence for the accuracy of biographical data: Long-term retest and observer ratings', *Personnel Psychology*, **39**, 791–809.
Sims, R.L. (1993), 'The relationship between academic dishonesty and unethical business practices', *Journal of Education for Business*, **68**, 207–12.
Spector, P.E., Fox, S., Penney, L.M., Bruursema, K., Goh, A. and Kessler, S. (2006), 'The dimensionality of counterproductivity: Are all counterproductive behaviors created equal?', *Journal of Vocational Behavior*, **68** (3), 446–60.
Stone, T.H., Jawahar, I.M. and Kisamore, J.L. (2010), 'Predicting academic misconduct intentions and behavior using the theory of planned behavior and personality', *Basic and Applied Social Psychology*, **32**, 35–45.
Stone, T.H., Kisamore, J.L. and Jawahar, I.M. (2008), 'Predicting students' perceptions of academic misconduct on the Hogan Personality Inventory Reliability Scale', *Psychological Reports*, **102**, 495–508.
Stone, T.H., Kisamore, J.L., Kluemper, D. and Jawahar, I.M. (2012), 'Whistle-blowing in the classroom', *Journal of Higher Education Theory and Practice*, **12** (5), 11–26.
Tzafrir, S.S. and Hareli, S. (2008), 'Employees' emotional reactions to promotion decisions: The role of causal attributions and perceptions of justice', *Career Development International*, **14**, 351–71.
Viswesvaran, C. and Ones, D.S. (2000), 'Perspectives on models of job performance', *International Journal of Selection and Assessment*, **8**, 216–26.
Whitley, B.E. Jr (1998), 'Factors associated with cheating among college students', *Research in Higher Education*, **39**, 235–74.
Wilson, K. and Gullone, E. (1999), 'The relationship between personality and affect over the lifespan', *Personality and Individual Differences*, **27**, 1141–56.

APPENDIX 26A.1 SCALE OF CONTENT AND COMPLETELY STANDARDIZED FACTOR LOADINGS

Cheating Behavior

Item	Loading
Copied a few sentences from a source but did not give credit	.56
Copied from another student and turned in as own	.63
Helped someone cheat on a test	.69
Collaborated on assignment that was supposed to be individual work	.66
Turned in work done by others	.55
Copied from another student on test	.76
Used notes on test without instructor's permission	.73
Received substantial help on assignment without permission	.58
Cheated on test in any way	.81
Used unfair methods to learn about a test	.79

Report Cheating

Item	Loading
I would report an incidence of cheating by a student whom I do not know	.94
I would report an incidence of cheating by a student whom I consider to be a friend	.82
It is important to report observations of academic dishonesty by other students	.67
Reporting instances of cheating is necessary to be fair to honest students	.60

Organizational Citizenship Behaviors – Interpersonal Helping

Item	Loading
I go out of my way to help co-workers with work-related problems	.71
I voluntarily help new employees settle into the job	.61
I frequently adjust work schedule to accommodate other employees' requests	.43
I always go out of the way to make newer employees feel welcome	.68
I show genuine concern and courtesy toward co-workers, even under the most trying business or personal situations	.63

Organizational Citizenship Behaviors – Individual Initiative

Item	Loading
For issues that may have serious consequences, I express opinions honestly even when others may disagree	.51
I often motivate others to express their ideas and opinions	.68
I encourage others to try new and more effective ways of doing their job	.82
I encourage hesitant or quiet co-workers to voice their opinions when they otherwise might not speak up	.69
I frequently communicate to co-workers suggestions on how the group can improve	.77

Organizational Citizenship Behaviors – Personal Industry

Item	Loading
I rarely miss work even when I have a legitimate reason for doing so	.54
I perform my job with unusually few errors	.75
I perform my job duties with extra special care	.69
I always meet or beat deadlines for completing work	.75

Counter Productive Work Behaviors – Sabotage	
Purposely:	
wasted your employer's material/supplies	.31
damaged a piece of equipment or property	.92
dirtied or littered your place of work	.44
Counter Productive Work Behaviors – Production Deviance	
Purposely:	
did work incorrectly	.62
worked slowly when things needed to get done	.53
failed to follow instructions	.59
Counter Productive Work Behaviors – Withdrawal	
Came to work late without permission	.56
Stayed home from work and said you were sick when you weren't	.68
Taken a longer break than you were allowed to take	.71
Left work earlier than you were allowed to	.48
Counter Productive Work Behaviors – Theft	
Stolen something belonging to your employer	.56
Took supplies or tools home without permission	.31
Put in to be paid for more hours than you worked	.49
Took money from your employer without permission	.96
Stole something belonging to someone at work	.93

27 Educating students for sustainable careers: in the classroom and beyond

Jon P. Briscoe

INTRODUCTION

The idea of sustainable careers is practical and very timely in an era in which careers may seem anything but sustainable. That said, the ephemeral nature of economic demands, vocational trends and so on make sustainability seem a distant prize. External situations and internal individual dynamics shift (as they always have – but with greater complexity and speed) across the lifespan (Erikson, 1980; Hall, 2002; Kegan, 1994), thus making sustainability an even greater challenge.

In this chapter, I will try to paint a picture of how career sustainability might be inculcated amongst and within individuals in classroom settings. As researchers and educators, we sometimes have only one shot at trying to influence our students, especially those in professional programmes. In such contexts, we rarely enjoy the in-depth consultation and one-on-one attention that a career coach or mentor might get. We may not have the attentive audience who are invested in their careers the way a group of outsourced employees (as one example) might be.

By the same token, we do enjoy some advantages as educators. We can legitimize the relevance and rigour of 'soft skills' such as self-awareness, learning, values clarification and career development. We can introduce scripts that students would not have thought of and we can challenge scripts that they may bring to their careers in a helpful way and in a safe setting.

Regardless of the strengths and weaknesses of the classroom setting for the development of career sustainability, it is the main and for some of us the only arena in which we apply the practical craft of our theoretical interests and insights into career practice. It seems very important to treat this venue seriously and to use it as an opportunity to present tools for career sustainability.

The chapter will primarily pertain to students who are in the midst of their careers rather than in college or recently graduated. This is because in my experience career insight and the ability to understand many of the available career tools as they relate to sustainability are heavily dependent upon real-world career experience.

Profile of My Students

The students I am teaching are workers first rather than students first. Frequently, they are going to graduate school part-time as they maintain a full-time career. Sometimes, they have suspended their career to pursue graduate work full-time, but the career is in full-view and is the primary motivation for further education in the great majority of cases. These students are often hungry for usable knowledge. They have been out long enough to know that the life and career plans they had imagined as adolescents and young adults often did not pan out, or they panned out but did not bring the anticipated satisfaction. In some ways, these students are ideal. They know that they don't know all they need to, and are in a process of unlearning as much as learning.

Often in business school (my teaching context) students are accustomed to spreadsheets and problems with answers that can be quantified. Most students are relieved and surprised to find themselves in a class that treats human values and potential as a critical piece to the puzzle of business, individual performance and personal well-being. However, a few may be confused and even dismissive of such content. A skilled and experienced teacher will be able to quickly establish the relevance of people-related principles – from strategic HR, to leadership, to group dynamics, to organizational behaviour – and finally to career development.

How My Research and Experience Inform My Teaching Perspective

I have been researching careers for about 13 years. Initially my attempts were to better measure protean and boundaryless careers (Briscoe et al., 2006). This led to closely observing differences in these measures across age cohorts, various types of students, managers and executives, and populations in different countries. A growing curiosity in international differences in terms of careers led me, Douglas (Tim) Hall, and Wolfgang Mayrhofer to found the 5C Group (Cross-Cultural Collaboration on Contemporary Careers) in order to study career success and career transitions around the world (Briscoe et al., 2012).

While the early stages involved several countries, I had direct contact with interview data collection and/or coding with colleagues in Malaysia, Mexico, South Africa and the United States. This allowed a high contrast of research participants and contexts. It allowed for great insight into how career success shifts across career stages and how context shapes career success. It enabled us to see why some people are more able to learn from career transitions than others.

PROTEAN PERSPECTIVE FOR A SUSTAINABLE CAREER

Careers are often judged on content. 'What do you do' is a euphemism in many countries for 'who are you' and 'why do you matter?' In a sustainable career, *process* is probably more important than *content*. How does one sharpen the saw (Covey, 1989) or recover from career setbacks (Hall, 1986)? How do we learn to make judgments on how 'knowing whom' relates to 'knowing how' and 'knowing why' (Arthur et al., 1995). One might have been extremely successful and even 'made it' by some measure of success, and yet not have the skills to move on when the time comes. One is easily reminded of prosperous professional athletes who never developed the skills to manage their resources or re-imagine their identities, or a downsized worker who does not know how to remake themself in a new role. Perhaps less dramatic but still distressing is the person who never questions their place in the world and taps into a sense of calling (Hall and Chandler, 2005).

Our goal as educators, I believe, is to give our students informed and meaningful choices when it comes to their careers. Part of this involves competency in their trade, whether it be construction, retail, management or accounting. But part of this involves knowing who they are. As Warren Bennis put it 'until you truly know yourself, strengths and weaknesses, know what you want to do and why you want to do it, you cannot succeed in any but the most superficial sense of the word' (1994: 40). A lack of self-knowledge can be fatal to a sustainable career because one might be executing a career plan that does not reflect one's innermost desires. In such a case a person is headed for a crash or, more dangerously, for success that is sustained but prevents them from realizing their true goals that have not been met, yet alone identified.

A sad example of this is the case of Chuck Barris, a wildly successful game show creator and host in the United States who made millions of dollars while changing the landscape of television programming. Late in life he lost an adult daughter to suicide. Six years after her death, he reflected on the emptiness of his external career (Derr and Laurent, 1987) and his regrets for not balancing his life in a way that would have let him know his daughter (Pearlman, 2004) whom he would later write about at the end of a deep and long post-mortem exploration (Barris, 2010). Externally, his success proved enduring. Internally, it had an expiration date as he never effectively reflected on his deepest priorities until it was too late.

Protean Combinations and Implications

While various career perspectives can be used fruitfully, I will use the one with which I am most familiar and which I have utilized primarily in my own teaching: the 'protean career'. Hall (1976) defined the protean career as a career in which the person's own definition of, and path toward, career success trump external defined definitions and paths toward career success. Today, but even more so at the time Hall originally wrote, a protean career meant one had to pay attention to process because the default process that an organizational career often structured was not necessarily one that matched a protean perspective (Hall, 2002).

More recently, Hall and I (Briscoe and Hall, 2006) specified that the protean career could be broken down into two primary components: a values-driven approach to the career and a self-directed career orientation. Clinically, these are offered as attitudinal constructs (Briscoe et al., 2006) but for a basic perspective it helps to understand that individuals who have a protean approach to their career know themselves and the values they need to express in their life and career to feel fulfilled (Katz and Kahn, 1978). They also take an independent and self-directed behavioural approach to impact their career in a way that allows them to be adaptive and perhaps creative in fulfilling their passion.

When thinking about these components of values-driven and self-directed career components, we labelled a protean career profile according to whether a person is high or low in any combination. Figure 27.1 depicts four possible quadrants: dependent, rigid, reactive and transformational.

A person who is not sure what they care about in their career nor what they need to do to tactically manage their career might be considered 'dependent'. Such a career posture is sustainable only if drifting is the persistent pattern and one is talented enough at drifting not to succumb to the challenges of survival. Happily I have encountered few people in this extreme predicament. One, interviewed during a study in Australia (Waters

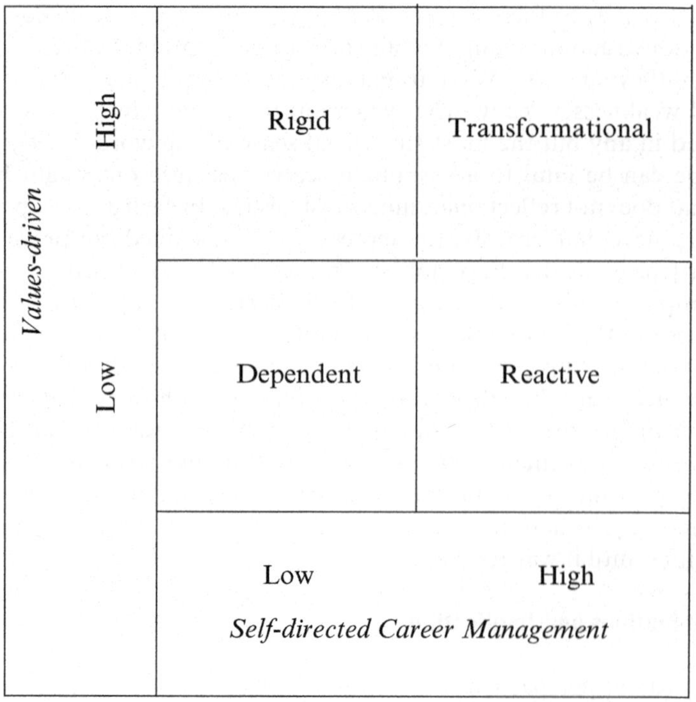

Source: Based upon Briscoe and Hall (2006).

Figure 27.1 Protean career combinations

et al., 2014), chased shiny objects from month to month and year to year such as 'a lass moving to Darwin', a 'bloke with a fishing boat', and whatever else seemed attractive at the time. I like to refer to him as 'Forrest Gump' without the charm (referring to the movie of the same name starring Tom Hanks). This posture is essentially surrendering agency and, in turn, sustainability.

We labelled as 'rigid' those who were highly values-driven but not very self-directed in terms of tactically managing their career. They know what they want, but they are not very good at getting it. Like the stereotype of academics in an 'ivory tower', rigid career actors can be impractical even while very cognizant of their values. In my first career development course I taught a middle-aged woman who felt disrespected in her job. She wanted more engagement, more respect, more status and more meaning. She was job hunting for a job that would allow this. One week she came to class with 'good news' and 'bad news'. The good news? She found a job opportunity with a boss who she felt would value and respect her with work that engaged her. 'What is the bad news?', I asked? 'It's an extra 20 minute drive' she said sadly. While I admittedly did not know what 20 minutes meant to her work–life balance, I felt stunned at how she weighed relief of career angst against a 20-minute commute.

I believe that the 'reactive' protean profile is the most problematic. In this orientation, a person is good at driving career behaviour toward their interests. However, they are not clear on the values driving their interests! Values are of course critical to effective self-leadership (Katz and Kahn, 1978; Bennis, 1994) as well as leadership (Burns, 1978; Seltzer and Bass, 1990; Walumbwa et al., 2008). But a non-protean perspective on values aligns one not with one's own, but with external values. This means that a person is willing to say 'how high' when an organization says 'jump', but they are not able to question or substitute the external value that prescribes the jump. The employer may be very pleased to have a yes man or woman loyal to their wishes. In my mind this is dangerous for both the person and the employer. Ethical behaviour, authentic leadership, and emotional intelligence will suffer. I believe many ethical and strategic failures such as Enron, Arthur Andersen, and market factors leading to the latest recession led to individual and corporate downfalls due to employees following the herd but not questioning the herd's values nor adequately examining their own. This posture may appear deceptively 'sustainable' because until a fall the person may not recognize that a values deficit is in play.

Hall and I ultimately concluded that a 'transformational' posture is ideal. This occurs when a person is both in tune with and committed to their personal career values and also tactically sophisticated in driving their career behaviour in a self-directed fashion. This means that the various career chapters or 'learning cycles' (Hall and Mirvis, 1994) one passes through are evaluated and managed according to personal values and self-directed, independent behaviours. While the histories of great leaders such as Ghandi and Mandela come to mind as examples of transformational careers, so also do practitioners attempting to balance meaning and growth in their vocational and private lives while tactically building a career that honours various life realms (Wrzesniewski and Dutton, 2001; Mainiero and Sullivan, 2005).

Protean Learning Process and Sustainable Careers

Beyond having the optimal combination of protean career dimensions outlined in the previous section, one has to use those dimensions to manage one's career in a sustainable way. A non-comprehensive list of career skills including protean as well as other skills might be identity exploration and awareness (Briscoe and Hall, 1999; Hall, 2002), values awareness and expression (Briscoe and Hall, 2006; DeFillippi and Arthur, 1994), adaptability and learning (Hall, 2002; DeFillippi and Arthur, 1994) and relationships (Hall et al., 1997; Arthur et al., 1995). These skills need to be utilized and engaged within and between career chapters and transitions for the individual to reap their benefits.

A helpful way of thinking about *process* is via the concept of career learning cycles (Hall, 1993; 2002). Considering the life span approach to career stages (Super, 1957; Super et al., 1996), Hall instead conceived of exploration, trial, establishment and mastery to occur not just across a career but within career segments he labelled 'career learning cycles'. This helped him and others (Hall and Mirvis, 1994; Hall and Chandler, 2005) understand career dynamics and career management in a relatively ephemeral context, realizing that attending to process is just as important within career stages as across them.

With Hall's learning cycle as a starting point, he and I (Briscoe and Hall, 2009) theorized about how one might become more protean with a deep look at process. We reasoned that higher levels of protean career orientation would make one more likely to explore career learning cycles. While failure experiences might naturally lead to

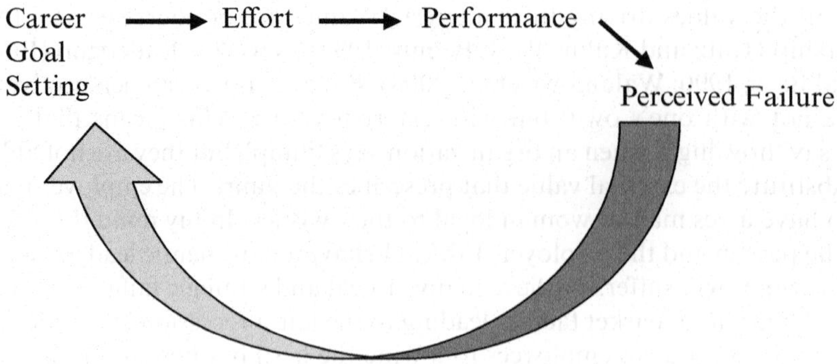

Figure 27.2 Single-loop career learning: failure response

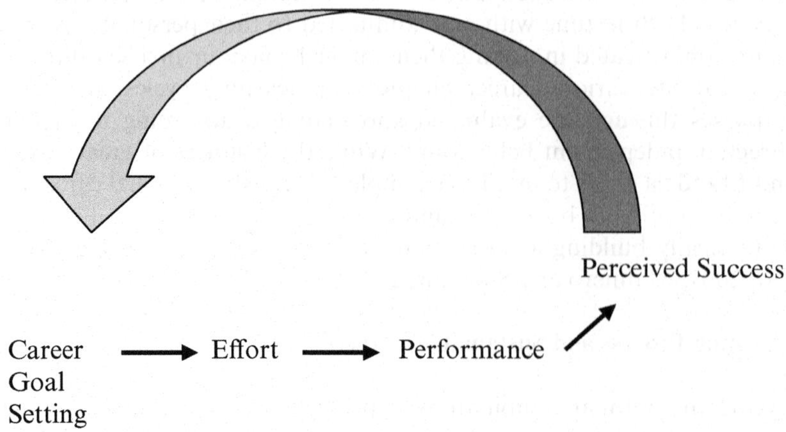

Figure 27.3 Single-loop career learning: success response

introspection on self and career, success experiences might ironically prevent one from deeply examining one's assumptions, identities and career tactics (Hall, 1986).

Responses to the career learning cycle that are merely reactive, perhaps adjusting tactics but not taking a deep look at values and identity or career behaviour and adaptability, and their respective underlying assumptions, we labelled as single loop 'failure' responses. Single loop 'success' responses, on the other hand, were those in which introspection was skipped due to the conclusion that 'all is well' based upon objective career success and external recognition. This can lead to eventual problems if the person's values and identity have not been adequately established, or if their career tactics were not sustainable due to personal or external factors.

We depicted protean double-loop learning as the process of examining self and career, including underlying assumptions, regardless of whether a career learning cycle is seen subjectively or objectively as a success or failure. This takes discipline of course. In my and colleagues' research, we find that career actors often work passively through their career scripts, only reflecting heavily when they 'have' to. For a person to reflect deliberately in a non-threatening context is an important but not commonly observed skill.

Recently published research (Waters et al., 2014) showed that protean attitudes in one longitudinal study were dynamic – perking up during unemployment, and decreasing after re-employment. This is encouraging in one sense since it implies people are able to adapt to career threats and opportunities in a functional fashion. However, they may not be reflecting proactively or in a disciplined fashion if a threat is not perceived.

Another study (Briscoe et al., 2009), not centred specifically on the protean career, indicated that reflecting at the end of the career learning cycle is valuable but not ideal. When comparing career transitions amongst sets of employees in six countries, it became clear that those who had either objective and/or subjective positive outcomes were able to reflect on self, career, learning and context *throughout* the career learning cycle, not just at the end. Very few people reflected through all stages, but we found that reflection was demonstrated at the beginning of career transitions, during stable career segments, and finishing career transitions.

An additional key element in a sustainable career recognized in protean and boundaryless careers is relationships. Positive relationships provide a 'secure base' which provides the career actor with a sense of safety and support that may give them new perspectives in addition to providing psychological comfort (Kahn, 1996). Whether they be formal mentoring or informal support and developmental relationships, our links to others provide meaning to our work and fulfil our core motivation (Deci et al., 1999).

PRINCIPLES TO GUIDE EDUCATION TOWARD SUSTAINABLE CAREERS

From the previous discussion of learning and reflection as applied in the context of career learning cycles it is possible to infer some principles that should guide teaching sustainable career management (see Box 27.1).

EDUCATIONAL APPROACHES TO THE SUSTAINABLE CAREER: IN THE CLASSROOM AND BEYOND

Several approaches to inculcating skills that might lead to a sustainable career will be reviewed. I don't claim these as comprehensive, but they represent a sample of approaches encountered in my own teaching efforts, those I have observed from others, and in the literature.

For each educational approach, I will explore their consistency with the principles outlined in the previous section; discuss their use, as well as advantages and disadvantages in the classroom; and discuss their potential use in the field by the student in their post-classroom life. In my own teaching, I think I have not done enough to give tools to students to replicate the classroom tools in their working lives. In that sense, I don't offer myself as an authority in these methods, but rather present my ideas in the hope that they will be useful to the career scholars community as we try to progress in helping our students achieve greater career sustainability.

BOX 27.1 PRINCIPLES OF EDUCATION FOR A SUSTAINABLE CAREER

1. An overarching principle of education for a sustainable career is that it produces self-directed career skills which allow a person greater capacity to understand, manage and shape their career.
2. Identity and values are key. Any teaching/learning approach that hopes to result in a more sustainable career for the student must have identity and values as a core focus. The student must have a grounding around who they are and which values are core to their identity and its expression (Briscoe, 2013; Hall et al., 1997). While this is a moving target, it must be a prioritized one for the student. A failure to do so means there is no bedrock upon which to judge 'knowing why', to use the intelligent career capital language, and then 'knowing how' in addition to 'knowing whom' can be tenuous as the person's natural and balanced career orbit is disrupted.
3. There must be an emphasis upon learning. This sounds obvious, but don't forget that many self-help books focus upon performance and advancement as if a focus upon such objective career success is a foregone conclusion. As shown with goal orientation (Button et al., 1996), a performance goal orientation where more certain success is sought leads to worse, not better performance than a mastery (or learning) goal orientation. A sustainable career is where learning is a constant factor.
4. Beyond learning, learning how to learn is a higher skill and priority. Hall (1986; 2002) and Briscoe and Hall (1999) refer to learning how to learn as a 'metacompetency' which allows one to develop various other important competencies. Just as learning needs to extend performance, learning to learn is necessary to constantly monitor one's own identity, needs and values, as well as to understand the ever-changing environment and closely linked adjustments in behavioural adaptation that provide success across the shifting canvas of one's career.
5. Experience is key. Experience is the fuel of learning and adaptation, as well as identity and values. As one's career and life unfold, more experience is acquired. However as has been stated, everyone has experience, but not everyone learns from it (source unknown).
6. Relationships matter. In spite of the independent nature of modern careers in the West, self-discovery, development, identity, competence and meaning occur in the context of relationships. Career development that forsakes relationships is only a shell of its potential.

I label the classroom approaches that I will explore here: 'Static assessment', '360° feedback', 'Skills development', 'Action learning', 'Structured introspection' (timelines, etc.), and 'Peer coaching'.

Static Assessment

Static assessment is a term I use to describe assessments that result in fixed numerical scores or values, or preset ordinal or categorical variables. Such assessments are based upon validated or non-validated academic and commercial measures, completed by the student and self-scored, scored in automated fashion, or assessed and interpreted by others.

A classic tool would be Holland's (1997) self-directed search model which gives output for helping compare personal values and preferences to occupational choices. In a similar vein, the Campbell Interest and Skills Survey or CISS (Campbell, 1995) helps students or others compare self-perceived skills and interests to those of existing people in specified occupations. Values assessments such as the Rokeach Values Survey (Rokeach, 1973) can also build basic awareness of one's priorities. Similar but more qualitative assessments include Schein's career anchor model (1990; 1996) and the intelligent career card sort or ICCS (Arthur et al., 2008). Schein's method has an option of relying upon qualitative interviewing. While it results in a specific categorical reference range, it allows for nuance and interpretation. The ICCS is a real breakthrough in that it relies upon a dynamic model of interdependent career competencies (knowing how, knowing why, and knowing whom). As with Schein's career anchor process, completing the Intelligent Career Card sort is designed to produce introspection in the process of producing categorical results.

Static, quantitative measures help clarify identity and values by offering contrast with others' values. The more qualitative and process-based assessments have the advantage of helping identity and values be discovered in part, even though they result in relatively static categories. They also offer more learning, and learning process advantages. The more numeric based assessments seem to result mainly in passive learning. A risk is that the student views their results in a static fashion and leaves them in the past as time moves on; or maybe relies upon that static point as a valid measure across time even as their life contexts or personal orientations may have changed.

In terms of helping the student make use of experience, static assessments seem limited. They may inspire experience but don't seem to help the student reflect upon experience. The Schein approach does seem potentially more powerful in terms of at least using experience to make diagnoses, and the ICCS, if used as its designers intended, would be helpful. Of the assessments briefly profiled in this section, the ICCS clearly seems to be the one (and maybe the only one) that would encourage a long-range engagement with and appreciation of how relationships enhanced career development. Finally, the ICCS has an advantage in that it is replicable across the career if the students choose to use it.

In the classroom a big advantage of static assessments is that they give some uniformity and comparison points for group discussion. They also provide a starting point for self-exploration when the student may not know where to start. A negative is that students may not receive a score they resonate with and may conclude that there is not much point in exploring a certain career dimension related to the assessment.

I think the biggest disadvantage to the *static* assessment is their fixed nature (more precisely the static nature of the outcomes). They may be too conclusive and too tidy. They may offer short-term answers when long-term exploration is more wisely sought and prescribed. We should develop future static assessments that produce them in a way that inspires reflection upon process, relationships and experience, and which can be easily and *meaningfully* replicated by our students months and years into their ongoing careers.

The advantages and limitations of static assessment as well as the other educational approaches reviewed in terms of how well they reflect the principles of sustainable careers are profiled in Table 27.1.

360° Feedback

360° feedback involves getting (typically) anonymous feedback from raters at different organizational levels on the focal person's performance, demonstration of certain skills or attributes and/or demonstration of valued character traits.

Table 27.1 Impact of educational approaches on the sustainable career

Educational approach	Principles						
	Produces self-directed skills	Focus on identity and values	Emphasis upon learning	Improves 'learning how to learn'	Experience is central	Relationships better understood and developed	Potential for approach *as typically practised* to be re-utilized by student beyond classroom?
	Impact level of educational approaches						
Static assessment	Low	Possible	Moderate (but passive)	Low	Very low	Possible	Low
360° feedback	Low	High if well explored	High	High if behavioural change initiated	Potentially	Strong potential	Low
Skills development	High	Strong potential	High	Strong potential	Potentially	Strong potential	Moderate to strong
Action learning	High	Strong potential	High	High	Very high	Strong potential	Good if educator prepares student
Structured introspection	High	High	High	High	Very high	High	Strong
Peer coaching	Strong potential	High	High	Strong potential	Potentially	High	Moderate, requires training to transfer to 'real world'

While this method is used extensively in the corporate world, it is used much less in classroom settings due largely to the monetary and temporal cost as well as the effort needed by the professor and/or student to manage the process. Nevertheless, feedback on performance, behaviours and perceived values is of course hugely relevant to career development.

In considering the principles for education methods aimed toward building sustainable careers, 360° feedback certainly helps people have a better sense of identity or awareness, as they can compare their own perceptions to others. This in and of itself is learning. If it leads to efforts to change and re-assess, it can even lead to 'learning to learn'. If the assessment is well designed, it should give the feedback receiver information on how to improve work relationships.

A probable limitation in a classroom setting of 360° feedback is that it is harder to mine experience and harder to monitor future experience. This is because the teacher's supervision and authority end with the semester in most cases. Programmes (such as an executive MBA programme) might structure extended rounds of feedback, or commercial outfits might offer multiple rounds as an offer to students.

While impractical for the reasons mentioned above, one big advantage of 360° feedback in the classroom setting is that the class can provide a relatively safe environment. The student is able to view their results in a learning mode, without the possible performance pressure that can come from a supervisor or performance review. Teachers are in an ideal position to be the student's advocate and to help them explore the feedback in terms of personal values and long-term career goals, not only the performance goals outlined by the organization. Also, when such feedback is very disappointing, a supportive teacher can put things into perspective and build the student toward future identities and possibilities.

In my own experience, I have found credible and relevant 360° feedback to be one of the most valued aspects of career or leadership development activities for my students. While the results are not objective, they are owned by (anonymous) sources outside of the student. It helps build the students' awareness and appreciation for what they need to do to reach their goals. For this reason it might be wise to employ 360° feedback where possible.

Skills Development

Skills development refers to activities in class that attempt to teach students new emotional, cognitive and behavioural tools for managing their careers. Because they are often process oriented, they have a special potential to help students develop more sustainable career skills and, in turn, sustainable careers.

Almost any of the assessments profiled in this chapter lead to greater self-awareness for the career actor. Sometimes heightened awareness of new career perspectives is enough to add new skills. In teaching protean and boundaryless career theory to my students, I was sometimes surprised that mere awareness of a new way of thinking was enough to motivate students to experiment with and add new approaches.

Since those early years teaching the protean and boundaryless career theories, I have developed scales to measure the associated theoretical constructs with colleagues (Briscoe et al., 2006). Beyond the research gains, having such tools in the classroom helped students move beyond theory to self-awareness. However, the next step was to move beyond self-awareness to training. Presenting case studies and dissecting one's own career experience allows students to see how the concept might apply in their own lives.

Beyond the protean scale, other instruments can also be considered to provide 'static' feedback while also developing process skills. Earlier the ICCS (Arthur et al., 2008) was profiled as providing a static set of output in its feedback. That is true, but it also teaches a process skill that can be repeated and recycled for future career cycles. Another assessment that heightens self and relationships awareness is the Development Network Questionnaire (Higgins, 2004). While it profiles relationship networks and how they can provide career and psychosocial support, it also teaches students perspectives for reconsidering, reprioritizing and expanding their networks.

There are many other skills-based approaches, but those reviewed here demonstrate the nature of skills-based approaches and some of their strengths. Turning to our principles for how to educate students toward sustainable careers, we can conclude that such skills-based approaches at least have the potential to enhance their identity and self-awareness. They certainly provide passive learning, but they also offer the chance for students to learn more about how they can learn more effectively. If applied to actual past or prospective future experiences, skills development can be very effective at helping students build more sustainable careers. As implied by the examples above, skills-based approaches are amenable to developing self-directed skills and greater appreciation and utilization of developmental relationships.

Skills development can be improved by providing tools that allow students to press 'repeat' in the future and reapply those skills to new career stages and career contexts. This might simply require re-thinking our episodic approach to career development and teaching students more for the long term, beyond our short time with them.

Action Learning

Action learning can be understood as reflection upon actions designed to improve or change something where the key outputs are the solution developed for a given problem or opportunity as well as the learning *about learning* that comes from it (Revans, 1982). Action learning is very impactful in corporate environments when used with real life applications, and aided by expert facilitation and advice that optimizes reflection and learning.

In a classroom environment focused upon individual development, it is a little harder to execute action learning because career learning cycles are often longer-term affairs than a semester, and serendipity does not always occur that would correlate a relevant career learning opportunity with an academic semester. Nevertheless, short-term learning might occur that is relevant to a piece of the career puzzle that students are occupied with.

In recent years I have begun to have students attempt a focused change in the course of the classwork. It could be purely career related, or it might be related to complementary focuses such as leadership development or emotional intelligence. The student will typically be educated about a topic such as authentic leadership. Then, they will choose some related behaviours to focus upon over a period of a few weeks. A writing assignment holds them accountable for their learning and increases the likelihood of substantive reflection. For some students this can be a powerful experience that causes them to rethink assumptions about themselves and their careers.

While action learning is in some ways limited due to time constraints, its selective utilization does offer some important features that can support principles of career education seeking to increase sustainable careers. First of all, it causes students to identify, question and perhaps modify their identity and values as they modify and examine their 'theories in use' (Argyris, 1976; 1991). It represents learning both explicitly and implicitly. It is one of the few methods that actually generate new and relevant experience in class. If taught well, it is replicable by the student and certainly can help them become more self-directed. It can also be used to enhance and improve relationships. So, in summary, action learning is a very promising tool for inculcating career sustainability.

STRUCTURED INTROSPECTION

Structured introspection is a deep-level examination of personal behaviour or identity and values that is structured toward a relevant and focused learning goal. The goal can be broad (sometimes comprising subsets of goals) or narrow. In my opinion, this is a place where career development and other complementary focuses (leadership development, for example) shine.

As with many other behaviours, our career behaviour and sense-making (Weick, 1996) can become scripted, routine and thus less accessible to awareness, let alone reflection. One job of a career educator is to help students make the invisible visible, and the unappreciated appreciated. This helps them develop greater agency over their career.

While I have cited them in other sections, structured methods such as the ICCS (Arthur et al., 2008), the Developmental Network Questionnaire (Higgins, 2004), and the Career Anchors interview (Schein, 1990) certainly guide structured introspection. Other methods such as job crafting (Wrzesniewski and Dutton, 2001) and discussion of character strengths (Seligman, 2004) can do the same, but they have an added benefit of focusing the student upon positives in their work and in themselves.

A timeline exercise in which the student points to important events, experiences, transitions, roles and relationships across the life-span can be very powerful. I usually practise with my class on a surrogate career via a case study before letting students start on their own. I find that while students sometimes need help generating the events on their timeline, they often need a second set of eyes to help them assign meaning to the points identified in the timeline. Making meaning is critical in making the timeline exercise relevant. Because some issues have been buried or taken for granted, their meaning may have been as well. Finally, in the timeline or similar exercises, it is also critical that the student learn to translate the insight they have earned into an action plan.

Structured introspection has several advantages when considering our principles supporting the education of a sustainable career. It is impressively tied to identity and values. It is very powerful. For this reason, ethical and professional considerations are needed on the part of the teacher. In one study in which colleagues and I (Briscoe et al., 2014) were researching changes in mood from before and after a structured introspection exercise that used authentic leadership and timelines, we found that both positive and negative moods rose. This is because accurate examination of the past is not all carefree or cathartic; it can bring up difficult memories or associations.

With the above in mind, it is critical to help the student understand the limits of career development and perhaps the boundaries. Not being a trained therapist, I am clear that while the exercises we do may be therapeutic, I am not trained to help the students in that manner, nor is it my role in the class. Students need to be encouraged to see their own adaptability skills being developed in difficult situations. Even the most difficult stories demonstrate how students in fact coped and succeeded. Some students are quite reluctant to see the good in themselves, and helping them to do so is a very helpful role the teacher can play. It also helps the students see themselves more accurately, which is of course good 'medicine' for effective career development.

Beyond identity and values, structured introspection is a strong tool for teaching learning and meta-learning. Use this tool in a way that will let the students use the process again in the future so as to be replicable. Structured introspection involves experience in all three time directions. . .past, present and future (at least anticipatory experience in the future). It can help the student more deeply appreciate relationships, and the relationship with the teacher and other students can teach healthy helping relationship skills.

Peer Coaching

Peer Coaching involves the use of students as coaches to one another around learning and developmental goals. Peer coaching does not exist in a vacuum, only in relation to the skill being targeted. In that sense I believe that peer coaching can be useful, no matter which of the methods covered in this chapter is used in career education.

One thing peer coaching does, if introduced correctly, is to educate the student on the proper role and boundaries involved in both giving and receiving feedback. Thus, as the student gives feedback, they simultaneously prepare to receive their own. This mutual role-playing is highly effective and primes the student for greater development. Peer coaching also introduces vulnerability and intimacy. Boundaries of functionality and relevance temper vulnerability and intimacy, but vulnerability can open up a student to stronger learning, and intimacy can result in greater levels of trust and support.

Parker et al. (2008) outline five critical qualities for successful career coaching: (1) equal status of partners; (2) focus on personal and professional development of both peers; (3) a focus upon real-life career situations in the peer-coaching; (4) an emphasis upon process as well as content to emphasize skill development; and finally (5) the peer coaching accelerates peer learning. Such ground rules and skills education must be given verbally but, more importantly, demonstrated behaviourally by the teacher.

Peer coaching is a powerful classroom tool for reinforcing all of the principles outlined earlier in the chapter to help educate students toward sustainable careers. Proper practice of peer coaching helps the student reflect upon their own identity and values. If using the guidelines outlined by Parker et al. (2008) in the paragraph above, peer coaching certainly emphasizes learning as well as learning to learn. In addition, real experience is the key subject of peer coaching in career development. Relationships are utilized perhaps to peak potential (for a classroom context) with peer coaching. If skills are made explicit and correctly taught and reinforced, peer coaching is a replicable skill that can be used to drive a self-directed career.

CONCLUSION

At the time of this writing the world was mesmerized about the loss of Malaysian Airlines Flight MH370, which departed from its flight plan for unknown reasons. There was a tremendous focus upon finding the 'black box' which would hopefully provide details of the final moments of the flight. A downside to the black box (at least circa 2014) is that it has limited recall and may not provide information on the events that led to the change of course well before the actual crash of the plane.

Being a professor with careers on his mind and maybe not enough else (!), my mind focused upon how career reflection can sometimes be like a black box. When a career problem presents itself, we may look at the current problems and options in an ephemeral time frame, not looking far enough back to find the cause of the current issues, nor perhaps forward to see whether similar problems can be avoided in the future.

To help ourselves and our students craft sustainable careers, we need to take the long view. In terms of identity, values, skills, experience, history and behaviours, we need to help students know themselves present and past, increase their level of skill in identifying options in their environment and responding to them, and creating ongoing individual capacity to respond to both predictable as well as unknown developments in the future.

I believe that the tools we need are already in our possession, but we must treat them and our students less in a 'black box' fashion and more as a tool kit that can be carried light and far, that can be used and re-used by the educated student practitioner. Perhaps the metaphor of a hunter or explorer who lives off the land is more appropriate in considering which tools might be 'given' to our students, and how such tools can be crafted for economy and durability. What is the compass? Does the student need to play defence and offence or neither (are they a hunter, an explorer, or something entirely different? Do they need maps, or mapmaking skills? Can they live off the land if they need to? Have we given them tools that they will be able to carry and use in the career commons as well as in the career wilderness?

The more I reflect upon the teaching of career development and sustainable careers, the more I am reminded of why I became interested in careers as a teaching and scholarly topic in the first place. Careers represent a key, if not *the* key intersection of life's priorities and are repositories of meaning, competence and identity. They serve as streams throughout life's narratives and, while changing, remain constant in one sense. They survive demotions, course corrections, child-rearing, jet-setting, divorce, calamity and even success. As teachers trying to increase career sustainability for our students, we are in a privileged position that I know we don't take lightly, and that I hope we can steadily improve through our own individual and shared career development and dialogue.

REFERENCES

Argyris, C. (1976), 'Single-loop and double-loop models in research on decision making', *Administrative Science Quarterly*, **21**(3), 363–75.

Argyris, C. (1991), 'Teaching smart people how to learn', *Harvard Business Review*, **69**(3), 99–109.

Arthur, M.B., P.H. Claman and R.J. DeFillippi (1995), 'Intelligent enterprise, intelligent careers', *The Academy of Management Executive*, **9**(4), 7–20.

Arthur, M.B., R.J. DeFillippi and V.J. Lindsay (2008), 'On being a knowledge worker', *Organizational Dynamics*, **37**(4), 365–77.
Barris, C. (2010), *Della: A Memoir of My Daughter*, New York: Simon and Schuster.
Bennis, W. (1994), *On Becoming a Leader*, Reading, MA: Perseus.
Briscoe, J.P. (2013), 'The expression and suppression of personal values in organizational contexts', Presentation at the Academy of Management annual meeting, Orlando, Florida, 13 August.
Briscoe, J.P. and D.T. Hall (1999), 'Grooming and picking leaders using competency frameworks: Do they work?', *Organizational Dynamics*, Autumn, pp. 37–52.
Briscoe, J.P. and D.T. Hall (2006), 'The interplay of protean and boundaryless careers: Combinations and implications', *Journal of Vocational Behavior*, **69**(1), 4–18.
Briscoe, J.P. and D.T. Hall (2009), 'Toward a self-sustaining career: Being and becoming protean through career learning', paper presented at the 2009 annual meeting of the Academy of Management, Chicago, IL, 10 August.
Briscoe, J.P., D.T. Hall and R.L. Frautschy DeMuth (2006), 'Protean and boundaryless careers: An empirical examination', *Journal of Vocational Behavior*, **69**(1), 30–47.
Briscoe, J.P., L.E. Waters and J. Unite (2014), 'Building positive and authentic leaders: An action-oriented approach with executives in training', Working paper, Department of Management, Northern Illinois University, DeKalb, IL.
Briscoe, J.P., K. Chudzikowski, B. Demel, W. Mayrhofer and J. Unite (2012), 'The 5C project: Our story and our research', in J.P. Briscoe, D.T. Hall and W. Mayrhofer (eds), *Careers Around the World: Individual and Contextual Perspectives*, New York: Routledge, pp. 39–55.
Briscoe, J.P., J. Unite, K. Chudzikowski, O. Colorado, B. Demel, D.T. Hall, M. Las Heras, W. Mayrhofer, B.B. Milikic, E. Ogliastri, M. Taniguchi, S. Yan and J. Zikic (2009), 'Orientations to career transitions: A cross-cultural framework for understanding their impact', paper presented at the annual conference of the European Group for Organization Studies, Barcelona, Spain, 2–4 July.
Burns, J.M. (1978), *Leadership*, New York: Harper & Row.
Button, S.B., J.E. Mathieu and D.M. Zajac (1996), 'Goal orientation in organizational research: A conceptual and empirical approach', *Organizational Behavior and Human Decision Processes*, **67**, 26–48.
Campbell, D.P. (1995), 'The Campbell Interest and Skill Survey (CISS): A product of ninety years of psychometric evolution', *Journal of Career Assessment*, **3**(4), 391–410.
Covey, S. (1989), *The Seven Habits of Highly Effective People*, New York: Simon & Schuster.
Deci, E.L., R.M. Ryan and R. Koestner (1999), 'A meta-analytic review of experiments examining the effects of extrinsic rewards on intrinsic motivation', *Psychological Bulletin*, **125**, 627–68.
DeFillippi, R.J. and M.B. Arthur (1994), 'The boundaryless career: A competency-based perspective', *Journal of Organizational Behavior*, **15**(4), 307–24.
Derr, C.B. and A. Laurent (1987), 'The internal and external careers: A theoretical and cross-cultural perspective', Working paper, European Institute of Business Administration.
Erikson, E.H. (1980), *Identity and the Life Cycle*, New York: W.W. Norton.
Hall, D.T. (1976), *Careers in Organizations*, Glenview, IL: Scott, Foresman.
Hall, D.T. (1986), 'Breaking career routines: Midcareer choice and identity development', in D.T. Hall and Associates, *Career Development in Organizations*, San Francisco, CA: Jossey-Bass, pp. 120–59.
Hall, D.T. (1993), 'The new "career contract": Wrong on both counts?', Technical Report, Boston: Boston University School of Management, Executive Development Roundtable.
Hall, D.T. (2002), *Protean Careers In and Out of Organizations*, Thousand Oaks, CA: Sage Publications.
Hall, D.T. and D.E. Chandler (2005), 'Psychological success: When the career is a calling', *Journal of Organizational Behavior*, **26**(2), 155–76.
Hall, D.T. and P.H. Mirvis (1994), 'Careers as lifelong learning', in A. Howard (ed.), *The Changing Nature of Work*, San Francisco, CA: Jossey-Bass.
Hall, D.T., J.P. Briscoe and K.E. Kram (1997), 'Identity, values and learning in the protean career', in C.L. Cooper and S.E. Jackson (eds), *Creating Tomorrow's Organizations*, London: John Wiley & Sons, pp. 321–35.
Higgins, M.C. (2004), 'Developmental network questionnaire (9-404-105)', Boston, MA: Harvard Business School Publishing.
Holland, J.L. (1997), *Making Vocational Choices: A Theory of Vocational Personalities and Work Environments* (3rd edn), Englewood Cliffs, NJ: Prentice Hall.
Kahn, W.A. (1996), 'Secure base relationships at work', in D.T. Hall (ed.), *The Career is Dead – Long Live the Career: A Relational Approach to Careers*, San Francisco, CA: Jossey-Bass, pp. 158–79.
Katz, D. and R.L. Kahn (1978), *The Social Psychology of Organizations* (2nd edn), New York: Wiley.
Kegan, R. (1994), *In Over Our Heads: The Mental Demands of Modern Life*, Cambridge, MA: Harvard University Press.
Mainiero, L.A. and S.E. Sullivan (2005), 'Kaleidoscope careers: An alternate explanation for the "opt-out" revolution', *The Academy of Management Executive*, **19**(1), 106–23.

Parker, P., D.T. Hall and K.E. Kram (2008), 'Peer coaching: A relational process for accelerating career learning', *Academy of Management Learning & Education*, **7**(4), 487–503.
Pearlman, J. (2004), 'The end game. Forget "the gong show", "the newlywed game", and all the rest. Chuck Barris just wants to make peace with his daughter's memory', Tribune Newspapers: Newsday, 31 May, available at http://articles.chicagotribune.com/2004-05-31/features/0405310115_1_gong-show-newlywed-game-dating-game.
Revans, R.W. (1982), *The Origin and Growth of Action Learning*, Brickley, UK: Chartwell-Bratt.
Rokeach, M. (1973), *The Nature of Human Values* (Vol. 438), New York: Free Press.
Schein, E.H. (1990), *Career Anchors: Discovering Your Real Values*, San Diego, CA: University Associates.
Schein, E.H. (1996), 'Career anchors revisited: Implications for career development in the 21st century', *The Academy of Management Executive*, **10**(4), 80–88.
Seligman, M.E. (2004), *Character Strengths and Virtues: A Handbook and Classification*, New York: Oxford University Press.
Seltzer, J. and B.M. Bass (1990), 'Transformational leadership: Beyond initiation and consideration', *Journal of Management*, **16**(4), 693–703.
Super, D.E. (1957), *The Psychology of Careers*, New York: Harper & Row.
Super, D.E., M.L. Savickas and C.M. Super (1996), 'The life-span, life-space approach to careers', in D. Brown, L. Brooks et al. (eds), *Career Choice and Development* (3rd edn), San Francisco, CA: Jossey-Bass, pp. 121–78.
Walumbwa, F.O., B.J. Avolio, W.L. Gardner, T.S. Wernsing and S.J. Peterson (2008), 'Authentic leadership: Development and validation of a theory-based measure', *Journal of Management*, **34**(1), 89–126.
Waters, L.E., J.P. Briscoe, D.T. Hall and L. Wang (2014), 'Protean career attitudes during unemployment and reemployment: A longitudinal perspective', *Journal of Vocational Behavior*, **84**(3), 405–19.
Weick, Karl E. (1996), 'Enactment and the boundaryless career: Organizing as we work', in Michael B. Arthur and Denise M. Rousseau (eds), *The Boundaryless Career: A New Employment Principle for a New Organizational Era*, New York: Oxford University Press.
Wrzesniewski, A. and J.E. Dutton (2001), 'Crafting a job: Revisioning employees as active crafters of their work', *Academy of Management Review*, **26**(2), 179–201.

28 Sustainable careers then and now[1]

Barbara S. Lawrence, Douglas T. Hall and Michael B. Arthur

Sustainable careers, those focusing on individuals' continuing employability in jobs that facilitate their personal development over time, have been the underlying ideology of careers research for many years. Certainly it was a concern of ours 25 years ago when we edited the *Handbook of Career Theory* (Arthur et al., 1989). However, until now, this philosophy has been largely implicit. The world of work has changed a good bit since 1989. Career opportunities and limitations have transformed dramatically and these changes support the need for making this philosophy explicit.

We live in a global knowledge economy: many products and services are sourced by an international workforce and aimed at global rather than national markets. In 1989, the Internet was in embryonic form and only available to a small group of academic researchers. It now conveys a major portion of all information available and connects people both inside and across countries. Economic booms and busts have become connected as well, so it matters if China devalues the yen or the countries in the European Union consider eliminating the euro. All of this has had an inevitable effect on the way people experience work over their lives. The chaotic nature of and interdependence between economic environments have made sustainable careers an increasingly salient concern for individuals and organizations.

Our goal in this chapter is not to provide any conclusions about sustainable careers but rather to explore some personal reflections. As a point of departure, we consider sustainable careers as including two components: employability and workability (De Vos and De Prins, 2014; De Vos and Gielens, 2014). Employability is the extent to which workers in any society have the opportunity to be employed, in both the short and the long term (Forrier and Sels, 2003, p. 642).[2] Workability is the extent to which jobs represent reasonable, long-term expectations from employees, without overambitious challenges in a job today that result in burnout tomorrow (De Vos and Gielens, 2014, p. 14). This long-term perspective presents substantial challenges. Sustainable careers require facilitating career growth and security for all workers, promoting the concept of individual career ownership throughout the workforce and pursuing a proactive, systemic approach to careers rather than capitulating to short-term challenges (De Vos and Gielens, 2014, pp. 14–15; Van der Heijden and De Vos, Chapter 1, this volume).

Each of us has engaged with these challenges through largely separate journeys over the last 25 years. To help arrive at our thoughts about sustainable careers we begin with how careers were understood theoretically before 1989, why we embarked on the journey that led to the *Handbook of Career Theory* and what has happened since. We follow with brief summaries of the work each of us pursued after the *Handbook*'s publication. Next, we offer our joint reflection on how our thoughts relate to sustainable careers. We conclude with some pointers for further research.

CAREER RESEARCH FROM 1950 TO TODAY

There are several excellent histories of careers research (for example, Moore et al., 2007; Sullivan and Baruch, 2009; Sullivan and Crocitto, 2007) that we will not repeat here. The following provides a selective overview of the conceptual developments that led to our own work on the *Handbook* and afterwards.

Looking backward, we see career theory and research as evolving during three time periods divided roughly as: 1950–1970 in which the focus was individuals *or* organizations *or* occupations;[3] 1970–1989 with a focus on individuals *within* organizations and occupations, and 1989 to the present, which expanded to focus on individuals *within, outside and across* organizations and occupations. Adding sustainable careers to this mix is defining a fourth stage in which the focus is on self-actualizing careers, careers that allow individuals to realize their full potential, and access to the social contexts which facilitate that realization.[4] It also includes the organizational side of the equation. What kinds of requirements do such careers place on organizations and society and to what extent can scenarios that enable both individual workers and organizations be designed? In this fourth stage, we see careers as emerging into a territory that more explicitly includes an ideological component: the more sustainable the career, the more self-actualized are individuals' experiences of them and the more effective individuals become in contributing to organizational performance. We view this development with enthusiasm and a sense of optimism towards the future of the field.

INDIVIDUALS *OR* ORGANIZATIONS *OR* OCCUPATIONS (1950–1970)

The Human Relations school of management inquiry, generally attributed to Roethlisberger and Dickson (1939), was the first to recognize that the best interests of organizations were wisely served by accommodating and tapping the best interests of employees. However, early careers research generally focused on either individuals and their careers or on the organizations and occupations in which they worked. In 1970, careers research in the United States and much of the rest of the world was weaning itself off post-WWII assumptions. William Whyte's (1956) *Organization Man* worked in and was committed to the requirements of large, hierarchical organizations. And although these organizations exhibited considerable diversity, including R&D laboratories, churches, aerospace firms and government agencies, employees operated with a common understanding of the expected relationship between individuals and the organizations in which they worked. As Whyte (pp. 3–4) noted:

> They are all, as they so often put it, in the same boat. Listen to them talk to each other over the front lawns of their suburbia and you cannot help but be struck by how well they grasp the common denominators which bind them. Whatever the differences in their organization ties, it is the common problems of collective work that dominate their attention.

Focus on Individuals' Careers

Early research on careers reflected these common problems. With life-time employment, large organizations could afford to study their human resources: what kinds of employees were most likely to be successful? What skills, knowledge and abilities were required for each job? In 1956, Douglas Bray (Bray et al., 1974) started what became a landmark, longitudinal study of management careers at AT&T.[5] The idea was to examine the nature versus nurture explanations for good managers (Howard and Bray, 1988, p. x in preface). One perspective held that good managers could be identified at hiring using their individual characteristics, whose later development was accomplished by 'maturing'. The other perspective maintained that good managers could develop through planned experiences, such as job rotation or training. The answer that both are important seems obvious today, but at the time, the idea that managers could be developed was rather new. The idea behind this work was to maximize the value of employees to their employers.

Another line of research focused on individuals and their initial choice of career. The idea was that individuals should choose careers in which their likes and dislikes of various kinds of work matched existing profiles of people in those occupations. Several vocational choice tests emerged of which the two oldest and most well known are the Strong Vocational Interest Inventory (Strong, 1926; 1927) and the Kuder Preference Record (Kuder, 1939). Given life-time employment, individuals' work was assumed to remain constant over time. If people switched jobs, it usually meant a change in position or organization, for instance, from a line to staff job, rather than a change in work, such as from a public school teacher to a truck driver. Thus, there was little interest in the time dimension of careers except for an acceptance that some people got promoted faster, and maybe worked the system better, than others.

Focus on Organizations or Occupations as Careers

Sociologists were also studying careers (for example, Caplow, 1953; Caplow and McGee, 1958) but using a different conceptual lens. Instead of focusing on individuals, they focused on the work environments in which individuals worked: their occupations and institutions. Much of this work focused on social stratification and its consequences, but one particular branch of sociology, the so-called 'Chicago School', emphasized the interplay between workers and their environments (Goffman, 1961; Hughes, 1958; 1962). Everett Hughes and colleagues such as Howard Becker and Anselm Strauss were looking at the effects of social context, such as socialization into the medical profession or becoming 'taxi dancers' – women paid to dance with men in twentieth-century dance halls – where role perceptions and identities developed over time (Becker, 1961; Cressey, 1932; Strauss, 1962). For instance, Becker's *Art Worlds* (Becker, 1982; 2008) examined the interstitial community of artists, suppliers, dealers and buyers that created the social context in which art was produced. This kind of work foreshadows current research, for instance, on institutional rules that link entrepreneurial careers in the US film industry (Jones, 2001).[6]

These research streams did not focus on sustainable careers. One prescribed individuals' careers as requiring fit with the organization, another that individuals' interests should fit those of others currently holding the occupation and the third focusing on the description and implications of occupational contexts. Some scholars did study topics that are central to sustainable careers, such as integrating effective organizational design with jobs fostering workers' psychological health (Argyris, 1964) and work and family issues (Bailyn, 1970; Dyer, 1955; Rapoport and Rapoport, 1965). Yet, for the most part, these efforts were not coordinated.

INDIVIDUALS *WITHIN* ORGANIZATIONS OR OCCUPATIONS (1970–1989)

Starting in the mid-1970s, a small group of scholars, initially working from US institutions at Boston University, Brigham Young University, Harvard Business School, Massachusetts Institute of Technology, the Naval Postgraduate School and the University of Southern California, coalesced around a new vision for career research. It represented a conceptual shift from careers as individual experiences that remained relatively constant to careers as individual experiences over time in which workers were explicitly situated within and influenced by the organizations in which they worked (Derr and Schein, 1978; Hall and Lerner, 1980). As noted by Schein: '(n)either organizational effectiveness nor individual satisfaction can be achieved unless there is a better matching of what the organization needs and what the individuals who spend their working lives in those organizations need' (1978, p. 243). This situated approach was more closely associated with sustainable careers. It established the deep connection between individual careers and social context as the phenomenon of interest.

There was in addition a shared sense that studying careers didn't fit solely in any of its traditional disciplines: vocational psychology (Super, 1957), career development (Osipow, 1968) or sociology (Hughes, 1958). The phenomenon seemed more complex than the explanations. With this in mind, the group started meeting semi-annually to explore a more interdisciplinary approach. Three landmark books were published by members of this group between 1976 and 1978: *Careers in Organizations* (Hall, 1976), *Organizational Careers: Some New Perspectives* (Van Maanen, 1977), and *Career Dynamics: Matching Individual and Organizational Needs* (Schein, 1978). The field had grown from studying either individuals in organizations *or* the occupations in which they worked, to individuals working *within* organizations or occupations.

Recognizing that it was important to disseminate these ideas through an open discussion within the academic community, the group reorganized and expanded in the summer of 1978 as the 'Careers Interest Group', a spinoff of the Organization Behavior Division of the Academy of Management. This interest group provided the meeting ground in which the three of us began working together.

We wanted to contribute to the momentum established by the 1970s and 1980s group and started the *Handbook of Career Theory* with two goals in mind. One was to review the historical underpinnings of career theory and the other was to add a more explicit interdisciplinary agenda to career research. For Part I, we invited a group of well-known scholars to summarize the current 'state of the art' in extant career-related disciplines. The flow of these nine chapters was meant to be evolutionary in that they were arranged chronologically, from psychology with person-occupation matching, sociology with careers as social roles, and then, what was more recent at the time, work on adult development with organizational and minority careers.

For Part II, the emerging perspective on careers meant that all work-related research was relevant. We wanted the *Handbook* to explore this territory because there was little work that focused across disciplines or levels of analysis. As we were not ourselves experts in many of these fields, we invited prominent scholars from other fields to apply their perspectives to careers and address a 'what if?' What kind of theory might we generate if we examined careers from the perspective of someone whose research involved labor–management relations, blue-collar workers or production and manufacturing? What if we applied ideas from anthropology about rites of passage? What if we examined careers from a political science perspective?

We used two attributes to define the terrain: the discipline in which the work was done and the level of analysis at which the work was conducted. These attributes included a large number of disciplines. A short list includes psychology, social psychology, sociology, anthropology, political science, strategy and economics. The levels of analysis also occupy a vast space, including individuals, mentors and mentees, couples, families, social networks, organizations, occupations, cultures, internal labor markets, industries, nations and probably others we didn't consider. The book concluded with three chapters written by scholars charged to encourage a dialogue across the past and future-looking perspectives on career theory.

INDIVIDUALS *WITHIN*, *INSIDE* AND *OUTSIDE* OF ORGANIZATIONS AND OCCUPATIONS (1990 TO PRESENT)

When we look back, we see the *Handbook* as another transition point, a first step in moving forward from the 1970s' and 1980s' work on individuals *within* organizations to the 1990s' work on individuals *within*, *inside* and *outside* of organizations and occupations (for example, Arthur and Rousseau, 1996). The book made several contributions to this transition. One was providing an enduring definition of career: 'The evolving sequence of individuals' work experiences over time' (Arthur et al., 1989, p. 8). We did not know what the future would bring, but moving forward required a definition with sufficient breadth to remain inclusive of unexpected metamorphoses in the work environment.

This definition, which focuses on individuals who work in any context, allows the social and economic conditions within which they work to change. It provides an umbrella for topics such as working identity (Ibarra, 1999; 2003), early career underemployment (Verbruggen et al., 2014), contingent workers (Barley and Kunda, 2005; Liden et al., 2003), human resource strategy and labor markets (Cappelli, 1999; 2008) as well as mechanisms that influence how careers are experienced, such as reference groups (Grote and Hall, 2013; Lawrence, 2006), structural holes (Burt, 1992), and resources and signaling (Castilla et al., 2013). In other words, independent of socio-economic, historical and technological change, this definition encompasses sustainable careers now and, to the extent possible, the future.

Another contribution was legitimizing the basic assumption established by scholars in the 1970s and 1980s that the phenomenon of interest is careers, independent of the scholar's academic background and that, as a result, career theory and research requires an interdisciplinary perspective. This does not mean that every study needs to be interdisciplinary: sometimes it is even difficult to decide what interdisciplinary means. Rather, it means that each should acknowledge its contribution to and place within this broad picture of the phenomenon. This is in keeping with viewing sustainable careers as a desirable perspective because it means our research requires that the needs of both individuals and organizations be considered. Most studies will not include both, but when there is only explicit empirical focus on one, we can still look for explicit discussion of the other.

In 2014, the literature suggests that all this activity since the 1970s has created a vibrant community. Yet many careers scholars feel careers research has not accomplished its interdisciplinary promise. There are good arguments on both sides surrounding the question of specialization versus generalizability. For this discussion, we define careers research loosely as research authored or inspired by scholars in the broader careers community identifiable by members' attachments to the Academy of Management (AoM), the European Group on Organization Studies (EGOS) or both.

Specialization

On the specialization side, scholars have been successful in creating a new, specialized field related to both organizational behavior and theory. While we were working on the book and after its publication, many developments helped consolidate and support these nascent ideas. The Careers Interest Group of the Academy of Management became a formal Division, and the growth in careers scholarship was underway. This burgeoning development produced a concurrent expansion in the breadth of the dialog. Examples include *The Boundaryless Career* (Arthur and Rousseau, 1996), the *Handbook of Career Studies* (Gunz and Peiperl, 2007), *The Psychology of Working: A New Perspective for Career Development, Counseling and Public Policy* (Blustein, 2006) and this volume.

As a quick check on the success of specialization, we examined articles with the word 'career' in their title, comparing those published in 1989 with those published in 2013.[7] We offer the following observations.[8]

First, interest in careers research seems to have increased dramatically. In 1989 there were 462 articles published with the word 'career' in their title. In 2013, that number increased by 250 percent to 1137. International interest has also grown dramatically. In 1989, the number of countries represented by authors of career articles was 23. In 2013, that number increased by 320 percent to 74. The list now includes a diverse set of countries including China, Uganda, Venezuela, Malta, Slovenia, Russia and Saudi Arabia. Moreover, the author list has become more diffuse by country. The proportion of articles whose authors come from the United States has declined from 52.3 percent in 1989 to 40.1 percent in 2013, which is a positive development because it indicates increasing international interest in the topic.

Second, the field has benefited from the growth of the Internet and its effect on global communication. As noted earlier, the Internet was nascent in 1989. In 2015, we take it for granted, with its connecting blogs and URLs used for discussion and debate, from professional association discussion boards to listservs devoted to specific topics, to organized social media such as Facebook, LinkedIn, and ResearchGate. In 2001 scholars convened the first careers track at the EGOS meeting. Careers scholars established and have maintained a regular presence at this conference since that time. Research connections between scholars in the United States and scholars from other countries have burgeoned.

Generalizability

On concerns for generalizability, there is less evidence of success. Most careers research is not published in mainstream organizational journals, such as the *Academy of Management Journal*, *Organization Science* and *Administrative Science Quarterly*. This means that it does not receive the same level of attention from the organizational behavior and organizational theory community as does work from other fields. Meanwhile, although this is a broad-brush assessment, much career-related research that has been published in these journals does not reference authors who are members of the careers community. Nor does the careers community reciprocate, although again, this is a broad-brush assessment. As noted by Jones and Dunn (2007, p. 437), 'Careers scholars . . . are yet to claim their role as a conceptual bridge and intellectual anchor' to organization studies.

In addition, much careers research remains focused on the psychological and vocational education components of careers. Using the same data as above, in 1989, 39.5 percent of all articles with 'career' in the title were classified as being published in psychology or educational research journals. In 2013, that proportion did not change, with 39.6 percent of all careers articles published in the two categories. So the ratio of psychological research to research from other disciplines remains constant. This precipitates two kinds of problems. One concerns the overall balance of disciplinary contributions to careers research, as psychological views are so dominant. The other concerns the way careers research is viewed by outside scholars, who may well feel excluded from the conversation.

IN WHAT DIRECTION DID THE EDITORS GO?

In each of our own lives, careers remain a central interest. However, while we all study careers, our work reflects the limitations above. We have focused on very different aspects of the subject. Michael has focused on career opportunities extending beyond organizational boundaries: how they help us view careers that are emerging and changing and how individuals can successfully approach these opportunities with agency. Tim has focused on protean careers, examining how people can maintain work lives that allow them to develop themselves at the same time as they respond to the new, increasingly chaotic pressures imposed by work environments. Barbara has focused on how social contexts constrain and facilitate individual development: how career-related norms emerge and how individuals acquire the reference groups through which they gather information and construe career-related meaning. Writing this chapter gave us the opportunity to think back and share our mostly separate journeys, and to reflect on their meaning. It also provided an opportunity to consider the strengths and weaknesses of specialization and generalizability.

Michael's Journey

After completing the *Handbook of Career Theory* (1989) Michael conducted an international study of human resource management in small to medium enterprises (SMEs). In investigating work on Japan, he quickly realized that the Japanese managerial 'salaryman' stereotype, popularized in Western management thought, applied to only a small proportion of the population. The average employment period for the supposedly privileged Japanese male worker was, in fact, only eight years. Similar or lower average employment rates applied in other countries. Large organizations commanded a limited and declining proportion of overall employment. What did this mean for assumptions about careers?

He went back to the *Handbook of Career Theory* (Arthur et al., 1989) and found inspiration in two chapters that spoke to the above question. In one, Gene Dalton spoke persuasively about organizations being dangerous, and particularly so when 'we expect things from [them] that they cannot deliver.' He went on:

> Organizations are dangerous because too often we have organized the jobs in them according to old models of efficiency without taking into account human needs. They are dangerous when we allow ourselves to think that some specialized knowledge or past achievement will make us secure; technology and organizational needs shift so rapidly that it is only our ability to learn and adapt that prepares us for the future (Dalton, 1989, p. 107).

In another chapter, Karl Weick and Lisa Berlinger examined the prospects for careers in 'self-designing' – that is, highly innovative – organizations. They concluded:

> To prepare oneself for a lifetime of learning and exploration is to become attached to processes rather than structures. Processes are harder to grasp, harder to count, harder to ascend, harder to change and harder to accumulate. Since careers are so often defined as tangible possessions and accomplishments, a shift toward self-designing careers is neither easy nor are there many models for how to do it (Weick and Berlinger, 1989, p. 326).

Thus, early on, Michael was concerned about how individuals could maintain sustainable careers in this dangerous environment. He and his colleague Robert DeFillippi were already thinking about how a stronger focus on interpersonal networking might further our understanding of careers when the theme for the 1993 Academy of Management meeting was announced: 'The Boundaryless Organization', a term popularized by Jack Welch, at that time CEO of General Electric. The two colleagues saw an opportunity and convened a small group to hold a symposium on 'boundaryless careers'. Extending the definition of career cited above, they defined boundaryless careers as 'sequences of work opportunities that go beyond the boundaries of any single organization.' (DeFillippi and Arthur, 1994, p. 307). However, they left room for other contributors to bring their own definitions.

Robert and Michael's own contribution to the symposium was to develop a view of career development based on three 'ways of knowing' (DeFillippi and Arthur, 1994) that later became known as the Intelligent Career Framework (Arthur et al., 1995). Robert led the way in developing the framework and in applying it to our understanding of project-based organizing (DeFillippi and Arthur, 1998; DeFillippi et al., 2006). Michael maintained a career perspective and developed the Intelligent Career Card Sort career exploration exercise with Polly Parker (Parker and Arthur, 2000) and joined a project to study patterns of new careers in a stratified sample of New Zealand workers (Arthur et al., 1999).

Michael then became interested in the interdependence between the subjective and objective sides of the career (Arthur et al., 2005), envisioning 'new directions' for boundaryless careers research (Tams and Arthur, 2010) and in arguing the advantages of an interdisciplinary approach to careers (Arthur, 2008; Khapova and Arthur, 2011). Most recently (Arthur, 2014), he has tied the strength of an interdisciplinary approach back to earlier work on careers at MIT in the 1970s, work that had a profound influence on the *Handbook of Career Theory*. He remains committed to overlapping agendas of helping people claim greater ownership of their (sustainable) careers, and promoting an interdisciplinary approach across both authorship and review phases of journal publishing.

Tim's Journey

Tim's work since the *Handbook of Career Theory* (Arthur et al., 1989) unfolded during the end of an era of downsizing and slow growth. In work organizations, delayering, successive bouts of Total Quality Management (TQM) and a focus on efficiency resulted in career plateauing for many employees. At the same time, the baby boom generation in the United States, born between 1946 and 1964, was entering midlife and mid-career. This entitled generation was expecting to experience both objective and psychological success in their careers. Unfortunately, they reached this career stage at exactly the wrong time. It was not a good time for career development as the standard career model was no longer sustainable (Hall, 1996).

Tim's concern was that if people cannot experience sustainable careers in the old ways, what new ways would facilitate these opportunities? Thus, he focused on alternatives to promotion as strategies for career growth. He had already edited a book in 1986 called *Career Development in Organizations* (Hall, 1986a), which explored the state-of-the-art of organizational career development programs. This book was part of the Society for Industrial and Organizational Psychology's (SIOP) 'New Frontiers' series and it was the top-selling volume in the series at the time, reflecting interest in the topic. In retrospect, though, that time was the beginning of the end of traditional career programs based upon advancement and the single-organization career.

Tim then turned to the many middle-career issues that resulted from the baby boom's demographic effects on careers. He had written a chapter on identity change and midcareer development (Hall, 1986b) that presented a recursive model showing how people develop routines in the early part of their careers that tend to create momentum and resistance to change. However, under certain conditions a person might experience a trigger event that precipitates the beginning of movement. The person might experiment with some new behavior, and it might be satisfying, leading to increased satisfaction, self-esteem and work involvement. These positive outcomes could feed back and positively affect the person's career goals, which in turn might produce more significant career and identity change. This theoretical model has not been tested, but Tim and his colleagues are planning studies on the topic.

In the 1990s Tim's work focused on leaders' careers, examining leadership succession, leader development, and organizational leadership programs. Most leadership writing does not consider leaders' personal development: they are a disadvantaged group in that sense. So he applied career theory to this group. The 'old contract' still applies to them.

Here in the 2000s, people seem to have lost sight of the whole person in organizational life. As a result, Tim has turned his thinking to the subjective career, work–life balance and pursuing individual career aspirations. He explored these ideas in his book, *Careers In and Out of Organizations* (Hall, 2002) and is currently delving deeper into issues of personal meaning, authenticity and identity. He is also exploring the role of national context, for example, with the 5C project, which is examining universal and country-specific factors, identifying global variations in the meaning of career and career success (Briscoe et al., 2012).

There are several recurring themes in Tim's work. The first is defining careers as a series of work-related experiences over the span of the person's life, which entails continuous learning and evolution. The second is examining the meta-competencies that keep the person learning and maintain his or her employability, identity and adaptability. The third is maintaining a focus on career development and success as activities that require joint pursuit by individuals and organizations. His attention to the current career issues facing individuals runs through all of these. He feels that at this point in the evolution of careers research we need more context-specific studies of careers; for example, more studies of specific occupations and types of work. We need to revisit the Chicago School and researchers such as Hughes, Becker and Strauss.

Barbara's Journey

Barbara's perspective on sustainable careers has always focused on how social and demographic structures influence career outcomes (Lawrence and Tolbert, 2007). These structures create boundaries that circumscribe the information individuals acquire and how they use it to interpret their careers. Interviewees kept telling her they made career decisions because '*they*', some abstractly defined category of others, would approve or disapprove of their choices (Lawrence, 2011). *They* was apparently a significant reference group: the ground from which people created what became figural at work. It created well-recognized opportunities but also insidious, unseen limitations. Perceptions of these referents were exerting significant impact on individuals' career outcomes (Lawrence, 2006).

Because this territory falls between the typical boundaries of individuals and organizations, capturing it involved seemingly unrelated work on age norms, career and organizational timetables, organizational demography, organizational fault lines and organizational reference groups. Integrating interview, survey and demographic data facilitated comparisons between individuals' perceptions and organizational reality. To what extent were individuals' perceptions accurate? A key difference between this work and other approaches is that the latter tend to examine what is common among individuals' career interpretations. For instance, Duberly et al. (2006) identify four career scripts that scientists draw on to account for career-related behaviors: organizational careerist, impassioned scientist, strategic opportunist and balance seeker. Instead, Barbara asks why many individuals who observe such scripts see them so differently.

Initially, her work focused on career timetables (Lawrence, 1984; 1988; 1990). People classified themselves as ahead-of-schedule, on-schedule or behind-schedule in their careers. It became clear that they created such norms even when, in reality, there were none. For instance, people in one organization observed that mid-level careers followed an age progression, with lower levels having younger managers than higher levels, even when actual organizational data showed no age differences (Lawrence, 1990). Yet these perceptions seemed to influence career satisfaction and performance.

The next question was, if perceptual differences exist and if they influence career outcomes, where do they come from? Some differences could be explained by individuals' demographic attributes, such as age and education, but the explained variation was not high. To explore this further, Barbara interviewed people in a wide variety of careers about how they evaluated their own careers. Some were engineers, physicians and lawyers in small and large organizations. Others worked in self-created jobs, such as putting together an independent movie production or developing, producing and selling skate boards through sponsorship in big tournaments. Consistently and independent of the kind of work they were involved in, people said they evaluated themselves by comparison with an abstract group of specific and also undefined others.

To better understand 'who is *they*?' Barbara conducted an ego-network study in a large organization. Her data included subjects' lists of the people each knew, reference groups averaging 50 names per subject. As expected, the composition of these groups was strongly related to subjects' demographic attributes. However, demographics consistently explained less variation in the attributes of subjects' close associations, people they worked with regularly, than distant associations, people with whom they worked infrequently or not at all. For instance, subjects' demographic attributes predicted 37 percent of the variation in the average age of their close associations, but 61 percent of the variation in their distant ones. Moreover, the composition of subjects' distant associations consistently explained more variation in their career outcomes, such as expected achievement, than their close associations. This, and her work on how these reference groups cluster (Lawrence and Zyphur, 2011), suggests that *they*, those referents out there that people perceive but don't work with, contribute significantly to the way people view their own careers.

Recently, she has started a study of geoscientists to examine the same phenomena in an open social context, in the sense that subjects work in different geoscience disciplines and at different institutions rather than in one common organization. Here the question is where scientists get the information that allows them to find collaborators from other disciplines.

The topic of sustainable careers emphasizes the intersection between individuals and their work environments. Moreover, it assumes that what goes on within this intersection is generalizable. Yet, individuals often experience a common, shared environment quite differently. Thus, Barbara believes that further research requires understanding why this occurs. Her work on 'who is *they*?' provides one source of these variations. However, the dialectic between structure, norms and outcomes is complex (Lawrence and Tolbert, 2007). This means that human resource policies that provide sustainable careers for some people do not provide the same opportunity for others. We need to learn how to design work in ways that maximize such careers for everyone.

MOVING FORWARD: A SHARED FOCUS ON SUSTAINABLE CAREERS

Drawing together our separate journeys, we consider some of the common themes in our work since the publication of the *Handbook*. As we discuss these themes, we will keep in mind the elements of sustainable careers as outlined by Van der Heijden, De Vos and their colleagues (De Vos and De Prins, 2014; De Vos and Gielens, 2014; Van der Heijden and De Vos, 2015).

First, all individuals who work have careers, since the career is defined as the sequence of work-related experiences the person has over his or her work life (Arthur et al., 1989). Thus, under the umbrella of 'career' we include all kinds of work and occupations, not just professionals.[9] The main issue, however, is not whether someone has a career or not, but rather what these careers will look like in the future, both to individuals and to institutions, given the many changes likely to unfold. How will people manage their careers and how will employers attempt to manage their employees' careers? Will employers see their employees as talents, as in interchangeable parts, or as unique individuals with full lives and complex potential to be developed, as well as a need for work to have meaning and purpose? It is this latter emotional and motivational aspect of work that provides sustainable personal commitment not only to excellent performance but also to ongoing growth and learning. This issue of career growth and the maintenance of commitment and purpose represents a major element of a career's sustainability.

A clear theme in our work since the *Handbook* is how individuals think about their careers in relation to the rest of their lives, how they learn and adapt and how much influence they exert over their careers relative to the influence of other actors and factors in the environment, such as reference groups. And, as De Vos and Gielens (2014) show, the issues of growth, without 'overambitious challenge' and life balance are also key in heading off burnout and alienation in the career.

It is also clear that people need education to support these sustainability factors. First, and most obviously, they need to learn the key knowledge, skills and abilities that prepare them for the present and future. Second, more than ever before, they need to understand their own strengths and weaknesses and how to use these to negotiate an increasingly chaotic work environment. Moreover, people need to develop the meta-competencies to empower them to be continuous learners: self-awareness and adaptability. They need to be able to recognize skill deficiencies on their own, before these gaps become problems, and they need to be able to self-correct and develop new skills and capabilities just in the course of their everyday work activities.

One important way that employers can facilitate the development of these career-sustaining qualities is through the conscious creation of work roles that represent *smart jobs* (Hall and Las Heras, 2010). Smart jobs are ones that *require* the development and exercise of the elements of employability simply in the successful performance of the job. If we think of the key elements of employability as self-awareness, adaptability and social capital (Fugate et al., 2004), this suggests that a smart job would be designed so that the person had to constantly be receiving feedback, from self and others, constantly reaching out to new people, such as customers, suppliers, teachers/coaches, superiors and subordinates and constantly finding new methods and strategies for doing the job. The *hoshin* method (Liker, 2004) for quality improvement and continuous learning is a long-standing example of a process for imbuing smart elements into people's jobs. More recent approaches focus more directly on the opportunities leaders have to promote smart jobs for subordinates (Dutton and Spreitzer, 2014) and teams (Ancona and Bresman, 2007; Edmondson, 2012).

At the same time, almost everyone wants some stability in their lives. Young people who don't have families often test the waters by moving from one job to another. But that doesn't last when they get tired of moving, start families, want benefits, predictable retirements and sufficient stability to do meaningful work that requires long-term commitment. Thus, despite the increased omnipresence of boundaryless careers that is required by today's labor markets, workers with families, relatives, or other attachments to a particular geographic location will continue to demand stable, meaningful careers. Some of this mobility may be gained by changing jobs but staying in the same family home, or in certain cases by telecommuting. However, a relatively high demand for work that lends itself to job crafting (for example, Tims et al., 2013; Wrzesniewski and Dutton, 2001), local work opportunities and social opportunities will persist.

Nevertheless, people have to deal with constant change and live through intermingled stages of learning, development and stability. Learning by definition involves change, losing competence in certain areas and growing competence in new areas. It also means feeling less successful in one's work during a growth cycle. Paradoxically, one has to learn to feel comfortable being uncomfortable, in trading off stability and possible decline for instability and potential future growth. Just as physical stretching can be good for sustaining the body, employability stretching is good for careers.

One other stretching activity that individuals need to learn is how to gauge work environments more accurately. People learn how and what work is valued by observing others: their organizations, family and society at large. When they see only a small portion of these environments, their self-perceptions and beliefs about future possibilities are similarly limited. An individual growing up in a rural community where no one goes to college frequently finds it difficult to imagine that there are more possibilities for his or her life. It is difficult to see beyond these taken-for-granted norms and we need to learn more about what generates them and how to design organizations in ways that facilitate achievable imagining.

CONCLUSION

The philosophy of sustainable careers has been implicit in much research since the Human Relations movement in the 1930s and in most of our own work since 1989. It seems unlikely that any person or corporate executive would disagree that sustainable careers are good for workers as well as organizations. The definition including workability and employability is a win–win. However, these attributes raise several questions about how we explore the subject. Sustainable careers represent an 'ideal type'. We may never be able to pin down what is or is not a sustainable career. Rather, we may need to identify more and less sustainable careers.

As in all career research, sustainable careers involve a time element. If we ask people whether their job is sustainable, their answer is likely to include their assessment of their career-to-date and their psychological contract with those responsible for the future.

They may also tell us that some portions of their careers were more sustainable than others. We've mentioned that different age groups have different career requirements. In addition, periods of discomfort from career learning and stretching may also be accompanied by the fear and stress induced by not knowing whether they will thrive in the future. These transitions, if successful, can easily be integrated into successful sustainable career stories. If they are not successful, then in addition to producing an unsustainable career situation, they are likely to create doubt in individuals' minds that continuous learning and stretching represent positive life developments.

Another topic that requires more attention is the social contexts within which careers are experienced, such as organizations, occupational communities, national cultures and industry regions. We noted earlier that careers research sports a rich history in psychology. Indeed much of our focus in this chapter has been about individuals: their agency in career decisions, the broadening opportunities available, the contradictions inherent in subjective and objective success and the meaning work holds at different times of life. However, in order for careers to be sustainable, they need to meet employers' needs as well as those of employees. Maintaining human resource policies that support sustainable careers is expensive and if an organization doesn't thrive, neither do sustainable careers.

There is also the question of who decides whether careers are sustainable when assessing how individuals' needs fit organizational needs. It's relatively easy to ask individuals whether they see themselves as experiencing a sustainable career. It's also easy to ask executives whether they think their organization is providing sustainable careers. However, it is similarly easy to imagine that employees and executives do not see sustainable careers similarly. Many executives have little idea of how their employees experience work and prefer to believe rather than find out whether their organization supports sustainable careers and, if it does, for whom.

In one organization studied by one of the authors, executives were puzzled and upset by the high turnover of their engineers. The executives were quite satisfied with their own careers and projected these experiences to those of their engineers. When asked, the engineers were leaving because they had been hired for their state-of-the-art skills, yet the company's products required only old technology. The company was hiring engineers for whom it could not provide a sustainable career. Certainly there is no organization in which all employees' needs for sustainability fit precisely with the organization's requirements for performance.

In conclusion, we offer a few thoughts on the four elements behind the definition of sustainable careers introduced by the editors of this volume. Regarding *time*, as career scripts become less clear they need more attention, which requires moving away from cross-sectional research designs. Regarding *social space*, expecting workers to move into new situations prompts us to consider their attendant risks. Turning to *agency*, we need to move from static to more dynamic models of careers that accommodate the emergent notion of adult identity development. This connects to *meaning*, which also calls for a more developmental view of people's career situations. All of these thoughts are more easily said than accomplished. Let us feel good about all the progress that's been made, as we realize there is much that still needs to be done!

NOTES

1. The authors would like to thank Ans De Vos and Beatrice Van der Heijden for their support and patience while writing this chapter. We also thank Lan Wang for her assistance in gathering and analyzing the bibliographic data and the Friedman Research Fund at Boston University for technical support.
2. Employability has also been defined as an individual-level construct (Fugate et al., 2004, p. 15). We prefer a work environment-level definition because employability then balances the individual-level focus of workability. Sustainability involves the tension between individuals and work environments, and workability and employability thus cover this basic territory.
3. We use the term 'organization' as a short-hand for the diverse social contexts in which people work, recognizing that many careers fall across or outside typical organizational boundaries. For instance, politicians operate in multiple, overlapping social contexts, their local communities, the regions they represent, and the governmental agencies they work for. This social context differs dramatically from that experienced by an employee who works in a single organization.
4. We use the term 'self-actualization' as originally posited by Maslow (1943): 'Even if all these needs are satisfied, we may still often (if not always) expect that a new discontent and restlessness will soon develop, unless the individual is doing what he is fitted for. A musician must make music, an artist must paint, a poet must write if he is to be ultimately happy. What a man *can* be, he *must* be' (p. 382).
5. See Howard and Bray's book (1988) for detail on the many follow-ups conducted on the original assessment group and a second cohort selected in the 1970s and early 1980s.
6. We acknowledge that this is a distinctly US perspective, representing what the authors know best. We do not claim that the same patterns prevailed elsewhere. However, as we observe later, it is interesting that a more global research agenda has developed in the recent past.
7. We thank Lan Wang at Boston University for the data presented here, which were obtained from the Web of Science.
8. These data have many limitations. For instance, many of these articles examine a specific individual's career or provide career advice for those pursuing a career rather than providing research on careers per se. Moreover, the Web of Science is not a complete archive of academic articles.
9. Perhaps some element of confusion here may derive that in some languages the word for occupation is sometimes translated as 'profession'. An example here would be *Beruf* in German, which many English speakers translate as 'occupation', while some German speakers translate it as 'profession'.

REFERENCES

Ancona, D.G. and Bresman, H. (2007). *X-Teams: How to Build Teams that Lead, Innovate, and Succeed.* Boston, MA: Harvard Business School.

Argyris, C. (1964). *Integrating the Individual and the Organization.* New York: John Wiley.

Arthur, M.B. (2008). Examining contemporary careers: A call for interdisciplinary inquiry. *Human Relations*, 61(2), 163–86.

Arthur, M.B. (2014). The boundaryless career at 20: Where do we stand and where can we go? *Career Development International*, 19(6), 627–40.

Arthur, M.B. and Rousseau, D.M. (1996). *The Boundaryless Career: A New Employment Principle for a New Organizational Era.* New York: Oxford University Press.

Arthur, M.B., Claman, P.H. and DeFillippi, R. J. (1995). Intelligent enterprise, intelligent careers. *Academy of Management Executive*, 9(4), 7–20.

Arthur, M.B., Hall, D.T. and Lawrence, B.S. (1989). *Handbook of Career Theory.* Cambridge, UK: Cambridge University Press.

Arthur, M.B., Inkson, K. and Pringle, J.K. (1999). *New Careers: Individual Action and Economic Change.* Thousand Oaks, CA: Sage.

Arthur, M.B., Khapova, S.N. and Wilderom, C.P.M. (2005). Career success in a boundaryless career world. *Journal of Organizational Behavior*, 26(2), 177–202.

Bailyn, L. (1970). Career and family orientations of husbands and wives in relation to marital happiness. *Human Relations*, 23(2), 97–113.

Barley, S.R. and Kunda, G. (2005). *Gurus, Hired Guns and Warm Bodies: Itinerant Experts in a Knowledge Economy.* Princeton, NJ: Princeton University Press.

Becker, H.S. (1961). *Boys in White: Student Culture in Medical School.* Chicago: University of Chicago Press.

Becker, H.S. (1982). *Art Worlds.* Berkeley, CA: University of California Press.

Becker, H.S. (2008). *Art Worlds and Collective Activity: 25th Anniversary Edition*. Berkeley, CA: University of California Press.

Blustein, D.L. (2006). *The Psychology of Working: A New Perspective for Career Development, Counseling, and Public Policy*. Mahwah, NJ: Lawrence Erlbaum Associates.

Bray, D.W., Campbell, R.J. and Grant, D.L. (1974). *Formative Years in Business: A Long-Term AT&T Study of Managerial Lives*. New York: Wiley.

Briscoe, J.P., Hall, D.T. and Mayrhofer, W. (2012). *Careers Around the World: Individual and Contextual Perspectives*. New York: Routledge.

Burt, R.S. (1992). Getting ahead. In R.S. Burt, *Structural Holes* (pp. 115–80). Cambridge, MA: Harvard University Press.

Caplow, T. (1953). The criteria of organizational success. *Social Forces*, 32(1), 1–9.

Caplow, T. and McGee, R.J. (1958). *The Academic Marketplace*. New York: Basic Books.

Cappelli, P. (1999). *The New Deal at Work*. Boston, MA: Harvard Business School Press.

Cappelli, P. (2008). Talent management for the 21st century. *Harvard Business Review*, March, 75–81.

Castilla, E.J., Lan, G.J. and Rissing, B.A. (2013). Social networks and employment: Mechanisms (Part 1). *Sociology Compass*, 7(12), 999–1012.

Cressey, P.G. (1932). *The Taxi-Dance Hall: A Sociological Study in Commercialized Recreation and City Life*. Chicago, IL: University of Chicago Press.

Dalton, G.W. (1989). Developmental views of careers in organizations. In M.B. Arthur, D.T. Hall and B.S. Lawrence (eds), *Handbook of Career Theory* (pp. 89–109). Cambridge, UK: Cambridge University Press.

De Vos, A. and De Prins, P. (2014). Towards a framework for sustainable career management. Paper presented at the Small Group Meeting on Age Policies, Antwerp, Belgium.

De Vos, A. and Gielens, T. (2014). System level practices to facilitate sustainable careers. Paper presented at the European Network on Career & AGE (Age, Generations, Experience), Seville, Spain.

DeFillippi, R.J. and Arthur, M.B. (1994). The boundaryless career: A competency-based perspective. *Journal of Organizational Behavior*, 15(4), 307–24.

DeFillippi, R.J. and Arthur, M.B. (1998). Paradox in project-based enterprise: The case of film-making. *California Management Review*, 40(2), 125–39.

DeFillippi, R.J., Arthur, M.B. and Lindsay, V.J. (2006). *Knowledge at Work: Creative Collaboration in the Global Economy*. Oxford, UK: Basil Blackwell.

Derr, C.B. and Schein, E.H. (1978). *Proceedings of the Career Research Conference*, 30 April–2 May, Cambridge, MA.

Duberley, J., Cohen, L. and Mallon, M. (2006). Constructing scientific careers: Change, continuity and context. *Organization Studies*, 27(8), 1131–51.

Dutton, J.E. and G.M. Spreitzer (2014). *How to Be a Positive Leader*. San Francisco: Berrett-Koehler Publishers.

Dyer, W.G. (1955). The interlocking of work and family social systems among lower occupational families. *Social Forces*, 34, 230–33.

Edmondson, A.C. (2012). *Teaming: How Organizations Learn, Innovate and Compete in the Knowledge Economy*. San Francisco: Jossey-Bass.

Forrier, A. and Sels, L. (2003). Temporary employment and employability: Training opportunities and efforts of temporary and permanent employees in Belgium. *Work, Employment and Society*, 17(4), 641–66.

Fugate, M., Kinicki, A.J. and Ashforth, B.E. (2004). Employability: A psycho-social construct, its dimensions and applications. *Journal of Vocational Behavior*, 65(1), 14–38.

Goffman, E. (1961). *Asylums: Essays on the Social Situation of Mental Patients and Other Inmates*. Garden City, NY: Anchor Books.

Grote, G. and Hall, D.T. (2013). Reference groups: A missing link in career studies. *Journal of Vocational Behavior*, 83(2), 151–71.

Gunz, H. and Peiperl, M. (2007). *Handbook of Career Studies*. Thousand Oaks, CA: Sage.

Hall, D.T. (1976). *Careers in Organizations*. Pacific Palisades, CA: Goodyear Publishing Company.

Hall, D.T. (ed.) (1986a). *Career Development in Organizations*. San Francisco, CA: Jossey-Bass.

Hall, D.T. (1986b). Breaking career routines: Midcareer choice and identity development. In D.T. Hall (ed.), *Career Development in Organizations* (pp. 120–59). San Francisco, CA: Jossey-Bass.

Hall, D.T. (1996). *The Career is Dead – Long Live the Career: A Relational Approach to Careers*. San Francisco, CA: Jossey-Bass.

Hall, D.T. (2002). *Careers In and Out of Organizations*. Thousand Oaks, CA: Sage Publications.

Hall, D.T. and Las Heras, M. (2010). Reintegrating job design and career theory: Creating not just good jobs but smart jobs. *Journal of Organizational Behavior*, 31, 448–62.

Hall, D.T. and Lerner, P. (1980). Career development in work organizations: Research and practice. *Professional Psychology*, 11(3), 428–35.

Howard, A. and Bray, D.W. (1988). *Managerial Lives in Transition: Advancing Age and Changing Times*. New York: Guilford Press.

Hughes, E.C. (1958). *Men and Their Work*. Glencoe, IL: Free Press.

Hughes, E.C. (1962). Good people and dirty work. *Social Problems*, 10(1), 3–11.

Ibarra, H. (1999). Provisional selves: Experimenting with image and identity in professional adaptation. *Administrative Science Quarterly*, 44(4), 764–91.

Ibarra, H. (2003). *Working Identity: Unconventional Strategies for Reinventing Your Career*. Boston, MA: Harvard Business School.

Jones, C. (2001). Co-evolution of entrepreneurial careers, institutional rules and competitive dynamics in American Film, 1985–1920. *Organization Studies*, 22(6), 911–44.

Jones, C. and Dunn, M.B. (2007). Careers and institutions: The centrality of careers to organizational studies. In H. Gunz and M. Peiperl (eds), *Handbook of Career Studies* (pp. 437–50). Los Angeles, CA: Sage.

Khapova, S.N. and Arthur, M.B. (2011). Interdisciplinary approaches to contemporary career studies. *Human Relations*, 64(1), 3–17.

Kuder, G.F. (1939). *Kuder Preference Record: Form A*. Chicago, IL: University of Chicago.

Lawrence, B.S. (1984). Age grading: The implicit organizational timetable. *Journal of Organizational Behavior*, 5(1), 23–35.

Lawrence, B.S. (1988). New wrinkles in the theory of age: Demography, norms and performance ratings. *Academy of Management Journal*, 31(2), 309–37.

Lawrence, B.S. (1990). At the crossroads: A multiple-level explanation of individual attainment. *Organization Science*, 1(1), 65–85.

Lawrence, B.S. (2006). Organizational reference groups: A missing perspective on social context. *Organization Science*, 17(1), 80–100.

Lawrence, B.S. (2011). The Hughes Award – Who is they? Inquiries into how individuals construe social context. *Human Relations*, 64(6), 749–73.

Lawrence, B.S. and Tolbert, P.S. (2007). Organizational demography and careers: Structure, norms and outcomes. In M. Peiperl and H. Gunz (eds), *Handbook of Career Studies* (pp. 399–421). Thousand Oaks, CA: Sage Publications.

Lawrence, B.S. and Zyphur, M.J. (2011). Identifying organizational faultlines with latent class cluster analysis. *Organizational Research Methods*, 14(1), 32–57.

Liden, R.C., Wayne, S.J., Kraimer, M.L. and Sparrowe, R.T. (2003). The dual commitments of contingent workers: An examination of contingents' commitment to the agency and the organization. *Journal of Organizational Behavior*, 24(5), 609–25.

Liker, J.K. (2004). *The Toyota Way*. New York: McGraw Hill.

Maslow, A.H. (1943). A theory of human motivation. *Psychological Review*, 50, 370–96.

Moore, C., Gunz, H. and Hall, D.T. (2007). Tracing the historical roots of career theory in management and organization studies. In H. Gunz and M. Peiperl (eds), *Handbook of Career Studies* (pp. 13–38). Thousand Oaks, CA: Sage Publications.

Osipow, S.H. (1968). *Theories of Career Development*. New York: Appleton-Century Crofts.

Parker, P. and Arthur, M.B. (2000). Careers, organizing and community. In M.A. Peiperl, M. B. Arthur, R. Goffee and T.L. Morris (eds), *Career Frontiers: New Conceptions of Working Lives* (pp. 99–121). Oxford, UK: Oxford University Press.

Rapoport, R.N. and Rapoport, R. (1965). Work and family in contemporary soceity. *American Sociological Review*, 30, 381–94.

Roethlisberger, F.J. and Dickson, W.J. (1939). *Management and the Worker*. Cambridge, MA: Harvard University Press.

Schein, E.H. (1978). *Career Dynamics: Matching Individual and Organizational Needs*. Reading, MA: Addison-Wesley Publishing Company.

Strauss, A. (1962). *The Professional Scientist: A Study of American Chemists*. Chicago, IL: Aldine Publishing.

Strong, E.K., Jr (1926). An interest test for personnel managers. *Journal of Personnel Research*, 5, 194–203.

Strong, E.K., Jr (1927). *Vocational Interest Blank*. Stanford, CA: Stanford University.

Sullivan, S.E. and Baruch, Y. (2009). Advances in career theory and research: A critical review and agenda for future exploration. *Journal of Management*, 35(6), 1542–71.

Sullivan, S.E. and Crocitto, M. (2007). The developmental theories: A critical examination of their continuing impact on careers research. In H. Gunz and M. Peiperl (eds), *Handbook of Career Studies* (pp. 283–309). Los Angeles, CA: Sage.

Super, D.E. (1957). *Scientific Careers and Vocational Development Theory*. New York: Teachers College, Columbia University.

Tams, S. and Arthur, M.B. (2010). New directions for boundaryless careers: Agency and interdependence in a changing world. *Journal of Organizational Behavior*, 31(5), 629–46.

Tims, M., Bakker, A.B. and Derks, D. (2013). The impact of job crafting on job demands, job resources, and well-being. *Journal of Occupational Health Psychology*, 18(2), 230–40.
Van Maanen, J. (1977). *Organizational Careers: Some New Perspectives*. New York: John Wiley.
Verbruggen, M., Van Emmerik, H., Van Gils, A., de Grip, A. and Meng, C. (2014). Does early-career underemployment impact future career success? A career path dependency perspective. Paper presented at the Academy of Management, Philadelphia.
Weick, K.E. and Berlinger, L.R. (1989). Career improvisation in self-designing organizations. In M.B. Arthur, D.T. Hall and B.S. Lawrence (eds), *Handbook of Career Theory* (pp. 313–28). Cambridge, UK: Cambridge Unversity Press.
Whyte, W.H. (1956). *The Organization Man*. New York: Simon and Schuster.
Wrzesniewski, A. and Dutton, J.E. (2001). Crafting a job: Revisioning employees as active crafters of their work. *The Academy of Management Review*, 26(2), 179–201.

Index

Title of publications are shown in *italics*.